BUDDHA ŚĀKYAMUNI

Padmasambhava, Guru Rinpoche

། །ཞིག་པ་ཆེན་པོ་མདོ་སྡེའི་རྒྱན་གྱི་དགོངས་དོན་
རྣམ་པར་བཤད་པ་ཐེག་མཆོག་བདུད་རྩིའི་
དགའ་སྟོན་ཅེས་བྱ་བ་བཞུགས། །

པདྨ་ཀཽ་རའི་སྒྲ་བསྒྱུར་མཐུན་ཚོགས་ནས་
སྒྲ་བསྒྱུར་ཞུས།།

A Feast of the Nectar of the Supreme Vehicle

*An Explanation of the
Ornament of the Mahāyāna Sūtras*

*Maitreya's Mahāyānasūtrālaṃkāra
with a commentary by Jamgön Mipham*

TRANSLATED BY THE
Padmakara Translation Group

SHAMBHALA
BOULDER
2018

Shambhala Publications, Inc.
4720 Walnut Street
Boulder, Colorado 80301
www.shambhala.com

© 2018 by the Padmakara Translation Group
All line drawings by Olivier Philippot.
Photograph of Kangyur Rinpoche by Matthieu Ricard.

All rights reserved. No part of this book may be reproduced
in any form or by any means, electronic or mechanical, including
photocopying, recording, or by any information storage and retrieval
system, without permission in writing from the publisher.

9 8 7 6 5 4 3 2 1

First Edition
Printed in the United States of America

♾ This edition is printed on acid-free paper that meets the
American National Standards Institute z39.48 Standard.
♻ Shambhala Publications makes every effort to print on recycled paper.
For more information please visit www.shambhala.com.

Shambhala Publications is distributed worldwide by
Penguin Random House, Inc., and its subsidiaries.

LIBRARY OF CONGRESS CATALOGING-IN-PUBLICATION DATA
Names: Asaṅga, author. | Maitreyanātha. | Mi-pham-rgya-mtsho, Jam-mgon Ju, 1846–
1912, writer of added commentary. | Comité de traduction Padmakara, translator.
Title: A feast of the nectar of the supreme vehicle: an explanation of the Ornament of the
Mahāyāna sūtras: Maitreya's Mahāyānasūtrālaṅkāra / with a commentary by Jamgön
Mipham; translated by the Padmakara Translation Group.
Other titles: Mahāyānasūtrālaṅkāra:. English
Description: First edition. | Boulder: Shambhala, 2018. | Includes bibliographical
references and index.
Identifiers: LCCN 2017019294 | ISBN 9781611804676 (hardcover: alk. paper)
Subjects: LCSH: Yogācāra (Buddhism)—Early works to 1800.
Classification: LCC BQ3002.E5 P33 2018 | DDC 294.3/85—dc23
LC record available at https://lccn.loc.gov/2017019294

The Padmakara Translation Group gratefully acknowledges
the generous support of the Tsadra Foundation
in sponsoring the translation and preparation
of this book.

Contents

Foreword by Jigme Khyentse Rinpoche — xiii

Translator's Introduction — xv

Ornament of the Mahāyāna Sūtras: The Root Verses

1. The First Chapter — 3
2. Establishing the Great Vehicle as the Buddha's Word — 5
3. Refuge — 9
4. The Potential — 13
5. The Spiritual Intent: Bodhicitta — 15
6. Practice — 19
7. Thatness — 21
8. Powers — 23
9. Full Maturation — 25
10. Enlightenment — 29
11. Interest — 41
12. Thorough Investigation — 45
13. Teaching the Dharma — 57
14. Practicing the Dharma — 61
15. Instructions and Follow-Up Teachings — 67
16. Skillful Activity — 75
17. Transcendent Perfections and Ways of Attracting Disciples — 77
18. Offering, Reliance, and Boundless Attitudes — 89
19. Elements Leading to Enlightenment — 99
20. Qualities — 113
21. Conduct and Consummation — 125

A Feast of the Nectar of the Supreme Vehicle: The Commentary

    Preamble, Title, and Translator's Homage   137

    Introduction   139

Part One: What Is to Be Established: Establishing the Great Vehicle as the Buddha's Word

    1. General Presentation   151

    2. Specific Explanations   155

Part Two: What Is to Be Specifically Known

    3. Refuge   171

    4. The Potential   183

    5. The Spiritual Intent: Bodhicitta   197

    6. Practice   221

Part Three: What Is to Be Reflected Upon

    7. Thatness   233

    8. Powers   249

    9. Full Maturation   259

Part Four: The Inconceivable, That Which Is beyond Reflection

    10. Enlightenment   279

    Recapitulation   339

Part Five: The Approach to Enlightenment

Preliminaries

    11. Interest   345

    12. Thorough Investigation   359

    13. Teaching the Dharma   447

14. Practicing the Dharma	473
15. Instructions and Follow-Up Teachings	491
Intermediate Summary	519

Main Explanation

16. Skillful Activity	521
17. Transcendent Perfections and Ways of Attracting Disciples	525
18. Offering, Reliance, and Boundless Attitudes	579
19. Elements Leading to Enlightenment	629
20. Qualities	731
21. Conduct and Consummation	797
Conclusion	843
Appendix 1: Structural Outline	847
Appendix 2: The Five Bodhisattva Paths and the Thirty-Seven Elements Leading to Enlightenment	863
Appendix 3: The Three Worlds and Six Realms	867
Glossary	871
Works Cited	887
Bibliography	891
Index	893

Foreword

Jigme Khyentse Rinpoche

In an age when science claims to have an answer for everything and is even attempting to prove the validity of Buddhist meditation, while many people's ideas about different religions and spiritual paths reduce these to simplistic and misleading stereotypes, it is hard to comprehend the true breadth and profundity of the Buddha's teachings. During his lifetime, Buddha Śākyamuni taught on countless occasions, on many different levels, and to different individuals, in order to help each particular person understand something that would bring him or her closer to enlightenment. For us to consider the vast scope of these teachings is as mind-blowing and awe-inspiring as gazing into the immensity of space.

In the *Sūtrālaṃkāra*, the Buddha's regent, Maitreya, brings this vast array of teachings together, arranging them in an orderly fashion and putting them into perspective so that we can begin to understand them and use them as a path to enlightenment. Of the three principal aspects of the path—view, meditation, and conduct—this text, like Shantideva's *The Way of the Bodhisattva* (*Bodhicaryāvatāra*), deals mainly with the view and conduct of the great bodhisattvas, whose sole aim is the enlightenment of all beings. Once we have an inkling of the extraordinary kindness and wisdom of these bodhisattvas, whom we can meet even today as our teachers, we can begin to infer that the incredible qualities and deeds that Maitreya describes are possible.

I hope that this translation of Maitreya's presentation, along with Mipham Rinpoche's clear explanation, will help readers to gain a glimpse of the Buddha's message in all its vastness, taking them beyond limited conceptions and inspiring them to practice the path it describes.

Translator's Introduction

Ornament of the Mahāyāna Sūtras is the longest and most wide ranging of the five treatises that Ārya Asaṅga received from the Buddha Maitreya and brought back from the Tuṣita heaven. It is also the work that perhaps most obviously testifies to Asaṅga's mission to spread the message of the Great Vehicle (Mahāyāna) at a time when the teachings, in particular the Abhidharma, were threatened with decline, for it serves as a veritable manifesto for the Great Vehicle, describing in detail the attractions of the bodhisattva path. Its beautiful descriptions of the qualities of the bodhisattva are widely quoted throughout Tibetan Buddhist literature, and in the monastic colleges of the Nyingma school it is included among the thirteen most important source texts studied in the curriculum. Many Tibetan masters have been inspired to write commentaries on it, among them the celebrated Nyingma scholar Jamgön Mipham (1846–1912), who was an outstanding proponent of the nonsectarian movement founded by such masters as Jamyang Khyentse Wangpo and Jamgön Kongtrul. It is his commentary, based on an authoritative Indian commentary, that we have chosen to translate here.

ĀRYA ASAṄGA AND THE FIVE TREATISES OF MAITREYA

The various traditional accounts of Asaṅga's life suggest that he was a man not so much born with a mission as conceived with a mission, for among the people deeply concerned with the situation of Buddhism in fourth-century India was his mother. As a young nun, she bemoaned the fact that she lacked the scholarship and eloquence of the paṇḍitas at the Indian Buddhist universities and the meditative accomplishments of Buddhist hermits. She realized, however, that there was one thing she could do that no paṇḍita could—bear children, even if it meant taking the drastic step of giving up her monastic vows. Praying fervently that her offspring would be able to make the teachings flourish once more, she proceeded, through successive liaisons with three men, to give birth to three sons who she hoped would fulfill that historic destiny. Of the three boys, the eldest was Asaṅga and the second was Vasubandhu, who later became Asaṅga's foremost disciple, and they were indeed to make their mark on the development of Indian Buddhism over the next few centuries.

Briefed by his mother, the young Asaṅga set about his appointed task with enthusiasm. His aim was to seek the help of the future Buddha, the bodhisattva Maitreya, and for this he decided to undertake a meditation retreat, practicing Maitreya's sādhana. After six years, however, his initial fervor had begun to wear off, for he had had not the slightest sign that he was accomplishing his goal. Not once had he even had a dream in which Maitreya appeared to him. Disillusioned, he abandoned his isolated retreat and set off back to the civilized world. On the way, he met a man rubbing an iron rod with a piece of cotton, apparently in the hope of making a needle from it. Amazed that anyone could put so much effort into such a futile endeavor, Asaṅga realized that it would be a mistake to give up so easily his infinitely more lofty ambition, and he returned to his cave with renewed faith.

Another three years of strenuous meditation, however, still produced no results, and once again he left his retreat, only to encounter a man stroking a massive rock with a feather. The rock, it turned out, was shading the man's house from the sun, and he was trying to remove it. Again, it was brought home to Asaṅga that in order to achieve his aim, he would need a lot more perseverance, and so he went back to his cave to continue meditating. But after a further three years of intensive practice, he had still not seen any signs of accomplishment. In all, twelve years had passed without a single auspicious dream, and Asaṅga finally decided that there was no point in carrying on. Utterly discouraged, he abandoned his retreat, this time, he thought, for good.

Arriving on the outskirts of a village, he came across a starving dog, dragging its maggot-infested hind legs behind it. Despite the dog's attempts to bite him, Asaṅga was overwhelmed by compassion, and for want of anything to feed the dog, he cut a piece of flesh from his own leg for it to eat. He then turned his attention to its appalling wounds, but soon realized that all attempts to remove the maggots might save the dog but would kill the maggots. The only solution he could think of was to use his tongue to coax the maggots out of the stinking flesh. Shutting his eyes, he bent down to do what he could to heal the animal, only to find himself licking the dust by the side of the road. When he opened his eyes, he found the dog had disappeared. In its place, before him stood Maitreya. His wonder at finally beholding the object of his practice, however, quickly gave way to resentment. "Where have you been all this time?" he demanded.

"I've been with you from the beginning," answered Maitreya, "but until now you were too obscured to see me. Now your compassion has cleared away your obscurations."

To prove his point, after healing the wound in Asaṅga's leg, he told Asaṅga to take him on his shoulder into the village. The villagers all thought the tattered beggar who kept on asking them what he had on his shoulder was mad, for they could see nothing. But one old woman, who was slightly less obscured than the others, did wonder what he was doing carrying a diseased dog around with him.

Now that Asaṅga had at last accomplished his practice and could communicate directly with Maitreya, the bodhisattva took him to the Tuṣita heaven, where he gave him the teachings that he subsequently brought back to earth and wrote down as the Five Treatises of Maitreya—*Ornament of the Mahāyāna Sūtras* (*Mahāyānasūtrālaṃkāra*), *Sublime Continuum* (*Mahāyānottaratantraśāstra-ratnagotravibhāga*), *Distinguishing the Middle from Extremes* (*Madhyāntavibhāga*), *Distinguishing Phenomena and Suchness* (*Dharmadharmatāvibhāga*), and *Ornament of True Realization* (*Abhisamayālaṃkāra*). The last of these is a guide to the Prajñāpāramitā sūtras and is therefore associated with the second turning of the wheel of the Dharma, the teachings given by Buddha Śākyamuni that emphasize emptiness, the absence of any permanent, independent, and single entity in phenomena. The other four treatises are generally said to belong to the teachings of the third turning, which include the doctrine of buddha nature and the three realities. Asaṅga is identified, in particular, with the Vast (or Extensive) Activity tradition,[1] and nowhere is this more clearly shown than in *Ornament of the Mahāyāna Sūtras*.

Overview of *Ornament of the Mahāyāna Sūtras*

In attempting to promote the message of the Great Vehicle to his potential audience, Asaṅga put the emphasis on vaunting its merits compared to those

---

1. The Vast Activity tradition includes the Yogācāra (Yogic Practice) and Mind-Only (Cittamātra) approaches and is often contrasted with the Profound View tradition of Nāgārjuna, associated with the Middle Way (Madhyamaka) teachings of the second turning of the wheel of the Dharma. One of the remarkable achievements of Mipham Rinpoche in this and other texts was to promote a synthesis of the two approaches, showing that they were compatible with each other.

of the Listener (Śrāvaka) schools and other, non-Buddhist, traditions. It is in this sense that *Ornament of the Mahāyāna Sūtras* serves not merely as a stand-alone text for presenting the Mahāyāna teachings but as a true ornament, highlighting the special features of the scriptures it adorns.

The text begins with three verses that serve as a synopsis for the whole of the rest of the text. Jamgön Mipham's explanation of these necessarily assumes a knowledge at least of the structure, if not the content, of all that follows, and it would have been easily understood by students at the monastic colleges (*shedras*) who traditionally would have learned the root text and probably the structural outline[2] by heart before studying the commentary with a learned instructor. The first few pages, therefore, demand a certain patience on the part of readers who are new to this text, as they attempt to understand the way in which *Ornament of the Mahāyāna Sūtras* is divided into its five parts, these being referred to in the root text only through their five corresponding metaphors contained in the second verse. Mipham draws on a number of Indian commentaries with varying interpretations of these opening verses in order to establish the structure of the text as a whole.

After introducing Maitreya's teaching in the three opening verses, Asaṅga, acting as a mouthpiece for Maitreya, sets about presenting his exposition of the Great Vehicle. His first task is to convince his audience that what he is offering are genuine Buddhist teachings. The vast majority of Buddhists in fourth-century India belonged to the various Listener schools, many of whose followers regarded the Great Vehicle tradition with deep suspicion. Only two centuries before, Nāgārjuna had rediscovered the Prajñāpāramitā sūtras, until then hidden in the realms of the nāgas, and now Asaṅga was presenting teachings that he claimed had been given to him in a celestial realm. These teachings must have struck many listeners as being precisely the sort of thing Lord Buddha had been referring to when he warned of the dangers of false doctrines and the fact that the Dharma would be destroyed from within. They would have seriously doubted that these teachings could truly be the words of the Buddha and not the inventions of some clever intellectuals. These doubts over the authenticity of the Great Vehicle teachings were still being addressed four centuries later by Śāntideva in the ninth chapter of *The Way of the Bodhisattva* (*Bodhicaryāvatāra*),[3] and

---

2. Mipham's structural outline (Tib. *sa bcad*) is reproduced in appendix 1.
3. *Bodhicaryāvatāra*, IX, 41–43.

the debate between the Mahāyāna and Theravāda schools has continued to the present day.

In the first two chapters, therefore, Asaṅga proceeds to establish that the Great Vehicle is an authentic Buddhist teaching. After reassuring his skeptical readers that despite the Mahāyāna's awe-inspiring teachings on emptiness and the unwelcome news that enlightenment will come only at the end of three measureless kalpas in cyclic existence, it is actually a sweet-tasting medicine that will cure all the ills of saṃsāra and grant perfect buddhahood, he goes on to clear away their doubts and objections one by one in chapter 2.[4]

Next, in the second part of the text, Asaṅga presents some specific differences between the Great Vehicle and other vehicles based on features common to both. He begins, in chapter 3, with refuge, for taking refuge is what defines someone as a Buddhist. Here, he is less interested in introducing the basics of what constitutes refuge or describing the Three Jewels than in explaining the superiority of Mahāyāna refuge relative to that of the listeners and solitary realizers.

While the chapter on refuge may have served to whet the appetites of the readers whom Asaṅga hopes to recruit into the Great Vehicle, the fourth chapter introduces a proviso, for engaging in the Great Vehicle path is not something that anyone can do. While it is true, as is explained in detail in the *Sublime Continuum*, that all sentient beings possess the buddha nature, the seed that can sprout and eventually blossom into perfect buddhahood, in practice, the degree to which that seed is ready to germinate varies according to different beings' accumulation of good or bad karma and the strength of their habitual propensities for particular paths. Thus there are some who naturally have the desire and perseverance to undertake the bodhisattvas' path to buddhahood and see it through to the end, others who only have the

---

[4]. It should be noted that the number of chapters in the root text appears to differ between the various versions—Sanskrit, Tibetan, and Chinese (see Robert Thurman's introduction to Maitreyanātha/Āryāsaṅga, *The Universal Vehicle Discourse Literature*, pp. xxxiv–xxxv). Furthermore, some commentators group Asaṅga's three opening verses and the three verses that follow in praise of the Great Vehicle together to form a prologue to the whole work. Mipham, however, classifies the three opening verses as an introduction ("How the Treatise Was Composed"), and the last three verses as a general presentation for part 1 ("Establishing the Great Vehicle as the Buddha's Word"), with specific explanations in the second chapter. To avoid part 1 seeming to begin in the middle of chapter 1 in the root text, we have followed Mipham's structural outline by classifying the three opening verses as an introduction, and the next three verses as chapter 1, the beginning of part 1.

potential to follow the listeners' path and become arhats, some who might change paths depending on circumstances, and yet others whose karma is so bad that they will seemingly never progress spiritually. Of all these, the potential for the Great Vehicle is obviously essential if one is to cultivate the mind intent on supreme enlightenment, which is the subject of the next chapter—bodhicitta. This is the mental attitude, the spiritual intent, that drives the entire path to enlightenment, and Asaṅga's aim in chapter 5 is to compare it with the inferior spiritual intent that motivates listeners and solitary realizers. This is followed by the sixth chapter, on the practice, the bodhisattvas' altruistic activity that is based on their bodhicitta.

Asaṅga's intention in this second part is to inspire enthusiasm for the Great Vehicle by impressing on potential followers the particular features that make it superior in terms of refuge, the bodhisattvas' potential, their bodhicitta, and their practice. He does this without going into the full details that characterize the path of the Great Vehicle, which he is saving for the fifth part of the text. In the meanwhile, there are still a number of salient features he wishes his readers to reflect upon before throwing themselves into the practice. These are addressed in parts 3 and 4. The three chapters in part 3 present the philosophical basis of the Great Vehicle by introducing the reader to thatness (chapter 7), the miraculous powers bodhisattvas obtain that enable them to benefit sentient beings (chapter 8), and an explanation of how bodhisattvas bring first themselves and then others to the state of maturation in which their potential for enlightenment can be fully exploited (chapter 9).

It is in his explanation of thatness that Asaṅga begins to present the mind-only teachings of the three realities or natures associated with the Buddha's third turning of the wheel of the Dharma. It is important to understand—and Mipham takes pains to point this out—that Asaṅga is not presenting here the philosophical tenets of later followers who are associated with the so-called Mind-Only school (Cittamātra), but rather the viewpoint of the scriptural mind-only teachings as the Buddha intended them to be understood. The Mind-Only tenet holders considered the self-illuminating nondual consciousness or reflexive awareness to exist ultimately, and it is this that is refuted by the Mādhyamikas in traditional explanations of the four Buddhist philosophical schools,[5] thereby relegating the Cittamātrins to

---

5. The four philosophical systems are the Vaibhāṣika, Sautrāntika, Cittamātra, and Madhyamaka.

the second position in this doxological hierarchy. But as Mipham already shows in his commentary on Śāntarakṣita's *Adornment of the Middle Way* (*Madhyamakālaṃkāra*), which presents a synthesis of the Cittamātra and Madhyamaka views, as long as the self-illuminating reflexive awareness is not considered to be ultimately real, the Cittamātra view is not incompatible with Madhyamaka. Indeed, Mipham refers to it as the "subtle, inner Madhyamaka," thus demonstrating that Asaṅga's view is no less profound than that of Nāgārjuna. Part 4, "The Inconceivable, That Which Is beyond Reflection," comprises a single chapter that provides a glimpse of the final result of the path, perfect enlightenment as a buddha (chapter 10).

These first four parts of *Ornament of the Mahāyāna Sūtras* represent less than one third of the text. The pattern of brief introduction followed by detailed explanation that characterizes not only Asaṅga's works but many of the treatises belonging to the Indian śāstra tradition is again evident in part 5, "The Approach to Enlightenment," which occupies the remainder of the text and can be said to provide an even more detailed explanation of the earlier chapters, still with a certain emphasis on the Great Vehicle's superiority. It covers the entire path, from the bodhisattva's initial interest in the Great Vehicle up to the consummate qualities of buddhahood. Jamgön Mipham divides this fifth part into two: preliminaries and the main explanation of the path. Broadly speaking, the preliminaries refer to the ways in which bodhisattvas first attain the path of seeing, by realizing emptiness directly. They then progress through the bodhisattva levels on the noble path.

Beginning with faith in the teachings, bodhisattvas proceed to receive and analyze these teachings, and then pass them on to other beings. At the same time, they put them into practice, continuing all the while to receive further teachings that will nurture their progress. In this way, through chapters 11 to 15, they prepare themselves for the vast activities of the bodhisattvas on the ten levels. It is these activities that are dealt with in detail in the so-called main explanation, which covers chapters 16 to 21 and takes up the entire second half of the text. The topics presented here include the bodhisattvas' skillful activity, the six transcendent perfections, the four ways of attracting disciples, venerating the buddhas, following a spiritual master, meditating on the four boundless attitudes, the thirty-seven elements leading to enlightenment (preceded by eight prerequisites for training in these), skillful means, retentive memory, aspirations, concentration, the four summaries of the Dharma (with detailed presentations of impermanence and no-self), the qualities that bodhisattvas gain, their conduct on the ten levels, and finally the consummate qualities of buddhahood. In this way, Asaṅga progressively reveals, through the text's five parts, first the hallmark, then the superior features, and finally the full glory of the Great Vehicle, as if "opening a chest of jewels."

Commentaries on *Ornament of the Mahāyāna Sūtras*

As with many of the other treatises that belong to the Indian śāstra tradition, *Ornament of the Mahāyāna Sūtras* presents many of its ideas obliquely, using key words and phrases that refer to subjects in the sūtras that would probably have been familiar to the Buddhists of the fourth century. It serves to make sense of the Buddha's teachings more by ordering and structuring the contents of the sūtras than by commenting on them explicitly in detail. Many of the verses in this text simply provide lists of terms and ideas, which are rarely immediately understandable to neophytes. It would seem likely that even among Asaṅga's followers there were some who needed further explanation, for within a generation, Vasubandhu, Asaṅga's half brother and principal disciple, had written a commentary on this treatise, the *Commentary on Ornament of the Mahāyāna Sūtras* (*Sūtrālaṃkārabhāṣya*), which makes up 261 pages in the Tibetan Tengyur collection of translated Indian treatises.

Asaṅga himself had written *The Stage of a Bodhisattva* (*Bodhisattvabhūmi*), which is thought by some to be his own commentary on *Ornament of the Mahāyāna Sūtras* on account of its almost identical chapter layout, though it is somewhat different in content. Vasubandhu's *Commentary* provided the basis for a much more detailed work, the definitive commentary composed by Ācārya Sthiramati,[6] Vasubandhu's foremost disciple and an expert on the Abhidharma. Mipham refers to this enormous text as the *"Great Commentary,"* no doubt as much in admiration at Sthiramati's elucidations as in reference to the work's length. Covering almost 1,100 densely printed pages, it is one of the longest works in the Tibetan Tengyur and must have remained the standard commentary on *Ornament of the Mahāyāna Sūtras* for many generations. The version in the Tengyur is, unfortunately, incomplete, ending abruptly and mysteriously halfway through the final chapter.

---

6. *Detailed Commentary of the Ornament of the Sūtras*, *Sūtrālaṃkāravṛttibhāṣya*, *mDo sde rgyan gyi 'grel bshad*.

In writing his own commentary on *Ornament of the Mahāyāna Sūtras*, Mipham took Sthiramati's commentary as a basis, though he admits that it is not easy to understand. While Sthiramati goes over Asaṅga's text line by line and even phrase by phrase, often with extraordinary thoroughness and clarity, without a structural outline his treatment of the text can make it difficult to see the wood for the trees, and some students may find his style excessively repetitive and long-winded ("this word means this, that phrase means such and such, this section is going to show . . ."). In order to adapt Sthiramati's commentary to the needs of his contemporaries, therefore, Mipham provided a structural outline through which readers could navigate the text without losing the general thread of Asaṅga's presentation. He then had to condense the two weighty volumes of the *Great Commentary* into a single tome while still providing an adequate level of explanation. This he achieved by cutting out many of Sthiramati's repetitive passages, as well as rephrasing some of his explanations, still leaving room for his own comments. His masterly compact syntactical structures do seem, however, to have assumed a certain familiarity on the reader's part with Sthiramati's work.

It should be remembered that in Tibet, commentaries like Mipham's were traditionally intended to serve as lecture notes, which the khenpos and instructors at the monastic colleges relied on for their detailed oral explanations, nourished by their extensive training and knowledge of the Indian commentatorial tradition, including Sthiramati's work. Only on the basis of such lectures could individual study of a text, as we are used to in the West, provide the necessary insight into the author's intentions. For our part, as translators, the task of translating Mipham's text into English would have been rendered significantly more difficult had we not been able to refer constantly to Sthiramati's commentary and, on occasion, to Vasubandhu's much shorter *Bhāṣya*.

Besides reducing the contents of the *Great Commentary* to a more manageable size, Jamgön Mipham had also to resolve a disparity between the two texts he had before him—namely, Asaṅga's root text and Sthiramati's commentary. The problem originated from their translation from Sanskrit into Tibetan. The root text had been translated in the eighth century by Śākyasiṃha and Kawa Peltsek (who had also translated Vasubandhu's *Bhāṣya*). The commentary, on the other hand, had been translated in the eleventh century by Municandra and Che Tashi, and by then the standards of translation, particularly concerning the translation of certain Sanskrit terms, had changed. The Tibetan translation of Sthiramati's commentary therefore differs from the accepted root text translation in the Tibetan Tengyur that Mipham's students would have been using, not only in its vocabulary but, in some cases, in its interpretation of the root text passages that Sthiramati quotes.

Mipham overcomes this difficulty by specifically pointing out major differences in interpretation and by indicating differences in terminology and vocabulary, providing both alternative versions. This approach helps to reveal nuances in the meaning of root passages and adds depth and clarity to the commentary. Readers who find themselves puzzled by his frequent use of alternative conjunctions between terms and phrases need to bear in mind that they can be largely accounted for by Mipham's desire to create a synthesis between these different translations. Some of these presentations of terminological alternatives found in Mipham's commentary are synonymous Tibetan translations of the Sanskrit and thus have been rendered by a single term in our English translation.

Certain comments by Mipham Rinpoche refer to specific points of Tibetan grammar or spelling. We have retained these in our translation not only for the sake of completeness but also for the benefit of readers who may wish to study the text in Tibetan. On occasion, Mipham breaks with the traditional requirement of this literary genre to include every one of the root text's words. This concerns, in particular, the repeated Tibetan connective particle *dang* used to separate items in a list, which he feels hardly needs including each time it occurs. It may be noted that in this English translation, the particle is frequently rendered by a comma.

A word-for-word translation of many of the root verses would make practically no sense to Western readers, and although no one should expect to understand *Ornament of the Mahāyāna Sūtras* without studying its commentaries, we have attempted to help the reader through the occasional addition of words taken from Jamgön Mipham's explanations. In doing so we have taken the liberty of imagining a version of the verses that might have resembled what Asaṅga himself understood of the cryptic text he received from Maitreya.

A certain amount of background knowledge is required of readers in order to understand this complex work. We have attempted to ease their task by providing footnotes and a glossary of some basic terms as well as terms that have specific meanings in the context of our translation, along with two charts that summarize the five paths and thirty-seven elements leading to enlightenment and the three worlds of cyclic existence. The bibliography includes a list of books that may help provide further information necessary to an understanding of the root text and Jamgön Mipham's commentary.

Acknowledgments

This translation was made at the request of our teachers Pema Wangyal Rinpoche and Jigme Khyentse Rinpoche, who also conferred the transmission of the root text and Mipham's commentary as well as answering some of our numerous questions. To them, first and foremost, we owe an immense debt of gratitude. We are also deeply grateful to Alak Zenkar Rinpoche, Khenchen Pema Sherab, Khenpo Sönam Tsewang, Khenpo Tenzin Norgay, and Khenpo Tseten for their unstinting help with many difficult points. In particular, we would like to thank Khenpo Shedrup Palden, who spent many hours going through almost two-thirds of the text with the principal translator, Stephen Gethin. Thanks are due too to his colleagues in the Padmakara Translation Group, John Canti, Helena Blankleder, Wulstan Fletcher, and Patrick Carré for their many helpful suggestions, and to Art Engle for sharing his knowledge of the Sanskrit text and his draft translation of Asaṅga's *Bodhisattvabhūmi*. Further suggestions were gratefully received from Claude Herail and Judith Wright who courageously read through the draft translation. As with our previous books, we are indebted to the Tsadra Foundation, without whose generosity this project would have been impossible, and to Nikko Odiseos, Casey Kemp, Tracy Davis, and the Shambhala Publications team, whose dedication and enthusiasm continue to ensure that the great classics of Buddhist literature are made available to the English-speaking world.

Despite receiving so much assistance with the translation of this difficult text, the principal translator is aware of the manifold shortcomings in his rendering of the root text and its commentary. All mistakes and misinterpretations are entirely his responsibility. Nevertheless, it is hoped that this version will in some way complement other existing and future translations, and that it may serve as a source of inspiration for anyone who wishes to emulate the extensive activities of the bodhisattvas.

THE ROOT VERSES

Ornament of the Mahāyāna Sūtras

Asaṅga's Classic Text Received from Maitreya

In Sanskrit
Mahāyāna-sūtra-alaṃkāra-nāma-kārikā

In Tibetan
Theg pa chen po mdo sde rgyan zhes bya ba'i tshig le'ur byas pa

Buddha Maitreya

I
The First Chapter

Homage to all the buddhas and bodhisattvas.

1. He who knows the meaning created a composition showing that meaning with flawless speech and phrasing
Out of natural compassion for suffering beings in order to free them from suffering.
For beings who follow the way expounded in the Supreme Vehicle,
He revealed the nature of five unexcelled metaphors:

2. The crafting of a piece of gold, the blossoming of a lotus flower,
Eating well-cooked food when starving,
Hearing good news, and opening a chest of jewels—
These illustrate the sublime delights the teachings set forth here will bring.

3. When those of natural and ornamented beauty behold themselves
Reflected in a glass, it brings them consummate delight.
So too, when the meaning of the Dharma, whose excellent words are always naturally full of virtues,
Is clarified, it brings the wise the greatest joy.

4. Like medicine that smells foul
Yet tastes quite sweet,
Know that the Dharma also has two aspects—
The meaning and the words.

5. This difficult Dharma, extensive and profound,
Is like a monarch—difficult to please;
Yet if pleased, it likewise will bestow
The riches of sublime qualities.

6. The purest, priceless jewel will not delight
   The eyes of those who cannot see its worth.
   This Dharma is the same for those who lack discernment.
   But for those who are their opposites, each will bring commensurate delight.

2

Establishing the Great Vehicle as the Buddha's Word

1. The Great Vehicle is shown to be the Buddha's word
   Because nothing adverse was predicted, it appeared at the same time,
   It is beyond the scope of intellectuals, it can be proven,
   Its existence or nonexistence depends on there being another vehicle,
   It is the antidote, and its words mean something different.

2. The vision of the buddhas is direct and clear;
   They act to keep the teachings safe;
   Their gnosis knows no impediment in terms of time;
   So they could never be indifferent.

3. Because it is incomplete and in contradiction,
   And is neither the method nor taught in that way,
   This vehicle of the listeners
   Is not what is known as the Great Vehicle.

4. Because its attitude, teachings,
   Application, support, and duration
   Conflict and are thus inferior,
   It is just that—a lesser vehicle.

5. The Great Vehicle is introduced in its own sūtras,
   And is evident in its own Vinaya;
   And because it is profound, because it is extensive,
   It does not contradict the true nature of things.

6. Intellectuals are held to be reliant, uncertain,
   Not comprehensive, confined to the relative, and wearied,
   And they relate to immature beings.
   That is why the Great Vehicle is not within their scope.

7. Because it is extensive, because it is deep,
   One is matured and nonconceptuality is realized.
   For this reason, both aspects are taught in the Great Vehicle,
   And it is this that is the means to the unsurpassable.

8. Beings' groundless fear of the Great Vehicle makes them suffer,
   Accumulating a great mass of negative karma over long periods of time.
   With no potential, evil companions, no virtue accumulated from the past, and an untrained mind,
   They are frightened by this Dharma here, and miss the great goal.

9. There is no other vehicle than the Great Vehicle, for it is utterly profound and it is concordant.
   Teaching a variety of things and continuously indicating them through numerous means,
   It does not mean exactly what is said, for the Lord's intention is exceedingly profound.
   If properly examined by the wise, this Dharma will not give them cause to fear.

10. The wise begin by listening, and on that basis they reflect;
    From proper reflection comes the gnosis whose object is the true meaning;
    From that, the noble path is reached, and thus is wisdom born.
    Without their having self-cognizant wisdom at that stage, how would they ever be convinced?

11. "I do not understand it." "Such profundities the Buddha cannot know."
    "Why should the profound be beyond the scope of intellectuals?"
    "Why will those who realize the profound meaning be liberated?"
    Such thoughts don't hold as reasons for being afraid.

12. The fact that those of lowly aspirations, of very base propensity,
    Who keep base friends for constant company
    Have no interest in this Dharma that perfectly explains
    The extensive and profound is proof of its superiority.

13. Adhering to what they have heard, they gain some discernment
    And despise anything else they hear.
    Ignorant of the rest of these boundless varied subjects,
    How could they ever be certain?

14. If one understands the words literally,
    One becomes proud and one's intellect declines.
    Rejecting the Excellent Words as a whole,
    One will be destroyed, obscured by anger toward the Dharma.

15. Negative states of mind are by nature harmful—
    It is wrong to have them even for illogical things,
    Let alone for teachings that one doubts.
    It's best, therefore, to be impartial, and thus free of fault.

3
Refuge

1. Because of four particular features by which they are classified—
   Universality, commitment, realization, and overpowering supremacy—
   Those who fully take refuge in the Three Jewels with the Supreme Vehicle in mind
   Are known as the greatest among those who have gone for refuge.

2. Why? At first it is difficult to make such a definite commitment,
   And practicing over many thousands of kalpas is hard;
   Because its accomplishment is of great benefit to beings,
   Taking refuge in this Great Vehicle is of the highest value.

3. Those who have set out to liberate all beings,
   Whose mastery is all-inclusive with regard to the vehicles and gnosis,
   And for whom nirvāṇa is the one taste of saṃsāra and peace—
   Such wise persons should be known for their universality.

4. They who, with much joy, strive for supreme enlightenment,
   Who perfectly undergo austerities without getting discouraged,
   Who will attain buddhahood and be the equal of all the buddhas—
   Those wise persons should be known for their supreme commitment.

5. They who are well born as the supreme children of the buddhas
   Have the intention, wisdom, merit, and compassion—
   The incomparable seed, mother, womb, and nurse.
   Those wise persons should be known for their supreme commitment.

6. Their bodies are fully adorned with all the marks,
   And they have gained the power to bring all beings to maturity;

They have acquired the great bliss of the buddhas, infinite and
    peaceful,
And know how to display great means in providing refuge for all
    beings.

7. On them all the buddhas have conferred the empowerment of great
       light rays,
    They have perfect, total mastery over phenomena,
    They know perfectly how to teach the Buddha's circle of disciples,
    And, establishing the precepts, they strive to correct and help.

8. Like a great minister, they penetrate the transcendent perfections,
    Constantly watch over the array of elements that lead to the great
       enlightenment,
    Perpetually hold the three secrets,
    And continually and unremittingly act for the good of many beings.

9. They have acquired a great heap of merit, supremacy in the three
       worlds, the greatest mundane happiness,
    Complete peace from the great mass of suffering, the bliss of supreme
       wisdom,
    The totality of virtues—the sublime eternal body, a mass of many
       dharmas—
    The reversal of habitual tendencies, and complete liberation from
       existence and peace.

10. The wise outshine the listeners and their followers
    On account of their virtue, which is vast; of great value; infinite,
       perpetual, and unceasing; and inexhaustible.
    That virtue—of mundane bodhisattvas, of supramundane
       bodhisattvas who bring beings to maturity,
    And of bodhisattvas who acquire mastery—is never brought to an end
       with the extinction of the aggregates.

11. Know that this refuge, the commitment of those who wish for
       buddhahood, arises out of compassion.
    It is the refuge of the wise, who thence attain omniscience and,
       undeterred by hardship, bring benefit and happiness.

For those who are certain of deliverance, it always has the qualities that all the vehicles depend on.
It is obtained formally and naturally. In these respects, it is supreme.

12. To go for refuge in this way has great value,
For those who do so will develop a host of boundless qualities.
Filled with thoughts of compassion for beings,
They spread the teachings of the peerless great and noble beings.

4
The Potential

1. Existence, supremacy, nature,
   Signs, categories of potential,
   Defects, benefits, and two analogies—
   These are the topics, each with four aspects.

2. In considering the differences in disposition,
   Interest, and practice,
   And the different results,
   The existence of different potentials can be stated with certainty.

3. Bodhisattvas' virtue is superior,
   Complete, of great purpose,
   And inexhaustible, and for these reasons
   Their potential is termed "supreme."

4. The potential is natural and evolving,
   The support and what is supported;
   It exists and does not exist.
   It should be understood as signifying "that which releases qualities."

5. Compassion prior to joining the path,
   Interest, resilience,
   And practicing perfect virtue—
   These are explained as being sure signs of the potential.

6. Fixed potential, unfixed potential,
   One that is not affected by conditions,
   And one that is affected—these in brief
   Are the four kinds of potential.

7. Habituation to defilements, evil friends,
   Poverty, and subjection to others' control—
   These in brief are threats to the potential;
   Know that there are four.

8. Should those with bodhisattva potential go to the lower realms,
   It is after a long time, and they are soon released,
   And even there they experience little suffering;
   Saddened by the plight of beings, they bring them to maturity.

9. Know that the potential is like a mine of gold,
   The source of infinite virtue,
   Endowed with gnosis and without contaminant,
   And the source, as well, of different powers.

10. Know that it is like a source of precious stones,
    For it is the cause of the great enlightenment;
    It is the source of great gnosis, of sublime concentration,
    And of benefit for many beings.

11. Some cannot but consistently follow evil ways;
    Others have completely destroyed virtuous ways.
    Some have no merit that is consistent with liberation,
    Have inferior virtue, or are deprived of the cause.

12. Without understanding it, bodhisattvas feel immense interest
    For the Great Dharma of the profound and extensive explanations
       taught in order to benefit others;
    They have the patience to practice it and will ultimately attain
       perfection, superior in two ways.
    Know that this comes from their natural possession of qualities and
       therefore from the developed potential.

13. That sublime potential is the healthy, perfect root
    That makes the tree of enlightenment grow, with its extensive
       qualities,
    Bringing bliss to beings and shading them from great misery,
    And bearing the fruit that gives oneself and others benefit and happiness.

5

The Spiritual Intent: Bodhicitta

1. Great in its enthusiasm, great in its undertaking,
   Great in its goal, and great in its outcome—
   The bodhisattva's intention
   Is the mental factor associated with two aims.

2. That spiritual intent is classified on the different levels
   In relation to interest, pure superior intention,
   Distinct full maturation,
   And likewise freedom from obscurations.

3. Its root is held to be compassion,
   Its intention is to constantly bring benefit to beings,
   Its interest concerns the teachings,
   And likewise its object is the quest for gnosis.

4. Determination to go higher is its means of progress;
   The vast vow is its support;
   Its counteragent is to wish
   And undertake to stop the path.

5. Its nature is merit and wisdom;
   Its benefit is that virtue grows;
   Its certain deliverance is held to be
   The constant practice of the transcendent perfections.

6. Its ultimate reach is the level,
   Brought about by application on each one, respectively.
   Know that with all these a bodhisattva's spiritual intent
   Is definitively established.

7. Bodhicitta arises unstably through the power of a friend,
   Or in a stable manner through the power of a cause,
   Of sources of good, of listening, and through habituation to virtue.
   This describes the bodhicitta that is revealed by someone else.

8. Born from attending the perfect buddhas
   And accumulating merit and wisdom,
   The gnosis without concepts with regard to phenomena
   Is therefore held to be sublime.

9. Because bodhisattvas have acquired realization of the sameness
   Of phenomena, of sentient beings,
   Of the deeds that benefit them, and above all of the buddha state,
   Their joy is particularly great.

10. Bodhicitta's birth, vastness,
    Associated enthusiasm, pure intention,
    Mastery of the remaining levels,
    And certain deliverance are the points that should be understood.

11. It is born from the seed of interest in the Dharma
    And from the mother of the highest transcendent perfection;
    The bliss that comes from concentration is its womb,
    And compassion is the nurse that nurtures it.

12. Bodhisattvas accomplish ten great aspirations,
    And so their bodhicitta should be known as vast.
    They are not discouraged by hardships over great lengths of time,
    And so their bodhicitta should be understood as enthusiastic.

13. Bodhisattvas realize that they are nearing enlightenment
    And they have gathered knowledge of its means,
    So their intention, you should understand, is pure.
    They master the methods of the other bodhisattva levels.

14. Keeping in mind the presentation of those levels,
    Bodhisattvas know them to be just concepts,
    And even in that regard, they have no concepts—
    Know that because of this deliverance is certain.

15. Bodhicitta should be understood to be like the earth,
    Or alternatively like fine gold,
    Or like the waxing moon;
    Or resembling fire.

16. Another way it should be known is like a great treasure,
    Or like a mine of precious jewels,
    Or like the ocean,
    Or else a diamond or mountain.

17. It is like a sovereign medicine,
    Or like a great friend;
    Or like a wishing jewel,
    Or like the sun.

18. Again, it is like the gandharva's song,
    Or understood to be like a king;
    Or also like a treasury,
    Or known to be like a busy road.

19. Know that it is like a vehicle;
    Bodhicitta is like a fount,
    Like delightful speech,
    And like the flow of a great river.

20. The bodhisattvas' bodhicitta
    Is taught as being like a cloud.
    Arouse, therefore, this spiritual intent,
    So rich in qualities, correctly and with joy.

21. Beings who lack a more worthy spiritual intent
    Are deprived of the happiness derived from having altruistic
        thoughts,
    From acquiring the corresponding means, from understanding the
        import of the great intention,
    And from seeing thatness; they thus proceed to peace alone.

22. As soon as the wise arouse the sublime intent,
    Their minds are completely restrained from committing infinite evils.
    Ever virtuous and loving, as they grow in both,
    They delight in experiencing both happiness and pain.

23. At that time, for others' sake,
    They accept hardship with no regard for their own bodies or lives.
    How could such beings do anything bad
    When others do them wrong?

24. Having realized that all things are like illusions
    And that taking birth is like going to a pleasure grove,
    In times of prosperity and times of trouble,
    They are not afraid of defilements or of suffering.

25. They delight in the ornaments that are their own qualities,
    In the festive fare of helping sentient beings,
    In the sublime location of their voluntary birth,
    And in the entertainment of miraculous displays.
    Such delights are not for those who do not embody compassion.

26. Striving for the sake of others, these lords of compassion,
    Even when in the Hell of Torment Unsurpassed, consider it to be delightful.
    How could such beings be afraid of the pains they suffer
    For the sake of others in existence?

27. Those who constantly rely on the teacher, great love,
    Are deeply pained by others' sufferings.
    When it is their duty to act for others,
    To have another person prompt them would be utterly disgraceful.

28. For those who are the highest of beings, carrying on their heads
    The great burden of sentient beings, it is not right to travel leisurely.
    Since they and other beings are fettered by all kinds of bonds,
    Their diligence should be multiplied a hundred times.

6

Practice

---

1. Great in terms of its basis, undertaking, and result—
   Such is held to be the practice of the buddhas' heirs:
   Great is their continuous commitment, great is their forbearance,
   And great is the goal that they must perfectly achieve.

2. Once they have acquired the attitude that others are equal to themselves,
   Or have a greater love for others than for themselves,
   Bodhisattvas thus think others' goals outweigh their own:
   Their own aim is that others' aims are fulfilled.

3. The compassionate ones, for the sake of others,
   Bring upon themselves the most terrible suffering;
   Ordinary folk are nothing like as ruthless
   In inflicting pain, even on their enemies.

4. Bodhisattvas correctly teach those who realize the lowest, middling,
   And supreme realities; they satisfy, induce,
   Help ascertain the meaning, ripen virtue,
   And likewise instruct, settle, and liberate minds;

5. They help accomplish extraordinary qualities;
   Likewise they bring birth in the family, predictions, empowerment,
   And the unsurpassable state of the tathāgatas' omniscience.
   In these thirteen ways they bring benefit to others.

6. Bodhisattvas give precise explanations to suit the individual,
   Are not pompous, not possessive, are learned,
   Patient, disciplined, very advanced, and inexhaustible.
   In these respects, the practice of the Conqueror's children is supreme.

7. Ordinary attached beings pursue great fear;
   Those who delight in existence have misconceived, transient bliss;
   Those who delight in peace completely pacify their own perpetuation;
   Those whose nature is compassion pacify all perpetuation,
      continuously.

8. Confused ordinary people striving for their own happiness
   Will always fail to achieve it and suffer instead.
   The steadfast, striving constantly for others' good,
   Will achieve the goals of both and thence nirvāṇa.

9. Whenever the children of the buddhas act,
   Whatever different sense objects they experience,
   Using appropriate and fitting words,
   They are actually acting to benefit beings.

10. The wise do not place any blame on those people
    Whose minds are ever helpless in the face of evil.
    "Without wanting to, they act ungratefully."
    Thus their compassion for ordinary people grows more and more.

11. With this practice, bodhisattvas outshine all existence and beings;
    They possess the highest peace,
    Increase the host of multifarious qualities,
    And, with loving thoughts, constantly gather beings.

7

THATNESS

---

1. It is not existent nor nonexistent, not the same nor different;
   Not produced nor destroyed, it will not diminish
   Nor increase; it cannot be purified
   Yet becomes perfectly pure—these are the characteristics of the ultimate.

2. The belief in a self does not constitute a self as such,
   And nor do the aggregates which abide in evil; their characteristics are not the same.
   Nor is there a self that is other than these two. It is produced erroneously.
   Freedom, therefore, is a simple error coming to an end.

3. How is it that beings rely on a mere delusion
   And do not realize the continuous nature of suffering?
   Unaware, although they are aware, they suffer, although there is no suffering;
   The nature of phenomena does not exist as such.

4. How, when beings can directly perceive things arising dependently,
   Do they believe in things being created by something else?
   Why do they not see what is there, yet see what is not there?
   What sort of darkness is that?

5. On the ultimate level, there is not the slightest difference
   Between peace and birth.
   Nevertheless, those who practice virtue, it is taught,
   Will bring an end to birth and thus gain peace.

6. Bodhisattvas, going beyond infinite merit and wisdom,
   Perfectly gather the accumulations, and then
   Reflect and gain perfect certainty with regard to the Dharma.
   As a result, they realize objects to be the products of expression.

7. Once they see that things are merely expressions,
   They dwell in the truth that it is mind alone that appears as those things.
   After that they gain direct realization
   Of the expanse of reality, free of the characteristics of duality.

8. From intellectual understanding that there is nothing other than the mind,
   They then realize that neither does the mind exist.
   Once the wise have seen that both do not exist,
   They abide in the expanse of reality devoid of those.

9. The power of nonconceptual gnosis in the wise
   Constantly extends to everything in equal measure,
   And clears away the dense jungle of the faults they bear,
   Like a universal antidote removing poison.

10. Settling their intelligence in the expanse of reality,
    The root of the excellent presentation, the sacred Dharma the capable ones have taught,
    The steadfast with that stream of mindfulness and knowledge that things are mere concepts
    Swiftly traverse the ocean of excellent qualities.

8

Powers

1. Beings' births, speech, minds, virtue and nonvirtue,
   Abodes, and deliverance—these are manifestly perceived.
   Such knowledge—all-pervading, of different kinds,
   And unimpeded—defines the powers of those who attain stability.

2. Having attained the utterly pure fourth dhyāna,
   And through its being imbued with nonconceptual gnosis,
   By keeping in mind the modes of application,
   They will achieve the supreme accomplishment of powers.

3. They dwell perpetually in the matchless, vast abode
   Of the noble, celestial, and pure states;
   Journeying in all directions, they make perfect offerings to the buddhas
   And inspire sentient beings to practice purity.

4. They see all universes, with their formation, their destruction,
   And their sentient beings, as magical illusions.
   Possessed of powers, they exhibit them
   As desired in apparent and varied forms.

5. Emitting rays of light to those who in the lower realms
   Are racked with pain, they take them to the higher realms.
   Rattling Māra's fine and lofty mansion,
   They terrify the demons and their gang.

6. In the midst of a supreme gathering,
   They demonstrate displays of boundless concentrations.
   And by manifesting in art, through birth, and as supreme manifestations,
   They act perpetually for beings' good.

7. Because of their mastery of the different kinds of gnosis,
   They display buddha fields as desired, and thus achieve purity.
   By proclaiming the name "Buddha" wherever the name "Buddha" is unknown,
   They send beings to other worlds.

8. Like birds whose wings are fully grown,
   They have the ability to bring beings to maturity;
   From the Buddha they receive high praise,
   And people take their words to heart.

9. Six kinds of preternatural knowledge, three kinds of knowledge,
   Eight perfect freedoms, and likewise eight kinds of perceptual domination,
   The ten powers of perceptual limitlessness, and boundless concentrations—
   These are the powers of those who have attained stability.

10. The wise who have acquired supreme power
    Give helpless beings their own independence;
    Constantly helping others is their sole joy;
    Steadfast as lions, they continue their activities within existence.

9

Full Maturation

1. Delight, faith, peace, compassion,
   Forbearance, a sharp mind, and power,
   Immunity to beguilement, and possession of the branches—
   These in great measure are the signs of a fully matured child of the buddhas.

2. The three (the sublime companion and the others),
   The utmost diligence, perfect consummation, and holding together the supreme teachings,
   With the purpose of maintaining the sacred Dharma on a vast scale—
   These are held to be the characteristics of perfect maturation in the compassionate.

3. Knowledge of good qualities, unshakable faith,
   Speedy attainment of concentration, and the experience of the result,
   With the purpose of creating confidence in the Teacher—
   These are held to be characteristics of perfect maturation in the buddhas' heirs.

4. Full restraint, the elimination of defiling thoughts,
   Freedom from obstacles, and delight in virtue,
   With the purpose of dispelling defilements in the buddhas' heirs—
   These are held to be characteristics of perfect maturation.

5. Being naturally kindhearted, seeing the sufferings of others,
   Completely eschewing inferior attitudes,
   Progressing, and taking birth as the best of beings—
   These are the signs of having fully matured compassion for others.

6. Natural steadiness, habituation through analysis,
   The ability to bear cold and other extreme sufferings,
   And progress and delight in virtue—
   These are held to be characteristics of fully matured forbearance.

7. Pure maturation, unforgetting recollection of what one has heard,
   Superior recognition of what is well explained and what is badly spoken,
   And readiness for the birth of great intelligence—
   These are the characteristics of having a fully matured, extremely sharp mind.

8. Developing the two elements through the two kinds of virtue,
   And thus becoming perfectly ready for the result to occur,
   Accomplishing everything one wishes, and becoming the greatest of beings—
   These are the characteristics of having fully matured attainment of power.

9. An attitude toward the excellent Dharma born of reasoned analysis,
   Constant freedom from obstacles created by demons,
   The acquisition of superiority, and refutation of opponents—
   These are the characteristics of having fully matured immunity to beguilement.

10. Having an accumulation of virtue, a suitable support for practicing diligence,
    And delight in perfect seclusion and virtue—
    These are the characteristics of perfectly matured possession of the branches
    For the children of the buddhas.

11. Since they are themselves mature in terms of these nine elements,
    They are fit to bring others to full maturity.
    Those in whom the stream of qualities is growing
    Are always the supreme friends of beings.

12. We say that boils that drip are "ripe,"
    And food when it is fit to eat.
    So too, it is taught that maturity in such individuals
    Refers to removal and employment with regard to two factors.

13. Bodhisattvas' maturation of living beings is explained as
    Maturation through riddance, and likewise full maturation,
    Perfect maturation, congruent maturation, excellent maturation,
    Maturation through realization, continuous maturation, and
       progressive maturation.

14. Unlike the buddhas' heirs, who, with their wish to help,
    Devote themselves to bringing all beings here to maturity,
    Fathers, mothers, friends, and relatives
    Never treat their children and friends so well.

15. Unlike loving bodhisattvas, who act in order to bring happiness and
       benefit,
    Caring affectionately for other sentient beings,
    Ordinary people feel no kindness for themselves,
    Let alone for others who depend on them.

16. There is nothing, including their bodies and possessions,
    That bodhisattvas will not give to others.
    They mature others by bringing them a double benefit,
    And, giving equally, they never tire of the virtues of generosity.

17. Establishing others in that which is steadfast, natural,
    Totally nonviolent, delightful, and careful,
    They benefit in two respects and mature others
    Through the continuity of the ripened effects and the qualities similar
       to the cause.

18. Thinking of others who harm them as benefactors,
    They are perfectly patient even with those who do them violent harm.
    With their knowledge of methods and their endurance of harm,
    They lead those who harm them to truly take up virtue.

19. The buddhas' heirs, relying on the utmost diligence,
    Perfectly mature hosts of sentient beings.
    If only for the sake of another's single virtuous thought,
    They will not lose heart even after ten billion kalpas.

20. Having attained unsurpassable mastery of the mind,
    They definitively overcome any desire for veneration from others.
    Causing others to aspire to the sublime teachings,
    They make their virtue perfectly increase.

21. Certain of the intended meaning of thatness,
    They completely clarify beings' doubts.
    Because of that, through their respect for the victors' teachings,
    They increase their own and others' virtuous qualities.

22. Thus bodhisattvas, through compassion, train all beings,
    Setting them in the higher realms or in the three virtues,
    In modest, supreme, and middling ways,
    For as long as the world exists.

10

Enlightenment

---

1. Through their undergoing countless hundreds of austerities,
   Accumulating countless stores of virtue
   For countless lengths of time,
   And exhausting countless obscurations,

2. Omniscience is attained,
   Free of all contaminating obscurations;
   As when a chest of jewels is opened,
   Buddhahood is perfectly revealed.

3. With awesome austerities undertaken, many hundred trials endured, and every merit gathered,
   The longest kalpas traversed, all obscurations of a being brought to an end,
   And with the subtlest veils on the levels destroyed, buddhahood is gained,
   As if a chest of jewels with magical powers were opened.

4. All phenomena are the enlightened state;
   No phenomena whatsoever exist.
   Although it is the nature of positive qualities,
   It cannot be expressed in such terms.

5. Because it is the cause of the jewel-like Dharma,
   It is like a mine of jewels.
   Because it is the cause of the crop of virtue,
   It is likened to a cloud.

6. The buddha state possesses all phenomena, or alternatively is devoid of all phenomena:
Because it gives rise to the extensive and vast jewel-like Dharma, it is like a mine of precious things;
Because it showers on beings the great rain of the well-explained, inexhaustible Dharma,
Thus causing living creatures' crop of virtue to flourish, it is like a cloud.

7. Constantly, against the whole host of defilements,
Against all kinds of negative actions,
And even aging and death,
The enlightened state gives complete protection.

8. Because it protects from every kind of trouble,
From the lower realms, from wrong paths,
From the view of the transitory composite, and from lesser vehicles,
It is the supreme refuge.

9. The enlightened state is the supreme, incomparable refuge.
For those who are subject to different kinds of danger, to the transitory composite and all other wrong views, to vehicles,
To the sufferings of the many forms of lower rebirth, and to ways that are not the proper means,
It gives protection from birth and death, and from all defilements and deeds.

10. It comprises the buddha bodies in which the enlightened qualities are fully complete,
The knowledge for training beings through the sacred Dharma,
And transcendent compassion for all beings—
That enlightened state is held to be the supreme refuge here.

11. Because, to the very end of the universe,
It wards off sentient beings' every difficulty
And brings them all that is perfect,
The enlightened state is held to be the great refuge.

12. The complete destruction of the seeds of defilement-related and
    cognitive obscurations, constantly present for great lengths of time,
    Eliminated through all kinds of extensive means,
    And the attainment of the transformed state possessed of the sublime
    qualities of virtue
    Is buddhahood, attained by the path of the gnosis of utterly pure
    nonconceptuality and immense scope.

13. Dwelling in that state, the Tathāgata,
    As if seated on the lofty king of mountains, watches over beings.
    If he has compassion even for those who delight in peace,
    Need one mention his compassion for other beings who delight in
    existence?

14. In that state, there is engagement, perfect engagement, nonengagement,
    Disengagement, perpetual engagement, dual and nondual engagement,
    Similarity, superiority, and universality.
    This is held to be the fully transformed state of the tathāgatas.

15. Just as space is accepted as being forever omnipresent,
    So too is enlightenment considered always omnipresent.
    Just as space is present in every kind of form,
    So too is enlightenment omnipresent in the host of sentient beings.

16. Just as in a broken pail
    The moon's reflection will not appear,
    To evil beings, likewise,
    The Buddha's form will not appear.

17. Just as a fire will either blaze
    Or else die down,
    Likewise, know that the buddhas too
    Appear or disappear.

18. Just as drums may sound
    Without their being struck,
    The teachings appear
    Without the buddhas deliberately teaching.

19. Just as the precious gem effortlessly
    Shines with its own light,
    So too, the buddhas, without thinking,
    Assuredly demonstrate their deeds.

20. Just as in space the activities
    Of the universe appear unceasingly,
    So too, in the untainted expanse of reality,
    The victors' deeds continue without end.

21. Just as all the time in space
    Things perish and things come into being,
    So too, in the untainted expanse of reality,
    The buddhas' activities grow and decrease.

22. Though no different before or after,
    Suchness free of all contaminating obscurations
    Is held to be the enlightened state;
    Neither is it pure nor is it impure.

23. When emptiness is completely purified,
    The sublime nature of no-self is attained;
    Thus the buddhas obtain the pure nature
    And they will therefore become the self of the Great Being.

24. It is not that the Buddha, therefore, exists,
    Nor can it be said that he does not exist.
    When questioned in such terms, it's said,
    The Buddha did not answer.

25. Just as it is for the fading of heat in an iron
    Or the disappearance of floaters in the eye,
    One cannot talk about existence or nonexistence
    In relation to the Buddha's mind and gnosis.

26. Because the buddhas in the untainted expanse of reality
    Are incorporeal, like the sky,
    And because they follow on from their previous physical forms,
    They are neither single nor multiple.

27. With regard to the strengths and other buddha qualities,
    Enlightenment is like a mine of precious gems.
    For the crop of beings' virtue,
    It is held to be like a great cloud.

28. Because merit and wisdom are perfectly complete,
    It is likened to a full moon.
    Because of its illuminating gnosis,
    It is likened to a great sun.

29. Just as the infinite rays of light
    Issuing from the sun's orb are intermingled
    And always perform the same functions,
    Lighting up the whole world,

30. Likewise, the infinite buddhas
    In the untainted expanse are considered to merge together,
    Performing their deeds in unison
    And making the light of gnosis shine.

31. When the sun gives forth a single ray of light,
    All the rays of light come forth.
    From this analogy, know that, likewise,
    The gnosis of all the buddhas manifests.

32. Just as the sun's rays
    Have no sense of "mine" in where they go,
    The gnosis of the buddhas too
    Has no sense of "mine" when it is applied.

33. Like a single ray of sunlight
    Making everything visible to beings,
    The buddhas' gnosis at once throws light
    On everything that can be known.

34. Just as the light of the sun's rays
    Is considered to be obscured by clouds,
    The gnosis of the buddhas
    Is obscured by sentient beings' faults.

35. Just as knots tied in a piece of cloth
    Produce a patchwork when it is dyed,
    On account of the force that propels it,
    The gnosis of liberation manifests more or less brightly.

36. To describe these profound points—
    The characteristics, way of abiding, and activities
    Of the buddhas in the uncontaminated expanse of reality—
    Would be to paint a picture in the sky.

37. Suchness is present in all, and not different,
    Yet purified it is the Tathāgata.
    Thus it is that all beings
    Are imbued with its essence.

38. The attainments of the listeners
    Outshine those of the worldly.
    Those on the level of the solitary realizers
    Outshine those of the listeners.

39. These cannot approach even a fraction
    Of the attainments of the bodhisattvas.
    And those do not compare with even a fraction
    Of the attainments of the tathāgatas.

40. For whom they are applied, and where,
    And how, to what extent, and for what length of time—
    On such grounds are the attainments of the buddhas
    Held to be inconceivable and immeasurable.

41. When the five sense organs are transformed,
    They perceive all the sense objects, and there arise
    Twelve hundred all-perceiving qualities,
    Which are obtained as the supreme attainment.

42. When the mind is transformed,
    It functions consistently with that attainment,
    And supreme attainment is obtained
    With regard to the uncontaminated nonconceptual gnosis.

43. When the apprehending subjects associated with the sense objects are transformed,
These are enjoyed in any way one wishes,
And to show this, supreme attainment is obtained
With regard to the purification of realms.

44. When conceptual thought is transformed,
Supreme attainment is obtained
Regarding gnosis and all activities,
At all times and without impediment.

45. When the support is transformed,
Supreme attainment is obtained
Of the nondwelling nirvāṇa,
The uncontaminated state of buddhahood.

46. When sexual activity is transformed,
Supreme attainment is obtained
In terms of dwelling in the buddhas' bliss
And being free of the defilements that relate to seeing women.

47. When the perception of space is transformed,
Supreme attainment is obtained
With regard to acquiring all the riches one wishes,
To moving unimpededly, and to taking different forms.

48. Thus, in the uncontaminated state of buddhahood
There are said to be infinite transformations,
With infinite attainments
Accomplishing inconceivable activities.

49. Here, in all the regions of the universe, by means of the victors' excellent explanations,
Those in the world who are growing in virtue proceed to the highest purity,
While those without a store of merit proceed to the sublime state of growth in virtue.
Thus the immature proceed ever to maturity, but there is never no one left.

50. Thus the steadfast in different worlds are always and forever attaining
    The great enlightenment, so hard to attain, marvelous, and endowed
        with sublime qualities,
    Eternal, stable, and a refuge for the unprotected.
    How amazing that is, and yet not at all amazing, for they have
        practiced the excellent way.

51. A buddha simultaneously displays a variety of deeds—
    In some places turning the Dharma Wheel in many hundreds of ways,
        in some taking birth, in others not appearing,
    In some showing different styles of birth, in some every kind of
        awakening, and in some the parinirvāṇa,
    And yet all these are demonstrated without moving from that state.

52. The buddhas never purposefully think, "I matured those beings,"
    Or "I will mature those," or "Now I'm maturing these."
    Yet constantly in all directions through the three approaches,
    They will bring beings to perfect maturity through virtuous practice.

53. Just as the sun, with its many rays shining in all directions throughout
        the universe,
    Effortlessly ripens all the numerous crops,
    The sun of the Dharma, with the universal light of the teachings
        bringing perfect peace,
    Brings sentient beings everywhere to maturity.

54. Just as from a single lamp many countless, infinite lamps
    Are lit and yet it does not go out,
    From one mature being many countless, infinite maturations
    Occur, yet that being is never spent.

55. Just as the great ocean can never have enough water
    Nor does it grow larger from the many great rivers flowing into it,
    The realm of enlightenment never has enough of the constant and
        unceasing
    Stream of pure beings entering it and grows no bigger—this is the
        greatest wonder in this world.

56. Its nature is the suchness of all phenomena
    Purified of the two obscurations.
    Its nature is inexhaustible power
    With regard to knowing the object and focusing on that knowledge.

57. Through knowledge of suchness and meditation,
    Using all kinds of means, enlightenment occurs
    And bears inexhaustible fruit,
    Forever giving rise to the two for all that lives.

58. Active in the skillful application
    Of manifestation through body, speech, and mind,
    Enlightenment possesses infinite concentrations,
    Powers of retention, and the two.

59. It is distinguished as the nature,
    The perfect enjoyment of the teachings, and the manifestation.
    All this describes the perfectly pure
    Expanse of reality of the enlightened state.

60. The bodies of the buddhas are classified as
    The natural body, the body of perfect enjoyment,
    And another, the body of manifestation.
    The first is the basis for the other two.

61. In all worlds the body of perfect enjoyment
    Varies on account of its retinues,
    Buddha fields, names, bodies,
    Enjoyment of the teachings, and activities.

62. The natural body is uniform,
    Subtle, and related to the latter body;
    It manifests enjoyments however they may be desired
    And so is held to be the cause of the wealth of perfect enjoyment.

63. The boundless manifestations of the enlightened state
    Are held to be the manifestation body.
    The fulfillment of the twofold goal
    Rests entirely on the two.

64. By constantly displaying artistic expression,
    Birth, great enlightenment, and the parinirvāṇa,
    The Buddha's manifestation bodies
    Are the great means for liberating beings.

65. Know that the bodies of the buddhas
    Are included in the three buddha bodies.
    The three bodies are taught as being the fulfillments
    Of one's own and others' goals along with their basis.

66. In terms of basis, intention,
    And activities, they are the same.
    In terms of nature, incessancy,
    And continuity, they are eternal.

67. There are only the unmoving mirrorlike gnosis
    And the three kinds of gnosis based on it—
    Equalizing, all-discerning,
    And all-accomplishing.

68. Mirrorlike gnosis is devoid of a sense of possession,
    Utterly impartial, and ever present;
    It is not ignorant with regard to all things that can be known,
    But never directed toward them.

69. Because it is the cause of all kinds of gnosis,
    It is like a great mine of gnosis.
    It is the enjoyment body itself,
    For the other kinds of gnosis appear as reflections in it.

70. The gnosis of equality is held to be
    Pure as a result of its cultivation with respect to sentient beings.
    To have entered the nondwelling peace
    Is said to be the gnosis of equality.

71. Constantly possessed of love
    And great compassion,
    It visibly reveals to sentient beings
    The Buddha's form according to their aspirations.

72. All-discerning gnosis
    Is never obstructed as to all there is to know;
    It is like a treasure house
    Of concentrations and powers of retention.

73. To the disciples in the retinue
    It displays all kinds of riches
    And makes the rain of the Great Dharma pour down,
    Removing all their doubts.

74. All-accomplishing gnosis
    Accomplishes beings' welfare
    In all worlds with multifarious manifestations,
    Infinite and inconceivable.

75. Know that those manifestations of the buddhas,
    Forever performing their deeds,
    Are inconceivable in every way—
    In their diversity, numbers, and realms.

76. Because of holding the teachings, because of an attitude of equanimity,
    Because of teaching the true Dharma,
    And because of accomplishing tasks,
    The four kinds of gnosis will properly arise.

77. Because there are different potentials, because there is benefit,
    Because of fulfillment, and because there is no beginning,
    The Buddha is not single; but, because in the uncontaminated state
    There are no distinctions, neither is he multiple.

78. That which does not exist
    Is held to be the sublime existence.
    Not conceptualizing in any way
    Is held to be the sublime conceptualization.

79. Meditation that does not look at aspects
    Is held to be the sublime meditation.
    The attainment of those who do not look
    To attain anything is also held to be sublime.

80. Those who have views concerning height, distance, attributes,
And their own superiority in terms of diligence—
Of these proud bodhisattvas
It is said, "They are far from enlightenment."

81. Those who regard all the aforementioned views
As mere conceptual constructs—
Of these bodhisattvas who are free from concepts
It is said, "They will attain enlightenment."

82. The rivers that have not reached the sea
Have different locations, different streams,
Little water, with different activities,
Providing for the needs of tiny creatures living in them.

83. Yet when they reach the ocean,
They all have one location, their water a single vast expanse,
With the same activity, an immense and constant source
For myriad marine creatures, providing all they need.

84. The steadfast who have not reached enlightenment
Have different supports, different intellects,
Little realization, and different activities;
They benefit and constantly provide for only a few beings.

85. Once buddhahood is reached, they all
Have but one support and a single great realization;
Their deeds blend as one, and eternally and abundantly
They fulfill the needs of vast hosts of beings.

86. Thus, because the enlightened state has incomparable virtuous qualities,
Because it is the cause of benefit and happiness,
And because it is the inexhaustible source of the highest bliss and virtue,
The wise should adopt the virtuous intention to attain enlightenment.

II
Interest

1. The following is a recapitulation:
   Introduction, establishing, refuge, potential,
   Likewise, spiritual intent,
   One's own and others' benefit, thatness,
   Powers, full maturation, and enlightenment.

2. Interest may be arisen, nonarisen, subjective, and objective,
   Received from a friend, natural, mistaken,
   Unmistaken, manifest, or otherwise nonmanifest,
   Produced from sound, investigative, and viewing,

3. Expropriable, mixed, unadulterated by counteragents,
   Inferior, vast, obscured, and unobscured,
   Diligent, nondiligent, with accumulation, and without,
   Firmly engaged, and advanced.

4. Abundant failure to keep faith in mind,
   Laziness, disturbed practice,
   Bad company, feeble merit,
   And keeping incorrect ideas in mind,

5. Carelessness, and little learning,
   Being satisfied with little learning and reflection,
   Pride in calm alone, and likewise, it is held,
   Failure to habituate,

6. Lack of disenchantment, and likewise disenchantment,
   Being obscured, lack of diligence,
   And failure to accumulate merit—
   These are recognized as obstacles to interest.

7. Great merit, absence of regret,
   Mental bliss, and great bliss,
   No wastage, stability,
   And similarly enhancement,

8. Direct realization of the nature of phenomena,
   The supreme attainment of one's own and others' goals,
   And quick preternatural knowledge—
   These are the benefits of interest.

9. The interest of the desirous is like a dog,
   That of those with concentration is like a turtle,
   That of those who achieve their own goal is like a servant,
   And that of those who achieve others' goal is like a king.

10. Just as a dog is constantly tormented by hunger and never satisfied,
    A turtle in the water remains completely withdrawn,
    A servant moves around, their body always cowed in fear,
    And a king governs his dominion by his edicts,

11. Similarly, you should always distinguish among the various kinds of interest
    Of those who are distracted, who remain withdrawn, who benefit themselves, and who bring benefit to others.
    The steadfast who properly understand that interest in the Great Vehicle is best
    Will, in this context, forever seek that same interest in it.

12. Sentient beings born as humans,
    In infinite numbers, in every instant,
    Attain perfect enlightenment,
    So do not give in to losing heart.

13. Just as merit grows
    From giving food to others
    But not from eating food oneself,
    The greater merit of which the sūtras speak

14. Is acquired from teaching
    The way of altruistic aims
    And not from teaching
    The way that is based on selfish goals.

15. And thus, if the wise constantly increase their interest
    In the vast doctrine of the great noble ones,
    They will gain immense and uninterrupted merit, their interest will grow,
    And they will attain buddhahood with all its boundless qualities.

12

Thorough Investigation

1. The scriptural collections are summarized as two or three,
   The reasons for which are held to be ninefold.
   Through habitual inclination, understanding, pacification,
   And full realization, they bring one to perfect liberation.

2. Sūtra, Abhidharma, and Vinaya
   Are considered to comprise, in brief, four points.
   The wise who know these
   Will obtain omniscience.

3. Because they relate the settings, nature,
   Subjects, and meanings, they are the "sūtras."
   Because it makes increasingly manifest, does so repeatedly,
   Overpowers, and brings understanding, it is the Abhidharma.

4. Because there are downfalls, and there is their source,
   Their recovery, and certain deliverance,
   And with regard to the individual, the edict,
   Detailed description, and definition, it is the Vinaya.

5. The point is held to be
   The teachings, the inner, the outer, and both.
   Two are discovered through two processes,
   And both by nonconceptuality.

6. Because, by means of mental verbalization, one has faith in the
      meaning as it is taught,
   Because one understands that the things that appear as objects
   Do so on account of such verbalization,
   And because the mind dwells on the nominal—

7. With the three wisdoms of listening and so on,
   One will discover the point of the teachings.
   Discovering the other three points
   Fully depends on those teachings, which were mentioned earlier.

8. The three families, the performance of deeds,
   Having an impaired or unimpaired support,
   Maintaining interest, and furthermore
   Acting with intense keenness;

9. Inferior and complete supports
   Which are verbal and nonverbal;
   Equivalent to knowledge,
   Having the cause and nature of yoga;

10. Considering things in combination
    And considering them separately,
    In five ways and seven;
    Fivefold complete knowledge of this;

11. Objects associated with meditation—
    Fourfold and thirty-sevenfold;
    The nature of the two paths;
    Two benefits, receiving,

12. Application, mastery,
    The lesser, and the extensive—
    These aspects of yogis' attentiveness
    Are held to include everything.

13. Delusion as to what is forever free of duality, its basis, and thatness
    (Utterly inexpressible and beyond elaboration)
    Should be recognized, eliminated, and, while accepted as intrinsically
       uncontaminated, completely purified.
    Thatness is held to be pure, free of defilements, like the sky, gold,
       and water.

14. Apart from that, there's not the slightest thing in beings that exists,
    Yet beings are all completely ignorant of this—their minds
    Reject what does exist and cling to what does not.
    Such is the enormity of the world's confusion.

15. Of false imagination,
    We say it is like a magical illusion;
    And of dualistic delusion,
    We say it is like the forms in a magical illusion.

16. In the same way that there is nothing in an illusion,
    We accept the ultimate truth.
    And in the same way that it is perceived,
    We accept the relative truth.

17. Just as when the illusions are not there
    And their causes are clearly seen,
    When transformation takes place,
    One perceives the false imagination.

18. Undeceived people
    Use the illusion's causes as they wish.
    So too, those who are diligent in the precepts, undeluded,
    Experience the transformed state as they please.

19. Though they are there in appearance,
    It is not that they really exist.
    Thus we say that in magical illusions and the like
    Things exist and do not exist.

20. It is not that what is there does not exist,
    Nor that what is not there exists.
    In magical illusions and the like
    We do not distinguish between their existence and nonexistence.

21. Similarly, if dualistic appearances exist there,
    It is not that they exist substantially.
    Thus, for forms and the like
    We say that they exist and do not exist.

22. It is not that what is there does not exist,
    Nor that what is not there does exist.
    With regard to forms and the like
    We say that there is no distinction between their existing and not existing.

23. It is in order to refute the extremes
    Of superimposition and repudiation,
    And in order to halt those who take the lower vehicles,
    That this has been asserted.

24. The cause of delusion and delusion itself
    Are held to be the perception of the material
    And the perception of the immaterial.
    Because the one does not exist, neither can the other.

25. Because the apprehension of the form of an elephant in a show of magic
    Is an illusion, we speak of two things.
    Although there are not two things in the same way that they appear there,
    There is the perception of duality.

26. Because the apprehension of the forms of skeletons
    Is an illusion, we speak of two things.
    Although there are not two things in the same way that they appear there,
    There is the perception of duality.

27. All phenomena that characterize delusion
    Exist like that and do not exist like that.
    There is no contradiction in their existing and not existing,
    So they are like magical illusions that are there but not there.

28. All phenomena related to the antidotes
    Do not exist like that and do exist like that.
    Because they do not exist as they seem, they are devoid of characteristics:
    They too are shown to be like magical illusions.

29. As in the defeat of an illusory king
    By another illusory king,
    Bodhisattvas, who have seen phenomena,
    Are without conceit.

30. The buddhas, sublimely awakened, said in their respective teachings
    That compounded phenomena should be understood as being like
       magical illusions, like dreams,
    Mirages, reflections, optical illusions, echoes, the reflection of the
       moon on water, and magical creations,
    Considering the six, the six, the two, the two groups of six, and each of
       the three.

31. Incorrect thinking, both incorrect and not incorrect,
    Nonconceptuality,
    And both nonconceptual and not nonconceptual—
    These are said to include all knowable phenomena.

32. From their own realm the two appear,
    Ignorance and defilements arise, and with them,
    The concepts that lead to birth,
    And this occurs in the complete absence of two substantial entities.

33. As a result of acquiring the particular point of the teachings
    And abiding in the mind's own expanse,
    Thatness manifests, free of dualistic appearances,
    As with a hide and an arrow.

34. The mind is held to appear dualistically,
    And in that manner it appears as attachment and the rest,
    Or else it manifests as faith and other qualities;
    But there are no defiling or virtuous phenomena.

35. The mind appears as various things
    And operates in a variety of forms.
    These appearances in the mind exist and do not exist,
    And are not therefore phenomenal.

36. In order to benefit sentient beings,
    The buddhas gave perfect explanations
    By classifying the exemplary subject,
    The essential quality, and the means of demonstration.

37. The mind and its views,
    Their condition, and the unchanging—
    These, in short, comprise the exemplary subject,
    Of which there are countless different kinds.

38. Its cause (the notion of names as things),
    The habitual tendencies to conceive such notions,
    And the consequent appearance of objects—
    Such is the imputed reality.

39. The appearance of names and objects
    Corresponding to objects and names,
    Which is the cause of false imagination,
    Is the imputed reality.

40. Having threefold appearance whose nature is the object,
    And threefold appearance whose nature is the subject,
    False imagination
    Is the dependent reality.

41. Nonexistence, existence,
    The sameness of existence and nonexistence,
    Not peace, peace, and freedom from concepts—
    Such is the fully present reality.

42. Having focused on the teachings that are consistent with the cause,
    One is properly attentive,
    One abides in the expanse of the mind,
    And one sees that objects exist and do not exist.

43. On that level, everything becomes sameness,
    The noble potential, utterly uncontaminated,
    Similar but superior,
    Neither diminishing nor increasing.

44. When the seeds are transformed,
    The perceptions of place, sense objects, and body
    Are transformed. That untainted expanse
    Is the support pervading all.

45. When the mind, apprehenders, and conceptualization
    Are transformed, there are four kinds of mastery—
    In nonconceptuality, fields,
    Gnosis, and activities.

46. These four kinds of mastery are gained
    On three levels—Immovable and the others.
    On one of these levels, two are gained,
    And on each of the others, one is gained.

47. The wise will understand that all existence is devoid of both kinds of self,
    And knowing the sameness of that state, they approach suchness in terms of mental apprehension.
    Then, as they keep the mind on mind-only, that perception too will disappear.
    This nonappearance is liberation, sublimely free of references.

48. When the foundation—accumulation—and the development are present,
    One will see that everything is just a name.
    And seeing that seeing of just a name,
    One then no longer sees even that.

49. The mind with its negative tendencies,
    Caught by the noose of belief in a self,
    Becomes totally immersed.
    By settling inward, we hold, it turns away.

50. Because things do not exist of themselves, and they do not exist as their own nature,
    And because they do not dwell in their own nature,
    And because they do not exist as they are apprehended,
    They are held to be devoid of intrinsic existence.

51. Each proposition being the basis for subsequent ones,
    Absence of intrinsic existence
    Establishes absence of production, absence of cessation,
    Primordial peace, and natural nirvāṇa.

52. With regard to a beginning, a same thing, otherness,
    Its own definition, itself, transformation,
    Defilement, and extraordinary knowledge,
    Acceptance that phenomena are unborn has been explained.

53. Because of similarity with regard to the path, no-self,
    And liberation, because of different potentials,
    Because of achieving both aspirations, because of manifestations,
    And because it is the ultimate, there is a single vehicle.

54. In order to draw some disciples on to it
    And to keep others properly on it,
    The perfect buddhas
    Teach uncertain disciples a single vehicle.

55. Listeners of unfixed potential are of two kinds:
    Those who have seen the truth of their vehicle and those who have not.
    Those who have seen the truth,
    Whether or not rid of attachment, are inferior.

56. Both have attained the noble path,
    And by transforming that attainment,
    They possess an inconceivable
    Birth of transformation in existence.

57. One, by the power of prayers of aspiration,
    Attains accomplishment by being born;
    The other, because of being a nonreturner,
    Attains accomplishment through manifestation.

58. Since these two, from repetition,
    Continue to think of themselves,
    They delight in nirvāṇa,
    So realization is slow.

59. Those who have not attained the goal
    Take birth when there is no Buddha and,
    Yearning to manifest, strive for concentration,
    By which means they will attain supreme enlightenment.

60. Without being diligent in the five sciences,
    Even the highest of noble beings will not attain omniscience.
    Therefore, in order to subjugate others, to care for them,
    And to know all things themselves, they are diligent in these.

61. Joy from considering the cause,
    Mindfulness of the support,
    The wish for a shared result,
    And a yearning for a similar enlightenment;

62. Joy on account of the four powers,
    True indefatigability,
    And the four aspects of practice with regard to
    Incompatible traits and their antidotes;

63. Clear faith, correct reception,
    A longing to give to others,
    Armor, prayer,
    True joy, and a sense of duty;

64. The highest genuine enthusiasm
    For obtaining power in the six perfections,
    For full maturation, making offerings,
    And following a teacher; and affection;

65. Shame and regret for having practiced badly
    Or not at all, delighting in the object,
    The notion of despair as an enemy,
    Introducing, and expressive intelligence;

66. Generosity and so forth being the support
    Of perfect enlightenment (not Īśvara and the others),
    Distinguishing the faults in incompatible traits
    And the qualities in their antidotes;

67. Joy from the memory of accumulation,
    Seeing the great point,
    And the wish for yoga, for nonconceptuality,
    For retention, and for encountering;

68. The obtainment of power for eliminating
    The seven kinds of wrong belief,
    And the four thoughts
    Of what is extraordinary and what is not;

69. Impartiality toward sentient beings,
    Being seen as a great being,
    Hoping for the recompense of good qualities in others,
    A threefold aspiration, and continuity;

70. In order to accomplish the Buddha's teaching,
    The intention to not fall short;
    Sadness with regard to beings who fail in that,
    And delight with regard to those who flourish;

71. Not having faith in fake meditation
    And having faith in the authentic,
    Attentiveness to refusal,
    Pleasure from predictions and certainty;

72. The intention to practice with a view to future lives,
    Looking to equality,
    And, on account of engagement in the highest Dharma,
    The conviction of one's own greatness—

73. Keeping in mind the virtue that results
    From the ten transcendent perfections
    Makes the potential within a bodhisattva
    Constantly unfold and grow.

74. Developing, possessed of superior mentality, and great—
    Such is held to be the thorough investigation of the steadfast.
    Their investigation is accompanied by factors to be eliminated,
    Is free of such factors, and is mastered.

75. Bodhisattvas' investigation is said to be
    Lacking the buddha body, body-associated, body-attained,
    And body-complete; and also with much pride,
    With subtle pride, and without pride.

76. The Dharma of the steadfast is the source
    Of qualities material and immaterial—
    The marks, and likewise freedom from disease—
    Of mastery in preternatural knowledge, and inexhaustibility.

77. Children of the buddhas should completely abandon
    The concepts of existence and nonexistence, of superimposition and negation,
    The concepts of unity and multiplicity, of intrinsic nature and particularity,
    And the concepts of clinging to names and objects as real.

78. Those who are thus intelligent and virtuous, relying on intense diligence,
    Correctly investigate the nature of the two truths.
    Thereby, they will forever become the teachers of beings
    And like an ocean be filled with good qualities.

13

Teaching the Dharma

1. If steadfast bodhisattvas joyously and forever give away immense gifts to beings who suffer—
The lives and riches they have won with such great difficulty and yet devoid of essence—
Need one mention their unstintingly giving of the vast Dharma that benefits beings in every way,
That is found with no great difficulty, and even when given away entirely grows inexhaustibly?

2. Because it is to be known by oneself, Lord Buddha did not teach the Dharma;
Yet with the breath of his teachings, rationally explained, the embodiment of compassion, like a python,
Draws beings onto the path, setting them perfectly in the mouth of total peace,
Utterly pure, vast, common, and inexhaustible.

3. Consequently, no practitioner's meditation is pointless,
And thus neither are the teachings of the sugatas pointless.
If one could see the meaning simply by listening, there would be no point in meditating,
And if one could practice meditation without having listened, there would be no point in teaching.

4. The teaching of sublime bodhisattvas
Occurs through transmission, realization, and mastery:
From the mouth, from form of every kind,
And from space it issues forth.

5. Extensive, doubt-dispelling,
   Acceptable, and indicative of both natures—
   This, a bodhisattva's teaching,
   Is said to be perfect.

6. The Dharma teaching of a sublime bodhisattva
   Is gentle, free of conceit, tireless,
   Clear, diversified, rational,
   Intelligible, disinterested, and universal.

7. The bodhisattvas' words are not faint,
   They are pleasing, well expounded, and conventional;
   They are appropriate, free of material motives,
   Moderate, and likewise abundant.

8. Because they indicate, and likewise explain,
   Correspond to the vehicle, are pleasurable,
   Conventional, and appropriate,
   Lead to certain deliverance, and are concordant—

9. The syllables uttered by the sublime bodhisattvas
   Are described, in short, as perfect.
   The speech of the sugatas is infinite;
   With sixty qualities, it is inconceivable.

10. With words, solid reasoning,
    Brief introductions, detailed explanations,
    The clearing of doubts, and much repetition,
    For those who understand when merely told the title or else from detailed presentations,

11. The buddhas teach, and their teaching
    Is pure, free of the three spheres;
    Know that it is devoid
    Of eight faults:

12. Laziness, incomprehensibility,
    Failure to set a time, lack of certainty,
    Failure to resolve doubts,
    Failure to stabilize freedom from doubt,

13. Discouragement, and stinginess—
    These are held to be faults in discourse.
    Because it is free of these,
    The buddhas' teaching is unexcelled.

14. Because it engenders faith, joy, and understanding,
    This Dharma is virtuous;
    Having twofold meaning and easy to retain,
    It teaches pure activity with four good qualities.

15. Having nothing in common with others,
    Completing the elimination of the defilements of the three worlds,
    Naturally pure, and decontaminating—
    Such is held to be pure activity with four good qualities.

16. Indirect teachings given for the purpose of introducing,
    Indirect teachings on reality,
    Indirect teachings connected with remedial methods,
    And indirect teachings expressed through metaphors—

17. These are the four kinds of indirect teachings,
    Given when the buddhas have in mind the listeners, reality,
    And likewise the suppression of faults
    And the expression of the profound.

18. Know that implied teachings are of four kinds,
    Implying sameness, another sense,
    And similarly another time,
    And with people's attitudes in mind.

19. Contempt for the Buddha and for the Dharma,
    Laziness, complacency,
    Indulgence in pride and in attachment,
    Remorse, and rejection by those of unfixed potential—

20. As the remedy to these obscurations in beings,
    The Buddha taught the Supreme Vehicle.
    With it, all the faults obstructing them
    Will be removed.

21. The best of wise beings who apply themselves
    To holding the *Two Stanzas*,
    By means of the words or meaning,
    Will acquire ten kinds of good qualities:

22. The fullest increase of their potential,
    The greatest happiness at the moment of death,
    Rebirth wherever they wish,
    And in all their lives, recollection of their past lives,

23. Meetings with the buddhas,
    Hearing the Supreme Vehicle from them,
    Endowment with interest and understanding,
    Acquisition of the two doors, and the swift attainment of enlightenment.

24. Thus, bodhisattvas with good intellects, who are tireless,
    Loving, renowned, and expert in the right procedures,
    Are excellent exponents. In teaching,
    They are brightly shining suns in the midst of humankind.

14

Practicing the Dharma

1. The wise, neither wrong
   Nor right with regard to the two,
   Fully know, by means of the three,
   The two kinds of no-self—individual and phenomenal.

2. Then, those who know the meaning
   Realize that all teachings are like a boat
   And give up being content with listening.
   Thus they are said to know the way.

3. With the knowledge of an ordinary person,
   They thus realize the two,
   And then, in order to perfect that knowledge,
   They practice the consistent way.

4. After that, on the first level,
   As the equals of all bodhisattvas in that state,
   They acquire the supramundane,
   Unsurpassable gnosis.

5. Having fully extinguished
   All the defilements that need to be eliminated by seeing,
   In order to eliminate cognitive obscurations,
   They apply themselves to meditation.

6. By the combined practice of gnosis,
   Conceptual and nonconceptual,
   On the remaining levels they continue
   To cultivate consistent realization.

7. The place in which the wise practice
   Is full of virtues—well supplied,
   A good place, a healthy place,
   With good company, and comfortable for yoga.

8. Recognize that learned bodhisattvas
   Who have seen the truth, who are skilled in discourse,
   Full of love, and never tire
   Are great and holy beings.

9. Excellent aim, excellent reliance,
   Excellent method, determination to be free,
   And excellent application—with these,
   One is said to have the right orientation.

10. A happy mind, and birth in freedom,
    Absence of disease, a capacity for concentration,
    And thorough discernment—
    All these result from merit gathered in past lives.

11. Besides the expanse of reality,
    There is nothing that exists.
    For this reason, the buddhas have it in mind
    That certain deliverance is attachment and the like.

12. Besides the expanse of reality,
    There is nothing that exists.
    So this, the wise accept, was the intended implication
    Of the teaching on defilement.

13. Because they properly approach
    Attachment and the like as suchness,
    They will be completely free from them:
    Thus they are delivered from them by means of them.

14. Even the most terrible sufferings of dwelling in the hell realms
    For beings' sake do not harm the buddhas' heirs at all.

The various good thoughts of those who follow lower vehicles,
Thinking of the defects and virtues of existence and peace, are harmful to the wise.

15. For the wise, staying in the hells does not forever
Prevent their vast and uncontaminated enlightenment.
Thinking of the complete coolth of benefiting oneself in the other vehicles
Brings great happiness, but it is an obstacle.

16. Phenomena do not exist yet are perceived;
Defilement does not exist and yet is purified;
Know that they are like magical illusions and so forth,
And likewise that they are like space.

17. Just as on a well-drawn picture
There are no different planes, yet there seem to be,
To the false imagination, duality,
Though never there, appears in different ways.

18. When muddy water becomes clear,
Its clarity is not something produced from the muddy state,
But rather the removal of the dirt contaminating it.
So it is with the purity of one's own mind.

19. The mind is held to be eternally natural clear light;
It is coarsened by adventitious faults.
The mind is ultimate reality, and there is no other mind but clear light.
We speak of this as the nature of mind.

20. Bodhisattvas feel for sentient beings
A heartfelt love as great as that
Felt for an only child—
Their constant wish is to bring them help.

21. Because it brings benefit to sentient beings,
    The fondness bodhisattvas feel does not become a downfall.
    But hatred in them will always violate
    And act against all beings.

22. Like doves who love their young the most,
    Staying with them and holding them close,
    With not the slightest place for anger,
    Are those whose hearts are full of love for beings, their children.

23. Because they love, there's never room for rage.
    Because they pacify, malice is out of place.
    Because they benefit, they never think deceitfully.
    Because they comfort, they'll never terrify.

24. Like the sick taking efficacious medicine,
    They enter saṃsāra.
    Like doctors for those who are ill,
    Bodhisattvas practice for sentient beings.

25. As with servants who will not work,
    Likewise do they treat themselves.
    As with merchants and their wares,
    Likewise do they use their pleasures.

26. As with dyers and their cloth,
    Likewise do they work on karmic acts.
    As with fathers and their infant sons,
    Likewise do they never injure beings.

27. As when one rubs two sticks to make a fire,
    Likewise do they practice hard and all the time.
    Like a trustworthy person,
    They practice their incomplete superior concentration.

28. In the same way as magicians,
    They practice with wisdom regarding phenomena.
    All these are held to show the how and the what
    Of the practice of the bodhisattvas.

29. Thus, armed with constant diligence on a vast scale,
   They make the greatest efforts to bring about a twofold maturation.
   Gradually, with supreme, nonconceptual intelligence devoid of contaminants,
   They proceed to the unsurpassable accomplishment.

15
Instructions and Follow-Up Teachings

1. After a measureless kalpa, there is certain deliverance,
   And faith grows ever greater.
   Like rivers flowing into the ocean,
   Virtuous activities lead to true completion.

2. The conquerors' heirs who have thus gathered the accumulations
   Are pure from the outset.
   They have perfect understanding and a virtuous mind;
   They apply themselves to meditation.

3. At that time, bodhisattvas in the stream of Dharma
   Will receive from the buddhas
   Extensive oral instructions
   For achieving a vast degree of sustained calm and gnosis.

4. Next, those who are diligent in the precepts begin by
   Contemplating just the names of the sūtras
   And other scriptures
   That clearly explain nonduality.

5. After that, step by step,
   They classify and analyze the contents.
   In each, they properly
   Examine their meaning.

6. Having become certain of the meaning,
   They summarize all the teachings.
   In order to achieve the point of those teachings,
   They then proceed to form an aspiration.

7. Continuously, with mental expressions,
   They should research and examine the teachings
   And analyze them with the attentiveness of the single taste
   In which expression is absent.

8. The summarization of the scriptures in their titles
   Should be understood as being the path of sustained calm.
   The path of profound insight
   Should be understood as the analysis of their meaning.

9. Know that the path of their union
   Is a combination of these.
   A dull mind has to be kept focused,
   And wildness must be subdued.

10. Then, when there is evenness with regard to the object,
    Bodhisattvas settle in equanimity.
    In all this, constancy
    And devotion are to be applied.

11. Once they direct the mind at the object,
    They should not be distracted from the continuity of that.
    They should quickly realize when they are distracted
    And draw the mind back onto the object.

12. The wise should gather
    The mind inward more and more.
    Then, because they see the virtues of this,
    They tame the mind in concentration.

13. Because they see the fault in distraction,
    They should pacify the disinclination to concentrate.
    Similarly, they should pacify covetousness
    And unhappiness, if these arise.

14. Then, those who are diligent in the precepts,
    By deliberately acting on their states of mind,
    Achieve natural concentration.
    From getting used to that, they no longer make deliberate effort.

15. Then, they gain great fitness
    Of the body and mind,
    And are known to have attentiveness.
    Having fostered it,

16. By progressing further,
    They attain the states of the actual concentrations.
    From striving for preternatural knowledge,
    They are purified and become supremely fit.

17. By using the preternatural powers
    Gained through concentration,
    In order to venerate and listen to
    Countless buddhas,
    They travel to different worlds.

18. Thus they venerate infinite buddhas
    For infinite kalpas.
    And because they have venerated them,
    Their minds become supremely fit.

19. And so they will obtain
    Five prelusive benefits.
    For those who are to become unsurpassable,
    Perfectly pure vessels,

20. All the negative tendencies of the body
    Will be exhausted in each instant.
    And all the time, the mind and body
    Will throughout be perfectly fit.

21. They will realize uninterruptedly
    The whole light of the Dharma.
    The signs of perfect purity
    Will be clearly seen without checking.

22. Similarly, in order to perfect the body of truth
    And attain perfect purity,
    The wise take hold of their causes,
    Constantly and in all situations.

23. Next, bodhisattvas like these
    Remain in evenness, and by doing so,
    No longer see any objects
    As anything other than mental expressions.

24. In order to enhance the light of Dharma,
    The steadfast apply themselves fully with diligence.
    The light of Dharma grows greater
    And they will remain in the state of mind-only.

25. Then, everything that appears as a sense object
    Will clearly appear as the mind.
    At that time, the distracting apprehension
    Of those things will be eliminated.

26. After that, only the distractions
    In the form of an apprehending subject are left.
    At that time, they quickly reach
    The concentration "with no obstruction."

27. Immediately after that,
    Distractions in the form of a subject are eliminated.
    The above are to be understood as being
    The successive stages of warmth and so forth.

28. Subsequently they acquire
    Unsurpassable supramundane gnosis,
    Nonconceptual, uncontaminated,
    And free of the two kinds of grasping.

29. This, their transformation,
    Is held to be the first level.
    Over a measureless kalpa
    They have become utterly pure.

30. Having gained perfect realization
    Of the expanse of reality, sameness,
    At that time they acquire the awareness
    That all beings are the same as themselves, all the time.

31. With regard to sentient beings, they are even-minded
    Concerning their lack of self, their suffering, their goal,
    And in not hoping for reward;
    With regard to other bodhisattvas, they are alike.

32. All things compounded in the three worlds
    Are false imagination.
    This they see by dint of gnosis,
    Utterly pure and free of duality.

33. By seeing the nature of nonexistence,
    Bodhisattvas are freed from the obscurations to be eliminated.
    Consequently, at that time they are said
    To have attained the path of seeing.

34. Because they know the emptiness of what does not exist,
    And likewise the emptiness of what does exist,
    And they know the natural emptiness,
    They are described as knowing emptiness.

35. The basis of absence of attributes
    Is said to be the complete exhaustion of concepts;
    The basis of absence of expectancy
    Is false imagination.

36. For the buddhas' children
    All the various elements leading to enlightenment
    Are said to be acquired forever
    Simultaneously with the path of seeing.

37. Knowing with wisdom that beings are simply compounded,
    And that the nonexistent self is simply the unfolding of suffering,
    They have eliminated the view of a useless self
    And acquire the view of the "great self," which is highly useful.

38. Such bodhisattvas, while not believing in a self, know that belief;
    While not suffering, they suffer terribly.
    They never hope for anything in return for all the benefit they bring,
    Any more than they would seek a recompense for doing themselves
        some good.

39. Through supreme liberation, their minds are free,
    Yet they are bound for ages by unending chains.
    Even if they see no end to suffering,
    They apply themselves and truly set to work.

40. The worldly cannot bear the pains they have in just one life,
    Let alone the sum of others' sufferings for the duration of the world—
    Never could they imagine such a thing.
    Bodhisattvas are quite the opposite of them.

41. The joy and love those bodhisattvas feel for beings,
    Their application, their never losing heart—
    These are the greatest wonders in all worlds;
    And yet, since bodhisattvas and beings are the same, there's not so
        much to marvel at.

42. Next, bodhisattvas
    Meditate on the two kinds of gnosis
    On the remaining levels, the path of meditation,
    And thereby fully purify themselves.

43. Nonconceptual gnosis
    Refines the qualities of buddhahood;
    The other, distinguishing gnosis,
    Brings sentient beings to maturity.

44. By completing two measureless kalpas
    They reach the end of the path of meditation;
    Having attained the final stage of meditation,
    Bodhisattvas receive empowerment.

45. Having gained the vajra-like concentration
That no concept can destroy,
They attain the ultimate transformation,
The unsurpassable level—

46. The absence of all contaminating obscurations,
The perfect accomplishment, from that abode,
Of deeds to benefit all beings,
And the perfect knowledge of all things.

47. Thus, from their always beholding the capable ones, who are difficult to see,
And from their unequaled listening, clear faith arises, and by dint of this,
Their minds will always be utterly content.
How could this not be highly beneficial?

48. To those who dwell at the door of the Dharma
The tathāgatas are always present, giving advice.
As if pulled by the hair, they are forcefully dragged
From the thicket of evil and brought to enlightenment.

49. The buddhas praise those who constantly apply themselves to their own fulfillment
And rebuke those who act wrongly. To the best of beings who devote themselves to stability and discernment,
The victors at this time properly explain all that hinders or favors progress in the practice of this, the sugatas' doctrine—
Things to be avoided and those to be embraced.

50. Purified by their vision, awakened with nonconceptuality,
They outshine the whole world,
Perpetually dispelling the greatest darkness
And shining on beings like huge suns rising.

51. Thus forever filled with the good that they have gathered,
And having constantly received extensive instructions from the buddhas,
Supreme bodhisattvas will acquire immense concentration of mind
And travel to the far shore of the ocean of virtues.

16

Skillful Activity

---

1. In summary, bodhisattvas have much interest,
   Investigate the teachings, explain them,
   Practice accordingly, and receive
   The perfect instructions and follow-up teachings.

2. Just as the base upon which the forests, beings,
   Mountains, and rivers rest is always the earth,
   So too the base for generosity and other forms of virtue
   Is said to always be the three activities of the wise.

3. Bodhisattvas, whose very nature is great diligence
   In all kinds of arduous deeds, which take many kalpas to complete,
   Will never be dispirited by their tasks here,
   Their physical, verbal, and mental activities.

4. Just as those who wish themselves good physically avoid
   Poison, weapons, thunderbolts, and enemies,
   Bodhisattvas direct their three kinds of activities
   Away from the two lower vehicles.

5. Continually free of concepts, they do not look at the three aspects
   Of the doer, the object, and the doing.
   So, because they are fully imbued with such skillful means,
   Their deeds are pure and transcend the infinitely good.

17

Transcendent Perfections and Ways of Attracting Disciples

1. One should know the number of perfections, their characteristics, order,
Etymology, aspects of the training,
Their classifications, their all-inclusiveness, the factors incompatible with them,
Their good qualities, and how their interrelationships are determined.

2. The transcendent perfections result in higher rebirths
With abundant wealth, a perfect body, a perfect entourage, and perfect achievement;
And also perpetual immunity to defilements
And absence of error in everything one does.

3. Applying themselves assiduously to the welfare of beings,
Bodhisattvas give, refrain from harm, and act patiently.
With concentration, liberation, and the basis of these,
They entirely achieve their own good.

4. They relieve the destitute, avoid all forms of harm,
Bear injury, are not discouraged by their task,
Make others happy, and give clear explanations.
Thus they fulfill the aims of others, and this is their own aim.

5. Bodhisattvas take no pleasure in possessions,
Have deep respect, are indefatigable in two respects,
Train spiritually, and are free of concepts—
The entire Great Vehicle amounts to this.

6. The path of nonattachment to sense objects,
    The path of restraint from the distraction of acquiring them,
    And the paths of never abandoning beings, of increasing,
    And again, of purifying obscurations—

7. These six transcendent perfections
    The Buddha has clearly explained in terms of the three trainings:
    Three perfections in the first, two in the last two,
    And one included in all three.

8. Generosity counters its opposite,
    Is endowed with nonconceptual gnosis,
    Fulfills all wishes,
    And ripens beings in three ways.

9. Discipline counters its opposite,
    Is endowed with nonconceptual gnosis,
    Fulfills all wishes,
    And ripens beings in three ways.

10. Patience counters its opposite,
    Is endowed with nonconceptual gnosis,
    Fulfills all wishes,
    And ripens beings in three ways.

11. Diligence counters its opposite,
    Is endowed with nonconceptual gnosis,
    Fulfills all wishes,
    And ripens beings in three ways.

12. Concentration counters its opposite,
    Is endowed with nonconceptual gnosis,
    Fulfills all wishes,
    And ripens beings in three ways.

13. Wisdom counters its opposite,
    Is endowed with nonconceptual gnosis,
    Fulfills all wishes,
    And ripens beings in three ways.

14. Because the next one arises in dependence on the preceding one,
    And each is superior to the former one,
    And because each is more subtle than the former one,
    They are taught one after the other.

15. One perfection banishes poverty,
    One obtains coolth, one puts an end to anger,
    One connects one to what is supreme, one keeps the mind focused,
    And one knows the ultimate—thus are they explained.

16. For all of them the training is described
    As relying on the substance,
    And similarly on attentiveness,
    On one's attitude, pure method, and mastery.

17. It is the giving-away of gifts,
    Springs from reliance on a rooted attitude,
    Results in a perfect body and riches,
    Cares for both oneself and others, leads to completion,

18. Is endowed with freedom from stinginess,
    And comprises the gifts of Dharma, of material gifts, and of freedom from fear:
    Knowing that such is generosity,
    The wise accomplish it perfectly.

19. It has six branches, springs from one's being imbued with the wish for ultimate peace,
    Bestows happy states and a stable mind,
    Supports, stills, and frees from fear,
    Brings about the accumulation of merit,

20. Is symbolically designated or naturally obtained,
    And is present in those who keep vows:
    Knowing that such is discipline,
    The wise accomplish it perfectly.

21. It endures, ignores, and understands,
    Springs from compassion and dependence on the Dharma,
    Is described as having five benefits,
    Brings benefit to both oneself and others,

22. Is fully endowed as the greatest of austerities,
    And is held to be of the above three kinds:
    Knowing that such is patience,
    The wise accomplish it perfectly.

23. It is the true delight in virtue,
    Springs from interest and determination,
    Increases qualities such as mindfulness,
    Is the antidote to defilement,

24. Is possessed of qualities such as the absence of attachment,
    And is of seven kinds:
    Knowing that such is diligence,
    The wise accomplish it perfectly.

25. It is the settling of the mind within,
    Springs from mindfulness and diligence,
    Gives rise to bliss,
    Brings mastery of preternatural powers and the ways of abiding,

26. Is the foremost of all practices,
    And is threefold for those who have it:
    Knowing that such is concentration,
    The wise accomplish it perfectly.

27. It correctly discerns knowable phenomena,
    Depends on concentration,
    Gives complete freedom from defilement,
    Provides sustenance through superior knowledge and perfect explanations,

28. Is highest of all the teachings,
    And is threefold for those who have it:
    Knowing that such is wisdom,
    The wise accomplish it perfectly.

29. All virtuous practices are to be understood
As distracted, meditational, or both.
These three each include
Two transcendent perfections.

30. In their generosity, bodhisattvas are
Unattached, unattached, unattached,
Quite without attachment,
Unattached, unattached, and unattached.

31. In their discipline, bodhisattvas are
Unattached, unattached, unattached,
Quite without attachment,
Unattached, unattached, and unattached.

32. In their patience, bodhisattvas are
Unattached, unattached, unattached,
Quite without attachment,
Unattached, unattached, and unattached.

33. In their diligence, bodhisattvas are
Unattached, unattached, unattached,
Quite without attachment,
Unattached, unattached, and unattached.

34. In their concentration, bodhisattvas are
Unattached, unattached, unattached,
Quite without attachment,
Unattached, unattached, and unattached.

35. In their wisdom, bodhisattvas are
Unattached, unattached, unattached,
Quite without attachment,
Unattached, unattached, and unattached.

36. The buddhas' children, when meeting those in need, will always give them something, even their own lives.
They do so out of compassion, with no hope of reward from others, and no interest in any desired result.
With that same generosity, they bring all beings to the three levels of enlightenment.
Since their generosity is imbued with gnosis, it remains unspent throughout all worlds.

37. The buddhas' children constantly undertake the three kinds of discipline whose nature is restraint and diligence.
They do not crave the higher realms and, even if they actually attain them, are not attached to such states.
With that discipline, they bring all beings to the three levels of enlightenment.
Since their discipline is imbued with gnosis, it remains unspent throughout all worlds.

38. The buddhas' children endure the most arduous tasks and all the harm that people do to them.
This is not because they seek the higher realms or are powerless, nor out of fear, nor with an eye for their own benefit.
With their unexcelled patience, they bring all beings to the three levels of enlightenment.
Since their patience is imbued with gnosis, it remains unspent throughout all worlds.

39. The buddhas' children do things with incomparable diligence, armor-like and applied,
Destroying their own and others' defilements and causing them to attain supreme enlightenment.
Through that very diligence, they bring all beings to the three levels of enlightenment.
Since their diligence is imbued with gnosis, it remains unspent throughout all worlds.

40. The buddhas' children, endowed with concentration, have
accomplished all kinds of concentrative states.
They who have attained the highest bliss of concentration
compassionately take lower births.
Through that very concentration, they bring all beings to the three
levels of enlightenment.
Since their concentration is imbued with gnosis, it remains unspent
throughout all worlds.

41. The buddhas' children have complete knowledge of everything there is
to know and of its nature.
They feel no attachment to nirvāṇa, not to mention to saṃsāra.
With that very gnosis they bring all beings to the three levels of
enlightenment.
Since their gnosis envelops all beings, it remains unspent throughout
all worlds.

42. Vast, disinterested,
Immensely beneficial, and inexhaustible—
Such are the four qualities that should be known
Of all the perfections such as generosity.

43. In seeing and being fulfilled, beggars
Are delighted, sad, and full of hope.
But even more so are the loving ones who give,
So they will always outshine those who beg.

44. Out of love, they constantly give to sentient beings
Their lives, possessions, and spouses,
And are overjoyed to do so.
How would they not maintain abstinence with regard to these?

45. Noble beings have no regard for themselves, are impartial,
Fearless, and full of love,
So how could they, who give everything away,
Do others harm and tell them lies?

46. Those with love who wish to help impartially,
    Who greatly fear that others might have pain,
    Who apply their minds to taming sentient beings,
    Have cast afar the three misdeeds of speech.

47. Those who've given everything away, who are compassionate
    And know full well that things arise dependently—
    How could they indulge
    In all the mind's defilements?

48. When those with love are harmed
    Or suffer helping others,
    They always find delight, thinking of the benefit.
    What, then, is there for them to bear?

49. They have no notion of other beings as others,
    And constant love for others more than for themselves;
    For beings, they undertake austerities, and so for those with loving tenderness
    Diligence is not hard, even if extremely difficult.

50. The concentration of three kinds of beings is held to have but little bliss:
    It is selfish bliss, with clinging, that loses its strength,
    Or is exhausted, and is associated with ignorance.
    A bodhisattva's concentration is just the opposite.

51. There is wisdom like one who fumbles in the dark,
    And wisdom like a light that has been concealed.
    These bear no comparison with the knowledge of the compassionate ones,
    The third wisdom, which is like the rays of the sun.

52. In terms of the individual, substance,
    Reason, dedication,
    Cause, gnosis, fields,
    And reliance, their generosity is supreme.

53. In terms of the individual, substance,
    Reason, dedication,
    Cause, gnosis, field,
    And reliance, their discipline is supreme.

54. In terms of the individual, substance,
    Reason, dedication,
    Cause, gnosis, field,
    And reliance, their patience is supreme.

55. In terms of the individual, substance,
    Reason, dedication,
    Cause, gnosis, field,
    And reliance, their diligence is supreme.

56. In terms of the individual, substance,
    Reason, dedication,
    Cause, gnosis, field,
    And reliance, their concentration is supreme.

57. In terms of the individual, substance,
    Reason, dedication,
    Cause, gnosis, field,
    And reliance, their wisdom is supreme.

58. Bodhisattvas feel the greatest joy
    When their generosity makes a single being happy,
    Even if it has brought them many kalpas of difficulty.
    No need is there to mention what they feel when this is not the case.

59. Because living beings desire wealth,
    The steadfast give them the very things they want.
    While humans seek riches for the sake of their bodies,
    Those very bodies the steadfast give away a hundred times.

60. When even giving their bodies brings them no mental pain,
    What need is there to mention lesser gifts?
    In this they are beyond the world, and from it they derive the greatest joy—
    The highest of all the joys experienced by those beyond the world.

61. The wise, by giving all, derive delight
    From the pleasure of those who were longing for those gifts.
    The beggars feel no similar delight
    When they receive the alms they begged.

62. The wise, impoverished by giving all they own,
    Think themselves enriched.
    The beggars, now the owners of all that wealth,
    Have no such feeling that they're rich.

63. The wise, when properly satisfying the needy with excellent gifts,
    Think of them as great benefactors.
    The beggars, once they have received great quantities of wealth,
    Have no such gratitude to the giver for what they've gained.

64. Just as they enjoy delicious fruit from a tree by the road,
    Beings partake greatly of a bodhisattva's riches,
    Using them unhesitatingly as they please.
    Yet no one but a bodhisattva has such wealth—the joy of generosity.

65. Diligence, it has been well taught, should be known
    For its importance, the reason for its importance, its different functions,
    Different aspects, categories in terms of individuals,
    And categories as the antidote to the four kinds of obstacles.

66. Of all the host of virtues, diligence is the best.
    When one relies on it, virtue is subsequently achieved.
    Through diligence, one instantly achieves the greatest happiness
    And all the qualities of this world and beyond.

67. Through diligence, one obtains the enjoyments one desires in saṃsāra.
    Through diligence, one gains changeable pure states.
    Through diligence, one transcends the transitory composite and is freed.
    Through diligence, one attains supreme enlightenment and buddhahood.

68. Furthermore, there is one diligence that leads to decrease and increase,
    One that has power over liberation, another that eliminates counteragents,
    One that realizes thatness, one that completely transforms,
    And diligence of great significance, which is variously defined.

69. First comes the diligence of virtue,
    Then the diligence of proper application,
    And the diligence of not being disheartened, overpowered, or content.
    All these aspects the buddhas have explained.

70. As for those people diligent in the three vehicles,
    Their attitudes and wisdom vary from limited through to vast,
    So there are further forms of diligence—lesser, middling, and best—
    These are applied to the lesser goal and the greater goal.

71. Those with diligence are never short of possessions.
    Those with diligence are not overwhelmed by defilements.
    Those with diligence are not overcome by loss of heart.
    Those with diligence are never short of attainments.

72. Because they are mutually inclusive, because of their subdivisions,
    Because of their very nature, and because they are causal,
    You should know that the six transcendent perfections
    Are determined as being in every way interrelated.

73. Generosity is considered to be the same.
    Teaching them, encouraging others to practice them,
    And practicing them oneself are termed
    Agreeable speech, helpful activity, and consistent behavior.

74. Since they are the methods for bringing beings benefit,
    For making them comprehend, for making them engage,
    And similarly for making them continue the practice,
    Know that there are four ways of attracting disciples.

75. The first turns beings into proper receptacles,
    The second makes them interested,
    The third makes them practice,
    And the fourth helps them train and purify themselves.

76. The four ways of attracting disciples
    Comprise two groups—
    Material and Dharma,
    Of which the latter includes the reference Dharma.

77. Know that they are categorized
    Into lesser, middling, and best ways of attracting,
    And the mostly unsuccessful, mostly successful,
    And entirely successful.

78. Those who are attracting a following
    Properly depend on these methods.
    This accomplishes all the goals of everyone
    And is highly praised as the best of means.

79. Attracting disciples in the past,
    In the future, and in the present
    Are all by these same means, which therefore constitute
    The path for ripening sentient beings.

80. Thus those whose minds are ever unattached to wealth,
    Who are peaceful, restrained, perfectly diligent, settled,
    And are free of concepts with regard to existence and objects
    Are they who gather a host of sentient beings.

18

Offering, Reliance, and Boundless Attitudes

1. In order to complete the two accumulations,
   Those whose minds are full of faith
   Offer to the buddhas robes and so forth,
   In both real and imagined ways.

2. The offering of one who has made the prayer
   That the coming of the Buddha be beneficial,
   Offered without conceptualizing the three spheres,
   Is a complete offering to the Buddha.

3. The different kinds of offerings include
   Bringing to maturity limitless sentient beings,
   Offering material things, and making offerings with the mind:
   Devotion, aspiration,

4. Compassion, patient forbearance,
   Correct practice,
   Focusing on the basics, realization,
   Liberation, and also suchness.

5. Offering has been explained
   In terms of the reason, dedication,
   Support, substance, cause,
   Gnosis, fields, and location.

6. Offerings are described in terms of
   Cause and result; self and others;
   Lesser and greater offerings,
   Which are two categories related to things acquired,

7. Veneration, and practice;
   Offerings made with pride and those without;
   And they are classified in terms of application,
   Transmigration, and aspiration.

8. Offerings made to the buddhas mentally are best,
   That is, with interest in the Dharma, the right mental state, and mastery,
   Supported by nonconceptual means,
   And in a single identity with all.

9. Reliance has been taught in terms of
   The support, basics, specific points,
   Dedication, cause, gnosis,
   Fields, and state.

10. Take as a teacher someone disciplined, peaceful, totally at peace,
    Possessed of superior qualities, diligence, and knowledge of the texts;
    Who has full realization, is skilled in explanation,
    Full of love, and indefatigable.

11. Follow the spiritual master with respect,
    With belongings, service, and practice.
    In accordance with those principles, the wise approach the spiritual master
    With a wish to know the Dharma, from time to time, respectfully.

12. With no desire for veneration and wealth,
    They dedicate their reliance for the sake of accomplishment.
    The steadfast practice all that they've been taught,
    And that is what makes the master truly pleased.

13. Having become learned in the three vehicles and having realized them,
    They strive hard to accomplish their own vehicle.
    The purpose is to ripen countless beings,
    And as well to train in pure fields.

14. They should rely fully on a spiritual master in order to possess the qualities
    For enjoying their share of the Dharma and not material gain.
    The wise follow a spiritual master by cause and effect,
    In progressing from the door of Dharma and outwardly,

15. By listening and with the yoga of mind,
    And with pride and without.
    The wise follow a spiritual master in terms of transmigration,
    Application, and aspiration.

16. Following the sublime spiritual master mentally is best—
    That is, with interest in the Dharma, the right mental state, and mastery,
    Supported by nonconceptual means,
    And in a single identity with all.

17. The pure states of the steadfast have abandoned countering agents,
    Are endowed with nonconceptual gnosis,
    Are applied to three kinds of objects,
    And bring sentient beings to maturity.

18. These attitudes of the steadfast are applied to
    Those who wish for happiness, those tormented by suffering,
    Those who are happy, and those with defilements,
    And to the treatises on these, and to their suchness.

19. It is because of suchness that love is nonconceptual,
    And because of its purity through attaining peace,
    Because of the two kinds of action,
    And because defilements have been exhausted.

20. These attitudes are termed wavering, unwavering,
    Savored with attachment, and not savored.
    The attitudes of bodhisattvas remain
    Unwavering and free of attachment.

21. In those who are, by nature, not concentrated,
    Who are lesser, middling, or on inferior levels,
    Whose motivation is inferior, or who have pride,
    Their love and so forth is inferior; in others it is superior.

22. The wise who abide forever in these pure states
    Are born in the world of desire.
    By means of them, they complete the accumulations
    And bring beings to maturity.

23. In all their lives, they will never part from pure states
    And will be free from their counteragents.
    Even when they are not paying heed,
    They will never be overwhelmed by circumstances.

24. Bodhisattvas who have the wish to harm,
    Who are cruel, unappreciative,
    And full of malice, attachment, and desire,
    Are affected by many kinds of negative consequences.

25. Because of defilements, they destroy themselves,
    Destroy sentient beings, and destroy their discipline.
    These degenerate beings have few resources
    And are disparaged by protectors and the Teacher alike.

26. Subject to arguments and unpleasant gossip,
    In other lives they will be born deprived of freedom;
    Since they will lose what they have acquired and what they have not,
    They'll suffer greatly in their minds.

27. All these faults never occur
    In those who abide properly in love and the other attitudes.
    Free of defilements, for the sake of sentient beings,
    They never abandon saṃsāra.

28. The thoughts of love and so forth
    That the Buddha's children have for sentient beings
    No being can feel, even for
    Their one and only perfect child.

29. Their compassion touches sentient beings
    Who are ablaze, who are overpowered by enemies,
    Who are oppressed by suffering or obscured by darkness,
    Who tread the hardest path,

30. Who are weighed down by great chains,
    Who are addicted to poisoned food,
    Who have completely lost the way,
    Who are following mistaken paths, and who are weak.

31. The rejection of harm, the seeds of supreme enlightenment,
    The creation of happiness and acceptance of pain,
    The cause for everything they desire, and the yielding of compassion
        itself—
    For the Buddha's children who rely on these qualities, enlightenment
        is not far off.

32. Those with compassion and the highest intelligence,
    Knowing that everything in saṃsāra is suffering
    And devoid of self, will never be discouraged,
    Nor will they be much troubled by its faults.

33. Those with tenderness, seeing the world's pain as their own,
    Know just what suffering is
    And the means for eliminating it.
    Though pained by it, they will never be discouraged.

34. This tenderness of those whose nature is compassion
    Is fourfold: natural, analytic,
    Related to former training,
    And acquired with the purity that weakens its counteragents.

35. That which is not uniform or constant, which is without superior intention,
Which lacks the means for accomplishment, and is neither free from attachment
Nor nonconceptual is not tenderness.
Those who thus have no tender love are not bodhisattvas.

36. That which possesses compassion, forbearance, intention,
Aspiration, taking birth, and the maturation of sentient beings—
The first being the root; the last, the sublime fruit—
Is the great tree of compassion.

37. If the root, compassion, is absent,
There will not be the forbearance to put up with hardship.
If the wise cannot endure suffering,
They will not have the intention to help beings.

38. Their minds devoid of that intention,
They will not pray for positive and pure rebirths.
And if they do not achieve a good rebirth,
They will never bring sentient beings to maturity.

39. Know that with love watering their compassion,
From their happiness when they suffer,
It expands and grows; and from proper attentiveness,
The great boughs grow and spread.

40. The unbroken stream of their aspirations,
Like leaves that are cast off and renewed,
Is fulfilled by two causes, as a result of which
The flowers and fruit bring benefit.

41. Since great compassion is the source of qualities,
Who would not have compassion for sentient beings?
Even though they thus feel pain for them,
Aroused through tenderness, it produces immeasurable bliss.

42. Those with tenderness, who are imbued with compassion,
    Do not even set their minds on peace,
    Let alone become attached
    To mundane bliss or their own lives.

43. Ordinary love is not beyond reproach,
    Nor is it supramundane.
    The love the wise feel in their tenderness
    Is irreproachable and has gone beyond the world.

44. It is the means for leading ordinary beings
    Dwelling in the gloom of ignorance
    And on the flooding waves of suffering.
    How could it not be free of fault?

45. If in this world, enlightened by themselves,
    The arhats do not have such love,
    What need to speak of anybody else?
    How could it not be supramundane?

46. Bodhisattvas do not suffer,
    Yet any pain they feel through tender love
    At first makes them afraid,
    But once they have arrived, it gives them the greatest joy.

47. The pain that comes through tenderness
    Will outshine every mundane happiness,
    And even those who've reached their goal don't have it.
    What could be more wonderful than that?

48. The steadfast, with their tender gifts,
    Create the bliss of generosity;
    The happiness of those who find enjoyment in the three worlds
    Cannot compare to even a fraction of that.

49. If, out of tenderness, for beings' sake
    They do not leave saṃsāra, suffering itself,
    What suffering will the compassionate ones
    Not accept in order to benefit others?

50. From the compassion, generosity,
    And wealth of those with tender hearts,
    The happiness that grows from love, from caring,
    And from their power to help will constantly increase.

51. This is like an exhortation to the weak:
    "With compassion you must expand and make it grow;
    By giving, you must ripen and bring happiness;
    You must lead them perfectly and guide."

52. Because of their compassion, suffering makes them suffer.
    Without creating happiness, how could they be happy?
    It is because of this that those with tender love,
    By making others happy, bring happiness upon themselves.

53. The compassionate always, as it were, instruct their generosity:
    "Do not desire happiness for yourself;
    Make others happy with gifts of your possessions.
    Otherwise, since I make no distinctions, happiness is also not for me."

54. "Their happiness makes me happy,
    So give beings gifts along with the result.
    If there is something you should do for me,
    Make the result wholly theirs."

55. "Even though those who give have no desire for wealth,
    They gain abundant riches and good things.
    It's not that I want such happiness,
    But like that I can continue to give."

56. "Constantly observe me
    Fully giving all I own with tender love.
    Thus you should know that the result
    Does not interest me at all."

57. "If you do not let go of the resulting benefits you will obtain,
    There'll never be any delight in giving gifts.
    If, for a single instant, you fail to give like that,
    Then there will be no true joy in generosity."

58. "You do not reward those who are not generous,
But it is not like me to look for recompense like that.
I do not have your hopes for something in return,
And so I give the resulting benefits entirely to others."

59. The tender generosity of bodhisattvas
Is free of shameful deeds, is based on purity,
Leads to happiness, and is protective,
Unquestioning, and without stain.

60. With tender love, bodhisattvas give everything
On a vast scale and of the best quality, constantly,
With joy, an absence of materialism, and purity,
Dedicating their generosity to enlightenment and to virtue.

61. While those with tender love, their minds sated with joy on three accounts,
Find great delight in giving everything away,
No similar delight will those who revel in those gifts
Derive from using all those things.

62. Tender love for the stingy, tender love for the unruly,
Tender love for those in turmoil, tender love for the careless,
Compassion for those beguiled by objects,
And compassion for those who mistakenly cling—

63. A bodhisattva's compassion
Comes from happiness and suffering and their cause;
A bodhisattva's compassion
Comes from its cause, the teacher, and its nature.

64. A bodhisattva's compassion
Is to be understood as equal on account of its attitude,
Its accomplishment, its absence of attachment,
Its nonconceptuality, and its purity.

65. The bodhisattvas' mental training in the four boundless attitudes
Is the best by virtue of their interest in the Dharma,
Their specific mental states, mastery,
Nonconceptuality, and oneness.

66. Thus, by developing deep faith in the bhagavāns
    And making constant, extraordinary offerings—material things as well as great veneration—
    By always following the beneficial friend who is possessed of many qualities,
    And through tender love for beings, they will gain every accomplishment.

19

Elements Leading to Enlightenment

1. A sense of shame has eliminated its opposite,
   Is coupled with nonconceptual gnosis,
   Has as its object lower paths that are merely free of wrongdoing,
   Matures sentient beings, and belongs to the steadfast.

2. When the counteragents
   Of the six perfections increase in them
   And the antidotes decrease,
   Bodhisattvas feel unbearably ashamed.

3. The steadfast are ashamed of being lazy
   About training in the six perfections,
   And also of indulging in activities
   Related to the defilements.

4. In those who are, by nature, not concentrated,
   Who are lesser, middling, or on inferior levels,
   Whose motivation is inferior, or who have a sense of "I,"
   Their sense of shame is inferior; in others it is superior.

5. From a lack of decency and improper ways, the wise
   Indulge in defilements, get angry,
   Forsake what is good, and become proud, as a result of which
   They oppress sentient beings and destroy their discipline.

6. They will be stricken with remorse,
   And will receive almost no respect.
   The hosts of faithful nonhumans
   And even the Teacher will ignore them.

7. Their fellow bodhisattvas will condemn them,
   And in this life the world will speak unpleasantly of them,
   While in other lives to come,
   They'll be reborn in realms devoid of leisure.

8. So all the good they have acquired
   And all that they have not yet gained
   Will fade away. Because of this they'll suffer,
   And their minds will never find true rest.

9. None of these misfortunes can occur
   For the buddhas' heirs who have a sense of shame.
   The skillful always take the best rebirth
   As human beings or as gods.

10. Wise beings with a sense of shame swiftly complete
    The accumulations that lead to perfect enlightenment.
    The buddhas' children will never grow weary
    Of bringing beings to maturity.

11. They will be forever free of shamelessness
    And never separate from the antidote.
    Such are the benefits
    Bodhisattvas with a sense of shame will gain.

12. The immature, though adorned in gorgeous clothes,
    Have no consideration and so are stained by faults.
    The buddhas' children clothed in a sense of shame,
    Though uncovered, are unstained by faults.

13. The buddhas' children, with their sense of decency,
    Are, like the sky, never tainted by ordinary concerns.
    Counted among the assembly of buddhas' children,
    Those who are adorned with a sense of shame are the loveliest.

14. With their sense of shame, bodhisattvas
    Love beings like a mother would her children.
    It is their sense of shame as well that constantly
    Protects them in saṃsāra from all kinds of faults.

15. Acceptance of everything,
    Refusal of everything,
    Nonengagement, and engagement
    Are the signs of decency in an upright individual.

16. The bodhisattvas' mental training in decency
    Is the best by virtue of their interest in the teachings,
    Their specific mental states, mastery,
    Nonconceptuality, and oneness.

17. A bodhisattva's steadfastness is far superior
    To that of those who are not bodhisattvas
    By virtue of its specific characteristics,
    Its categories, and its immutability.

18. Their diligence, concentration, and wisdom
    Correspond to strength of mind, endurance, and stability.
    On account of these three, bodhisattvas
    Apply themselves without fear.

19. Through a lack of courage, wavering, and ignorance
    There is fear of all there is to do.
    So know that the three innate states
    Are included in the word "steadfastness."

20. The steadfastness of the steady arises
    Naturally, through their aspirations,
    In their lack of concern,
    In the face of sentient beings' ingratitude,

21. In their hearing of the profound and of the extensive,
    With regard to beings who are hard to train,
    And with regard to the inconceivable buddha bodies.
    It arises in the face of their different austerities,

22. In their not abandoning saṃsāra,
    And in their freedom from defilements there.
    It is unequaled by other beings,
    So bodhisattvas are considered the greatest of steadfast beings.

23. Like the king of mountains assailed by butterflies,
    Garuḍas, and the ocean,
    The steadfast are not shaken by evil company,
    By suffering, or by hearing the profound.

24. Bodhisattvas' indefatigability is incomparable
    And based on three things: their insatiable thirst for listening,
    Their great diligence, and their suffering.
    Relying on their sense of shame and their steadfastness,

25. The indefatigability of the wise—
    Those who yearn for the great enlightenment—
    Is held to be, on the different levels,
    Imperfect, perfect, and utterly perfect.

26. Because of its basis, its purpose,
    Effects, specific characteristics,
    Inexhaustibility, and perfectly accomplished result,
    Steadfast bodhisattvas' knowledge of the treatises

27. Is far superior.
    Contained in their concentration and their powers of retention,
    It brings sentient beings to maturity
    And serves to hold the sacred Dharma.

28. Steadfast bodhisattvas' knowledge of the world—
    Of physical and verbal conventions,
    And, mentally, of the truth—is without equal.
    It is superior to that of other beings.

29. The steadfast are always smiling;
    They always speak straightforwardly.
    This is in order to make beings fit vessels
    So that they accomplish the sacred Dharma.

30. Because two truths state
    How worlds continuously come into being,
    And two how they will disappear,
    Such knowledge is known as knowledge of the world.

31. In order to dispel the former and achieve the latter,
    The wise apply these truths.
    Because the wise know all truths,
    They are described as "knowers of the world."

32. The teachings taught in the scriptures,
    The meaning they imply,
    The authoritative ultimate meaning,
    And its inexpressible attainment—

33. These are taught here to prevent
    Rejection, literal understanding,
    Understanding the truth incorrectly,
    And attaining something expressible.

34. Through their interest, thorough analysis,
    Learning how things are from others,
    And inexpressible gnosis,
    The steadfast will never fail.

35. On account of their knowledge of classifications,
    Characteristics, phrasing, and gnosis,
    The bodhisattvas' four kinds of perfect knowledge
    Are considered to be without equal.

36. The teaching and the means for teaching it
    By those who diligently teach
    Are shown by just the topics and their meanings,
    The languages, and their knowledge of these.

37. Because they indicate the topics, because they explain them,
    Because they bring about the complete acquisition of both,
    And because they reply to objections,
    There are four kinds of perfect knowledge.

38. This is complete knowledge
    Consequent on the direct cognition of sameness;
    Clearing away every kind of doubt,
    It is termed "perfect knowledge."

39. The bodhisattvas' accumulations
    Of merit and wisdom are without equal.
    With the one, they attain the highest states in saṃsāra;
    With the other, they circle without defilements.

40. Generosity and discipline are the accumulation of merit;
    Wisdom is that of wisdom;
    The other three are both;
    Five, in part, are wisdom too.

41. When continuity in the practice is achieved,
    Virtue is repeatedly accomplished.
    The accumulations of the steadfast
    Serve to accomplish all goals.

42. In order to enter, to be free from characteristics,
    To act spontaneously,
    To be empowered, and to reach the ultimate,
    The steadfast accomplish the accumulations.

43. The meditation of the wise
    On close mindfulness
    Is unequaled in fourteen respects,
    And therefore far superior to that of nonbodhisattvas.

44. On account of the support, the antidotes,
    And likewise the introduction,
    Object, attentiveness,
    And attainment, their practice is superior;

45. It is so on account of its compatibility,
    Full engagement, complete knowledge, birth,
    Greatness, culmination,
    Practice, and perfect accomplishment.

46. The genuine restraints of the steadfast
    Are unmatched by beings.
    They are practiced as the remedies for
    Faults in the practice of close mindfulness.

47. In order to make use of saṃsāra,
    Get rid of hindrances,
    Discard misplaced attentiveness,
    Enter the levels,

48. Dwell in the absence of attributes,
    Receive predictions,
    Bring sentient beings to maturity,
    Receive empowerment,

49. Purify the universe,
    And reach the ultimate,
    Wise bodhisattvas practice these genuine restraints
    As the antidotes to counteragents.

50. On the basis of keenness,
    They practice the yoga with special points,
    Described as the antidote
    In all the practices of genuine restraint.

51. Steadfast bodhisattvas' four bases of miraculous powers,
    Endowed with superior characteristics,
    Are brought into play in order to accomplish
    All their own and others' aims.

52. With the support, detailed classification,
    Means, and full accomplishment,
    The bases of miraculous powers of the steadfast
    Are fully presented.

53. They are described as being
    Based on transcendent concentration,
    With four categories and means,
    And six kinds of full accomplishment.

54. One of these means is the application of effort,
    The second acts as an aid,
    The third directs the mind,
    And the fourth is an antidote.

55. These result in the accomplishment of powers of vision,
    And of instructions, different displays,
    Aspirations, powers,
    And the acquisition of qualities.

56. Enlightenment, activities, supreme learning,
    Sustained calm, and profound insight
    Should be known as being the objects of faith and the others
    In the sense of these bringing the accomplishment of those goals.

57. Faith and the others lead to the bodhisattva levels
    But are considered to be associated with defilement.
    Because they weaken their counteragents,
    They are termed irresistible forces.

58. The branches of enlightenment are classified as such
    For those who have entered the levels.
    This is because they have realized sameness
    With regard to phenomena and all beings.

59. In order to conquer unconquered knowledge,
    They specifically practice mindfulness.
    Their perfect discernment destroys
    Every conceptualized attribute.

60. They apply their diligence
    In order to realize everything swiftly.
    As the light of Dharma grows,
    They are forever filled with joy.

61. Because they are free of all obscurations,
    They are fully fit and thus accomplish bliss.
    Their concentration gives rise
    To all the wealth they could desire.

62. With evenness, they abide
    At all times as they wish;
    In their postmeditation and nonconceptual states,
    They remain constantly sublime.

63. Courageous beings with such qualities
    Are compared to the universal emperor;
    They are constantly surrounded by the branches of enlightenment
    As if by his seven precious attributes.

64. These are the nature branch and the source branch,
    Third, the branch of certain deliverance,
    Fourth, the branch of benefit,
    And the threefold branch of absence of defilements.

65. After that, bodhisattvas follow up
    Their realization of the nature as it is,
    They realize its presentation
    And apply that presentation,

66. They purify the three acts,
    And they cultivate the antidotes
    To factors that obscure knowledge,
    The path, and extraordinary qualities.

67. Because, on the basis of right abiding,
    The mind settles on the mind,
    And because phenomena are perfectly discerned,
    There is sustained calm and profound insight.

68. These are held to be universal, partial,
    Not partial, and causal.
    Related to realization and to certain deliverance,
    Devoid of attributes, not deliberate,

69. Completely purifying, and perfectly pure—
    The yoga of sustained calm and profound insight of the steadfast
    Is universal for all levels;
    It is this that accomplishes everything.

70. Skill in completing the Buddha Dharma,
    In bringing sentient beings to full maturation,
    In swift attainment, in accomplishing activities,
    And in not interrupting the path—

71. The means employed by bodhisattvas
    On all levels are without equal:
    By relying on such skill in means,
    They accomplish every kind of goal.

72. The powers of memory that come through maturation,
    Habitual listening, and concentration
    Are respectively lesser and greater,
    The greater itself being threefold.

73. That of the wise who have not yet entered
    And that of those who have entered, albeit on impure levels,
    Are lesser and middling.
    The power of memory of those on pure levels is greater.

74. Bodhisattvas who repeatedly
    Rely correctly on these
    Constantly teach others the sacred Dharma
    And retain it themselves.

75. The prayers of the steadfast
    Are accompanied by a yearning intention,
    Aroused by gnosis,
    And on all levels they have no equal.

76. They are to be known as the cause,
    Bringing accomplishment through their mere intent;
    They thus bear fruit the moment they are conceived
    And in the future are fulfilled.

77. They are diverse, great, and, on ever higher levels
    Until enlightenment, pure;
    Thus it is that bodhisattvas' goals,
    Their own as well as others', are fully accomplished.

78. The domains of the three kinds of concentration are
    The two kinds of no-self,
    The support of belief in a self,
    And the permanent elimination of the latter.

79. From the very nature of subjects and objects,
    You should know these concentrations are of three kinds.
    They take the form of nonconceptuality,
    Rejection, and perfect joy.

80. In order to completely know,
    To eliminate, and to realize,
    The concentrations such as emptiness
    Are declared to be three.

81. With the wish to benefit beings,
    The four summaries of the Dharma
    Were taught to bodhisattvas
    As the causal basis for concentration.

82. For the steadfast, these four signify
    Nonexistence, conceptualization,
    Simple imputation,
    And the complete extinction of concepts.

83. Impermanence is established because of an impossibility, because things arise from causes,
    Because of a contradiction, because things do not last by themselves,
    Because of an absence, because the nature of things has been determined,
    Because of their succession, and because of cessation;

84. Because of visible transformation,
    Because of cause and result,
    Because of being seized, because of ownership,
    And because of following purity and beings.

85. Life at the beginning, during growth,
    During development, related to the substantial supports,
    During change, and during maturation,
    Likewise inferior and superior lives,

86. Lives with light and without light,
    In the process of migration to other places,
    With seeds, and without seeds,
    And in manifestations—

87. These are the fourteen aspects of life.
    Considering these, because of causes and measurable differences,
    The unreasonableness of there being no point in development,
    The impossibility of a support,

88. The impossibility of things persisting,
    The final immutability of things that do not disintegrate in the beginning,
    And the impossibility, likewise, of inferior and superior births
    And of radiant and nonradiant lives,

89. Because of the absence of migration, the impossibility of persistence,
    And the impossibility of final aggregates,
    And because they follow the mind—for all these reasons,
    All compounded phenomena are momentary.

90. The elements and the six objects
    Are described as being momentary
    Because water dries up and its level rises;
    Because wind, by nature, moves, rises, and drops;

91. Because earth is related to those elements;
    And because it undergoes four kinds of transformation.
    Colors, smells, tastes, and physical sensations are similar,
    And so, like them, they are momentary.

92. Because fire burns in dependence on fuel,
    Because sound is observed to grow louder,
    Because imperceptible forms follow the mind, and because of the answers to questions—
    For these reasons, external phenomena too are momentary.

93. An individual is to be expressed
    As existing as a designation; it is not substantial.
    It cannot be perceived, is a mistaken notion,
    And is the cause of the defilement process and the defilements.

94. On account of two faults, it cannot be described
    As identical to or different from the aggregates,
    For they would then be the self
    Or it would be a substantial thing.

95. If it exists substantially, it is necessary to provide
    The reason why it cannot be described.
    To say that it cannot be described as being the same or different
    Without giving a reason is inadmissible.

96. In considering what are their defining characteristics,
    What ordinary people can see, and what is written in the treatises,
    It is incorrect to compare the self and aggregates to fire and firewood,
    Saying that they are both and inexpressible, for they are two.

97. Because consciousness comes into being when the two conditions are present,
    Anything that is not those conditions serves no purpose.
    For that reason, the self will never be anything—
    From that which looks to that which is liberated.

98. If the self were a ruler,
    It would never let impermanence or unwanted things occur.
    You have to establish its functions and attributes.
    And it would invalidate the three aspects of perfect awakening.

99. Because of three faults,
    Its activity in looking and so forth is not spontaneous,
    Nor is it a contributory condition of these functions;
    It has no activity in looking and the like.

100. Because it is not the agent, because they are impermanent,
And because they would operate all at once or constantly,
The functions of looking and so forth
Could never occur spontaneously.

101. Similarly, because its activity would continue as it was before,
Or would dissolve and be impermanent,
And no third alternative is possible,
It cannot be a contributory condition.

102. Thus all phenomena are devoid of a self,
And ultimately are emptiness.
To conceive of a self
Is explained as a fault and nothing else.

103. The specific distinctions between the stages
Of defilement and purification,
And the particular differences between their beginning and continuing,
Were taught in terms of individuals.

104. No need is there to develop the belief in a self—
We have been accustomed to it from time without beginning.
If individuals existed, everyone would be effortlessly liberated,
Or there would be no liberation.

105. Thus bodhisattvas who constantly possess
All these excellent qualities
Not only do not forsake their own goal
But they also accomplish the goals of others.

20

Qualities

---

1. Their own bodies they give away,
   And relinquish their abundant wealth to keep the vows of discipline;
   They're patient with those who are downcast,
   And, with no regard for their bodies or their lives,

2. They diligently strive;
   They do not savor the bliss of concentration,
   And, in their wisdom, have no concepts—
   Such are considered the wonders of the wise.

3. To be born in the tathāgata family,
   Receive predictions and empowerment,
   And fully attain enlightenment too—
   These are held to be most marvelous.

4. In view of their freedom from attachment, their compassion,
   And likewise their attainment of the highest meditation
   And their attitude of sameness,
   Their dedication to those perfections is not so very wondrous.

5. With regard to themselves, their wives,
   Their children, and their companions,
   Sentient beings are nothing like the wise,
   Whose love for all that lives is so immense.

6. In their impartiality to all in need,
   Their faultless discipline,
   Patience in all respects,
   Great diligence for the sake of all,

7. Their constant virtuous concentration,
   And nonconceptual wisdom—
   In all these the bodhisattvas' attitude of sameness
   Should thus be known.

8. Making beings fit vessels,
   Establishing them in discipline,
   Patiently enduring harm,
   Traveling in order to benefit,

9. Introducing them to this doctrine,
   Removing their doubts—
   All this is held to be the benefit
   The wise bring to sentient beings.

10. Constantly caring for sentient beings
    With an attitude that considers them all the same,
    They give birth to the noble levels,
    Cause virtue to grow,

11. Protect from wrongdoing,
    And help them train in what they have heard.
    With these five activities, the buddhas' heirs
    Are like mothers to beings.

12. Constantly causing faith to be born
    In all sentient beings,
    They teach them superior discipline and the like,
    Connect them to perfect liberation,

13. Pray to the buddhas on their behalf,
    And eliminate their obscurations.
    So with these five activities, the buddhas' heirs
    Are like fathers to beings.

14. They keep secret those teachings
    That are unsuitable for beings,
    Reproach them for lapses in the training,
    Praise them for excellence,

15. Give them instructions,
    And warn them of demons.
    With these five activities, the buddhas' heirs
    Are like kinsfolk to beings.

16. Having no confusion in their own minds
    Concerning defilement and purity,
    They give all that is abundant and perfect,
    Both mundane and beyond;

17. Never discouraged and unwavering,
    They always wish beings' benefit and happiness.
    With these five activities, the buddhas' heirs
    Are like friends to beings.

18. Forever diligent in the task
    Of bringing beings to maturity,
    They speak of perfect deliverance,
    Patiently bear all kinds of ingratitude,

19. Bestow the two kinds of excellence,
    And are expert in the means for achieving these.
    With these five activities, the buddhas' heirs
    Are like servants for beings.

20. They wish that others may acquire
    The acceptance that phenomena are unborn,
    They teach all vehicles,
    Prepare them for the accomplishment of yoga,

21. Maintain a lovely countenance, and never look for
    Reciprocal help or karmic recompense.
    With these five activities, the buddhas' heirs
    Are like teachers for beings.

22. Those who are extremely diligent in benefiting beings
    Help them complete the accumulations,
    Swiftly bring those who have accumulated merit to liberation,
    Make them eliminate incompatible factors,

23. And connect them to all excellence,
    Mundane and supramundane.
    With these five activities, the buddhas' heirs
    Are like preceptors for beings.

24. Because they are not attached to wealth,
    Keep faultless discipline,
    Are full of gratitude,
    And apply themselves to the practice,

25. Beings who in that way undertake
    The six transcendent perfections
    Similarly benefit
    Bodhisattvas in return.

26. For beings and themselves, bodhisattvas always wish
    For increase, decrease,
    Maturation, progress on the levels,
    And unsurpassable enlightenment.

27. In their absence of fear, their correct intent,
    The removal of doubts,
    And their use of the instructions on practice,
    The buddhas' heirs are never wasteful.

28. Generosity without expectation,
    Discipline with no desire for higher rebirth,
    Patience with all in every respect,
    Diligence in gathering all good qualities,

29. Likewise, concentration that is not intended for the formless world,
    And wisdom possessed of skillful means—
    Those who are steadfast in these six perfections
    Are applying them authentically.

30. Attachment to pleasure, violations,
    Pride, indulging in pleasure,
    Savoring, and concepts
    Result in diminution for the steadfast.

31. The antidotes to these,
    For bodhisattvas who use them,
    Are to be understood as their opposites,
    And therefore as favorable, enhancing qualities.

32. Making a show, pretense,
    Putting on a serene face,
    Likewise applying oneself from time to time,
    Remaining calm in body and speech,
    And being superbly eloquent—
    All these are divorced from accomplishment;

33. They are explained as not being
    The authentic practices of the bodhisattvas.
    The practices of those who apply themselves to their opposites
    Are explained as being authentic.

34. The wise, on all the levels,
    Practice generosity and the others
    And thereby correct
    The six counteragents in beings.

35. Specifying the individual and the time,
    The predictions the wise receive are twofold.
    There are predictions of enlightenment, of predictions,
    And also ones that are described as "great,"

36. Which are for those who have gained acceptance of the unborn,
    Who have abandoned pride and effort,
    And are of the same nature
    As the buddhas and their children.

37. Again, it is in terms of their buddha field, name,
    Time, the name of the kalpa,
    Their following, and the duration of their doctrine
    That predictions are said to be made.

38. For the wise, at all times,
    Abundance, birth, indefatigability,
    Perpetual training, unimpaired concentration,
    The accomplishment of their deeds,
    And spontaneous acceptance
    Will certainly be obtained.

39. Making offerings, taking the precepts properly,
    Compassion, cultivating virtue,
    Likewise, carefulness in lonely places,
    And insatiability in study—
    These are the definite duties
    Of the steadfast on all the levels.

40. To know the defects of desire,
    Examine mistakes,
    Willingly take on suffering,
    Cultivate all forms of good,

41. Avoid savoring bliss,
    And be free of concepts
    Are the perpetual duties
    Of the steadfast on all the levels.

42. The gift of Dharma, pure discipline,
    The attainment of acceptance that phenomena are unborn,
    Diligence in the Great Vehicle,
    Dwelling in the last of the dhyānas, endowed with compassion,
    And wisdom—these are the most important aspects
    Of the transcendent perfections for the wise.

43. For the steadfast on all levels,
    The presentation of the sciences
    In specific sections such as the condensed discourses
    Is what is called the presentation of the teachings.

44. The truth is presented on the basis of
    Seven aspects of suchness.
    Rational application and vehicles
    Are presented respectively as being of four and three kinds.

45. Properly keeping things in mind,
    The correct view that possesses the result,
    Discernment with valid cognition, and the inconceivable
    Are to be understood as the four kinds of rational application.

46. Distinguished by their attitude,
    Teachings, application,
    Accumulations, and accomplishment,
    There are held to be three vehicles.

47. Names and objects
    Are reciprocally investigated as being adventitious;
    The two kinds of designation
    Are investigated as being no more than that.

48. Because of nonconceptuality with regard to everything,
    There are four kinds of true gnosis.
    These enable the steadfast
    To accomplish all their goals on all levels.

49. The causes of bondage—
    The support, enjoyments, and seeds—
    Here bind the mind, mental factors,
    And the body, along with the seeds.

50. Conceptual structures placed before the mind
    And those that are naturally present—
    The wise destroy them all,
    Thus attaining supreme enlightenment.

51. With the knowledge that perceives suchness,
    The elimination of dualism,
    And the direct perception of residual negative tendencies,
    The wise are held to bring an end to these.

52. With the gnosis that perceives suchness
    They meditate on the absence of distinct aspects
    And directly perceive existence and nonexistence,
    This being referred to as "mastery over thought."

53. For the immature, the true state of things is concealed
    And everywhere the untrue state of things appears.
    For bodhisattvas, that has been dispelled,
    And everywhere the true state of things appears.

54. Know that what does not exist and what exists
    Does not appear and does appear.
    Such is transformation:
    Because they can act as they please, they are free.

55. The vast object, which always appears
    To be the same in kind at different moments,
    Creates an obstacle.
    So, fully recognizing this, they eliminate it.

56. The objects that are to be brought to full maturity, to be purified,
    To be attained, that are ready to be brought to maturity,
    And that are to be authentically taught
    Are the immeasurable objects of the wise.

57. The birth of bodhicitta,
    Acceptance of the unborn,
    The lesser uncontaminated eye,
    And the exhaustion of taints,

58. The long duration of the sacred Dharma,
    Detailed knowledge, resolution, and enjoyment—
    These are the results of the explanations
    Of the wise who are so engaged.

59. The greatness of its reference,
    And likewise of its twin accomplishment,
    Its gnosis, diligent application,
    Its skill in means,

60. Its great consummation,
    And great buddha activities—
    It is because it possesses these forms of greatness
    That the Great Vehicle is so described.

61. This is summarized as the potential, interest in the teachings,
    And likewise arousing bodhicitta,
    Practicing the transcendent perfections,
    Entering the flawless levels,

62. Bringing beings to maturity,
    Purifying the universe,
    Realizing the nondwelling nirvāṇa,
    Attaining supreme enlightenment, and displaying enlightened activities.

63. Some bodhisattvas are interested,
    Others have pure superior intention,
    Conceive attributes, are without attributes,
    And practice without deliberate effort—
    These five should be understood
    As referring to the bodhisattvas on all the levels.

64. One who is unattached to pleasure, pure in the three deeds,
    Who overpowers anger, strives for sublime qualities,
    Never moves from the practice, and sees profound thatness
    Is a bodhisattva who delights in enlightenment.

65. One who wants to help, intends no harm,
    Willingly accepts others' harm,
    Is steadfast, careful, and learned
    Is a bodhisattva who strives for others' good.

66. One who knows the defects of keeping things for oneself,
    Who is without attachment, and never holds a grudge,
    Practices yoga, is expert in the special points, and is without wrong views
    Is a bodhisattva who is perfectly settled inwardly.

67. One who is full of love, maintains the virtues of a sense of shame,
Who happily accepts suffering, is unattached to personal well-being,
Gives priority to mindfulness, and is a master of perfect equipoise
Is a bodhisattva who is never at odds with the vehicle.

68. One who dispels suffering, never causes pain,
Who accepts suffering, is unafraid of difficulties,
Is liberated from suffering, and has no concepts of misery
Is a bodhisattva who willingly takes on suffering.

69. One who gets no joy in certain ways, delights in natural ways,
Despises other ways, and is diligent in virtue,
Has mastered the teachings, and is not obscured with regard to phenomena
Is a bodhisattva for whom the Dharma is the most important thing.

70. One who is careful with possessions, careful in discipline,
Careful to remain on guard, careful in virtue,
Careful with bliss, and careful with regard to phenomena
Is a bodhisattva who is careful with regard to the vehicle.

71. One who is ashamed of showing disrespect, ashamed of the slightest fault,
Ashamed of not being patient, ashamed of failing,
Ashamed of distraction, and ashamed of lower views
Is a bodhisattva who is ashamed of other vehicles.

72. For now and the hereafter, through equanimity,
Application, attainment of mastery,
Appropriate teaching, and the great result,
Bodhisattvas engage in benefiting beings.

73. Bodhisattvas are known by different names:
Hero of Enlightenment, Great Hero,
Wise One, Supremely Brilliant One,
Child of the Buddhas, Foundation of the Victorious Ones,
Victor, Sprout of the Victors;

74. Powerful One, Most Exalted One,
    Pilot, Supremely Famed One,
    Compassionate One, One of Great Merit,
    Mighty Lord, and likewise, Truthful One.

75. Because of five particularities—their excellent realization of thatness,
    Their perfect realization of the great goal, their realization of everything,
    Their constant realization, and their realization of means—
    They are called bodhisattvas.

76. Because of their subsequent realization of the self,
    Realization of subtle views, realization of the various consciousnesses,
    And realization of all as being false imagination,
    They are called bodhisattvas.

77. Because of their realization of the unrealized,
    Realization of the subsequent realization, realization of nonsubstantiality,
    Realization of production, and realization of the unknown,
    They are called bodhisattvas.

78. Because of their realization that objects do not exist,
    Realization of ultimate truth, realization of all objects,
    Realization of the totality of objects, and realization of the realized,
        realizer, and realization,
    They are called bodhisattvas.

79. Because of their realization of the accomplishment,
    Realization of the abode, realization of the womb, realization of the
        stages,
    And realization of bringing about realization and dispelling doubts,
    They are called bodhisattvas.

80. For the wise, intelligence is acquired, unacquired,
    Or fully present; realized or consequently realized;
    Used for teaching or beyond expression; with an "I" or with the "I"
        destroyed;
    And either immature or fully mature.

21

Conduct and Consummation

1. Compassionate, soft-spoken,
   Steadfast, openhanded,
   And able to comment on the profound intention—
   These are the marks of the wise.

2. For they are caring, inspire interest,
   Are not discouraged, and attract in two ways.
   It should thus be understood that there are five signs,
   Which are related to their intention and application.

3. Bodhisattvas always
   Become lay universal emperors,
   And in all those births
   They work for beings' good.

4. On all the levels, the wise
   Take ordination by receiving the vows,
   By obtaining them naturally,
   Or otherwise, by displaying ordination.

5. Those who've taken ordination
   Have boundless good qualities;
   Thus those diligent in the precepts
   Are superior to lay bodhisattvas.

6. On each and every level, steadfast bodhisattvas
   Wish to bring beings pleasant results in future lives,
   They wish to introduce them to virtue in this life,
   And they wish that they may attain nirvāṇa.

These constitute their superior intention for sentient beings,
Which is said to be impure, pure, or utterly pure.

7. On each and every level, the wise
Take care of beings through prayers of aspiration,
By having the attitude of sameness, by becoming sovereigns,
And by attracting a following.

8. The wise are said to take birth
Through the power of their actions,
And also through their prayers,
Concentration, and mastery.

9. The states of abiding and the levels themselves
Are described in terms of characteristics, individuals, training,
Aggregates, accomplishment, signs,
Etymological definitions, and attainment.

10. The sublime realization of emptiness;
The persistence of deeds, which are never wasted;
Rebirth in the world of desire
After dwelling in the intense bliss of concentration;

11. Then, full dedication to saṃsāra
Of the elements conducive to enlightenment;
With defiling factors absent from the mind,
The full maturation of sentient beings;

12. Protection from defilement
When taking birth through specific intention;
The path of the single certainty of the absence of attributes,
Connecting to the path of single progress;

13. Spontaneous accomplishment of the absence of attributes,
And purification of the universe;
Subsequent accomplishment
Of the maturation of sentient beings;

14. Concentrations and powers of retention;
    And perfect purity, enlightenment—
    Presented thus, the defining characteristics
    Of the levels can be known.

15. The bodhisattvas on these levels are those with perfectly pure view,
    Those with extremely pure discipline, those who are settled in evenness,
    Those who are rid of pride with regard to the Dharma, who have no pride with regard to
    Distinctions between mindstreams and between defilement and purity,

16. Those who have acquired the mental capacity for instantaneous realization,
    Those who dwell in equanimity and purify fields, those who are skilled in ripening beings,
    And those who have great powers, have perfected the body,
    Are skilled in clear display, and receive empowerment.

17. After truly realizing ultimate reality,
    They train here in superior discipline,
    Superior mind, and superior wisdom.
    The object of wisdom is twofold:

18. The suchness of phenomena, and the processes
    That operate from not knowing and knowing that suchness.
    These are the objects of wisdom
    On which they dwell on the two levels.

19. Training and meditating
    Leads to four further results:
    Dwelling in the absence of attributes
    With deliberate effort is the first result.

20. Doing the same without deliberate effort
    And purifying everything as a buddha field
    Is the second result.
    Then there is the accomplishment of maturing beings,

21. And the accomplishment of concentrations and powers of retention,
    Which constitutes the supreme result.
    These four results
    Are directly related to the four levels.

22. Having truly realized ultimate reality,
    Here, they purify the aggregate of discipline,
    After which they purify the aggregates
    Of concentration and wisdom.

23. On the other levels
    They purify liberation from four obscurations
    And the gnosis of liberation
    From even the impeding obscurations.

24. All the levels should be understood
    As levels of nonaccomplishment and accomplishment.
    And those of accomplishment are again held to be
    Levels of nonaccomplishment and accomplishment.

25. Their accomplishment is to be understood from
    Keeping the system in mind,
    From knowing that it is all thought,
    And from nonconceptuality with regard to that.

26. Because they can only be known personally,
    And because they are the domain of the buddhas,
    The training and its accomplishment
    On all the levels are inconceivable.

27. They have clear vision and interest,
    Are undaunted and never weak-minded,
    Are independent of others,
    Have understood everything perfectly,

28. Are even-minded toward all,
    Are never influenced, have no attachment,
    Know the means, and take birth within the retinue—
    These are considered the signs on all the levels.

29. Never lacking determination, bodhisattvas have no attachment, no
    hostile feelings, no anger, no laziness,
    No intentions that are not loving and compassionate, and they are not
    carried away by wrong understanding and concepts.
    Their minds are not distracted; they are not carried away by happiness,
    nor affected by suffering.
    They follow spiritual masters, devote themselves to listening, and are
    diligent in making offerings to their teachers.

30. They who know the supreme means share with others
    The vast entirety of the merit they have gathered and dedicate it daily
    to perfect enlightenment.
    Born in excellent places, they constantly practice virtue and revel in
    the qualities of preternatural knowledge.
    Know that they are treasuries of qualities surpassing all the buddhas'
    children.

31. On all the levels, overall,
    There are five benefits for the wise,
    Related to sustained calm,
    To profound insight, and to both.

32. When they see they are approaching enlightenment
    And accomplishing beings' goals,
    They will feel the greatest joy.
    Because of that, it is called Perfect Joy.

33. Because they are free of the contamination of broken vows and
    misplaced efforts,
    This level is called Immaculate.
    Because they make the great light of Dharma shine,
    It is called Luminous.

34. Because they have the hotly burning light,
    This Dharma leading to enlightenment,
    This level, burning up the two,
    Is known as Radiant.

35. Because they bring sentient beings to maturity
    And also guard their own minds,
    It is difficult for the wise to train,
    So it is called Hard to Conquer.

36. As bodhisattvas rely on transcendent wisdom,
    Both saṃsāra and nirvāṇa
    Become clearly manifest here,
    So this level is called Clearly Manifest.

37. Because it is connected to the sole path to tread,
    This level is known as Far Progressed.
    Because it is unmoved by the two kinds of apprehension,
    It is called Immovable.

38. Because of their excellent intelligence, with perfect knowledge,
    That level is Perfect Intellect.
    Because the immensity of their sky-like minds is filled
    With the two like clouds, it is Cloud of Dharma.

39. Because they constantly and joyfully abide
    In the various practices of virtue,
    The levels of those bodhisattvas
    Are considered to be "states of abiding."

40. On them, the fears of countless beings are removed;
    On them, there's ever higher progress.
    For these reasons, those immeasurable states
    Are considered to be levels.

41. Attainment of the levels is fourfold:
    By means of interest,
    By engagement in activities,
    By realization, and by accomplishment.

42. The four activities of the steadfast
    Were taught in accordance with a sūtra
    In order to inspire beings interested in the Great Vehicle,

To inspire those interested in lower vehicles,
To inspire those interested in both,
And in order to subdue beings.

43. To you possessed of love for sentient beings,
Who wish them to encounter and be free,
Who wish them to never be deprived,
And who wish for their benefit and happiness, I pay homage.

44. Capable One, definitively released from all obscuration,
Dominant over all worlds,
Your knowledge pervades all that can be known.
To you whose mind is free, I pay homage.

45. To you who destroy every defilement
In all sentient beings,
Who act to overcome defilements
And are imbued with love for those with defilements, I pay homage.

46. Spontaneous, free of attachment,
Without impediment, constantly in meditation—
To you who give answers to all questions,
I pay homage.

47. With regard to what is explained—the support and supported—
And what is used to explain—your words and knowledge—
Your mind is always unimpeded.
To you, excellent teacher, I pay homage.

48. Proceeding and knowing all activities,
You give excellent instructions,
In their languages, on the comings and goings of beings
And their certain deliverance. To you, I pay homage.

49. When beings see you,
They all know you to be a holy being.
To you, the mere sight of whom
Creates faith, I pay homage.

50. To you who have mastery
In assuming, abiding, and relinquishing,
In manifestation and transformation,
In concentration, and in gnosis, I pay homage.

51. To you who vanquish the demons
That utterly deceive sentient beings with regard to
The means, refuge, purity,
And certain deliverance by the Great Vehicle, I pay homage.

52. To you who, for your own and others' sake,
Show gnosis and elimination,
Teach certain deliverance and what hinders it,
And will never be crushed by tīrthikas and others, I pay homage.

53. Never on your guard nor forgetful,
You speak boldly in the midst of your disciples;
To you who have eliminated the two defilements
And gather a following, I pay homage.

54. Omniscient One, all the time,
Whenever you move, whenever you stay,
You have no activities in which you are not omniscient.
To you who truly merit that name, I pay homage.

55. In acting for the sake of all beings,
You are never untimely,
So your deeds are always meaningful.
To you who are never forgetful, I pay homage.

56. In all worlds, six times during the night and day,
You look upon each and every being,
Manifesting great compassion.
To you whose intention is to help, I pay homage.

57. To you who surpass
All the listeners and solitary realizers
In your conduct, realization, gnosis,
And activities, I pay homage.

58. With the three buddha bodies, you have attained
    Great enlightenment, in all aspects.
    To you who remove the doubts of all beings
    On every plane, I pay homage.

59. To you who have no grasping, commit no fault,
    Are undisturbed, never stay still,
    Never stir, and are free from elaborations
    With regard to all phenomena, I pay homage.

60. He has accomplished ultimate truth,
    Having been definitively released from all the levels.
    He is the highest of all beings
    And acts to liberate all sentient beings.

61. Possessing unequaled, inexhaustible qualities,
    He appears in worldly realms, and in maṇḍalas,
    But is completely invisible
    To gods and humans.

62. Nevertheless, through his power,
    In accordance with the fortunes of beings
    And for as long as the world endures,
    The stream of his deeds will never cease.

The poem entitled "Ornament of the Mahāyāna Sūtras" was composed by Ārya Maitreya. It was translated, corrected, and finalized by the learned Indian abbot Śākyasiṃha and the great reviser and translator Venerable Peltsek and others. At a later date the paṇḍita Parahita, the great brahmin Sajjana, and the monk-translator Loden Sherab explained it with a few corrections and produced a definitive version.

THE COMMENTARY

A Feast of the Nectar of the Supreme Vehicle

An explanation of the
Ornament of the Mahāyāna Sūtras

BY JAMGÖN MIPHAM

ĀRYA ASAṄGA (FOURTH CENTURY CE)

Namo mañjuśrīkumārabhūtaya

To the incomparable Teacher, King of the Śākyas,
The Regent, Lord of the Ten Levels, Invincible Protector,[1]
His beloved disciple, Ārya Asaṅga,
And to him who was inspired by his words, the sublime scholar
 Vasubandhu,
To the glorious Sthiramati, his foremost student,
The host of supreme beings in the lineage that came down from them,
And to the spiritual masters, gracious explicators of this path,
Respectfully I pay homage.
With total reverence for these, the Great Regent's Excellent Words,
This feast of the Supreme Vehicle teachings he gave for all beings,
I shall explain them with others' good in mind.
Come now and feast upon the nectar of the highest way.

Here is a clear, easy-to-understand explanation of the extraordinary scriptural text entitled *Ornament of the Mahāyāna Sūtras*, one of the Five Treatises of Maitreya that the great charioteer Asaṅga, having attained the concentration of the stream of Dharma,[2] received in person from the regent Maitreya ("Invincible Protector") in the Dharma palace of Tuṣita. It has four topics: the title, the translator's homage, the actual text, and the conclusion.

The Title

>In Sanskrit: *Mahāyāna-sūtra-alāṃkāra-nāma-kārikā*
>In Tibetan: *Theg pa chen po mdo sde rgyan zhes bya ba'i tshig le'ur byas pa*

---

1. Tib. *rgyal tshab sa bcu'i dbang phyug mi pham mgon*. These are all epithets of Maitreya.
2. Tib. *chos kyi rgyun gyi ting nge 'dzin*, the concentration of bodhisattvas on the path of joining that leads to their attaining the first bodhisattva level.

The Sanskrit title is *Mahāyāna-sūtra-alāṃkāra-nāma-kārikā*, which in Tibetan is *Theg pa chen po mdo sde rgyan zhes bya ba'i tshig le'ur byas pa* (meaning "A composition in verse entitled *Ornament of the Mahāyāna Sūtras*").

This treatise is an ornament that illuminates, by means of five unexcelled metaphors, the intended meaning of the sūtras of the Great Vehicle (so called because of seven features that make it great).[3] It was therefore given the title: "Ornament of the Sūtras." And since it was melodiously expressed in verse, it is "a composition in verse."

Translator's Homage

Homage to all the buddhas and bodhisattvas.

The scriptural source text was translated into Tibetan by the great translator Kawa Peltsek, who began with the translator's homage: "Homage to all the buddhas and bodhisattvas."

The Actual Text

The third topic, the actual text, consists of two parts: (1) an account of how the treatise was composed and (2) an explanation of the main text of the treatise.

---

3. Tib. *chen po bdun*. These seven aspects of the greatness of the Great Vehicle are described below, ch. 20, vv. 59 and 60.

Introduction

How the Treatise Was Composed

> He who knows the meaning created a composition showing
>   that meaning with flawless speech and phrasing
> Out of natural compassion for suffering beings in order to
>   free them from suffering.
> For beings who follow the way expounded in the Supreme Vehicle
> He revealed the nature of five unexcelled metaphors: (I, 1)
>
> The crafting of a piece of gold, the blossoming of a lotus flower,
> Eating well-cooked food when starving,
> Hearing good news, and opening a chest of jewels—
> These illustrate the sublime delights the teachings set forth
>   here will bring. (I, 2)

The author of this text was he who knew the meaning of the Mahāyāna sūtras and gave an explanation showing that meaning to others, with flawless speech and phrasing. His purpose was that all sentient beings should be liberated from suffering, and the causal basis was his natural compassion,[1] great compassion for beings who suffer. The method that he taught was the Dharma as expounded in the Supreme Vehicle. The individuals for whom he taught it were those who follow the Supreme Vehicle—namely, beings who are taking the Mahāyāna path to reach their goal, or the host of Mahāyāna practitioners. As to the manner in which he taught, he revealed the nature of five unexcelled metaphors (unexcelled because they contain the meaning of the Great Vehicle), in which the words and their meanings are perfectly connected.

What are these five? A skillful goldsmith's fashioning of earrings and the like from gold. A lotus flower coming into full bloom. A starving person

---

1. Sthiramati explains: "since bodhisattvas are the nature of compassion."

eating delicious, perfectly prepared food. Hearing good news that makes one happy. And opening a chest of all kinds of jewels. Such are the sublime joys that the explanations in this treatise—this Dharma of the Great Vehicle—produce.

It is because the five metaphors are used to clarify the intended meaning of the Mahāyāna sūtras that we speak of them in this context as an "ornament of the sūtras." It is essential to recognize the significance of these five, for they summarize the whole of this treatise, and they will therefore be explained below.

In this context, let us look at what the great being Sthiramati says in his commentary. According to him, this treatise explains all the profound and extensive practices of the bodhisattvas, which can be summarized under three headings: what to train in, how to train, and who is training. The first of these, what one trains in, can be condensed into seven objects in which one trains: one's own welfare, others' welfare, thatness, powers, bringing one's own buddha qualities to maturity, bringing others to maturity, and unsurpassable perfect enlightenment. How one trains is in six ways: by first developing a great interest in the teachings of the Great Vehicle, investigating the Dharma, teaching the Dharma, practicing the Dharma in accord with the teachings, persevering in the correct instructions and follow-up teachings, and imbuing one's physical, verbal, and mental activities with skillful means. Those who train are the bodhisattvas, of whom there are ten categories: those who are of the bodhisattva type, those who have entered the Great Vehicle, those with impure aspirations, those with pure aspirations, those whose aspirations are not matured, those whose aspirations are matured, those with uncertain realization, those with certain realization, those who are delayed by a single birth,[2] and those who are in their last existence. The names of all these bodhisattvas are Heroes of Enlightenment, Great Heroes, The Wise, and so on, as explained in the text.[3] These points, says Sthiramati, constitute the approach taken in this treatise.

He goes on to describe how the elements in the first two verses ("He who knows the meaning...") can be explained respectively in terms of the seven

---

2. Bodhisattvas on the tenth level who will attain buddhahood in their next rebirth. Sthiramati gives the bodhisattva Maitreya as an example.

3. See page 787.

cases taught in the texts on grammar—namely, the nominative, accusative, instrumental, purposive, causative, appendant, and intentional cases.[4]

Here, what he calls the purposive denotes the fourth case, the dative, as is also explained in the grammars—using the example of "giving": "giving for someone's benefit" denotes the purpose. What he calls the causative case refers to the ablative. His "appendant case" is the sixth case, the genitive: according to some grammars, the Sanskrit word *hasti* indicates a hand or appendage, as in "the hand of Chöjin." The intentional case, in this context, is not the fourth grammatical case, the dative, but signifies the locative, in the sense that since this text is intended for individuals in the Mahāyāna, it depends on (or is located in) those individuals. In some grammars, the seventh case is called *nimittasaptami*, the attributive case. On this basis, putting the emphasis on the accusative, the long commentary explains the first verse as follows.

What is the agent or entity that is doing the ornamenting? It is "He who knows the meaning," the Mahāyāna sūtras constituting the entity or basis that is ornamented. How are they ornamented? With this treatise, in its enabling us to understand the meaning of the Mahāyāna sūtras. How does he engage in the action of ornamenting those sūtras (the object) with this treatise? By indicating their meaning. With what means? With flawless speech and phrasing. For what purpose does it so ornament them? "To free them from suffering." What is the causal factor out of which it arises? It arises "out of natural compassion for suffering beings." What is it connected with? "The way expounded in the Supreme Vehicle," showing that this treatise is related to the Mahāyāna scriptures in the same way that a branch is connected to a tree. And on what kind of person does it depend? On "beings who follow that way": since it is intended for Mahāyāna individuals, it depends on their mind streams, like a bird sitting on a tree. The explanation in the long commentary appears to be difficult to understand, so here I have given a summary to clarify the main points.

Alternatively, if we explain this verse mainly stressing the instrumental case, it can be understood as follows. The agent who composed this treatise is indicated by "He who knows the meaning," that is, the regent Ajitanātha,

---

4. Mipham Rinpoche's grammatical analysis of the first verse requires a knowledge of Tibetan and Sanskrit grammar. Although the cases do not correspond exactly with those in English grammar, we have employed these terms for the sake of simplicity.

Lord of the Ten Levels,[5] who understood and perceived the intended meaning, just as it is, of all the sūtras of the Great Vehicle and thereby gained *perfect knowledge of all the meanings*. What did he create? He "created a composition showing that meaning," that is, he produced a composition indicating the whole meaning of the sūtras, composed by the power of his *perfect knowledge through unbounded intelligence and ability*. With what sort of instrument? "With flawless speech and phrasing," uncontaminated by obscurations—that is, with perfectly pure speech to express it, related to the *perfect knowledge of each and every aspect of the Dharma*, and with the *perfect knowledge of the languages*, the different languages of beings. For what purpose? In order to free all sentient beings from suffering. Out of what motivation or causal factor? Out of the great compassion that the Great Regent, whose nature is wisdom and compassion, has for all beings who are suffering. Now, is this treatise, whose composition comes from such a perfect cause, related to, or does it belong to, the Great Vehicle or the Lesser Vehicle? It is of "the way expounded in the Supreme Vehicle," meaning that it belongs to and is related to the Great Vehicle. And for whom is it intended—on whose mind streams will it depend? For bodhisattvas, beings who are following the way of the Supreme Vehicle.

Flawless speech, in short, comprises eight branches: (1) It is "civilized"—that is, it concerns the city of liberation, or it comprises well-known phrases; (2) it is sweet sounding, melodious, and pleasing; (3) it is clear, with fine phrases and words; (4) it confers knowledge; (5) its meaning is entirely comprehensible; (6) it is worth listening to, being endowed with great meaning—the meaning of the sacred Dharma—and disinterested,[6] and it makes one's faith grow more and more; (7) it is not discordant and is pleasant and inspiring; and (8) it is limitless—it is so vast in scope that a learned scholar could never reach the end of it. The first of these eight is flawless in terms of what such speech concerns; the next two in terms of its nature; and the remaining five in terms of its effect.

Flawless phrasing also comprises eight branches: (1) "The words and letters are rational"—the names, phrases, and letters are connected in the right order; (2) they are "connected, having the right meaning"—they match the meaning or accomplish the meaning; (3) they are "accordant"—they

---

5. Tib. *rgyal tshab sa bcu'i dbang phyug mi pham mgon po*, i.e., the bodhisattva Maitreya.
6. Tib. *rten pa med pa*, lit. "without support." According to Sthiramati, this means that it is not based on attachment to gain and honor.

present the meaning properly; (4) they are "appropriate"—the phrases and letters are clear; (5) they are "agreeable"—that is, they are to one's liking; (6) they are "fitting"—they suit the audience's mentality; (7) they are "apt"—they are to do with the Dharma and are meaningful and timely; and (8) they comprise the "branches for sustained diligence"—"sustained diligence" referring to diligence that brings about learning and does so constantly, and "branches" referring to the possession of the correct view and so on. All these indicate that everything the author says is meaningful.

What are the points illustrated by the five unexcelled metaphors? The great master Vasubandhu speaks of five points:

- that which is to be established;
- that which is to be specifically known;
- that which is to be reflected upon;
- that which is inconceivable;[7]
- and full accomplishment[8]—the object of realization that can only be known personally along with the actual approach to enlightenment.[9]

As to the intended meaning of these synoptic terms, there are a number of points of view put forward by the Indian masters. The master Sthiramati speaks of three classifications that associate these five terms with the five categories, the three realities and the three kinds of individual. These can be summarized as follows.

The five categories include all the subjects of the Great Vehicle and can therefore be associated with the above terms. These five categories are name, reason, conception, suchness, and nonconceptual gnosis. (1) With regard to the first of these, inasmuch as they express all phenomena by names, beings cling to them as objects; but inasmuch as these expressions are no more than names, the objects *have to be established* as not existing. (2) The reason for labeling things with names is that there are the appearances—as

---

7. Tib. *bsam gyis mi khyab pa*, lit. "cannot be pervaded by thought or reflection," in contrast to the previous point, which can be reflected upon (*bsam par bya ba*).
8. It should be noted here and throughout the discussion that follows that the same Tibetan term (*yongs su grub pa*) is used for this fifth point and for the third of the three realities, the fully present reality.
9. Tib. *byang chub kyi phyogs dang mthun pa'i ngo bo nyid*, lit. "the very nature of the elements that lead to enlightenment." This term covers the whole of part 5 (chapters 11–21) and not simply the elements leading to enlightenment (*byang chub phyogs mthun*) described in chapter 19.

the apprehended-object aspect—of the dependent reality. These are *what have to be specifically known* as dependent appearance through the power of the mind. (3) Conception is what appears as the apprehending-subject aspect of the mind and mental factors: it refers to the eight consciousnesses, which are the actual dependent reality. It is *what has to be reflected upon* by one's determining its nature. These three are associated with the first three metaphors respectively. (4) Suchness is the fully present reality: unless it is known personally, it is *inconceivable*. When suchness is directly realized on the first bodhisattva level, it gives rise to joy at the certainty of attaining enlightenment, as if one were hearing good news. (5) The elements that lead to enlightenment, above all the nonconceptual gnosis, are held to be what is indicated by the fifth metaphor. According to the *Compendium of the Great Vehicle*, if one were to ask what the *full accomplishment* is like, it is to be recognized by the four qualities of the purity aspect: the natural purity, or suchness; the uncontaminated purity, which is suchness free of all obscurations; the path purity that makes one attain the latter and comprises the elements that lead to enlightenment; and that which gives rise to it, the referential purity, that is, the Mahāyāna teachings.

Of the three realities, the imputed reality is what is to be established (as having no existence). The other four of the above five points—that which is to be specifically known, and so on—are associated with the dependent arising of the defilement and purity aspects, the essential nature (both related to dependent reality), the unchanging fully present reality, and the unmistaken fully present reality.

With regard to the three kinds of individual, Sthiramati teaches in terms of the uncomprehending, the doubtful, and those with wrong beliefs, for whom the Great Vehicle has first to be established as the Buddha's word, and so on. But for fear of being too long, I will not write about this here.

The master Jñānaśrī taught that associating the five points (what is to be established and so on) with the five categories (name, reason, and so forth) is not acceptable. His tradition has two approaches, one in which the five metaphors are associated with the earlier lines, "He who knows the meaning . . . ," and the other in which they are associated with the later sections, "Establishing the Great Vehicle as the Buddha's Word," and so on. This second approach is that followed by Vasubandhu and is as follows.

What is to be established is threefold: establishing the Great Vehicle as the Buddha's word, establishing the object of one's spiritual intent[10] as

---

10. I.e., enlightenment, or, in other words, the Buddha.

INTRODUCTION — 145

the supreme refuge, and establishing that the perpetuating cause is the Mahāyāna potential. What is to be specifically known is twofold: the spiritual intent and accomplishing the twofold goal. What is to be reflected upon is, in this case, thatness in its profound aspect (rather than its extensive aspect). The inconceivable is twofold: powers and full maturation. Full accomplishment refers to enlightenment. All this, says Jñānaśrī, can be understood from the words in the root text, "The chapter on establishing," and "opening a chest of jewels." It is also indicated in the Recapitulation.[11]

How one trains covers the chapters from "Interest" (11) through to "Instructions and Follow-Up Teachings" (15). Using the same scheme as above, Jñānaśrī explains that what is to be established corresponds to the chapters from "Interest" (gained from the Great Vehicle being established as the Buddha's word) through to "Practicing the Dharma" (11–14). What is to be specifically known is the instructions and follow-up teachings (15). What is to be reflected upon corresponds to the vast skill in means, comprising the ways of attracting disciples, the transcendent perfections (17); boundless attitudes, offering, and reliance (18), and so on; and the elements on the path leading to enlightenment (19). The inconceivable corresponds to qualities (20). Full accomplishment, which is the point of realization, corresponds to the chapter on consummation (21).

Excellent though these explanations are, and by the most learned of scholars, a more convenient and easily understood way to associate the five metaphors with the entire body of this treatise is as follows.

What is to be established. Establishing the Great Vehicle as the Buddha's word, which is like beating gold to produce an ornament, frees one from ignorance, wrong understanding, and doubts with regard to its being the Buddha's word, and gives rise to delight at being able to enjoy the Great Vehicle.

What is to be specifically known refers to the distinguishing features of the Great Vehicle, namely, its refuge, potential, spiritual intent, and practice. Now, of course, the listeners also take refuge in the Three Jewels; they have a potential—that of the lower vehicle; they develop a spiritual intent, albeit for their own state of peace and happiness; and, as the path, they practice the three trainings. But when one knows the specific differences that make the Great Vehicle superior to those lower vehicles, one acquires a greater

---

11. The recapitulation in the root text at the beginning of chapter 11. Jñānaśrī, in his *Sūtrālaṃkāra-piṇḍārtha*, adds that all this corresponds to "what one trains in," the first of the three headings mentioned earlier. This is now followed by "how one trains."

enthusiasm for the Mahāyāna path, because of which one feels the same sort of delight at being Mahāyāna-minded as at a lotus bud blossoming.

What is to be reflected upon, once one has understood these specific differences between the greater and lesser vehicles and entered the Great Vehicle, is the meaning of thatness taught in the Great Vehicle, the miraculous powers of the Mahāyāna bodhisattvas, and the manner in which their faculties are brought to full maturation. By reflecting on these, one will oneself engage in gaining certainty as to the meaning of thatness, in the powers that enable one to accomplish the two bodhisattva goals, and in the methods for fully maturing one's faculties to accomplish the latter, for the experience of obtaining any of the qualities of knowing thatness, accomplishing great powers, and maturing one's own faculties gives rise to the same delight as eating deliciously prepared food.

The inconceivable refers to enlightenment. Generally speaking, thatness too is inconceivable, for unless it is known personally we cannot imagine what it is like; but this does not contradict the fact that we can conceive of it in a general manner by hearing of it and reflecting on it simply in terms of its characteristics. Thus, although there is nothing more inconceivable than the inconceivable activities of a buddha, or than any others of the four things he taught as being inconceivable,[12] in this case we are determining the nature of enlightenment. By doing so, even though we have not at present achieved even a fraction of the good qualities of such inconceivable enlightenment, we know that once we have entered the path of the Great Vehicle, they will one day be attainable. And knowing this is like hearing or reading good news in a letter—a letter from the king, for example, saying, "He has rewarded you with such and such honors." Even if one does not actually have the reward at the time one hears the news, one feels delighted, in the certainty that one will receive it in due course. Thus, since enlightenment is the full accomplishment, the point of realization which can only be known personally, it is inconceivable. On the other hand, all the elements of the path that are the causal factors for accomplishing that enlightenment constitute what we call the approach to enlightenment, and so all the chapters

---

12. The four things that are inconceivable are described by Sthiramati as the inconceivable activities of the buddhas; the karma of beings; the actions of jewels, mantras, and medicines; and the yogi's sphere of activity. On page 260 below, Mipham lists them alternatively as the karma of beings, the power of mantras and medicines, the Tathāgata's wisdom, and the yogi's sphere of activity.

that come after the Enlightenment chapter are to be associated with the analogy of opening a chest of jewels.

One might think that the analogy of opening a chest of jewels would actually indicate enlightenment, and that it is therefore inappropriate to associate that analogy with the elements leading to enlightenment. But it is wholly appropriate, because the result of perfectly completing the elements leading to enlightenment—that is, of the path—is indeed enlightenment, so even though enlightenment is the ultimate thing to be indicated by the analogy of opening a chest full of jewels, the Enlightenment chapter in this context is about determining that inconceivable enlightenment by study and reflection. This, therefore, corresponds to the stage illustrated by the analogy of hearing the news in a letter, "You are going to be given a huge chest completely full of priceless jewels"; and it is on the path of no more learning that one realizes buddhahood, which is like opening a chest filled to the brim with all the jewel-like buddha qualities—the strengths and so forth. Individuals on the path of learning, however, only know that it is like that: they have not actually realized it, and so for them its exact nature is inconceivable. But the inconceivable is still what has to be reflected upon, so there is no contradiction here.

Having considered unsurpassable enlightenment in this way, to attain enlightenment one then practices the profound and extensive path in its entirety, beginning with interest. During this period, as one realizes the temporary qualities of the paths and levels, in due order, one receives the respective jewels in one's hand, as it were, and in that way the qualities of the paths and levels of that bodhisattva grow more and more vast, and the experience of those qualities right up until one reaches the buddha level is like actually opening the chest of jewels. The analogy, therefore, indicates the whole path from interest up to the result.

> When those of natural and ornamented beauty behold themselves
> Reflected in a glass, it brings them consummate delight.
> So too, when the meaning of the Dharma, whose excellent words are always naturally full of virtues,
> Is clarified, it brings the wise the greatest joy. (I, 3)

Some people might wonder, since the Buddha's teachings naturally possess all the qualities of perfection, both in their words and in their meanings, why is it necessary to embellish them with a treatise? It is true that an attractive woman who is adorned with different kinds of precious ornaments naturally has all the virtues of beauty. But if that person, with all her jewelry, looks at herself in a clear mirror, when she sees the image of her bejeweled form, she will feel especially great delight. So it is too for the Buddha's teachings, which are always endowed with boundless natural good qualities—for all his Excellent Words are virtuous in the beginning, middle, and end; they are perfect and complete in their words and meanings; they are endowed with the four qualities of pure conduct; and they are therefore particularly sublime. This treatise brings together in one text the extensive points in all the Buddha's varied teachings and arranges them in perfect order, setting forth without error each of the intended meanings of the Victorious One by investigating the profound aspects that are difficult to understand. As a result, the wise and learned have no difficulty in gaining certainty in the meaning of the Buddha's words, and they feel the greatest joy on hearing this treatise, as one would at seeing a reflection in a mirror that highlights beautiful features. It is in this sense that this treatise is an ornament, illuminating the intended meanings of the sūtras.

The Main Text of the Treatise

The explanation of the main text of the treatise that now follows is divided into five parts: (1) what is to be established; (2) what is to be specifically known; (3) what is to be reflected upon; (4) the inconceivable—that which is beyond reflection; and (5) the actual approach to enlightenment.[13]

---

13. The above explanation of how *Ornament of the Mahāyāna Sūtras* was composed makes up the first half of chapter 1 in Kawa Peltsek's translation, which we have entitled "Introduction." The first of the five sections that make up the main text, "What Is to Be Established," comprises the second half of the original chapter 1 (now entitled "chapter 1," which is a general outline) and chapter 2, which discusses specific details. We have, however, retained the original verse numbers.

PART ONE
WHAT IS TO BE ESTABLISHED

Establishing the Great Vehicle as the Buddha's Word

I

A General Presentation of Establishing the Great Vehicle as the Buddha's Word

Like medicine that smells foul
Yet tastes quite sweet,
Know that the Dharma also has two aspects—
The meaning and the words. (I, 4)

Some medicines smell so horrible that one can hardly put one's nose to them, and yet they taste delicious and are highly efficacious, healing one's ailments and doing one's body much good. There are similarly two sides to the teachings of the Great Vehicle—namely, the meaning and the written words. In considering the words alone, when immature people with small minds and lowly aspirations hear in the Mahāyāna scriptures that everything is devoid of essence and that one must stay in saṃsāra for up to three measureless great kalpas, undertaking great austerities such as giving away one's head and limbs, they take fright and reject these teachings as they would sweet-tasting, potent medicines on account of their pungent, unpleasant smell. This is the fault of the individual and not of the Mahāyāna teachings. For if we use reasoning to ascertain their meaning properly, we will see that although the teachings say that all phenomena are empty of an essential nature, they fully accord with presentations of conventional truth and are not indicating that things do not exist conventionally. In other words, they mean that things do not exist in the way they are imputed to exist by ordinary, immature beings. But they are not teaching that there is no dependent reality and no fully present reality, for the former exists conventionally and the latter is ultimate truth. As for remaining in saṃsāra and undertaking austerities, on account of their extraordinary skillful means and wisdom, bodhisattvas are able to accomplish these without any difficulty. So because understanding the meaning of the teachings will make us more interested in the Great Vehicle, this verse advises us not to reject it merely on the basis of the words and without realizing their underlying meaning.

> This difficult Dharma, extensive and profound,
> Is like a monarch—difficult to please;
> Yet if pleased, it likewise will bestow
> The riches of sublime qualities. (I, 5)

Now although the Mahāyāna path requires forbearance in undertaking immense austerities, a boundless accumulation of merit on a vast scale, and practice over long periods of time, these are good qualities in the Great Vehicle and not defects. Why? These teachings of the Great Vehicle, which are difficult (being extremely hard to obtain and, moreover, difficult for lesser beings to apply), extensive (on account of their infinite aspects such as the levels and transcendent perfections), and profound (being difficult to comprehend), are like kings. In ordinary life, it is hard to please great monarchs with small acts. But if one serves them with great deeds that really delight them, one will be rewarded by vast riches and wealth. Similarly, even though the Great Vehicle is difficult to accomplish for individuals of modest capacity, if it is practiced with a combination of skillful means and wisdom, it bestows the inexhaustible riches of sublime qualities such as the ten strengths and the four fearlessnesses.[1]

> The purest, priceless jewel will not delight
> The eyes of those who cannot see its worth.
> This Dharma is the same for those who lack discernment.
> But for their opposites, each will bring commensurate
>   delight. (I, 6)

Again, even though the Mahāyāna teachings have sublime qualities, people with meager understanding and interest in them do not know that. This is illustrated by the analogy of a jewel of the finest quality. Priceless though it is, if it were to fall into the hands of uneducated people who know nothing about jewels, they would not be able to see its true worth. A cowherd

---

1. For the ten strengths and four fearlessnesses, see chapter 21, pp. 836 and 837.

or other lowly person, instead of being thrilled, would therefore throw it away, thinking, "What good is this to me?" In the same way, undiscerning people do not derive any satisfaction from these teachings or consider them anything to marvel at. On the other hand, their opposites—those who are discerning and have vast aspirations—will, like people who know about jewels and take delight in the finest stones, derive the greatest joy from this Great Vehicle and take a keen interest in pursuing it.

This completes the explanation of the first chapter of *Ornament of the Mahāyāna Sūtras*.

2

Specific Explanations of Establishing the Great Vehicle as the Buddha's Word

The specific explanations comprise two sections: (1) different arguments to counteract wrong ways of thinking and (2) instructions on getting rid of wrong beliefs with regard to the Great Vehicle.

1. Different Arguments to Counteract Wrong Ways of Thinking

> The Great Vehicle is shown to be the Buddha's word.
> Because nothing adverse was predicted, it appeared at the same time,
> It is beyond the scope of intellectuals, it can be proven,
> Its existence or nonexistence depends on there being another vehicle,
> It is the antidote, and its words mean something different.
> (II, 1)

The followers of the Listeners' Vehicle say that the three scriptural collections of the listeners are the Buddha's word but that the Great Vehicle is not. They claim that the latter was made up after the Buddha's parinirvāṇa by tīrthikas and intellectuals under the influence of demons attempting to damage the Buddha's doctrine. And, they go on to say, the Buddha himself declared that it is necessary to distinguish between what is and what is not the Buddha's word, between teachings of the unwholesome and teachings of what is great. Any teachings that are introduced in the Sūtra Collection, appear in the Vinaya, or are not in contradiction with the true nature of things according to the Abhidharma are teachings of what is great; such teachings are the Buddha's word. Their opposite, teachings of the unwholesome, are the way of demons and tīrthikas. That being the case, the explanation in the Mahāyāna texts that the aggregates, sense spheres, and senses-and-fields are devoid of essence conflicts with the sūtras of the listeners' scriptures that teach the aggregates and sense spheres as existing. In the listeners' Vinaya, it is taught that to declare that there is no Buddha, Dharma, or Saṅgha constitutes a downfall: the explanations in Mahāyāna texts that they do not exist do not appear in their Vinaya. The listeners' scriptures teach that dependent arising, which by nature involves birth and cessation, leads in its forward order to saṃsāra and in the reverse order to nirvāṇa, whereas the Mahāyāna texts state that all phenomena are unborn and unceasing. Furthermore, while the listeners' scriptures state that it is by eliminating real obscurations on the paths of seeing and meditation that one attains nirvāṇa, the Mahāyāna texts teach that the obscurations to be eliminated and the antidotes eliminating them have no essential reality and that phenomena are by nature nirvāṇa. So on these and other points the Mahāyāna texts contradict the true nature of things according to the Abhidharma. On all these grounds, say the listeners, the Great Vehicle is not the Buddha's word.

They go on to point out that if people of modest capacity practice just this Listeners' Vehicle for their own good, they will attain the result of listener; those of middling capacity, by training for one hundred kalpas, will become rhinoceros-like solitary realizers; and if individuals of superior faculties, who are able to endure the sufferings of saṃsāra, train for three measureless kalpas, they will accomplish buddhahood. But apart from the vehicle of the listeners, they say, there is no other Great Vehicle.

There are eight different arguments in reply to the above objections:

(1) If the Mahāyāna were not the Buddha's word and were a doctrine that would have an adverse effect on his teachings, surely the Buddha would previously have predicted it, saying, "This is what will happen in the future." But he did not.

(2) Both the Great and Lesser Vehicles appeared at the same time, when the Buddha was present in this world, and there can be no certainty in the claim that the Great Vehicle appeared later.

(3) Since profound and extensive teachings like those on the levels, transcendent perfections, and emptiness are beyond the scope of such intellectuals and tīrthikas, the latter would have been incapable of composing them.

(4) If, then, the teachings on the levels, transcendent perfections, and

similar topics were composed by some other buddha—someone who had the same realization of the levels and perfections—this proves that such teachings could also be the Buddha's word.

Besides, it is well known that at the time Lord Buddha, the King of the Śākyas, taught the Dharma to the listeners, he spoke of the three vehicles—this is not disputed. It is the Buddha himself who taught the three vehicles, for it is established that he is the teacher who knew the paths of the three kinds of individual in their entirety. This is why the root verse says, "Its existence or nonexistence depends on there being another vehicle."

(5) If there is a so-called Great Vehicle separate from the Listeners' Vehicle, there must also be a Listeners' Vehicle. The fact that one can strive for peace for one's own sake, something that is not taught in the Great Vehicle, the path for achieving buddhahood, is the proof that there is also a Listeners' Vehicle. And if (6) there were no Great Vehicle other than the Listeners' Vehicle, there could not be a Listeners' Vehicle either, because it is impossible to have a single vehicle posited as two, a greater and a lesser. Since there would not then be a separate path for accomplishing omniscient buddhahood, buddhahood would be impossible, and without a buddha it is impossible that even the Listeners' Vehicle would have been taught. Put another way, since it is impossible for listeners to become buddhas, there would not even be a Listeners' Vehicle, which comes to the same thing.

If there is a Great Vehicle, then it is reasonable to suppose that when the Buddha appeared in the world, he would have taught it to those disciples who were of the Mahāyāna family,[1] for he is omniscient and compassionate, taking all three kinds of beings as his disciples. It follows, therefore, that Lord Buddha himself taught a Great Vehicle, so a Great Vehicle must exist. And if it exists, because we know of no great vehicle other than the unmistaken teachings on the levels, transcendent perfections, emptiness, and so forth, these teachings must be the Great Vehicle expounded by the Buddha. They cannot have been composed by intellectuals.

(7) Another reason is that the teachings of the Great Vehicle constitute the antidote to the two obscurations. If there were no Great Vehicle, then however much one trained in realizing the individual no-self, which is all that is taught in the Listeners' Vehicle, one would not eliminate the cognitive obscurations, and there would therefore be no way to accomplish omniscient buddhahood.

---

1. Tib. *theg chen rigs can*, that is, those who had the Mahāyāna potential (see chapter 4).

(8) The teachings that there is no Buddha, no path, no result, no birth, no cessation, and so on, do not, as the words appear to suggest, negate their existing in relative truth. These teachings were given in order to convey other meanings or express other intentions, and they are not therefore in contradiction with the nature of things.

> The vision of the buddhas is direct and clear;
> They act to keep the teachings safe;
> Their gnosis knows no impediment in terms of time;
> So they could never be indifferent. (II, 2)

One might argue that just because the Buddha did not predict it, one cannot be certain that the Mahāyāna is not a false teaching. (1) The buddhas, being free of all attachment and obstruction with regard to everything there is to be known, have the eye of gnosis that sees all phenomena directly. That there is something they do not know is, therefore, impossible. (2) They possess timely compassion, acting to preserve the doctrine for beings' benefit, so they would be watching out for any event that could be detrimental to the teachings and would not remain indifferent by failing to predict it. (3) Their unclouded wisdom-vision penetrates even the whole of the past, present, and future. So for these three reasons, one cannot accept the argument that a buddha might act indifferently and fail to make predictions.

> Because it is incomplete and in contradiction,
> And is neither the method nor taught in that way,
> This vehicle of the listeners
> Is not what is known as the Great Vehicle. (II, 3)

Moreover, one cannot attain buddhahood by training for a long time in the Listeners' Vehicle alone. While the path of the Great Vehicle is the one that accomplishes the twofold goal (one's own and others'), the accomplishment of others' goals is lacking in the Listeners' Vehicle, which is thus incomplete. The fact that listeners, out of fear and disenchantment with saṃsāra, strive to attain freedom from attachment and peace for themselves is in contradiction with accomplishing others' good. And while the method for attaining unsurpassable enlightenment comprises, above all, both wisdom (the realization of the two kinds of no-self) and great compassion (the wish that all sentient beings be freed from suffering), following the Listeners'

Vehicle is not such a method, and the method is not taught in that way.[2] For this reason, this vehicle of the listeners is not what we call the Great Vehicle, for it conflicts with the Great Vehicle.

> **Because its attitude, teachings,**
> **Application, support, and duration**
> **Conflict and are thus inferior,**
> **It is just that—a lesser vehicle. (II, 4)**

In what way does the Listeners' Vehicle conflict with the Great Vehicle? Its attitude is to keep one's own goal in mind. It teaches the listeners' path consistent with that attitude, in order to obtain mere peace for oneself. Its application involves diligently practicing such a path. The support to be relied upon is inferior in that listeners do not undertake the two accumulations on a vast scale. And its time span is short, for one can attain its ultimate fruit in as little as three lifetimes. Hence, these five aspects (attitude, teaching, application, support, and time) being lesser compared to those of the Great Vehicle, the Listeners' Vehicle is in every respect, by the very nature of its path, just that—a lesser vehicle compared to the Great Vehicle, so how could it be a great vehicle?

> **The Great Vehicle is introduced in its own sūtras,**
> **And is evident in its own Vinaya;**
> **And because it is profound, because it is extensive,**
> **It does not contradict the true nature of things. (II, 5)**

To find fault with the Mahāyāna teachings in their not being introduced in the sūtras and so on makes no sense. The fact that the Mahāyāna scriptures do not agree with some of the listeners' sūtras and other texts does not prove that the Great Vehicle is not the Buddha's word. Even the sūtras of the different listeners' orders do not agree with one another, so to think, "The Mahāyāna does not agree with the sūtras and other scriptures that we

---

2. Tib. *de ltar ma bstan*. Mipham explains the root text is "not taught in that way" simply by inserting the word *thabs* ("the method"). Both Vasubandhu and Sthiramati show that this statement answers the listeners' claim that although the bodhisattvas' path is not directly taught in the Listeners' Vehicle, it is indicated therein using different terms. But no, says Maitreya, the method of the Great Vehicle is not so taught in the Listeners' Vehicle, and it cannot be claimed that the Listeners' Vehicle is the Great Vehicle.

accept" is a shortcoming in the listeners' own thinking, not in the Mahāyāna teachings. Because they have not realized the profound intended meaning of the sūtras, they believe that there is a contradiction, but in fact there is no contradiction between the Buddha's earlier and later teachings. Even the Great Vehicle accepts that phenomena like the Three Jewels and the aggregates, sense spheres, and senses-and-fields exist for immature beings— conventionally or as mere imputations. It is because the listeners would be unable to understand that these phenomena (which they say are in every respect truly existing and undelusory) ultimately have no intrinsic nature that in the Listeners' Vehicle the Buddha spoke of subjects such as birth, cessation, defilement and purity, obscurations to be eliminated, and antidotes from the point of view of relative, conventional truth, and that he did not teach that phenomena have no intrinsic nature. But at no time did he teach that they were *not* without intrinsic nature and *not* empty, for in the Listeners' Vehicle too he spoke of the five aggregates being hollow and insubstantial, like magical illusions ("Form is like a bubble about to burst," and so on).[3]

There is, therefore, no contradiction. From its own point of view, the Great Vehicle, which is more profound and extensive than the Listeners' Vehicle, has all three sections that teach the three superior trainings— namely the Sūtra section, Vinaya, and Abhidharma. It is introduced in its own Sūtra section. It is evident in its own Vinaya, which relates to defilements specific to the Great Vehicle. And because it unmistakenly indicates the profound and extensive teachings, it is not in contradiction with the true nature of things as taught in the Mahāyāna Abhidharma.

> **Intellectuals are held to be reliant, uncertain,**
> **Not comprehensive, confined to the relative, and wearied,**
> **And they relate to immature beings.**
> **That is why the Great Vehicle is not within their scope. (II, 6)**

Earlier it was said that the Mahāyāna teachings are beyond the scope of intellectuals. You might argue that there is no certainty in this, and that intellectuals can write anything. This is not the case. Those we call intellec-

---

3. In other words, the Great Vehicle accepts the same relative truths as the Listeners' Vehicle, while in the Listeners' Vehicle the Buddha referred to emptiness, so the two vehicles are not contradictory as the listeners would suppose.

tuals apply their gross and subtle analyses only to things that come within their own limited sphere of vision. They are incapable of penetrating profound points that conflict with their own ordinary ways of thinking, and this is why they are called intellectuals. Such intellectuals are held to be reliant on evidence based on others' explanations or what they see for themselves, and they only practice analysis. Instead of ascertaining everything that can be known,[4] they reflect only on the superficial meanings that their own intellects can accept, so they can neither encompass phenomena in all their multiplicity nor understand that the profound nature of things is emptiness. Their scope is that of relative truth, confined to what they are capable of knowing with their own ordinary senses and minds. Incapable of fathoming the ultimate condition of things, the profound and extensive, for they lack the courage, these wearied individuals[5] relate to ordinary, immature beings. That is why the Great Vehicle, which teaches truths that are extremely profound and difficult to understand and infinitely vast, is not the object of intellectuals. The Dharma expounded by the Buddha is imbued with omniscient gnosis, and therefore it transcends all the aforementioned definitions of intellectuals—relying on others' logical principles and so on. It is inconceivable. Such a Dharma, therefore, could not possibly originate in the teachings of intellectuals and tīrthikas. Subjects like the levels, transcendent perfections, and emptiness that are explained in the Mahāyāna scriptures have never been seen in their texts in the past, and it is impossible that they will ever appear there in the future either.

Were you to ask, "If the method for attaining buddhahood is not taught in the Listeners' Vehicle,[6] how is it that it is taught in the Great Vehicle?" the answer is given in the following verse.

> **Because it is extensive, because it is deep,**
> **One is matured and nonconceptuality is realized.**

---

4. Although Sthiramati comments that, unlike the Buddha's teachings, which remain the same all the time, intellectuals' knowledge changes with time and so is uncertain or inconstant, Mipham here appears to interpret the intellectuals' uncertainty as an inability to ascertain all knowable phenomena and relates it to their noncomprehensiveness and being confined to the relative.

5. Tib. *skyo ba can*. According to Sthiramati, they are "wearied" in the sense that their words and courage have failed them.

6. This question arises from the statement in verse 3 above: "it is neither the method nor taught in that way."

> For this reason, both aspects are taught in the Great Vehicle,
> And it is this that is the means to the unsurpassable. (II, 7)

Because the Mahāyāna teaches the full extent of things, the extensive subjects of the levels, transcendent perfections, and so forth, and because it teaches the true nature of things, profound emptiness, one's stream of being is fully matured through the accumulation of merit (the extensive aspect), and nonconceptual gnosis arises through the realization of emptiness (the profound aspect). For this reason, both the profound and extensive aspects are taught in the Great Vehicle, and it is this that is the means for accomplishing unsurpassable enlightenment.

It is said that the listeners, striving for their own sake to achieve peace from the sufferings of saṃsāra, know only the no-self of the individual, and therefore their gnosis (the realization of the nature of things), compared to that of a Mahāyāna practitioner, is as minute as the space eaten out by a weevil inside a mustard seed. As for their realization of all things in their multiplicity, by the power of their aspiration for knowledge, they can only know, through examination, things that are not too remote in space or time. And although they have not realized the boundless qualities of the sacred Dharma, they are able to realize no-self from the meaning of just a single verse on the essence of dependent arising and achieve their result. In the Great Vehicle, the gnosis of the profound aspect is nonconceptual transcendent wisdom, and since it realizes everything that is to be known, it is as vast as space. It is the subject that knows the countless, extensive topics of the five sciences and of the three vehicles that make up the inner science of the Buddhist teachings. A Mahāyāna practitioner's accumulation of merit is as boundless as the water in the ocean, compared to which the accumulation of merit of someone practicing the Listeners' Vehicle is a mere puddle in a cow's hoofprint.

2. Instructions on Getting Rid of Wrong Beliefs Regarding the Great Vehicle

> Beings' groundless fear of the Great Vehicle makes them suffer,
> Accumulating a great mass of negative karma over long
>   periods of time.
> With no potential, evil companions, no virtue accumulated
>   from the past, and an untrained mind,
> They are frightened by this Dharma here, and miss the great
>   goal. (II, 8)

Beings of modest capacity are afraid of the Great Vehicle, though it is not something to be afraid of. This causes them mental distress and makes them hostile to the Dharma. As a result, they accumulate an enormous amount of negative karma and in the future will be tormented for long periods of time by the sufferings in the hells. The cause underlying this fear and rejection of the Mahāyāna is that they do not have the Mahāyāna potential. There are also the contributory conditions of their being taken on by the wrong sorts of companions (ones who are hostile to the Great Vehicle), of their having failed to accumulate merit in the past and thus being incapable of any interest in the Great Vehicle, and of their not having trained their minds in the profound meaning in the present life. As a result, they become afraid of these Mahāyāna teachings and, failing to respect the Mahāyāna teachings when they are present here, they will miss the great goal. This verse, therefore, is an instruction to guard oneself at all costs against these shortcomings by acquainting oneself with them and maintaining a careful attitude.

> There is no other vehicle than the Great Vehicle, for it is
>   utterly profound and it is concordant.
> Teaching a variety of things and continuously indicating
>   them through numerous means,
> It does not mean exactly what is said, for the Lord's
>   intention is exceedingly profound.
> If properly examined by the wise, this Dharma will not give
>   them cause to fear. (II, 9)

There is no Supreme Vehicle other than that Great Vehicle, in any realm or age, for its intent is extremely profound and it concurs with all beings' aspirations or with all aspects of knowledge. ("Concurs" is also explained as meaning that the Great and Lesser Vehicles appeared at the same time.)[7] It teaches the various aspects of the extensive Dharma—the levels, transcendent perfections, elements leading to enlightenment, aggregates, sense spheres, and senses-and-fields, what is correct and what is incorrect, and so forth. And it repeatedly and continuously demonstrates each of the teachings, such as that on emptiness, in numerous sūtras with different words and meanings. Because these were taught using implied teachings and indirect teachings and the words used to explain them are, for the most part, not to be taken literally, Lord Buddha's intention is extremely profound. For this

---

7. This is the author's own note.

reason, if the wise examine them properly, the teachings of the Great Vehicle will not make them afraid. Instead, they will feel all the more wonder and respect. This verse, therefore, advises us to examine the Great Vehicle and not to reject it without having done so.

> The wise begin by listening, and on that basis they reflect;
> From proper reflection comes the gnosis whose object is the true meaning;
> From that, the noble path is reached, and thus is wisdom born.
> Without their having self-cognizant wisdom at that stage, how would they ever be convinced? (II, 10)

Even if people do examine it, however, they might still not be convinced. This verse shows that this is because they have not developed an approximate understanding, let alone direct self-cognizant wisdom, with regard to the profound meaning. At this stage of the entrance to the Dharma, one begins by listening to the teachings, and on that basis one will keep their meaning in mind—reflecting on the teachings or keeping them in mind is impossible without having heard them. From properly keeping them in mind, there arises the gnosis of acceptance of a bodhisattva on the path of earnest aspiration that takes the true meaning as its object.[8] From that, the first level on the noble path is attained, and thence the gnosis or wisdom of the ten levels is born. At that time, however, what it is that realizes the profound true meaning is never an ordinary person's mind but self-cognizant wisdom. So unless one has that self-cognizant wisdom, how can one be convinced with any other, intellectual, understanding? Forms cannot be seen without eyes to see them, even if one has ears and other sense organs.

> "I do not understand it." "Such profundities the Buddha cannot know."
> "Why should the profound be beyond the scope of intellectuals?"
> "Why will those who realize the profound meaning be liberated?"
> Such thoughts don't hold as reasons for being afraid. (II, 11)

---

8. Tib. *yang dag pa'i don*, in other words, emptiness, the object of right view.

For this reason, even if one does not completely understand the meaning of the Great Vehicle, it is not right to reject it. It is wrong to think, "Because I don't understand it, it is not the true Dharma." We do not understand it because we have not accumulated enough merit and we therefore do not have the good fortune to realize the profound meaning—like blind people who cannot see even in broad daylight.

Neither is it right to think that things that are too profound for us cannot be understood by the Buddha either. We are obscured as to the true meaning; the Buddha possesses gnosis free from all obscuration. So why would something we do not understand not be understood by the Buddha? People with blurred vision cannot see minute objects, but this is not the case for someone with the divine eye.

Do not think, "Even if it is profound, why should it not be within the scope of intellectuals?" If it were no better than mere intellectual knowledge, then why would the buddhas need to attain profound, manifest enlightenment?

"Why will those who realize the profound meaning—that there is no birth and no cessation—be liberated, while intellectuals who analyze things with the valid cognition of direct perception and inference will not?" This sort of reflection is no reason for fearing the Great Vehicle. If one could be liberated merely by investigating things with direct perception and inferential logic, all sentient beings would be liberated from the beginning. This, however, is not the case, for they are bound by attachment to things. If they knew that things have no intrinsic existence, they would be liberated. Intellectuals who think like that believe their own understanding to be valid and have rejected the profound meaning of the Dharma perceived by the great noble beings. Like the frog in the fable of the frog in the well[9] and like a blind person competing against someone who can see, they are extremely foolish, for they swear by their own invalid thinking and repudiate valid cognition.

The fact that those of lowly aspirations, of very base propensity, Who keep base friends for constant company

---

9. This fable is related in Patrul Rinpoche, *The Words of My Perfect Teacher*, 140. The frog in the story could not conceive of an expanse of water any larger than the well he lived in. When he arrived at the edge of the ocean, he was overcome by its immensity and died from shock.

> Have no interest in this Dharma that perfectly explains
> The extensive and profound is proof of its superiority. (II, 12)

As a result of their very base potential or propensity,[10] reinforced by the fact that they are surrounded by base companions who are averse to the Great Vehicle, people with lowly aspirations have no interest in these teachings that explain in an unmistaken way the profound and extensive meaning. Therein lies the proof of the Great Vehicle's superiority. Because it is beyond the scope of inferior beings, the wise know that it is a teaching that is out of the ordinary.

> Adhering to what they have heard, they gain some discernment
> And despise anything else they hear.
> Ignorant of the rest of these boundless varied subjects,
> How could they ever be certain? (II, 13)

Adhering to what they have heard, non-Mahāyānists have acquired a little bit of discernment in analyzing whether something is valid or invalid. And yet, instead of analyzing profound teachings that are unfamiliar to them, they scorn anything else they hear—that is, the Mahāyāna—without having examined it. This is wrong. Why? Because without knowing the infinite variety of subjects in the Great Vehicle, with all their implications, one will be ignorant as to whether the rest of the teachings are valid or invalid, as to whether they are the Dharma or not. How can you be certain?[11] Without properly understanding the meaning, you cannot be sure of the difference between what to accept and what to reject.

> If one understands the words literally,
> One becomes proud and one's intellect declines.
> Rejecting the Excellent Words as a whole,
> One will be destroyed, obscured by anger toward the
>   Dharma. (II, 14)

> Negative states of mind are by nature harmful—
> It is wrong to have them even for illogical things,

---

10. That is, the potential for lower vehicles. See chapter 4.
11. I.e., how can non-Mahāyānists be certain that the Great Vehicle is not the Buddha's word.

**Let alone for teachings that one doubts.
It's best, therefore, to be impartial, and thus free of fault. (II, 15)**

If we take those passages in the sūtras that say, "There is no form, there is no sound . . . ," incorrectly, without knowing their intended meaning, and we think that we have definitely understood or fully comprehended them, as if they meant what the words indicate, we will become conceited, saying to ourselves, "I know what that phrase means," and because we have not understood the correct meaning, our discernment will deteriorate. This sort of thing will lead to our rejecting other teachings of the Buddha's Excellent Words as well. It is therefore destructive for us, for by getting angry at the profound teachings we will accumulate serious obscurations.

The reason for this is that the mental fault of anger is naturally harmful. Unlike physical and verbal actions, which can be transformed by their motivation, it is by its very nature negative. It is inappropriate to get angry at something unpleasant that might harm one, or even at illogical objects such as bits of charred wood, for in the Mūlasarvāstivādin *Sūtra Like a Saw*,[12] the Buddha said, "Monks, it is not right to get angry at a piece of charred wood, let alone at a body that possesses consciousness." So one need hardly mention that it is out of place to get angry at teachings about which one is skeptical and regarding which one is unable to determine whether or not they are the true Dharma. For as Lord Buddha said, if one has rejected the Mahāyāna teachings, one will repeatedly experience truly terrible suffering in the Hell of Torment Unsurpassed for many kalpas, during which time numerous world systems will be formed and destroyed. This is why, even though they may not feel interested in a teaching that they do not really understand, it is better for those who wish the best for themselves to remain impartial, rather than dishonoring it by getting angry or disrespectful, for they will then not be at fault.

This completes the explanation of the meaning of the second chapter of *Ornament of the Mahāyāna Sūtras*, the chapter on establishing the Great Vehicle.

---

12. Tib. *nyan thos kyi gzhung sog le lta bu'i mdo*. Mipham has copied the name of this source from Sthiramati's commentary. It most probably belonged to the Mūlasarvāstivādin canon, which is no longer extant, so we have not been able to trace the sūtra. Passages similar to the one quoted here are to be found in the Vinaya section of the Kangyur and in the *Parinirvāṇa-sūtra*.

Having thus established the Great Vehicle as the Buddha's word, we now come to what is to be specifically known—namely, the differences between the Great and Lesser vehicles. Although there are many ways of classifying these, they are explained here in terms of the particular features of the four topics of refuge, potential, spiritual intent, and practice, beginning with the potential, which is the cause, and the refuge, which is the initial entrance to the path. From this we can understand the differences in the various attitudes and their application.

PART TWO
WHAT IS TO BE SPECIFICALLY KNOWN

ĀRYA ASAṄGA AND THE BUDDHA MAITREYA

3
Refuge

This chapter has three sections: (1) particular features; (2) the nature of the refuge that has those features; and (3) a concluding summary. The first of these is divided into two: (1) a brief presentation of the four particular features and (2) a detailed explanation of these four points.

1. Particular Features
a. Brief Presentation of the Four Particular Features

> Because of four particular features by which they are classified—
> Universality, commitment, realization, and overpowering supremacy—
> Those who fully take refuge in the Three Jewels with the Supreme Vehicle in mind
> Are known as the greatest among those who have gone for refuge. (III, 1)
>
> Why? At first it is difficult to make such a definite commitment,
> And practicing over many thousands of kalpas is hard;
> Because its accomplishment is of great benefit to beings,
> Taking refuge in this Great Vehicle is of the highest value.
> (III, 2)

The refuge of the followers of the Great Vehicle is superior on account of four particular features: their universality, for they have undertaken to liberate all sentient beings and so on; their commitment ("to attain buddhahood"); their realization of the two kinds of no-self; and the fact that they outshine worldly beings and listeners and solitary realizers. On account of the particularity of these four general points or divisions, anyone who has fully taken refuge in the Three Jewels with the goal or manner of the Supreme Vehicle specifically in mind is to be known as foremost among those who have gone for refuge—superior to those who have taken refuge in mundane beings such as Brahmā and Īśvara and to the listeners and solitary realizers who have taken refuge in the Three Jewels for their own benefit.

Why is this? Because it is difficult in the beginning for ordinary beings to be definite in vowing and praying: "In order to free all sentient beings from saṃsāra and set them in liberation and omniscience, I will attain unsurpassable, perfect enlightenment as a buddha." Of the numerous beings there are, those who make this kind of aspiration related to their spiritual intent are extremely rare. Then, once they have given rise to this spiritual intent, it is difficult to accomplish, for its application involves giving away their bodies, their possessions, and so forth in order to attain unsurpassable enlightenment and completely liberate sentient beings, and it takes many thousands of kalpas. When they accomplish unsurpassable enlightenment as buddhas, they benefit all sentient beings until the end of time, so it is very meaningful. This is why it is of the greatest value to take this Great Vehicle as the path and rely on it as a refuge.

b. Detailed Explanation of These Four Points in Order
i. Universality

> **Those who have set out to liberate all beings,**
> **Whose mastery is all-inclusive with regard to the vehicles**
>   **and gnosis,**
> **And for whom nirvāṇa is the one taste of saṃsāra and peace—**
> **Such wise persons should be known for their universality.**
>   (III, 3)

The particular feature of universality is fourfold, related to sentient beings, vehicles, gnosis, and nirvāṇa, in that order. Bodhisattvas are engaged in liberating the whole infinity of sentient beings. They have realization of all three vehicles. They have mastered the universal gnosis that is the realization of the two kinds of no-self. And they have realized the expanse of nirvāṇa as the one taste of saṃsāra and peace and embrace the whole of nirvāṇa or knowable phenomena (for through their wisdom and compassion they do not remain in the extremes of existence and peace).[1] These wise beings are to be understood in this context as universal. The listeners do not possess this particular feature.

ii. Commitment

This section is divided into two: (1) the actual commitment and (2) analogies indicating the virtues of that commitment.

(1) The Actual Commitment

> They who, with much joy, strive for supreme enlightenment,
> Who perfectly undergo austerities without getting discouraged,
> Who will attain buddhahood and be the equal of all the buddhas—
> Those wise persons should be known for their supreme commitment. (III, 4)

Bodhisattvas rejoice many times from the depth of their hearts in the Buddha's qualities (his strengths, fearlessnesses, and so forth) and have the intention of striving for supreme enlightenment, so they are distinguished by their aspiration. From the level of earnest aspiration and through the ten levels, they perfectly undergo austerities such as giving away their bodies and so forth and willingly accepting suffering, without ever getting discouraged from accomplishing the path, so they are distinguished by their practice. Having attained perfect buddhahood, they will be indistinguishable in their elimination and realization from all the buddhas and will become their equal in Body, Speech, and Mind, so they are distinguished by their result. In this way, the wise are to be known for their supreme commitment or pledge.

(2) Analogies Indicating the Virtues of That Commitment

There are two analogies: that of a prince and that of a great minister.

---

1. In other words, they embrace or pervade the whole of the nondwelling nirvāṇa (*mi gnas myang 'das*).

(a) The Analogy of a Prince for One Who Is Born into the Supreme Buddha Family

> They who are well born as the supreme children of the buddhas
> Have the intention, wisdom, merit, and compassion—
> The incomparable seed, mother, womb, and nurse.
> Those wise persons should be known for their supreme commitment. (III, 5)

Like the son of a universal emperor, who possesses four perfections—his seed; his sublime mother, who is a queen of noble lineage; her womb, which is free of such defects as disease; and the nurse who brings him up—bodhisattvas are known as the high-born children of the unbroken lineage of the tathāgatas. Listeners, on the other hand, are not known as children of the Buddha: they are disciples born from his Speech.[2] Bodhisattvas born as the supreme children of the buddha bhagavāns have aroused the mind intent on unsurpassable enlightenment. They have the transcendent wisdom that is the realization of no-self. They possess the accumulation of both merit and wisdom. And they have the compassion that never abandons any sentient being. These four qualities are analogous to the incomparable father's seed, the incomparable mother, the incomparable womb, and the incomparable nurse respectively. Wise bodhisattvas born from these qualities should be understood as having made the supreme commitment. Because of that pledge to accomplish unsurpassable enlightenment, they are born into the family of the tathāgatas, like a true imperial prince.

> Their bodies are fully adorned with all the marks,
> And they have gained the power to bring all beings to maturity;
> They have acquired the great bliss of the buddhas, infinite and peaceful,
> And know how to display great means in providing refuge for all beings. (III, 6)

---

2. It is said that the Buddha's children comprise his actual son Rāhula, the son of his Body; the listeners, who are the children of his Speech; and the bodhisattvas, who are the children of his Mind.

Again, one who is born as the son of a universal emperor has four qualities that make him superior to ordinary persons. His body is ornamented with distinctive marks. He subjugates other, minor monarchs and governs them well. He acquires the wealth of a prince. And he is well versed in royal ways and in all branches of science and culture. Analogous to these four qualities are those of the bodhisattvas. Everything about them is pleasing, their bodies being adorned with all the major and minor marks of excellence. The latter are more extraordinary than the marks of a worldly universal emperor in three respects: they are lasting,[3] they are more brilliant, and they are perfectly complete. Through the strength of their wisdom, bodhisattvas have gained the physical, verbal, and mental power to mature all sentient beings by establishing them in virtue. They have acquired the inexhaustible, and therefore infinite, great bliss of the buddhas, at peace from the defilements. And in drawing all beings out of suffering and establishing them in everlasting bliss, they will become a refuge for all beings, knowing how to display the great means as it is and in its entirety, or to display the infinite facets of skillful means and wisdom.

> **On them all the buddhas have conferred the empowerment of great light rays,**
> **They have perfect, total mastery over phenomena,**
> **They know perfectly how to teach the Buddha's circle of disciples,**
> **And, establishing the precepts, they strive to correct and help. (III, 7)**

The son of a universal emperor bearing all the marks of perfection possesses four other qualities. He has been empowered by his father as the crown prince. He is expert in the critical appraisal of his duties. He is accomplished in the physical, vocal, and intellectual arts. And he rules his subjects and court by subjugation and protection.[4] So it is with bodhisattvas who commit themselves to unsurpassable enlightenment. On the tenth level, all the buddhas bestow on them the great light rays empowerment. The unobstructed gnosis they obtain as a result of that empowerment gives them perfect and

---

3. Tib. *yul na gnas pa*. The univeral emperor's marks disappear when he dies. A bodhisattva's marks are stable and permanent.
4. Sthiramati: "he punishes offenders and helps and rewards those who do well."

total mastery over all phenomena, as they are and as many as there are. They know perfectly how to display miracles and teach the Dharma to all the Buddha's circle of disciples. And by establishing the training in superior discipline, they correct wrongdoers and help and care for those who act properly.

(b) The Analogy of a Great Minister

> Like a great minister, they penetrate the transcendent
>   perfections,
> Constantly watch over the array of elements that lead to the
>   great enlightenment,
> Perpetually hold the three secrets,
> And continually and unremittingly act for the good of many
>   beings. (III, 8)

Unlike the listeners, these bodhisattvas are the ones who watch over the Buddha's Mahāyāna teachings and the secrets of his Body, Speech, and Mind. To illustrate this by an analogy, a great minister who has become the king's most trusted confidant can go into the queens' quarters and other parts of the king's inner court; he keeps watch over all the treasury; he is privy to the king's secret discussions; and he has authority to give orders to others. Like the great minister with his four privileges, bodhisattvas penetrate the Buddha's teachings, engaging in the practices of the Great Vehicle such as the ten transcendent perfections. They constantly take care of or watch over the treasury in which all the elements leading to great enlightenment are spread out and displayed. They perpetually hold the three secrets of the Buddha's Body, Speech, and Mind. (Vajrapāṇi, for example, is said, in the *Sūtra of the Inconceivable Secrets*, to have remained constantly in the presence of Lord Buddha, both when the latter was a bodhisattva and when he attained buddhahood, and he knew even the secrets of the Buddha's Body, Speech, and Mind that others did not know.)[5] And they are always working unceasingly for the good of numerous beings.

   5. Sthiramati explains these three secrets as follows. With the secret of the body, during famines or epidemics the great bodhisattvas manifest as huge fish on which beings can feed, or as celestial doctors. Through the blessings of their secret speech, walls, trees, and space resound the teachings of the sacred Dharma. The blessings of their secret mind enable dull beings to realize the profound points of the Dharma.

iii. Realization

> They have acquired a great heap of merit, supremacy in the
> three worlds, the greatest mundane happiness,
> Complete peace from the great mass of suffering, the bliss of
> supreme wisdom,
> The totality of virtues—the sublime eternal body, a mass of
> many dharmas—
> The reversal of habitual tendencies, and complete liberation
> from existence and peace. (III, 9)

Realization can be summed up as the realization that the individual and phenomena are devoid of self, but it is treated here in greater detail in terms of eight excellent qualities: (1) In the beginning, when bodhisattvas develop an interest in the Mahāyāna teachings, they acquire an immense mass of merit, as limitless as space and sentient beings. (2) Having developed interest, they then arouse the mind intent on unsurpassable enlightenment, and at that moment they become exalted, superior to all the beings in the three worlds. (3) When they intentionally take birth in saṃsāra for their own and others' sakes, they experience boundless worldly happiness, with all the pleasures of gods and humans. (4) On the first level, they attain direct realization of the expanse of reality, at which point they acquire the state of mind of the equality of self and others. Having seen that they will be able to accomplish their own and others' goals, they feel exceedingly joyful and completely quell the great mass of suffering for themselves and others,[6] for at that time they are free from the five kinds of fear—of having nothing to live on, of not being praised, with regard to their retinue,[7] of falling into the lower realms, and of death and transmigration. They thus quell their own suffering and reduce these same five fears in sentient beings too. (5) When, on the eighth level, they attain the "acceptance that phenomena are unborn," they spontaneously achieve the great vision of nonconceptual gnosis and abide in the bliss of the highest state of mind.

---

6. The "great mass of suffering" (Tib. *sdug bsngal gyi phung po chen po*) refers to suffering in its gross aspects. Until bodhisattvas attain enlightenment, they are still subject to the most subtle forms of suffering.

7. "Fear with regard to their retinue": bodhisattvas are not afraid of not having a retinue, and they are not afraid of being bettered in any way by their followers and unable to answer their questions.

Having passed these five stages and the ten levels, they obtain the following three qualities on the level of buddhahood. (6) They have completed the totality of virtue, the eternal body of Dharma that endures until the end of saṃsāra, utterly exalted and supreme above worldly beings, listeners, and solitary realizers, a mass of many countless untainted qualities or teachings (sūtras and so forth).[8] (7) They have driven away forever the habitual tendencies related both to the defilements and to cognitive obscurations. And (8) they have attained the nondwelling nirvāṇa, complete liberation from the extremes of both existence and peace.

iv. Overpowering Supremacy

> The wise outshine the listeners and their followers
> On account of their virtue, which is vast; of great value;
>   infinite, perpetual, and unceasing; and inexhaustible.
> That virtue—of mundane bodhisattvas, of supramundane
>   bodhisattvas who bring beings to maturity,
> And of bodhisattvas who acquire mastery—is never brought
>   to an end with the extinction of the aggregates. (III, 10)

These wise bodhisattvas surpass the listeners and solitary realizers together with their many followers on account of four kinds of virtue. The virtue of bodhisattvas dwelling on the level of earnest aspiration up to the supreme mundane level is not like that of the listeners, which leads to a partial nirvāṇa, but it is also the cause for their entering saṃsāra to benefit all sentient beings. It is therefore because of the vastness[9] of their virtue that bodhisattvas outshine all the listeners.

From the first level up until the seventh, they outshine all the listeners on account of the great value of their virtue, for it leads to the attainment of unsurpassable enlightenment.

On the three pure levels, with the spontaneous accomplishment of nonconceptual gnosis, all their sources of good grow and mature like fruit rip-

---

    8. Mipham provides here two possible interpretations ("qualities" and "teachings") for the root text's "dharmas" (Tib. *chos*).

    9. Tib. *rgya chen po*. Although Mipham's text appears to read "because of its being a great cause" (*rgyu chen po*), we have followed Sthiramati and the Derge edition of the root text here.

ening. Infinite qualities such as the strengths and transcendent perfections develop. And bodhisattvas perpetually and unceasingly perform the deeds of the buddhas and expound the Dharma. So on this account, again they outshine the listeners.

On the level of buddhahood, they acquire the ultimate perfection of qualities such as the strengths, fearlessnesses, and distinctive qualities, and since these can never come to an end in the expanse without residual aggregates, they again outshine the listeners.[10]

Thus the virtue of those who have taken the Mahāyāna refuge—that is, of those who arouse bodhicitta on the path of earnest aspiration up to the supreme mundane level; of those who bring beings to full maturity by the purity of their superior intention from the supramundane second level up to the seventh; and of those who acquire perfect mastery in four respects (nonconceptuality and so on) on the three pure levels—is especially sublime because it does not come to an end in the nirvāṇa without residual aggregates as is the case for the listeners and solitary realizers.

2. The Refuge Itself That Has the Above Particular Features

> Know that this refuge, the commitment of those who wish
> for buddhahood, arises out of compassion.
> It is the refuge of the wise, who thence attain omniscience
> and, undeterred by hardship, bring benefit and happiness.
> For those who are certain of deliverance it always has the
> qualities that all the vehicles depend on.
> It is obtained formally and naturally. In these respects, it is
> supreme. (III, 11)

This refuge of followers of the Great Vehicle is the desire for buddhahood: it is the aspiration of those who wish to accomplish the reality of the Buddha in whom they have gone for refuge, making the promise or commitment "Just as this Buddha is the refuge of all sentient beings, may I too attain buddhahood in order to remove the sufferings of all sentient beings." This is the *essence* or *nature* of the refuge. For the listeners it is to take refuge in

---

10. Tib. *phung po lhag med kyi dbyings*. See "nirvāṇa without residual aggregates" in the glossary.

the Buddha, Dharma, and Saṅgha in order to protect themselves, thinking, "May I be liberated from the suffering of saṃsāra."

You should understand that this commitment, "May I accomplish buddhahood," comes from the loving, compassionate wish that all sentient beings be freed from suffering. The *cause*, therefore, of the Mahāyāna refuge is compassion.

From taking refuge in this way, bodhisattvas attain the ten levels one after the other and obtain the gnosis that knows everything there is to be known. This is the *result* of taking refuge, the resultant refuge.

Having attained buddhahood, they bring benefit and happiness to all beings for as long as space endures. Even while training on the path, bodhisattvas are tireless in undergoing all kinds of hardships for the benefit of sentient beings. These constitute the *effects* of refuge. Sthiramati's commentary and others explain that beings are brought benefit in this life materially and by being introduced to virtue, and are brought happiness in other lives by being set in pleasurable human and celestial rebirths and in nirvāṇa. Elsewhere these are explained as the happiness of the higher realms in this life and the benefit of ultimate excellence in future lives. Yet another explanation refers to temporary happiness and ultimate benefit.

The *property* of the refuge is that, for individuals who are certain of deliverance through the paths of the lesser and greater vehicles, it always possesses the qualities that all three vehicles rely on. The Mahāyāna refuge embraces all three vehicles, and therefore teaching that vehicle and its elements to any beings who have faith in any of the three vehicles frees them from suffering or brings them definitive deliverance. So in having the qualities relied on in all vehicles, it is the refuge and protector of the three Buddhist families,[11] the beings of these different families relying on or placing their trust in their respective vehicles.

There are two categories or *forms of implementation* for this taking refuge: refuge obtained formally and that obtained naturally. The first is the refuge obtained through one's own verbal promise and through the words and other signs of preceptors and instructors. This is the gross refuge that comes about through communication. Refuge obtained naturally refers to direct realization of the truth of ultimate reality on the first bodhisattva level, which from then on cannot possible fail. This kind of refuge is what we

---

11. Tib. *rigs can gsum*, lit. "three potential-holders." The three Buddhist families are the listeners, solitary realizers, and bodhisattvas.

call the profound or subtle refuge obtained naturally. Arousing bodhicitta similarly has two aspects.

This refuge of the wise (bodhisattvas) that possesses these six aspects—essence or nature, cause, result, effects, property, and implementation—is the best, far superior to the refuges of mundane beings and of supramundane beings such as listeners and solitary realizers.

3. Concluding Summary

> To go for refuge in this way has great value,
> For those who do so will develop a host of boundless qualities.
> Filled with thoughts of compassion for beings,
> They spread the teachings of the peerless great and noble beings. (III, 12)

Taking this Mahāyāna refuge in the way described above is of immense value. This is because in that way one accomplishes both one's own and others' goals. Those who have taken refuge will increasingly develop a host of immeasurable qualities, from progressively accomplishing the levels and paths up to acquiring the qualities of buddhahood (the strengths, fearlessnesses, unceasing spontaneous activities, and the rest), thus completely fulfilling their own goal. And, to fulfill others' goals, they will attain perfection in thought and deed, for they are filled with the attitude of compassion for the whole infinity of these beings, which they then implement by extensively teaching and explaining in the ten directions the Mahāyāna teachings of the peerless great noble beings, the buddhas and bodhisattvas, thereby setting beings in perfect liberation, in temporary and everlasting happiness.

This completes the explanation of the third chapter of *Ornament of the Mahāyāna Sūtras*, the chapter on refuge.

Whichever path we follow of any of the three vehicles, it begins with refuge. Those who follow the path are confident that their respective path is the way to perfect liberation that will free them forever from the sufferings of saṃsāra. They therefore also consider those who teach that path to be sublime sources of refuge, and this is how they set out on the path. Those, on the other hand, who do not truly accept the Three Jewels as their refuge lack the good fortune to be Buddhists. It is for this reason that the refuge is explained first.

Now, although the greater and lesser vehicles are both similar in that their followers take refuge in the Three Jewels, it happens that there are three kinds of beings—some take refuge in the Great Vehicle, for example, while others take refuge in the lesser vehicles. You might wonder what the reason is for this, and it is in order to resolve such questions that the Refuge chapter is followed by a chapter on the potential. Since beings who possess the supreme potential are those who arouse the mind that is set on unsurpassable enlightenment, it is this spiritual intent that is dealt with next. There then follows an explanation of the practice, that is, the actual application of the attitude of bodhicitta. This is the first of two chapters on practice, and it is simply a general exposition of the differences that are to be specifically known between the practice of the Great Vehicle and that of the lesser vehicles. The chapter on practice that comes later is an explanation of the actual practice as distinct from study. Having noted this, we will now proceed with the main subject.

4

The Potential[1]

This chapter is divided into three sections: (1) an explanation of having the potential; (2) an explanation of how the potential may be lacking; and (3) a concluding summary of the chapter, praising the supreme potential of the Great Vehicle. The first of these has two parts: a synoptic introduction and a detailed explanation of each its points in order.

1. An Explanation of Having the Potential
a. Synoptic Introduction

> Existence, supremacy, nature,
> Signs, categories of potential,
> Defects, benefits, and two analogies—
> These are the topics, each with four aspects. (IV, 1)

There are eight general points: (1) the existence of the different potentials; (2) the supremacy of the Mahāyāna potential over these different potentials; (3) the nature of that potential; (4) the signs of that potential; (5) categories of the potential; (6) the obscurations or defects that prevent the potential from being awakened; (7) the benefits of the potential; and (8) two analogies for the potential, gold and precious stones. Each of these eight is explained in terms of four aspects.

---

1. The meaning of the Tibetan term *rigs* includes both a potential and the expression of that potential, hence its translation as "family," "kind," "spiritual lineage," etc. In genetic terms it would mean both the gene and the genotype, though here, of course, a person's spiritual potential and makeup is not something that is inherited from parents but is rather the continuity of spiritual karma. We have therefore translated the term as "potential" and occasionally as "type," depending on the context.

b. Detailed Explanation of Each of the Points in Order
i. The Existence of Different Potentials

> In considering the differences in disposition,
> Interest, and practice,
> And the different results,
> The existence of different potentials can be stated with
>   certainty. (IV, 2)

How can one see that there are different potentials? There is a great variety of different potentials or dispositions in beings' characters. (Here "disposition," "seed," and "potential" are simply different words for the same thing.) Sentient beings' dispositions take all sorts of different forms. Some indulge in attachment, others are predominantly hateful, ignorant, proud, and so forth. And there are different spiritual types—some are listeners, some are solitary realizers, others are followers of the Great Vehicle. So it is clear that there are different kinds of potential. And for each of these different kinds of beings—beings who are predominantly full of attachment, and so on—there are again many different variations. The *Sūtra of the Myrobalan* states:

> Were you to count each type of being using a pile of myrobalan fruits one league high and one league in circumference, saying, "This one represents the beings who have the listener potential, this one those with the solitary-realizer potential, this one those who have the potential for indulging in attachment," and so on, that pile of myrobalan fruits (or pellets) would quickly be used up. But you will never be finished with counting the different types of beings.

Because of these different potentials or dispositions, there is also a whole variety of different interests. Even with regard to one thing—food—there are countless different tastes, beginning with some people's taste for sweet things and others' preference for sour foods. If we consider the path to liberation too, there are differences. Some people, whether or not they are taught by a spiritual master, have faith in the Listeners' Vehicle and not in the Great Vehicle. Similarly, there are differences in beings' ability, or inability, to practice the transcendent perfections. And in terms of the resultant liberation, there is the lesser enlightenment of the listeners, the middling enlightenment of the solitary realizers, and the supreme enlightenment of the Great Vehicle.

Considering these four arguments, therefore, it can definitely be said that there are different kinds of potential. If there were not different potentials or dispositions—in other words, if there were no differences in the cause—there would not be different interests, practices, and results either. The fact that this is not the case proves that there are different dispositions.

ii. The supremacy of the Mahāyāna potential

> Bodhisattvas' virtue is superior,
> Complete, of great purpose,
> And inexhaustible, and for these reasons
> Their potential is termed "supreme." (IV, 3)

The Mahāyāna potential is what causes the Mahāyāna practitioners' sources of good to be clear and pure, being free of the two obscurations, and it is therefore superior to the potential of practitioners in the lower vehicles. It is what causes all their sources of good associated with the levels, the transcendent perfections, and the final result (the ten strengths and so forth) to be complete. It is what causes that good to be of great purpose, for it gives rise to the fulfillment of both one's own goal and other beings' goals. And even when the nirvāṇa without residual aggregates has been attained, it is what causes that good (the strengths, fearlessnesses, and so forth) never to be exhausted until the end of saṃsāra.[2] For these four reasons, the Mahāyāna potential is described as supreme, for the listeners do not have these four aspects of virtue (superior on account of their being pure and clear and so on)—their potential does not act as the causal factor that produces the same kind of virtue.

iii. The Different Categories of the Nature of That Potential

> The potential is natural and evolving,
> The support and what is supported;
> It exists and does not exist.
> It should be understood as signifying "that which releases qualities." (IV, 4)

---

2. Even though one has attained the final result, buddhahood, the cause is never spent but continues to function as the qualities of buddhahood.

There are two kinds: the naturally existing potential and the developed potential or evolving potential. The former is the support, the latter what is supported, hence these four different terms.

The naturally existing potential, according to the Cittamātra point of view, is something that sentient beings have naturally "obtained" since time without beginning and that acts as a quality of their six sense powers.[3] It is like their nature or character. Without it having been created or fabricated by anyone, they all possess the seed of true enlightenment. It is because one possesses that seed that one can have the good fortune to attain perfect enlightenment. The Cittamātrins give the analogy of different ores: some kinds of rock contain gold, others contain iron or copper, and the one cannot change into the other. In their tradition they speak of five types of being: those who have the potentials of the three vehicles,[4] those of unfixed potential, and those without potential, who are forever deprived of the seed of liberation. This is also the system presented in this treatise.

Even the Mādhyamikas do not deny that these five types can exist temporarily. It has been taught that as long as listeners fixed in their aim to attain nirvāṇa have not obtained the result of their particular path, the buddhas cannot prevent them from doing so even if they try.[5] Also, there are beings with a lot of attachment who never think of wanting to abandon saṃsāra, and in that situation even the buddhas cannot act to establish them on the path of liberation.[6] Both these kinds of beings must exist—how otherwise would there be individuals who have obtained the listeners' enlightenment and also beings who still have not attained liberation despite the advent of numerous buddhas (for there are sentient beings until the very

---

3. In his *Bodhisattvabhūmivyākhā*, Sāgaramegha gives three explanations for Asaṅga's describing the naturally existing potential as a quality of the six sense powers. The first is that this seed or potential for developing virtuous qualities cannot be described as either identical with or distinct from conditioned entities; the six sense powers are the particular conditioned entities with which it is associated. Second, the six sense powers are the inner causes for developing virtuous states of mind, so the potential for generating those virtuous qualities is identified with them. Third, when an individual completes the spiritual path and is transformed into an enlightened being, the six sense powers represent the substantive entities that will become the name and form aspects of that enlightened being.

4. I.e., three types of being, each with the fixed potential for one of the three vehicles.

5. The listeners here are of "fixed potential," and even the buddhas cannot persuade them to change to another path such as that of the Great Vehicle.

6. These are beings "without potential."

end of saṃsāra)? So from one point of view, the Cittamātrins' position is not untenable.

On the other hand, the basic nature of sentient beings' minds cannot be anything other than the unborn, natural clear light, the essence of the sugatas. Just as heat is the nature of fire, the essence of the sugatas is the true nature of the mind. So since this true nature cannot but be present in every single being, according to the Mādhyamika position, there are no beings who are permanently without potential. Even this treatise states in one verse—"Suchness is present in all"—that all beings have the essence of the Tathāgata.[7] And where it says,

> The mind is ultimate reality, and there is no other mind but clear light.
> We speak of this as the nature of mind.[8]

it is referring to the fact that in the ultimate truth, the naturally existing potential is the true nature of the mind, the natural state that is the union of clarity and emptiness, as is extensively explained in the *Sublime Continuum*. We will not discuss the meaning of these terms in detail here.

What we call the developed potential refers to the fully accomplished potential. When a bodhisattva, in whom the naturally existing potential is present, meets a spiritual master, arouses the mind intent on unsurpassable enlightenment, and is engaged in practicing the bodhisattva activities, at that time we speak of the evolving or fully accomplished potential.

The *Great Commentary* gives further explanations of these two terms simply as categories. When those who have the bodhisattva potential have practiced the Mahāyāna path from the beginning, we speak of the natural potential. For those with the bodhisattva potential who have entered the Listeners' Vehicle and later, on account of a spiritual master, enter the Great Vehicle, we speak of the accomplished potential. The first of these terms is also used for beings of fixed potential, while the second is used to describe beings of unfixed potential who are guided by a spiritual master and are definitely established as the Mahāyāna type.

In this regard, potential signifies a cause, so when just the naturally existing potential is present, it exists simply as the nature of a cause, and not

---

7. See ch. 10, v. 37.
8. See ch. 14, v. 19.

as the nature of a result. "It exists and does not exist" is therefore stated simply in terms of causation.[9] It is in dependence on the naturally existing potential that the evolving potential arises, so the evolving potential, with respect to the former, is a result. On the other hand, since the subsequent stages of the path happen from the evolving potential, it is also a cause. The naturally existing potential is the cause of everything up to the qualities of buddhahood—the ten strengths, and the rest—for it is in dependence on it that the path and result occur.

A derivational gloss of the Sanskrit word for potential, *gotra*, interprets it as a contraction of *guṇa* ("excellent qualities") and *tāra* ("to release"), and it should therefore be understood as signifying "that which releases qualities," for it is this potential that brings out and perfects all excellent qualities, from those of arousing bodhicitta, through those of the stages of earnest aspiration and the ten levels, up to the qualities of buddhahood.

iv. The Marks or Signs of the Potential

> **Compassion prior to joining the path,**
> **Interest, resilience,**
> **And practicing perfect virtue—**
> **These are explained as being sure signs of the potential. (IV, 5)**

The marks or signs of the potential are extremely numerous, but they can be summarized as four. Just as we know from smoke that there is fire, we can know that individuals who have these four signs are people who have the Mahāyāna potential, as follows.

Even before joining or entering the Great Vehicle, in other words, even before they have aroused the mind intent on supreme enlightenment, such people, on seeing beings suffering, spontaneously feel compassion. Simply on hearing the extensive and profound teachings of the Mahāyāna, even if they do not understand what they mean, they naturally feel an inspired interest. When they hear of the difficult practices they will have to undertake for other beings' sake, instead of getting discouraged and wondering, "How could I possibly do that?" they have the mental resilience to think, "How marvelous that is!" And they are naturally enthusiastic about the virtuous practices of the six transcendent perfections and find joy in practicing

---

9. As Vasubandhu points out in his commentary (*Sūtrālaṃkāra-vyakhya*), it exists as a cause; it does not exist as a result.

them. These are said to be definite signs of the Mahāyāna potential. Beings who do not have that potential are quite the opposite in character.

v. A Further Classification of the Potential

> Fixed potential, unfixed potential,
> One that is not affected by conditions,
> And one that is affected—these in brief
> Are the four kinds of potential. (IV, 6)

The categories of the potential are as follows.

The fixed potential is that of beings who are definitely established on one or other of the three paths—listener, solitary realizer, or bodhisattva. Until they attain their respective enlightenment, whatever they do, they will not attain any other kind of enlightenment. They are like distinct substances such as stone or gold or silver.

The unfixed potential is that of beings who may, on encountering one of the three vehicles, convert to that vehicle and thus change in potential. They are like certain rocks that can be transformed, by smelting, refining, or special chemical processes, into gold, silver, or copper.

Thus, it is said of the fixed potential that it cannot be affected by conditions, because even if a spiritual master teaches people of fixed potential a different path, on account of their particular potential, until they have attained their respective level of enlightenment, they will not apply themselves to attaining any other kind of enlightenment.

The unfixed potential, on the other hand, can be affected by conditions, for just as white cloth will hold red or any other colored dye with which it is brought into contact, those of unfixed potential will obtain the result of the path that any spiritual master they meet teaches them.

In short, then, there are these four kinds of potential. This is the general case, but in this context, we should consider two kinds of beings who follow the Mahāyāna—those of fixed potential for the Great Vehicle and those of unfixed potential who are affected by circumstances—because it is the Mahāyāna potential that we are discussing at present.

vi. Threats to the Potential

> Habituation to defilements, evil friends,
> Poverty, and subjection to others' control—

> These in brief are threats to the potential;
> Know that there are four. (IV, 7)

What we call threats to the potential are the obscurations or defects that prevent one from engaging in virtuous practice even if one has the potential. They are (1) long-term habituation to the defilements such as attachment, aversion, and bewilderment; (2) falling under the influence of bad company, with people who commit negative actions, and so getting involved in negative activities; (3) material deprivation, as a result of which, rather than practicing virtue, one performs negative actions;[10] and (4) being dominated by kings, powerful officials, gangsters, and so forth, and thus being deprived of the freedom to avoid negative actions and perform positive actions. In short, therefore, the threats to the potential are to be understood as fourfold.

vii. The Benefits or Excellence of the Mahāyāna Potential

> Should those with bodhisattva potential go to the lower realms,
> It is after a long time, and they are soon released,
> And even there they experience little suffering;
> Saddened by the plight of beings, they bring them to maturity. (IV, 8)

If beings with the listener or solitary-realizer potential and those who have no potential for liberation commit serious negative actions such as the five crimes with immediate retribution, they are reborn in the hells as soon as they die. On the other hand, if those with the bodhisattva potential commit crimes with immediate retribution and other such actions, their going to the lower realms and experiencing the result of their negative actions is postponed for many years or kalpas and occurs long afterward. For them, such actions do not have the power to ripen promptly as they do for beings with other potentials. This is explained in the commentary. The reason for this is that, because of the Mahāyāna potential, even if one engages in negative actions, one feels ashamed and remorseful: the fact that one does not take

---

10. Sthiramati specifies that as a result of poverty, one is unable to practice generosity and so forth, and one commits negative actions in order to procure what one needs.

pleasure in them makes it difficult for one to rapidly experience the fully ripened effect of one's negative actions in the same way that other sentient beings do.

Also, other sentient beings, when they are reborn in the lower realms, have to stay there for as long as it takes for the life span in the hell or other realm to be completed. Beings with the bodhisattva potential, however, are quickly liberated without having to stay that long.

Moreover, in the lower realms, they suffer only a little and are able to escape, as was the case for King Ajātaśatru. He had killed his father, a stream enterer, yet he experienced the fully ripened effect of this crime with immediate retribution—rebirth in the hells—for only as long as it takes for a yo-yo to rebound.

Even as they are experiencing the sufferings in the lower realms, they are saddened at the beings helplessly tormented there on account of their actions. This causes them to feel great compassion for other beings who are suffering just as they are and to establish those beings in virtue and bring them to full maturity—as in the stories of Daughter, the son of Vallabha, and that of the strongman Bakshita.[11] Others who are suffering in the lower realms and are not of the bodhisattva type experience every kind of extreme torment. In such situations they can only feel anger and hatred for each other.

These, then, are the four virtues that come from having the Mahāyāna potential.

viii. Two Analogies
(1) Gold

> **Know that the potential is like a mine of gold,**
> **The source of infinite virtue,**
> **Endowed with gnosis and without contaminant,**
> **And the source, as well, of different powers. (IV, 9)**

The Mahāyāna potential is to be understood as being like a gold mine or source of gold. A mine of pure or fine gold has four qualities. It is the basis

---

11. The story of Daughter is related by Patrul Rinpoche in *The Words of My Perfect Teacher*, 224. The story that precedes it on the same page is that of Bakshita, the name the Buddha had in a previous life in the hells.

or source of large quantities of gold, the source of gold that gleams with light, the source of gold free of all impurity, and the source of gold that can be worked. Similarly, like a mine or source of fine gold, from which countless hundreds of thousands of gold coins can be minted, the bodhisattva potential is the source of boundless virtue—the transcendent perfections, levels, strengths, fearlessnesses, and so forth. Just as pure gold shines with a beautiful golden light, the bodhisattva potential too is the basis or support that shines with the light of gnosis, enabling one to know unmistakenly the general and specific characteristics of all phenomena. Just as gold that comes from a gold mine does not have the slightest impurity or contamination, and even if burned has an even greater luster, the bodhisattva potential too is the basis of nirvāṇa, uncontaminated by defilements. And like gold produced from a gold mine, which even when beaten can be worked without cracking or disintegrating, this bodhisattva potential is also the source of clairvoyant powers that can be used to fulfill all desires.

(2) Precious Stones

> Know that it is like a source of precious stones,
> For it is the cause of the great enlightenment;
> It is the source of great gnosis, of sublime concentration,
> And of benefit for many beings. (IV, 10)

The bodhisattva potential should be understood as being like a "potential" or "domain," meaning "source," of the finest gems such as beryls, sapphires, and rubies. There are four reasons for this.

Just as a jewel mine or domain is not a source of iron and trinkets, but rather an abundant and perfect source of all kinds of precious things such as beryls, diamonds, pearls, and so forth, the bodhisattva potential is not the support or basis for the listeners' and solitary realizers' enlightenment, but rather the cause that produces the great enlightenment, free of all obscurations, that occurs immediately after the vajra-like concentration.

The bodhisattva potential is also the source of the vast gnosis that shines with the light of the four kinds of gnosis—mirrorlike gnosis and the others—like sublime gems that are brightly and beautifully colored.

Again, the bodhisattva potential is the source of the most extraordinary concentrations—the concentration of Brave Progression, the concentration of the Sky Treasury, and so forth—like the finest perfectly shaped gems.

And just as from a jewel mine innumerable multicolored jewels are produced, or just as the finest jewels are priceless and can therefore provide for numerous beings, the bodhisattva potential is the source of benefit for many beings, bringing them everlasting happiness.

2. An Explanation of How the Potential May Be Lacking

There are two kinds of beings whom we refer to as "lacking the potential": those who lack the potential in that the cause of liberation is absent in that particular situation and those who lack the potential in that they will never attain liberation.

> **Some cannot but consistently follow evil ways;**
> **Others have completely destroyed virtuous ways,**
> **Some have no merit that is consistent with liberation,**
> **Have inferior virtue, or are deprived of the cause. (IV, 11)**

For the first of these two kinds of beings who lack the potential, four cases are described. Although they are not permanently deprived of the potential, they are incapable, in that particular situation, of developing the path to liberation, as if they had no potential, and so this inferior kind of being is described in negative terms, in the same way that one might speak of someone with no children apart from bad ones as being childless.

What are these four cases? Some people may have the Mahāyāna potential, but because of the intensity of their defilements, they necessarily follow ways that are consistently evil, indulging in acts such as the crimes with immediate retribution. Even though they have the potential, it is as if in that situation the potential is lacking, for they lack the good fortune to transcend suffering, and they are therefore referred to as "lacking the potential."

Some people, as a result of being guided by an evil teacher,[12] acquire wrong views, believing that there is no such thing as cause and effect and no liberation. This completely destroys their sources of good related to virtuous paths or severs the root of merit. As long as they retain those views, there is no seed for liberation, and so in this case they are described as "lacking the potential."

Again, some beings perform tainted positive actions simply in order to

---

12. Tib. *mi dge ba'i bshes gnyen*, lit. "a friend in evil," the opposite of a spiritual friend.

experience the samsaric happiness of gods, humans, and the like as the fully ripened effect. However, since they do not have any merit consistent with liberation in the form of positive actions imbued with the intention to strive for liberation, they will not attain nirvāṇa even after many kalpas, and for this reason we speak of them as "lacking the potential."

Then there are certain beings who have only inferior, or very few, sources of good consistent with liberation. In such a situation, they lack any accumulation of merit and wisdom sufficiently powerful to accomplish higher qualities. These beings too are referred to as "lacking the potential."

In all these four cases, although these beings have the Mahāyāna potential, they are in the clutches of powerful adverse circumstances and, the causal factor[13] being weak, the potential is not awakened. For this reason, they will not attain enlightenment for a long time—that is, until their situations change. This is why these inferior beings are spoken of in negative terms as "lacking the potential."

"Deprived of the cause" refers to beings who, unlike the above four cases, are permanently deprived of the cause for attaining liberation and are therefore described as "lacking the potential."

3. Concluding Summary of the Chapter, Praising the Supreme Potential for the Great Vehicle

> **Without understanding it, bodhisattvas feel immense interest**
> **For the Great Dharma of the profound and extensive explanations taught in order to benefit others;**
> **They have the patience to practice it and will ultimately attain perfection, superior in two ways.**
> **Know that this comes from their natural possession of qualities and therefore from the developed potential.**
> **(IV, 12)**

Simply from hearing the Mahāyāna teachings that were taught in order to benefit other beings—both the profound explanations that teach emptiness and the extensive explanations that teach the levels, transcendent perfections, strengths, fearlessnesses, and so forth—even without understanding

---

13. I.e., their virtue or merit.

precisely what they mean, those who have the Mahāyāna potential feel immensely inspired. They have the patience to undergo hardships in practicing the transcendent perfections, as a result of which they will complete the accumulation of merit and wisdom and finally attain the great enlightenment, the sublime result that is superior to both worldly attainments and the supramundane attainments of the listeners and solitary realizers. That attainment, it should be understood, comes from the very fact that bodhisattvas possess the qualities of the naturally existing potential and thence, through their correctly accomplishing virtue, from the developed potential.

> That sublime potential is the healthy, perfect root
> That makes the tree of enlightenment grow, with its
>   extensive qualities,
> Bringing bliss to beings and shading them from great
>   misery,
> And bearing the fruit that gives oneself and others benefit
>   and happiness. (IV, 13)

Like a great tree with its trunk, flowers, and so forth, the sublime tree of unsurpassable enlightenment displays the whole vast array of qualities such as the ten strengths. It brings sentient beings to the great untainted bliss and puts them at peace from their enormous suffering, as in the cool shade of a tree that refreshes those afflicted by the heat, affording them physical and mental ease. And its fruit brings benefit and happiness to oneself and other beings like the delicious fruit from a fruit tree. For that tree to grow, for it to provide shade, and for the fruit to ripen, the root must be healthy, solid, and undecayed. That root is the supreme potential.

This completes the explanation of the fourth chapter of *Ornament of the Mahāyāna Sūtras*, the chapter on the potential.

5

The Spiritual Intent: Bodhicitta[1]

This chapter has four sections: (1) definition; (2) classification; (3) analogies; and (4) a praise of the benefits and advantages of bodhicitta.

1. Definition

> **Great in its enthusiasm, great in its undertaking,**
> **Great in its goal, and great in its outcome—**
> **The bodhisattva's intention**
> **Is the mental factor associated with two aims. (V, 1)**

The bodhisattva's spiritual intent is defined in terms of its greatness in four respects and of the two aims it considers. It is great in its enthusiasm—in listening to, reflecting upon, and meditating on the teachings of the Great Vehicle with armor-like diligence and joyfully undergoing austerities in practicing the path for countless kalpas in order to benefit others, without turning back. It is great in its undertaking—in its diligence in application, practicing as if one has donned armor. It is great in its goal—in perfectly achieving both one's own and others' goals. And it is great in the result that emerges—the attainment of unsurpassable enlightenment. These are its four particular qualities.

In essence, bodhicitta is the mental factor of intention in a bodhisattva's mind. What, then, are bodhisattvas thinking of or considering in arousing bodhicitta? They are thinking of attaining great enlightenment themselves

---

1. Tib. *sems bskyed*, lit. "the mind or attitude that is aroused intent on enlightenment." This chapter deals mainly with *byang chub mchog tu sems bskyed*, the bodhisattva's spiritual intent to attain supreme enlightenment (that is, buddhahood), which we have generally rendered as the widely used Sanskrit term *bodhicitta*, this being generally familiar to Western followers of the Tibetan Mahāyāna tradition. Where the term *sems bskyed* is used to refer to the listeners' or solitary realizers' intentions to attain their respective levels of enlightenment as arhats, we have translated it as "spiritual intent."

and of bringing benefit and happiness to all other sentient beings. Thus, any thought that arises concomitant with the mental factor of intention possessing these two aims—namely, focusing on enlightenment and on the welfare of beings—is what we call bodhicitta. In short, it is a commitment—the thought and aspiration "For the sake of all sentient beings, I shall attain unsurpassable enlightenment."

2. Classifications

There are three ways in which bodhicitta is classified: (1) in terms of the different levels; (2) in terms of eleven elements of these different kinds of bodhicitta; and (3) in terms of bodhicitta acquired formally and that acquired naturally.

a. Classification in Terms of the Different Levels

> That spiritual intent is classified on the different levels
> In relation to interest, pure superior intention,
> Distinct full maturation,
> And likewise freedom from obscurations. (V, 2)

Bodhicitta on the different levels (beginning with the level of earnest aspiration) is classified as follows. Bodhicitta on the level of earnest aspiration, that is, on the paths of accumulation and joining, is developed by means of interest, based simply on faith, and it is therefore known as the bodhicitta that arises through interest.

On the first to seventh levels, it is known as the bodhicitta with pure superior intention—"superior intention" because bodhisattvas have acquired the state of mind that realizes that they themselves and others are the same, and their minds are therefore trained to the extent that there is no distinction between their own and others' welfare; and "pure" because it is uncontaminated by subject-object duality.

From the eighth level up to the tenth, it is known as the fully matured bodhicitta, because on these levels bodhisattvas have acquired spontaneous nonconceptual gnosis, and the transcendent perfections are therefore practiced effortlessly and spontaneously. It is in this respect that it is held to be distinct from the previous kinds of bodhicitta.[2]

---

2. Here Mipham is commenting on the word "distinct" (Tib. *gzhan*, lit. "other") in the root verse.

Similarly, on the level of buddhahood, it is known as bodhicitta free of all obscurations, because it is the ultimate, resultant bodhicitta: the two kinds of obscuration and the habitual tendencies have all been eliminated.

b. Classification in Terms of Eleven Elements of These Different Kinds of Bodhicitta, Beginning with the Root

> **Its root is held to be compassion,**
> **Its intention is to constantly bring benefit to beings,**
> **Its interest concerns the teachings,**
> **And likewise its object is the quest for gnosis. (V, 3)**

What is the root of bodhicitta? It is held to be compassion, for it is from the compassionate desire to dispel sentient beings' suffering that one has the wish to attain enlightenment for the sake of sentient beings. Without compassion for sentient beings, one is like a listener, striving for the nirvāṇa in which one is completely at peace from one's own suffering.

What is its intention? It is to think—constantly, until the end of saṃsāra—of the benefit of all sentient beings in this life and forever.

Similarly, the interest associated with bodhicitta is an interest in the profound and extensive teachings of the Great Vehicle.

As for the object on which bodhicitta focuses, it is the quest to obtain the nonconceptual gnosis that is the perfection of the two kinds of no-self, by hearing, reflecting, and meditating upon the teachings of the Great Vehicle.

> **Determination to go higher is its means of progress;**
> **The vast vow is its support;**
> **Its counteragent is to wish**
> **And undertake to stop the path. (V, 4)**

Determined progress from the level one is on to a higher level is the vehicle or means of proceeding for bodhicitta, because it is by means of determination that one rises higher and higher.

The bodhisattva's vow that involves the three kinds of discipline—namely, avoiding negative actions, gathering virtue, and benefiting others—is the support for bodhicitta.

Stopping the Mahāyāna path and arousing the spiritual intent for the nirvāṇa of the lesser vehicles interrupts or counteracts bodhicitta, the intent for supreme enlightenment. If that counteragent arises in one's mind and one voluntarily continues in that vein, it will obstruct the arousing of bodhicitta. (In some versions, this fourth line appears to be absent.)[3]

> **Its nature is merit and wisdom;**
> **Its benefit is that virtue grows;**
> **Its certain deliverance is held to be**
> **The constant practice of the transcendent perfections. (V, 5)**

The great compassion that is the wish to take all beings beyond suffering[4] represents the accumulation of merit; the wisdom that realizes emptiness and knows that in ultimate truth there is nothing to be taken beyond suffering represents the accumulation of wisdom. These two accumulations constitute the nature of bodhicitta. (The Tibetan syllable *te* here is a continuative particle.)[5]

The growth of merit and virtue as far as the reaches of space, of beings, and of worlds is the benefit of bodhicitta.

How does arousing bodhicitta bring release from saṃsāra? Constant application to the six transcendent perfections in order to be definitively released from the three worlds and attain unsurpassable enlightenment is held to be its certain deliverance.

> **Its ultimate reach is the level,**
> **Brought about by application on each one, respectively.**
> **Know that with all these a bodhisattva's spiritual intent**
> **Is definitively established. (V, 6)**

---

3. This is the author's own note.
4. That is, to take them to nirvāṇa (Tib. *mya ngan las bzla ba*).
5. Mipham appears to be referring here to the continuative particle *te* at the end of the first line of the root text in the Tibetan translation of Sthiramati's commentary, linking the first line to the second. In Kawa Peltsek's translation of the root text, the particle *gyi* is used at the end of this line, effectively incorporating both lines in the category of "benefit" and omitting "nature" as a separate item in this list of elements, making a total of ten rather than eleven such elements. A literal translation of Kawa Peltsek's root verse, as commented by Vasubandhu, might therefore read, "The growth of virtue, whose nature is merit and wisdom, is its benefit." Mipham appears to be pointing out that although the first line leads on to the second, they nevertheless refer to separate elements.

What is the ultimate reach of those different kinds of bodhicitta?[6] The ultimate reach of bodhicitta is the level. How is that? Application on each of the ten levels completes each one, and from this we speak of the "ultimate reach" of that particular kind of bodhicitta. In other words, when one completes the ten transcendent perfections, beginning with completing transcendent generosity on the first level and ending with completing transcendent gnosis on the tenth level, one is said to "reach the ultimate point" of the ten levels. For this reason, the full accomplishment of a transcendent perfection with the respective kind of bodhicitta is its ultimate reach on that level; and the ultimate reach of bodhicitta on the path of training is the final stage of the tenth level. The ultimate result is the buddha level.

This presentation of the bodhisattva's spiritual intent in terms of these eleven points is to be understood as being the definitive, or unquestioned, or established explanation.

c. Classification in Terms of Bodhicitta Acquired Formally and That Acquired Naturally

Bodhicitta aroused from the level of earnest aspiration up to the supreme mundane level is bodhicitta acquired formally. This refers to the commitment expressed in the words of the bodhicitta vow that is taken through the power of one's own merit and of the spiritual master. Bodhicitta aroused on the first level upward is what is known as bodhicitta acquired naturally.[7] These two categories are otherwise termed relative bodhicitta (which is the spiritual intent to attain unsurpassable enlightenment) and ultimate bodhicitta (which is the realization of one's own mind being free of conceptual elaboration or the realization of the truth of ultimate reality—whichever term we use, they both refer to the same thing: nonconceptual gnosis). Once one attains the bodhisattva levels, one will realize the inseparable union of relative and ultimate bodhicitta.

To begin with we shall describe the different ways in which bodhicitta acquired formally or revealed by another arises.

---

6. I.e., the different kinds described in the previous section.

7. Tib. *chos nyid kyis thob pa*. The term *chos nyid* has a wide range of meanings depending on context. Here it includes the notion that ultimate bodhicitta is aroused with the realization of the ultimate reality. Thus, this kind of bodhicitta could also be called "bodhicitta acquired through realization of the ultimate reality."

> Bodhicitta arises unstably through the power of a friend,
> Or in a stable manner through the power of a cause,
> Of sources of good, of listening, and through habituation to virtue.
> This describes the bodhicitta that is revealed by someone else. (V, 7)

- Bodhicitta aroused through the prompting of a spiritual friend is what we call "bodhicitta aroused through the power of a friend."
- Bodhicitta aroused because of the presence of the bodhisattva potential arises through the power of a cause.
- Bodhicitta aroused in this life on account of one's having aroused bodhicitta, practiced the Mahāyāna teachings, and gathered the accumulation of wisdom in previous lives arises through the power of one's sources of good.
- Bodhicitta aroused by anyone as a result of listening to the Mahāyāna teachings (as did many gods and humans in the past who aroused the mind intent on unsurpassable enlightenment when Lord Buddha taught the Great Vehicle) arises through the power of listening.
- And bodhicitta is aroused through habituation to the virtuous act of listening to the Mahāyāna teachings and reflecting on them in this life.

Of these five, the first is unstable since it is possible to revert from it;[8] the last four arise in a stable manner. These five describe the bodhicitta revealed by another.

Ultimate bodhicitta is explained in the next seven verses.

> Born from attending the perfect buddhas
> And accumulating merit and wisdom,
> The gnosis without concepts with regard to phenomena
> Is therefore held to be sublime. (V, 8)

On the level of earnest aspiration, for as long as one measureless great kalpa, bodhisattvas make offerings to the perfect buddhas and attend them by listening to their teachings, reflecting, and meditating. And they fully gather

---

8. The bodhicitta vow one has received from a spiritual friend may be given up, for example.

the two accumulations of merit and wisdom, embodied in the six transcendent perfections. As a result of this, there arises the gnosis free from dualistic concepts of phenomena—subject and object, permanence and impermanence, and so on. This sublime realization is held to be the sublime bodhicitta or ultimate bodhicitta.

> Because bodhisattvas have acquired realization of the sameness
> Of phenomena, of sentient beings,
> Of the deeds that benefit them, and above all of the buddha state,
> Their joy is particularly great. (V, 9)

This ultimate bodhicitta arises when the first level is attained, and as a result bodhisattvas feel extremely joyful, which is why that level is called Perfect Joy. Why do they feel so joyful at that time? Because they acquire the state of mind that realizes the sameness of the aggregates and all other phenomena. And in the same way, they acquire the state of mind that realizes the sameness of all sentient beings, the state of mind that realizes the sameness of the deeds to be performed for their benefit, and, above all, the state of mind that realizes the sameness of the buddhas' body of truth (dharmakāya.) It is from acquiring this fourfold realization of sameness that the bodhisattvas' joy is particularly great.[9]

Because they have realized that there is no difference between phenomena, oneself, others, and the buddhas, and that all these are the same in being by nature the expanse of reality, they understand the nature of phenomena and therefore have no fear of saṃsāra. And from not thinking of others' welfare as any different from their own, from seeing that they will accomplish beings' welfare, from realizing that they will be of benefit to all beings, and from realizing that they are approaching the buddha level, they feel immensely joyful.

> Bodhicitta's birth, vastness,
> Associated enthusiasm, pure intention,
> Mastery of the remainder,
> And certain deliverance are the points that should be
>   understood. (V, 10)

---

9. Far greater, comments Sthiramati, than the happiness of acquiring worldly riches or attaining the listeners' nirvāṇa.

The ultimate bodhicitta is to be known by six topics: its birth, vastness, enthusiasm with regard to the latter, pure intention, mastery of the remainder, and certain deliverance. This brief exposition is now followed by an explanation of each of these points.

> **It is born from the seed of interest in the Dharma**
> **And from the mother of the highest transcendent perfection;**
> **The bliss that comes from concentration is its womb,**
> **And compassion is the nurse that nurtures it. (V, 11)**

First, its birth has four aspects, indicated by analogy with the way in which womb-born beings take birth in the world. Interest in the teachings of the Supreme Vehicle is the seed. The highest of the transcendent perfections, transcendent wisdom that is the realization that all phenomena are empty, is, as it were, the mother from which it is born. The bliss of the trained flexibility that comes from one-pointed concentration is like a perfectly healthy womb. And the great compassion is like a nurse, holding one back from the precipice of the listeners' nirvāṇa and nurturing virtuous ways. It is in arising from these four causes that bodhicitta is born.

> **Bodhisattvas accomplish ten great aspirations,**
> **And so their bodhicitta should be known as vast.**
> **They are not discouraged by hardships over great lengths of time,**
> **And so their bodhicitta should be understood as**
> **enthusiastic. (V, 12)**

Second, whereas the listeners give rise to their spiritual intent for their own sake, bodhisattvas arouse bodhicitta for the sake of both themselves and others, accomplishing ten great aspirations, and for this reason their bodhicitta is to be known for its vastness. These ten great aspirations are as follows: (1) to make offerings to all the buddhas; (2) to fully hold all the sacred teachings; (3) to manifest in all kinds of physical forms to teach beings; (4) to enter all kinds of buddha fields; (5) to complete all the transcendent perfections; (6) to bring all sentient beings to maturity; (7) to purify realms as buddha fields; (8) to act in harmony with the bodhisattva activities; (9) to be beneficial in all their activities; and (10) to attain great enlightenment.

These aspirations have countless hundreds of thousands of attendant aspirations, and they are all accomplished with ten limitless objects: the realm of sentient beings; the realm of the universe; the realm of space; the totality of the sacred teachings; likewise nirvāṇa; the coming of the buddhas; the gnosis of the buddhas; the thoughts in sentient beings' minds; the accomplishment of the entire scope of the buddhas' gnosis; and, summarizing these nine, what is known as the realm of the continuum of the universe, of the continuum of the Dharma, and of the continuum of gnosis. It should be understood that these ten pervade the whole of space and time without limit, and that it is on such a scale that bodhisattvas engage in displaying manifestations according to their aspirations.

Third, whereas the listeners' enthusiasm goes no further than the achievement of their own goal, bodhisattvas never tire of performing all kinds of difficult activities that others are incapable of doing in order to achieve both their own and others' goals, and this over immense periods of time—up to three measureless kalpas. For this reason, the ultimate bodhicitta should be understood as incorporating enthusiasm.

> Bodhisattvas realize that they are nearing enlightenment
> And they have gathered knowledge of its means,
> So their intention, you should understand, is pure.
> They master the methods of the other bodhisattva levels. (V, 13)

Fourth, the listeners go no further than eliminating the obscurations of defilements and thereby attaining their respective result. Bodhisattvas, on the other hand, realize that they are approaching unsurpassable enlightenment in which the two obscurations have been purified, and they also gain knowledge of the means for attaining buddhahood. For this reason, you should understand that their intention is pure.

Fifth, the listeners, in eliminating the imputational and innate defilements related to the three worlds, go no further than mastering the levels of stream enterer, once-returner, nonreturner, and arhat. Bodhisattvas, when they attain the first level and so on, know how to attain the other, higher remaining levels and their respective qualities, which is why we speak of "mastery of the remainder."

> Keeping in mind the presentation of those levels,
> Bodhisattvas know them to be just concepts,
> And even in that regard, they have no concepts—
> Know that because of this deliverance is certain. (V, 14)

Sixth, by leaving behind the previous levels and proceeding to the subsequent ones, bodhisattvas rise from one level to the next and are definitively released. While keeping in mind the arrangement, on the relative, conventional level, of the level's defining characteristics (such as, on the first level, the completion of transcendent generosity, and the twelve sets of a hundred qualities—beholding a hundred buddhas, and so forth), they also know that that level's characteristics are merely posited by one's own mind on account of one's concepts, and nothing else. And, without conceptualizing even that concept that they are "the mind-only" or "mere concepts," they dwell in nonconceptual gnosis and will proceed beyond the first level to the second. This should similarly be understood for the other levels as well, and it is how we should understand certain deliverance from one level to the next.

3. Analogies for Arousing Bodhicitta

The next six verses provide analogies for arousing bodhicitta. Beginning from when one arouses bodhicitta for the first time on the level of earnest aspiration, and up until the tenth level, the different instances of arousing bodhicitta are associated with twenty-two similes, in which the essential aspects of the Mahāyāna path are complete, and which are related to the eighty inexhaustible qualities—determination, intention, and so forth.[10]

> **Bodhicitta should be understood to be like the earth,**
> **Or alternatively like fine gold,**
> **Or like the waxing moon;**
> **Or resembling fire. (V, 15)**

(1) First, the bodhicitta associated with determination—the determination to attain unsurpassable enlightenment—is the sole support or basis for giving rise to all the elements of the Mahāyāna path (from intention, applica-

---

10. The eighty inexhaustible qualities, which appear in the *Sūtra of the Teaching of Akṣayamati* (*Akṣayamatinirdeśa-sūtra*), are called inexhaustible because they exist inexhaustibly in bodhisattvas. They are determination, intention, application, superior (altruistic) intention, the six transcendent perfections, the four boundless attitudes, the five kinds of preternatural knowledge, the four ways of attracting disciples, the four kinds of perfect knowledge, the four reliances, the two accumulations, the thirty-seven elements leading to enlightenment, sustained calm and profound insight, the powers of retention and brilliant eloquence, the four summaries of the Dharma, the single path to be trodden, and the body of truth.

tion, superior intention, and the transcendent perfections through to skill in means) and all the qualities of the Mahāyāna result—the ten strengths, four fearlessnesses, eighteen distinctive qualities, and so forth. It is therefore comparable to the great earth, which is the support for all the grass, trees, medicinal fruits, and grain.

(2) Next, and based on the previous spiritual intent, is the bodhicitta associated with the unchanging good intention to bring benefit and happiness to sentient beings. It is like fine gold, whose color and properties do not alter even when tested by flaming, cutting, and rubbing.

(3) The bodhicitta associated with increasing the two accumulations by thorough application to the transcendent perfections is like the waxing moon.

(4) Next, the bodhicitta associated with the superior intention that can shoulder the responsibility for others' welfare is to be understood as being like fire. The more firewood there is, the more the fire will naturally burn and spread. In the same way, bodhisattvas' intention to attain the next stage, whether it is from the stage of warmth to the peak stage on the path of joining, or from the tenth level to buddhahood, enables them to acquire correspondingly greater qualities.

In other source texts, the waxing moon is given as the simile for superior intention, and fire as the simile for application. These four apply to ordinary beings, from those who first arouse bodhicitta up to those on the supreme mundane level.

> **Another way it should be known is like a great treasure,**
> **Or like a mine of precious jewels,**
> **Or like the ocean,**
> **Or else a diamond or mountain. (V, 16)**

(5) Next, the bodhicitta associated with transcendent generosity is to be understood as being like a great treasure. A great treasure is described as being of four kinds—conch, lotus, great lotus, and so on—and also of nine kinds, but stated simply, it is an inexhaustible treasure of jewels. In a place where there is such a treasure, however much food, clothes, and other necessary things are produced from it, it never runs out. Generosity satisfies the material and spiritual needs of countless sentient beings in the same way, for a bodhisattva's generosity never ever comes to an end, even in the expanse of nirvāṇa without residual aggregates.

(6) Another kind of bodhicitta, that associated with transcendent discipline, is like a source or mine of all sorts of precious stones. In the same way that an infinite variety of precious gems can be extracted from such a place, from the bodhicitta associated with a bodhisattva's discipline all the infinite gem-like qualities of the path and result of the Great Vehicle emerge—the levels, transcendent perfections, elements leading to enlightenment, strengths, fearlessnesses, and all the rest.

(7) The bodhicitta associated with transcendent patience is to be understood as being like the ocean. Even if the ocean is stirred up by boats, fish, large marine creatures, and the like, its waters will never become clouded, and its depths are not moved. In the same way, no unpleasant conditions such as austere practices and being wronged by others are capable of sullying a bodhisattva's patient mind.

(8) Further, the bodhicitta associated with transcendent diligence is like a diamond, for just as a diamond is not affected by anything—fire, water, cutting, grinding, and so forth—a bodhisattva's bodhicitta cannot be damaged by the dart of laziness.

(9) The bodhicitta associated with transcendent concentration is like the king of mountains, Mount Meru, which cannot be moved even by any of the winds of the four directions, for a bodhisattva's concentration is unmoved by distracting thoughts.

> It is like a sovereign medicine,
> Or like a great friend;
> Or like a wishing jewel,
> Or like the sun. (V, 17)

(10) The bodhicitta associated with transcendent wisdom is like the king of elixirs or medicines. Merely from the sight of that medicine, or the touch, smell, or taste of it, all illnesses caused by wind, bile, and phlegm disorders are cured. Similarly, the transcendent wisdom that comes from listening, reflecting, and meditating cures all the maladies of the defilement-related and cognitive obscurations.

(11) Next, the bodhicitta associated with the four boundless attitudes is to be understood as being like a great friend. True friends help one throughout the three times, in moments of pleasure, moments of pain, and in moments of neither; they never abandon one. Similarly, compassion draws beings out of their misery when they are suffering. Love makes them happy when they

are unhappy. Joy rejoices at their happiness and helps them to never lose it. And in thinking, "May they not be attached to being happy," "May those who are suffering not be averse to suffering," impartiality makes their minds settle without attachment or aversion.

(12) The bodhicitta associated with the five kinds of preternatural knowledge is like the wishing gem, which is the source of everything one could need or wish for. With the miraculous eye, bodhisattvas can see all forms and, through their knowledge of deaths and births, they can tell the future. With the miraculous ear, they can hear all sounds. By knowing others' minds, they are conscious of sentient beings' different mental states. By remembering past lives, they know what happened in their own and others' former series of lives. And by means of the preternatural power of miraculous transformation, they display many kinds of miracles, such as manifesting in various forms. In this manner, with their preternatural knowledge and power, they are able to fulfill all their own and others' wishes.

(13) Again, the bodhicitta associated with the four ways of attracting disciples is to be known as being like the sun. Just as the sun makes the various crops ripen, bodhisattvas ripen beings' mind streams by attracting beings and introducing them to virtue. They attract the miserly with their generosity, and similarly the hateful by speaking agreeably, the confused by means of helpful activity, and the proud by means of consistent behavior. More generally, they use the four ways of attracting disciples to attract all sentient beings and then introduce them to virtue.

> Again, it is like the gandharva's song,
> Or understood to be like a king;
> Or also like a treasury,
> Or known to be like a busy road. (V, 18)

(14) Further, the bodhicitta associated with the four kinds of perfect knowledge (knowledge of phenomena, of meanings, of languages, and of brilliant eloquence) is like the sweet song of a gandharva. Because bodhisattvas possess the four kinds of perfect knowledge, they can correctly answer, with endless confidence and eloquence, and in each being's language, the different questions that different sentient beings wish to understand regarding different phenomena and meanings, thus completely satisfying their minds. This bodhicitta, therefore, is like the song of a gandharva, which is so beautiful that whoever hears it is delighted and contented.

(15) Another kind of bodhicitta, associated with the four reliances, is to be understood as being like a king. Since the king has dominion over the land, his subjects are unable to do anything other than what he has commanded, and his words do not, therefore, go to waste. Similarly, a bodhisattva who has the four reliances (reliance on the meaning rather than the words, on the teaching rather than the person, on the ultimate meaning rather than the expedient meaning, and on gnosis rather than intellectual knowledge) is able to know all the intended meanings taught by the Tathāgata without mistake and thus to realize the true meaning of the Buddha's words without their being wasted. To illustrate this with an analogy, someone who serves their king well will be rewarded with dominion and wealth: their service will not have been wasted. Whereas if they serve him badly, their service will go to waste, for they will lose their dominion and life. In the same way, someone who relies only on the person, on the words, on the expedient meaning, and on intellectual knowledge will see their reliance wasted. For those who rely on the teaching, the meaning, the ultimate meaning, and gnosis, the meaning of the Buddha's words will not be wasted.

(16) Similarly, another kind of bodhicitta, associated with the two accumulations of merit and wisdom, is like a treasury. Just as a treasury can contain an inestimable quantity of grains or coins and so forth, the equivalent bodhicitta has an infinite accumulation of merit and an infinite accumulation of wisdom.

(17) The bodhicitta associated with the thirty-seven elements that lead to enlightenment is like a highway on which all kinds of beings, the great and the lowly, have traveled in the past, are traveling at present, and will travel in the future. For these thirty-seven elements that lead to enlightenment are the road by which all the listeners, solitary realizers, and bodhisattvas of the past, present, and future arrive at their respective resultant enlightenment. The highway and the road to enlightenment are to be understood, therefore, as equivalent.

> Know that it is like a vehicle;
> Bodhicitta is like a fount,
> Like delightful speech,
> And like the flow of a great river. (V, 19)

(18) The bodhicitta associated with sustained calm and profound insight is like a vehicle or conveyance. In the same way that a conveyance such as

a horse, elephant, or carriage takes the loads it is carrying wherever one wishes, the combination of sustained calm (in which the mind remains one-pointedly concentrated without being distracted) and profound insight (in which one unmistakenly realizes the truth) enables one to attain the correct realization of all phenomena, exactly as they have been established and as many as have been established, and to arrive at the ultimate result.

(19) The bodhicitta associated with both infallible memory and inexhaustible confidence and eloquence is like a fountain. However much water one draws from it, a public spring or fountain never runs dry, and the water never ceases to flow. Similarly, for bodhisattvas who have gained the power of retention, the teachings they have heard in the past will never be lost through being forgotten; through their eloquent confidence, they can elaborate on the teachings anew, and however much they teach, it will never come to an end.

(20) The bodhicitta associated with the four summaries of the Dharma—namely, that all compounded things are impermanent, all tainted phenomena are suffering, all phenomena are devoid of self, and nirvāṇa is peace—is like delightful speech. Take the example of someone who is unhappy at being separated from their relatives and possessions and is told, "You will find your relatives and possessions"; or of someone who is afraid of dying and receives advice on how their life can be saved; or of someone who wants something and hears advice on how to obtain it—these, in short, are words that are right: they are comforting and of happy import. For such people, they are words that bring delight. Similarly, the words one hears that express the four summaries of the Dharma constitute the nectar-like perfect Dharma, the path that leads to peace beyond suffering. By hearing it, one is relieved of the limitless sufferings of saṃsāra, one realizes the nature of the true Dharma, and one attains the state of everlasting happiness. So this bodhicitta makes fortunate individuals replete as if with nectar and gives rise to the most marvelous joy in their minds.

(21) The bodhicitta associated with the single path to tread is like the flow of a great river. A great river proceeds effortlessly and flows by itself into the sea. Similarly, when, on the eighth level, bodhisattvas acquire the great acceptance that phenomena are unborn and nonconceptual gnosis is effortlessly and spontaneously achieved all the time, both in formal meditation and in the postmeditation periods, there is no difference in the mind streams and activities of the bodhisattvas who have reached that level; they are all mingled and equivalent in what is referred to as the single path to

tread. Their own completion of the path to buddhahood and the bringing of sentient beings to maturity are undertaken effortlessly and spontaneously.

> The bodhisattvas' bodhicitta
> Is taught as being like a cloud.
> Arouse, therefore, this spiritual intent,
> So rich in qualities, correctly and with joy. (V, 20)

(22) In the children of the victorious ones, the bodhicitta associated with the skill in means is taught as being like a cloud. As with the rain falling onto the earth from a huge cloud and giving rise to the crops and various other kinds of earthly riches, for bodhisattvas in whom skillful means and wisdom are united, this bodhicitta gives rise to the deeds they display (from descending from the Tuṣita heaven through to the parinirvāṇa)[11] and to the various qualities of benefit and happiness of the higher realms and awakening.

As these twenty-two similes show, the bodhisattvas' bodhicitta is rich in excellent qualities, so you should arouse this spiritual intent for supreme enlightenment correctly, with deep faith and joy.

4. In Praise of the Benefits and Advantages of Bodhicitta

The next eight verses are a praise of bodhicitta, used as an instruction for applying it. The first describes how those who do not have the Mahāyāna spiritual intent lack four kinds of happiness.

> Beings who lack a more worthy spiritual intent
> Are deprived of the happiness derived from having altruistic thoughts,
> From acquiring the corresponding means, from understanding the import of the great intention,
> And from seeing thatness; they thus proceed to peace alone.
> (V, 21)

Ordinary people, listeners, and solitary realizers, who do not have the atti-

---

11. I.e., the twelve deeds of a buddha.

tude that befits the great, or "a more worthy attitude"—that is, the spiritual intent for supreme enlightenment that befits the bodhisattvas and tathāgatas—lack four kinds of happiness.

For bodhisattvas there is the happiness of the courageous intention to bring other sentient beings to perfect elimination (the elimination of the two obscurations) and to perfect realization (the realization of the two kinds of no-self). In fact, bodhisattvas derive greater pleasure from managing to help a single sentient being in some small way than from attaining their own goal, so one need hardly mention their joy at establishing beings in perfect elimination and realization. This boundless, unflawed[12] happiness that arises from accomplishing the perfect goal of infinite sentient beings is lost for listeners and solitary realizers because they lack that intention.

Similarly, from knowing and acquiring all kinds of different means for accomplishing benefit and happiness for sentient beings, bodhisattvas feel sublimely happy. For the listeners and solitary realizers, there occurs some limited happiness from merely knowing the means for their own liberation from the sufferings of saṃsāra, but it is not the vast joy that is the bodhisattva's.

Bodhisattvas derive the most sublime happiness both from establishing the import of the Buddha's thinking[13] as taught in the Great Vehicle (the profound meaning by nature free from elaboration, the fact that all phenomena are not born and do not cease) and from realizing, as they are, the profound intentions indicated by his words—that is, of the implied teachings and indirect teachings. Listeners and solitary realizers have nothing like that happiness: they experience the happiness of knowing only the no-self of the individual and their limited path.

Bodhisattvas obtain the inexhaustible great bliss, as vast as space, of seeing, just as it is, the ultimate or supreme thatness of all phenomena, emptiness, the great evenness. This is something the listeners and solitary realizers do not have. They have realized only the no-self of the individual, and so they have no realization of thatness as it is with regard to outer objects, which, for them, exist.

Thus, deprived of these four kinds of happiness, for they have not aroused the spiritual intent for supreme enlightenment, listeners and solitary real-

---

12. Tib. *mchog tu kha na ma tho ba med pa*, lit. "utterly free of unwholesomeness," that is, of wrongdoing, of pride, etc.

13. Tib. *dgongs pa chen po*, lit. "the great intention."

izers will proceed to the nirvāṇa that is merely complete peace from the sufferings of saṃsāra and is the absence of the perpetuating aggregates. This shows that it is better to give up any inclination for the listeners' and solitary realizers' result and to arouse the mind intent on supreme enlightenment.

The second of these verses shows that when the ultimate bodhicitta is born, there is no fear of being discouraged by the lower realms and the sufferings of saṃsāra.

> As soon as the wise arouse the sublime intent,
> Their minds are completely restrained from committing
>   infinite evils.
> Ever virtuous and loving, as they grow in both,
> They delight in experiencing both happiness and pain.
> (V, 22)

The moment that "the wise"—that is, bodhisattvas who have the gnosis that is the realization of no-self—first give rise to the ultimate bodhicitta, the supreme spiritual intent for unsurpassable enlightenment, their minds are completely bound against doing any evil, in the way of actions that harm any of the infinite sentient beings and the infinite nonvirtuous actions of the body, speech, and mind. And they acquire a natural restraint[14] against ever doing them in the future. Since they have obtained the vow[15] to commit no evil action whatsoever, they have no fear of going to the three lower realms.

Bodhisattvas who have aroused bodhicitta are continuously increasing both their virtuous activities and their compassion for beings, so they perform positive actions and are loving toward beings all the time. For this reason, they are not only joyful when they are experiencing bliss but also pleased when they experience pain, and so they never fear getting discouraged. They are happy when, on account of their virtue, they experience the many joys of celestial and human existence, and they are happy when, with their burgeoning love, they gladly take upon themselves numerous sufferings in the three lower realms—heat and cold and suchlike—for the sake of other suffering beings. Such bodhisattvas will never become discouraged

---

14. Tib. *chos nyid kyi sdom pa*.

15. Tib. *sdom pa*, lit. "restraint." Although this term is often translated as "vow," in this context the realization of ultimate bodhicitta automatically prevents bodhisattvas from committing nonvirtuous actions, without their making a formal vow.

by saṃsāra. This verse, therefore, counsels willing acceptance without ever turning one's back on bodhicitta.

> At that time, for others' sake,
> They accept hardship with no regard for their bodies or lives.
> How could such beings do anything bad
> When others do them wrong? (V, 23)

Third, one might think that when one remains here in saṃsāra, it must be hard to put up with the manifold ingratitude of sentient beings. Surely, even bodhisattvas would get discouraged and fail in their virtuous activities. But at such times, bodhisattvas who have reached the levels and who with great compassion cherish others more than themselves have no regard for their own bodies or lives but give away these very things to benefit other beings. They willingly assume or accept intense suffering from extreme hardships such as giving away their heads and limbs for other beings' sake over many kalpas. How could bodhisattvas like that ever begin to do anything bad, such as retaliating when other beings kill them or otherwise harm them? It is quite impossible for them to do so. For this reason, you should take an interest in arousing their spiritual intent.

> Having realized that all things are like illusions
> And that taking birth is like going to a pleasure grove,
> In times of prosperity and times of trouble
> They are not afraid of defilements or of suffering. (V, 24)

Fourth, however well or badly things go for them here in saṃsāra, bodhisattvas never turn back from their bodhisattva activities. On account of their accumulation of wisdom—the realization that all outer and inner phenomena are like magical illusions, like dreams, and so on—and of their accumulation of merit, bodhisattvas, for beings' sake, take birth wherever they wish in the celestial and human realms. In doing so, they realize that abandoning their previous body and taking another rebirth is like going to a beautiful pleasure grove. When things go well, even if they are the sovereigns of gods and humans, they have no fear of the fetters of defilements such as attachment, as we shall see later. This is because, as mentioned above, they perceive all phenomena as magical illusions. Similarly, even when things go badly, when death befalls them and they have to leave behind their celestial or human bodies and possessions, these bodhisattvas have no fear of the pain of leaving them behind. This is because they know that these too are like magical illusions, and that rebirth is like going to a pleasure grove. This, therefore, is an instruction showing that since bodhisattvas never fall back from the path whatever pleasure or pain befalls them, you should certainly train on the path to enlightenment.

> **They delight in the ornaments that are their own qualities,**
> **In the festive fare of helping sentient beings,**
> **In the sublime location of their voluntary birth,**
> **And in the entertainment of miraculous displays.**
> **Such delights are not for those who do not embody compassion. (V, 25)**

The fifth of these verses expands on what is meant by realizing that taking birth is like going to a pleasure grove, as was just mentioned. The analogy refers to the fact that gods and humans who go to a delightful pleasure grove do so with four aims in mind: to bathe and beautify themselves with ornaments; to enjoy different kinds of food and drink in a picnic; to pass the time there in agreeable surroundings; and to enjoy a variety of entertainments. In anticipation of these four pleasures, they make the decision to go to the pleasure grove, and there is no changing their minds. In the same way, when bodhisattvas pass from one life to the next, it is in order to embellish their own mind streams more and more with the ornaments of their own excellent qualities—generosity, discipline, powers of retention, concentration, wisdom, and so forth. Their delight, wherever they are reborn, at benefiting the beings there is analogous to the pleasures of a picnic. Their taking birth wherever and in whatever physical form they wish is analogous to staying in a delightful location. And using their five kinds of preternatural knowledge to display all kinds of miraculous feats there is analogous to taking part in various kinds of entertainment. In this way, bodhisattvas who take birth again and again in existence savor four delights analogous to the pleasures that mundane beings experience in the four activities of going to a pleasure grove: the delight of being adorned with the ornaments of excellent qualities; that of feasting on the food of benefiting others; that of lingering in a sublimely pleasant garden where they can benefit others; and that of performing their various miraculous displays. These four delights are absent in others who are not bodhisattvas, the very embodiments of compassion:

even the noble listeners and solitary realizers do not have them, let alone mundane beings. For this reason, you should certainly arouse bodhicitta, because the qualities of bodhisattvas who have aroused bodhicitta are particularly sublime.

> **Striving for the sake of others, these lords of compassion,
> Even when in the Hell of Torment Unsurpassed, consider it
>   to be delightful.
> How could such beings be afraid of the pains they suffer
> For the sake of others in existence? (V, 26)**

Sixth, how is it that bodhisattvas do not recoil and lose heart in the face of painful experiences such as giving away their bodies? As a result of realizing that all phenomena are devoid of self, bodhisattvas are completely free of attachment to their own interests. Their aim is to bring benefit in this life and happiness forever to other sentient beings who do not have such realization, and to this end they exert themselves constantly in practicing the six transcendent perfections. These bodhisattvas—"lords of compassion," for others' suffering makes them suffer too—will stay in the Hell of Torment Unsurpassed themselves when it will benefit others, and even that they consider to be blissful and pleasant. It does not arouse in them the slightest regret. How could beings like that be afraid of the pain of giving their bodies, limbs, and the like when it is in order to benefit other beings in this world? This verse demonstrates their capacity to willingly accept intense suffering. (In Sthiramati's commentary, this part of the root verse has been translated as: "the pains that befall them in dependence on others?"[16] The meaning, however, is the same.) Thus, it is because bodhisattvas have such marvelous qualities that they are not afraid of any sufferings whatsoever in this existence. Rather, they wholly rejoice in it and willingly accept it. And since their joy never diminishes, they are never discouraged. For this reason, you should put the path to enlightenment into practice.

Seventh, bodhisattvas are the great "unacquainted" friends of all beings.

---

16. The Tibetan translation of the last two lines of this verse in Sthiramati's commentary reads: *gzhan la brten pa'i sdug bsngal 'byung ba yis / srid pa dag na de 'dra ga la skrag* ("How could such beings in existence be afraid of the pains that befall them in dependence on others?"). Compare this with Kawa Peltsek's translation: *de 'dra ba dag srid na gzhan rten phyir / sdug bsnal 'byung ba rnam kyi ga la 'jigs.*

That is to say, they do not help them on account of previous acquaintance—for example, because those beings have pleased them in the past by serving them, making them material offerings, worshipping them, and so on, or because they are related by family or friendship in this life. Rather, it is in their character to naturally feel love and compassion for other beings, and they therefore, as a matter of course, devote themselves to beings' welfare. They do not need to be prompted by others, as the following verse shows:

> **Those who constantly rely on the teacher, great love,**
> **Are deeply pained by others' sufferings.**
> **When it is their duty to act for others,**
> **To have another prompt them would be utterly disgraceful. (V, 27)**

Bodhisattvas constantly rely on the great compassion and kindness in their streams of being. For them it is like a master reminding them, in the same way that a master might remind a disciple to adopt right actions and abandon wrong actions. Other beings' sufferings cause them greater distress than a mother feels when her child falls sick. So, when it is their job to dispel other beings' sufferings and bring them to happiness and virtue, to fail to do so themselves and to have to be urged to do so by someone else would be extremely shameful, for it would be contrary to the bodhisattva way. It would be as shameful as it would be, even to ordinary people, if a wealthy man were not to give his destitute mother the smallest thing when he saw her and had to be prompted by someone else's saying, "She's your mother. Give her something to eat!" What a disgrace it would be, how unprincipled they would say he was, if he did not give some small thing even when urged to do so. In the same way, great love is the bodhisattvas' master who, as it were, keeps on reminding them. For that master's followers not to engage in love's objectives would be utterly shameful. Thus, since bodhisattvas are naturally loving and do not need other beings to prompt them, they engage in the welfare of other beings without any need to be urged to do so. This verse, therefore, implicitly praises this quality, the fact that it is impossible for them to cease caring for beings' welfare, and it is thus an instruction to work for the benefit of beings.

> **For those who are the highest of beings, carrying on their heads**
> **The great burden of sentient beings, it is not right to travel**
>   **leisurely.**

**Since they and others are fettered by all kinds of bonds,
Their diligence should be multiplied a hundred times. (V, 28)**

The eighth of these verses is an instruction on the need for bodhisattvas to be especially diligent. Even in ordinary life, those who have to travel a long way carrying a big load need to concentrate and go quickly. If they take it too easy, it will be difficult for them to reach their destination. Similarly, since bodhisattvas have given rise to the intention to attain the great enlightenment in order to liberate all sentient beings in unsurpassable enlightenment, they should, as the most excellent of beings carrying on their heads the great burden of all sentient beings, proceed to the state of great enlightenment as they have undertaken to do. To fall prey to the laziness of postponement and proceed or set out on the path in a leisurely manner, instead of speedily applying diligence in practicing the six transcendent perfections that lead to enlightenment, is not at all becoming. Even listeners, who have set out to cut the bonds of karma and defilements for their own sake alone, hasten to make efforts as if lighting a fire by rubbing two sticks together rapidly and continuously, and they attain their own resultant enlightenment in three or seven lifetimes. Bodhisattvas have to remove the bonds of karma and defilements that are present in their own mind streams and those of all beings, and so, since they and other sentient beings are at present completely bound by all kinds of different fetters, and in particular the three obscurations (karmic obscurations, obscurations of defilements, and obscurations due to the fully ripened karmic effect),[17] their diligence should be a hundred times greater than that of the listeners and solitary realizers.

This completes the explanation of the fifth chapter of *Ornament of the Mahāyāna Sūtras*, the chapter on the spiritual intent.

---

17. The three obscurations or fetters are as follows, according to Sthiramati, who bases his explanation on the *Abhidharmakośa*: (1) being fettered by the karma of the five crimes with immediate retribution; (2) being fettered by intense defilements such as attachment and hatred; and (3) being fettered by rebirth in the three lower realms, in the northern continent of Uttarakuru, or as an insensate god in the world of form (*'du shes med pa'i lha*). See also Longchen Yeshe Dorje, Kangyur Rinpoche, *Treasury of Precious Qualities, Book 1*, 441n14 (for this and the other references to this work below, readers of the 1st edition without the root text will need to subtract 90 from the page numbers in the revised edition).

6

Practice

Having thus aroused bodhicitta, it is necessary to put one's undertaking into practice, so there now follows an explanation on the practice, the fourth topic of what is to be specifically known. This is divided into three: (1) a general exposition on perfectly accomplishing the twofold goal; (2) specific explanations of how to accomplish others' goals; and (3) a concluding summary showing the greatness of the practice.

1. General Exposition of the Perfect Practice for Accomplishing the Twofold Goal

> Great in terms of its basis, undertaking, and result—
> Such is held to be the practice of the buddhas' heirs:
> Great is their continuous commitment, great is their forbearance,
> And great is the goal that they must perfectly achieve. (VI, 1)

On account of its possessing three great aspects—the great basis, great undertaking, and great result—the practice of the children of the victorious ones is held to be superior.

Great basis refers to the fact that since the practice happens through first arousing the spiritual intent for supreme enlightenment ("I must liberate all sentient beings into unsurpassable enlightenment"), the basis of the practice is that bodhicitta, which is thus explained as being the great basis. This is a great and everlasting commitment, an engagement in the welfare of all sentient beings, and in this respect the practice is virtuous in the beginning.

Great undertaking refers to the fact that, from the level of earnest aspiration up to the tenth level, the practice is undertaken with boundless joy at completing the Buddha's path oneself and bringing sentient beings to maturity. Because bodhisattvas never get discouraged, it involves great forbearance and is thus virtuous in the middle.

From attaining the result, the great unsurpassable enlightenment, bodhisattvas fulfill their own goal and perform the deeds of perfectly accomplishing the great goal of all sentient beings until the end of saṃsāra. In this respect, the practice is virtuous in the end.

The listeners and solitary realizers have none of these three great qualities.

2. Specific Explanations of the Practice for Accomplishing Others' Goals

The specific explanations comprise six sections: (1) how bodhisattvas engage in benefiting others; (2) categories of altruistic activity; (3) the highest altruistic activity; (4) the superiority of the bodhisattvas' practice; (5) the uninterrupted nature of the practice; and (6) not being discouraged by others' ingratitude.

a. How Bodhisattvas Engage in Benefiting Others

> Once they have acquired the attitude that others are equal to themselves,
> Or have a greater love for others than for themselves,
> Bodhisattvas thus think others' goals outweigh their own:
> Their own aim is that others' aims are fulfilled. (VI, 2)

> The compassionate ones, for the sake of others,
> Bring upon themselves the most terrible suffering;
> Ordinary folk are nothing like as ruthless
> In inflicting pain, even on their enemies. (VI, 3)

Once bodhisattvas have acquired the state of mind that realizes the sameness of themselves and all sentient beings (or the attitude of loving others more than oneself, of caring for them more than oneself), subsequently, more than wanting to eliminate defilements and suffering and to accomplish mundane and supramundane happiness for themselves, they think mainly or above all of achieving these two things for others. For such bodhisattvas, there is no difference between what is fulfillment for themselves and what is fulfillment for others: they are the same.[1]

Another explanation is that on the level of earnest aspiration, where their

---

1. Alternative translation: For such bodhisattvas, what is their own goal? What are others' goals? There is no difference: they are the same.

compassion and discernment is aspirational, bodhisattvas train in equalizing and exchanging themselves and others and thus acquire the attitude that they and sentient beings are the same. And when they attain the first level, they realize the truth of the omnipresent expanse of reality and thereby realize the very sameness of themselves and others. It is then that the attitude of caring for others more than themselves becomes a reality, as they think of those sentient beings who do not have that same realization that they themselves have achieved, and who wander for ages, hardly able to bear the intense sufferings of delusion.

Thus it is that bodhisattvas, whose very nature is compassion, give away their kingdoms, their bodies, and so forth for the sake of other sentient beings, and in doing so they bring upon themselves the most terrible suffering. Ordinary assailants, murderers, and the like do not perpetrate such acts of physical violence and mutilation anything like so ruthlessly, even on their own enemies.

b. Categories of Altruistic Activity

> Bodhisattvas correctly teach those who realize the lowest, middling,
> And supreme realities; they satisfy, induce,
> Help ascertain the meaning, ripen virtue,
> And likewise instruct, settle, and liberate minds; (VI, 4)
>
> They help accomplish extraordinary qualities;
> Likewise they bring birth in the family, predictions, empowerment,
> And the unsurpassable state of the tathāgatas' omniscience.
> In these thirteen ways they bring benefit to others. (VI, 5)

What do bodhisattvas do to benefit others, and how? There are thirteen different ways in which they work for others' good:

(1) Bodhisattvas know, by means of their miraculous ability to tell all, the minds of the three kinds of beings (namely, those who have the listener potential and are the lowliest of the different kinds of beings, or ones of least stature; those who have the solitary-realizer potential, who are middling; and those who have the bodhisattva potential, who abide by the supreme reality).[2] With this knowledge, they use their miraculous power of explana-

---

2. Sthiramati explains here that listeners realize the lesser reality or emptiness (*chos nyid*), solitary realizers the middling reality, and bodhisattvas the supreme reality.

tion to correctly teach the appropriate antidote for each one—teaching, for example, meditation on ugliness for those with attachment.

(2) By displaying the miraculous power of magical transformation, they cause the tīrthikas and others who do not have faith in these teachings to have faith, and then introduce them to the correct doctrine, thus making them content.

(3) They bestow on ordinary people the refuge in the Three Jewels and induce them to take the five basic precepts.

(4) They dispel the doubts of those who have not understood the teachings related to their family, that is, of one of the three vehicles, and help them ascertain the meaning of their respective Dharma.

(5) They induce those in whom sources of good have not ripened to practice the six transcendent perfections, thereby causing the sources of good related to the six perfections to ripen.

(6) Similarly, they instruct or give relevant advice to those who wish to practice concentration but do not have the necessary instructions.

(7) They help those who have received instructions on concentration to achieve the settling of their minds in one-pointed absorption.

(8) They help those who do not have profound insight to give rise to wisdom and develop the intelligence[3] to attain the result of their respective vehicle. In other words, they free their minds from doubt and other obscurations.

(9) They help those who have not yet acquired them to accomplish extraordinary qualities such as the union of sustained calm and profound insight, preternatural powers, the elements that lead to enlightenment, and the powers of perceptual limitlessness.

The ways described above benefit beings in the common vehicle. The ways in which beings[4] are benefited in terms of the uncommon Great Vehicle are as follows.

(10) On the first level, they are caused to be born in the buddha family.[5]

(11) On the eighth level, because they have now attained the "acceptance that phenomena are unborn," they naturally receive predictions from the

---

3. Tib. *blo gros byed pa*. This expression, copied from Sthiramati, appears to be a synonym for *lhag mthong*, "profound insight," though perhaps with the spelling *blo gros 'byed pa*.

4. "Beings" in this case refers to bodhisattvas on the bodhisattva levels.

5. Having attained the first level, bodhisattvas cannot revert to having the potential of lower vehicles.

tathāgatas, who tell them, "Fortunate child, in such and such a buddha field, at such and such a time, you will be known as the tathāgata called —."

(12) On the tenth level, they are empowered with light rays from all the buddhas of the ten directions as the Buddha's regents, kings of Dharma.

(13) On the buddha level, Universal Light, the acquisition of the four kinds of gnosis places them in the unsurpassable state of the knowledge of the tathāgatas.

c. THE HIGHEST ALTRUISTIC ACTIVITY

> Bodhisattvas give precise explanations to suit the individual,
> Are not pompous, not possessive, are learned,
> Patient, disciplined, very advanced, and inexhaustible.
> In these respects, the practice of the Conqueror's children is
>   supreme. (VI, 6)

Bodhisattvas' altruistic activity is at its highest when it is beneficial for others and does not go to waste.

It is by teaching the Dharma in tune with each of the three kinds of beings that one will benefit them. The *Heap of Jewels* states, "It is a mistake for a bodhisattva to expound the profound and extensive teachings to those of the listeners' and solitary realizers' vehicles." Teachings that are not in tune with their respective characters will not benefit them and are not, therefore, the best means for accomplishing their goals. Consequently, since any of the three kinds of beings have attachment and the other defilements in greater or lesser degrees, the correct way to teach them is to teach the antidotes precisely, giving beings with attachment the teachings on ugliness, those with aversion the teachings on love, those with bewilderment the teachings on dependent arising, and so on.

Even if bodhisattvas have acquired numerous special qualities such as miraculous powers, they refrain from giving themselves airs on account of these—physically, verbally, or mentally (thinking, "I am so good."). This is the most effective way of helping others. On the other hand, contriving to make oneself attractive and bearing oneself pompously, indulging in boastful talk, and having conceited thoughts will not greatly benefit others.

By displaying miracles and teaching the Dharma, bodhisattvas may tame beings and establish them on the path, but they never have partial and possessive thoughts like, "These are my disciples; it is I who tamed them."

By means of their learning in the teachings of the three vehicles, bodhisattvas enable others who have not gained realization to gain realization, they enable those with erroneous ideas to counteract them, and they enable those with doubts to dispel them.

For others' sake, they patiently put up with difficulties such as heat and cold, hunger and thirst, and ingratitude.

By controlling their body, speech, and mind and being disciplined, bodhisattvas are able to make others disciplined as well. It is said in a sūtra, "Unless I am liberated myself, I cannot liberate other sentient beings. Likewise, if I am not peaceful, I cannot make others peaceful. If I am not disciplined, I cannot make others disciplined."

"Very advanced"[6] and "inexhaustible" both refer to the practice of bodhisattvas who have entered the levels. It is by placing others too on the levels that bodhisattvas who have attained the levels benefit sentient beings. Those who have entered the levels, from the first level up to the buddha level, are known as "very advanced." Apart from bodhisattvas, ordinary people and listeners and solitary realizers are unable to enter those levels, so bodhisattvas are said to be more advanced than they are. As explained above, bodhisattvas on the first level, who are "born in the family,"[7] are able to benefit other sentient beings by causing them also to be born in the buddha family. Similarly, just as their own nonconceptual gnosis ripens from their having received predictions, they are able to bring others too to that state of gnosis. Likewise, having obtained empowerment, they are able to bring others to the same level as their own. And having acquired omniscient gnosis when they attain buddhahood, they are able to establish other sentient beings in it as well.

"Inexhaustible" refers to the fact that, for the following four reasons, a bodhisattva's practice is never exhausted and will never come to an end. Since there is no end to sentient beings to be liberated, the bodhicitta that is aroused for their sake never comes to an end. Since bodhicitta is inexhaustible, the intention is never exhausted. Since the intention is inexhaustible, the compassion that comes from the intention is never exhausted. And since compassion is inexhaustible, the skillful means and wisdom in acting for the sake of sentient beings are never exhausted.

---

6. Tib. *shin tu ring song*, lit. "very far gone."
7. That is, the tathāgata or buddha family.

It is in these respects that the practice of the children of the victorious ones, because it is engaged in benefiting others, is at its highest.

These eight qualities—teaching to suit the individual, and so on—enable bodhisattvas to accomplish the thirteen different ways of benefiting others as follows. In teaching precisely, in tune with each being, they teach correctly. By not putting on airs, they make beings content. By being unpossessive, they induce beings to enter the Dharma. By means of their learning, they help beings ascertain the meaning. By being patient, they help them ripen their sources of good. By means of their discipline, they instruct, settle, liberate minds, and help accomplish extraordinary qualities. Their being advanced is related to the last four: birth in the family, predictions, empowerment, and establishment in the unsurpassable state of the knowledge of the tathāgatas. Their inexhaustible qualities apply generally.

d. The Superiority of the Bodhisattvas' Practice

> Ordinary attached beings pursue great fear;
> Those who delight in existence have misconceived, transient bliss;
> Those who delight in peace completely pacify their own perpetuation;
> Those whose nature is compassion pacify all perpetuation, continuously. (VI, 7)

Ordinary beings in the world of desire, who are full of desire and attachment to the five sense pleasures, indulge in them. This is their "practice." Because of it, they will experience great fear in this life and their whole series of lives, which is why they are said to "pursue great fear." Beings in the two higher worlds (the worlds of form and formlessness) practice concentration—mental absorption. Since their delight in their respective levels of existence does not transcend the suffering of everything composite, their bliss is a misconception, samsaric by nature, transient and unstable. It is out of attachment to that bliss that they practice such concentration. The listeners and solitary realizers, who delight in pacifying the sufferings of saṃsāra, engage only in completely pacifying the perpetuation of subsequent existences for their own streams of being, and that is what they practice. As for the practice of those who embody compassion—that is, bodhisattvas—with wisdom they pacify the whole perpetuation of suffering in themselves and others, and with compassion they never forsake sentient beings but constantly remain in saṃsāra to benefit others. Their practice is therefore superior to the above-mentioned practices of mundane beings and supramundane listeners and solitary realizers.

> **Confused ordinary people striving for their own happiness**
> **Will always fail to achieve it and suffer instead.**
> **The steadfast, striving constantly for others' good,**
> **Will achieve the goals of both and thence nirvāṇa. (VI, 8)**

Mundane, ordinary confused beings never give a single thought to others' welfare, but instead work themselves to the bone with all kinds of activities such as farming, business, and womanizing in order to achieve happiness for themselves. Yet they always fail to achieve the unqualified, perfect happiness they so want for themselves. Instead, even in this life, they suffer from heat, cold, hunger, thirst, and the like. Because they are ever looking for things they have not yet got, and what they have got is deteriorating, they encounter numerous difficulties, physical and mental. And in other lives, they will suffer in many different ways in the lower realms and elsewhere.

Steadfast bodhisattvas, who are constantly diligent in benefiting others, will, for the time being, benefit both themselves and others in their experiencing many kinds of happiness in this life and the next. And ultimately, they will attain the nondwelling nirvāṇa. At that time they will achieve the completion of their own goal, the great bliss that can never fade, and, to fulfill others' goals, they will gain the inexhaustible activities that bring benefit and happiness for as long as there are sentient beings.

e. The Uninterrupted Nature of the Practice

> **Whenever the children of the buddhas act,**
> **Whatever different sense objects they experience,**
> **Using appropriate and fitting words,**
> **They are actually acting to benefit beings. (VI, 9)**

Other people, when they are not deliberately trying, do not actually accomplish anything, but this is not the case for bodhisattvas. The power of their bodhicitta, both in intention and in action, is such that even when they are without concerns—when they are asleep, for example—their sources of good are constantly increasing. Not only at times when they are actually using their body, speech, and mind to benefit beings by practicing generosity and the other five transcendent perfections, but even in their normal activities—moving around, walking, lying down, and sitting—they are acting for beings' good in the prayers of aspiration they are making mentally. Whatever activities the buddhas' children are engaged in, at those times, whichever of the various objects of the six senses they perceive, they are in reality making prayers of aspiration to benefit beings, using appropriately worded prayers to suit the situation, so that even their indeterminate activities all become beneficial for sentient beings. In this way they make full use of skillful means, as taught in the *Sūtra of the Perfectly Pure Sphere of Activity*. When they enter a town, bodhisattvas pray: "May all sentient beings enter the city of supreme liberation." When they set out on a journey: "May all beings set out on the path of the Great Vehicle." When they climb a flight of steps: "May all beings ascend the staircase to liberation." When they wash: "May all beings' karmic actions and defilements be purified." When they light a fire: "May the fire of gnosis consume all beings' thoughts." And so on. In so dedicating each of their activities, praying that all beings may obtain happiness and perfect liberation through the corresponding purificatory factors, bodhisattvas never cease to work for others' benefit.

f. Not Being Discouraged by Others' Ingratitude When Acting for Their Benefit

> The wise do not place any blame on those people
> Whose minds are ever helpless in the face of evil.
> "Without wanting to, they act ungratefully."
> Thus their compassion for ordinary people grows more and
>   more. (VI, 10)

Bodhisattvas are endowed with wisdom (the unmistaken realization of the nature of all phenomena) and with great compassion for sentient beings. Ordinary people's minds are constantly rendered powerless by the evils of attachment, aversion, and bewilderment, the root of which is the belief in a nonexistent self. So when they strike or insult or hold wrong views against a wise bodhisattva, the bodhisattva does not consider that it is their fault, but realizes that they are like deranged people making trouble for others and even committing suicide. Without wanting to be, they are slaves to their defilements, and this is why they are acting in this ungrateful manner. Bodhisattvas do not, therefore, feel angry or discouraged with regard to these ungrateful beings. Their compassion grows ever stronger as they think, "I must free these beings from those evils."

3. Concluding Summary Showing the Greatness of the Practice

> With this practice, bodhisattvas outshine all existence and beings;
> They possess the highest peace,
> Increase the host of multifarious qualities,
> And, with loving thoughts, constantly gather beings. (VI, 11)

With this practice, bodhisattvas triumph over all the three worlds of existence and the five classes of beings and possess sublime peace, the nondwelling nirvāṇa. They increase the mass of multifarious qualities such as the levels, transcendent perfections, strengths, and fearlessnesses more and more. And, with their loving intentions, they constantly gather beings and never forsake them. The bodhisattva's practice thus has four kinds of greatness: those of outshining all beings, attaining the nondwelling nirvāṇa, increasing in excellent qualities, and never forsaking sentient beings. This is the import of everything that has been explained above.

This completes the explanation of the sixth chapter of *Ornament of the Mahāyāna Sūtras*, the chapter on practice.

Because it has been taught that the practice leads to the nondwelling nirvāṇa, and it is not possible to attain the nondwelling nirvāṇa without realizing thatness, the chapter on practice is now followed by an explanation of the chapter on thatness.

PART THREE
WHAT IS TO BE REFLECTED UPON

ĀRYA STHIRAMATI (SIXTH CENTURY CE)

7
Thatness

The chapter on thatness contains three sections: (1) the defining characteristics of thatness; (2) establishing the two kinds of no-self; and (3) the stages by which thatness is realized.

1. The Defining Characteristics of Thatness

> **It is not existent nor nonexistent, not the same nor different;**
> **Not produced nor destroyed, it will not diminish**
> **Nor increase; it cannot be purified**
> **Yet becomes perfectly pure—these are the characteristics of**
>   **the ultimate. (VII, 1)**

The defining characteristic of thatness, which is to be realized personally, is that it is free from four extremes: existence, nonexistence, one-and-the-sameness, and distinctness. How? Like the imputed reality and the dependent reality, the ultimate, thatness, is not existent. And, being the fully present reality, it is not nonexistent.

There are no other so-called phenomena than the phenomena of the dependent reality, of the profound, inner dependent arising. The belief that they exist in the way they appear—that is, in the dualism of subject and object—constitutes the imputed reality. That is how they appear to be, and immature, ordinary beings cling to them as if they existed in the way they appear. Yet they have never, from the very beginning, existed as dualistic phenomena, as subject and object. But while not existing in that way, the fully present reality does exist in that, being the actual condition of things or ultimate truth, it is emptiness—which exists as the positive conclusion,[1]

---

1. Tib. *yongs gcod du grub pa*. Just as sound, for example, is "positively" established as

in conventional terms, of there being nothing in something, the latter therefore being affirmed as empty.

Since the so-called imputed and dependent realities and the truly existent reality are not one and the same, they are not identical or indistinguishable. On the other hand, since they are not distinct, they are not different. This is also stated in the sūtra *Unraveling the Intent*:

> The compounded world and the ultimate
> Are characterized as being neither the same nor distinct.

The imputed reality is a mistake and does not really exist; the dependent reality is dualistic appearance, which is the basis of the imputed reality. The fully present reality, on the other hand, is unmistaken and devoid of duality. They are not, therefore, one and the same, but are respectively phenomena and their true nature.[2]

In that case, are they different? No, they are not. The fact that the dependent reality is intrinsically devoid of dualistic subject-object imputations is the fully present reality, and there is no other so-called fully present reality different from that: the true nature of the dependent reality (the phenomenon imbued with that nature) is the fully present reality. If these two were distinct, the dependent reality could never be devoid of the duality of subject and object, so their being different does not hold. Just as one cannot separate compounded phenomena and impermanence, nor fire and heat, these two realities should be understood as not existing separately.

The ultimate fully present reality has, from the beginning, never been produced nor been destroyed or made to cease. Its very nature is that, from the very beginning, it has never arisen through causes and conditions, so how could it perish? Even with time, there is no difference in it before, when we are in saṃsāra, or afterward, when we are in nirvāṇa: without ever diminishing or increasing, it remains exactly as it is. Just as the sky does not grow bigger when there are clouds or smaller when there are none, suchness does not diminish with the diminution of the defilement aspect or increase with the growth of the purity aspect. And, since its very nature is inherently perfectly

---

impermanent by the negation of its permanence, emptiness is positively established by the negation of the existence of subject and object.

2. Tib. *chos can dang chos nyid*, Skt. *dharmin* and *dharmatā*. The phenomena that have or are imbued with the true nature or reality, and the true nature or reality itself, which is emptiness.

pure, there is no "repurifying" it—it is like the sky, or high-quality gold, or water, or crystal, which are naturally pure. As far as its nature is concerned, there is no question of removing contaminants. However, just as the sky can become free of passing clouds, gold free of tarnish, water free of suspended particles, and crystal free of dirt, the fully present reality, as a result of the removal of the two adventitious obscurations, becomes perfectly pure and uncontaminated.

These, then, are the defining characteristics of the ultimate. This nondual ultimate nature is thus indicated by five points: it is neither existent nor nonexistent; it is not the same nor different; it is not produced or destroyed; it does not grow or diminish; and it is neither pure nor impure.

According to the Mādhyamikas, it is not that all the phenomena that appear through the power of dependent arising are not existent on the relative, conventional level, nor that they are existent on the ultimate level; nor even that they are both existent and nonexistent. On the ultimate level, nonexistence is the true nature of phenomena that exist conventionally. So, apart from simply being distinguished by name, these two do not, in fact, exist as two distinct entities: they are like fire and its heat, or molasses and its sweetness. Could there, then, be a third possibility—that thatness is something that is neither existent on the relative level nor nonexistent on the ultimate level? No. There is no valid means of cognition that provides a proof for a third alternative that is neither a phenomenon nor an empty true nature. Such a third possibility could never be the intrinsic or true nature of conventional phenomena. The Mādhyamikas thus assert freedom from the four extremes (existence, nonexistence, both, and neither), freedom from all conceptual elaboration, the inseparability of the two truths—the inseparability of phenomena and their true nature—which has to be realized personally. This true nature free from conceptual elaboration is always the same in being devoid of production, destruction, diminution, and expansion. It has not as much as an atom's worth of the characteristics of dualistic phenomena such as purity and impurity.

Now, the Cittamātra approach speaks of all phenomena being nothing other than simply the appearances of the mind, and it asserts that only the clear and aware consciousness of the dependent reality, the basis of perception, exists substantially. If the Cittamātrins' final standpoint is the assertion that this consciousness is only a substantially existent entity inasmuch as it is the cause for all conventional phenomena appearing, and that apart from this assertion they are not claiming that it exists substantially as a truly existing entity in ultimate truth, then they are not at all in contradiction with the Mādhyamika tradition. On the other hand, if they were to assert that it is truly existent in ultimate truth, they would be contradicting the Mādhyamika approach. It seems, therefore, that it is just this particular point that needs to be examined as a source of contention (or otherwise) for the Mādhyamikas.

In the cycle of teachings of Maitreya and the writings of the great charioteer Asaṅga, whose thinking is one and the same, it is taught that individuals on the level of earnest aspiration first understand that all phenomena are simply the mind. Subsequently they have the experience that there is no object to be apprehended in the mind. Then, at the stage of the supreme mundane level on the path of joining, they realize that because there is no object, neither is there a subject, and immediately after that, they attain the first level with the direct realization of the truth of ultimate reality devoid of the duality of subject and object. As for things being only the mind, the source of the dualistic perception of things appearing as environment, sense objects, and a body is the consciousness of the ground of all, which is accepted as existing substantially on the conventional level but is taught as being like a magical illusion and so on since it appears in a variety of ways while not existing dualistically. For this reason, because this tradition realizes, perfectly correctly, that the nondual consciousness is devoid of any truly existing entities and of characteristics, the ultimate intentions of the charioteers of Madhyamaka and Cittamātra should be considered as being in agreement.

Why, then, do the Mādhyamika masters refute the Cittamātra tenet system? Because self-styled proponents of the Cittamātra tenets, when speaking of mind-only, say that there are no external objects but that the mind exists substantially—like a rope that is devoid of snakeness, but not devoid of ropeness. Having failed to understand that such statements are asserted from the conventional point of view, they believe the nondual consciousness to be truly existent on the ultimate level. It is this tenet that the Mādhyamikas repudiate. But, they say, we do not refute the thinking of Ārya Asaṅga, who correctly realized the mind-only path taught by the Buddha.

There is nothing inappropriate in saying this. If there are Tibetan scholars who accept that even listeners who have seen the truth are no different from the Mādhyamikas in having realized both kinds of no-self, it goes without saying that the great charioteer Asaṅga had realized the true intention of Madhyamaka, because he was a noble being.[3]

---

3. As a noble being or *ārya*, one who has attained the bodhisattva levels, he had directly realized emptiness.

Generally speaking, the Mādhyamikas are content to establish definitively that dependently arising phenomena are not produced. But although there is no obligation to accept the Cittamātra tenets, I feel it is all for the good if one can understand the essential point that although the great charioteers of the Madhyamaka and Cittamātra who founded the paths of the profound and extensive teachings appear to present them differently, their ultimate intentions are in perfect agreement in the expanse of gnosis—as we shall see. On this very subject of dependent arising, Ārya Asaṅga explains in the *Compendium of the Great Vehicle* and other texts that it is of two kinds: dependent arising related to discerning the essential nature, and dependent arising related to discerning the pleasant and unpleasant. The first of these explains how all appearances proliferate from the ground of all. This is the subtle, inner dependent arising, to be realized by bodhisattvas who have mastered the subtle, profound meaning. It is therefore more profound than dependent arising related to discerning pleasant and unpleasant, which is the gross, outer dependent arising that is taught in terms of the twelve links.

In a similar vein, the sūtras of the ultimate teachings and the profound tantras of the Mantrayāna also state that there are no phenomena apart from the mind, and that the roots of both saṃsāra and nirvāṇa lie in the mind. Because of the mind, the phenomena of saṃsāra and nirvāṇa arise; if there were no mind, there would be no saṃsāra and no nirvāṇa. How? It is by the power of the mind that defilements create karma, subsequently producing the process of defilement that is saṃsāra. And it is with the mind that one gives rise to the wisdom of the realization of no-self and to compassion, practices the Mahāyāna path, and thereby achieves buddhahood, whose nature is the five kinds of gnosis, the transformation of the eight consciousnesses, and the ground of all. It is with the mind, too, that the listeners and solitary realizers realize the no-self of the individual and attain nirvāṇa, beyond the suffering of grasping at existence. So the roots of defilement and purity depend on the mind. Anyone who is a Buddhist has to accept this.

Moreover, it is said, "If one definitively establishes that mind is devoid of intrinsic existence, one will realize the Mahāyāna path with little difficulty." And the *Tantra of Vairocana's Enlightenment* teaches that this is one of the most crucial points on the path. Furthermore, in the *Jeweled Lamp of the Middle Way*, a treatise that summarizes the key points of the whole of Madhyamaka, the master Bhavya,[4] who was renowned as a great scholar in the land of India, explains that the Yogācāra Madhyamaka is known as

---

4. Bhavya is another name for the sixth-century Indian master Bhāvaviveka.

the subtle, inner Madhyamaka, and that the Madhyamaka of those who accept external objects is known as the obvious, outer Madhyamaka. He also clearly states that when it comes to the actual practice, the Yogācāra Madhyamaka is the more profound—even Glorious Candrakīrti practiced in that way.

So, if this so-called "self-illuminating nondual consciousness" asserted by the Cittamātrins is understood to be a consciousness that is the ultimate of all dualistic consciousnesses,[5] and it is merely that its subject and object are inexpressible, and if such a consciousness is understood to be truly existent and not intrinsically empty, then it is something that has to be refuted. If, on the other hand, that consciousness is understood to be unborn from the very beginning, to be directly experienced by reflexive awareness, and to be self-illuminating gnosis without subject or object, it is something to be established. Both the Madhyamaka and Mantrayāna have to accept this. If there were no reflexively aware gnosis, or mind of clear light, it would be impossible for there to be a mind that realizes the truth of the ultimate reality on the path of learning; and at the time of the path of no more learning, the nirvāṇa without residue, the Buddha would have no omniscient gnosis. And in that case there would be no difference between the Buddha's nirvāṇa and the nirvāṇa of the lower vehicles, which is like the extinction of a lamp, so how could one talk about the Buddha's bodies (kāyas), different kinds of gnosis, and inexhaustible activities?[6]

To sum up, thatness, which is the actual condition of all phenomena, is the completely unbiased union of appearance and emptiness,[7] to be realized personally. If one realizes that it never changes in any situation, whether in the ground, path, or result, one will be saved from the abyss of unwholesome, extremist views.

---

5. Tib. *gzung 'dzin can gyi rnam shes*, consciousnesses involving a perceived object and perceiving subject.

6. This point marks the end of Mipham's discussion of the essential relationship between Madhyamaka and Cittamātra that started with Asaṅga's remarks on dependent arising. In the Tibetan, the sentence encouraging one to understand this relationship occurs here, at the end of the discussion, whereas we have considered it more appropriate, in English translation, to use it to introduce the discussion.

7. "Unbiased" means that it does not tend to one aspect more than the other, to appearance more than emptiness, or vice versa.

2. Establishing Thatness: Proving the Two Kinds of No-Self by Reasoning
a. Proving the Absence of Self in the Individual

> **The belief in a self does not constitute a self as such,**
> **And nor do the aggregates which abide in evil; their characteristics are not the same.**
> **Nor is there a self that is other than these two. It is produced erroneously.**
> **Freedom, therefore, is a simple error coming to an end. (VII, 2)**

What we call the individual self, apart from simply being erroneously conceived without examination or analysis, does not in fact exist, because neither the belief in a self, nor the aggregates, nor anything other than them is a self. The "I" implicit in the view of the transitory composite or belief in a self is not a self, because the belief in a self is a mental phenomenon, and it is therefore compounded, impermanent, not all-pervading, and productive of the three kinds of karmic actions (virtuous, nonvirtuous, and indeterminate)—quite different in its defining characteristics from the self that the tīrthikas imagine, which is defined as uncompounded, permanent, all-pervading, and not productive of karmic actions.

The five aggregates, which are the support for the view of the transitory composite, are also taught as not being, by nature or in their characteristics, a self. According to Sthiramati's commentary, "abodes of evil"[8] refers to the aggregates—in their being the basis of the view of the transitory composite, which is the root of all defilements (hence "evil"), and in their being the abodes for that belief; or, alternatively, in their being produced by the negative tendencies of defilements. Some translations[9] have "that which abides in evil,"[10] which refers to the aggregates in the sense that they are the abode of defilements and suffering. Whatever the case, the five aggregates are not a self, for reasons similar to those just mentioned: they are impermanent, compounded, nonpervading, productive of karmic actions, and multiple, and they are therefore quite different, in their defining characteristics, from

---

8. Tib. *ngan pa'i gnas*.
9. I.e., different Tibetan translations from the Sanskrit.
10. Tib. *ngan par gnas*. This is the version in Kawa Peltsek's translation.

the self that happens in and of itself.[11] The latter is not the new product of causes and conditions, and it is all-pervading, permanent, nonproductive of karmic actions, and single.

There is no so-called self that is other than these two—that is, the view of the transitory composite that is the subject, and the five aggregates that are the object. Apart from these two, it is impossible to observe any other self-existing, either by the valid cognition of direct perception or by that of inference.

This refutation of the self-imputed by non-Buddhists also refutes the conceived object of the innate notion of "I." Sentient beings have only a single "I," not several, and from time without beginning until the end they consider that they are a single being. By making use of the three kinds of analysis just mentioned, we will realize that such a self is merely an invention.

Why, then, if there is no self, do all sentient beings think "I"? It is not because the self exists that they think "I." It is simply because of the delusion or mistaken, erroneous idea that it exists when it does not that they give rise to the thought that it exists—in the same way that they might take a rope to be a snake, or see a young woman in a dream.

One might argue, "If there is a self, then being bound by defilements in saṃsāra and being liberated when those bonds are cut makes sense. But if there is no self, who is liberated? Making an effort to liberate oneself, in that case, makes no sense." We are not striving to liberate an existent self. Take the analogy of someone mistaking a rope for a snake: they are terrified, but when they see that there is no snake there, they are extremely relieved. Similarly, because we think there is a self, when in fact there is none, we accumulate defilements and karmic actions and continuously undergo the experience of saṃsāra and suffering. Consequently, once we have the true wisdom to realize that there is no self, karma and defilements are stopped, and we thereby attain liberation. So what we call "liberation" is simply the cessation of a deluded idea or error in one's mind stream: it is not that an existent self is liberated. If a self existed, we could never reverse the belief in a self, and if we could not get rid of that, there would be no stopping karmic actions and defilements. Because of attachment to a self, we would continuously engage in saṃsāra.

---

11. Tib. *bdag ngo bo nyid kyis byung ba*, the self proposed by many non-Buddhist philosophers.

b. Showing the Absence of Self in Phenomena

> How is it that beings rely on a mere delusion
> And do not realize the continuous nature of suffering?
> Unaware, although they are aware, they suffer, although there is no suffering;
> The nature of phenomena does not exist as such. (VII, 3)
>
> How, when beings can directly perceive things arising dependently,
> Do they believe in things being created by something else?
> Why do they not see what is there, yet see what is not there?
> What sort of darkness is that? (VII, 4)

How is it that people who rely on what is merely a delusion—the erroneous idea that a self and phenomena exist—do not realize that they are maintaining a continuity whose nature is the various sufferings caused by that delusion (birth, aging, and so forth), and that they are simply persisting in their own deluded idea? It is because, as will be explained below, they are blanketed by the great darkness of not seeing the nature of things that is there while they mistakenly see what is not there. They do not have the untainted gnosis that realizes that what constitutes saṃsāra is suffering and delusion, and they are therefore said to be lacking awareness or not correctly aware. They *are* aware in the sense that they experience happy, painful, and neutral feelings with the tainted cognition that apprehends things mistakenly.

Whichever of the three feelings they experience, these are never anything other than suffering. Painful feelings constitute suffering by nature,[12] happy feelings comprise the suffering of change, and neutral feelings comprise the suffering of everything composite. In truth, there is no experience of suffering, because there is no self to experience it and because the phenomena being experienced also do not truly exist. In what way do they not exist? Although the nature or essence of phenomena (which are comprised in the aggregates, sense spheres, and senses-and-fields) exists only to the extent that they appear, it is like a magical illusion, a dream, a mirage. It is not that ultimately there is a nature or essence of these phenomena that exists.

---

12. I.e., the suffering of suffering, or suffering upon suffering.

Things do not in fact exist in the way they appear, and they are therefore devoid of self, empty; they exist as emptiness.

Why is this? External entities are produced from causes and conditions such as the four elements, seeds, and so forth. Internal entities—that is, sentient beings' aggregates—are produced through the coming together of causes and conditions such as ignorance and conditioning factors. How is it, then, that when they can directly experience and perceive all phenomena, external and internal, arising in dependence on the coming together of their respective causes and conditions, foolish people believe these things to arise through having been created (or through being created) by something else—Īśvara or a self, for example? Why, instead of seeing the fact of dependent arising that is intrinsic to all phenomena, do they see in them something else—a creator such as a self or Īśvara—even though it does not exist? What kind of darkness is this? To most people, darkness is something that conceals things that are there and makes them invisible. It never makes things that are not there visible! And yet, because of the darkness of ignorance present in beings' minds, they fail to see the evident interdependent production of things that is there as their very nature and, instead, see something that is not there—other-production. What a strange, novel kind of darkness that is!

> On the ultimate level, there is not the slightest difference
> Between peace and birth.
> Nevertheless, those who practice virtue, it is taught,
> Will bring an end to birth and thus gain peace. (VII, 5)

When we speak of "self" in this context, it is not only explained as being another word for an individual, and similarly for sentient being, life, man, human being, and so on.[13] The word also applies to the nature of phenomena: the so-called phenomenal self is used to signify the essence or nature of phenomena.[14] The tīrthikas make the mistake of clinging to the individual self and claiming that the resulting bondage is liberation. And the listeners

---

13. "Life" (Tib. *srog*) refers to the "living soul" (Skt. *jiva*) of Jainism. "Man" and "human being" are references to the celestial being Manu (Tib. *shed can*) in Hindu mythology who, on account of his merit running out, fell to earth, and to the human race that he fathered (Tib. *shed bu*, Manu's offspring).

14. "Essence" and "nature" are, of course, used here in the relative sense.

too are mistaken in their clinging to the phenomenal self and then claiming that their bondage by the nature of phenomena is liberation, for they have not understood the nature of phenomena.[15] According to the explanations of the Great Vehicle, all phenomena are the same in being nondual, though it is nevertheless acceptable to speak of saṃsāra and nirvāṇa and of bondage and liberation. Thus, with regard to what appears as the phenomena of saṃsāra and nirvāṇa, on the ultimate level, or from the point of view of their actual condition, there is not the slightest difference between peace, that is, nirvāṇa (which is the cessation of ignorance and, as a result, the cessation of everything up to aging and death) and birth in saṃsāra (which is the arising, on account of ignorance, of conditioning factors and the rest up to the arising of aging and death).[16] Since all the phenomena of saṃsāra and nirvāṇa are the same in being intrinsically nonarising and nonceasing, the nature of saṃsāra itself *is* nirvāṇa.

If that is the case, then what is the difference between ordinary people who are in saṃsāra and noble beings who have attained nirvāṇa? It is not that there is a difference in samsaric and nirvanic selves and phenomena that exist on the ultimate level, but that beings are ordinary or noble as a result of whether or not they have realized that the self and phenomena are devoid of essence. On the ultimate level, saṃsāra and nirvāṇa *are* the same, but it is nevertheless taught that those who complete their training in the virtuous practice of realizing the way things are (that is, impermanence, suffering, and the no-self of the individual) put an end to rebirth in saṃsāra and attain the peace of the listeners and solitary realizers. And when those who undertake the virtuous actions of the six transcendent perfections imbued with nonconceptual gnosis complete the path, they also put an end to rebirth in a subtle mental body[17] and thereby attain the nondwelling nirvāṇa in which they are at peace from even the mere habitual tendencies of saṃsāra.

---

15. The listeners have realized the no-self of the individual but not that of phenomena: they are still bound by their belief that phenomena have intrinsic existence, for they have not realized the fact that phenomena are empty by nature.

16. For a complete list of the twelve links of dependent arising, see the glossary.

17. Tib. *yid kyi rang bzhin gyi lus*, the subtle mental body that arhats have, caused by their minds' latent propensity for ignorance. See Kunzang Pelden, *The Nectar of Manjushri's Speech*, 341–42.

3. The Stages by Which the Ultimate, Thatness, Is Realized

> Bodhisattvas, going beyond infinite merit and wisdom,
> Perfectly gather the accumulations, and then
> Reflect and gain perfect certainty with regard to the Dharma.
> As a result, they realize objects to be the products of expression. (VII, 6)

Bodhisattvas, followers of the Great Vehicle, obtain their result through the paths of accumulation, joining, seeing, and meditation by means of the nonconceptual gnosis that realizes no-self in all phenomena, as follows. For one measureless kalpa, bodhisattvas "go beyond" the accumulations of merit and wisdom, which are infinite in nature. These comprise making offerings to the tathāgatas and listening, reflecting, and meditating, and practicing the six transcendent perfections. Bodhisattvas "go beyond"[18] them in the sense of gathering them until one measureless kalpa is completed or, alternatively, of perfectly gathering the accumulations that enable them to go beyond that to the noble levels. By means of the absorption of sustained calm that comes with reflecting properly on impermanence, suffering, emptiness, and no-self, and through the profound insight that definitively, without any doubt, ascertains them, they gain perfect certainty with regard to the points taught in the sūtras and other teachings in the Buddhist scriptures. These first three lines describe the path of accumulation.

As a result of gathering the accumulations like this and reflecting and gaining certainty with regard to the teachings, they realize that all external objects—forms, sounds, pillars, vases, and so forth—are simply nomenclatural; that is, they are simply taken to be this or that by the conceptual mind on the basis of names, and apart from this they have nothing to do with names, their real nature being inexpressible. This is the stage of warmth, known as the attainment of wisdom perceptions.

> Once they see that things are merely expressions,
> They dwell in the truth that it is mind alone that appears as those things.
> After that they gain direct realization
> Of the expanse of reality, free of the characteristics of duality. (VII, 7)

---

18. Tib. *pha rol*, lit. "going to the other side."

Once these bodhisattvas have understood especially that things are merely nominal expressions or conceptualizations as this or that, they see that things appear from the mind. This is the stage of the peak, known as the concentration of increasing wisdom perceptions.

Having understood that the phenomena perceived as the object aspect are the mind itself appearing as those objects, like objects in a dream, and that there are no external objects that are other than the mind, their minds rest perfectly in the nature of mind-only. This is the stage of acceptance, known as the concentration that has partially penetrated thatness, because with regard to thatness free from subject and object, they realize the absence of intrinsic existence of only one aspect—the object.

After that, they gain direct realization of the expanse of reality that is free from the dualistic characteristics of subject and object and they attain the path of seeing. How?

> **From intellectual understanding that there is nothing other than the mind,**
> **They then realize that neither does the mind exist.**
> **Once the wise have seen that both do not exist,**
> **They abide in the expanse of reality devoid of those. (VII, 8)**

At the stage of acceptance, having understood intellectually that there are no objects or outer phenomena other than the mind, they then realize that if the apprehended object does not exist, neither does the apprehending mind; subject and object are mutually dependent, so if there is no object, there is no subject either. This is the supreme mundane level, the immediately preceding concentration.

In the very instant after that, once the wise have realized that both subject and object are devoid of intrinsic existence, nonconceptual gnosis becomes a reality: with self-cognizant wisdom, they directly realize the expanse of reality that does not possess the characteristics of the dualistic phenomena of subject and object. This eliminates the defilement-related and cognitive obscurations to be eliminated by the path of seeing.

> **The power of nonconceptual gnosis in the wise**
> **Constantly extends to everything in equal measure,**
> **And clears away the dense jungle of the faults they bear**
> **Like a universal antidote removing poison. (VII, 9)**

We come next to the path of meditation, on which the wise bodhisattvas' nonconceptual gnosis extends equally to everything (or to all external and internal phenomena), constantly, from the second level up to the tenth. It is applied evenly, without things being conceived as subject or object, without duality. It is this that clears away the dense, jungle-like mass of faults that the bodhisattva has accumulated from time without beginning and that are so difficult to recognize and to eliminate—the obscurations of defilements, cognitive obscurations, and dualistic habitual tendencies resting on that bodhisattva's mind stream or consciousness of the ground of all, which is associated with the dependent reality. Like a powerful antidotal medicine, of which only a few drops poured into a vial of poison transforms it all into medicine, and whose mere smell or taste counteracts all poisons, the nonconceptual gnosis completely removes the poison-like subtle obscurations that are to be eliminated through the path of meditation and enables the great nonconceptual gnosis of the Buddha's level to manifest.

> Settling their intelligence in the expanse of reality,
> The root of the excellent presentation, the sacred Dharma
>   the capable ones have taught,
> The steadfast with that stream of mindfulness and
>   knowledge that things are mere concepts
> Swiftly traverse the ocean of excellent qualities. (VII, 10)

The sacred Dharma, containing twelve branches including the sūtras, was expounded by the buddhas, the capable ones who have vowed to refrain forever from all negative action with body, speech, and mind. It is virtuous in the beginning, middle, and end and is therefore an excellent presentation. The ultimate root of the meanings of all these teachings is for bodhisattvas to place their wisdom or intelligence on the expanse of reality, this also being referred to as "root mind," because they focus on the single meaning of all the sūtras combined. In that way, during formal meditation their stream of mindfulness contemplating the expanse of reality becomes more and more refined. And in postmeditation, they are steadfast in their knowledge that there are no phenomena other than the mere concepts of their own minds—that they are the mind alone—and in the knowledge that this mind too is devoid of intrinsic existence. These bodhisattvas will swiftly, in no time at all, perfect the ocean-like resultant qualities—the strengths, fearlessnesses, and so forth—and attain buddhahood, that is, the stage of no more training.

Most versions of the root text have "movements of recollection" (*dran rgyu*) here, but this is a scribal error, because in Sthiramati's *Great Commentary*, and also where this passage is quoted in the *Compendium of the Great Vehicle*, there is "stream of mindfulness" (*dran rgyud*).

This completes the explanation of the seventh chapter of *Ornament of the Mahāyāna Sūtras*, the chapter on thatness.

This explanation of thatness that is to be realized is followed by an explanation on accomplishing the extraordinary qualities used to bring others to maturity—the chapter on powers.

8
Powers

The chapter on powers is divided into seven sections describing their (1) essence; (2) causes; (3) results; (4) functions; (5) qualities; (6) categories and employment; and (7) the greatness of the qualities of these powers.

1. The Essence of the Powers

> Beings' births, speech, minds, virtue and nonvirtue,
> Abodes, and deliverance—these are manifestly perceived.
> Such knowledge—all-pervading, of different kinds,
> And unimpeded—defines the powers of those who attain stability. (VIII, 1)

"Birth" by implication includes death and refers to the knowledge of sentient beings' deaths, of where they will be reborn, and of how many lives they will have, from now until they attain nirvāṇa. This is the preternatural knowledge of death and birth by means of the divine eye.

"Speech" refers to knowledge of all the sounds and utterances of all sentient beings, the preternatural knowledge gained through the divine ear.

"Mind" refers to knowing the eighty-four thousand or so mental activities of sentient beings, the preternatural knowledge of others' minds.

"Virtue and nonvirtue" refers to the preternatural knowledge of previous lives, in other words, knowing the habitual tendencies that beings have from time without beginning in saṃsāra for doing or giving rise to positive and negative actions; and knowing also where they have taken birth in their previous lives, what karmic actions they have accumulated, what happiness and suffering they will have experienced, how long they have lived, and so on.

"Abodes" is the world in which buddhas, bodhisattvas, listeners, solitary realizers, and sentient beings dwell, and it refers to the knowledge of miraculous powers—for instance, passing unhindered to a particular place in order to make offerings to the buddhas and to benefit sentient beings.

"Deliverance" refers to the preternatural knowledge of the exhaustion of taints, which is the means by which beings may be certainly delivered from saṃsāra.

These six kinds of preternatural knowledge are clearly and directly experienced, like the fresh fruit of the emblic myrobalan[1] placed in the palm of the hand. When we speak of them here, we are referring to the fact that bodhisattvas have acquired fully manifest powers through mastery of the six kinds of preternatural knowledge. Their different kinds of preternatural knowledge are far superior to those of mundane sages and listeners and solitary realizers. In what way? They extend everywhere to all the worlds in the ten directions and to all times, and for each of the six kinds of preternatural knowledge there are infinite further categories, which are brought into play without impediment. That is the difference in the powers of bodhisattvas who have gained stability or mastery in using preternatural knowledge. This description of the nature or essence of the different kinds of preternatural knowledge will now be followed by an explanation of the causal factors that produce it.

2. The Causal Factors That Lead to Preternatural Knowledge

> Having attained the utterly pure fourth dhyāna,
> And through its being imbued with nonconceptual gnosis,
> By keeping in mind the modes of application,
> They will achieve the supreme accomplishment of powers.
> (VIII, 2)

The various forms of preternatural knowledge come from three causal factors:

(1) In terms of their level, bodhisattvas need to have attained the concentration of the fourth dhyāna, which is utterly pure on account of its being without the predominant faults of craving, defiled views, pride, and doubt, and on account of the bodhisattvas' fitness to do whatever they wish through their having acquired mastery of the different modes of meditative absorption—skipping stages, proceeding in order, and proceeding in the reverse order.

---

1. The structure of the jelly-like seeds can be seen through the transparent skin.

(2) Then, as a contributory factor, this is imbued with nonconceptual gnosis.

(3) As for the way preternatural knowledge is thus accomplished, it is from correctly keeping in mind the relevant points of each of the different kinds of preternatural knowledge, or the features that enable one to attain this or that preternatural knowledge as they have been presented.[2] The relevant points are what bodhisattvas think of or keep in mind when they wish to achieve preternatural knowledge. According to the sūtras, when they wish to achieve the preternatural knowledge of the divine eye, they concentrate on pervading all the directions with their vision and seeing all forms without obscuration. When they wish for the knowledge and ability to perform miracles, they concentrate on making their bodies very light and transforming them as they please. When they wish for the preternatural knowledge of the divine ear, they concentrate on numerous different sounds and on actually perceiving all sounds. To know others' minds, they concentrate on the many states of mind in others and on actually perceiving all their mental activities. Similarly, they focus on the past and on the truth and liberation.[3]

It is through these causal factors that bodhisattvas, the highest beings among those who accomplish powers with the six kinds of preternatural knowledge, achieve their extraordinary preternatural knowledge, for they are backed by nonconceptual gnosis and so on.[4]

3. The Results of Accomplishing Preternatural Knowledge

> They dwell perpetually in the matchless, vast abode
> Of the noble, celestial, and pure states;
> Journeying in all directions, they make perfect offerings to the buddhas
> And inspire sentient beings to practice purity. (VIII, 3)

---

2. I.e., in accordance with their presentation in the sūtras.

3. These last two refer to bodhisattvas' knowledge of former lives and knowledge of the exhaustion of taints respectively.

4. As Sthiramati points out, these causes are what make the bodhisattva's six kinds of preternatural knowledge superior to those of listeners, solitary realizers, and mundane beings.

As a result of accomplishing the different kinds of preternatural knowledge, bodhisattvas dwell in the noble states of the three doors of perfect liberation, along with the four truths, the levels, and the transcendent perfections, and especially in emptiness and the absorption of cessation. They dwell in the celestial states of the four dhyānas and the four formless absorptions, and especially in the fourth dhyāna. And they dwell in the pure states, the concentrations of the four boundless attitudes, especially compassion. Their so dwelling is superior in that it is beyond compare, extremely vast in scope, and constant. With their powers of preternatural knowledge, bodhisattvas travel throughout the ten directions and make perfect offerings to the buddhas. And by means of miraculous displays, they inspire sentient beings, causing pure sources of good to arise in their minds. In these three respects,[5] the result of their accomplishing the different kinds of preternatural knowledge is superior to that of such beings as listeners and solitary realizers.

4. The Functions of Preternatural Knowledge

> **They see all universes, with their formation, their destruction,**
> **And their sentient beings, as magical illusions.**
> **Possessed of powers, they exhibit them**
> **As desired in apparent and varied forms. (VIII, 4)**

The activity of seeing with the preternatural knowledge of the divine eye is to see all the universes in the ten directions—the physical universes with their formation and final destruction, along with all the sentient beings living in them—as being devoid of intrinsic existence, like a magical illusion, a mirage, or a dream.

The activity of showing miracles is as follows. Bodhisattvas who have mastery in whichever of the six kinds of preternatural knowledge they wish, or who possess the ten powers, exhibit these as they wish, in whichever form and with whichever means will benefit sentient beings (or alternatively, as beings wish—in accord with their aspirations). They also authentically demonstrate a whole variety of different activities, clearly visible or apparent, such as blazing with fire, flying in the sky, making the earth tremble, and inserting the entire cosmos of a billion universes into a mustard seed.

---

5. I.e., the bodhisattvas' matchless and vast ways of abiding, their making offerings to the buddhas, and their inspiring beings to virtue.

> Emitting rays of light to those who in the lower realms
> Are racked with pain, they take them to the higher realms.
> Rattling Māra's fine and lofty mansion,
> They terrify the demons and their gang. (VIII, 5)

Furthermore, bodhisattvas emit rays of light in all directions. As a result, the moment that the light touches the hell beings, hungry spirits, and animals, who have gone to evil states of extreme misery and pain, their sufferings are soothed and they gain faith, whereupon they immediately transmigrate from those realms and go to the higher realms of gods and humans.

These light rays shake the abode of Māra, a soaring, many-storied palace beautifully decorated with countless precious stones, along with the demons and their henchmen living there, terrifying them and deterring them from their devilish deeds.

> In the midst of a supreme gathering,
> They demonstrate displays of boundless concentrations.
> And by manifesting in art, through birth, and as supreme manifestations,
> They act perpetually for beings' good. (VIII, 6)

Regarding the activity of display, in the midst of a supreme gathering—a gathering of the Tathāgata and principal bodhisattvas—a bodhisattva who has acquired powers may enter meditative absorption in infinite concentrations such as the concentration of Brave Progression, the Illusion-Like concentration, and the Sky Treasury concentration, demonstrating a variety of boundless displays, like the displays through concentration demonstrated by Mañjuśrī, Avalokiteśvara, and others as mentioned in the sūtras.

As for the activity of manifestation, by manifesting in art, through birth, and as supreme nirmāṇakāya manifestations, bodhisattvas remain for the sake of the beings in the ten directions, not temporarily but all the time. An example of manifesting in art is that of a nirmāṇakāya manifesting as a gandharva playing the vīṇā in order to convert the gandharva Supriya.[6] Nirmāṇakāyas who manifest through birth appear in the same physical

---

6. The gandharva Supriya (Tib. *dri za rab dga'*) was a celestial musician who was particularly proud of his fine voice and the music he made on his six-stringed vīṇā (Indian lute). The Buddha, manifesting as a vīṇā player, made a much more beautiful sound with only a one-stringed vīṇā, and thus crushed Supriya's pride.

form as Indra and other celestial beings, or even as yakṣa spirits, animals, and so forth, by taking birth among them. Supreme nirmāṇakāya manifestations are those who appear as supreme nirmāṇakāya buddhas demonstrating transmigration from the Tuṣita heaven and so on, the attainment of full enlightenment, and the parinirvāṇa. Nirmāṇakāyas who manifest in art are also referred to in Sthiramati's commentary as nirmāṇakāyas who manifest in action. These manifest as artists and artisans, potters, musicians, and the like, manifesting a variety of different arts and, in doing so, benefiting sentient beings.

The *Great Commentary* speaks of six activities of preternatural knowledge, which it explains as the activity of seeing, that of showing miracles, the two activities of light rays (drawing beings out of the lower realms and intimidating the demons), the activity of display, and that of manifestation.

> **Because of their mastery of the different kinds of gnosis,**
> **They display buddha fields as desired, and thus achieve purity.**
> **By proclaiming the name "Buddha" wherever the name**
>   **"Buddha" is unknown,**
> **They send beings to other worlds. (VIII, 7)**

Furthermore, bodhisattvas who possess the six kinds of preternatural knowledge purify everything as a buddha field. Those who possess the ten powers, because of their mastery of the different kinds of gnosis, are able to display buddha fields of whatever color beings wish (crystal, gold, and so forth), and similarly of whatever shape, layout, and size the beings to be converted desire. Their obtaining such utterly pure buddha fields is therefore described as purifying the container.

In any world where the name "Buddha" and the words "Dharma" and "Saṅgha" are unknown, they authentically proclaim the name "Buddha" and the names or words "Dharma" and "Saṅgha." By doing so, they cause beings to develop faith and send them to other buddha fields where the Three Jewels are present. This is explained as purifying the beings or contents.[7]

These verses explaining their activities are followed by the fifth section showing how these preternatural powers possess special qualities.

---

7. This is a traditional reference to the universe as the container and the beings within it as the contents.

5. The Qualities of Possessing Preternatural Knowledge

> Like birds whose wings are fully grown,
> They have the ability to bring beings to maturity;
> From the Buddha they receive high praise,
> And people take their words to heart. (VIII, 8)

Bodhisattvas have three qualities by virtue of their preternatural knowledge: they are able to bring sentient beings to maturity, they are highly praised, and their words are worth taking to heart.

Just as birds whose wings are all fully developed can fly through the air, going wherever they wish without any difficulty, bodhisattvas who have acquired the six kinds of preternatural knowledge gain the supreme ability to bring sentient beings to maturity without difficulty by gathering them with the four ways of attracting disciples and establishing them in virtue.

Furthermore, such bodhisattvas, by asking the Buddha relevant questions, will be praised by him, saying, "Fortunate child, yours is an excellent question," and in various other ways.

Since they have preternatural knowledge, they know others' minds and thus act accordingly. And because people delight at their miraculous displays and other bodhisattva qualities, whatever the bodhisattvas tell them is worth taking to heart, so that no one ever disobeys them.

6. Categories of Preternatural Knowledge and Power and How They Are Used to Benefit Beings

> Six kinds of preternatural knowledge, three kinds of
>   knowledge,
> Eight perfect freedoms, and likewise eight kinds of
>   perceptual domination,
> The ten powers of perceptual limitlessness, and boundless
>   concentrations—
> These are the powers of those who have attained stability.
>   (VIII, 9)

The first category of powers comprises the six kinds of preternatural knowledge described above, from the clairvoyance of the miraculous or divine eye to the preternatural knowledge of the exhaustion of taints.

The second category comprises the three kinds of knowledge: that is, skill in knowing the past, present, and future by means of the preternatural knowledge of former lives, of death and rebirth, and of the exhaustion of taints.

The third category comprises the eight perfect freedoms: the three perfect freedoms of "form beholding form," of "nonform beholding form," and of "beholding excellence or beauty"; the four perfect freedoms with regard to the formless states—infinite space and the others; and the perfect freedom of the absorption of cessation.

Similarly, the fourth category comprises the eight kinds of perceptual domination: (1) perceiving oneself to be embodied, having control over smaller physical forms, whether beautiful in color, ugly, or sublime; (2) having control similarly over larger physical forms; (3) perceiving oneself as being disembodied, having control over smaller and (4) larger physical forms; and (5–8) having control over the four colors blue, yellow, white, and red.

The fifth category comprises the ten powers of perceptual limitlessness: those of earth, water, fire, and wind; blue, yellow, white, and red; limitless space; and limitless consciousness.

These perfect freedoms and powers of perceptual domination and limitlessness constitute the path of training thoroughly in manifestation by means of concentration. A bodhisattva begins this with the perfect freedoms, accomplishes it with the different kinds of perceptual dominance, and masters it even more with the powers of perceptual limitlessness, so these are all categories of powers.

Finally, the sixth category comprises the boundless concentrations of the Great Vehicle, such as the concentration of Brave Progression, the Illusion-Like concentration, and the Sky Treasury concentration, which also form part of a bodhisattva's powers.

All the six categories described here constitute the powers that enable bodhisattvas who have attained stability to bring sentient beings to maturity, for they all have the capacity or power to do that.

7. Conclusion Showing the Greatness of the Qualities of the Bodhisattvas' Powers

> The wise who have acquired supreme power
> Give helpless beings their own independence;

Constantly helping others is their sole joy;
Steadfast as lions, they continue their activities within existence. (VIII, 10)

This concluding summary in praise of the greatness of acquiring powers such as the six kinds of preternatural knowledge indicates their greatness in three respects: their great power, great joy, and great fearlessness with regard to existence.

Bodhisattvas who have acquired powers have gained mastery in the ten powers, or pure gnosis, so they are referred to as "the wise who have acquired supreme power."[8] Beings who have fallen under the influence of karma and defilements have not the slightest choice, in this life, but to engage in whatever those influences lead them to do. And in their subsequent lives too, they will never be their own masters, for they will have to go, against their will, wherever their deeds and defilements propel them. Yet, because of their power, bodhisattvas can use miraculous displays and other bodhisattva powers to tame those beings and give them the independence of the bodhisattva condition, establishing them in virtue so that, bit by bit, those beings too are able to become their own masters, like the bodhisattvas. This is the greatness of the bodhisattva's powers in terms of power.

Bodhisattvas never think of their own good, but always delight solely in helping others. This is the greatness of their powers in terms of joy.

Like lions living in wooded hills and caves, who have no fear of any wild animals as they wander through the forest, bodhisattvas who have acquired stability and are their own masters are not afraid of anyone—demons, tīrthikas, or anyone else—even when they stay in the three worlds of existence for the sake of sentient beings. Since they have not the slightest fear of being tainted by defilements and of suffering, they continue to act here in existence with the confidence and fearlessness of their complete stability.

This completes the explanation of the eighth chapter of *Ornament of the Mahāyāna Sūtras*, the chapter on powers.

---

8. "The wise" here translates the Tibetan *blo dang ldan*, lit. "possessing a mind," which Mipham qualifies thus: *blo ni shes rab bo*, "'mind' means 'wisdom.'" For the ten powers, see *Treasury of Precious Qualities*, appendix 5.

9
Full Maturation

Since the special qualities of a bodhisattva—acquiring powers, and so on—are achieved through maturing the mind stream, this is now explained. There are two parts to this chapter: (1) maturing oneself and (2) bringing others to maturity. The first of these is divided into a brief introduction and a detailed explanation.

1. Maturing Oneself
a. Brief Introduction

> Delight, faith, peace, compassion,
> Forbearance, a sharp mind, and power,
> Immunity to beguilement, and possession of the branches—
> These in great measure are the signs of a fully matured child
>   of the buddhas. (IX, 1)

There are nine factors that a bodhisattva has brought to a high degree of maturity: (1) delight in the Mahāyāna teachings; (2) faith in the spiritual master who teaches them; (3) peace in having very few defilements and the power to eliminate them; (4) compassion for sentient beings; (5) forbearance in putting up with difficult practices for one's own and others' sake; (6) a sharp or lucid mind, able to grasp the Mahāyāna teachings correctly by listening and reflecting, on the path of earnest aspiration; (7) possession of power, that is, the capacity to remain unaffected by defilements and to realize emptiness, chiefly through having gathered the accumulations; (8) immunity to being beguiled away from the path by demons, tīrthikas, and the like; and (9) possession of all five of the branches that eliminate defilements—faith, freedom from dishonesty, freedom from pretension, good health, and a powerful abode or support. These nine brought to a high degree of maturity are the defining characteristics of a fully matured child of the buddhas.

b. Detailed Explanation

The above nine factors are now explained in detail, in the same order.

i. Delight

> The three (the sublime companion and the others),
> The utmost diligence, perfect consummation, and holding
>   together the supreme teachings,
> With the purpose of maintaining the sacred Dharma on a
>   vast scale—
> These are held to be the characteristics of perfect maturation
>   in the compassionate. (IX, 2)

Fully matured delight arises from three causal factors: the "sublime companion," indicating the spiritual master, and "the others," referring to listening to the teachings and properly keeping their meaning in mind. (The Tibetan word *dang* in the root text has the function of inclusion: although some such phrase connectors are not specifically mentioned in the commentary, they are to be understood).[1]

The essence or nature of fully matured delight is twofold: to have the utmost diligence in constantly listening to the Mahāyāna teachings, reflecting on them, and meditating on them; and to have perfect mastery of them, that is, to be free from doubts with regard to the profound and inconceivable points in the Great Vehicle, beginning with what the Buddha referred to as the four things that are inconceivable—namely, beings' karma, the power of mantras and medicines, the Tathāgata's gnosis, and the yogi's sphere of activity.

Its effect is that one brings together the best of the teachings, the Great Vehicle, and preserves them from being lost—that is, one prevents the teachings from disappearing by teaching and practicing oneself and by protecting others who are studying and practicing.

---

1. As a rule, commentaries of this kind include every one of the words in the root text. An exception has been made in the case of this verse, where the different items listed are separated in the root text by the Tibetan *dang* (translated as "and" or by the use of commas). Mipham is pointing out that we should understand the word "and" between each of the sentences commenting on these items, even though it does not appear in print. See also Translator's Introduction, page xxiv.

Its purpose, in brief, is to enable one to extensively hold the sacred Dharma of the Great Vehicle.

These are held to be the defining characteristics of a compassionate bodhisattva's perfectly matured delight in the Great Vehicle.

ii. Faith

> **Knowledge of good qualities, unshakable faith,**
> **Speedy attainment of concentration, and the experience of the result,**
> **With the purpose of creating confidence in the Teacher—**
> **These are held to be characteristics of perfect maturation in the buddhas' heirs. (IX, 3)**

The causal factor that makes faith arise is knowing the qualities of our teacher, the Buddha. Its nature is the acquisition of unshakable faith. When one gains irreversible faith in the Teacher, one's mind is undivided, inseparable from the Teacher. This occurs genuinely on attaining the first level, when one will acquire unshakable faith in the Three Jewels through knowing them. The effect of matured faith is that it enables one to rapidly attain Mahāyāna concentrations such as the concentration of Brave Progression and to experience the result of concentration, the different kinds of preternatural knowledge. Its purpose is to create perfect confidence in the Sublime Teacher. These are held to be the defining characteristics of a bodhisattva's faith being perfectly matured.

iii. Peace

> **Full restraint, the elimination of defiling thoughts,**
> **Freedom from obstacles, and delight in virtue,**
> **With the purpose of dispelling defilements in the buddhas' heirs—**
> **These are held to be characteristics of perfect maturation.**
> **(IX, 4)**

The causal factor that results in fully matured peace is to be sustained by mindfulness and vigilance and to thereby completely restrain one's senses from pursuing their objects and avoid throwing oneself into negative activities. Its essence is to abandon thoughts related to defilements. Its effect is that one has no obstacles to training in the antidotes to the defilements and negative actions, and one delights in practicing virtue—that is, the six transcendent perfections. The purpose of perfectly matured peace in children of the buddhas is to dispel their defilements. These are held to be the defining characteristics of their perfectly matured peace.

iv. Compassion

> Being naturally kindhearted, seeing the sufferings of others,
> Completely eschewing inferior attitudes,
> Progressing, and taking birth as the best of beings—
> These are the signs of having fully matured compassion for others. (IX, 5)

Fully matured compassion arises from three causal factors: a predominance of naturally tender feelings for sentient beings on account of one's potential; the object-related condition[2] of seeing other beings suffering; and completely eschewing even the intention of lower vehicles, the desire for the listeners' and solitary realizers' nirvāṇa. The nature or essence of fully matured compassion is that it grows more and more, because the compassion one gains on the levels is greater than that on the paths of accumulation and joining, and one's compassion on the second level is greater than that on the first level, and so on. Its effect is that one obtains a body as the best of beings, that is, one acquires the support of a body whose qualities excel those of sentient beings; and, once the first level is attained, one acquires the major and minor marks. These are the defining characteristics in the buddhas' children of fully matured compassion for others.

v. Forbearance

> Natural steadiness, habituation through analysis,
> The ability to bear cold and other extreme sufferings,

---

2. Tib. *dmigs rkyen*. One of four kinds of conditions or secondary causes, the object-related condition refers to the object of one's meditation or practice. In this case, it is by focusing on other beings' suffering that compassion arises. See also *Treasury of Precious Qualities*, 459n114.

> And progress and delight in virtue—
> These are held to be characteristics of fully matured
> forbearance. (IX, 6)

The factors that produce fully matured forbearance are the natural possession, on account of one's potential, of a steady, patient disposition that willingly accepts suffering without getting discouraged; and habituation, through analysis, to the meaning of the teachings one has received. Such teachings include those that show that when one is harmed by someone else, it happens as a result of one's own deeds; that the other person cannot help doing it; that all phenomena arise from causes and conditions; that there is no self and no perpetrator; that all phenomena are devoid of intrinsic existence and are like illusions, and so on. The essence of fully matured forbearance is the ability to put up with even the greatest sufferings of heat, cold, others' ingratitude, and the like without being adversely affected or turning back. Its effect is to make one's good qualities increase more and more and to make one take delight in applying oneself wholeheartedly and without second thoughts to virtue, that is, to the six transcendent perfections. These, then, are held to be the characteristics of fully matured forbearance.

vi. A Sharp Mind

> Pure maturation, unforgetting recollection of what one has
> heard,
> Superior recognition of what is well explained and what is
> badly spoken,
> And readiness for the birth of great intelligence—
> These are the characteristics of having a fully matured,
> extremely sharp mind. (IX, 7)

The causal factor that brings about a fully matured, sharp or lucid mind is what is known as "pure maturation": because of the ripening of one's virtuous deeds in previous lives—listening to the sacred Dharma, reflecting, and so forth—one has gained a body endowed with wisdom and with all the faculties complete. Its essence is recollection, as a result of which one does not forget the points that one has heard, reflected on, and so forth; and similarly wisdom, as a result of which one has the gnosis that is able to distinguish proper, excellent explanations from ones that are incorrectly taught and badly expressed. Because of these two—recollection and wisdom—the mind is never mistaken and is referred to as a sharp mind. The effect is that once the cause of that sharp mind has been created with mundane recollection and wisdom, it grows in the mind and one is fit for the birth of the great intelligence of the noble levels. These are held to be the characteristics of a fully matured, extremely sharp mind.

vii. Power

> Developing the two elements through the two kinds of virtue,
> And thus becoming perfectly ready for the result to occur,
> Accomplishing everything one wishes, and becoming the greatest of beings—
> These are the characteristics of having fully matured attainment of power. (IX, 8)

What causes fully matured power to develop is mainly practicing the two kinds of virtue, related to the accumulations of merit and wisdom, thereby developing the two elements or seeds of these two kinds of virtue present in the ground of all, as if moistening seeds to make them sprout.

Its nature or essence is that when those two elements are developed, they act as the support through which one becomes supremely fit for directly giving rise to the result of the noble path in the Great Vehicle. Sthiramati, in his commentary, gives this line as "Supreme fitness as the support for giving rise to the result" and says that the support is the support or body in which one attains the noble path. Whichever the case, becoming fit to attain the noble path in that support is the full maturation of power.

Its effect is that when one possesses fully matured power, one has the capacity to accomplish whatever one desires for the benefit of sentient beings and so on, and one will therefore accomplish everything one wishes. And by obtaining the most excellent body and possessions on account of one's accumulated merit, and obtaining the most extraordinary wisdom on account of one's accumulated wisdom, one becomes the greatest of beings.

Possession of these three—cause, essence, and effect—is characteristic of the acquisition of power being fully matured.

viii. Immunity to Beguilement

> An attitude toward the excellent Dharma born of reasoned
>   analysis,
> Constant freedom from obstacles created by demons,
> The acquisition of superiority, and refutation of opponents—
> These are the characteristics of having fully matured
>   immunity to beguilement. (IX, 9)

The causal factor that produces fully matured immunity to beguilement is the use of the four kinds of rational application to investigate the intended meaning of the excellent Dharma of the Great Vehicle ("excellent" because it correctly teaches profound and extensive subjects) and thereby to determine its meaning and acquire an attitude free of doubts. Its essence is that one never has any obstacles created by demons. As a result of confidence in the meaning of the profound teachings, one gains certainty, and demons and tīrthikas are unable to draw one away from that path. Its effect is that by acquiring superior certainty (compared to others') in the points taught in the Great Vehicle and so forth, one is able to establish the correct teaching tradition and to refute others' tenets that appear to be the Dharma but are incorrect. According to Sthiramati's commentary, "the acquisition of superiority" also means that one's reasoned analysis becomes increasingly better. Possession of these three—cause, essence, and function—is characteristic of fully matured immunity to beguilement.

ix. Possession of the Branches

> Having an accumulation of virtue, a suitable support for
>   practicing diligence,
> And delight in perfect seclusion and virtue—
> These are the characteristics of perfectly matured possession
>   of the branches
> For the children of the buddhas. (IX, 10)

When we speak of full maturation in possessing the five branches of elimination, "elimination" refers to the fact that once one has gained direct realization of the expanse of reality on the first level, the duality of subject and object is eliminated. And the five factors (faith and the others mentioned above)³ that assist in this are known as "branches of elimination." How are these five fully matured in terms of their cause, nature, and function?

The causal factor that fully matures the branches of elimination is the accumulation of virtue, that is, of merit and wisdom. This is related to faith.

The nature of the branches of elimination (which, of the five, is related to good health) is "a suitable support for practicing diligence," "support" referring to one's body. In other words, when one is performing positive actions, one is never not up to it physically.

The effect of the branches of elimination is twofold: delight in perfect seclusion (seclusion in the avoidance of all distracting preoccupations, and the bodhisattvas' supreme seclusion from such things as having in mind their own welfare) and delight in the perfect virtue of listening to the Mahāyāna teachings, reflecting on them, and meditating on them. Delight in seclusion is related to freedom from dishonesty and freedom from pretension; delight in virtue is related to wisdom.⁴

These five branches of elimination brought to maturity are the defining characteristics of full and perfect maturation of possession of the branches in a child of the buddhas.

c. Summary

The summary is divided into two sections: (1) maturing oneself and (2) an analogy for maturation.

i. Maturing Oneself

> Since they are themselves mature in terms of these nine elements,
> They are fit to bring others to full maturity.
> Those in whom the stream of qualities is growing
> Are always the supreme friends of beings. (IX, 11)

Through delight and the other eight elements that have just been explained, bodhisattvas become the fully mature embodiment of the Buddha's teach-

---

3. Faith, freedom from dishonesty, freedom from pretension, good health, and a powerful support.

4. Sthiramati's commentary mentions "wisdom" here as the fifth of the five branches, in place of the "support" listed in the commentary on the first verse above.

ings, and they then have the quality of being fit to bring other sentient beings to full maturity. For by maturing themselves, they are able to bring others to maturity. In them the stream of all the qualities of the six transcendent perfections grows greater and greater. Constantly bringing other sentient beings to maturity, they are "the supreme friends of beings." This verse shows that maturing oneself has two virtues: it is the basis for maturing others, and it enables the body of one's own qualities to grow.

ii. An Analogy for Maturation

> We say that boils that drip are "ripe,"
> And food when it is fit to eat.
> So too, it is taught that maturity in such individuals
> Refers to removal and employment with regard to two
>   factors. (IX, 12)

To make an analogy for what we call maturation, in ordinary life, abscesses and food are said to be ripe when they respectively drip pus and are fit to eat. If one lances an abscess that is not ripe with pus, no pus will drip out and one will not have done the condition any good. If it is ripe with pus, the time is right for lancing the abscess, since it is ready to drip pus, and we therefore say the abscess is ripe. When fruits such as grapes are unripe, or food, even though prepared, is not well cooked, they are inedible, while when they are ripe to perfection, they can be enjoyed.

Similarly, for a person with the five aggregates, maturity refers to ability with respect to two factors—being able to remove factors that have to be eliminated and being able to employ remedial factors. Just as boils and so on are sore when they are ripe and full of pus, and are healed by the pus being drained, so it is for someone with this bodily support who is able to eliminate defilements such as attachment and is thereby healed. And just as food that is ripe can be enjoyed, so it is when that person is able to live constantly in virtue and practice it. Such a person is what we call "fully matured."

However much delight one takes in the Mahāyāna teachings, if that delight is not mature, one will not be able to practice them wholeheartedly, following a spiritual master and listening to, reflecting on, and meditating on the teachings. But when delight is fully matured, one is able to hold the sacred teachings. The same is true for the other eight factors, for when they are fully matured, one is able to actually put each one into effect. It has therefore been said that in order for bodhisattvas to complete the qualities of the Mahāyāna path and result in their own mind streams and to bring sentient beings to maturity, which is by increasing faith and the other fully ripened faculties, they have to fully train in these faculties in a timely manner. Accordingly, in order for beings with fewer faculties to become ones with intermediate faculties, and for those with intermediate faculties to become beings with greater faculties, it is very important that they train completely from one faculty to the next. When they develop these faculties, they will realize what they had not previously realized and will obtain what they had not previously obtained. Their excellent qualities will vastly increase all the way up to the level of buddhahood.

2. Bringing Others to Maturity

This section is divided into three parts, which deal with (1) categories; (2) intention; and (3) application.

a. Categories

> Bodhisattvas' maturation of living beings is explained as
> Maturation through riddance, and likewise full maturation,
> Perfect maturation, congruent maturation, excellent
>   maturation,
> Maturation through realization, continuous maturation,
>   and progressive maturation. (IX, 13)

Bodhisattvas are considered to bring beings to maturity in eight different ways: (1) They mature sentient beings in ridding them of defilements such as attachment. Similarly, (2) they bring to full maturity all those who possess the potentials of the three vehicles. (3) They bring them to perfect maturity, for unlike beings who are brought by mundane paths to the maturity of the higher worlds but then fall back again, those who are matured by the three vehicles do not regress. (4) They mature them consistently or fittingly by giving disciples appropriate teachings suited to their mind streams—for example, teaching ugliness to those with attachment. (This maturation is different from the previous ones.)[5] (5) They mature them excellently, that

---

5. Mipham is explaining here the significance of the Tibetan word *gzhan* (lit. "another") in the root text, rendered by a comma in our translation.

is, carefully and concentratedly, impartially and with respect for others. (6) They mature them through their superiority or through their realization—that is, having attained the first level themselves, they establish others on that level. (7) They mature them continuously, by constantly and unerringly teaching beings the path taught by the buddhas. And (8) they mature them progressively, beginning from the level of earnest aspiration all the way up to the tenth level.

b. The Special Qualities of Their Intention

> Unlike the buddhas' heirs, who, with their wish to help,
> Devote themselves to bringing all beings here to maturity,
> Fathers, mothers, friends, and relatives
> Never treat their children and friends so well. (IX, 14)

Bodhisattvas, with their intention to benefit—their wish to set all sentient beings in temporary and ultimate happiness—are engaged in bringing all beings here in saṃsāra to maturity. Unlike them, fathers, mothers, relatives, and friends in ordinary life have no such excellent intentions for their own children and friends. Why is this? Because although parents and so on love their own children and friends, and although they are able to help them a little bit—on a temporary level, in this life—they are incapable of developing the intention or wish to establish them in virtue, the cause of lasting happiness. And in some cases they even introduce them to negative activities.

> Unlike loving bodhisattvas, who act in order to bring
>   happiness and benefit,
> Caring affectionately for other sentient beings,
> Ordinary people feel no kindness for themselves,
> Let alone for others who depend on them. (IX, 15)

When those who are the embodiment of love act in order to benefit other sentient beings, they lovingly desire to make other beings happy, immediately and forever. Unlike them, ordinary people do not even want to be kind to themselves, let alone to other beings who are dearest to them. Of course, ordinary people love themselves, but as a result of the negative actions (killing, stealing, and the like) that they perform out of ignorance in order to be happy in this life, they are punished by the authorities in this life and achieve much suffering in future lives. Similarly, by killing themselves and practicing unwholesome forms of asceticism such as acting like a dog or an ox, they bring suffering upon themselves in this life and the next, and since they do not know the way to lasting happiness, they are unable to undertake it. Bodhisattvas' love for all sentient beings is a love that wishes them every kind of virtue and everlasting happiness.

c. The Special Qualities of Their Application

This part covers the next seven verses, six verses that deal with maturation through the six transcendent perfections and a concluding verse that serves as a summary.

i. Generosity

> There is nothing, including their bodies and possessions,
> That bodhisattvas will not give to others.
> They mature others by bringing them a double benefit,
> And, giving equally, they never tire of the virtues of generosity. (IX, 16)

Bodhisattvas bring sentient beings to maturity with generosity in three ways: giving everything, giving equally, and giving without ever being satisfied.

There is absolutely nothing, not the slightest thing, that bodhisattvas will not give if they see that their own bodies and possessions will benefit others. They give away everything that it is in their power to give. And their generosity brings benefit not only by the gift of those things. That same generosity in this life helps the recipients in this life by completely fulfilling their wishes. And by establishing them in virtuous ways and bringing them to maturity, it benefits them in future lives and sets them in lasting happiness by sowing the seed of liberation. Their generosity thus brings sentient beings to full maturity by benefiting them in two ways—in the short term and the long term.

In being generous, bodhisattvas give equally, with the same attitude to everyone, and without making any distinctions between good and bad, between high and low status, or between those who are close and those who are distant.

And they never consider it sufficient to give a few things, for a few years or kalpas. Even if they give until the very end of saṃsāra, they will never be satisfied with the virtues of generosity.

ii. Discipline

> Establishing others in that which is steadfast, natural,
> Totally nonviolent, delightful, and careful,
> They benefit in two respects and mature others
> Through the continuity of the ripened effects and the
>   qualities similar to the cause. (IX, 17)

"Steadfast" in this verse refers to perpetual discipline—that is, the keeping of one's vows not for a short time but forever, until there are no sentient beings left. The translation of Sthiramati's commentary has "perpetual."[6] Then there is natural discipline, by which bodhisattvas shy away from negative actions and practice positive actions on account of their natural disposition resulting from previous habituation. Total nonviolence toward beings refers to perfect discipline in not committing any of the ten negative actions even in one's dreams. This is gained on the second level. Natural delight refers to the discipline of superior realization: as a result of realizing the truth on the first level, bodhisattvas automatically acquire the discipline that delights the noble beings, and by doing so they naturally reject everything that is nonvirtuous and they delight in virtue. Carefulness refers to faultless discipline, through which not even sullying downfalls or subtle mistakes occur in any of the bodhisattva's conduct.

Having themselves observed this supreme discipline with its five aspects, bodhisattvas introduce other beings to such discipline and doubly benefit them—for this life and future ones, or in the immediate term and forever. And by thus introducing them to discipline, they bring others to maturity, for the fully ripened effect of discipline is that one obtains a continuous series of rebirths with a pleasing body—for example, as a celestial or human

---

6. In other words, Sthiramati's commentary refers to this aspect of discipline as "perpetual" (Tib. *rtag pa*) instead of "steadfast" (Tib. *brtan pa*, as in Kawa Peltsek's translation of the root verse). Sthiramati gives two alternative interpretations for "perpetual": until the bodhisattva reaches the heart of enlightenment (and not just for this life) or for the duration of one's life (and not intermittently).

being; and the qualities similar to the cause are the continued taking of vows in all one's future lives.

iii. Patience

> Thinking of others who harm them as benefactors,
> They are perfectly patient even with those who do them violent harm.
> With their knowledge of methods and their endurance of harm
> They lead those who harm them to truly take up virtue.
> (IX, 18)

When other sentient beings act adversely toward bodhisattvas, in greater or lesser degrees, even up to physical harm and killing them, those bodhisattvas think, "Because of this, I can perfect my patience," and they consider that those beings are helping them as if they were spiritual teachers. Bodhisattvas with this sort of attitude endure even the most violent injuries, such as their flesh and bones being hacked to pieces, so there is no need to mention their putting up with minor wrongs. Not only do they know these methods for cultivating patience, as just explained, and the methods of detailed analysis and so on,[7] but they also know that affording immediate and long-term benefit to others who harm them is the way to bring them to maturity, and because of this they patiently endure the harm inflicted on them. By these means they induce those who harm them to genuinely take up virtue, and they thereby bring them to maturity.

iv. Diligence

> The buddhas' heirs, relying on the utmost diligence,
> Perfectly mature hosts of sentient beings.

---

[7]. The methods of detailed analysis are briefly referred to on page 263 above in the section on forbearance, where mention is made of the teachings that show that when one is harmed by someone else, it happens as a result of one's own deeds, and so on. See also the chapters on patience in Shantideva, *The Way of the Bodhisattva (Bodhicaryāvatāra)*, trans. Padmakara Translation Group (Boston: Shambhala Publications, 2008); its commentary, Kunzang Pelden, *Nectar of Manjushri's Speech*; and Gampopa, *Ornament of Precious Liberation*, trans. Ken Holmes, in *Stages of the Buddha's Teachings: Three Key Texts* (Somerville, MA: Wisdom Publications, 2015).

> If only for the sake of another's single virtuous thought,
> They will not lose heart even after ten billion kalpas. (IX, 19)

Children of the buddhas rely on the utmost diligence, whether armor-like diligence or diligence in application, never stopping or being satisfied in their work for beings' welfare, and it is by means of such diligence that they bring infinite hosts of sentient beings to perfect maturity. Thus, when they see another being whom they can one day bring to maturity and who has the potential to give rise to a virtuous thought for a single instant—a single generous thought, for example—they will apply their efforts for as long as it takes to achieve that, even if it is for ten billion kalpas, without getting the slightest bit discouraged.

v. Concentration

> Having attained unsurpassable mastery of the mind,
> They definitively overcome any desire for veneration from others.
> Causing others to aspire to the sublime teachings,
> They make their virtue perfectly increase. (IX, 20)

Bodhisattvas who have acquired "mastery of the mind" have mastered their minds through concentration. When they gain the six kinds of preternatural knowledge, as explained earlier, and in particular the extraordinary concentrations of the buddhas and bodhisattvas, the concentration of Brave Progression and others, they attain unsurpassable mastery of mind. Having done so, they definitively overcome any desire to be honored, held in high repute, and similarly venerated by others on account of their having those good qualities. Utterly devoid of any such motivation, they inspire others to take an earnest interest in the sublime Buddha's teachings and cause the virtue in their mind streams, the transcendent perfections, to grow perfectly—all this by displaying miracles, by teaching the Dharma in accord with others' mind streams through knowing their thoughts, and by other powers of preternatural knowledge.

vi. Wisdom

> Certain of the intended meaning of thatness,
> They completely clarify beings' doubts.

> Because of that, through their respect for the victors'
> teachings,
> They increase their own and others' virtuous qualities. (IX, 21)

By the power of their wisdom, bodhisattvas determine the profound intended meaning of thatness, without any doubts, and gain perfect certainty—that is, having properly understood all the ultimate, expedient, explicit, and implied teachings, they become masters at discerning thatness. They can thus also clarify and completely dispel the doubts of those beings who are perplexed as to thatness and the meaning of the explicit and implied teachings. Because of their having that kind of wisdom, bodhisattvas themselves respect the buddhas' teachings, and, by introducing other sentient beings to that wisdom, they cause them too to respect the buddhas' teachings and thus bring them to maturity. By doing so, they make the virtuous qualities in their own and others' mind streams flourish.

vii. Summary

> Thus bodhisattvas, through compassion, train all beings,
> Setting them in the higher realms or in the three virtues,
> In modest, supreme, and middling ways,
> For as long as the world exists. (IX, 22)

Thus it is that bodhisattvas, through their compassion, work for the benefit of all beings. They bring beings to temporary maturity by causing them to obtain happy rebirth as celestial beings and humans. Even individuals without potential, when they encounter a bodhisattva, are introduced to the ten positive actions and thereby temporarily brought to maturity in the higher realms.[8] "In the three virtues" refers to bodhisattvas' introducing beings to the virtue related to liberation, that is, lasting happiness in the three kinds of enlightenment: in other words, they set the three kinds of beings[9] on their respective paths.

---

8. Mipham is commenting here on the significance of the Tibetan particle *'am* (meaning "or"), which in other versions of the Tibetan root text appears as *'ang* (meaning "and" or "also").

9. The three kinds of beings (Tib. *rigs can gsum*) are those that have the potentials for the paths of the listeners, solitary realizers, and bodhisattvas.

As to how they set beings in the Great Vehicle in particular, it is by bringing those with a modest accumulation of merit and wisdom to maturity on the path of earnest aspiration, by bringing those with the greatest accumulation to maturity on the three pure levels, and by bringing those with middling accumulation to maturity on the first to seventh levels.

For how long do they bring beings to maturity? For as long as the world exists they will engage in doing so, and thereby train beings. All the space there is, is filled with sentient beings, and space and sentient beings exist until the end of time. That is how long bodhisattvas will train beings by bringing them to maturity—in other words, endlessly.

This completes the explanation of the ninth chapter of *Ornament of the Mahāyāna Sūtras*, the chapter on full maturation.

Although the nine factors of maturation are mainly shown in relation to the level of earnest aspiration, in general, for a bodhisattva the ultimate point of the levels and of the maturation of faculties is the attainment of great enlightenment at the end of the tenth level. For this reason, the chapter on full maturation is followed by an explanation of the result, great enlightenment.

Part Four
The Inconceivable, That Which Is Beyond Reflection

JAMGÖN MIPHAM (1846–1912)

10

Enlightenment

This chapter has three parts: (1) a brief introduction in terms of enlightenment being the ultimate attainment; (2) a detailed explanation of its nature; and (3) in summary, an instruction on arousing bodhicitta with unsurpassable enlightenment in mind.

1. Brief Introduction in Terms of Enlightenment Being the Ultimate Attainment

This brief exposition is indicated by two verses, with a third verse explaining their meaning.

> Through their undergoing countless hundreds of austerities,
> Accumulating countless stores of virtue
> For countless lengths of time,
> And exhausting countless obscurations, (X, 1)

> Omniscience is attained,
> Free of all contaminating obscurations;
> As when a chest of jewels is opened,
> Buddhahood is perfectly revealed. (X, 2)

There are countless "hundreds" (meaning a great many) of difficult practices and efforts that bodhisattvas make on the path with the six transcendent perfections—giving away their bodies and possessions and so forth. The listeners and solitary realizers have no such hardships. As we read in the sūtras, "The eyes that I have given away for the sake of sentient beings, all put together, would be higher than Mount Meru; the blood I've spilled is more copious than the oceans in the four directions. . . ." And there are similar descriptions in the sūtras of the countless austerities they undertake with discipline, patience, and so on. By means of the transcendent perfections, levels, and elements leading to enlightenment, they accumulate countless positive actions. They exert themselves diligently over incalculable lengths of time. And they bring to exhaustion countless obscurations.

Because of this, they attain the state of gnosis that knows all that is to be known, free of all contaminating obscurations. As when a casket full of all kinds of precious things is opened and the various jewels in it become visible, the ultimate fruit, buddhahood, is truly revealed.

The meaning of these two verses is summarized as follows.

> **With awesome austerities undertaken, many hundred trials endured, and every merit gathered,**
> **The longest kalpas traversed, all obscurations of a being brought to an end,**
> **And with the subtlest veils on the levels destroyed, buddhahood is gained,**
> **As if a chest of jewels with magical powers were opened. (X, 3)**

In that bodhisattvas have gone through hundreds of ordeals that no one else would be able to face, in immense numbers of different kinds, their austerities are countless. There is no putting a number to the levels, elements leading to enlightenment, and transcendent perfections, yet they have fully accumulated the whole entirety of wondrous virtuous practices that completely transcend the listeners' and solitary realizers' sources of good, and so their virtue is boundless. As for their having practiced over incalculable periods of time, it is not for a short, intermediate kalpa, nor for one great kalpa or even a hundred or so great kalpas, but for three measureless kalpas—a period of time so long that it cannot be fathomed by ordinary minds. In what way are the obscurations countless? Obscurations are present in the mind streams of all beings, so when the obscurations a being has had in all its lives since time without beginning are classified in terms of defilement-related obscurations, of cognitive obscurations, of the forms they take, and of their objects, the obscurations a bodhisattva has exhausted are limitless and countless.

As to the way in which they are free of all contaminating obscurations, with the different kinds of gnosis of the ten levels they have successively destroyed the corresponding obscurations to be eliminated on each level. And having destroyed even the subtle cognitive obscurations (the habitual tendencies to ignorance) with the vajra-like concentration, they have attained buddhahood—the completion of elimination and the ultimate point of realization. As with the opening of a casket containing all kinds of precious things with the power to grant every need and wish, the ultimate qualities of the fruition—the strengths, fearlessnesses, distinctive qualities, and so forth—have become manifest.

2. Detailed Explanation of the Nature of Great Enlightenment

The detailed explanation is divided into (1) a general exposition in terms of ten qualities and (2) a presentation of the great enlightenment that possesses those qualities under six headings.

a. A General Exposition in Terms of Ten Qualities

The ten qualities are those of (1) inconceivability; (2) the fulfillment of the two goals; (3) enlightenment being the supreme refuge; (4) transformation; (5) all-pervasiveness; (6) the performance of deeds spontaneously and nonconceptually; (7) inestimable profundity; (8) its unchanging essence; (9) its boundless attainments; and (10) bringing sentient beings to maturity. The first two of the ten qualities are indicated separately with one verse each and then dealt with together in a third verse comprising a common explanation.

i. The Quality of Inconceivability

> All phenomena are the enlightened state;
> No phenomena whatsoever exist.
> Although it is the nature of positive qualities,
> It cannot be expressed in such terms. (X, 4)

The enlightened state[1] does not exist dualistically as an apprehending subject or apprehended object, or as existent or nonexistent—it is inconceivable.

---

1. Throughout this chapter we have sometimes chosen to translate the Tibetan term *sangs rgyas* as "enlightened state" rather than as the Sanskrit *Buddha* so as to avoid the limited sense that might result from "Buddha" being understood in its connotation as an individual enlightened being.

For at the time of enlightenment, the dualism of an apprehending subject and apprehended object has been eliminated; and since it does not exist as an imputed, subject-object reality, while existing in terms of the fully present reality, it transcends existence and nonexistence. What we call "Buddha" is suchness free of the two kinds of self and unadulterated by adventitious contaminants. Hence we read in the *Sūtra of the Ornament of the Light of Gnosis*:

> Phenomena, forever nonarisen, are the Tathāgata;
> All phenomena are like the Sugata.

In other words, the Buddha is the body of truth, the state devoid of arising and cessation. And for this reason, the *Diamond Cutter Sūtra* states:

> Those who see me as a physical form,
> Who perceive me as sound,
> Have entered the wrong path.
> Such people are not seeing me.
> View the Buddha as suchness.
> The guides are the body of truth.
> The ultimate reality is not something that can be known,
> So these are not objects of knowledge.

If we consider things from the point of view of the actual nature of suchness, all phenomena, however they appear, are also by nature the enlightened state, for there is no phenomenon whatsoever that is anything other than the expanse of reality, suchness. If there were, it would not be the case that all phenomena are devoid of intrinsic nature and are unproduced. Alternatively, we could also say that there are no phenomena whatsoever that exist in the way they are imputed by immature, ordinary beings.

The enlightened state occurs through the accomplishment of the levels, transcendent perfections, and elements leading to enlightenment. And when enlightenment has been attained, its nature is that of all the untainted positive qualities—the levels, transcendent perfections, elements leading to enlightenment, strengths, fearlessnesses, and so forth. Nevertheless, it is not possible for a subject conceptualizing such things as the transcendent perfections by imputing them as this or that in dualistic terms of a subject and object to say, "The enlightened state is like this." Even though the enlightened state is by nature generosity, for example, no dualistic attributes such as the three concepts of a buddha who gives, a recipient, and a gift are present. The enlightened state is not an object that can be conceived by a dualistic imputing consciousness.

ii. THE QUALITY OF FULFILLMENT OF THE TWO GOALS

> Because it is the cause of the jewel-like Dharma,
> It is like a mine of jewels.
> Because it is the cause of the crop of virtue,
> It is likened to a cloud. (X, 5)

As we have seen, the enlightened state, on account of its nondual nature, is inconceivable. And yet its power is the spontaneous fulfillment of the two goals. How is that? The enlightened state is the causal factor that creates the causes and conditions for the boundless jewels of the Dharma of transmission that is expounded and of the Dharma of realization that comprises the ten strengths, the four fearlessnesses, and all the other qualities. Like a source or mine of all kinds of precious substances, the Buddha has attained the fulfillment of his own goal. And because the enlightened state is the causal factor that ripens the crop of virtue in all beings, the Buddha, who is held to be like a cloud, has the power to fulfill others' goals.

There now follows an explanation of the above two verses:

> The buddha state possesses all phenomena, or alternatively is
>   devoid of all phenomena:
> Because it gives rise to the extensive and vast jewel-like
>   Dharma, it is like a mine of precious things;
> Because it showers on beings the great rain of the well-
>   explained, inexhaustible Dharma,
> Thus causing living creatures' crop of virtue to flourish, it is
>   like a cloud. (X, 6)

The enlightened state possesses all dharmas that are to be known or, there again, is devoid of all phenomena. Since all phenomena are no different from the ultimate reality, suchness, it is endowed with all phenomena—this being considered from the point of view of the multiplicity of phenomena. Alternatively, from the point of view of the nature of phenomena, it is devoid of all phenomena, for suchness has none of the attributes of dualistic subject-object phenomena. Because this enlightened state beyond duality gives rise to the jewel-like Dharma—the extensive Dharma of transmission of the Great Vehicle and the immeasurably vast Dharma of realization comprising the levels, transcendent perfections, strengths, fearlessnesses, and the rest—it is like a source or mine of precious things.

By showering down on all beings the great rain of Dharma (which is well explained in that it is virtuous in the beginning, middle, and end, and inexhaustible in that if its meaning is realized once, it is never exhausted until the end of saṃsāra, or alternatively, in that there is no end to the number of its topics), it causes the seeds of untainted transcendent virtue to grow like a crop, on a vast scale, in hosts of living creatures. For this reason, it is like a cloud.

iii. The Quality of Being the Supreme Refuge

This section is divided into three parts: (1) the accomplishment of one's own goal; (2) the accomplishment of others' goals; and (3) establishing the enlightened state as the incomparable refuge on account of its twofold accomplishment.

(1) The Accomplishment of One's Own Goal

> Constantly, against the whole host of defilements,
> Against all kinds of negative actions,
> And even aging and death,
> The enlightened state gives complete protection. (X, 7)

When one has gone for refuge in the Buddha, that enlightened state gives one complete protection from all kinds of defilements such as ignorance and craving, from all negative activities, tainted actions such as the ten negative actions and the five crimes with immediate retribution, and even from aging and death. This is not for a short period or from time to time, but all the time. In the enlightened state, the three components of the defilement aspect—defilements, karmic actions, and life or rebirth—never occur, so when beings who take refuge in the Buddha attain the resultant refuge, they fulfill their own goals and thus become their own refuge. Mundane beings who, stricken by fear, flee to the mountains, to caves and similar places and seek refuge there, or turn for protection to worldly monarchs, minor mundane gods, Brahmā, Īśvara, and the like, cannot enjoy the same sort of protection.

(2) The Accomplishment of Others' Goals

> Because it protects from every kind of trouble,
> From the lower realms, from wrong paths,
> From the view of the transitory composite, and from lesser vehicles,
> It is the supreme refuge. (X, 8)

In the enlightened state, there are five ways in which other beings too are protected: (1) The Buddha gives protection from every kind of worldly trouble. Through the blessings of the Tathāgata, the blind can see, the deaf can hear, the insane regain their senses, and all kinds of sickness, failed harvests, and other such blights are removed simply by the Buddha visiting a village. And even praying to him removes all kinds of evil. (2) Furthermore, the minute the rays of light emitted by the Tathāgata touch the inhabitants of the hells and other lower realms, all their sufferings are appeased and they are reborn in the higher realms. And even thinking of the Buddha or hearing his name in the hells brings liberation from those realms. (3) With regard to tīrthikas and others who are engaged in improper austerities and disciplines[2] that are not the means for gaining liberation, the Buddha draws them away from those paths and sets them on the path to the higher realms and liberation. (4) Again, he protects those who hold the view of the transitory composite, the view of "I" and "mine," by teaching them the individual no-self and setting them in the listeners' and solitary realizers' nirvāṇa. (5) And by introducing the Great Vehicle to beings of unfixed potential who have begun following the listeners' or solitary realizers' paths, or wish to do so, he gives protection from lesser vehicles. For all these reasons, the Buddha is the supreme refuge of other beings.

---

2. Such ascetic practices as lying on cinders, lying on thorns, and jumping off cliffs (Sthiramati).

(3) Establishing the Enlightened State as the Incomparable Refuge, on Account of Its Twofold Accomplishment

The next three verses each address one of the following three topics: the main presentation, the fact that the enlightened state is the supreme refuge, and the fact that it is the great refuge.

> The enlightened state is the supreme, incomparable refuge.
> For those who are subject to different kinds of danger, to the
>   transitory composite and all other wrong views, to vehicles,
> To the sufferings of the many forms of lower rebirth, and to
>   ways that are not the proper means,
> It gives protection from birth and death, and from all
>   defilements and deeds. (X, 9)

To summarize the points presented above, the enlightened state cannot be compared to other refuges: it is held to be supreme among all refuges, superior to mundane refuges and superior even to the refuge of supramundane beings who go for refuge in the partial nirvāṇa that is the listeners' and solitary realizers' state of peace. What is the reason for this? The enlightened state is a refuge for those who are subject to all the various fearful afflictions here in saṃsāra, to the different wrong views such as the view of the transitory composite, to involvement in the lesser vehicles, to the sufferings of the many forms of rebirth in the lower realms, and to involvement in ways that give no means of liberation. It protects them forever from birth and death and from all the defilements and karmic actions that are their causes. In some editions of the root text, "lower realms" appears instead of "deeds." This should be understood as referring to the defiling deeds that lead to rebirth in the lower realms—deeds such as the crimes with immediate retribution and the ten negative actions.

> It comprises the buddha bodies in which the enlightened
>   qualities are fully complete,
> The knowledge for training beings through the sacred Dharma,
> And transcendent compassion for all beings—
> That enlightened state is held to be the supreme refuge here. (X, 10)

The reason it is the supreme refuge is that it is the consummation of one's own goal and others' goals. When enlightenment is attained, the three buddha bodies, in which the strengths and all the other qualities of fruition are fully complete, represent the ultimate fulfillment of one's own goal. As for others' goals, their ultimate fulfillment is achieved both through wisdom and through great compassion. Wisdom refers to the unobstructed knowledge and ability to introduce beings to the sacred Dharma—the sūtras and the other eleven branches of the teachings—and by that means to thoroughly train them, liberating their mind streams by teaching them in accordance with their dispositions, faculties, and aspirations. Great compassion is transcendent, unremitting love and compassion for all beings. It is because it possesses the qualities of the consummation of the two goals that the enlightened state is held to be the supreme refuge here in existence.

> **Because, to the very end of the universe,**
> **It wards off sentient beings' every difficulty**
> **And brings them all that is perfect,**
> **The enlightened state is held to be the great refuge. (X, 11)**

It is the great refuge because, for as far as the universe extends, for as long as the universe endures, it has the power to drive away and cure forever every one of the problems that afflict all beings and to make them acquire all that is perfect, both mundane and supramundane. This is why the enlightened state is asserted to be the great refuge.

iv. The Quality of Transformation

This section is divided into (1) an explanation of transformation itself and (2) an explanation of its superiority.

(1) An Explanation of Transformation Itself

> **The complete destruction of the seeds of defilement-related**
> **and cognitive obscurations, constantly present for great**
> **lengths of time,**
> **Eliminated through all kinds of extensive means,**
> **And the attainment of the transformed state possessed of**
> **the sublime qualities of virtue**
> **Is buddhahood, attained by the path of the gnosis of utterly**
> **pure nonconceptuality and immense scope. (X, 12)**

The habitual tendencies or seeds of the defilement-related and cognitive obscurations have been continuously and inseparably present in one's stream of consciousness for a great length of time—since the beginning of saṃsāra, to which there is no beginning. With regard to eliminating these, from the first level up to the tenth level, they are completely destroyed or eliminated by the supreme supramundane gnosis. This gnosis is the result of an immense accumulation of merit and wisdom and is as utterly vast as space in its absence of concepts. And it is through having all kinds of aspects—or, alternatively, by means of all its different kinds—that it destroys those seeds, for on each level there are nine kinds of gnosis (greater-great, and so forth).[3] The object (namely, the five aggregates) is transformed into the utterly pure expanse of reality and the subject (consciousness) into nonconceptual gnosis. Alternatively, the empty nature of all phenomena is transformed into the utterly pure expanse of reality, suchness; and the eight consciousnesses into the four kinds of gnosis. These five processes constitute what we call "transformation."

In short, although all impure appearances—the outer world that appears as the place, the eight consciousnesses that appear as the subject, and what appears as the body—naturally exist as thatness from the very beginning, we fail to see their intrinsic nature as it is, for it has been veiled by the two obscurations. This failure is eliminated with the path, the "transformation" of the boundless, infinite appearances, distinguished by their perfect purity. Although, from the point of view of the nature of phenomena, they are free of subject-object duality and have never moved from the state of evenness, while from the point of view of the multiplicity of phenomena, all things that can be known appear distinctly like the appearances in a magical illusion, they are the same, devoid of one-sided attributes.

One who has attained this transformation, which is endowed with the sublime, untainted virtuous qualities such as the strengths and fearlessnesses ("sublime" because they are qualities the listeners and solitary realizers do not have), is known as a buddha, whose very nature is attained by the path, training in two kinds of gnosis. These are the realization, by means of the utterly pure[4] nonconceptuality in the bodhisattvas' meditative equipoise,

---

3. Nine kinds of gnosis: great, middling, and little, each divided into greater, middling, and lesser.

4. Tib. *rab tu dag pa* (as in Kawa Peltsek's translation of the root verse) or *shin tu dag pa* (as in the translation of Sthiramati's commentary).

that all phenomena are devoid of reference, like the "surface" of the sky; and the so-called "gnosis of immense scope"[5] or pure mundane gnosis in the postmeditational phase, which sees that although the infinite knowable phenomena appear, they are like magical illusions and so forth. At the time of enlightenment, there is no difference between meditation and postmeditation, and by means of the great spontaneous or inconceivable gnosis, all phenomena are beheld simultaneously as they are and in their multiplicity.

(2) An Explanation of Its Superiority

This explanation has two parts: (1) how the Buddha's transformation is superior to the listeners' and solitary realizers' transformation and (2) ten divisions of the qualities of the Buddha's transformation.

(a) How the Buddha's Transformation Is Superior to the Listeners' and Solitary Realizers' Transformation

> **Dwelling in that state, the Tathāgata,**
> **As if seated on the lofty king of mountains, watches over beings.**
> **If he has compassion even for those who delight in peace,**
> **Need one mention his compassion for other beings who delight in existence? (X, 13)**

Abiding in that untainted expanse that is the state of transformation, the Buddha, the One Who Has Gone to Suchness[6] (for he has arrived at or realized that "such" is the nature of the expanse of reality), is like someone who looks in the ten directions from the top of Mount Meru, the highest of all mountains, and can see all forms, near and far, good and bad. For in the same way, the Tathāgata, seated atop the lofty peak that is the Buddha's state of complete transformation, far above the listeners' and solitary realizers' transformation, watches over all beings with his great compassion. His great compassion extends even to the listeners and solitary realizers, those who delight in the peace of nirvāṇa for their own sake. In not working

---

5. Tib. *shin tu yul chen po'i ye shes*, lit. "the gnosis of the extremely great object."
6. Tib. *de bzhin gshegs pa*, Skt. *tathāgata*.

for the welfare of sentient beings, with whom they have been related since time without beginning in saṃsāra, the listeners and solitary realizers lack great compassion, and since they do not have the great wisdom that has realized the no-self of phenomena, they are unable to get rid of cognitive obscurations and have therefore not acquired omniscient gnosis. This is why the Buddha has compassion even for them. This being so, one need hardly mention his love and compassion for other beings in saṃsāra who delight in existence, the abode of suffering, for they are not free from the three kinds of suffering.

(b) Ten Divisions of the Qualities of the Buddha's Transformation

> In that state, there is engagement, perfect engagement, nonengagement,
> Disengagement, perpetual engagement, dual and nondual engagement,
> Similarity, superiority, and universality.
> This is held to be the fully transformed state of the tathāgatas. (X, 14)

"In that state," meaning in the Buddha's state of complete transformation, there are the following extraordinary qualities: (1) Engagement in others' welfare, in always acting exclusively for the benefit of sentient beings. (2) Perfect engagement, in that the Buddha's transformation is the greatest of all qualities, greater than the transformation of worldly beings and supramundane beings—that is, listeners and solitary realizers. (3) Nonengagement, in that the Buddha's transformation never engages in the three causal factors that, in ordinary beings, give rise to defilements: the presence of the related object,[7] thinking of it incorrectly, and not having eliminated latent defilements. (4) Disengagement, in that once that transformation is attained, it is impossible to ever engage in defilements and nonvirtuous activities. (5) Perpetual engagement, for that transformation is attained once and for all and is applied all the time, unceasingly, it being impossible for it to diminish until the end of saṃsāra. Alternatively, total engagement, in that all the

---

7. The object that will give rise to a specific defilement: for example, an enemy, who will give rise to hatred.

antidotes to the defilement process are applied.[8] (6) Dual engagement, in that the Buddha first displays enlightenment and finally displays the parinirvāṇa. Having attained buddhahood, in all the world systems in the ten directions, at all times, by means of supreme nirmāṇakāya manifestations, the Buddha displays great enlightenment in order to train beings. (7) Nondual engagement, in that on the ultimate level the Buddha does not engage in the two—that is, since he has realized that saṃsāra and nirvāṇa are the same, he remains in neither. (8) Similarity, in that simply from the point of view of complete liberation, of having eliminated the defilements together with their seeds, the Buddha is like or similar to the listeners and solitary realizers. (9) Superiority, in that specifically the Buddha's transformation is superior to that of the listeners and solitary realizers on account of the elimination of cognitive obscurations and of his qualities such as the strengths and fearlessnesses. (10) Universality, in that it applies to all vehicles, for the Buddha teaches sentient beings the Dharma of the three vehicles in accordance with their individual potentials, faculties, and aspirations.

That which is described in terms of these ten categories is held to be the tathāgatas' state of complete transformation. For this reason, it should be understood that the Buddha's state of transformation is endowed with the highest qualities and is applied on a vast scale, for it acts as every kind of remedy.

v. The Quality of All-Pervasiveness

This section is divided into (1) the main explanation and (2) clarification of a doubt.

(1) The Main Explanation of How the Enlightened State Pervades All Entities of Time and Space

> Just as space is accepted as being forever omnipresent,
> So too is enlightenment considered always omnipresent.
> Just as space is present in every kind of form,
> So too is enlightenment omnipresent in the host of sentient beings. (X, 15)

---

8. These are two alternative interpretations of the Tibetan term *kun 'jug*.

Just as space is considered to be omnipresent in all things (vases and the rest), all the time, throughout past, present, and future, in the same way the untainted expanse of reality that is the transformed, enlightened state is also held to be omnipresent all the time in all entities, past, present, and future. Since none of the phenomena included in the three times are outside the scope of suchness, and since that expanse is perfectly pure in nature, there is no difference, in terms of their essential nature, between how they are at the time of buddhahood and how they were before.

Just as space is omnipresent in and pervades everything that is form without distinction, whether long or short, white or red, good or bad, or in between, in the same way, the expanse of the enlightened state too pervades the mind streams of the whole host of sentient beings, whether good, bad, or neither, and is naturally present as their true nature. The enlightened state is by nature the expanse of reality, totally purified of adventitious contaminants. When, on the first level, one realizes the nature of the omnipresent expanse of reality, one acquires the state of mind that realizes the sameness of oneself and all beings. Whatever one is, beings are too. Whatever beings are, one is oneself as well. When bodhisattvas who have realized that there is no difference between themselves and all beings and that all are equal complete their gradual training on the ten levels and attain the buddha level, they completely realize that all sentient beings are naturally perfectly enlightened. It is in this sense that the transformed state is omnipresent in the host of sentient beings.

(2) Clarification of a Doubt

> **Just as in a broken pail**
> **The moon's reflection will not appear,**
> **To evil beings, likewise,**
> **The Buddha's form will not appear. (X, 16)**

> **Just as a fire will either blaze**
> **Or else die down,**
> **Likewise, know that the buddhas too**
> **Appear or disappear. (X, 17)**

If the nature of the enlightened state is thus present in all sentient beings and there is no difference between them, why is it that all beings do not always see the nature of the enlightened state that is the true nature of their own minds, and why do they not see the Buddha's form body either? The fact that they cannot see it shows that beings' minds are veiled by obscurations and they are not therefore suitable vessels for perceiving the Buddha. To illustrate this with an analogy, although the orb of the moon is there in the sky, its reflection will not appear in a vessel that is broken and has no water in it. Similarly, evil beings, who have failed to gather the accumulations of merit and wisdom in their mind streams and are obscured by their defilements and the negative deeds they have committed, are like broken vessels containing no water. They lack the clear water of faith and concentration, and therefore they cannot perceive either the nature of the enlightened state or the Buddha's form. The term "rūpa"[9] in this verse is used to mean both "nature" and "form."

So the fact that the Buddha's form body is visible to some and invisible to others is not because it does not pervade everything. It appears wherever there are trainable beings who have accumulated sufficient merit and wisdom to see the Buddha, and it does not appear to those who have not. Just as a fire either flares up in the presence of fuel or dies down and stops burning when there is none, you should understand that so it is for the buddhas' form bodies. At times when there are beings to be trained, they appear—that is, they attain enlightenment and remain alive. And in those places and times in which there are no suitable beings to be trained, they pass into nirvāṇa and are no longer visible.

vi. The Quality of Performing Deeds Spontaneously and Nonconceptually

The way in which the buddhas perform their deeds spontaneously and nonconceptually is shown in the next four verses, indicating the four ways in which they appear: teaching the Dharma, demonstrating a whole variety of deeds, acting unceasingly, and being more or less active. When the listeners, after exerting themselves for their own benefit, attain nirvāṇa, their activities cease. The buddhas' activities, for others' benefit, are quite different in that they are accomplished spontaneously, without any notion of effort, and are unceasing.

---

9. *Rūpa*, the Sanskrit word for "form."

> Just as drums may sound
> Without their being struck,
> The teachings appear
> Without the buddhas deliberately teaching. (X, 18)

When Indra is going to enjoy the pleasures of the five senses, without anyone beating it, the great drum created through the gods' merit makes a sound signaling his delight in the five pleasures. When he is going to stop enjoying them, it signals that he is turning away from the five sense pleasures. When he is victorious over the demigods, the sound of the gods' victory occurs. And when he is carefree, there emerges the sound of the teachings on impermanence and so forth.[10] So it is with the victorious ones, perfect buddhas, who dwell in the untainted expanse of reality and have no ordinary thoughts: without their making any effort or deliberately thinking, "I will give such and such a person this or that teaching," there arises a whole variety of teachings in accord with each being's individual aspirations.

> Just as the Precious Gem effortlessly
> Shines with its own light,
> So too, the buddhas, without thinking,
> Assuredly demonstrate their deeds. (X, 19)

Just as the Precious Gem[11] shines effortlessly, emitting its own light in all directions, when the buddhas act for the sake of sentient beings, without intending or thinking, "I will do this or that," they spontaneously, like that gem, surely display a variety of physical, verbal, and mental activities for the sake of beings to be trained.

> Just as in space the activities
> Of the universe appear unceasingly,
> So too, in the untainted expanse of reality
> The victors' deeds continue without end. (X, 20)

---

10. I.e., the four seals or summaries of the Buddha's teaching: all compounded things are impermanent, all that is tainted is suffering, all phenomena are without self, and nirvāṇa is peace (Sthiramati).

11. Tib. *nor bu rin po che*, Skt. *maṇi-ratnam*, one of the seven attributes of royalty possessed by a universal emperor.

Just as in space the formation, duration, and destruction of the universe, and the activities of beings (moving around, sitting, and so on) appear in unceasing continuity, similarly, even though the buddhas remain in the perfectly pure abode of the untainted expanse of reality, without their moving from that state, the activities of the victorious ones continue unceasingly in the ten directions and until the end of time.

> **Just as all the time in space**
> **Things perish and things come into being,**
> **So too, in the untainted expanse of reality,**
> **The buddhas' activities grow and decrease. (X, 21)**

Unceasing though they are, the buddhas' activities appear to grow and diminish, to be undertaken and not undertaken, depending on the beings to be trained. Here in space, all the time there are some things, external or internal, that have come into being and remain and then decline. Things that were there before are destroyed—forests, houses, and so forth burn down. Beings die. And there are other things, external and internal, that come newly into being. In the same way, in the untainted expanse of reality, depending on the beings to be trained, the buddhas' activities of manifesting their form bodies in this world and so on appear to be newly produced, and those previously present appear to diminish.

vii. The Quality of the Inestimable Profundity of the Expanse That Is the Enlightened State

The following sixteen verses cover three points: (1) profound characteristics; (2) profound abiding; and (3) profound activities.

(1) Profound Characteristics

The four characteristics described in this section, those of (1) perfect purity; (2) the enlightened state being the sublime "self"; (3) inexpressibility; and (4) perfect liberation are indicated by one verse each.

(a) The Characteristic of Perfect Purity

> **Though no different before or after,**
> **Suchness free of all contaminating obscurations**

> Is held to be the enlightened state.
> Neither is it pure nor is it impure. (X, 22)

Suchness, the perfectly pure nature, is no different from one moment to the next—from the condition of an ordinary individual up to enlightenment. The essential nature of emptiness, which is naturally clear and radiant, never changes. We nevertheless hold that suchness completely uncontaminated by adventitious obscurations is what we call the enlightened state, while when it is contaminated by adventitious obscurations we do not call it the expanse of the enlightened state. It is naturally pure, pure from the very beginning: it is not that it has become pure, nor that it is impure on account of subsequent adventitious contamination. Such is the profundity of the characteristic of perfect purity. People of meager intelligence find this difficult to understand, for they think that if it is pure and uncontaminated from the very beginning, why are sentient beings not enlightened? And that if beings are only enlightened at a time in the future when the contaminants are purified, then it cannot be naturally pure from the very beginning.

(b) The Characteristic of the Enlightened State Being the Sublime "Self"

> When emptiness is completely purified,
> The sublime nature of no-self is attained;
> Thus the buddhas obtain the pure nature
> And they will therefore become the self of the Great Being.
>   (X, 23)

When this naturally radiant state of emptiness is completely purified of the adventitious contaminants that are its own appearances, one attains the sublime nature or intrinsic nature or essence that is the actual condition or nature of things, devoid of both the individual self and the phenomenal self. Thus the buddhas have obtained the utterly pure nature, and for this reason they are said to become the "self" of the Great Being, the suchness that is the unmistaken condition of things. This is not the self that is the conceived object of the belief in the two kinds of self, for there is no such self in reality. Suchness devoid of the two kinds of self, free from the extremes of existence and nonexistence, is the unmistaken actual condition of things, and so when it is actualized, it is the highest self, what we call the "self of the Great Being."[12]

(c) The Characteristic of Inexpressibility

> It is not that the Buddha, therefore, exists,
> Nor can it be said that he does not exist.
> When questioned in such terms, it's said,
> The Buddha did not answer. (X, 24)

It is not that the Buddha therefore exists as an individual or a phenomenon. Nor can one say that he does not exist as suchness beyond conceptual elaboration. People with dualistic minds maintain the conventional idea that the Buddha is a transient human being and wonder whether or not the Buddha will come again once he has passed into nirvāṇa, and whether or not he exists after passing away. It is said that when he was asked such questions, posed in terms of these two conceptual extremes,[13] the Buddha did not answer, for the Buddha is beyond the extremes of existence and nonexistence and we cannot say that he comes or does not come. Were one to ask whether the manifestation body will appear again in the world or not, it will come again and again, wherever and whenever there are beings to be trained, and it exists as long as there are beings—but not in the same way as sentient beings, who die and then reappear. Those who wonder whether or not a sentient being will appear after it dies ask, "Will the Buddha come again or not?" thinking that he is like ordinary beings who die and are reborn. But for the Buddha there is no real birth or coming, for he is the nature of suchness.

(d) The Characteristic of Perfect Liberation

> Just as it is for the fading of heat in an iron
> Or the disappearance of floaters in the eye,

---

12. Great Nature, or Great Being, (Tib. *bdag nyid chen po*) is also used as a general epithet for a buddha.
13. The conceptual extremes of coming and not coming, of existing and not existing. The tīrthikas who asked these questions could not see any other alternative to these two possibilities.

> One cannot talk about existence or nonexistence
> In relation to the Buddha's mind and gnosis. (X, 25)

Perfect liberation, being by nature suchness, is similarly profound, and likened to the cooling of an iron heated in the fire and to the removal of floaters in the eye. One cannot say that reduction of heat exists in a cool iron, because now, when the iron is cool, the heat has already ceased and is no longer present, so how can we say that its reduction exists? It is like the child of a barren woman. Nor can one talk about there being no reduction of heat in the iron, because if at that time the heat were not reduced, the iron would still be hot. The same argument can be applied to the question of whether or not the disappearance of floaters exists in the eye.

As in these examples, one cannot say whether the extinction of the fire of desire (analogous to the heat) in the Buddha's perfectly liberated mind (analogous to the iron) exists or does not exist, nor whether the disappearance of the floaters of ignorance exists or does not exist in the eye of the Buddha's gnosis, the wisdom of perfect liberation. When the mind is liberated and wisdom is liberated, the heat of attachment and the floaters of ignorance have already ceased to be and do not now exist, so one cannot talk about their extinction or disappearance existing. Nor can one talk about them not existing either, because the liberated mind and the liberated wisdom are present after the former states. When we think of this in terms of the continuity of the mind with its phases of impurity and purity, we speak of elimination and perfect liberation. But considered in terms of the nature of suchness, being free from the very beginning, when it is realized on the level of buddhahood, there is no new liberation.

Freedom from the defilements that are eliminated through the paths of seeing and meditation is what we call the perfect liberation of the mind. And the correct recognition of perfect liberation as perfect liberation is what we call the perfect liberation of wisdom. This is explained in the commentary. We can also speak of the perfect liberation of wisdom in terms of the cognitive obscurations having been eliminated. In fact, it is the gnosis that is perfectly freed of the two obscurations.

(2) Profound Abiding

> Because the buddhas in the untainted expanse of reality
> Are incorporeal, like the sky,

> And because they follow on from their previous physical forms,
> They are neither single nor multiple. (X, 26)

Since the buddhas who dwell in the untainted expanse of reality are the same in being the body of truth, suchness, like the sky, and therefore do not have individual, separate bodies, nor do they have a sense of self, there is not a multitude of different buddhas. But neither is there a single Buddha, because in the past, when they were practicing the bodhisattva activities from the level of earnest aspiration up until the tenth level, they had individual bodies, and we conventionally call their resultant attainment "buddhas" by virtue of the fact that they follow on from their having been multiple, distinct bodhisattvas. This manner in which the Buddha—who is single *and* multiple—abides in the untainted expanse of reality is therefore very profound, for it is difficult to understand.

(3) Profound Activities

There are ten categories of profound activities. This section ends with a verse summarizing the three aspects of profundity.

(a) Activities Related to Enlightenment, Like a Mine of Gems

> With regard to the strengths and other buddha qualities,
> Enlightenment is like a mine of precious gems. (X, 27ab)

In performing the activities that are the source of the Buddha's qualities—the ten strengths, four fearlessnesses, and so forth—great enlightenment is like a source of all sorts of precious substances.[14]

(b) The Activity of Bringing Sentient Beings to Full Maturity

> For the crop of beings' virtue
> It is held to be like a great cloud. (X, 27cd)

---

14. Activities such as teaching the Dharma are the source of the Buddha's qualities being obtained by others.

In making the virtuous crop of the six transcendent perfections ripen in beings' mind streams, great enlightenment is like a great cloud sending down rain.

(c) The Activity Leading to Ultimate Perfection

> Because merit and wisdom are perfectly complete,
> It is likened to a full moon. (X, 28ab)

On the level of buddhahood, the accumulation of merit and wisdom has been brought to ultimate completion, so it is likened to the full moon. This refers to the activity of leading to ultimate perfection, which is as complete as the fullness of the moon at full moon, without the slightest incompleteness.[15]

(d) The Activity of Teaching the Dharma

> Because of its illuminating gnosis,
> It is likened to a great sun. (X, 28cd)

Since the rays of light of the Buddha's omniscient gnosis, teaching the Dharma, illumine the minds of sentient beings in the ten directions and cause them to see the truth, the enlightened state is likened to a "great sun." There is, of course, only one sun in a world system of four continents, and so it cannot be termed great or small, but because the sun of enlightenment lights up infinite world systems in the ten directions, it is exemplified by the novel idea of a "great sun."

(e) Activities Such as Manifestation

> Just as the infinite rays of light
> Issuing from the sun's orb are intermingled
> And always perform the same functions,
> Lighting up the whole world, (X, 29)
>
> Likewise, the infinite buddhas
> In the untainted expanse are considered to merge together,

---

15. This activity is that of bringing beings to ultimate perfection.

> Performing their deeds in unison
> And making the light of gnosis shine. (X, 30)

The infinite rays issuing from the sun's orb are not separate and distinct but mingled together, always performing the same functions—causing the crops to ripen, drying up mud, and so on—without each having a different task. Its light illumines the whole world. In the same way, the infinite buddhas (so styled by virtue of their following on from their former bodies) dwelling in the perfectly pure, untainted expanse of reality are considered to be merged indistinguishably into a single taste as the nature of the body of truth, suchness. They act in unison to benefit beings to be trained, making the light of gnosis shine on all sentient beings in the ten directions. When a single buddha performs the activities of manifesting, bringing sentient beings to maturity, and so forth, because there are no distinctions in the body of truth, in fact all the infinite buddhas are performing that very activity, for they are mingled together. The doers, their deeds, and their gnosis are all but one, and indistinguishable. This verse shows that all the Buddha's deeds—manifesting, teaching the Dharma, bringing beings to maturity, performing miracles, and the rest—are the activity of all the buddhas combined.

(f) ACTIVITIES OF THE MANIFESTATION OF GNOSIS

> When the sun gives forth a single ray of light,
> All the rays of light come forth.
> From this analogy, know that, likewise,
> The gnosis of all the buddhas manifests. (X, 31)

When a single ray of sunlight shines forth, all the light rays shining in other directions shine forth simultaneously. By analogy, when a single one of all the buddhas gives rise to gnosis in, for example, answering beings' questions, it should be understood that all the different instances of gnosis of infinite other buddhas are applied simultaneously and arise as one with that same gnosis.

(g) NONCONCEPTUALITY IN THE BUDDHAS' ACTIVITIES

> Just as the sun's rays
> Have no sense of "mine" in where they go,

> The gnosis of the buddhas too
> Has no sense of "mine" when it is applied. (X, 32)

Wherever they penetrate, the sun's rays have no sense of "mine"—they do not think, "I will penetrate here" or "I must illumine this." In the same way, when the buddhas' gnosis is applied to beings' benefit and happiness, there is no notion of "I" and "mine." It is applied spontaneously, without concepts.

(h) The Activity of Instantly Knowing Multifarious Aspects

> Like a single ray of sunlight
> Making everything visible to beings,
> The buddhas' gnosis at once throws light
> On everything that can be known. (X, 33)

Just as a single ray of sunlight, wherever it falls, makes everything in that place instantly visible to beings, similarly the buddhas' gnosis instantly illumines everything there is to be known in the three times and the ten directions. It knows everything at the same time. This is not limited knowledge that knows some things earlier and some things later, or when it knows certain things does not know others. It knows everything there is to be known in a single instant, just as in a clear mirror all the forms reflected there appear together and not at different times.

(i) The Activity of Gnosis Being Inaccessible

> Just as the light of the sun's rays
> Is considered to be obscured by clouds,
> The gnosis of the buddhas
> Is obscured by sentient beings' faults. (X, 34)

Although the sun's rays shine everywhere, it is generally accepted that when they are obscured by such things as clouds and the walls of houses and caves, there is no light. In the same manner, the rays of the light of gnosis that the buddhas send everywhere are obscured by beings' faults and do not illuminate them. Because of these faults, which make them unsuitable vessels for seeing the buddhas' nirmāṇakāya manifestations, for hearing the teachings, and so on, the buddhas' gnosis does not penetrate them.

(j) Differences in the Activity of Gnosis Despite Equality in Terms of Perfect Liberation

> Just as knots tied in a piece of cloth
> Produce a patchwork when it is dyed,
> On account of the force that propels it,
> The gnosis of liberation manifests more or less brightly.
> (X, 35)

Even the listeners and solitary realizers have realized the untainted expanse that is perfect liberation from the suffering of saṃsāra. However, the gnosis within the expanse of perfect liberation may manifest more or less brightly depending on the propelling force of former aspirations and the accumulation of merit and wisdom made on the path of learning, like a knotted white cloth that has been dyed. As long as the cloth remains knotted, it looks as if it has taken the dye, but once the knots are undone they reveal a white design, so that the same cloth is a patchwork of brightly colored and colorless sections. The listeners and solitary realizers are perfectly liberated in having brought to exhaustion the defilements that are the root of suffering in saṃsāra. The buddhas too are perfectly liberated from saṃsāra in having brought to exhaustion the obscurations deriving from the defilements together with their habitual tendencies. But because they have eliminated the cognitive obscurations, made aspirations in the past, and obtained the great gnosis through completing the two accumulations, the activity of their gnosis in ripening beings' enlightened element[16] manifests unceasingly, in their sending forth emanations and so on. This is something the listeners and solitary realizers do not have.

(k) Concluding Summary of These Three Aspects of Profundity

> To describe these profound points—
> The characteristics, way of abiding, and activities
> Of the buddhas in the uncontaminated expanse of reality—
> Would be to paint a picture in the sky. (X, 36)

The four profound characteristics of the buddhas who dwell as one taste in

---

16. Tib. *khams*, i.e., the buddha nature (Skt. *tathāgatagarbha*) present in every being.

the uncontaminated expanse of reality, their profound abiding, and their ten profound activities have been explained thus by the Buddha, but they are as difficult to describe as painting a picture in the sky. Using concepts to illustrate the sky-like expanse of reality free of conceptual elaboration, saying, "It is like this," is like painting a picture in the sky—the paint will not stick. Nevertheless, those who have confidence in the inconceivable can paint a picture in the sky.[17] This, we should understand, is how utterly extraordinary these three aspects of profundity are.

All the above is an explanation of the enlightened state's quality of profundity.

viii. The Quality of Its Unchanging Essence—The Changeless Expanse of Reality, Suchness

> **Suchness is present in all, and not different,**
> **Yet purified it is the Tathāgata.**
> **Thus it is that all beings**
> **Are imbued with its essence. (X, 37)**

This expanse of reality, suchness, the true nature of all phenomena, is present in the minds of all sentient beings from the beginning, and no different in any of them. Yet that suchness, purified of adventitious contaminants, is nothing other than the Tathāgata. Thus all sentient beings too are imbued with the essence of that radiant nature, suchness. This essence of the sugatas, the untainted expanse, is free of all change, of increase and decrease, throughout past, present, and future. For these reasons it is also established that the ultimate, perfectly pure body of gnosis of the tathāgatas is permanent, stable, peaceful, and unchanging.

ix. The Quality of Its Boundless Attainments

This section is divided into (1) the superiority of the Buddha's attainments and (2) an enumeration of different categories of those attainments.

---

17. In similar vein, it is said that such was the Indian master Candrakīrti's realization that he could draw milk from the painting of a cow.

(1) The Superiority of the Buddha's Attainments

> The attainments of the listeners
> Outshine those of the worldly.
> Those on the level of the solitary realizers
> Outshine those of the listeners. (X, 38)
>
> These cannot approach even a fraction
> Of the attainments of the bodhisattvas.
> And those do not compare with even a fraction
> Of the attainments of the tathāgatas. (X, 39)
>
> For whom they are applied, and where,
> And how, to what extent, and for what length of time—
> On such grounds are the attainments of the buddhas
> Held to be inconceivable and immeasurable. (X, 40)

The listeners' attainments of the accumulation of merit and wisdom and preternatural knowledge outshine such attainments as mundane beings' two accumulations and rishis' preternatural knowledge. In comparison, the attainments of those on the solitary realizers' level outshine even the listeners' attainments, being superior and vaster. The wealth of qualities the solitary realizers have cannot compare with even a fraction, even a hundredth or a thousandth, of the bodhisattvas' accumulation of merit and wisdom, preternatural knowledge, and other attainments; they do not approach them in terms of analogies, numbers, or cause. The bodhisattvas' attainments cannot compare with even a fraction of the tathāgatas' transcendent attainments—their completion of the two accumulations and their infinite qualities such as preternatural knowledge, strength, and fearlessness. While it is true that the bodhisattvas' qualities are utterly boundless, they are quite different in magnitude compared to the buddhas' wealth of good qualities, like a single tiny particle of dust compared to infinite world systems.

The reason for this is that the beings for whose welfare the perfect buddhas' attainments are applied are boundless, for they are not applied to benefiting a certain number of beings—one being, or a hundred—but to benefiting all the boundless beings there are. Where they are applied is boundless, for they are applied in the infinite universes filling space. How they are applied is infinite, on account of the boundless bodies of manifestation (those who manifest in art, those who manifest through birth, and supreme nirmāṇakāya manifestations) and diversified skillful manifestations displayed according to the dispositions of beings to be trained. The extent of their application is infinite, for since the buddhas work for the benefit and happiness of all sentient beings, there is no calculating the extent of the benefit they do. And the duration of their application is infinite, for the buddhas engage in benefiting others for as long as there are still beings—and to beings there is no end. Thus, because the buddhas' attainments are so profound, being beyond the scope of the listeners and solitary realizers in terms of whom they are applied to, where, how, to what extent, and for how long, they are said to be inconceivable, beyond the imagination. And, on account of their vastness, the numbers of their categories are immeasurable.

(2) An Enumeration of Different Categories of Those Attainments

There are eight verses showing seven different kinds of attainment that come through transformation, along with how infinite these attainments are.

> When the five sense organs are transformed,
> They perceive all the sense objects, and there arise
> Twelve hundred all-perceiving qualities,
> Which are obtained as the supreme attainment. (X, 41)

When the sense organs—the eye and the others—are transformed into the pure state, each sense organ interacts with all the objects of the sense organs, and there arise twelve hundred qualities of perceiving all objects, which will be obtained as the supreme attainment. Previously, when the sense organs had not been transformed, the eye only saw forms, but it could not perceive the objects of the other sense organs—sound and the rest. When they have been transformed, the eye is able to apprehend everything—forms, sounds, smells, tastes, and physical sensations—and it is therefore able to interact with all the sense objects. Speaking of one hundred and twelve qualities,[18]

---

18. There appears to be a disparity here between the root verse's twelve hundred (Tib. *brgya phrag bcu gnyis*) and the one hundred and twelve (*brgya rtsa bcu gnyis*) mentioned by Sthiramati, though the *White Lotus Sūtra* that he refers to speaks of twelve hundred. Mipham explains these two different numbers in the sentences that follow.

Sthiramati's commentary mentions that even a single sense organ will have one hundred and twelve qualities, for which one should refer to the *Sūtra of the Questions of Dhāraṇīśvararāja* and the *White Lotus Sūtra of the Sacred Dharma*. Some people say that these refer to the one hundred and twelve qualities obtained by adding together the major and minor marks.[19] Others say that they are the qualities related to the level and so on. But these are not qualities of the sense organs, and therefore they are not relevant in this context. It is then evident that the twelve hundred qualities must be as explained in the above-named sūtras. Moreover, it appears that one can count them as follows. Each of the five sense objects can be split into six directional aspects,[20] and each of these again into ten aspects corresponding to the ten directions, making sixty such aspects in all. Beginning with the eye (and not counting the eye seeing forms, since that is not an extraordinary feature of the eye), its apprehension of the four objects—sounds, smells, tastes and physical sensations—multiplied by sixty makes two hundred and forty qualities for the eye. Adding all five sense organs together, we get 1,200 qualities, making twelve groups of one hundred. Although it is said in the *White Lotus Sūtra* that the flesh organs, which are produced through the merit of upholding that teaching,[21] apprehend everything—forms and so on—in all directions, it would be worth checking this point again in detail by referring to the sūtra, but in this general context it may not be relevant.[22]

One might wonder how the sense organ can be transformed if, as here in the Cittamātra tradition, neither a material sense organ nor form as an object exists. This is answered by the following quotation.

> Whatever seeds one has
> Are the source of anything that appears to the consciousness,
> And these are termed the twofold senses-and-fields,
> As the Capable One has explained.

---

19. The thirty-two major marks and eighty minor marks of a buddha.
20. The six directional aspects are north, south, east, west, above, and below.
21. Lit. "that Dharma," i.e., the Mahāyāna teachings.
22. The flesh organs—for example, the flesh eye (Tib. *sha'i mig*)—refer not to the organs we have as ordinary beings (*tha mal pa'i sha'i dbang po*) but to those of noble beings (*sha'i dbang po yongs su dag pa*). Mipham notes, however, that the numbers of qualities mentioned in this sūtra, in referring to flesh organs, present a specific case and so may not be relevant to the present discussion.

Accordingly, from the consciousness of the ground of all that has the habitual tendencies of an apprehending subject and an apprehended object there appear the six outer and inner senses-and-fields. The inner seed that is the support for the eye consciousness arising is held to be the "eye," and the apprehended object that arises from the eye consciousness and appears as form is what we call "form." It is similar for the other senses. Thus, from the point of view of appearance, there is a classification into two, the outer and inner senses-and-fields. At that time,[23] the mistaken inner attachment is eliminated by the unmistaken gnosis, and transformation thereby takes place.

> **When the mind is transformed,**
> **It functions consistently with that attainment,**
> **And supreme attainment is obtained**
> **With regard to the uncontaminated nonconceptual gnosis.**
> **(X, 42)**

"Mind" here is not what the listeners call "mind," that is, the mind organ that comes immediately after the six consciousnesses. What the Mahāyāna tradition calls "mind" is the defiled mind consciousness, which we hold to be the support of the mental consciousness, just as the eye organ, for example, is the support of the eye consciousness. As long as this defiled mind consciousness is not transformed, it has the view of an "I," whereas when it is freed of the concepts of "I" and "mine," it is transformed into the gnosis of equality, and it then functions in a way consistent with the attainment of the five transformed sense organs, in the same way that the mind interacts with all the sense objects in common even when it is untransformed. Sublime mastery will be obtained in the gnosis free of the concepts of subject and object and completely uncontaminated by defilement-related and cognitive obscurations.

> **When the apprehending subjects associated with the sense**
> **objects are transformed,**
> **These are enjoyed in any way one wishes,**
> **And to show this, supreme attainment is obtained**
> **With regard to the purification of realms. (X, 43)**

---

23. I.e., at the time of enlightenment.

When the consciousnesses of the five senses (the apprehending subjects associated with the five sense objects—form and the rest) are transformed, the objects of the sense consciousnesses are enjoyed in whatever way one wishes. In order to show this, one will obtain supreme mastery in displaying perfectly pure realms like the Blissful Realm[24] just as one wishes. In his commentary, Sthiramati says, "When the six sense objects from form through to phenomena and the five sense consciousnesses are transformed...." The individual impure sense consciousnesses are not conscious of anything other than their respective objects, but when they are transformed, each of them is conscious of all objects.

> When conceptual thought is transformed,
> Supreme attainment is obtained
> Regarding gnosis and all activities,
> At all times and without impediment. (X, 44)

When conceptual thought, that is, the mind consciousness, is transformed, one will obtain supreme mastery at all times in the unobstructed gnosis that knows everything there is to be known and in all activities such as displaying manifestations without impediment.

> When the support is transformed,
> Supreme attainment is obtained
> Of the nondwelling nirvāṇa,
> The uncontaminated state of buddhahood. (X, 45)

When the support, that is, the consciousness of the ground of all, is transformed, one will dwell in the uncontaminated abode of the enlightened state and obtain the supreme attainment of the nirvāṇa that does not dwell in the extremes of saṃsāra and nirvāṇa.

> When sexual activity is transformed,
> Supreme attainment is obtained
> In terms of dwelling in the buddhas' bliss
> And being free of the defilements that relate to seeing women. (X, 46)

---

24. Tib. *bde ba can*, Skt. *sukhāvatī*, the buddha field of Amitābha.

When sexual activity, the joining of the male and female organs, is transformed, one will obtain mastery in remaining in the bliss of concentration free from the conceptual elaboration that obscures enlightenment and in being without the defilement of desire on seeing members of the opposite sex.

> **When the perception of space is transformed,**
> **Supreme attainment is obtained**
> **With regard to acquiring all the riches one wishes,**
> **To moving unimpededly, and to taking different forms. (X, 47)**

When the perception of space is transformed, one will obtain supreme mastery in acquiring the concentration of the Sky Treasury, getting everything one thinks of from space; mastery in moving without impediment through the air, and even through mountains, rocks, and so forth; and mastery in taking different physical forms—that is, when one wishes to be visible, making one's physical form appear from space, and when one wishes to be invisible, using the concentration of dissolving the body to make everything physically disappear like space.

> **Thus, in the uncontaminated state of buddhahood**
> **There are said to be infinite transformations,**
> **With infinite attainments**
> **Accomplishing inconceivable activities. (X, 48)**

Thus, as indicated by the above explanations, there are as many boundless transformations into perfectly pure appearances as there are infinite aspects that can be known—environmental appearances, physical appearances, consciousnesses, and sensory objects such as forms. For this reason, in the uncontaminated state of enlightenment there are said to be infinite transformations, with infinite qualities or powers that are attained and that accomplish inconceivable benefit and happiness for beings to be trained. It is from having acquired such boundless qualities and attainments that the buddhas bring sentient beings to maturity, as we shall see next.

x. The Quality of Bringing Sentient Beings to Maturity[25]

This section is divided into seven parts: (1) how beings are brought to maturity; (2) the individuals that are brought to maturity; (3) the various deeds or means by which beings are brought to maturity; (4) nonconceptuality in maturing beings; (5) impartiality in maturing beings; (6) maturing beings in a chain reaction; and (7) how maturation continues unceasingly without ever reaching a sufficiency and without increase or diminution.

(1) How Beings Are Brought to Maturity

> Here, in all the regions of the universe, by means of the
>   victors' excellent explanations,
> Those in the world who are growing in virtue proceed to the
>   highest purity,
> While those without a store of merit proceed to the sublime
>   state of growth in virtue.
> Thus the immature proceed ever to maturity, but there is
>   never no one left. (X, 49)

When enlightenment is attained, how are sentient beings brought to maturity in this world of beings to be trained? Not in a few parts of the boundless universe, but in the infinite regions of the ten directions. Who brings them to maturity? The victorious ones. By what means? By clearly expounding the sacred Dharma, the Excellent Words. In what manner are they brought to maturity? Those in the world who, from the level of earnest aspiration up to the tenth level, are growing in the virtuous practices of the six transcendent perfections are brought to maturity in progressing higher and higher up to the sublime purity that is nirvāṇa. Beings who have not aroused bodhicitta and have not set out on the path—that is, mundane beings who have not accumulated merit in the past—are brought to maturity in arousing bodhicitta, starting to practice the path, and thereby progressing to the most excellent state of growing in virtue. Thus the buddhas

---

25. As Sthiramati points out, the earlier chapter dealt with bodhisattvas bringing beings to maturity while they are practicing on the path. The present section deals with how buddhas bring beings to maturity once they are enlightened.

bring to maturity those beings who are not mature, and in this way they eternally and unceasingly engage or proceed in the activities of bringing sentient beings to maturity. That is not to say, however, that there will be an end to sentient beings, with all having been brought to maturity and none left behind. Beings are infinite in number, so they do not decrease, and because the expanse of reality is unborn, it does not grow. Although all phenomena are devoid of intrinsic existence, they do exist as mere appearance, and so it is impossible for the appearance aspect of defilement and purity to come to an end.

(2) The Individuals That Are Brought to Maturity

> Thus the steadfast in different worlds are always and forever attaining
> The great enlightenment, so hard to attain, marvelous, and endowed with sublime qualities,
> Eternal, stable, and a refuge for the unprotected.
> How amazing that is, and yet not at all amazing, for they have practiced the excellent way. (X, 50)

Countless sentient beings have been brought to maturity as just described, and thus bodhisattvas, the steadfast individuals who are brought to maturity in the different regions of all the different worlds, are all the time—in each second of each day, forever and unceasingly—attaining the great enlightenment, the unsurpassable result that is extremely difficult to obtain. It is endowed with the strengths and all the other sublime qualities. It is something to be marveled at compared to the attainments of mundane beings, listeners, and solitary realizers. Once attained, it is eternal, for it exists until the end of saṃsāra. It is stable, for it never deteriorates. It is the refuge of those who have no protection from the torments of saṃsāra, helping them attain nirvāṇa, the end of all their sufferings. And, as has just been mentioned, it is constantly being attained by numerous individuals, one after another, in each second of every day. How utterly amazing that is. And yet, there is nothing at all amazing about it, for those bodhisattvas, fully mature individuals, have aroused bodhicitta, practiced the excellent way of the profound and extensive path—the two accumulations embodied in the six transcendent perfections—and obtained the result. That a sublime cause should give rise to a sublime result is perfectly natural.

(3) The Various Deeds or Means by Which Beings Are Brought to Maturity

> A buddha simultaneously displays a variety of deeds—
> In some places turning the Dharma Wheel in many hundreds of ways, in some taking birth, in others not appearing,
> In some showing different styles of birth, in some every kind of awakening, and in some the parinirvāṇa,
> And yet all these are demonstrated without moving from that state. (X, 51)

Buddhas simultaneously—that is, not sequentially—display a whole variety of deeds. In some places they turn the wheel of the Dharma, which comprises many hundreds of different approaches or teachings—that is, many varied subjects (the aggregates, sense spheres, and senses-and-fields, dependent arising, the truths, levels, transcendent perfections, and so forth) in many hundreds of different formulations (chapters, verses, and the like). At the same time, in some buddha fields, they demonstrate the deed of descending from the Tuṣita heaven and taking birth in Jambudvīpa; in other buddha fields they "do not appear," meaning that they do not demonstrate the twelve deeds of a buddha but assume the guise of a bodhisattva.

In some buddha fields they demonstrate the various deeds of birth, the activities of the bodhisattva's series of lives. In certain worlds they benefit beings by practicing transcendent generosity, giving away their various bodies and possessions. Similarly, they demonstrate the practices of transcendent discipline, patience, diligence, concentration, and wisdom. And they demonstrate a variety of modes of birth—good, bad, and neither good nor bad.

In some buddha fields they display the deed of attaining unsurpassable great enlightenment, in some they demonstrate attaining the solitary realizers' enlightenment, and in others the listeners' enlightenment, demonstrating all three forms of enlightenment depending on the different beings to be trained. Sthiramati says in his commentary that they demonstrate great enlightenment. In some buddha fields they demonstrate passing into nirvāṇa.

Although they display all these deeds simultaneously, and not sequentially, the buddhas never move even the slightest bit from the perfectly pure expanse of reality, the untainted state, suchness. These deeds are all performed effortlessly and spontaneously.

(4) Nonconceptuality in Maturing Beings

> The buddhas never purposefully think, "I matured those beings,"
> Or "I will mature those," or "Now I'm maturing these."
> Yet constantly in all directions through the three approaches,
> They will bring beings to perfect maturity through virtuous practice. (X, 52)

The buddhas do not make a deliberate effort and think, "In the past, I brought those beings to maturity"; "These ones I shall bring to maturity in the future"; and "At present, I am maturing these ones." And yet, boundlessly in all directions without restriction, constantly until the end of time, they will use the different approaches of the three vehicles to bring infinite beings to maturity through the practice of untainted virtue.

(5) Impartiality in Maturing Beings

> Just as the sun, with its many rays shining in all directions throughout the universe,
> Effortlessly ripens all the numerous crops,
> The sun of the Dharma, with the universal light of the teachings bringing perfect peace,
> Brings sentient beings everywhere to maturity. (X, 53)

The sun, with its many rays of light shining throughout the universe, not just in one direction but everywhere, ripens numerous crops, effortlessly. In the same way, the sun of the enlightened state, endowed with the countless teachings of the Twelve Branches of Excellent Speech, impartially brings beings in all the boundless regions of the universe to maturity with the universal light of the Dharma that shows the way to nirvāṇa, the state in which all suffering has been completely removed.

(6) Maturing Beings in a Chain Reaction

> Just as from a single lamp many countless, infinite lamps
> Are lit and yet it does not go out,
> From one mature being many countless, infinite maturations
> Occur, yet that being is never spent. (X, 54)

Although one would lose count of the great many lamps that are to be lit from a single lamp, that first lamp does not go out as more and more are lit. Similarly, from a single buddha who has attained ultimate maturity there arise a host of mature bodhisattvas, each of whom brings many beings to maturity, and those matured beings again bring others to maturity, one after another in succession, until the end of time, so that there occur infinite, countless maturations. And yet the buddha's maturation is never spent; such a stream of maturation never comes to an end.

(7) How Maturation Continues Unceasingly without Ever Reaching a Sufficiency and without Increase or Diminution

> Just as the great ocean can never have enough water
> Nor does it grow larger from the many great rivers flowing into it,
> The realm of enlightenment never has enough of the constant and unceasing
> Stream of pure beings entering it and grows no bigger—this is the greatest wonder in this world. (X, 55)

Although many kinds of rivers and streams flow from all directions into the great outer ocean,[26] constantly and unceasingly, for the ocean there can never be enough, and there is always room for the rivers to flow in. And however many great rivers flow into it, it will never grow larger. In the same way, for the realm or expanse of the enlightened state, the untainted state, suchness, there will never be enough of the infinite number of listeners,

---

26. "Great outer ocean" refers to the ocean surrounding Mount Meru according to the traditional Indian cosmology.

solitary realizers, and bodhisattvas whose obscurations have been purified and who are constantly and unceasingly entering nirvāṇa, and yet it will not grow larger. This is the most amazing and wondrous thing in this world.

b. A Presentation of Great Enlightenment in Terms of Six Aspects

The above description of great enlightenment in terms of its ten different qualities is now followed by a presentation of the great enlightenment that possesses those qualities, explained in terms of six aspects, beginning with its nature.[27] This is divided into (1) the actual presentation and (2) a specific explanation of its manifestations.

i. The Actual Presentation

Since the next four verses, in summary, describe the utterly pure expanse of reality, it is this that is explained first, followed by an explanation of the four kinds of gnosis, beginning with mirrorlike gnosis. This accords with the order in the *Sūtra on Buddhahood*, which states, "Buddhahood embodies five elements: the perfectly pure expanse of reality, mirrorlike gnosis, the gnosis of equality, all-discerning gnosis, and all-accomplishing gnosis." These are thus established in this treatise by the following summary.

> **Its nature is the suchness of all phenomena**
> **Purified of the two obscurations.**
> **Its nature is inexhaustible power**
> **With regard to knowing the object and focusing on that**
> **knowledge. (X, 56)**

The nature of all knowable phenomena—compounded, uncompounded, tainted, and untainted—is emptiness free of all extremes, and this is what we call suchness. It is their unmistaken actual condition, the ultimately authentic, the ultimate truth. Within the nature of suchness, there are no differences whatsoever, but in terms of the various conditioned phenomena that have that nature we nevertheless speak of "phenomena." And although there is no difference between the suchness of the buddhas and that of sen-

---

27. The six aspects are nature, cause, result, activity, properties, and categories.

tient beings, we refer to the suchness in the mind streams of beings, with their adventitious contaminants of mistaken perception, as "suchness with contaminants." Since the adventitious obscurations can be eliminated and the ultimate reality never changes, when the defilement-related and cognitive obscurations in the mind stream of an individual being are completely purified, that nature, the utterly pure expanse of reality, is what we call the Buddha's enlightenment. These first two lines indicate the transformation of suchness.

That enlightened being acquires the inexhaustible power of nonconceptual gnosis which, in meditative equipoise, takes as its object that same perfectly pure expanse of reality; and he or she acquires the inexhaustible power of focusing with the postmeditational gnosis on that nonconceptual gnosis. That postmeditational gnosis knows unmistakenly the mode of the nonconceptual gnosis. The translation of this line in Sthiramati's commentary is "Knowing the object and focusing on it," meaning that the object, the nonconceptual gnosis that is the transformed nature of the dependent reality, the consciousness of the ground of all, is correctly known with the postmeditational gnosis; "focusing on it" means focusing on the expanse of reality with nonconceptual gnosis. The way of commenting word-for-word here is different, but the meaning is the same: the attainment of the double inexhaustible power is explained as two kinds of gnosis, referring to meditation and postmeditation. In short, because on the level of buddhahood there is no alternation of meditation and postmeditation, with a single gnosis there is the nonconceptual vision of the nature of phenomena and the omniscient knowledge that sees all phenomena in their multiplicity, and this is held to be its nature, the attainment of inexhaustible power in these two. There is, therefore, no difference between phenomena and their true nature, the ultimate reality. At the stage of ultimate transformation, without moving from the vision of the true nature of phenomena as it is, one also spontaneously and effortlessly knows all phenomena in their multiplicity. This mastery of the two kinds of knowledge, which is the body of the essential nature (*svabhāvikakāya*) or body of truth, is a characteristic of the great enlightenment. All this is the *nature* of great enlightenment.

> **Through knowledge of suchness and meditation,**
> **Using all kinds of means, enlightenment occurs**
> **And bears inexhaustible fruit,**
> **Forever giving rise to the two for all that lives. (X, 57)**

The *cause* that makes one attain or realize great enlightenment is as follows. By hearing about, reflecting on, and meditating on suchness in accordance with the teachings on emptiness in the Mahāyāna sūtras, one determines it conclusively. Subsequently, by accumulating merit and wisdom on the level of earnest aspiration, and by meditating, one first gives rise to supramundane gnosis, the direct knowledge of suchness, and attains the first bodhisattva level. After that, meditation, using all the different kinds of methods up until the end of the tenth level, leads correctly to enlightenment.

The *result* of enlightenment is the production of both immediate benefit and long-term happiness at all times for the infinity of sentient beings. And it bears inexhaustible fruit for as long as saṃsāra lasts.

> Active in the skillful application
> Of manifestation through body, speech, and mind,
> Enlightenment possesses infinite concentrations,
> Powers of retention, and the two. (X, 58)

Similarly, the *activity* of great enlightenment lies in its function of skillful methods of activity or application in manifestation—appearing physically, verbally teaching the Dharma, and mentally conferring blessings. The skillfully applied activity of physical manifestation is appearance as a buddha to benefit beings and manifestation in all kinds of bodies such as those of gods and nāgas. Likewise, there is the skillfully applied activity of verbal manifestation, the sound of the Dharma arising directly, or from the sky, walls, trees, and so forth; and the activity of mental manifestation, whereby, through the Buddha's blessings, even the dull-witted could understand the meaning of the profound teachings, and Śāriputra, Subhūti, and others were inspired to expound the Perfection of Wisdom. "Application" here means activity; "skillful" refers to knowledge of the means for performing such manifestations, or alternatively to the activity of manifestation becoming the means for training beings.

Great enlightenment possesses infinite concentrations such as the concentration of Brave Progression and the Sky Treasury concentration; infinite powers of retention,[28] such as Inexhaustible Caskets and Infinite

---

28. *gzungs kyi sgo dpag tu med pa*, lit. "infinite doors of the power of retention" (Skt. *dhāraṇī*), meaning the ability to remember and therefore expound an infinite variety of teachings that serve as entrances through which beings may eliminate their particular defilements.

Doors; and both the infinite accumulations—those of merit and wisdom. Its *properties*, then, are infinite powers of retention, concentrations, and twofold accumulations.

> It is distinguished as the nature,
> The perfect enjoyment of the teachings, and the manifestation.
> All this describes the perfectly pure
> Expanse of reality of the enlightened state. (X, 59)

The *categories* of great enlightenment are distinguished as the natural body or body of truth, from the point of view of its essential nature; the body of perfect enjoyment of the Mahāyāna teachings, from the point of view of its appearance; and the body of manifestation, from the point of view of its activity for others' benefit.

This presentation in terms of these six aspects describes the perfectly pure expanse of reality of the enlightened state, for it determines great enlightenment, the perfectly pure expanse of reality, in terms of its nature and the other five topics.

ii. A Specific Explanation of Its Manifestations

The specific explanation is divided into (1) an explanation of the supports, the three buddha bodies, and (2) an explanation of the four kinds of gnosis that are supported. The first of these is further divided into a brief introduction and a detailed explanation.

(1) An Explanation of the Supports, the Three Buddha Bodies
(a) Brief Introduction

> The bodies of the buddhas are classified as
> The natural body, the body of perfect enjoyment,
> And another, the body of manifestation.
> The first is the basis for the other two. (X, 60)

The buddhas' bodies (*kāyas*) are categorized as follows. The "natural body" is the body of truth (*dharmakāya*). When the contaminants related to subject and object present in the consciousness of the ground of all are eliminated, the latter is transformed into the mirrorlike gnosis that beholds the expanse of reality as it is. From the point of view of suchness, it is spoken of as the natural or essential body, and from the point of view of gnosis it is referred to as the body of truth. These two are the ultimate nature and phenomena inseparable, and therefore, whichever way it is explained, this buddha body should be understood to be the realization of the utterly pure fundamental nature, which is union.[29] We should not understand it as the appearance aspect on its own. This is, in general, the sublime intended meaning of all the scriptures.

As for the body of perfect enjoyment (*saṃbhogakāya*), when the defiled mind consciousness is transformed into the gnosis of equality and the mind consciousness is transformed into all-discerning gnosis, this body enables bodhisattvas who have entered the bodhisattva levels to have full enjoyment of the Mahāyāna teachings.

There is another buddha body apart from these—the manifestation body (*nirmāṇakāya*), which results from the transformation of the five sense consciousnesses and brings to maturity the beings of Jambudvīpa and elsewhere by displaying transmigration from the Tuṣita heaven and other such deeds.

The first, the body of truth, is the support or basis of these last two, which comprise the form body. From that utterly pure great enlightenment the two buddha bodies appear to pure and impure beings destined to be trained.

(b) Detailed Explanation

The detailed explanation has two parts: (1) individual explanations of the three buddha bodies and (2) an explanation of the inclusiveness, equality, and eternity of the buddha bodies.

(i) Individual Explanations of the Three Buddha Bodies
1. The Body of Perfect Enjoyment

> In all worlds the body of perfect enjoyment
> Varies on account of its retinues,
> Buddha fields, names, bodies,
> Enjoyment of the teachings, and activities. (X, 61)

---

29. I.e., the union of appearance and emptiness.

In all completely pure worlds there are gathered different retinues of bodhisattvas—that is, different retinues of many differently named bodhisattvas. The buddha fields too have different aspects and colors (crystal, gold, beryl, and so on) and different names. Take, for example, the buddha fields of Vairocana, Amitābha, and other buddhas. Their bodies too are different in appearance: some are white in color, others yellow, and so on. As for the full enjoyment of the teachings, they explain a whole variety of different Mahāyāna subjects: some explain transcendent wisdom, others the ten levels, and so forth. And with regard to their activities, some disciples, depending on their attitudes, see them as physically huge, while some see them as quite small. The same is true with regard to their colors and to the teachings they give in accord with their disciples' aspirations. In all these respects, the body of perfect enjoyment appears variously, never in a single, definite form.

2. THE NATURAL BODY OR BODY OF TRUTH

The natural body is uniform,
Subtle, and related to the latter body;
It manifests enjoyments however they may be desired
And so is held to be the cause of the wealth of perfect
    enjoyment. (X, 62)

The natural body of truth is entirely uniform and undifferentiated: there is no appearance that is incompatible with the nature of the utterly pure expanse of reality possessed of the two purities. It is "subtle," because it is not within the domain of listeners, solitary realizers, and the like. It is related to the body of perfect enjoyment in that the body of truth is the causal factor for appearance as the body of perfect enjoyment. In what way? The body of perfect enjoyment having arisen from the cause, as it were,[30] that is the body of truth, it manifests as enjoyment, in any way that is desired, of the Mahāyāna teachings for bodhisattvas who have entered the levels. So that body of perfect enjoyment is held to be the cause of those bodhisattvas attaining the wealth of perfect enjoyment or being able to perfectly enjoy the teachings, because it is through the body of perfect enjoyment that all

---

30. Tib. *rgyu mthun pa*. The body of truth is referred to as the "cause" of the body of perfect enjoyment, but this should not be understood as being a cause in the conventional sense, as something compounded, like a seed giving rise to a sprout.

the Mahāyāna teachings are complete in the minds of those bodhisattvas present in the retinue of the body of perfect enjoyment. How? The enjoyment in whatever way is desired of both the outer enjoyments (the perfectly pure buddha field) and the inner enjoyments (the teachings of the Great Vehicle) is brought about by the body of perfect enjoyment.

3. The Buddha's Manifestation Body

> **The boundless manifestations of the enlightened state**
> **Are held to be the manifestation body.**
> **The fulfillment of the twofold goal**
> **Rests entirely on the two. (X, 63)**
>
> **By constantly displaying artistic expression,**
> **Birth, great enlightenment, and the parinirvāṇa,**
> **The Buddha's manifestation bodies**
> **Are the great means for liberating beings. (X, 64)**

All the infinite manifestations that benefit beings in whatever ways are appropriate are held to be the manifestation body. This does not refer only to the supreme nirmāṇakāya manifestation. Manifestations in the form of different kinds of beings such as gods are also said to be the manifestation body. The fulfillment of the two goals—that is, the fulfillment of one's own goal and fulfillment of others' goal—depends entirely and at all times on the two buddha bodies: the body of perfect enjoyment and the manifestation body. Having finally attained one's own goal, buddhahood, one constantly dwells in perfectly pure buddha fields propagating the feast-like teachings of the Great Vehicle to pure retinues. This, the ultimate reach of the form body, is the body of enjoyment. And in bringing other, impure beings to maturity by means of the manifestation body, one fulfills others' goals. This is expressed in terms of the principal aspects.[31]

In the body of truth there is no distinction between one's own and others' good: it is the basis for the arising of the two buddha bodies for the fulfillment of the two goals. The manifestation body, on the other hand, has four categories, based on the ways in which it benefits others: constantly, until

---

31. It is in the two form bodies, and not in the body of truth, that the fulfillment of one's own and others' goals is actually apparent.

the end of time, it displays manifestations of art, birth, great enlightenment, and parinirvāṇa. The manifestation-body buddhas are thus the great means for liberating beings in the expanse of nirvāṇa. They manifest in art by appearing as artisans such as joiners, potters, and musicians. They manifest in birth by descending from the Tuṣita heaven and taking birth in royal or priestly families, and so forth. They manifest great enlightenment by demonstrating the attainment of buddhahood, and the parinirvāṇa by demonstrating the final nirvāṇa, as Sthiramati describes. This has also been explained above.[32]

(ii) An Explanation of the Inclusiveness, Equality, and Eternity of the Buddha Bodies

> Know that the bodies of the buddhas
> Are included in the three buddha bodies.
> The three bodies are taught as being the fulfillments
> Of one's own and others' goals along with their basis. (X, 65)

The bodies of all the buddhas are to be understood as being included in the three buddha bodies. These three buddha bodies refer to the body of perfect enjoyment and the manifestation body, which accomplish one's own and others' goals, and the body of truth, which is the basis of these two. The truth body of all the buddhas is a single unity; infinite bodies of enjoyment are included in the body of enjoyment; and infinite bodies of manifestation are included in the body of manifestation. There is nothing that is not included in the three buddha bodies.

> In terms of basis, intention,
> And activities, they are the same.
> In terms of nature, incessancy,
> And continuity, they are eternal. (X, 66)

It has been taught that all the tathāgatas are equal. This means that the buddhas are the same in three respects: Their basis or abode is the same, for in the body of truth, the utterly pure expanse of reality, they are equal and undifferentiated. Their intentions are equal, for there is no difference in

---

32. See ch. 8, v. 6.

the magnitude or excellence of the intentions of any of the enjoyment-body buddhas. They all have a single intention: to bring benefit and happiness to all sentient beings. And their activities are equal, for the activities of all the manifestation bodies are the same in training beings, and the manifestations of all the buddhas occur together, as explained earlier.

It has also been taught that the buddha bodies of all the tathāgatas are eternal. They are eternal in three respects: The body of truth is essentially or naturally eternal because it is by nature devoid of birth and cessation. The enjoyment-body buddhas are eternal in that there is never any interruption in their teaching the Dharma. And the manifestation-body buddhas are eternal in their continuity; they are eternal in that even when they are not visible to some beings, they are visible to others, and in this manner they will appear continuously until the end of saṃsāra.[33] It is for these reasons that the buddhas' three buddha bodies are said to be eternal.

(2) An Explanation of the Four Kinds of Gnosis That Are Supported

This section is divided into four parts: (1) a brief introduction; (2) a detailed explanation of each of the four kinds of gnosis; (3) an explanation of the causes for acquiring the four kinds of gnosis; and (4) an explanation showing that the culmination of all paths is the Buddha's gnosis.

(a) Brief Introduction

> There are only the unmoving mirrorlike gnosis
> And the three kinds of gnosis based on it—
> Equalizing, all-discerning,
> And all-accomplishing. (X, 67)

Mirrorlike gnosis, the transformation of the consciousness of the ground of all, never moves from the perfectly pure expanse of reality; it endures until the end of saṃsāra without arising and engaging.[34] The three kinds of gnosis abide in and are dependent on that mirrorlike gnosis, and since they do arise and engage, they are moving. What are these three kinds of gnosis? The

---

33. Sthiramati's explanation is that when the nirmāṇakāya manifestations are not appearing in some worlds, they are appearing in others.

34. Tib. *'byung 'jug*, arising and engaging with an object.

defiled mind consciousness transformed, which is the gnosis of equality; the mind consciousness transformed, which is all-discerning gnosis; and the five sense consciousnesses transformed, which is all-accomplishing gnosis. Thus, there are just four kinds of gnosis, the transformations of the eight consciousnesses.

(b) Detailed Explanation of Each of the Four Kinds of Gnosis
(i) Mirrorlike Gnosis

> **Mirrorlike gnosis is devoid of a sense of possession,**
> **Utterly impartial, and ever present;**
> **It is not ignorant with regard to all things that can be known,**
> **But never directed toward them. (X, 68)**

In mirrorlike gnosis everything that can be known appears, and yet there are no concepts of subject and object, no "I" and concept of self, and no deliberate effort, and therefore no sense of possession. It is comparable to a mirror in which multiple reflections appear, yet the things reflected have no existence in the mirror; there is no concept of those reflections and no deliberate effort to produce them. It is not as if mirrorlike gnosis penetrates some places and directions and not others. It penetrates all places without bias and is therefore completely impartial. Since it arises throughout the three times, it is ever present. Since it is free of both defilement-related and cognitive obscurations, it is not ignorant with regard to any knowable objects but realizes the nature of things as they are. As for its aspect, since it never apprehends knowable phenomena conceptualizing them as this or that and taking them to be real, it is not directed toward its objects, because although things appear, there are no biased concepts of attributes.

> **Because it is the cause of all kinds of gnosis,**
> **It is like a great mine of gnosis.**
> **It is the enjoyment body itself,**
> **For the other kinds of gnosis appear as reflections in it. (X, 69)**

Because it is the cause of all the other kinds of gnosis, it is like an oceanic source of all the jewels of gnosis. It is referred to as the enjoyment body itself, because it is the ultimate basis of designation for the buddhas of perfect enjoyment. It is called mirrorlike gnosis because, just as in a clear mirror everything appears reflected, absolutely everything there is to know appears to this gnosis. And the three kinds of gnosis—the realization of sameness with regard to the nature of things, the realization of each and every one of them distinctly, and the spontaneous accomplishment of beings' welfare—appear as reflections or specific aspects that are based on and depend on it. This is why it is called mirrorlike gnosis.

(ii) The Gnosis of Equality

> The gnosis of equality is held to be
> Pure as a result of its cultivation with respect to sentient beings.
> To have entered the nondwelling peace
> Is said to be the gnosis of equality. (X, 70)

> Constantly possessed of love
> And great compassion,
> It visibly reveals to sentient beings
> The Buddha's form according to their aspirations. (X, 71)

When the realization gained on the first bodhisattva level that oneself and sentient beings are the same is cultivated up the tenth level, thereby eliminating even the most subtle habitual tendencies of the "I" and concept of self, it is said to become the pure gnosis of equality of the buddha level. This refers to the equality and inseparability of saṃsāra and nirvāṇa that does not dwell in the directions or extremes of existence and peace. The stilling of the dualistic concepts of existence and peace is held to be the essence of the gnosis of equality.

It is endowed at all times with love and great compassion. And its function lies in the buddhas displaying themselves to sentient beings in all kinds of bodily colors and shapes in accordance with each being's individual inclinations.

(iii) All-Discerning Gnosis

> All-discerning gnosis
> Is never obstructed as to all there is to know;
> It is like a treasure house
> Of concentrations and powers of retention. (X, 72)

> To the disciples in the retinue
> It displays all kinds of riches
> And makes the rain of the Great Dharma pour down,
> Removing all their doubts. (X, 73)

All-discerning gnosis is the gnosis that, at all times, has unobstructed knowledge of all the specific and general characteristics of all knowable phenomena. It is like a treasure house of infinite concentrations and infinite powers of retention.

Its function is to display to the whole circle of disciples in the Buddha's retinue the outer riches of enjoyable qualities—all the abundant and perfect riches of a pure buddha field with its adornments and layout (the ground made of jewels, the wish-fulfilling trees, the rivers of nectar, the inestimable palace) and massed clouds of offerings of untainted forms, sounds, fragrances, tastes, and physical sensations. And, by authentically displaying the inner riches of the Dharma, the specific and general characteristics of all the profound and extensive teachings, it makes the great rain of the Mahāyāna teachings pour down, removing all the disciples' doubts.

(iv) All-Accomplishing Gnosis

> All-accomplishing gnosis
> Accomplishes beings' welfare
> In all worlds with multifarious manifestations,
> Infinite and inconceivable. (X, 74)

> Know that those manifestations of the buddhas,
> Forever performing their deeds,
> Are inconceivable in every way—
> In their diversity, numbers, and realms. (X, 75)

All-accomplishing gnosis accomplishes the goals of all sentient beings in all the infinite worlds by means of a whole variety of different manifestations of body, speech, and mind, infinite in number and inconceivable. The reasons the buddhas' manifestations are multifarious, infinite, and inconceivable, as has just been mentioned, are as follows.

They are multifarious on account of the diversity of deeds or activities that they perform all the time for the welfare of beings, who have different natures, faculties, and degrees of interest. In benefiting beings, the buddhas manifest in the form of buddhas, and similarly as listeners, solitary realizers, bodhisattvas, gods, and every other kind of being, and they work in all sorts of ways for beings' benefit. In short, it is because they display a boundless variety of different manifestations that these are described as multifarious. Furthermore, since these manifestations are beyond counting in hundreds or thousands, they are spoken of as infinite. Their realms, that is to say, the worlds in which they benefit beings, are not limited to one or a hundred, but exceed in number the grains of sand in the Ganges; they display and manifest an immense infinity of boundless realms in the ten directions. The buddhas' manifestations are therefore to be understood as being in every way inconceivable.

(c) The Causes for Acquiring the Four Kinds of Gnosis

This section has two parts: (1) the ripening causes and (2) the cause for attaining complete purity. The first of these is divided into two: the main explanation and additional points.

(i) The Ripening Causes
1. Main Explanation

> Because of holding the teachings, because of an attitude of equanimity,
> Because of teaching the true Dharma,
> And because of accomplishing tasks,
> The four kinds of gnosis will properly arise. (X, 76)

If, when one is an ordinary being, one follows a spiritual master and holds the Mahāyāna teachings by listening to them, reflecting on them, meditating on them, and so on, this will act as the cause for acquiring mirrorlike gnosis, for as a result of this cause, the ground of all will gradually be transformed and turned into mirrorlike gnosis. So the first phrase in this verse should be understood as meaning "Because of one's holding the Dharma, mirrorlike gnosis will arise." The other three phrases are to be understood following the same principle. Because of one's cultivating an attitude of equanimity when one is an ordinary being, training one's mind in having as loving an attitude toward all beings as one has toward oneself, the gnosis of equality will arise. On the level of earnest aspiration, if one teaches other sentient beings the true Dharma, without mistake—as one has heard it—all-discerning gnosis will arise as a result. Similarly, because of one's doing beings' work for them, the all-accomplishing gnosis will arise. Thus from these four causal factors the four kinds of gnosis will properly arise. To obtain these four unsurpassable kinds of gnosis, therefore, we should, while we are ordinary beings, arouse the mind turned toward supreme enlightenment and practice these four causal factors as much as possible, dedicating our practice to the attainment of each of these kinds of gnosis, as the case may be. The interdependence of cause and effect is such that our efforts will never be wasted but unfailingly result in our acquiring those different kinds of gnosis.

2. Additional Points

One might argue that if, when individual beings obtain these unsurpassable kinds of gnosis in this way and they become as many buddhas, with as many different mind streams, then those buddhas too must be specifically characterized individuals, and their aggregates, sense spheres, and senses-and-fields must be multiple phenomena with specific characteristics and therefore compounded and impermanent. In that case, how can it be valid for the Buddha to say that noble beings are classified as uncompounded and not as compounded? If they are no different when they attain enlightenment, what, one might wonder, would be the point in each being's practicing the path and attaining the result?

As long as there is the belief in individuals and phenomena, there appear individuals with different mind streams and the multiple different phenomena of their aggregates, sense spheres, and so forth. However, in ultimate truth, there are no intrinsically existent phenomena or individuals: there is only radiant emptiness, the nature of the two kinds of no-self. When this is realized as it is, one is free of the belief in intrinsically existent individuals and phenomena, so that on the level of buddhahood, the buddhas are the omniform, inconceivable body of gnosis, the nature of the expanse of reality. They do not have any of the characteristics and aspects that the ordinary mind believes to be inherently existing individuals and phenomena. It is therefore taught that while the buddhas are no different in ultimate truth, on the conventional level they are designated differently. This is the subject of the following verse.

> Because there are different potentials, because there is benefit,
> Because of fulfillment, and because there is no beginning,
> The Buddha is not single; but, because in the uncontaminated state
> There are no distinctions, neither is he multiple. (X, 77)

Some people say that when a buddha attains enlightenment in one world, at that time no other buddhas will be born or appear in any of the other worlds in the ten directions, so that there is no more than one buddha in the whole universe, and he therefore benefits beings by producing other manifestations in other worlds. Others say that from time without beginning in saṃsāra there has only ever been one Buddha, and that he alone performs the various buddha activities for beings' benefit in all the buddha fields. Yet others say that there is not just one buddha who has attained the ultimate level but many different truth bodies rid of the "I" and the concept of self and devoid of the two obscurations.

Neither of these two unequivocal claims—that there is only one Buddha or that there are multiple buddhas—is correct, for the following reasons. There are infinite sentient beings in the universe who possess the potential for accomplishing buddhahood, and there are therefore many different potentials acting as causes. So it would not be logical for the result to be only a single buddha—just as it would be illogical to say that only one grain out of a whole pile of grain has the potential to produce a shoot, while the others do not.

Just as anyone can be filled and nourished with well-cooked food, anyone who gathers the two accumulations will have the benefit of attaining buddhahood. But if there were no more than one buddha, there would be no point in many individuals gathering the two accumulations in order to attain buddhahood. That too does not follow, so there cannot be only one buddha.

When the buddhas first arouse the mind turned toward unsurpassable enlightenment, they take the vow to attain the great enlightenment themselves and then to bring sentient beings to enlightenment, and this promise is completely fulfilled on the level of buddhahood. If there were only one buddha and no other sentient beings attaining enlightenment apart from him, that buddha would not bring even a single being to buddhahood, and therefore the initial promise would never be fulfilled. So again, if the buddhas' pledges to benefit beings are to be completely fulfilled, there cannot be only one buddha.

Up to this point this verse refutes those who say that there is only one buddha in the world and there are no other buddhas in other worlds. It has been said that two universal emperors or two buddhas cannot appear in a single world system at the same time, but this refers to a single world system with four continents. In the *Compendium of the Great Vehicle* it is stated that one buddha like the supreme manifestation body King of the Śākyas manifests in a great cosmos of a billion worlds as many times as those billion four-continent worlds, with a manifestation-body buddha appearing in each one simultaneously, entering his mother's womb and so on. This would refute those who say, with regard to time, that there is only one Buddha from time without beginning.

It is impossible to attain enlightenment without gathering the accumulations of merit and wisdom. And the two accumulations do not just happen by themselves without another buddha transmitting the relevant instructions. So there must have been another buddha before that one, and others before him. And therefore, just as saṃsāra is without beginning, there can be no beginning to buddhas either. For this reason, we cannot accept that there has been no more than one buddha from time without beginning. And it is an established fact that there are many buddhas who have come, one after another in succession. For all the above-mentioned reasons, therefore, there is not only one single buddha but numerous buddhas, infinite in number.

Nevertheless, when one attains the sublime, untainted expanse, the utterly pure expanse of reality uncontaminated by the two obscurations, in that state there are no distinctions at all: the enlightened state is classified or established as uncompounded suchness endowed with the two purities. So in those terms the enlightened state is not multiple either, for everything is the same taste—simply the expanse of reality, suchness, the natural radiant light, devoid of characteristics, as has already been explained.

(ii) The Cause for Attaining Complete Purity

What brings about the attainment of omniscience—self-originated gnosis, great enlightenment, characterized by nonduality—is the five transcendent perfections and especially the most important transcendent perfection, transcendent wisdom, which makes the other transcendent perfections pure. So there now follows an explanation of transcendent wisdom, the cause for obtaining the ultimate great gnosis.

> That which does not exist
> Is held to be the sublime existence.
> Not conceptualizing in any way
> Is held to be the sublime conceptualization. (X, 78)

The imputed reality of subject and object and so forth, being a nonexistent, dualistic concept, is held in ultimate truth to be the fully present reality or suchness—the true, correct, actual condition of things—the highest form of existence. This is indicated from the point of view of the object.

The nonconceptual gnosis that does not in any way have as its object elaborated conceptual constructs is held to be the sublime conceptualization, for it is the wisdom that conclusively determines the nature of the ultimately authentic. The actual nonconceptual gnosis is obtained when one attains the first level.

That objectless freedom from all elaborated conceptual constructs is the perfectly pure view of the Great Vehicle. It is what is meant by the passage in the Perfection of Wisdom that says that not seeing anything is the highest form of seeing.

> Meditation that does not look at aspects
> Is held to be the sublime meditation.
> The attainment of those who do not look
> To attain anything is also held to be sublime. (X, 79)

Because the meditation does not look at any subject or object, it is held to be the highest form of meditation, for bodhisattvas meditate in accord with the way things truly are—thatness. Genuine freedom from the three concepts of a meditator, an object of meditation, and an act of meditating occurs on the second to tenth levels, while on the level of earnest aspiration the meditation is emulative.[35]

Even with regard to the qualities of the result, buddhahood, there is nat-

---

35. Ordinary beings' meditation on emptiness is a surrogate meditation (Tib. *rjes mthun pa*), since although it may resemble meditation on emptiness and serves as a means to realizing emptiness, it is not the genuine thing (Tib. *mtshan nyid pa*).

urally no conceptualization, and so the attainment of those who, correctly, do not have the view that attainment is something truly existent is also sublime. As long as one has not eliminated the belief that what is to be attained is something real, one will not attain enlightenment. But from the realization of the nature of "nonattainment," buddhahood will be attained. Again in the Perfection of Wisdom it is taught that nonabiding is the highest form of abiding, and nonattainment is the highest of attainments.

Thus it has been taught that by recognizing that all the elements of the ground, path, and result are of the same taste in suchness devoid of all elaborated conceptual constructs, one obtains the great gnosis of enlightenment, the result. But if one has any notion of attributes, one remains far from the resultant transcendent perfection of wisdom and will not attain it. If, on the other hand, one realizes the absence of attributes, one will swiftly attain it.

> Those who have views concerning height, distance, attributes,
> And their own superiority in terms of diligence—
> Of these proud bodhisattvas
> It is said, "They are far from enlightenment." (X, 80)

> Those who regard all the aforementioned views
> As mere conceptual constructs—
> Of these bodhisattvas who are free of concepts
> It is said, "They will attain enlightenment." (X, 81)

Bodhisattvas who are proud and full of concepts consider the highest qualities (that is, buddha qualities) to be real things and attributes, or they see unsurpassable enlightenment endowed with marvelous qualities such as the ten strengths as weighty, for it is difficult to accomplish. (This alternative explanation follows Sthiramati's commentary, in which the word *guru* is translated in the sense of "weighty," rendering this verse: "Those who see weight, distance, attributes, and their own diligence.") They regard enlightenment as far away, because it requires that they practice for three measureless great kalpas. They see in it the attributes of an object that has to be meditated on. And they think that because they are making diligent efforts to attain unsurpassable enlightenment, they are much better than others. Such bodhisattvas are referred to as "a long way from unsurpassable enlightenment." Until they are free of such conceptualization and pride, they will never gain the correct path for attaining enlightenment.

Since all the conceptualized views that have just been mentioned are in fact no more than simple imputations and personal concepts, bodhisattvas free of the concepts of real attributes, who have realized that all phenomena are merely one's own mind, and who regard or see that mind without any concept of it as a thing or attribute, are described as "gaining unsurpassable enlightenment," because as a result of that absence of concepts they will rapidly acquire the acceptance that phenomena are unborn.

(d) Showing That the Culmination of All Paths Is the Buddha's Gnosis

It cannot be denied that when one is an ordinary being, on account of one's concepts one perceives different individuals and all sorts of different phenomena. Yet apart from their merely being classified by means of concepts or labeled by concepts, in fact, there are no phenomena that exist intrinsically and individually. So it is by gradually purifying those very concepts with nonconceptual gnosis that suchness (which is the complete stilling of the various conceptual elaborations such as individuals and phenomena) is progressively purified of the concepts of subject and object that obscure it until one attains the state of evenness, the expanse of reality, suchness, in which there are no differences. This is illustrated as follows.

> The rivers that have not reached the sea[36]
> Have different locations, different streams,
> Little water, with different activities,
> Providing for the needs of tiny creatures living in them. (X, 82)

> Yet when they reach the ocean,
> They all have one location, their water a single vast expanse,
> With the same activity, an immense and constant source
> For myriad marine creatures, providing all they need. (X, 83)

Before the earth's rivers reach (or enter) the sea,[37] they are separated by the lands they flow through and so flow through different places—in the east,

---

36. Lit. "gone under the earth." See the following note.
37. Lit. "before the rivers reach the ocean under the earth." The ocean here is seen from the point of view of ancient Indian cosmology, in which Mount Meru and the four conti-

in the south, and so on. And they take different forms—great rivers like the Ganges and Sindhu, their tributaries, and smaller rivers and streams. Moreover, the water flowing in them is very little compared to that in the ocean. It also has different effects: some water gives rise to wind disorders, some predisposes to bile disorders, and some causes diseases related to phlegm, and so on. Different beings use it for different purposes—for watering the fields, bathing, and the like. And that water fulfills the needs of the tiny creatures like frogs, tadpoles, and larvae that live in it.

But when those rivers reach the sea, they all mingle with it and become one great ocean, resting not on different places but on the single golden ground. It is a single, vast mass of water whose breadth and depth are hard to measure. All the water in the ocean has the same salty taste, and in the way it flows it all behaves in the same manner in spreading and collecting.[38] And for the many kinds of large and small animals—crocodiles, whales, and the like—that inhabit the ocean's waters, it is a perpetual, abundant source of all they need.

> The steadfast who have not reached enlightenment
> Have different supports, different intellects,
> Little realization, and different activities;
> They benefit and constantly provide for only a few beings.
>   (X, 84)
>
> Once buddhahood is reached, they all
> Have but one support and a single great realization;
> Their deeds blend as one, and eternally and abundantly
> They fulfill the needs of vast hosts of beings. (X, 85)

By analogy with the above, steadfast bodhisattvas who have not entered ultimate enlightenment have different individual bodies composed of the five aggregates. They have different mental powers and intellects—sharp

---

nents are located above the ocean, as it were, floating upon it. Despite this incompatibility with modern ideas, the analogy here remains applicable.

38. Tib. *spro zhing sdud pa*. Our literal translation "spreading and collecting" covers several interpretations. It could refer to the ebb and flow of the ocean's tides, to the characteristic property of water to spread over surfaces and also to collect in depressions, and to the evaporation of the sea forming clouds, producing rain and eventually rivers, which finally collect again in the sea.

and dull, excellent and poor, powerful and weak—and since they have not got rid of all obscurations and therefore lack omniscient gnosis, their realization, compared to the Buddha's, is very slight. Their activities too are different, for they engage in generosity, for example, only when it is the moment to do so. In working for the good of a few beings destined to be trained by them, they may fulfill the needs of those beings, but they do not benefit countless sentient beings in the ten directions as does the Buddha.

When all those bodhisattvas enter the state of ultimate enlightenment, whose nature is the perfectly pure expanse of reality and the four kinds of gnosis (mirrorlike gnosis and the others), the support or abode is the same, the one perfectly pure expanse of reality, and apart from this they do not have different bodies with distinct sets of aggregates. They all have great realization, with direct knowledge of everything there is to be known: there are no distinctions between sharp or dull faculties but only one state of omniscient gnosis. The activities of all of them are no different, but blended into one, eternally and unceasingly fulfilling the needs, abundantly and inexhaustibly, of the boundlessly, immeasurably vast hosts of the infinite sentient beings in the ten directions of space, ensuring their benefit and happiness.

3. Concluding Summary of the Chapter with a Verse in Praise of Great Enlightenment as an Instruction for Arousing Bodhicitta

> Thus, because the enlightened state has incomparable virtuous qualities,
> Because it is the cause of benefit and happiness,
> And because it is the inexhaustible source of the highest bliss and virtue,
> The wise should adopt the virtuous intention to attain enlightenment. (X, 86)

As has been explained, the enlightened state, from its own point of view, possesses incomparable untainted positive qualities—the transcendent perfections, the qualities associated with enlightenment, the strengths, the fearlessnesses, and so on. From other beings' point of view, it is the cause of benefit and happiness. And it is the inexhaustible source of the highest bliss (lasting freedom from suffering) and virtue (lasting freedom from the negative actions that bring suffering) that constitute the result. For all these reasons, advises Maitreya, the wise should properly adopt in their minds the virtuous spiritual intent to gain that supreme, unsurpassable enlightenment.

This completes the explanation of the tenth chapter of *Ornament of the Mahāyāna Sūtras*, the chapter on enlightenment.

Recapitulation Listing the First Ten Chapters

> The following is a recapitulation:
> Introduction, establishing, refuge, potential,
> Likewise, spiritual intent,
> One's own and others' benefit, thatness,
> Powers, full maturation, and enlightenment. (XI, 1)[1]

The first chapter, the chapter on why this work is called "Ornament of the Sūtras" has five verses. Establishing the Great Vehicle as the Buddha's word is indicated by fifteen verses. This is followed by twelve verses on the refuge. The potential is covered in thirteen verses, and similarly the spiritual intent by twenty-seven verses.[2] In the chapter on the practice for accomplishing one's own and others' goals, three verses are devoted to benefiting oneself and six to benefiting others. Thatness or the true meaning is described in ten verses. Powers are described in ten verses. Full maturation of oneself and sentient beings has twenty verses. Enlightenment completes this section with eighty-seven verses.

This recapitulation of the first ten chapters refers to the first four of the five unexcelled metaphors. These chapters cover establishing the path, the Great Vehicle, as the Buddha's teaching; the spiritual potential, which is the basis; refuge, the root of the path; bodhicitta, the spiritual intent that is the particular feature of the Mahāyāna path; its application, the practice; the particular factors that enable accomplishment—the powers and maturation; and enlightenment, the result that is accomplished. All these are described in general terms, constituting an introductory explanation of how

---

1. In the root text, this verse is included in the eleventh chapter.
2. This number, copied from Sthiramati, appears to be one short of the twenty-eight verses that we have counted for this chapter. The chapter on full maturation similarly contains twenty-two verses, and not twenty.

to gain knowledge of the particular features of the Mahāyāna path in which one is to be trained, along with its result, and thus to lay the foundation of the path.

Next there comes an explanation of how one is to be trained,[3] that is, of the actual approach to enlightenment, which is the means for realizing the result, unsurpassable enlightenment. This refers to the fifth unexcelled metaphor, which will be explained from this point onward. The whole first section up until the recapitulation, in describing the general features of the Mahāyāna path that is to be followed, explains the four sections (what is to be established, and the others) so that one can follow the path without hesitating and without mistaking the way, like a horse that is shown a straight course. In the context of the five metaphors, enlightenment, the inconceivable, which might otherwise be thought of as like opening a chest of jewels, is also the object of reflection on what is to be attained, and so it is treated as being like hearing good news. Actually opening the chest of jewels, as it were, corresponds to the level of buddhahood, but the means or cause for realizing it, which actually opens the chest, is the path constituting the elements that lead to enlightenment. "Elements that lead to enlightenment" should be understood as a general term covering Interest through to Conduct[4] and not only in the specific sense of the thirty-seven elements leading to enlightenment.

To help us understand what enlightenment is and what it is that leads to enlightenment, the tenth chapter describes enlightenment (the fully present reality, the ultimate realization that can only be known personally), and the next ten chapters comprise the so-called approach to enlightenment, the means or path for accomplishing enlightenment. By practicing the elements leading to enlightenment, one traverses the ten levels and gains their particular qualities: all these, up to the realization of the ultimate qualities—the four boundless attitudes of the enlightened state, its perfect freedoms, powers of perceptual limitlessness, perceptual domination, ten strengths, and so forth—are what are to be understood by the fifth metaphor. Thus, this section describing the approach to enlightenment comprises the eleven remaining chapters, from the chapter on interest up to that on conduct. They are related to the five indicative stages of yoga as follows. The five chap-

---

3. This corresponds to the second of Sthiramati's three headings (what one trains in, how to train, and who is training). See page 140.

14. I.e., chapters 11 through 21.

ters from "Interest" through to "Instructions and Follow-Up Teachings" correspond to the foundation; the four chapters "Skillful Activity" through to "Elements Leading to Enlightenment" correspond to development; the chapter on qualities corresponds to the mirrorlike stage; the concluding verses on the ten levels in the Conduct chapter correspond to vision; and the verses on the ultimate qualities of the result correspond to the support.

After this general explanation, we come now to the fifth principal section in the structural outline, the approach to enlightenment, which comprises four subsections: (1) the preliminaries, in five chapters beginning with the Interest chapter; (2) the main explanation, in four chapters beginning with "Skillful Activity"; (3) the temporary qualities of the practice in the Qualities chapter and up to the explanation of the ten levels in the Conduct chapter; and (4) an explanation of the ultimate qualities that are the qualities of the result. These four correspond to the fifth of the five unexcelled metaphors, "opening a chest of jewels."

The first of these subsections contains five chapters: one chapter on interest (the cause); three chapters on the practice (investigating the Dharma, teaching the Dharma, and practicing the Dharma); and one chapter on the instructions and follow-up teachings that enhance the latter.

PART FIVE
THE APPROACH TO ENLIGHTENMENT

Kyabje Kangyur Rinpoche, Longchen Yeshe Dorje (1897–1975), manifestation of Ārya Asaṅga and disciple of Jamgön Mipham

PRELIMINARIES

II

INTEREST

In the beginning when we set out on the path, it is necessary to give rise to interest,[1] for as it is said in the sūtras:

> The root of all that is virtuous
> Is interest, so the Capable One has declared.

It is by relying on the development of interest at the beginning of every positive activity that we will accomplish virtue. But without interest, we will never engage in any kind of virtue. We must therefore cultivate interest, for as we read in the *Sūtra of the Precious Lamp*:

> Developing faith, like a mother leading her children,
> Preserves all good qualities and makes them grow;
> It dispels our doubts and rescues us from all the rivers.
> Faith points us to the city of bliss.
> Faith is unsullied; it brings clarity of mind;
> Ridding us of pride, it is the root of respect.
> Faith is a treasure, a jewel, the perfect base;
> Like a hand, it is the root for gathering good.

And,

> Faith keeps us off demonic paths;
> It shows us the sublime path to liberation.

---

1. According to Sthiramati, the terms *mos pa* (often translated as "interest"), *dad pa* (faith), and *yid ches* (trust or confidence) all mean the same in the context of this chapter. We have nevertheless adhered to separate translations for these terms, generally translating *mos pa* in its widest sense as "interest." However, the term "interest" should be understood here in the sense of faith as a committed interest arising from confidence in its object's qualities, and much more than simply casual interest or curiosity.

An unspoiled seed in the field of good qualities,
Faith grows into the tree of enlightenment.

Accordingly, it is the chapter on interest that is taught first. This comprises (1) a general description of the categories of interest with an exposition of the twenty-six categories of interest, the sixteen obstacles to interest, and the eleven benefits of having interest, followed by (2) a specific explanation of interest in the Great Vehicle, in two sections: showing by similes the superiority of interest in the Great Vehicle, and instructions on following the Great Vehicle enthusiastically without getting discouraged.

1. General Description of the Categories of Interest
a. Twenty-Six Categories of Interest

> **Interest may be arisen, nonarisen, subjective, and objective,**
> **Received from a friend, natural, mistaken,**
> **Unmistaken, manifest, or otherwise nonmanifest,**
> **Produced from sound, investigative, and viewing, (XI, 2)**

> **Expropriable, mixed, unadulterated by counteragents,**
> **Inferior, vast, obscured, and unobscured,**
> **Diligent, nondiligent, with accumulation, and without,**
> **Firmly engaged, and advanced. (XI, 3)**

In general, the mental factor of confidence that something is true and as it is—for example, the karmic law of cause and effect, the four noble truths, or the Three Jewels—is what we call "faith" or "interest." And like the aggregate of form—which term is used for forms past, present, future, near, far, and so on—interest too is taught as being of different kinds, corresponding to its object, time, aspect, and so on.

Faith that has arisen in the past or is now present is known as *arisen interest*.

Future faith is called *nonarisen interest*.

Subjective interest is the mental factor "interest" itself[2] and is known as internal interest. Interest that is apprehended refers to previously arisen

---

2. Of the fifty-one mental factors, interest (Tib. *mos pa*) is the second of the five object-ascertaining factors. See also *Treasury of Precious Qualities*, appendix 4.

interest, which, when it is considered, is savored as being good and makes one feel happy: it is what we call *objective interest*. Because it is a different interest, which has been made the object, it is designated "external interest."

Interest in the training as taught by a spiritual friend is known as *interest received from a friend*. This is gross interest. Interest that arises from one's having the seed of faith and devotion and from the strength of one's potential[3] is known as *natural interest*, also termed "subtle interest."

Confidence and faith in the explanations of the tīrthika doctrines that the self and beings exist is known as *mistaken interest*. This is the wrong kind of interest. Confidence and faith in the Buddha's Excellent Words that teach impermanence, suffering, and no-self is known as *unmistaken interest*. It is the right kind of interest.

Interest that arises manifestly through the gathering of all the causes and conditions that give rise to interest is known as *manifest interest*. It is termed "proximate interest." Interest that has not at present manifestly arisen through the gathering of the causes and conditions that give rise to interest is known as *nonmanifest interest*. It differs from the previous kind of interest simply from the point of view that it should arise when the causes and conditions are gathered. It is termed "distant interest."

Interest that comes from listening to teachings that arouse one's faith is *interest produced by or from sound*. Interest that arises through using reasoning to examine the meaning of the teachings that one has heard is known as *the interest of investigation* through reflection. The interest originating from realizing the meaning of the teachings through meditation is the interest of the view or *interest that looks at the meaning*.

If, despite having developed faith, one is drawn onto other paths by tīrthikas, negative forces, and the like, such changeable faith is known as *expropriable interest*. This is a lesser kind of interest. When faith alternates with moments of lack of faith, the resulting mixture is known as *mixed interest* and is termed "middling." When one has nothing but faith, continuously, with no unfaithful thoughts, one has *interest unadulterated by counteragents*; this is a greater kind of interest.

Interest in the listeners' and solitary realizers' paths for the sake of perfect peace just for oneself is known as *inferior* or *lesser interest*. Interest in the

---

3. Tib. *rigs*. This could refer not only to the potential for enlightenment, that is, one's spiritual family, but also more literally to one's ordinary family, whose faith will naturally inspire and influence one's own faith.

teachings of the Great Vehicle, the path to the nondwelling nirvāṇa that spontaneously accomplishes the two goals, is *vast interest*.

All along the path, beginning from the stage of warmth on the path of earnest aspiration, one's interest in obtaining more and more extraordinary qualities may be interrupted by defilements such as attachment. One's interest is then *obscured interest*. Interest without such interruptions is known as *unobscured interest*.

Interest that arises uninterruptedly through diligence (both devoted application and constant application) is called *diligent interest* or endowed interest. Interest not endowed with such diligence is called *nondiligent interest* or unendowed interest.

Interest accompanied by the accumulations of merit and wisdom over one measureless kalpa on the level of earnest aspiration, which leads to one's gaining realization of the expanse of reality on the first bodhisattva level, is known as *interest with accumulated merit*. Interest that is not accompanied by such accumulations is known as *interest without accumulated merit*. In general, it is because of one's possessing or not possessing the accumulations of merit and wisdom that one's interest in the Great Vehicle will be vast and stable or weak and unstable.

The interest of bodhisattvas from the first level up to the seventh is called *firmly engaged interest*. This is because there is no diminution or deterioration in their interest. The interest of bodhisattvas dwelling on the pure levels, from the eighth level to the tenth level, is called *advanced interest*, because they have spontaneous, nonconceptual interest and have therefore advanced far beyond the level of conceptual thoughts and effort.

These two verses describing the different categories of interest are now followed by an explanation of the sixteen obstacles to interest.

b. Sixteen Obstacles to Interest

> Abundant failure to keep faith in mind,
> Laziness, disturbed practice,
> Bad company, feeble merit,
> And keeping incorrect ideas in mind, (XI, 4)

An abundant or predominant failure to keep faith in the Dharma in mind is an obstacle to arisen interest, because even if one has given rise to interest in the past and present a few times, if one does not preserve the flow of that interest by keeping it in mind, one's faith will evaporate.

Laziness is an obstacle to nonarisen faith, because faith does not arise in lazy people who make no effort to develop it.

"Disturbed practice" is explained as attachment to the object from thinking of faith developed in the past, and attachment to the subject, the present interest that apprehends the latter. These interrupt the practice of concentration, which consists in proper attentiveness without clinging to subject and object. This is an obstacle to both objective and subjective interest.

"Bad company" refers to evil companions—*un*spiritual friends. It impedes interest received from a friend, because even if one already has the interest received from a virtuous friend, it goes to waste on account of the anti-Buddhist ways taught by evil companions, and because the interest that comes from being instructed by a spiritual friend cannot arise in someone who is guided by evil companions.

A feeble accumulation of sources of good is a hindrance to natural interest, because even if one has the potential and the seed of interest, one's interest in the Mahāyāna teachings and so on will not emerge if one has not accumulated a great deal of merit.

Keeping incorrect ideas in mind—that things are permanent, happy, pure, and endowed with a self—hinders unmistaken interest, for one cannot then realize correctly that things are impermanent and so forth.

> **Carelessness, and little learning,**
> **Being satisfied with little learning and reflection,**
> **Pride in calm alone, and likewise, it is held,**
> **Failure to habituate, (XI, 5)**

Carelessness obstructs manifest interest. Manifest interest arises through one's not having attachment, aversion, and bewilderment, and through diligence. These four conditions constitute carefulness, while attachment, aversion, bewilderment, and laziness constitute carelessness and therefore prevent manifest interest from arising.

Receiving only a little teaching on limited topics—for example, hearing only the expedient teachings taught in the sūtras but not the ultimate teachings on emptiness and so on—hinders sound-produced interest. Since one cannot know about a subject that one has not studied, one will not have any faith in it. And people who have not heard the ultimate teachings are afraid of profound subjects like emptiness and do not have faith in them.

Considering that it is sufficient to hear the teachings without needing to reflect and meditate, and being satisfied with hearing only a few teachings on any subject without needing to study extensively both hinder investigative interest. As a result of such complacency, one cannot develop the interest deriving from the wisdom that comes from reflection; even if one develops it a little, one will not be able to develop it completely and on a vast scale.

Failure to reflect on the meaning of the teachings one has heard, or even if one does reflect a bit, to be satisfied with reflecting on them only a little and not very extensively is also, as in the previous case, an impediment to the investigative interest that comes from reflection. In short, if one thinks that it is enough to listen to a few teachings and to reflect on them a little bit, the interest that comes from reflection will not arise or, even if it arises a bit, it will be prevented from doing so properly and completely.

Pride in calm alone refers to being content with sustained calm alone and becoming self-satisfied, considering that it is enough simply to calm distracting thoughts without developing profound insight. This is an impediment to the interest of the view or interest that comes from meditation, because without profound insight, sustained calm on its own will not result in one's realizing the truth. Moreover, failure to apply oneself to meditation, thinking that reflection alone is sufficient, is also a hindrance to the interest of the view. "View," from the Sanskrit word *dṛśa*, also has the meaning of "seeing": by meditating, settling the mind in evenness, one sees the truth.

"And likewise, failure to habituate" means that, as in the previous case, failure to accustom oneself to interest again and again, or to blend it with one's mind, is a hindrance to both expropriable interest and mixed interest. As a result of not training one's mind again and again in interest, any interest one has is liable to be ravished away by other circumstances, and one's faith will alternate with lack of faith. The opposite of failure to integrate interest is thoroughly familiarized interest, which makes it hard for one's interest to be expropriated by circumstances, and also hard for occasional lack of faith to occur. For this reason, it is asserted that the obstacle to these two is not habituating one's mind to interest.

> **Lack of disenchantment, and likewise disenchantment,**
> **Being obscured, lack of diligence,**
> **And failure to accumulate merit—**
> **These are recognized as obstacles to interest. (XI, 6)**

Lack of disenchantment with saṃsāra hinders interest in the lesser vehicles because if one is attached to saṃsāra and does not weary of it, one will not strive for peace and happiness.

Similarly, being solely disenchanted with saṃsāra is an obstacle to interest in the Extensive Vehicle. This is because, in being fed up with saṃsāra and wanting to abandon it completely, one strives for one's own peace, like the listeners.

Being obscured, which was explained above with obscured interest, is an obstacle to unobscured interest.

Lack of diligence hinders diligent interest.

Failure to accumulate merit and wisdom is an obstacle to the arising of interest with accumulated merit.

The above explains only sixteen obstacles that need to be recognized. This is because five kinds of interest—namely, mistaken, nonmanifest, obscured, nondiligent, and without accumulated merit—are already permeated by incompatible factors, so there is no need to mention separate obstacles for them. In addition, three kinds of interest—unadulterated, firmly engaged, and advanced—are free from counteragents that hinder them, and so there are no obstacles to them. Subjective interest and objective interest share a single hindrance, as do expropriable interest and mixed interest. This makes ten fewer kinds of interest, bringing the number of factors that impede interest to sixteen.

It is also possible to count a total of eighteen obstacles by counting two hindrances for the interest that gives rise to reflection (namely, being content with merely hearing the teachings and being content with hearing only a few teachings) and by separating the hindrances to the interest that gives rise to meditation (namely, being content with only reflecting on the teachings and having pride in mere calm). However, in terms of the kinds of interest that are hindered, it is better to count them as sixteen. Thus, although these sixteen factors do not correspond to each of the different kinds of interest, in general they obscure all forms of interest and are therefore to be avoided.

c. Eleven Benefits of Having Interest

> Great merit, absence of regret,
> Mental bliss, and great bliss,
> No wastage, stability,
> And similarly enhancement, (XI, 7)

Present interest infinitely increases the great merit of faith in the Dharma.

Past interest, that is, past interest in the Mahāyāna teachings, is meritorious, and so in the present too it is not a cause for regret.

As a result of obtaining the concentration that realizes the absence of intrinsic existence in the object—that is, partial realization of thatness, where there is no attachment to the external object as substantially existent—one acquires mental bliss.

With the interest related to realization of the absence of intrinsic existence in the subject, one gains the great bliss of the concentration of the supreme mundane level or "immediately preceding concentration."[4]

With the interest received from a friend, provided it is not interrupted by circumstances, one obtains the benefit of one's merit not being wasted.

Natural interest, if not obstructed, leads to one's sources of good becoming stable and not diminishing.

In the same way as the above, unmistaken interest, evident interest, sound-produced interest, investigative interest, the interest of the view, expropriable interest, and unadulterated interest (seven in all), if not hindered by counteragents, each have the benefit of being self-enhancing. Middling unmistaken interest, for example, gives rise to great unmistaken interest, and so on.

> Direct realization of the nature of phenomena,
> The supreme attainment of one's own and others' goals,
> And quick preternatural knowledge—
> These are the benefits of interest. (XI, 8)

Interest unadulterated by counteragents, if not hindered, leads to direct realization of the nature of phenomena and attainment of the first bodhisattva level.

Interest in the lesser vehicles, if not interrupted by anything else, leads to the attainment of nirvāṇa, the goal of peace for oneself.

Interest in the Great Vehicle, if unobstructed, yields the supreme attainment of both one's own and others' goals.

Unobscured interest, diligent interest, interest with accumulated merit, firmly engaged interest, and advanced interest (five in all), if free of obstruct-

---

4. Tib. *de ma thag pa'i ting nge 'dzin*, the concentration immediately preceding the attainment of the path of seeing.

ing conditions, lead to one's gaining the qualities of quick preternatural knowledge. With the first three, one obtains the sharpest faculties, while with the last two one swiftly acquires omniscient gnosis.

These eleven explanations concern the benefits of interest.

For six kinds of interest—mistaken, nonevident, future, obscured, and nondiligent interest, and interest without accumulated merit—the benefits are not described because any possible benefits they might have are included in the benefits of faith; future interest has not yet arisen; and mistaken interest and others constitute obstacles.

Apart from distinguishing each of these benefits individually, you should recognize that in general the benefits of interest are also those of faith, so make an effort to develop faith.

2. Specific Explanation of Interest in the Great Vehicle
a. Showing by Similes the Superiority of Interest in the Great Vehicle

> **The interest of the desirous is like a dog,**
> **That of those with concentration is like a turtle,**
> **That of those who achieve their own goal is like a servant,**
> **And that of those who achieve others' goal is like a king.**
> **(XI, 9)**

A simile for the interest of beings full of desire—inhabitants of the world of desire who are attached to and enjoy the five external sense pleasures—is that it is like a dog. The interest of mundane beings who have abandoned external distractions by means of the concentrations of the worlds of form and formlessness and dwell in states of inner equipoise is like a turtle. The interest of listeners and solitary realizers, who obtain liberation for themselves from the sufferings of saṃsāra, is like a servant. And the interest of bodhisattvas, who benefit all other sentient beings, is like a king.

The meaning of these similes is explained in detail in the next two verses.

> **Just as a dog is constantly tormented by hunger and never satisfied,**
> **A turtle in the water remains completely withdrawn,**
> **A servant moves around, their body always cowed in fear,**
> **And a king governs his dominion by his edicts, (XI, 10)**

> Similarly, you should always distinguish among the various
> 	kinds of interest
> Of those who are distracted, who remain withdrawn, who
> 	benefit themselves, and who bring benefit to others.
> The steadfast who properly understand that interest in the
> 	Great Vehicle is best
> Will, in this context, forever seek that same interest in it.
> (XI, 11)

In what way is interest like a dog? Dogs are constantly hungry, forever afflicted by their desire for food and by the lack of it; their appetites are insatiable. A turtle, fearful of the other creatures in the water, retreats into its shell and stays there. The servant of a king or other master goes about the tasks their master has set them with their body constantly cowed, out of fear of displeasing or disobeying him. And a king, with the orders he gives, maintains his authority over the lands under his dominion as he pleases.

In the same way, taking these similes in order, the inhabitants of the world of desire, like dogs, spend their whole time in carefree distraction, indulging in the pleasures of the senses; dominated by their desires, they wander helplessly.

Those in the two higher worlds, afraid of being distracted from the experience of those states, concentrate their mental functions inward and dwell only on that, with no mental affinity for the profound and extensive Dharma that teaches the nature of knowable phenomena. The interest they have is like a turtle drawn into its shell.

The listeners and solitary realizers, who devote themselves only to benefiting themselves, are terrified of the sufferings of saṃsāra. They are afraid that if they slightly transgress the precepts of the Tathāgata, the Sovereign of the Dharma, which constitute the means for attaining liberation from that saṃsāra, the path to liberation will be obscured and they will obtain unpleasant fully ripened effects. So they apply great effort to the means for swiftly liberating themselves from saṃsāra. Their interest is like that of a servant.

The bodhisattvas' interest is like a king. Just as a king has dominion over his kingdom on account of his accumulation of merit in the past, bodhisattvas, because of their great wisdom and compassion, are untainted by the defects of saṃsāra even though they dwell in saṃsāra. And while they do not dwell in the one-sided extreme of peace, they have, rather, transcended the state of peace. They thus have dominion over both saṃsāra and nirvāṇa, and they fulfill the perfect goal of benefiting both themselves and all other sentient beings, now and forever. So the bodhisattva's interest is far superior to the interests of mundane beings in the world of desire and in the two higher worlds and of supramundane beings like listeners and solitary realizers. For this reason, of all the different varieties of interest in beings' natures, you should always know that bodhisattvas' interest, their faith in the Great Vehicle, is *the* most exalted. Because they know that, steadfast bodhisattvas have properly understood that interest in the Great Vehicle taught by the Buddha is superior to others, and, in this context of setting out on the path with interest, they are forever pursuing interest in the teachings of the Great Vehicle.

This explanation illustrating the superiority of such interest is followed by instructions on following the Great Vehicle enthusiastically without getting discouraged, which has three parts: (1) following the Great Vehicle without getting discouraged; (2) following it enthusiastically because it gives rise to immense merit; and (3) a summary on following the Great Vehicle in terms of three virtues.

b. Instructions on Following the Great Vehicle Enthusiastically without Getting Discouraged
i. Following the Great Vehicle without Getting Discouraged

> **Sentient beings born as humans,**
> **In infinite numbers, in every instant,**
> **Attain perfect enlightenment,**
> **So do not give in to losing heart. (XI, 12)**

In the Great Vehicle, when one is on the path, one has to willingly assume the difficult practices of giving away one's head and limbs and so forth and of having no fear with regard to the sufferings of saṃsāra, and it is by doing so that one accomplishes the result, buddhahood, with all its marvelous qualities. Nevertheless, you should never be discouraged and think, "This is the domain of a few great beings; how can an ordinary human being like me achieve that?" Why? "Sentient beings born as humans" are the best support for accomplishing enlightenment. They are superior in this respect even to those born as celestial beings. Humans do attain buddhahood, and not just some, not just a few. Many infinite human beings have attained buddhahood. Nor is this possible only occasionally. Right now, with every instant that passes, in the boundless universes in the ten directions, there are infinite bodhisattvas attaining unsurpassable perfect enlightenment. So never give in to losing heart and thinking, "I'll never be able to get enlightened." Instead, encourage yourself as follows: "In being born human, I am just the same as other human beings. By training gradually on the Mahāyāna path from the stage of earnest aspiration onward, they gain the power of wisdom and compassion: they understand the sufferings of saṃsāra to be like magical illusions, and they perfect the force of great compassion that never, ever abandons sentient beings. At that time, not only do they not think of the bodhisattva's practice as being difficult, but they experience the greatest, purest joy, with which no mundane bliss can possibly compare, and they attain the great goal, buddhahood. Why should I not do likewise? Those bodhisattvas also started off as ordinary beings like myself, but after following the teachings of the Great Vehicle, that is how they have ended up."

ii. Following the Great Vehicle Enthusiastically because It Gives Rise to Immense Merit

> Just as merit grows
> From giving food to others
> But not from eating food oneself,
> The greater merit of which the sūtras speak (XI, 13)
>
> Is acquired from teaching
> The way of altruistic aims
> And not from teaching
> The way that is based on selfish goals. (XI, 14)

If simply having an initial interest in the Mahāyāna teachings is a source of boundless benefits, one need hardly mention the benefits of practicing them properly. Why should that be so? Because they are the teachings that show how to achieve others' goals. Just as there is increasing merit in giving food to other beings but none in eating food oneself, teaching others the Great Vehicle, the path that is the basis for helping other sentient beings, and developing interest in the Great Vehicle oneself give rise to the greater merit that has been mentioned in the sūtras. The benefit acquired by expounding a single verse of the Mahāyāna teachings, for example, is far superior to that of offering to the tathāgatas infinite buddha fields filled with the seven precious attributes of royalty. Likewise, although there are certainly excellent benefits to be derived from teaching the lower vehicles that are the basis for one's own good, they do not procure benefits like those of teaching the Great Vehicle.

iii. A Summary on Following the Great Vehicle in Terms of Three Virtues

> And thus, if the wise constantly increase their interest
> In the vast doctrine of the great noble ones,
> They will gain immense and uninterrupted merit, their interest will grow,
> And they will attain buddhahood with all its boundless qualities. (XI, 15)

Thus, if wise bodhisattvas constantly develop greater interest in the extensive Dharma, the path of "the great noble beings" (that is, of the noble beings of the Great Vehicle), an unbroken stream of immense merit will be produced. Their interest will grow greater and greater up to the tenth level. And finally, they will attain unsurpassable great enlightenment, with all its boundless good qualities.

This completes the explanation of the eleventh chapter of *Ornament of the Mahāyāna Sūtras*, the chapter on the attitude—faith or interest in the Great Vehicle.

12

Thorough Investigation

On its own, interest, as described in the previous chapter, is not sufficient. It is necessary to use the wisdom gained through listening, reflecting, and meditating to investigate what one is interested in—namely, the profound and extensive teachings of the Great Vehicle—so that one acquires a wide knowledge of the teachings and gains certainty as to what they mean. This is why there now follows the chapter on investigating the Dharma, which has five sections: (1) the Dharma that has to be investigated; (2) the different forms of attentiveness used in investigation; (3) specific kinds of thorough investigation; (4) the results of investigating the Dharma; and (5) a concluding summary verse.

1. The Dharma That Has to Be Investigated

This section has two parts: (1) investigating the Dharma of transmission that is to be expounded and (2) investigating the Dharma whose meaning is to be realized. The first of these is divided into three: (1) thorough investigation of the subject, the Buddha's Excellent Words; (2) thorough investigation in discovering the point, the meaning indicated by the three scriptural collections; and (3) thorough investigation of the investigator, attentiveness.

a. Investigating the Dharma of Transmission That Is to Be Expounded
i. Thorough Investigation of the Subject, the Buddha's Excellent Words

> The scriptural collections are summarized as two or three,
> The reasons for which are held to be ninefold.
> Through habitual inclination, understanding, pacification,
> And full realization, they bring one to perfect liberation. (XII, 1)

The subject that we have to examine with the three kinds of wisdom is the Dharma that comprises the collections of the Buddha's Excellent Words. The Sanskrit word *piṭaka*, meaning a basket, is used for these collections because a great many topics are collected within them. In India the term is also used for a large measure, capable of holding many small measures. And in this context too, what we call the scriptural collections include numerous topics.

The categories of these collections may be summarized as three—the Sūtra Collection, Vinaya Collection, and Abhidharma Collection—or, alternatively, as two: namely, the bodhisattvas' collection, or Great Vehicle, and the listeners' collection, or Lesser Vehicle. The etymological definition of the term "collection"—as something in which numerous points are collected—has just been explained.

A detailed classification of the Buddha's Excellent Words comprises twelve branches, described as condensed, melodious, prophetic, verse, spoken with a purpose, contextual, biographical, historical, concerning his past lives, very detailed, marvelous, and establishing a truth. Of these, the very detailed teachings and those concerning his past lives belong to the bodhisattvas' collection, and of the rest there are some that are for the most part common to the Listeners' Vehicle and Great Vehicle and some that belong mainly to the listeners' collection. These twelve branches are all included in the three collections.

The Reasons for Defining Three Scriptural Collections

The reasons for defining three collections are held to be nine: three with regard to elimination, three with regard to the training, and three with regard to knowledge.

The first of these concern the dispelling of three defilements. The antidote that dispels the defilement of doubt[1] with regard to phenomena such as the aggregates, sense spheres, and senses-and-fields is the Sūtra Collection. For those who do not understand the general and specific characteristics of the aggregates, the sense spheres, the senses-and-fields, dependent arising, the truths, the levels, the transcendent perfections, and so forth, and who are uncertain about them, the Sūtra Collection defines and describes these topics, so that they definitely understand them and are freed of their doubts.

The Vinaya is the antidote that dispels the secondary defilements related

---

1. Tib. *the tshom*, often also translated as "indecision" or "hesitation."

to the pursuit of two extremes—merit-sapping pleasures[2] and debilitating austerities.[3] In order to prevent his disciples from acting, through attachment to pleasure, like laypeople in the pleasurable use of all kinds of fault-associated articles, the Buddha forbade activities that give rise, through wrong, worldly behavior, to radical defeats, residual faults, downfalls, minor faults, and the like.[4] He did permit the basic necessities for living, such as the alms bowl and the Dharma robes, which are not associated with negative activity. Any harmless articles[5] that contribute to physical well-being, acting as antidotes to ascetic practices that inflict fatigue and pain on one's body, such as the tīrthikas' penances, lying on hot ashes or thorns, going naked, fasting, and acting like a dog or a cow, are permitted for all who have taken ordination. Fully ordained monks who keep the vows and possess good qualities are permitted to enjoy delicious food, wear richly designed clothes, and stay in beautifully designed and decorated mansions with many rooms. Even if they enjoy such pleasures, there is no fault in their conduct provided that they are free of attachment and self-importance. On the other hand, if they have any attachment and self-importance, then even the observance of eating stale, unappetizing food and wearing robes made of rags picked off refuse heaps and the like constitutes faulty conduct. Thus, in the avoidance of articles that lead to faults and the use of things in which there is no fault, the Vinaya is the antidote that dispels the two extremes.

The Abhidharma Collection is the antidote to arrogant, self-centered views. What we call arrogant view is being proud of having received just a little bit of teaching and being attached to lax discipline, as a result of which one does not seek much teaching from a spiritual master. Since the general and specific characteristics of phenomena are determined in the Abhidharma, by studying it one will get rid of the different kinds of arrogance resulting from distorted views and inverted discipline and eliminate all sorts of wrong views.

Next, with regard to the training, there are the three trainings. The training in superior discipline comprises the perfect discipline of the prātimokṣa

---

2. Tib. *'dod pa bsod nyams kyi mtha'*, attachment to pleasure as a result of which one's merit declines.

3. Tib. *dka' tshegs ngal dub kyi mtha'*.

4. These refer to the precepts of full monastic ordination—namely, the four radical defeats, thirteen residual faults, thirty downfalls requiring rejection, four faults to be specifically confessed (not mentioned here), and the one hundred and twelve wrong actions (or minor faults). See *Treasury of Precious Qualities*, 290.

5. Tib. *yo byad sdig med*, articles free of negative actions and therefore karmically harmless.

common to all vehicles and the Mahāyāna discipline of avoiding negative actions, gathering virtue, and benefiting beings. The training in superior concentration comprises the eight common concentrations of the dhyānas and formless absorptions[6] and the uncommon concentrations of the bodhisattvas, such as the concentration of Brave Progression. And the training in superior wisdom comprises the four noble truths common to all vehicles and the extraordinary nonceptual gnosis of the Great Vehicle. All these three trainings are presented in the Sūtra Collection. The trainings in discipline and concentration are set forth in the Vinaya, for if one conducts oneself in accordance with what appears in the Vinaya, one is keeping discipline, and through having nothing to regret and so forth, one will gradually achieve concentration.[7] The Abhidharma determines without error the general and specific characteristics of phenomena, and it is from this that wisdom, the correct knowledge of the characteristics of phenomena, is born.

In terms of knowledge, we speak of two aspects to the explanations in the Sūtra Collection—the terms and the topics; or alternatively, the topics (the aggregates, sense spheres, senses-and-fields, and so forth) and their meanings (the four kinds of implied teachings and four kinds of indirect teachings); or again, the basic way (the ten positive actions by which one attains the higher realms) and the ultimate way (the thirty-seven elements leading to enlightenment and so on by which one attains nirvāṇa).[8] These are explained in the Sūtra Collection. The Vinaya is said to accomplish both these aspects, for by being diligent in subduing the defilements one actualizes them both or puts them into practice and thereby accomplishes them. And by means of the Abhidharma, which teaches these two without error and ascertains them definitively, one masters one's knowledge of them.

---

6. Tib. *bsam gzugs kyi ting 'dzin brgyad*, the concentrations of the four dhyānas of the world of form and of the four absorptions of the formless world.

7. Sthiramati: "If one keeps discipline, one will have no regrets; if one has nothing to regret, one gains physical relaxation; if one is physically relaxed, one will experience states of bliss; when one experiences states of bliss, the mind will become one-pointed, and one will thus achieve concentration."

8. The Tibetan terms for the two aspects referred to in this paragraph are respectively *chos* and *don*, both words with a wide range of meaning, as can be seen from the three alternative meanings given here. It is clearly impossible to provide a single English translation for either of them in this context.

The Purpose of Investigating the Teachings in the Three Scriptural Collections

It is by thoroughly investigating the three collections and putting them into practice using the three kinds of wisdom that one's mind stream is brought to perfect liberation. Listening plants in one's mind stream a habitual inclination for the path to liberation. Reflection brings understanding through one's gaining certainty with regard to the meaning of the collections. And meditation based on sustained calm pacifies distracting thoughts and, through profound insight, results in full realization of thatness.

Points by Which the Three Scriptural Collections Are Classified, and Their Etymological Definition

> Sūtra, Abhidharma, and Vinaya
> Are considered to comprise, in brief, four points.
> The wise who know these
> Will obtain omniscience. (XII, 2)

The Sūtras, Vinaya, and Abhidharma, if considered in brief, are each held to comprise four points. A wise bodhisattva, by gaining a thorough knowledge of all three collections of the Great and Lesser Vehicles and training on the path will attain omniscience. The listeners do not seek omniscience and therefore do not know the entirety of the three collections, but even by knowing the meaning of a single verse that teaches just the individual no-self, they will, with their own path, obtain the gnosis of exhaustion and nonarising.[9]

What are the four points that summarize each of the three collections?

> Because they relate the settings, nature,
> Subjects, and meanings, they are the "sūtras."
> Because it makes increasingly manifest, does so repeatedly,
> Overpowers, and brings understanding, it is the
>   Abhidharma. (XII, 3)

---

9. Tib. *zad mi skye shes pa'i ye shes*. This is the listeners' ultimate wisdom, their equivalent of the Mahāyāna's omniscience (*thams cad mkhyen pa*), resulting from the exhaustion of defilements and the fact that they will no longer arise.

The Sūtra Collection is summarized by the following four points: (1) the "setting," by which is meant the situation or historical background in which a sūtra originated, which comprises three points—the place where a teaching was given (Śrāvastī, for example), the buddha who expounded it, and the disciples who requested the teaching and for whom it was given; (2) the nature of the two truths; (3) subjects such as the aggregates, sense spheres, senses-and-fields, and dependent arising; and (4) their meanings, divided into implied and explicit, indirect, and so on. Because these are mentioned concisely, we speak of "sūtras," the Sanskrit word *sūtra* signifying that they contain these points in a complete and condensed (or "packaged") form.

The Sanskrit word *abhi* means "manifest."[10] (1) *Abhimukha* means "increasingly manifest." By unmistakenly determining the meaning of the truths, the elements leading to enlightenment, dependent arising, and so forth, the Abhidharma makes nirvāṇa increasingly manifest. (2) Similarly, it clearly demonstrates phenomena, repeatedly dividing and subdividing each one into different categories—material and immaterial, tainted and untainted, and so on. (3) By means of logical discussion and debate, it manifestly outshines all opponents. And (4) by means of reasoning and ascertainment it determines the points in the sūtras, so that they are clearly understood. For these reasons, we speak of the "Abhidharma."

> Because there are downfalls, and there is their source,
> Their recovery, and certain deliverance,
> And with regard to the individual, the edict,
> Detailed description, and definition, it is the Vinaya. (XII, 4)

The Vinaya, meaning "that which tames," is classified by means of the following four points:

(1) Five classes of downfalls: the radical defeats, residual faults, gross faults, downfalls,[11] and faults to be specifically confessed; or alternatively, radical defeats, residual faults, downfalls, faults to be specifically confessed, and wrong actions.

---

10. Tib. *mngon pa*. In the sentences that follow, we have also used the synonym "clear" in its adverbial form, "clearly."

11. Tib. *ltung byed*. These are specific breaches for fully ordained monks—as distinct from "downfalls" (Tib. *ltung ba*) as a general term for all faults in discipline; they include "downfalls requiring rejection" and "mere downfalls."

(2) The cause for these downfalls arising or occurring, which is fourfold: ignorance of the characteristics of these downfalls; defilements; carelessness; and failure to respect the precepts.

(3) Recovery from downfalls—by feeling regret from reflecting on what one has done and by vowing never to commit them in the future.

(4) Deliverance from downfalls or certain deliverance, of which there are seven aspects, as follows.

Confession. This is to openly acknowledge and confess in the presence of one or four or more fully ordained monks.

Accepting what one has to do as punishment. After committing a radical defeat, without the intention of concealing it, and subsequently feeling regret, a monk confesses it and is made to accept the punishment—being sent to the end of the row of all the monks and given his food last, and so on. He is thus given the precepts again.

Deliverance by dispensation. An example of this is that although Lord Buddha did not allow eating after midday, in certain circumstances he gave monks permission to eat at other specified times.

"Waiver." It is said that Lord Buddha once said to Ānanda, "When I pass into nirvāṇa, remember that apart from the fundamental precepts that I have laid down, the minor precepts may be waived." However, when the Buddha passed into nirvāṇa, Ānanda, overcome with grief, did not manage to inquire about this. Subsequently, Mahākāśyapa and the other compilers of the teachings said to him, "Why didn't you ask?" and punished him. Based on the Buddha's saying, "The minor precepts are to be waived," according to the Sarvāstivādin tradition the assembled Saṅgha can apparently grant exemption from the minor precepts. But in fact there has never been any exemption by the Saṅgha from the precepts in the past, nor is there at present. This is as stated in Sthiramati's *Great Commentary*.

Transformation of the body.[12] This refers to downfalls of fully ordained monks or nuns who have changed sex. For monks there are four radical defeats and for nuns there are eight radical defeats; monks have fewer defeats and downfalls, while nuns have more.[13] Take the case of a monk who changes sex into a nun. He may have committed a downfall when he

---

12. Tib. *gnas sam rten 'gyur ba*. The body is the location (*gnas*) or support (*rten*) of the prātimokṣa vows.

13. Fully ordained monks, or bhikṣus, must observe 253 precepts; fully ordained nuns, or bhikṣuṇīs, must observe 364 precepts.

was a monk, but if it is not a downfall common to both monks and nuns and is one that can be confessed only by a monk, because of having changed into a woman he will be delivered from the fault even if he has not performed the ritual of confessing the fault. The same principle applies to a nun who changes sex.[14]

Deliverance through correct realization. By examining the four summaries of the Dharma—compounded phenomena are impermanent, and so on—and, with wisdom, seeing the truth in them, one will be delivered from minor wrongdoings.

Certain deliverance by attaining ultimate reality. When one sees the truth,[15] one is liberated from the minor faults one committed in the past, and by attaining ultimate reality, in which state future misdeeds are impossible, one will be delivered from downfalls.

As well as these four points, there are four other points that are used in classifying the Vinaya: (1) The person for whom a precept was prescribed. For example, it was for Sudinna that the precept prohibiting sexual intercourse was prescribed for the first time. (2) The edict. When the monks told Lord Buddha that someone had committed such and such a fault, he spoke to the Saṅgha members and prescribed a precept as follows: "O monks, from now on monks are not allowed to do such and such a thing." (3) The detailed description of the edict. This comprises a precise and detailed explanation of the precept. And (4) an exact or conclusive definition, for each of the five groups of downfalls, of the point at which something will or will not constitute a downfall.

All this defines the Vinaya.

ii. Thorough Investigation in Discovering the Point, the Meaning Indicated by the Three Scriptural Collections

We have so far seen that the subject to be investigated is the three scriptural collections, the Dharma of transmission. We now have to look into discovering the point, as shown in the next three verses.

---

14. The monk's vow to abstain from sexual intercourse with a woman, for example, is not a precept common to both monks and nuns, because for a nun sexual intercourse with a woman does not constitute a radical defeat. Killing, on the other hand, is a radical defeat for both monks and nuns.

15. I.e., when one is an ārya, a noble being on the noble path.

The point is held to be
The teachings, the inner, the outer, and both.
Two are discovered through two processes,
And both by nonconceptuality. (XII, 5)

Because, by means of mental verbalization, one has faith in
    the meaning as it is taught,
Because one understands that the things that appear as objects
Do so on account of such verbalization,
And because the mind dwells on the nominal— (XII, 6)

With the three wisdoms of listening and so on,
One will discover the point of the teachings.
Discovering the other three points
Fully depends on those teachings, which were mentioned
    earlier. (XII, 7)

Here "discovering the point" means "realizing the point." In what way? Having investigated and discovered our subject, the teachings, we determine their meaning and know them to mean this or that.

There are held to be four objects of investigation here: (1) The different teachings in the Mahāyāna scriptural collections are the object of the three wisdoms—those that come from listening, reflecting, and meditating. (2) The inner object comprises one's own aggregates or the six apprehending inner sense powers. (3) The outer object comprises the six apprehended outer sense fields not included in one's own mind stream. (4) "Both" refers to the phenomena of the defilement and purity aspects included in both outer and inner.

Of these, two points (not conceptualizing outer and inner objects) are discovered by means of two processes: proper consideration of the outer apprehended object and of the inner apprehending subject. That is, when the suchness of the outer object is realized, one discovers the outer point, and when one directly recognizes the suchness of the inner object, one discovers the inner point. The discovery that there are no apprehended objects apart from the mind is the discovery that occurs at the stage of acceptance, and the discovery that there is no existent apprehending subject is the discovery that occurs at the stage of the supreme mundane level.

How is the suchness of "both" discovered? When one has no concepts of subject and object, one realizes suchness directly and attains the first level; one thus discovers the point of both and discovers the nonconceptual suchness of all phenomena. At the stages of warmth and crown or peak, the direct realization of ultimate reality is not acquired, so the teachings do not speak of "discovering the point" at these stages. I think this is because actually discovering the point implies direct realization free of the uncertainties associated with an indirect understanding of suchness.[16] Although in emptiness there are no distinctions at all, as far as phenomena are concerned,[17] we use the conventional terms of discovering the point of outer realization, of inner realization, and of both.

As for the manner in which one discovers the point of the teachings, by means of "mental verbalization"—that is, with the conceptual mind—one acquires great mental clarity or faith with regard to the points explained in the texts of the scriptural collections, and one then retains their meaning accordingly. This is what we call "discovering the point of the teachings with the wisdom that comes from listening." By listening attentively to the teachings given by a preceptor or instructor and thinking about the meaning, one gains confidence, knowing, when the teacher says, for example, "All these names, phrases, and letters are only appearances in the mind," that that is how it is.

Phenomena such as pillars and vases are merely labeled as such as a result of the habits of mental expression, and apart from that, their ultimately true nature is inexpressible: they are nothing more than one's own conceptual structures. To understand this with the wisdom that comes from reflection is to discover the point of the teachings with the wisdom that comes from reflection.

The mind related to the wisdom of meditation "dwells on the nominal"—that is, name as opposed to form[18]—whose basis is the mind and mental factors. In brief, all phenomena are appearances in the mind; they are imputed by the mind and established by the power of the mind. There is nothing else that exists apart from that, and they are therefore only mind. This mind dwells in suchness free of dualistic concepts of subject and object, empty and radiant. This, then, is to discover the point of the teachings with the wisdom that comes from meditating.

---

16. I.e., the indirect understanding of suchness that one has on the stages of warmth and peak before gaining direct realization.

17. Tib. *chos can*.

18. "Name" (Tib. *ming*) refers to the immaterial as opposed to the material (*gzugs*).

Thus, with the three wisdoms that come from listening, reflecting, and meditating one will discover the point of the teachings of the scriptural collections. First, by means of the names one hears, the meanings they express are conveyed to the mind. Then, by reflecting on those meanings, one acquires certainty. Finally, by meditating on them, one directly experiences them. It is by means of these three that one discovers the point or true meaning of the sacred Dharma.

The three aspects (outer, inner, and both) of discovering the point depend entirely on discovering the point of the teachings, which earlier were mentioned first, because if, having listened to the teachings and reflected on their meaning, one does not meditate on them, it is impossible to realize suchness, the nonconceptual nature of outer, inner, and both.

iii. Thorough Investigation of the Investigator, Attentiveness

This topic is covered by the next five verses.

> **The three families, the performance of deeds,**
> **Having an impaired or unimpaired support,**
> **Maintaining interest, and furthermore**
> **Acting with intense keenness; (XII, 8)**

Once one has discovered the point, it is necessary to acquire concentration by repeatedly keeping it in mind,[19] so this will now be explained. There are eighteen categories of yogis' attentiveness, beginning with attentiveness associated with the three families, attentiveness in performing deeds, and so forth. The first of these, "the three families," is a brief introduction, and the remainder comprise a detailed explanation of particular kinds of attentiveness:

(1) Attentiveness associated with the three families. The three families are those of the listeners, solitary realizers, and followers of the Great Vehicle. Those who have the fixed potential of the listeners consider and keep in mind the four noble truths. Those who have the fixed potential of the solitary realizers consider and keep in mind dependent arising, which is the

---

19. Throughout this section, the Tibetan expression *yid la byed pa* has been translated either as "attentiveness" or as "keep in mind."

teaching related to their path. Those who have the fixed potential of the bodhisattvas consider and keep in mind the two kinds of no-self.

(2) Attentiveness associated with performing activities. This is indicated by "the performance of deeds" and refers to performing deeds that accumulate merit. It is the attentiveness of those on the level of earnest aspiration who are accumulating merit and wisdom for a single measureless kalpa, which leads to attaining the first bodhisattva level.

(3) Attentiveness associated with different kinds of supports or conditions. This is shown by "having an impaired or unimpaired support." Impaired supports or situations are those of laypeople: the abundance of their worldly activities adversely affects their attentiveness. The opposite is true for those who have taken monastic ordination and who therefore have unimpaired supports.

(4) Attentiveness associated with maintaining interest is indicated by "maintaining interest." It is by remembering the Buddha that one maintains one's interest. This involves recalling the Buddha's extensive qualities as mentioned in the sūtras or remembering the Buddha in seven ways as summarized in the *Compendium of the Great Vehicle* as follows: (a) remembering that since the buddha bhagavāns possess the preternatural power of unimpededly entering all worlds, they have mastery over all phenomena; (b) remembering that the tathāgatas possess the eternal body, which is forever uncontaminated; (c) remembering that similarly, because they have eliminated all the defilement-related and cognitive obscurations, the tathāgatas are free of shameful deeds; (d) remembering that all the tathāgatas' deeds are spontaneous and unceasing; (e) remembering that the tathāgatas have dominion over great untainted riches such as pure buddha fields; (f) remembering that the tathāgatas are unstained—that is, untainted by the defects of the eight ordinary preoccupations; and (g) remembering that, since they bring sentient beings to maturation and liberation by skillfully displaying perfect enlightenment and the parinirvāṇa, the tathāgatas are great benefactors.

(5) Attentiveness associated with enthusiasm. This is indicated by "furthermore acting with intense keenness," which is different from the previous one. Having recalled the Buddha, one has an intense, keen confidence in him—that is, confidence that the Buddha is the ultimate refuge, has exhausted all defects, has perfected all good qualities, spontaneously accomplishes the two goals, and possesses the three buddha bodies; confidence that the Dharma is the authentic teaching for realizing the path and the

cessation; and confidence that the members of the Saṅgha who are following the authentic path will cross the swamp of saṃsāra and are true objects of offering.

> Inferior and complete supports
> Which are verbal and nonverbal;
> Equivalent to knowledge,
> Having the cause and nature of yoga; (XII, 9)

(6) Attentiveness associated with remaining in concentration. This is indicated by "inferior and complete supports which are verbal and nonverbal." There are two kinds of supports or conditions: one that relies on the "all-sufficing preparation" of the first dhyāna and is termed "inferior," and one that relies on the actual concentration of dhyāna, from the first to the fourth, and is termed "complete." For the actual concentration of dhyāna, the preparatory stages and the rudimentary stage of the first dhyāna have both gross and subtle discursiveness and are therefore termed "verbal"—verbal because the causal factor that activates speech is gross and subtle discursiveness. The extraordinary actual first dhyāna, which is free of gross discursiveness but still possesses subtle discursiveness, also belongs to the first category. The actual concentrations of the second dhyāna onward are free of both gross and subtle discursiveness and therefore termed "nonverbal." Sthiramati's commentary states that the preparatory stage and the first dhyāna possess both gross and subtle discursiveness; in the second and intermediate dhyānas there is no gross discursiveness but there is subtle discursiveness; and the third and fourth constitute concentration with neither gross nor subtle discursiveness.

(7) Attentiveness associated with knowledge. This is indicated by "equivalent to knowledge, having the cause and nature of yoga," which appears in Sthiramati's commentary as "That which perfectly possesses gnosis, the nature of yoga and its cause." The state of mind that is equivalent to, or perfectly endowed with, the gnosis or knowledge that arises through meditation is what we call the attentiveness associated with knowledge. That knowledge is the nature of yoga or of sustained calm and profound insight, whose cause is associated with the wisdom that comes from listening and reflecting. In short, the yoga of sustained calm and profound insight meditation that comes from the immaculate cause of listening and reflecting is the attentiveness associated with knowledge.

> **Considering things in combination**
> **And considering them separately,**
> **In five ways and seven;**
> **Fivefold complete knowledge of this;** (XII, 10)

(8) Attentiveness associated with considering the teachings in combination. This is indicated by "considering things in combination . . . in five ways." Considering the teachings in combination takes five forms: considering them summarized from the sūtras; considering them together in a summary or synoptic verse; considering them together in introductory instructions; considering them together in points one has committed to memory; and considering them together in an explanation. Of these five, the first consists of (a) summarizing the topics taught in the sūtras—the *Sūtra of the Ten Levels*, for example—and keeping them in mind in a general manner; (b) summarizing the topics taught in each chapter into a few points and in that way keeping them in mind; (c) summarizing the main subject in the form of a general outline comprising, for example, the introduction, main body of the text, and concluding summary, and considering that; (d) condensing the points of meditation that one has memorized into a simple point; and (e) in teaching others, condensing the teachings in the same way.

In short, this is to keep in mind the topics of the sūtras, the intermediate summaries or synoptic verses, and introductory summaries, and to keep in mind the points one has heard and that one teaches similarly condensed.

The points taught in all the Mahāyāna sūtras can be condensed into two: profound and extensive. The profound teachings can be summarized as suchness devoid of dualistic conceptual constructs such as subject and object, and self and other. Even though they are extensively explained in terms of different aspects, ultimately that is what they boil down to. The extensive teachings can all be summarized as ground, path, and result. The ground includes the two truths; the path includes the two accumulations; and the result includes the two buddha bodies. Thus the teachings are considered in combination.

(9) Attentiveness associated with considering things separately. This is indicated by "considering them separately . . . in seven [ways]." There are seven different ways in which things are considered separately: (a) considering names—"pillar" and "pot," for example; (b) considering phrases—indicating particularities by combining them with names (a *tall* pillar, a *new* pot, for example); and (c) considering letters—con-

sidering the consonants and vowels that are the basic components of all names.

Here one is considering these three different categories of expresser, considering that in any sūtra there are so many phrases, names, and letters indicating this and that meaning. There are no treatises, mundane or supramundane, that comprise anything other than names, phrases, and letters. Although they indicate meanings, they do so by the power of the mind's communicative activity: all names, phrases, and letters originate from the mind and are mere labels imputed by the mind. It is in the knowledge of this that they are applied to things that are inexpressible.[20]

From the point of view of what these three express, with regard to the fully present reality, there are two categories: (d) considering the no-self of the individual and (e) considering the no-self of phenomena. And with regard to the dependent reality: (f) considering that material phenomena and the body, which constitute the dependent reality appearing as the object, are respectively multiple and impermanent, and impure and subject to suffering; and (g) considering that the immaterial mind and mental factors, which constitute the dependent reality appearing as the subject, are suffering and impermanence.

(10) Attentiveness associated with the certainty of complete knowledge is indicated by "fivefold complete knowledge of this." Complete knowledge of the object of concentration is fivefold: (a) the basis that is to be completely known, which is the four truths; (b) the points that are to be completely known, which are their sixteen subdivisions—impermanence and the others; (c) the means for gaining complete knowledge, which is the two paths of seeing and meditation; (d) the result of complete knowledge, which is perfect liberation; and (e) the perfect knowledge of that perfect liberation, which is to see the gnosis that sees perfect liberation. Stated otherwise, having considered the five perpetuating aggregates (the basis), one knows that they are in fact suffering, impermanence, no-self, and emptiness. What makes one know this perfectly is the eightfold noble path—in other words, perfect knowledge comes on the paths of seeing and meditation. The result attained by that path is the perfect liberation of the mind through the elimination of defilements. And there arises the gnosis that beholds that perfect liberation. In fact, this refers to complete knowledge of the four noble truths.

---

20. For example, we use language to talk about such inexpressible topics as emptiness.

Objects associated with meditation—
Fourfold and thirty-sevenfold;
The nature of the two paths;
Two benefits, receiving, (XII, 11)

(11) Attentiveness associated with the object of meditation, which is indicated by "objects associated with meditation." The four objects of meditation (or objects associated with meditation) are meditation on the individual no-self, meditation on the no-self of phenomena, meditation on the object of seeing, and meditation on the object of knowing. Of these, the first—realizing that the five aggregates are impermanent and so on[21]—is also what the listeners meditate on. The second—that all phenomena are devoid of intrinsic nature—is what bodhisattvas meditate on. Seeing refers to the eight instants of acceptance (of the sixteen instants of gnosis on the path of seeing), and knowing to the eight instants of knowing. Alternatively, seeing can refer to sustained calm and knowing to profound insight.

The thirty-seven objects of meditation are the thirty-seven elements leading to enlightenment, which are as follows. The four close mindfulnesses comprise mindfulness of the body and impurity; of feelings and suffering; of the mind and impermanence; and of consciousness and the fact that all phenomena are devoid of self.

The four genuine restraints are (a) training in attainment, that is, in developing the three superior trainings where they have not yet been developed; (b) training in stability, that is, further developing and enriching the three trainings once they have been developed; (c) "training in expulsion," that is, being diligent in eliminating any counteragents to the three trainings that may arise; and (d) "training in the antidote," that is, meditation on ugliness, love, and dependent arising in order to prevent any negative factors from arising.[22]

Next, there are the four bases of miraculous powers: keenness, which is to keep in mind the antidote to complacency; diligence, keeping in mind the antidote to distraction and doubt; mindfulness, keeping in mind the antidote to mental excitation by concentrating the mind; and analysis, keeping in mind the antidote to dullness and low spirits.

21. Tib. *mi rtag sogs bzhi*, i.e., impermanent, suffering, empty, and no-self.
22. As Sthiramati points out, meditation on ugliness is the antidote to attachment, meditation on love is the antidote to aversion, and meditation on interdependence is the antidote to bewilderment.

Of the five powers that are the object of meditation, faith is to keep confidence in mind. Similarly, diligence is to make effort, mindfulness is to not forget, concentration is to stabilize the mind, and wisdom is to discern perfectly.

Keeping in mind the five irresistible forces is what overcomes counteragents to these five powers.

As for the seven elements of the path of enlightenment, in the case where enlightenment means the gnosis of exhaustion and nonarising,[23] they are the seven elements, beginning with mindfulness, that lead to that. Alternatively, they are the seven elements (mindfulness and the others) that lead to enlightenment in the sense of the nondual gnosis attained on the path of seeing. These constitute what has been described as "the meditation in which authentic enlightenment dawns."[24] These seven elements leading to enlightenment are (a) unforgetting mindfulness as an element leading to perfect enlightenment; (b) the perfect discernment of phenomena as an element leading to enlightenment, and which knows things without error; (c) diligence, that is, delight in virtue; (d) joy, a happy frame of mind; (e) serviceability and fitness in body and mind; (f) evenness, resting in a state of equilibrium; and (g) concentration, a settled state of mind.

The eightfold noble path is comprised of the following elements: (a) Right view is referred to[25] as training in freedom from doubt. It particularly involves meditating repeatedly, on the different levels of the path of meditation, on the expanse of reality that one realized definitively, without any doubt, on the first bodhisattva level. (b) Right thought is referred to as training in realizing the level of complete purification. From the level of earnest aspiration, listening, reflection, and meditation are gradually developed until, on the first bodhisattva level, the expanse of reality is realized directly. This is known as the level of complete purification, because, having risen out of formal meditation, one knows, "By completely purifying myself, I have realized what the expanse of reality is like." (c) Right speech is referred to as training in making other people understand correctly. (d) Right conduct is referred to as training in observing the discipline that the noble beings yearn for, for it is the discipline that pleases the noble beings.[26]

---

23. I.e., the listeners' enlightenment.
24. "Enlightenment" here refers to the realization on the first bodhisattva level.
25. I.e., in Sthiramati's commentary.
26. By means of right conduct, one inspires others, including the noble beings of the lower vehicles, to observe the same discipline.

(e) Right livelihood is referred to as training in cutting back on one's lifestyle, that is, making do with few possessions and avoiding wrong means of livelihood.[27] (f) Right effort is referred to as training in habituation to the path that one has attained by thorough training in previous lives. By practicing from the level of earnest aspiration up to the first bodhisattva level, one acquires, on the first level, superior diligence, and subsequently, up to the tenth level, one cultivates increasingly enhanced diligence. (g) Right mindfulness is referred to as training in not forgetting the special points for abiding in Dharma. When one concentrates one-pointedly on the expanse of reality, which is what is meant here by "Dharma," one trains in not forgetting the three special points or antidotes for dispelling low spirits and wildness, should these occur. The three special points are the special point of sustained calm, the special point of maintaining one's concentration or encouraging oneself, and the special point of equanimity. If the meditation becomes wild, one should calm it by practicing the special point of sustained calm. If low spirits and dullness occur, they should be corrected by concentration on the special point of encouraging oneself. When one is neither low-spirited nor wild, one should keep in mind the special point of equanimity and rest with the mind in its natural state, without movement. (h) Right concentration is referred to as training in the transformed state of meditation without special points. Once one is free of low spirits and wildness, there is no need to rely on the three special points, and one thus acquires the compassion of transformed, effortless meditation.

(12) Attentiveness associated with the nature of the two paths. This is indicated by "the nature of the two paths." The above meditation comprises the two paths of sustained calm and profound insight. Relying on undistracted sustained calm, one then, by means of the profound insight that perfectly discerns phenomena, realizes the nature of phenomena, as it is.

(13) Attentiveness associated with excellence or benefits. This is indicated by "two benefits." Attentiveness has two kinds of benefit: dispelling negative tendencies and dispelling defiled views. Negative tendencies are also of two kinds: physical negative tendencies that lead to negative actions such as killing, taking what is not given, unchaste conduct, lying, and so forth; and mental negative tendencies that move the mind toward attachment, aversion, and bewilderment, which are themselves the causal factors that lead

---

27. Sthiramati explains this as not seeking more than the alms bowl, Dharma robes, and suchlike that are mentioned in the scriptures, and not living by craft and deceit.

to indulging in negative actions. These negative tendencies are dispelled by keeping in mind and assimilating the no-self of phenomena. Defiled views, of which there are five—the view of the transitory composite, the view of extremes, wrong views, and the two views of superiority[28]—are dispelled by assimilation of the individual no-self.

(14) Attentiveness associated with correctly receiving instructions and follow-up teachings.[29] This is indicated by "receiving." Someone who has the Mahāyāna potential, has aroused the bodhicitta, and has attained the concentration of the stream of Dharma[30] on the level of earnest aspiration, then receives (and holds) from the buddhas and bodhisattvas the instructions on the concentration that leads to attaining the first level. This is known as attentiveness associated with correctly receiving.

Application, mastery,
The lesser, and the extensive—
These aspects of yogis' attentiveness
Are held to include everything. (XII, 12)

(15) Attentiveness associated with application. This is indicated by "application." The result of receiving the instructions is their application on the path, and such application is of five kinds.

First is application in investigating numbers. This is to consider how many names, phrases, and letters and how many verses and so forth there are in the instructions one has received—that is, in the texts of the Twelve Branches of Excellent Speech (the sūtras and so forth) that constitute the object of concentration.

Second is application in investigating the two aspects of their occurrence or usage. With regard to the occurrence of the above expressers, letters are the bases or precursors of all names and phrases, and since they comprise just fifty vowels and consonants, letters are considered to be finite in number. Names and phrases are considered to be infinite: there is no limit to their occurrence or usage, for in a scripture such as the *Perfection of Wisdom*

---

28. I.e., doctrinal superiority and ethical superiority. For details of these five defiled views, see *Treasury of Precious Qualities*, 381.

29. Tib. *gdams ngag rjes bstan*. This forms the subject of chapter 15, in which it is considered in detail.

30. See note 2, page 137.

in One Hundred Thousand Lines there are a very great many names and phrases, and there are many hundreds of thousands of sūtras like it.

Third is application in investigating conception. This is to understand unmistakenly the names and phrases of the instructions and so on that one has received ("The name for that is so-and-so, and its meaning is such and such"), associating names and their meanings. For example, when one says or thinks the name "vase," one associates it with its meaning, "a bulbous container for pouring water." On the basis of the general sound-image of the name, its specific characteristics appear as the object of the mind, and from fixating on its specific characteristics, one understands the meaning from the name and conceives the meaning. And when one sees the specific characteristics, one affixes the name to the object-image, thinking, "This is the name for that," and conceives the name.

Fourth is application in investigating order. In the conventional world, once one is accustomed to labeling things with different names—vase, woolen cloth, person, horse, and so forth—when they are mentioned correctly by their respective names, and before fixation on their respective meanings occurs, the thing's name arises in the mind, and from that one conceives the meaning.

These four kinds of application (of investigating numbers and so on) constitute the method, once one has listened to the teachings on the path of accumulation, for discovering the point of the teachings.

Fifth, application in perfect realization refers to the path of joining and subsequent paths, and for this there are eleven categories, whose realization is termed "application in perfect realization." With regard to these eleven categories, there are four on the path of joining, one on the path of seeing, and six comprising two in terms of what is to be realized, two that are superior and inferior, and two as categories of postmeditation.

The four on the path of joining are as follows. At the stage of warmth, one realizes that the imputation of meaning to name and of name to meaning (despite the fact that there is no essential connection between name and meaning) is merely the mind establishing "name" and "meaning" by superimposition. This is known as "the perfect realization that name and meaning arise adventitiously." At the peak stage, one recognizes that the dualistic phenomena of subject and object, although not existing intrinsically as subject and object, appear perceptibly (or actually appear) on account of the mind and mental factors, as if they did exist as such, and that they are merely conceptual structures. They are like the two moons that we perceive when we look at the moon and press one eye. Realizing this is known as "perfect realization of conceptual structures that actually appear." "Conceptual structure" here refers to the cause of appearances and is so termed because it is understood that the cause of such appearances is the mind. At the stage of acceptance, one ceases to conceptualize the six sense objects (or six objects) from forms through to phenomena and does not conceive an apprehended object. This perfect realization is what we call "perfect realization in not conceiving an object." On the supreme mundane level, one fully understands that the six consciousnesses that subjectively apprehend and conceive the six sense objects have no intrinsic existence, and this is known as "perfect realization in not conceiving a conceiver."

Following on immediately from this realization beyond the concepts of both subject and object, one attains the path of seeing and the first bodhisattva level. The realization one has at that time of the all-embracing expanse of reality, the ultimate reality devoid of the duality of subject and object, is termed "perfect realization of the expanse of reality."

On the listeners' path of seeing, there is what we call "perfect realization of the individual no-self." This is the direct realization only of the lack of individual self in the five aggregates and corresponds to the attainment of the result of stream enterer. On the bodhisattvas' path of seeing, there is not only the realization of the individual no-self but also what we call the "perfect realization of the no-self of phenomena," for both the five aggregates and illusion-like appearances are devoid of intrinsic existence.

The "perfect realization of those with limited intentions" refers to listeners who have attained the four results (stream enterer and the others)[31] and to solitary realizers—"limited" because they have achieved only their own goal and have not realized the no-self of phenomena. The "perfect realization of great beings with vast intentions" is that of bodhisattvas on the tenth level and of the tathāgatas, because they have completely realized their own and others' goals and the two kinds of no-self.

"Perfect realization of the arrangement of the qualities of assimilation" refers to assimilating the expanse of reality on the path of seeing, on the first bodhisattva level, as a result of which one realizes the twelve sets of one hundred special qualities—having a vision of one hundred buddhas in a single instant, and so forth. This is the perfect realization of the arrangement of qualities, which is realized by those with the correct view. "Perfect

---

31. See "four results of the Listeners' Vehicle" in the glossary.

realization of the qualities so arranged" refers to realizing the elements to be trained in from the second level up to the tenth, through which one assimilates and realizes the arrangement in which the corresponding twelve hundred sets of special qualities increase a thousandfold and more.[32] This is realized by the perfect realization of those on the path of meditation.

In Tibetan commentaries, these last six are associated only with the path of meditation, but we can see that this does not at all fit the thinking of Vasubandhu and Sthiramati.

(16) Attentiveness associated with mastery. This is indicated by "mastery." Keeping mastery in mind has three aspects: mastery in the purification of obscurations deriving from the defilements, mastery in the purification of both defilement-related and cognitive obscurations, and mastery in the accomplishment of extraordinary qualities. First, defilements such as attachment prevent one from attaining liberation in nirvāṇa. One therefore eliminates them by realizing the individual no-self on the paths of seeing and meditation so that they do not arise in the future. This much the listener and solitary-realizer arhats also have. Second, the cognitive obscurations that conceive of the phenomena of subject and object as intrinsically existing prevent one from obtaining omniscient gnosis, and one therefore eliminates both defilement-related and cognitive obscurations so that they never occur again. This is achieved by means of the Mahāyāna path. Third, one eliminates the factors that prevent one from obtaining the extraordinary qualities—the six kinds of preternatural knowledge, the ten strengths, four fearlessnesses, and the other qualities—and realizes these qualities, attaining mastery in the perfect purification that is the full accomplishment of good qualities.

(17) Attentiveness associated with the lesser vehicles, the paths of the listeners and solitary realizers.

(18) Attentiveness associated with the Great Vehicle, the extensive path of the bodhisattvas.

These make up the eighteen categories of yogis' attentiveness, which are held to include everything that they keep in mind, in all vehicles, greater and lesser.

---

32. Bodhisattvas on the second level gain twelve hundred thousand special qualities, those on the third gain twelve hundred million qualities, and so on.

b. Investigating the Dharma Whose Meaning Is to Be Realized

Investigating the Dharma of realization is divided into eleven sections: (1) investigating the thatness of phenomena; (2) investigating the illusion-like nature of phenomena; (3) investigating knowable phenomena; (4) investigating defilement and purity; (5) investigating mere awareness; (6) investigating different realities; (7) investigating perfect liberation; (8) investigating absence of intrinsic existence; (9) investigating the acceptance that phenomena are unborn; (10) investigating the intention in teaching a single vehicle; and (11) investigating the five sciences.

i. Investigating the Thatness of Phenomena

> **Delusion as to what is forever free of duality, its basis, and thatness**
> **(Utterly inexpressible and beyond elaboration)**
> **Should be recognized, eliminated, and, while accepted as intrinsically uncontaminated, completely purified.**
> **Thatness is held to be pure, free of defilements, like the sky, gold, and water. (XII, 13)**

The investigation of the thatness of the phenomena that lead to defilement or to purity has to be understood in terms of the three realities—imputed, dependent, and fully present. Although thatness is forever devoid of the duality of subject and object, we perceive things dualistically as subject and object. This is the imputed reality. The ground or support of deluded dualistic perception—even though there is no such subject-object duality—is the dependent reality. The nature that cannot be expressed by speech in any way and that is beyond the elaborations of discursive thought is the fully present reality. This is the actual condition of all phenomena—thatness. This, being devoid of the phenomena of subject and object and therefore beyond conceptual elaboration, can only be known personally. Thus, the imputed reality should be recognized as not existing, like the snake one might imagine on seeing a rope.[33] The impure dependent reality has to be eliminated,

---

33. In poor light, a rope on a path may easily be mistaken for a snake. There is no snake there, but one's imagination imputes a snake.

for the appearances of subject and object present in the dependent reality are what has to be purified. The fully present reality, which is accepted as being intrinsically uncontaminated, has to be purified of adventitious contaminants. "Intrinsically uncontaminated" means that it is in its very nature, from the beginning, devoid of any impurity, in the same way that, in terms of their very nature, the sky is unclouded, gold is naturally pure, and water is naturally limpid. Nevertheless, it is accepted that when the fully present reality is obscured by adventitious defilements, like clouds in the sky, mud on a piece of gold, or impurities in water, we do not realize that. Once it is free of the defilements, its perfect purity is realized.

> Apart from that, there's not the slightest thing in beings that exists,
> Yet beings are all completely ignorant of this—their minds
> Reject what does exist and cling to what does not.
> Such is the enormity of the world's confusion. (XII, 14)

Now, in terms of the way things are on the ultimate level, there is nothing existent in the elements that constitute beings other than the ultimate reality,[34] the fully present reality—not even an atom's worth of subject and object. Everything dwells in the state of that true nature. However, none of the beings in the three worlds have realized that ultimate reality. Their minds are completely ignorant of that actual condition of things, and they cling to the phenomena of subject and object. Thus it is that, completely rejecting the apprehension of something that does exist—the fully present reality, the fundamental nature intrinsic to phenomena—they take to be real something that does not exist, the imputed reality. Such is the enormity of the error that ordinary, ignorant beings make.

ii. INVESTIGATING THE ILLUSION-LIKE NATURE OF PHENOMENA

> Of false imagination,
> We say it is like a magical illusion;
> And of dualistic delusion,
> We say it is like the forms in a magical illusion. (XII, 15)

---

34. In the Tibetan here, "beings" are qualified as conditioned phenomena (Tib. *chos can*, Skt. *dharmin*) in contrast to the unconditioned ultimate reality that is their true nature (Tib. *chos nyid*, Skt. *dharmatā*).

Even though things do not exist in thatness, the experience of them does exist simply in their appearing. Phenomena perceived as subject and object all appear, but they have no intrinsic existence; they are like the things that appear in a magical illusion. Through the power of the spells that a magician intones over pebbles and other props, the images in a magical illusion actually appear in the form of horses, elephants, and the like. In the same way, the cause of the dualistic perceptions of subject and object, that is, the mind and mental factors that appear as the false imagination of subject and object, is described as being the nature of the dependent reality. And just as the forms—the bodies, limbs, colors, and so forth—of the horses, elephants, and so on that appear in the illusion look as if they are those of real horses and elephants, the dualistic delusions of subject and object are the very nature of the imputed reality. While not existing, the delusion of an object and the delusion of a subject are dualistically imputed, in the same way that a rope is mistaken for a snake.

> **In the same way that there is nothing in an illusion,**
> **We accept the ultimate truth.**
> **And in the same way that it is perceived,**
> **We accept the relative truth. (XII, 16)**

Just as it is accepted that there are no horses, elephants, or whatnot in the pebbles, sticks, and so forth over which the magician chants spells in a magical illusion, so too, the true nature of things—in which there has never been, since the very beginning, either subject or object—is accepted as being the ultimate truth or actual condition of things, the unmistaken nature of phenomena, which we therefore call the fully present reality. And just as it is accepted that the horses, elephants, and so forth are perceived because of the spell on the props in a magical illusion, all dualistic appearances with subject and object are accepted as being the relative truth.

> **Just as when the illusions are not there**
> **And their causes are clearly seen,**
> **When transformation takes place,**
> **One perceives the false imagination. (XII, 17)**

When the horses and elephants and other illusions that are conjured up by means of the magical spells are not there, the pebbles, sticks, and so on from which those visions are produced are directly and clearly seen. Similarly, when the habitual tendencies of subject and object are eliminated and the consciousness of the ground of all is transformed, just as there are no horses and elephants that appear, there is no perception of subject and object, and with the gnosis of meditative equipoise one sees the fully present reality, thatness. With the gnosis of the postmeditation, as is the case for the pebbles and sticks that are directly seen, one perceives the false imagination, the dependent nature, which is the basis of the dualistic perceptions of subject and object, and one will realize that the three worlds are simply the mind.

> **Undeceived people**
> **Use the illusion's causes as they wish.**
> **So too, those who are diligent in the precepts, undeluded,**
> **Experience the transformed state as they please. (XII, 18)**

To people whose vision is not distorted by the substances and spells used in the trick, the horses and elephants of the illusion do not appear. On the contrary, those people know that the props are just pebbles and sticks, and they use them as they wish, undeludedly. Similarly, undeluded bodhisattvas diligent in the precepts, who have attained the path that is the antidote to delusion, can experience the pure dependent nature, the transformation of the deluded appearances of dualistic apprehension, as they please—meaning that having seen things to be like a magical illusion, they are free to enjoy them without attachment, fear, and so on.

> **Though they are there in appearance,**
> **It is not that they really exist.**
> **Thus we say that in magical illusions and the like**
> **Things exist and do not exist. (XII, 19)**

Although the mere appearances that take the form of those horses and elephants in the magical illusion are present in their causes (the pebbles and sticks, for example), there have never been any real, substantial horses or elephants in them. Thus, in magical illusions, dreams, and so forth, mere appearances are present, so we cannot say that they do not exist; and because we say that they do not exist in the way they appear, neither can we say that they do exist.

> **It is not that what is there does not exist,**
> **Nor that what is not there exists.**

> In magical illusions and the like
> We do not distinguish between their existence and
>   nonexistence. (XII, 20)

One might think that it is impossible for phenomena to both exist and not exist or to be neither existent nor nonexistent, and that consequently one has to assert at least one or the other. The mere appearances that exist in appearing as a magical illusion are not nonexistent. If the appearances were nonexistent, no horses and elephants would appear, so they would not exist even deceptively, and there would be no basis for perceiving the illusion.

Nor have those appearances, which have no substantial existence, ever existed. If they did, they would not be deceptive, and it would be as if the horses and elephants were real. For this reason, the appearances of magical illusions are described on a single basis—both existing and not existing—without any distinction or contradiction: they are a combination of both appearance and emptiness.

> Similarly, if dualistic appearances exist there,
> It is not that they exist substantially.
> Thus, for forms and the like
> We say that they exist and do not exist. (XII, 21)

Similarly, although mere dualistic appearances exist in the dependent nature, it is not that there are things that exist dualistically in the way they appear to do. Thus, external forms, sounds, and so forth are described as existing as mere appearances and as not existing in the way they appear.

> It is not that what is there does not exist,
> Nor that what is not there does exist.
> With regard to forms and the like
> We say that there is no distinction between their existing
>   and not existing. (XII, 22)

Why is that? The mere appearances as those things are present there; it is not that they do not exist. But they do not exist as the objects—form and so forth—that seem to appear. Like the two moons that appear when one presses one's eye, they have never been established as existing. Therefore, with regard to forms and so on, we say that their existence and nonexistence are indistinguishably combined, as has just been explained, without falling into either extreme, as is shown in the analogy of the magical illusion.

> It is in order to refute the extremes
> Of superimposition and repudiation,
> And in order to halt those who take the lower vehicles,
> That this has been asserted. (XII, 23)

Thus, no distinction is made between existence and nonexistence: things exist merely in appearance, but they do not exist in the same way as they appear. This teaching is the Middle Way, and it is in order to refute the extremes of superimposing the imputed reality, saying it exists, and of repudiating the dependent reality, the basis of appearance, saying it does not exist, that *Distinguishing the Middle from Extremes* states:

> The false imagination exists,
> But there is no duality there.[35]

and,

> That is the Middle Way.[36]

When one realizes that, one knows that although the phenomena of subject and object appear, they are like magical illusions and have no intrinsic existence. One then has no fear of saṃsāra, nor is one attached to nirvāṇa. Those who fear samsaric suffering and seek nirvāṇa to rapidly quell their suffering use the lower vehicles to proceed to that peace. So it is in order to prevent them from engaging in the extreme of peace that we assert things in terms of freedom from the two extremes.

> The cause of delusion and delusion itself
> Are held to be the perception of the material
> And the perception of the immaterial.
> Because the one does not exist, neither can the other. (XII, 24)

---

35. The first line refers to the impure dependent reality, the second to the fact that subject and object (in that dependent reality) have no real existence.

36. *Distinguishing the Middle from Extremes*, I, 1 (first two lines) and 2 (last line).

Although neither subject nor object exists, the cause of dualistic delusion and the delusion itself are held to be the perception of the material and the perception of the immaterial. The cause of delusion is the perception of material phenomena that appear seemingly distinct from the mind arising in the form of the five sense organs and the five sense objects. In a dream, although the forms such as horses, elephants, women, and so forth that appear as the objects of one's own senses are one's own mind appearing as the object aspect, one does not know this and one considers them to be real apprehended objects that are something other than the consciousness. Their appearing as external objects is the cause of delusion. This being so, the nature of delusion itself is held to be the perception of something immaterial, for it is the dualistic apprehension of things as subject and object by the six consciousnesses—the eye consciousness and so on. Thus, even though there is the illusion of two things, there is no apprehending object that is distinct from an apprehending subject, and therefore, conversely, neither can there be a subject to apprehend that object, for from the point of view of either of these two, if the one is not present, there cannot be the other either. In fact, everything is devoid of both subject and object.

> Because the apprehension of the form of an elephant in a show of magic
> Is an illusion, we speak of two things.
> Although there are not two things in the same way that they appear there,
> There is the perception of duality. (XII, 25)

One might argue that if, in that case, material sense organs such as the eyes do not exist, and objects such as forms do not exist, there would be no cause for the sense consciousnesses, and they could not therefore arise. How can this be consistent with the undeniable fact that subject and object nevertheless appear?

Although subject and object do not exist, the validity of dualistic appearance is established both by examples familiar to ordinary people and by examples given in the treatises. As to the first kind of example, when one sees the form of an elephant in a magical illusion, one then apprehends it with the respective consciousness. That apprehension is a meaningless appearance and therefore a deceptive illusion. It is for this reason that the illusory object (the form of the elephant that is apprehended) and the consciousness apprehending it are spoken of as being two. Although there are no subjects and objects in the way that they apprehend and are apprehended in the illusion, the deluded mind merely perceives them as two—subject and object—and for ordinary beings they do exist.

> Because the apprehension of the forms of skeletons
> Is an illusion, we speak of two things.
> Although there are not two things in the same way that they appear there,
> There is the perception of duality. (XII, 26)

Now, to take the example in the treatises, yogis who meditate on the repulsive nature of things practice a clear visualization of people as skeletons. There are not actually any skeletons there: they are an illusion, so we just *speak* of subject and object. Although there is neither subject nor object in the way that the perception of the skeletons appears to the subject, it is as if there is a mental state that perceives them as two.

> All phenomena that characterize delusion
> Exist like that and do not exist like that.
> There is no contradiction in their existing and not existing,
> So they are like magical illusions that are there but not there.
>   (XII, 27)

> All phenomena related to the antidotes
> Do not exist like that and do exist like that.
> Because they do not exist as they seem, they are devoid of characteristics:
> They too are shown to be like magical illusions. (XII, 28)

What do the above examples show? Although the phenomena of defilement and purity that appear to the consciousness of the dependent nature do not exist dualistically as subject and object, they exist as two merely in appearance. Any unfavorable, defiling factors that characterize delusion are included in karma, defilements, and their fully ripened effects, and they all, as in the examples just explained, exist as mere deluded appearances, but they do not exist in the way they are imputed to do by immature beings. For this reason, there is no difference or contradiction in their being both existent and nonexistent. They are thus like magical illusions that are there in appearance but are not really there.

All the remedial factors—that is, the teachings explained in the sūtras and so forth, the elements of the path such as the close mindfulnesses and transcendent perfections, and qualities of the result such as the ten strengths—also do not exist in the way that they are dualistically imputed by immature beings as subject and object. And they do exist inasmuch as they simply appear. Although they appear, they do not exist in the same way as they appear. For that reason they are devoid of any intrinsic essential nature or attributes, and therefore they too are shown to be like magical illusions. As is taught in the Perfection of Wisdom, "All phenomena are like magical illusions and dreams; even nirvāṇa is like a magical illusion, a dream."

> **As in the defeat of an illusory king**
> **By another illusory king,**
> **Bodhisattvas, who have seen phenomena,**
> **Are without conceit. (XII, 29)**

If the phenomena associated with the process of defilement and those associated with the process of purification are both like magical illusions, how, one might wonder, does the purification process eliminate the defilement process? Suppose that in a magical illusion the illusion of a weak king, together with his court, is overthrown by the illusion of another, powerful king and his court and turned out of his palace. The mind related to defilements such as the belief in a self is analogous to the weak king in the illusion. It dwells in the consciousness of the ground of all, which is analogous to the king's palace. And the attendant mental factors are analogous to the weak king's court. As long as the antidote has not arisen, all the defiling phenomena will occur at the behest, as it were, of the weak king. Now, the more powerful king in the illusion (that is, the mind related to the purification process, comprising the wisdom of the realization of no-self, faith, and other virtuous elements), together with his court (mental factors), annihilates the phenomena associated with the defilement process and wins the kingdom, gaining command over all untainted phenomena in the palace of the transformed ground of all. Thus it is that bodhisattvas, who have seen that all the phenomena of the defilement process and purification process are appearances devoid of the dualism of subject and object, like magical illusions, eliminate the defilement aspect and develop the purity aspect, yet they are free of pride and not conceited about having done so.

There now follows an explanation of the Buddha's teaching that all phenomena are like the eight similes of illusion.

> The buddhas, sublimely awakened, said in their respective teachings
> That compounded phenomena should be understood as being like magical illusions, like dreams,
> Mirages, reflections, optical illusions, echoes, the reflection of the moon on water, and magical creations,
> Considering the six, the six, the two, the two groups of six, and each of the three. (XII, 30)

The buddhas are sublime in being fully awakened or in having authentic knowledge and are therefore superior to the listeners and solitary realizers. (Here, the translation in Sthiramati's commentary reads, "The buddhas, sublime knowers...") They are said to be fully awakened because they have awoken from the sleep of ignorance and developed their understanding with regard to knowable phenomena.[37] The repetition of the word "buddhas" in the original verse is not, therefore, redundant, since the first "buddhas" is to be understood as meaning buddhas in general, referring to the basis of predication, and the second as referring to their predicated properties, that is, to their realization—in this case, sublime realization.[38] These perfectly and fully enlightened buddhas, our teachers, taught in their sūtras and other scriptures that all compounded phenomena are to be understood as being like a magical illusion, a dream, a mirage, a reflection, an optical illusion, an echo, the reflection of the moon on water, and a miraculous apparition. Although these can all be used generally as analogies for the fact that phenomena are appearances that lack true existence, they are also used specifically, as follows.

The six inner sense faculties are like magical illusions. In what way?

---

37. Mipham is here describing the etymology of the Tibetan word for Buddha (*sangs rgyas*), where *sangs* signifies "awakened" and *rgyas* means "developed."
38. The repetition that Mipham refers to in the Tibetan root verse, which reads *sangs rgyas rnams sangs rgyas mchog rnams*, might, without the help of a commentary, be translated literally as "The buddhas, sublime buddhas." This repetition is less clear in our English translation of this line, which follows Mipham's commentary.

Although there are no sense organs, identities, sentient beings, or vital force appearing as the humans, horses, elephants, and so on in a magical illusion, it seems as if there are sentient beings with sense organs, minds, and vital force. In the same way, beings who appear to have eyes and the other sense organs that constitute the six inner sense faculties are also taught as being without life, individuality, and so forth.

The six outer sense fields—forms and the other objects of the senses—are like the appearances in a dream. They are to be understood as in a dream, where the experiences of enjoying forms (men and women, for example), sounds, smells, flavors, physical sensations, and mental objects appear, but there are no separate objects actually there.

"The two" refers to the mind and mental factors. There is no water in a mirage, but because the mirage is blue, shimmers, and so on, at a distance it gives the impression of water, whereas when one gets closer there is absolutely nothing there. In the same way, although the mind and mental factors make one cling to different phenomena with the idea that they are pillars, vases, men, women, blue, yellow, white, red, and so forth, these phenomena, when examined closely, are multiple, impermanent, and so forth, and there are no complete entities there to cling to.

"The two groups of six" refers to the two groups of six senses-and-fields, that is, the inner sense faculties and outer sense fields, which are compared to a reflection and an optical illusion. The six inner sense faculties are like reflections. Like a reflection appearing in a mirror on account of the figure in front of the mirror, our present six sense faculties appear, but they are unreal, like the reflection, for they manifest from the karmic tendencies produced by the six sense faculties of previous lives acting like the figure in front of the mirror. The six outer sense fields are like optical illusions. What we call an optical illusion is any perception in which the eye is deceived by conditions: a cairn looking like a person, the two moons that appear when one eye is pressed, one's own shadow appearing as another creature, hairs and so on appearing in one's vision, the mountains seeming to move when one is in a boat, and many other such visual tricks. In this context, however, it was taught that it should be understood as referring to the effect of a shadow. In the same way that a shadow is cast by an umbrella, a body, or whatever, the six outer sense fields are, as it were, the shadows cast by the six inner sense faculties. From the consciousness of the ground of all the six inner sense faculties (the eye and the others) manifest, and from them the outer sense fields appear in the form of the sense objects.

"Considering... each of the three" refers to the verbal activity of expounding the Dharma, the mental activity of resting in meditative absorption, and the physical activity of intentionally taking birth, these three being compared to an echo, the reflection of the moon on water, and a magical creation respectively. All teachings are like an echo, in the sense that an echo, while not existing in the same way as the original sound,[39] does exist as the audible object of the ear. Although the reflection of the moon appears in clear water, it is insubstantial. Similarly, when one is one-pointedly absorbed in concentration, the mind is not muddied by distracting thoughts and is therefore like clear water, in which the reflection of whatever one is meditating on—the four truths, points to be recollected, the powers of perceptual limitlessness, the different kinds of perceptual domination, and so forth—clearly appears. Intentional rebirths in saṃsāra are like magical creations, which though they appear successively in different places do so without attachment or aversion; for when bodhisattvas take birth in a succession of lives, one after the other, for the sake of sentient beings, they are free from attachment and aversion.

iii. Investigating Knowable Phenomena

Incorrect thinking, both incorrect and not incorrect,
Nonconceptuality,
And both nonconceptual and not nonconceptual—
These are said to include all knowable phenomena. (XII, 31)

Knowable phenomena can be summarized as mundane phenomena and supramundane phenomena. These two will now be examined.

"Incorrect" thoughts are those that are incompatible with attaining the expanse of reality and the nonconceptual gnosis. They comprise all thoughts with subject and object in the three worlds.

Then there are thoughts that are "both incorrect and not incorrect." All forms of proper thinking with respect to the practices of the level of earnest aspiration—from the time when, as an ordinary being, one carefully listens to the sacred teachings and reflects on them up to the highest mundane level—comprise, at this stage, the concepts of subject and object and are

---

39. Lit. "does not exist as the nature of sound," that is, it is not a sound produced by a person calling.

therefore incorrect. But since they can lead to realizing the expanse of reality and supramundane gnosis, they are, in a sense, the causes of such realization, so they are also not incorrect.

"Nonconceptuality" refers to having no concept of the expanse of reality as an object and of the supramundane gnosis as its subject, because there are no concepts of subject and object with regard to these two.

What we call "both nonconceptual and not nonconceptual" refers to the pure mundane gnosis present in the postmeditation after the nonconceptual gnosis attained in meditation. Because it considers the nonconceptual gnosis whose object is the expanse of reality, it is devoid of subject and object; or, since it is obtained after the nonconceptual gnosis, it is similarly free of clinging to subject and object. It is therefore nonconceptual. But because all phenomena are thought of as being illusion-like and mirage-like, with distinct general and particular characteristics, it is also not nonconceptual.

All knowable phenomena are said to be included in these four. There being no phenomena that are other than just the mind, everything that can be known is included in these four states of mind and in the expanse of reality.

iv. INVESTIGATING DEFILEMENT AND PURITY

> **From their own realm the two appear,**
> **Ignorance and defilements arise, and with them,**
> **The concepts that lead to birth,**
> **And this occurs in the complete absence of two substantial entities. (XII, 32)**

Let us now examine the nature of the defilement aspect (which comprises defilements, karmic actions, and birth or maturation) and the realm of the purity aspect (which comprises the noble path and nirvāṇa). Here "realm" has the same meaning as seed and cause. The consciousness of the ground of all, with its dualistic habitual tendencies, is what is referred to by "their own realm." From it, subject and object appear as two. When this happens, ignorance—the misunderstanding of the nature of things—and other defilements such as attachment, also arise, and with them the concepts of apprehended objects (forms and so forth) and of a consciousness that apprehends them. Again and again, one takes birth and enters saṃsāra. Even while one has this dualistic perception, the two substantial entities of subject and object are completely absent[40]—that is, from the very beginning they have never existed as two separate things. But because of the deluded mind, they appear as two things and are grasped at as two, thus giving rise to saṃsāra. To understand this is to investigate the nature of the defilement aspect.

> As a result of acquiring the particular point of the teachings
> And abiding in the mind's own expanse,
> Thatness manifests, free of dualistic appearances,
> As with a hide and an arrow. (XII, 33)

Next let us investigate the nature of the purity aspect. Individuals who have acquired the particular point of the teachings on the level of earnest aspiration, as explained above,[41] abide in the mind's own expanse, the dependent nature, or the expanse of reality that is the actual condition of things, and thereby attain the first bodhisattva level. Then, on the levels of the path of meditation, they train in the yoga of sustained calm and profound insight associated with that realization. As a result, thatness will manifest more and more, free of the dualistic appearances of subject and object, until the buddha level is attained.

How can we illustrate this? Because their minds are tainted by the delusion of dualistic perceptions and clinging, beings are unable to achieve the perfect liberation of mind from defilements and the perfect liberation of wisdom from ignorance. Bodhisattvas, by realizing that subject and object do not exist and meditating on that with sustained calm and profound insight, achieve both those aspects of liberation. As with hide that has been damaged by alcohol and the like and become hard and unyielding, their proud, stubborn minds are rendered soft and supple by the oil and water of sustained calm. And as with a bent arrow, their minds, which have become warped by wrong views such as the belief in a self and eternalistic and nihilistic views, so as to be incompatible with the actual condition of things, are straightened by being heated in the fire of profound insight.[42] In this way, by correcting the distorted mind with the path and accomplishing the path

---

40. Tib. *rnam par spangs pa*, lit. "completely eliminated or abandoned."
41. See ch. 12, vv. 6–7.
42. The reference here is to the traditional heat treatment of bamboo arrows to straighten them.

without error, they attain, on the buddha level, the liberation of mind and the liberation of wisdom that nothing can impair.

v. INVESTIGATING MERE AWARENESS[43]

> The mind is held to appear dualistically,
> And in that manner it appears as attachment and the rest,
> Or else it manifests as faith and other qualities;
> But there are no defiling or virtuous phenomena. (XII, 34)

What we call "mind-only" is held to refer to the fact that there is nothing more than the mind and mental factors, there being no external objects. There are two approaches concerning the word "only": one that excludes matter but does not exclude mental factors, and that of certain Cittamātrins who accept only the mind and exclude both mental factors and matter. In this context, "mind-only" is accepted as referring to both. According to the first, "mind," referring to the eight consciousnesses (beginning with the consciousness of the ground of all) together with the mental factors, appears as subject and object; apart from the mind there are no outer apprehended objects different from it. According to the second approach, the mind itself appears as subject and object, and besides that there are neither mental factors nor subject and object that exist. Both these explanations appear in Sthiramati's commentary: the first approach considers the mind and mental factors to be substantially distinct; the second considers that they are not.

In this way, the mind is held to appear as the phenomena of defilements (attachment, aversion, and the rest) or as faith, diligence, and so forth, but apart from the mind there are no other so-called defiling phenomena or virtuous phenomena.

> The mind appears as various things
> And operates in a variety of forms.
> These appearances in the mind exist and do not exist,
> And are not therefore phenomenal. (XII, 35)

Thus, the mind, the ground of all, appears as different apprehended phenomena and operates in a variety of forms of apprehending subject. But

---

43. The Tibetan term *rnam rig pa*, "mere awareness," is a synonym for Cittamātra or "Mind-Only."

these manifestations in the mind as subject and object exist merely in appearance; they do not in fact exist in the way they appear. They do not therefore exist as various kinds of phenomena that are distinct from the mind: all phenomena are merely appearances in the mind, and they therefore exist only as the mind.

vi. Investigating Different Realities

> In order to benefit sentient beings,
> The buddhas gave perfect explanations
> By classifying the exemplary subject,
> The essential quality, and the means of demonstration. (XII, 36)

In order to benefit sentient beings by helping them develop unclouded knowledge of the nature of knowable phenomena, the buddhas perfectly explained the distinctions between the exemplary subject, the essential quality, and the means of demonstration for this.[44] These will now be described.

The exemplary subject on the basis of which the respective essence or nature of the three realities is to be demonstrated boils down to the five bases of knowable phenomena: the basis of form, the basis of the main mind, the basis of the attendant mental factors, the basis of nonassociated conditioning factors, and the basis of noncompounded phenomena. The form basis comprises the ten senses-and-fields with form, that is, the five sense organs and the five objects. The mind basis comprises the eight

---

44. The essential quality or characteristic (Tib. *mtshan nyid*, translated in some contexts as "definition") of fire, for example, is heat. A candle flame, or the gas ring of a stove, may be the exemplary subject (*mtshan gzhi*) taken for the purpose of the investigation, on the basis of which fire in general will be qualified as hot. The means of demonstration (*mtshon pa*) is the thing or process that will show that fire is hot. Similarly, impermanence may be investigated as being an essential quality (*mtshan nyid*) of compounded phenomena, using a table as the exemplary subject (*mtshan gzhi*). In the present investigation, five exemplary subjects are taken, representing all knowable phenomena, and will be shown to have three kinds of essential quality, the three realities. What will show this is the five stages of the path, or, as Sthiramati succinctly puts it, the development of wisdom. These three terms are slightly different from the trio of terms more often used in logical investigation—*mtshan nyid*, the definition or characteristic; *mtshon bya*, the subject, or rather, the name, being defined or characterized; and *mtshan gzhi*, the thing that exemplifies the latter and is used as the basis for investigating it. We point this out because the translation of Tibetan in Sthiramati's commentary uses the term *mtshon bya* for *mtshan gzhi*, though as Mipham points out below, this does not make any substantial difference to the argument in this case.

consciousnesses. The mental-factors basis comprises the fifty-one mental factors. The basis of nonassociated conditioning factors is exemplified by the twenty-three nonassociated conditioning factors that are taught—acquisition, nonacquisition, and so forth.[45] Noncompounded phenomena are four: cessation through analysis, cessation without analysis, space, and suchness.

> The mind and its views,
> Their condition, and the unchanging—
> These, in short, comprise the exemplary subject,
> Of which there are countless different kinds. (XII, 37)

"Mind" here indicates the mind basis. For the mind to look at an object, there must all be present the object, sense organ, and attentiveness, so "and its views" indicates the mental factors, the five sense organs, and the five sense objects. Attentiveness to the object's observable quality indicates the mental-factors basis, and the five sense organs and five objects (forms, sounds, smells, tastes, and physical sensations) together indicate the form basis. "Their condition" indicates the condition of the mind, mental factors, and matter, that is, the basis of nonassociated conditioning factors, which belong to the compounded phenomena that are neither matter nor mind, and which are designated acquisition, nonacquisition, similarity of state, vital energy, the state of an ordinary being, and so on. "Unchanging" indicates the basis of noncompounded phenomena, which by definition never change into anything else, for, not being compounded by causal conditions, they are without formation, duration, and destruction. These five bases together constitute the exemplary subject. There are no knowable phenomena that are not included in these five, so they are held to be the exemplary subject for establishing the three realities.

According to Sthiramati's commentary, "mind" refers to the mind that appears as the object (that is, the five sense organs and five sense objects) and to the mind that appears as the subject (namely, the six consciousnesses). "And its views" indicates the mental factors, apparently in the sense that because their nature is to illuminate and to move, they engage with the object.

---

45. For the fifty-one mental factors and twenty-three nonassociated conditioning factors, see *Treasury of Precious Qualities*, appendix 4.

(In some translations, the term "subject" is also used for "exemplary subject."[46] Since they constitute what is to be demonstrated as having the three realities, both translations come to the same thing.)

If we subdivide the different categories of exemplary subject within these five, they are infinite, and each of them has countless further specific kinds. Distinguished in terms of individual beings (their minds, forms, and so forth) and different times and places, they are as limitless as the number of knowable phenomena.

The essential quality of these five exemplary subjects can be summarized as threefold: the imputed reality, the dependent reality, and the fully present reality. It is in terms of the dualistic appearance of phenomena, of the cause of their appearing so, and of their not existing dualistically that there are three realities or natures. These will now be explained.

The Imputed Reality

> Its cause (the notion of names as things),
> The habitual tendencies to conceive such notions,
> And the consequent appearance of objects—
> Such is the imputed reality. (XII, 38)

Even though outer objects do not exist, at the mere appearance that gives rise to the concept of a pillar, vase, or similar object that one expresses by name, there is the notion of this or that thing, and there is then the notion of believing that it truly exists ("This is a pillar, that is a vase . . ."). It is because of this that imputation occurs. This notion of name and attributes is one aspect of the imputed reality. Similarly, the habitual tendencies created by the elaboration of these imputations are also included in the imputed reality, because they are the cause of false imagination. Through the maturation of habitual tendencies that we have built up since time without beginning, objects such as pillars, vases, horses, elephants, and so forth actually appear. While those who are used to using language apprehend those things associating them with their names, even those who have no training in linguistic conventions, and who may not give things names, seem potentially able to associate objects with names. This too is the imputed reality.

---

46. Tib. *mtshon bya* (also translated as the object defined, definiendum, the object characterized) and *mtshan gzhi* respectively.

In short, through the awakening of the habitual tendency to conceptually elaborate the whole variety of phenomena that appear dualistically, we apprehend the different phenomena that appear dualistically as names and attributes and cling to their existing in the same way that they appear. This is the imputed reality.

> The appearance of names and objects
> Corresponding to objects and names,
> Which is the cause of false imagination,
> Is the imputed reality. (XII, 39)

The precise definition of "imputation" is given by the first two lines: "The appearance of names and objects corresponding to objects and names." A name such as "vase" gives rise to a corresponding image of the object—a bulbous article. Even if we do not actually see the object, merely from the name "vase" being uttered we grasp at the existence of the object, a bulbous article: the name is the cause of false imagination. Conversely, when we see a bulbous article, we grasp at the existence of the name ("This is a vase"): the object has become the cause for false imagination. In reality, there is no inherent connection between the name and the object, but because of adventitious concepts, we superimpose a name on the object that appears in the form of attributes. As a result, when we think of the name, we imagine the object and we superimpose the object on the name. Apprehending things in this way by associating names with the attributes of objects, and vice versa, we grasp at different phenomena individually (and separately), and this becomes the cause of false imagination. This, then, is held to be the imputed reality—imputed, that is, by the mind that dualistically apprehends separate subjects and objects.

The Dependent Reality

> Having threefold appearance whose nature is the object,
> And threefold appearance whose nature is the subject,
> False imagination
> Is the dependent reality. (XII, 40)

What is the dependent reality? The first "threefold appearance" in the root verse refers to the apprehended object—form—and comprises the three appearances of place, sense objects, and body. The second "threefold appearance" refers to the apprehending subject—the mind and mental factors—and comprises the three appearances of mind, apprehender, and conceptualization.

Place refers to appearance as our environment, the world. Sense objects refer to the six outer objects—forms, sounds, smells, tastes, physical sensations, and mental objects. Appearance as the body refers to the six sense organs—the eye, ear, nose, tongue, body, and mental faculty.

Appearance as the mind refers to the defiled mind consciousness, which, in considering the ground of all, views it as a self. The apprehender refers to the five sense consciousnesses from the eye consciousness to the body consciousness. Conceptualization refers to the mind consciousness because it demarcates the various objects and creates the concept of them as this or that. The second three appearances are said to have the nature of the subject, and the first three to have that of the object. All these six appearances are present as the seedlike habitual tendencies in the consciousness of the ground of all, which, when awakened, simply appear as in a dream, but apart from that they do not exist separately as subject and object. Nevertheless, they are perceived dualistically as if they did exist, and this leads to false imagination, the mind and mental factors of the three worlds. This is the dependent reality. As we read in the *Sūtra on the Descent into Laṅka*:

> One's body, possessions, environment, and the like
> I declare to be just the mind.

Thus, the mind (comprising the consciousness of the ground of all that is the basis of everything that appears as external and internal phenomena, together with its seven attendant consciousnesses) and mental factors are what we refer to as the "dependent reality," "dependent" because it is in dependence on (and through the domination of) the habitual tendencies related to defilement that things appear as subject and object.

The Fully Present Reality

> Nonexistence, existence,
> The sameness of existence and nonexistence,
> Not peace, peace, and freedom from concepts—
> Such is the fully present reality. (XII, 41)

What is the fully present reality? It is the expanse of reality, the nature of emptiness. In that the imputed reality of subject and object does not exist, it is nonexistence. And in that the nature of suchness devoid of duality exists, it is existence. Suchness, as the absence of subject and object, exists; and while suchness exists, the duality of subject and object does not exist. So even though we may speak of two—existence and nonexistence—they are not different but mutually inclusive: the fully present reality is sameness. By excluding duality, one determines suchness. And if one determines suchness, one excludes duality. Existence and nonexistence, in this sense, are therefore mutually inclusive and no different. From the point of view of its being adulterated by adventitious contaminants, the fully present reality is not peace; from the point of view of its own nature, it is naturally pure, radiant light, and therefore peace. Beyond the reach of the intellect, it is free of all the conceptual elaborations of subject and object, and therefore nonconceptual. Such is the fully present reality.

The Five Indicative Stages of Yoga

> Having focused on the teachings that are consistent with the cause,
> One is properly attentive,
> One abides in the expanse of the mind,
> And one sees that objects exist and do not exist. (XII, 42)

What makes known or demonstrates the fact that these three realities apply to the five bases are the five indicative stages of yoga: foundation, development or establishment, the mirrorlike stage, vision, and abode or support. It is by means of these five that the nature of the imputed reality (which is to be known as a mere superimposition on phenomena), that of the dependent reality (the false imagination related to appearances as subject and object, which is to be eliminated), and that of the fully present reality (the ground that is to be purified) are clearly indicated or made known as objects of the mind. These five will now be described.

The buddhas, having realized the two kinds of no-self, teach what they have realized, and for this reason the Twelve Branches of Excellent Speech are known as the "teachings that are consistent with the cause," because they are consistent with the path of realization that the buddhas have realized, or because they are the cause for attaining it. Those who wish to realize thatness begin, on the path of accumulation, by considering these teachings that are consistent with the cause for realizing the expanse of reality. Listening properly to the Excellent Words, they then reflect on their meaning and train in them. This is what we call the foundation. It is the cause for first engaging in the teachings or the foundation on which the subsequent indicative stages of yoga are based.

After considering the meaning of the Excellent Words in this way, one proceeds to be "properly attentive," referring to the establishment or developmental basis. On the path of joining, one practices being properly attentive, as a result of which one gains in meditative experience, and at this stage of warmth one understands that phenomena cannot be expressed by name. At the stage of the peak, one understands that the sense objects are like magical illusions. At the stage of acceptance, one realizes that there are no objects to be apprehended. And at the supreme mundane level, one realizes that there is no subject to apprehend them. In this way one's ascertainment of suchness gradually grows better and clearer. This is known as the developmental basis because it gives rise to the path of seeing. It is also known as establishment, because it establishes the mind in proper attention, that is, it establishes in the mind the habitual tendencies for realizing supramundane qualities.

The mirrorlike stage is indicated by "One abides in the expanse of the mind." The expanse of the mind that is the dependent reality is suchness devoid of duality, and this is therefore realized directly[47] at the time of the path of seeing, on the first bodhisattva level, when, with gnosis, all knowable phenomena are clearly and manifestly seen as the nature of suchness, like reflections appearing clearly in a mirror. Some authorities explain the mirrorlike stage as occurring from the greater path of accumulation until the supreme mundane level, when one's realization of emptiness is still indirect, but the explanation in Sthiramati's commentary that it is on the first level is better.

Vision is indicated by "One sees that objects exist and do not exist." From the second level up to the tenth, with the supramundane gnosis one sees existent phenomena as existing, and nonexistent phenomena as not existing. This is the unmistaken perception of the nature of things, which is why we speak of "vision." "Existent phenomena" refers to the dependent reality, which exists as the nature of relative truth, and to the fully present reality,

---

47. Tib. *mngon sum du gnas pa*, lit. "one dwells manifestly" in suchness.

which exists as the nature of ultimate truth. Both these are thus seen as existing. The imputed reality, being apprehended by the deluded mind, is seen as not existing, like the horns of a rabbit.

The abode or support is indicated by the whole of the next verse:

> **On that level, everything becomes sameness,**
> **The noble potential, utterly uncontaminated,**
> **Similar but superior,**
> **Neither diminishing nor increasing. (XII, 43)**

On the level of ultimate buddhahood, all phenomena will become sameness. All the buddhas who have entered the untainted expanse become the same in body, speech, and mind, and all phenomena too are similarly realized as being a single flavor, the nature of the great sameness. This perfectly pure nature, the expanse of reality, thatness, the actual condition of all phenomena, is what is referred to as the "potential of the noble beings,"[48] also known as "the essence of the sugatas" and "the ultimately authentic." That expanse is free of contamination by the two kinds of obscuration and is therefore an utterly uncontaminated state of transformation. Simply in terms of the defilement-related obscurations having been eliminated, buddhahood is similar to the liberation that the listeners and solitary realizers have. But it is superior to the listeners' and solitary realizers' liberation in five respects. The cessation of the defilement aspect does not diminish the expanse of reality, nor does the growth of the purity aspect cause it to increase. It is always the same, neither increasing nor decreasing, neither waxing nor waning. From that state of sameness, it never moves. This is what is referred to as the abode or support.

Liberation is common to all enlightened individuals, and in being liberated from saṃsāra the listeners and solitary realizers are the same as the buddhas, who are also similarly liberated. Nevertheless, the buddhas' liberation is superior in five respects: in their extraordinary purity, the complete purity of their realms, their attainment of the body of truth, their perfect enjoyment of the Mahāyāna teachings, and the deeds their manifestation bodies perform to benefit beings and their unceasing activities. In the first place, the listeners and solitary realizers have not eliminated the cognitive obscurations, so they are not as pure as the buddhas. Moreover, even though

---

48. Tib. *'phags pa'i rigs*. Here the "potential" has, of course, been realized.

they have eliminated the seed of defilements, they have not eliminated the subtle habitual tendencies. For this reason, even when they have attained the arhat level, because of their previous habitual tendencies from being born as monkeys, they may run and jump like monkeys; because of their previous tendencies as courtesans, they may look at their faces by looking in mirrors, or on the side of their alms bowls, and so on. So, although they do not have the defilements of such rebirths, they do have their habitual tendencies. The buddhas, on the other hand, do not have even the most subtle of the two kinds of obscurations and are therefore superior in terms of purity.

The buddhas, having trained in purifying their fields of perception, can display the array of completely pure buddha fields, with their ground of jewels, wish-fulfilling trees, rivers of nectar, and so forth. The listeners are unable to do this, so the buddhas are superior on account of their completely pure fields.

By realizing the two kinds of no-self, the buddhas attain the body of truth—the great sameness, suchness. The listeners and solitary realizers, with their realization of the individual no-self, have no more than just the "body" of liberation.[49]

The buddhas have attained the body of perfect enjoyment, as a result of which they, together with their retinues of tenth-level bodhisattvas, have perfect enjoyment of the Mahāyāna teachings, unceasingly, for as long as saṃsāra lasts. This is something the listeners and solitary realizers do not have.

Displaying supreme nirmāṇakāya manifestations and other manifestations of their body, speech, and mind, the buddhas, until the end of time, never cease their activities in bringing benefit and happiness to all sentient beings. This is not the case for the listeners and solitary realizers.

Of these five indicative stages of yoga, the first four are stages of the causal yoga, while the fifth is the stage of the resultant yoga. "Yoga" means the union of sustained calm and profound insight. These five stages of yoga reveal how the three realities apply to the five bases, for they help us to understand all phenomena—the five aggregates and uncompounded phenomena, along with suchness—in three ways: the dualistic subject-object imputations of immature beings, dualistic appearance, and nonduality.

---

49. Tib. *rnam par grol ba'i lus*, this being a state of wisdom rather than a physical state, but nevertheless inferior to the state of wisdom that is the Buddha's dharmakāya, or body of truth.

Some authorities associate the five bases with the three realities as follows. They associate form and nonassociated conditioning factors with the imputed reality, mind and mental factors with the dependent reality, and noncompounded phenomena with the fully present reality. But this is slightly incorrect. It should be understood that for each of the five bases there are all three realities—for example, form can be distinguished as imputed form, dependent form, and form qualified by its true nature (ultimate reality) or the true nature of form. The same applies to all five bases.

vii. Investigating Perfect Liberation

Investigating perfect liberation is covered by six verses.

The elimination of defilements and suffering and the realization of nirvāṇa by means of the noble path is perfect liberation; and to examine the means by which one will attain nirvāṇa is what we call "investigating perfect liberation."

> **When the seeds are transformed,**
> **The perceptions of place, sense objects, and body**
> **Are transformed. That untainted expanse**
> **Is the support pervading all. (XII, 44)**

Because the various habitual tendencies associated with defilement-related and cognitive obscurations or dualistic habitual tendencies are present in the consciousness of the ground of all, the latter is referred to as "the one with all the seeds." As a result of the ground of all that comprises such seeds being transformed and freed of the contaminants of subject and object, the three kinds of appearances that arise from those seeds are also transformed—namely, the appearance of the place or environment, the appearances of the six sense objects, and the appearances of the six sense organs as the body. When these are transformed, the environment is no longer impure, with thorny ravines, precipices, and the like, but is perceived as a jeweled universe. The sense objects become the six untainted pleasures of the senses to be enjoyed—beautiful wish-fulfilling trees, pools of nectar, and the like. The body becomes like the Buddha's body, with each of the sense organs able to perform the functions of all the senses, the perfect, infinitely powerful, vajra-like body, utterly pure and endowed with the twelve sets of one hundred qualities.

That untainted expanse of reality of the transformed ground of all is the location or support of perfect liberation, and it therefore pervades all the extraordinary qualities of transformation. An alternative explanation is that since the listeners, solitary realizers, and bodhisattvas all enter that expanse of perfect liberation, it is the universal support.

> When the mind, apprehenders, and conceptualization
> Are transformed, there are four kinds of mastery—
> In nonconceptuality, fields,
> Gnosis, and activities. (XII, 45)

The results of transforming the defiled mind consciousness, the consciousnesses of the five apprehending sense doors, and the conceptual mind consciousness are now dealt with in order. By transforming the defiled mind consciousness, one will master nonconceptuality. When it is not transformed, it conceives of the ground of all as a self, but when it is transformed, it takes the transformed, nonconceptual ground of all as its object and one thus acquires mastery of nonconceptuality. When the consciousnesses of the five apprehending sense doors are transformed, instead of perceiving ordinary impure objects of experience, one has mastery over completely pure fields. And when the conceptual mind consciousness is transformed, one will master both gnosis and activities. By thus acquiring the four kinds of perfect knowledge, one achieves mastery in gnosis, and through the power of one's preternatural knowledge, one achieves mastery in enlightened activities. This has been taught as being the same as in the section on transformation above.[50] Thus it is that the four kinds of mastery are acquired.

> These four kinds of mastery are gained
> On three levels—Immovable and the others.
> On one of these levels, two are gained,
> And on each of the others, one is gained. (XII, 46)

These four kinds of mastery are gained on the three levels beginning with the eighth level, Immovable. On one, the eighth level, one acquires the first two masteries, mastery of nonconceptuality and mastery of fields. And on

---

50. See above, ch. 10, vv. 42–44.

the others, one obtains mastery of gnosis (on the ninth level) and mastery of activities (on the tenth), these two levels therefore being described as having one mastery each.

> The wise will understand that all existence is devoid of both kinds of self,
> And knowing the sameness of that state, they approach suchness in terms of mental apprehension.
> Then, as they keep the mind on mind-only, that perception too will disappear.
> This nonappearance is liberation, sublimely free of references. (XII, 47)

Perfect liberation can also be explained in other ways. Wise bodhisattvas have realized the one taste of the two kinds of no-self (individual and phenomenal) in everything that belongs to or exists in the three worlds. In other words, by recognizing that they are devoid of the two kinds of imputed self, they have dispelled the extreme of superimposition. And when they know that the realization of no-self is not a complete vacuum, with nothing there at all, but the same as and not different from the illusion-like dependent nature and the fully present reality, suchness, devoid of the two kinds of self, they have dispelled the extreme of nihilistic repudiation. Knowing this middle way, bodhisattvas approach thatness in terms of the merely mental apprehension of such a path, and train their minds in this again and again.[51] This attentiveness to thatness in terms of mere mind occurs from the stage of warmth until the stage of acceptance. Then, by keeping the mind on the knowledge that everything is just the mind, they realize that even though things appear as the object, there is no intrinsically existent object, and that similarly even though the mind-only appears as the subject, the subject (like the object) does not exist either, and they then attain the concentration of the supreme mundane level—though there is no perception here of a subject attaining it. Once they have seen that both subject and object are equivalent and have no existence whatsoever, the conceptual elaborations of subject and object never appear in any way. This is liberation from all conceptual thought, the gnosis of the noble beings, the unmistaken fully present reality utterly free of all references.

51. Although thatness transcends the mind, the bodhisattva approaches it in terms of freedom from the two extremes, conscious all the while that such an approach is "mind-only."

> When the foundation—accumulation—and the
>   development are present,
> One will see that everything is just a name.
> And seeing that seeing of just a name,
> One then no longer sees even that. (XII, 48)

Another way of explaining perfect liberation is as follows. When one possesses the merit and wisdom accumulated over one measureless kalpa in the past, at this time both the foundation stage of accumulation in having listened to the Mahāyāna teachings, reflected on them, and meditated on them, and the developmental stage of properly keeping in mind impermanence, suffering, emptiness, and no-self on the path of earnest aspiration are present, and as a result, one attains the stages of warmth and the peak on the path of joining. At this point one will see that all phenomena have simply been labeled with names by the mind, and that apart from that they are merely conceptual constructions and have no existence as specifically characterized phenomena. The phenomena that are the object of such imputation do not exist but are merely labeled by the imagination: apart from just the mind and mental factors (the aggregates that are the basis of name, as opposed to form), there are no objects outside. When one realizes this, one attains the stage of acceptance on the path of joining, at which time one accepts that reality is devoid of external objects. Having seen this, one subsequently, at the stage of supreme mundane realization, no longer sees the subject that apprehends things as just names or mere mind. Thus, from one's no longer seeing both subject and object, the mirrorlike and vision stages occur, and finally one attains the state of sameness on the level of buddhahood, which is perfect liberation.

> **The mind with its negative tendencies,**
> **Caught by the noose of belief in a self,**
> **Becomes totally immersed.**
> **By settling inward, we hold, it turns away. (XII, 49)**

This verse shows yet another way of explaining perfect liberation. "Mind" in this case refers to the mind and mental factors, including the consciousness of the ground of all. That mind is accompanied by negative tendencies, of which there are two kinds: negative tendencies of the body (that is, nonvirtuous actions such as taking life) and those of the mind (attachment, aversion, and bewilderment); or alternatively, the negative habitual tendencies of obscurations deriving from the defilements and those of cognitive obscurations. The cause of negative tendencies is the belief in an individual self and the belief in a phenomenal self. Once caught in this noose of belief in a self, the mind enters fully into saṃsāra. In short, as long as the mind that is accompanied by the negative tendencies of defilement-related and cognitive obscurations accumulated by the two kinds of belief in a self has not abandoned these two beliefs, one accumulates habitual tendencies in the mind and is born in saṃsāra. By settling inward, it is held, that mind turns away. In what way does the mind settle inward? The distracted mind that attaches to the object is gathered in, into the mind itself, and rests peacefully, perfectly settled within. Once one has realized that it is just the mind that subjectively apprehends the nonexistent object and that the mind too is nonexistent, one is free of both subject and object. One therefore no longer accumulates habitual negative tendencies and one's mind turns away from entering saṃsāra. This is what we call perfect liberation.

Although Sthiramati's commentary does not give any other significance to these four different explanations of perfect liberation apart from their being different presentations, they represent the investigation of perfect liberation from four different points of view. The first gives a definition of liberation in terms of transformation. The second explains it from the point of view of the path to liberation. The third explains it in terms of the successive stages by which liberation takes place. The fourth shows that liberation or the absence of liberation depends on the mind: when there is bondage, it is the mind that is bound; when there is liberation, it is the mind that is liberated. On the other hand, the claims of non-Buddhists that one is liberated at God's behest, for example, and those of the Nirgrantha Jains that liberation has a material form are illogical. Without getting rid of the mind's bonds, it is impossible ever to be liberated. But if one eliminates the bonds of the two kinds of belief in a self, one will attain liberation.

viii. Investigating Absence of Intrinsic Existence

> Because things do not exist of themselves and they do not
>   exist as their own nature,
> And because they do not dwell in their own nature,
> And because they do not exist as they are apprehended,
> They are held to be devoid of intrinsic existence. (XII, 50)

It is taught in the sūtras that all phenomena are devoid of intrinsic existence; they are by nature nirvāṇa. This section explains how this is related to the three realities. "All phenomena," put briefly, are included in the three natures or realities—the imputed reality, the dependent reality, and the fully present reality. The dependent reality is the continuity of instants of the mind and mental factors appearing as subject and object. These have the three characteristics of compounded phenomena: they come into existence, continue to exist, and cease to exist. Now, the past, which has already ceased, is, by definition, not the present. The future, by definition, has not come into existence at the present time and therefore does not exist. And as for the present, which apparently continues to exist, it has, by definition, already been produced and it will not continue to exist for a second instant. For these three reasons, it is held that phenomena are devoid of substantial existence or intrinsic nature. This examination of the lack of intrinsic nature in terms of production and cessation is similar to the listeners' own explanation of emptiness and the lack of intrinsic existence.

To explain further the dependent reality's absence of intrinsic production, "because things do not exist of themselves" indicates that the dependent reality appears interdependently. Things do not come into being of themselves but arise in dependence on causes and conditions. Their arising has no intrinsic existence, and so they are said to be devoid of intrinsic existence. This refutes the Samkhyas' assertion that there is a primal substance from which everything else is produced, or that results exist at the time of their cause and are produced of themselves, it being impossible for them to come into being if they were absent at the time of the cause.

"They do not exist as their own nature" means that things that have ceased to exist do not arise again as their former nature, indicating that their disintegration is nothing more than things simply ceasing to exist—unlike what the Samkhyas say, that something that is destroyed does not become completely nonexistent but remains latent in the expanse of the primal substance.

"And because they do not dwell in their own nature" shows that because all present phenomena that have arisen do not persist into the second instant, there is no continuing to exist. This is different from the tīrthikas' assertion that things are not destroyed by momentariness: for them, once things have arisen, they remain the same as long as they last, until they are finally destroyed.

"And because they do not exist as they are apprehended"[52] refers to the imputed reality, which appears as two things and is thus imputed as two things. These are incorrectly imputed as subject and object, as purity, happiness, permanence, a self, and so forth. Apart from being simply the conceived object of the deluded mind, like a rope mistaken for a snake, it has never, even slightly, existed in the way that it is apprehended by that mind and is therefore referred to as being devoid of essence. It is in this way that the dependent reality and the imputed reality are held to be devoid of intrinsic existence.

> Each proposition being the basis for subsequent ones,
> Absence of intrinsic existence
> Establishes absence of production, absence of cessation,
> Primordial peace, and natural nirvāṇa. (XII, 51)

Each proposition, beginning with the absence of intrinsic existence, is the basis for establishing subsequent propositions, beginning with the absence of production. Thus, absence of intrinsic existence establishes absence of production: the fact that it is impossible for something devoid of intrinsic existence to come into being proves its absence of production. Absence of production proves absence of cessation. And anything that neither comes into existence nor ceases to exist must be peace from the beginning, uninvented by anyone. And the fact that it is impossible, in primordial peace, for there to be suffering or the cause of suffering, establishes natural nirvāṇa.

Thus, having shown the three ways in which the dependent reality is devoid of intrinsic existence and the one way in which the imputed reality is devoid of intrinsic existence, the Buddha taught that all phenomena that appear as subject and object are devoid of intrinsic existence, and for this reason, all phenomena are devoid of production, are devoid of cessation, are peace from the very beginning, and are by their very nature nirvāṇa. He was referring here to the fully present reality. So, although the dependent reality appears as production and cessation, it appears to come into being interdependently through the gathering of causes and conditions, but it is

---

52. We have translated this clause in the root verse as it appears in Kawa Peltsek's translation (*bzung bzhin de med phyir*). Mipham appears to quote it as, "And because they do not exist as subject and object" (*bzung 'dzin de med phyir*). The commentary that follows shows that these two versions come to the same thing.

by its very nature uncreated. The imputed reality is, by definition, uncreated or devoid of intrinsic existence. And the fully present reality is the ultimate nature, present since the beginning but devoid of intrinsic production and cessation. We should understand that it is with these three in mind that the Buddha spoke of the absence of intrinsic existence, absence of production and cessation, and so forth.

ix. Investigating the Acceptance That Phenomena Are Unborn

> With regard to a beginning, a same thing, otherness,
> Its own definition, itself, transformation,
> Defilement, and extraordinary knowledge,
> Acceptance that phenomena are unborn has been explained.
>   (XII, 52)

When, in the sūtras, the Buddha spoke of "acquiring the acceptance that phenomena are unborn," what was he talking about? What he called "the acceptance that phenomena are unborn" is the mental tolerance to accept the eight ways in which phenomena are without production.[53] These will now be explained.

The first category is acceptance that phenomena are unborn from the beginning. It is inappropriate to consider that there is a beginning to saṃsāra, that saṃsāra started at a specific moment. Saṃsāra was not invented by anyone, even by Īśvara, Brahmā, or any other so-called creator. From time without beginning it has been produced through the succession, one after another, of the twelve links of dependent arising, and one will therefore never find a beginning to saṃsāra. So when one accepts that saṃsāra has never had a beginning, a time when it came into being, one acquires the acceptance of that point.

Here in saṃsāra, once something has already come into being, that same thing does not come into being again. Having come into being, it ceases, and since it is then no more, being nonexistent, it cannot come into existence again. So to accept that once arisen, the same thing does not arise again is the second category.

---

53. Acceptance (Tib. *bzod pa*) in this case refers to the third category of transcendent patience, the ability to face the profound truth without fear.

Next is "otherness." In this saṃsāra, similar aggregates, sense spheres, and senses-and-fields that were commonly known before will come into being again and again. But there are no new, unprecedented phenomena not included in the aggregates, sense spheres, and senses-and-fields, and no new, unprecedented kinds of sentient beings that can come into being. This is the third category.[54]

The imputed reality, by definition, is unborn. Like the horn of a rabbit that has never come into existence, it too is unborn. Accepting this is the fourth category.

The dependent reality does not come into being of itself, for it arises in dependence on causes and conditions. Acceptance that it is unborn is the fifth category.

The fully present reality has not been produced through transformation. Like space, it is impossible to turn it into something else. Acceptance of this is the sixth category.

Noble arhats,[55] having eliminated all the defilements that have to be eliminated through the paths of seeing and meditation, acquire the gnosis of exhaustion, and they know that the process of defilement will never occur again. Acceptance of this point is the seventh category.

The extraordinary or specific knowledge that they are exhausted and will not arise is the truth body of the buddhas, in which the two obscurations do not arise again. Or, put another way, the truth body of all the buddhas is a single nature; there are not different truth bodies. There is no arising of the body of truth, inconsistently and distinctly, with some, former buddhas arising in one kind of truth body and other, future buddhas arising in another kind of truth body. Acceptance of this manner in which the body of truth is unborn constitutes the eighth category.

This is how acceptance of the nonarising of phenomena is explained—as acceptance of the eight kinds of nonarising described here. There are three general categories in acquiring acceptance, according to the way in which one accepts the nonarising of phenomena—lesser, middling, and great.

---

54. Whereas in the second category, it is accepted that a person who is reborn is not actually the same person, in this category it is accepted that similar kinds of beings (humans, for example) or phenomena (for instance, cups) can reoccur and appear to be another person or cup.

55. "Arhat" here refers to any noble being, whether listener or bodhisattva, who has "conquered the enemies" (Tib. *dgra bcom pa*), that is, eliminated the defilements, and not just to someone who has attained the final goal of the Listeners' Vehicle.

When one attains the stage of acceptance on the path of joining, one's acceptance is through an indirect understanding of the meaning of nonarising. This is lesser acceptance. On the path of seeing, the first bodhisattva level, it is through direct realization that one accepts nonarising, which is the middling stage. On the eighth level, nonconceptual gnosis is fully matured so that in both meditation and postmeditation one never moves from the knowledge that all phenomena are primordially unborn, and one thus acquires the great acceptance of the nonarising of phenomena.

It has been taught that nonreturning bodhisattvas[56] who have acquired acceptance are referred to as "predicted as buddhas," and the eighth level in particular is called the "level of prediction." However, when necessary,[57] those who possess the Mahāyāna potential and those who have just aroused the bodhicitta are also predicted as buddhas. What we call acceptance of the nonarising of phenomena is mainly explained as the acceptance that there are no phenomena other than the expanse of reality and that all phenomena are therefore unborn from the very beginning.

x. Investigating the Intention in Teaching a Single Vehicle

This topic is covered by seven verses.

> **Because of similarity with regard to the path, no-self,**
> **And liberation, because of different potentials,**
> **Because of achieving both aspirations, because of manifestations,**
> **And because it is the ultimate, there is a single vehicle. (XII, 53)**

Why is it that some sūtras speak of three vehicles and others of one vehicle? In the sūtras, there are the ultimate teachings and the expedient teachings. The Cittamātra system maintains that the explanations in terms of three vehicles are ultimate teachings, while those that speak of a single vehicle are expedient teachings given with a particular intention. What, then, was

---

56. Tib. *phyir mi ldog pa'i byang sems*, bodhisattvas who cannot possibly revert to lower vehicles.
57. "When necessary": for example, in order to encourage someone to follow the Mahāyāna path.

the Buddha's intention in saying that ultimately there is no more than one vehicle? In doing so, he had the following seven points in mind:

(1) He did not mean that there are not three paths or vehicles and three resultant enlightenments. In that the true nature of those who follow the three vehicles, of their respective paths, and of the results is none other than a single expanse of reality, he meant that the spiritual journey is equivalent.

(2) He meant that all those who follow the three vehicles are the same in that they realize the same individual no-self.

(3) He had in mind that the result of the three vehicles is equivalent in that it is perfect liberation from karma, defilements, and suffering.

(4) He meant that there are individuals of unfixed potential in different vehicles following the listeners' and solitary realizers' paths who then enter the Great Vehicle.

(5) He meant that there is no more than a single vehicle because both aspirations are achieved—the buddhas' aspiration to realize the sameness of themselves and all sentient beings, and the aspiration that listeners and solitary realizers of fixed potential who have practiced the bodhisattvas' activities in the past regain when they want to give them up and are encouraged by the Tathāgata, so that they think, "I too will become a buddha."[58]

(6) Intending to show beings to be trained by such means how to attain nirvāṇa by the Listeners' Vehicle, the Buddha said things like, "I have gone completely beyond suffering many hundreds of times through the Listeners' Vehicle." He was referring to buddha manifestations as listeners, and in that such manifestations and actual listeners both appear to attain nirvāṇa by the Listeners' Vehicle, he spoke of just one vehicle. This is also true for bodhisattvas who manifest as listeners: they do not actually realize the listeners' nirvāṇa but attain buddhahood.

(7) He had in mind that the ultimate vehicle is the Great Vehicle alone, and there is no other.

So it was with these points in mind that the Buddha spoke of a single vehicle and not of three. The *Great Commentary* explains these in considerable detail, but for fear of their being too complicated and difficult to grasp, I have summarized the key points to make them easier to understand.

---

58. Although such listeners and solitary realizers are firmly committed to their respective paths, they never completely give up the idea of attaining buddhahood, so in this respect there is only one vehicle.

> In order to draw some disciples on to it
> And to keep others properly on it,
> The perfect buddhas
> Teach uncertain disciples a single vehicle. (XII, 54)

What is the reason for teaching that there is a single vehicle? It is in order to draw certain listeners of unfixed potential and solitary realizers of unfixed potential into the Great Vehicle. Then there are others, bodhisattvas of unfixed potential, who have entered the Great Vehicle. But when they see the evil ways of sentient beings—they see them doing harm even when they are helped, harming others even when they have not been harmed, harming beings for no reason, and so on—they despair of saṃsāra and want to enter the listeners' nirvāṇa. So it is also in order to keep these bodhisattvas on the right path and prevent them from turning away from the Great Vehicle. For these reasons, the perfect buddhas explain to disciples of unfixed potential that there is a single vehicle. As a result of such explanations, the disciples realize that even if they follow the listeners' path, once they have attained its result they will in any case have to enter the Great Vehicle, so it is better for them to follow the Great Vehicle from the start and not give it up. They are thus prevented from turning back from the bodhisattva path. Listeners of unfixed potential are referred to as being of "listener potential" on account of their having practiced the listeners' activities in the past. The same applies, mutatis mutandis, to those with the other two kinds of potential.

> Listeners of unfixed potential are of two kinds:
> Those who have seen the truth of their vehicle and those who
>   have not.
> Those who have seen the truth,
> Whether or not rid of attachment, are inferior. (XII, 55)

Listeners of unfixed potential, having entered the Great Vehicle, will attain enlightenment, and for them there are two categories: (1) stream enterers, once-returners, and nonreturners who have seen the truth that is the point of their own vehicle[59] and (2) ordinary beings at the level of earnest aspiration who have not seen the truth. Those who have seen the truth are again divided into nonreturners who are rid of the attachment of the world of

---

59. According to Sthiramati, their vehicle in this context refers to the four noble truths.

desire; and stream enterers and once-returners who are not. These two latter categories (of those who have seen the truth and are free or not free of attachment) may have entered the Great Vehicle, but they have dull faculties and take a long time to attain the result of buddhahood, so they are inferior compared to those who have entered the Great Vehicle as ordinary beings.

> Both have attained the noble path,
> And by transforming that attainment,
> They possess an inconceivable
> Birth of transformation in existence. (XII, 56)

Noble listeners have turned their backs on existence and attained the noble path by which they will no longer take birth in existence. If they enter the Great Vehicle, they have to be reborn in saṃsāra and accomplish completion, maturation, and purification for three measureless kalpas. So how, having achieved the path that brings existence to an end, can they be reborn in saṃsāra? For both kinds of noble beings who have seen the truth, those that are free from attachment and those that are not, that untainted act— their attainment of the noble path, which is the antidote to existence in the three worlds—does not lead to their realizing the listener result but instead is transformed by their prayers of aspiration into the cause for their taking birth again in existence. So they have a transformation birth, inconceivable to the intellectual mind, and it is in this way that they take birth in saṃsāra in one life after another and undertake the practices of completion, maturation, and purification.

How, one might ask, can the noble path act as the cause for taking birth in saṃsāra when it involves turning one's back on saṃsāra and is the very antidote that brings existence to an end? In the commentary it is stated that although it is true that with the noble path alone one is not born in saṃsāra, nonreturners (who have the defilements of the two higher worlds) and stream enterers and once-returners (who have not exhausted the defilements of the world of desire to be eliminated by the path of meditation and have the defilements of the two higher worlds) dedicate the noble path to being born in saṃsāra and, because of this, they create the cause with defilements and will be born in saṃsāra. But in our view, the untainted action of attaining the noble path can never change into a tainted action: it is impossible for an untainted action to become tainted and for a positive action to become a negative one. Instead, having already abandoned saṃsāra by means of this untainted path, they give up the intention of striving for the peace of nirvāṇa for themselves and now, as a result of maintaining the aspirations that create birth in saṃsāra, possess an inconceivable transformation birth instead of achieving the listener result. You should understand that it is because of their aspirations that they take birth, and on account of their untainted action, the birth they obtain is not like birth as an ordinary person but an inconceivable transformation birth.

The Buddha allows listeners of unfixed potential who are not free of the attachment of the world of desire to continue using the path of profound insight to meditate that saṃsāra is suffering and nirvāṇa is peace as if to attain nirvāṇa. He then joins them to the path of meditation on the great compassion, fixing their gaze on saṃsāra, and they take birth in saṃsāra through compassion, at which point they are referred to as "fully dedicated to existence." These are noble beings who have seen the truth, so they are not repeatedly reborn in saṃsāra like ordinary beings, who are helplessly driven by their karmic actions and defilements, but take an inconceivable transformation birth.

> One, by the power of prayers of aspiration,
> Attains accomplishment by being born;
> The other, because of being a nonreturner,
> Attains accomplishment through manifestation. (XII, 57)

How do these noble beings take birth? Of those who are not free of the attachment of the world of desire and those who are free, the ones who are not free of attachment are stream enterers and once-returners. Out of their compassion for suffering beings, they pray, "Wherever I wish to benefit beings, may I be reborn there," and by the power of that prayer they actually take birth in those places.[60] Having taken birth, they bring benefit and happiness to sentient beings, and by doing so accumulate merit and wisdom and ultimately attain buddhahood.

The others, who are free of the attachment of the desire world, will not return to the world of desire, and because of this, although they do not themselves take birth in the world of desire, they display birth in saṃsāra through the manifestations of their concentration. They thus accumulate merit and wisdom and finally attain buddhahood.

---

60. They take an "authentic" birth (Tib. *skye ba mtshan nyid pa*), in contrast to the nonreturners, who display birth through manifestation.

> Since these two, from repetition,
> Continue to think of themselves,
> They delight in nirvāṇa,
> So realization is slow. (XII, 58)

For those who have seen the truth through the listeners' path (both those who are free of the attachment of the desire world and those who are not), the force of repetition, that is, of their previous former habituation, is such that they constantly prefer their own welfare, and they therefore delight in nirvāṇa. For this reason, it is said, they are slow to realize the result of the Great Vehicle.

> Those who have not attained the goal
> Take birth when there is no Buddha and,
> Yearning to manifest, strive for concentration,
> By which means they will attain supreme enlightenment. (XII, 59)

The Buddha's disciples in the Listeners' Vehicle who have not attained the goal of seeing the truth, who are of unfixed potential (ordinary beings or individuals on the level of earnest aspiration), and who have entered the Great Vehicle leave the human realm in the world of desire when they die and are reborn among the long-lived gods. There they remain for long periods of time. Then, when our teacher, the Buddha, is no longer in this world and his doctrine has disappeared, they will again take birth in the world of desire. Born in the world of desire, they will take no pleasure in the sense objects, and on the strength of their former habituation to the Buddha's teachings, they will realize the noble path without having a spiritual master, like the solitary realizers. Subsequently, with a yearning to create manifestations, they will put their efforts into achieving the dhyānas of the world of form. Relying on such concentration, they will emanate manifestations and, benefiting sentient beings in the three worlds, they will complete the accumulations of merit and wisdom and finally attain supreme enlightenment. As we read in the *Sūtra of the Lion's Roar of Śrīmālādevī*:

> First the fire sets alight the fuel,
> Then it spreads throughout the land.

When he spoke this metaphor, the Buddha had in mind three states: first they become listeners, then solitary realizers, and finally perfect buddhas.

Thus, it is possible, according to this tradition that holds that there are three final goals and vehicles, for beings of unfixed potential to enter the Great Vehicle and thence attain buddhahood. On the other hand, those who have the fixed potential to become listeners and solitary realizers will never attain buddhahood, while beings without potential will never have the chance to attain the enlightenment of the listeners and solitary realizers, let alone buddhahood. As for listener and solitary-realizer arhats, when they are in the state of nirvāṇa without residue their five aggregates are discontinued forever, so it is impossible for them to enter the Great Vehicle.

The Mādhyamikas maintain that all sentient beings have the essence of the sugatas[61] and can therefore attain buddhahood; there are no beings who do not have that potential. Since the nature of the mind is radiant light and it is possible to remove the adventitious contaminants, even listeners and solitary realizers who have temporarily reached the respective levels of enlightenment of their two vehicles and have entered nirvāṇa without residue will attain buddhahood. Aroused by the tathāgatas' rays of light, they will emerge from the expanse of cessation and, having taken an inconceivable transformation birth, they will reach the culmination of completion, maturation, and purification. In the end, this is what really happens, as is also taught in the *Sublime Continuum*.

As these two approaches accord with different individuals' natures, faculties, and aspirations, they are both taught in the sūtras, and it is impossible to deny the existence, in terms of temporary situations, of the paths and results of the three vehicles, or equally of beings without potential. So in this context, this is how things are to be explained.

xi. Investigating the Five Sciences

> Without being diligent in the five sciences,
> Even the highest of noble beings will not attain omniscience.
> Therefore, in order to subjugate others, to care for them,
> And to know all things themselves, they are diligent in
>   these. (XII, 60)

It is by removing misconceptions and becoming learned with regard to all knowable phenomena (both their nature and their multiplicity) that bodhi-

---

61. Skt. *sugatagarbha*, the buddha nature.

sattvas, followers of the Great Vehicle, attain omniscience, so they need to train well in all the sciences. Listeners desirous of peace and happiness are able to attain the listeners' enlightenment even by realizing the meaning of a single verse about the path for severing the root of existence, so they do not involve themselves in such extensive knowledge.

All knowledge, mundane and supramundane, can be summarized in just five sciences, which comprise the following:

(1) The treatises on the science of grammar. To begin with, all the Vedas, tenet systems, and so on require a knowledge of the subjects that is based on the words used to describe them, so these treatises present the correct way in which speech, which is made up of names, phrases, and letters, is constructed using names, grammatical connectors, and so on.

(2) The treatises on the science of logic that distinguish without error the true and mistaken meanings of what is being taught, or treatises that unmistakenly indicate the methods of valid cognition by direct perception and inference.

(3) The treatises on the various arts of ordinary beings. These follow mundane traditions of arts and crafts—physical arts and sports, and manual crafts such as calligraphy; vocal proficiency in the seven musical tones and in religious and secular speaking; and the theoretical knowledge of proper and improper worldly manners, of the eight kinds of examination,[62] and so on, to mention a few.

(4) The treatises on the eight branches of the science of medicine or the maintenance of good health. These include general presentations on "restoring health," that is, the correction of imbalances (due to diet and the like) of the wind, bile, and phlegm elements naturally present in all beings' bodies through mastery in four branches—the causes of disease, the nature of disease, the remedies for treating illness, and the methods for preventing illness from occurring in the future. They also include specialized medicine—the treatment of diseases particular to women and children; the remedial treatment of unexpected illnesses caused by external causes such as poisoning, weapon injury, and possession by negative forces; sexual treatments that increase semen and maintain sexual health; and antiaging treatments and

---

62. The eight kinds of examination refer, for example, to a king's ability to examine men (with a view to their suitability as servants), women (as potential wives), land, lakes and water, garments, gems and precious substances, horses, and elephants.

the promotion of long life by skillful techniques such as "taking the essence" on the basis of good health.

(5) The treatises on the "inner science" or the perfect, sacred Dharma that teaches a correct understanding of the nature of knowable phenomena, as they are and as many as there are, and indicates the path to the everlasting happiness of liberation and omniscience.

All the texts of the five minor sciences and others are included in these five. Without being diligent in these five sciences and mastering them, even the highest noble beings of the Great Vehicle, who are far superior to the noble beings of the lesser vehicles, will never attain omniscience. Why? Because omniscience means knowing everything there is to know, and it is the five sciences that encompass everything there is to know. So it is impossible to be omniscient without knowing these five. This is why even on the level of earnest aspiration, beings with the Mahāyāna potential, with their naturally sharp faculties and vast attitude and wisdom, are diligent in the five sciences, which encompass all branches of knowledge, and they dedicate them to attaining omniscient gnosis. As a result, and in similarity with the cause, they repeatedly train in this over many, many lives. Once they have attained the bodhisattva levels, the power of their concentration and gnosis is such that they have no difficulty in knowing all there is to know, and they habituate themselves to this over countless lives. Noble beings of the Great Vehicle are therefore especially diligent and learned in the five sciences. It is important to understand that it is impossible for them not to be learned. You must never have the sort of improper notion that once one has become a supreme noble being, one has to start learning the five sciences from scratch.

At the stage of training, bodhisattvas' abundant and unclouded knowledge of the five sciences may be called "omni-science,"[63] in much the same way as one might speak of having "all the medicines" when the necessary medicines are all there, or similarly of "everybody." But it is on the buddha level, when that causal knowledge is consummated, that they truly know everything encompassed by the five sciences and that they fully acquire the epithet "omniscient."

By mastering the five sciences, anyone earnestly applying themselves to pursuing the bodhisattva's work in benefiting others will be able to achieve others' welfare and attain omniscience. For this reason, bodhisattvas are extremely diligent in learning these five sciences, studying the sciences of

---

63. Tib. *rig gnas thams cad mkhyen pa*, lit. "knowledge of all sciences."

grammar and of logic so that they can use words and meanings to subjugate others—tīrthikas and the like—who teach perverse views, training in the sciences of the arts and medicine in order to care for beings generally and specifically, and learning the inner science or sacred Dharma in order to correctly know for themselves the nature and multiplicity of all phenomena. This is also taught in the *Sūtra in Repayment of Kindness*, in which the Buddha spoke of the need to train in each of the sciences (the sūtras and the other eleven branches of the sacred Dharma, the science of reasons or proofs, the science of grammar, the science of medicine, and the science of mundane arts) and then declared, "If bodhisattvas do not train in the five sciences, they will never acquire the gnosis of unsurpassable, perfect, omniscient enlightenment. This is why, to attain unsurpassable enlightenment, one must train in the five sciences."

2. The Different Forms of Attentiveness Used in Investigation

There now follows an explanation of the different forms of attentiveness[64] with which bodhisattvas investigate the Dharma and which cause the potential for transcendent perfection to grow. These are indicated in the next thirteen verses, beginning with attentiveness to joy from considering the cause, attentiveness in mindfulness of the support, attentiveness in wishing for a shared result, attentiveness in yearning for the same enlightenment, attentiveness associated with joy on account of one's powers, attentiveness associated with indefatigability, and attentiveness associated with abandoning incompatible traits and employing antidotes (making seven in all), and continuing from attentiveness associated with clear faith and so forth through to attentiveness associated with one's own superiority. It is from having kept all these in mind that the potential for transcendent perfection in one's mind stream will unfold.

> **Joy from considering the cause,**
> **Mindfulness of the support,**
> **The wish for a shared result,**
> **And a yearning for a similar enlightenment;** (XII, 61)

---

64. Or put another way, the different factors that are kept in mind in investigating the Dharma.

First, there is "joy from considering the cause." Bodhisattvas, who are individuals in whom the Mahāyāna potential is present, begin by examining to see whether or not they have the potential for buddhahood, the potential or seed for being able to accomplish the six transcendent perfections. From this they know that they have the cause for wanting to attain buddhahood and to practice the transcendent perfections. Because they repeatedly keep in mind their delight at this, thinking, "I have the good fortune for attaining buddhahood," the seed of transcendent perfection present in the ground of all will develop.

So it is with "mindfulness of the support." Those people in whom the potential is present subsequently arouse the mind set on unsurpassable enlightenment. Since this is the foundation or support for the transcendent perfections, they rejoice, thinking, "By arousing the bodhicitta I will complete the transcendent perfections." From their constantly remembering that support, their spiritual intent, with unforgetting mindfulness and wisdom, again, the potential for transcendent perfection will develop.

After that the bodhisattvas "wish for a shared result." Practicing the six transcendent perfections, they desire the ripened effects of the transcendent perfections not for themselves alone but to be shared with others. Keeping this dedication in mind also makes the potential for transcendent perfection grow.

After that comes "yearning for a similar enlightenment." This is the yearning, "Just as the buddhas of the past, present, and future, having practiced the six transcendent perfections, realize unsurpassable enlightenment, may I too, by practicing the six transcendent perfections, actually attain buddhahood." This too makes the potential for transcendent perfection unfold.

Thus you should know that attentiveness to these four—joy from considering the cause, being mindful of one's spiritual intent, wishing the result of practicing the transcendent perfections to be shared with all sentient beings, and the unsurpassable attainment—makes the seeds of the six transcendent perfections that are present in the element of one's own ground consciousness grow more and more, and that in the same way all the different kinds of attentiveness that follow make the potential for transcendent perfection grow, and that this takes place in the given order. The root text here mentions these very succinctly.

> **Joy on account of the four powers,**
> **True indefatigability,**

And the four aspects of practice with regard to
Incompatible traits and their antidotes; (XII, 62)

"Joy on account of the four powers" refers to keeping in mind the joy that arises from the four powers once one has seen that one has them, as will be explained below. "True indefatigability" refers to keeping in mind the fact that if one possesses these powers, one will certainly never despair of completing the path to buddhahood oneself and maturing sentient beings. And with regard to incompatible traits and their antidotes, there are four aspects to keeping in mind the abandoning of stinginess and other factors incompatible with the transcendent perfections and the employment of their antidotes (generosity and the rest) in order to accomplish unsurpassable enlightenment without ever getting discouraged.

The four powers are the power or ability to abandon factors incompatible with the transcendent perfections; the power to ripen the accumulations with antidotes—that is, with the transcendent perfections; the power to benefit oneself and other beings; and the ability one gains, on account of the fully ripened effect and the effect similar to the cause, to accomplish the transcendent perfections in the future.

What is the power of abandoning incompatible traits? It is the ability to see that generosity can dispel stinginess, and similarly to abandon the factors incompatible with each of the other transcendent perfections—namely, lax discipline, anger, laziness, distraction, and aberrant understanding.

Maturing the accumulations is seeing that with the six transcendent perfections the accumulations of merit and wisdom are gathered and ripened. Generosity, discipline, and patience are related to the accumulation of merit, wisdom and concentration to the accumulation of wisdom, and diligence to both of these.

How does one benefit oneself and others? By taking pleasure in giving generously and not regretting it, one benefits oneself now and in the future, and the gifts one makes benefit others. Similarly, with discipline and patience one ceases to harm others; with diligence one accomplishes others' good; by the power of concentration, one dispels others' illnesses, disasters in bad years, and so forth; and by teaching the Dharma with wisdom, one benefits others—there is no need to mention the benefit to oneself.

What are the fully ripened effects and the effects similar to the cause that occur in the future? As a result of generosity, one will be wealthy. As a result of discipline, one will be reborn as a human or celestial being. As a result of patience, one will be beautiful and have a large retinue of excellent followers.

Because of diligence, one will accomplish all one's tasks completely. Concentration will result in good physical health and a workable mind. And as a result of wisdom, one will be learned in all the sciences. These are all fully ripened effects. The effects similar to the cause are such that wherever one is reborn in one's future lives, one will take pleasure in practicing generosity and each of the other transcendent perfections and accomplish them, and by this means one will benefit oneself and bring others to maturity.

These, then, are the four powers.

Attentiveness associated with indefatigability comprises never getting discouraged in bringing sentient beings to maturity through the four ways of attracting disciples, and never getting discouraged in bringing the Buddha's teachings to maturity or perfection in oneself by following a spiritual master, listening to the sacred Dharma, and so forth. Despite beings' ingratitude, despite the heat and cold, hunger and thirst, exhaustion, and the rest that one may suffer when one practices the transcendent perfections oneself and subsequently sets others to practicing them, rather than getting discouraged, one can never have enough of practicing the Dharma.

Attentiveness associated with abandoning incompatible traits and employing antidotes involves four practices: (1) confessing traits, should they occur, that are incompatible with the transcendent perfections—traits from stinginess through to aberrant understanding that lead to negative actions; (2) rejoicing at one's own and others' application of the antidotes—generosity and the other five perfections; (3) praying to the tathāgatas to turn the wheel of the extensive and profound Dharma, the teachings on the transcendent perfections; and (4) fully dedicating all one's own and others' positive actions, beginning with the above three (confession, rejoicing, and prayer), to the attainment of unsurpassable enlightenment. As we read in the sūtras:

> I confess all my negative actions.
> I rejoice in all sources of good.
> All the buddhas I exhort and pray.
> May I and others obtain the sublime, unsurpassable gnosis.

> **Clear faith, correct reception,**
> **A longing to give to others,**
> **Armor, prayer,**
> **True joy, and a sense of duty;** (XII, 63)

Again, by one's keeping in mind the different kinds of attentiveness that are indicated in this verse—attentiveness associated with clear faith, attentiveness associated with correct reception, and so on—the potential for transcendent perfection will develop.

"Clear faith" refers to keeping in mind clear faith, which is to develop an untainted attitude with regard to the teachings on the six transcendent perfections and the transcendent perfections themselves (or alternatively, to the causal transcendent perfections and their result). In short, one keeps in mind the confidence that the six transcendent perfections are the foundation of all completion, maturation, and purification, and that boundless good qualities are their result. "Correct reception" refers to attentiveness in correctly receiving instructions, that is, with that kind of faith, seeking the teachings on the transcendent perfections and receiving them correctly. "A longing to give to others" refers to keeping in mind the delight or longing to give others those teachings. These three are related to the study of the teachings.

"Armor" refers to attentiveness to the donning of armor[65] in practicing the transcendent perfections on an infinite scale. "Prayer" refers to keeping in mind prayers of aspiration that in all one's lives the conditions for completing the six transcendent perfections—the spiritual master, one's relatives and friends, body, possessions, and so forth—may all be present so that one may practice the transcendent perfections continuously on a vast scale. "True joy" refers to keeping in mind a heartfelt delight in practicing the transcendent perfections, which are the cause for attaining unsurpassable enlightenment, throughout all one's lives. These three refer to engaging in the transcendent perfections according to the instructions one has received.

After these comes attentiveness associated with the possession of skillful means, indicated by "a sense of duty." In not only actually training in the transcendent perfections oneself but also rejoicing in others' practice of the transcendent perfections, deriving pleasure from them and appreciating them, one keeps in mind one's task of completing the transcendent perfections.

> The highest genuine enthusiasm
> For obtaining power in the six perfections,

---

65. "Armor" usually refers to the armor of patience and diligence.

> For full maturation, making offerings,
> And following a teacher; and affection; (XII, 64)

Four kinds of enthusiasm to be kept in mind are indicated in this verse. They are enthusiasm for obtaining power in the six transcendent perfections, enthusiasm for bringing sentient beings to full maturity, enthusiasm for making offerings to the tathāgatas, and enthusiasm for following the spiritual master.

With regard to the first, within each of the six transcendent perfections there are again six transcendent perfections: for generosity there is the generosity of generosity, the discipline of generosity, and so on through to the wisdom of generosity, making thirty-six in all. So the first factor to be kept in mind is enthusiasm for obtaining the power to be able to practice the transcendent perfections in that way. How does this subdivision of each perfection into six work? When one practices each transcendent perfection, one is practicing that particular transcendent perfection—the generosity of generosity, for example. At the same time, in practicing each transcendent perfection one is benefiting others, so in that respect one is practicing generosity. In that each perfection involves avoiding negative actions, undertaking positive actions, and bringing benefit to beings, one is practicing discipline. From the point of view of one's patiently bearing harm at that time, one is practicing patience. Making an effort to practice this or that transcendent perfection is its diligence aspect. Keeping the mind focused one-pointedly without being carried away by counteragents is the concentration aspect. And in terms of one's correctly knowing the cause and result of the respective transcendent perfection on the conventional level and remaining free from the three concepts of subject, object, and action on the ultimate level, one is practicing wisdom.

"Full maturation" refers to the second enthusiasm to be kept in mind—enthusiasm for practicing the six transcendent perfections in the form of the four ways of attracting disciples and thus bringing sentient beings to full maturation.

"Offering" refers to the third enthusiasm that is to be kept in mind—enthusiasm for making offerings to the tathāgatas, both in making material offerings and venerating them with transcendent generosity, and in offering one's practice of the other five transcendent perfections.

"Following" refers to the fourth enthusiasm to keep in mind—enthusiasm for following the spiritual master who teaches the unerring way of the transcendent perfections.

Thus keeping in mind the "highest genuine enthusiasm" for the transcendent perfections, for attracting disciples, for making offerings, and for following a teacher makes the potential for transcendent perfection grow.

After that, there is keeping in mind heartfelt affection, indicated by "affection." This comprises love, compassion, sympathetic joy, and impartiality, as will be explained in the section below on the boundless attitudes.[66] Compassion refers to arousing compassion for those who have traits incompatible with the six transcendent perfections or who suffer as a result of that, and not only feeling compassion but also doing one's best to dispel their suffering and introducing them to the transcendent perfections, through which traits like stinginess are abandoned, so that they no longer experience suffering. Love involves wishing that sentient beings be happy, and there again, not simply feeling love but also introducing them to the transcendent perfections that are the cause of happiness. Sympathetic joy involves rejoicing from the bottom of one's heart when sentient beings who possess generosity and other causes of happiness, or who are happy as the result of the latter, are happy, and introducing them to virtue and the transcendent perfections so that they will never be unhappy. Impartiality is to be without attachment and aversion, and therefore to think, "May those who are happy never feel attachment" and "May those who suffer (for example, from having their possessions appropriated by others) never feel aversion," and to give them teachings on the transcendent perfections so as to free them from attachment and aversion.

> Shame and regret for having practiced badly
> Or not at all, delighting in the object,
> The notion of despair as an enemy,
> Introducing, and expressive intelligence; (XII, 65)

Keeping in mind a sense of shame is indicated by "shame and regret for having practiced badly or not at all." This refers to shame and regret at, for example, never having practiced the transcendent perfections, and at what we call "having practiced badly or disgracefully," that is, not having practiced them completely, and having practiced them with stinginess and with lower paths in mind.

"Delighting in the object" refers to keeping delight in mind—one-pointed,

---

66. See ch. 18.

undistracted delight as one continuously practices the transcendent perfections. This is also known as keeping stability in mind.

"The notion of despair as an enemy." When one is engaging in generosity and the other transcendent perfections, one may feel depressed and not wish to practice. To think of this as an enemy, since it is an obstacle to attaining unsurpassable enlightenment, is to keep in mind not getting discouraged.

"Introducing" is explained as follows. Thinking that one will protect sentient beings by teaching them the path related to the six transcendent perfections, to introduce those to be trained to the treatises that teach the relevant scriptural tradition is what is known as "keeping introduction in mind." This is as described in the chapter on elements leading to enlightenment.

"Expressive intelligence" represents keeping expression in mind, that is, giving explanations in accord with beings' individual particularities as receptacles for the teachings. This refers to mundane knowledge in assessing people's minds. Below, the chapter on elements leading to enlightenment deals with knowledge of the truth rather than of what happens on the mundane level: this is ultimate knowledge.

> **Generosity and so forth being the support**
> **Of perfect enlightenment (not Īśvara and the others),**
> **Distinguishing the faults in incompatible traits**
> **And the qualities in their antidotes; (XII, 66)**

"Generosity and so forth being the support of perfect enlightenment (not Īśvara and the others)" refers to keeping in mind the support, knowing that the six transcendent perfections—generosity and the rest—are the foundation of perfect enlightenment and that Īśvara, Brahmā, and other gods are not supports for attaining enlightenment. This arises through the wisdom associated with the four reliances.[67]

"Distinguishing the faults in incompatible traits and the qualities in their antidotes" refers to keeping discrimination in mind; that is, knowing and keeping in mind, with the perfect knowledge of meanings, the fact that there are faults and qualities in the two—incompatible traits and antidotes. In stinginess and other incompatible traits there are faults such as future poverty. And in generosity and the other transcendent perfections there are good qualities, which are the opposite of those faults.

67. See ch. 19, v. 32.

> **Joy from the memory of accumulation,**
> **Seeing the great point,**
> **And the wish for yoga, for nonconceptuality,**
> **For retention, and for encountering; (XII, 67)**

Joy from remembering that one has gathered the two accumulations is indicated by "Joy from the memory of accumulation." This refers to keeping in mind one's delight from having remembered that one has gathered the accumulations—the accumulation of merit through generosity, discipline, and patience; the accumulation of wisdom through concentration and wisdom; and the diligence in each of these by giving with generosity and so on.

Keeping in mind one's seeing the great point is indicated by "seeing the great point." Generosity and the other transcendent perfections constitute the point, for they are the elements that lead to enlightenment. The culmination of nonconceptual gnosis being great enlightenment, generosity and the other transcendent perfections are the cause of that great enlightenment, so it is by completing them that one attains great enlightenment. This is why they are seen as being the great point.

"Yoga" refers to keeping yoga in mind—that is, meditating on the union of sustained calm and profound insight in order to complete the six transcendent perfections.

"Nonconceptuality" refers to nonconceptual gnosis, which is the means for completing the transcendent perfections. What makes one have nonconceptual gnosis is what we call "keeping in mind the wish for nonconceptuality." Put another way, when one actually practices, one's prayers of aspiration that one may engage in the transcendent perfections nonconceptually will be fulfilled, so we speak of keeping in mind the wish for nonconceptuality.

The above points, from the two accumulations up to nonconceptuality, are dealt with in the same order in the chapter on elements leading to enlightenment.

"Retention" refers to keeping retention in mind, that is, retaining both the teachings that describe the transcendent perfections and their meaning, without forgetting them. This comes about through infallible memory.

"The wish for encountering" refers to keeping in mind the obtainment of conditions, and amounts to prayers of aspiration—wishing and praying that wherever one is born, one will encounter spiritual masters and other conditions for completing the transcendent perfections.

The obtainment of power for eliminating
The seven kinds of wrong belief,
And the four thoughts
Of what is extraordinary and what is not; (XII, 68)

"The obtainment of power for eliminating the seven kinds of wrong belief" refers to attentiveness in obtaining the power to get rid of the seven kinds of wrong belief in order to train in the transcendent perfections. These seven mistaken or wrong beliefs are eliminated by the three concentrations and the four summaries of the Dharma. The belief that the phenomena of imputed reality exist when they do not; the belief that the fault-ridden phenomena of saṃsāra have good qualities such as being permanent;[68] and the view held by immature beings that nirvāṇa, rather than being full of good qualities, is like an abyss devoid of good qualities (for they fear it entails the extinction of the self)—these are the three mistaken beliefs. The antidotes that eliminate them are the three concentrations on emptiness, absence of expectancy, and absence of attributes respectively. The belief that compounded phenomena are permanent, the belief that tainted phenomena are happiness, the belief that there is a self in phenomena, and the belief that nirvāṇa is not peace are the four wrong beliefs. The antidotes for eliminating these are the four summaries of the Dharma—respectively that all compounded phenomena are impermanent, that all tainted phenomena are suffering, that all phenomena are empty and devoid of self, and that nirvāṇa is peace. Keeping all these in mind makes the potential for transcendent perfection grow.

    The detailed explanations of the six factors to be kept in mind from clear faith to true joy (verse 63) correspond to the six chapters on interest, investigating the Dharma, teaching the Dharma, practicing the Dharma, the instructions, and follow-up teachings. "A sense of duty" (verse 63) corresponds to the chapter on skillful activity (chapter 16). "Obtaining power in the six perfections" (verse 64) corresponds to the section on the six transcendent perfections in the chapter on transcendent perfections (chapter 17); and "full maturation" corresponds to the section on the four ways of attracting disciples in the same chapter. The next three, "offering," "following," and "affection," are as they appear in the chapter on offerings, reliance,

---

68. This is to hold that samsaric phenomena, which are characterized by impermanence, suffering, impurity, and no-self, are permanent, happy, pure, and a self.

and boundless attitudes (chapter 18). The factors to be kept in mind from "shame" through to "eliminating the seven kinds of wrong belief" (verses 65–68) are as they appear in order in the chapter on elements leading to enlightenment (chapter 19).

Then there is an explanation of two factors to be kept in mind with regard to what is extraordinary and what is not extraordinary, indicated by "four thoughts of what is extraordinary and what is not." There are four thoughts to be kept in mind about what is extraordinary and four about what is not extraordinary. Keeping these in mind also makes the potential for transcendent perfection grow. It is to be understood that in the same way all the different kinds of attentiveness make the potential for the ten transcendent perfections grow, as is shown by the single verse (73) at the end of this section, "Keeping in mind the virtue that results from the ten transcendent perfections. . . ." There is no need to repeat this in each individual case.

What are the four extraordinary thoughts? As indicated by "Their own bodies they give away . . . ,"[69] in the Qualities chapter, they are as follows: (1) It is extraordinary to think that in practicing the transcendent perfections, bodhisattvas give up things that are very difficult to give up, giving away or renouncing their bodies for the sake of their own practice of generosity, abandoning all the wonderful things they have—their bodies, family, and the like—for the sake of their discipline, and so on through to having no concepts in their practice of wisdom. (2) We can also marvel at the length of time, for it is an extraordinary thought that they practice the extensive activities of the transcendent perfections for three measureless kalpas. (3) Even when they are practicing the six transcendent perfections, they do not hope for any personal reward in this life, which again is something quite amazing. (4) Similarly, it is quite extraordinary that they do not hope for any ripened karmic fruit in future lives.

Other explanations for these four are also mentioned in the scriptures—being born in a good family, and so on.

The four unextraordinary thoughts are as follows: (1) Just as there is nothing very extraordinary in a crop of rice growing from planting rice grain, for this is the very nature of the interdependence of cause and effect, there is no great wonder in obtaining the boundless qualities of enlightenment as the result of practicing the boundless transcendent perfections. (2) It would be quite surprising if, by considering oneself and others not equal, one were to

---

69. Ch. 20, v. 1.

benefit others as much as oneself. But since, through long habituation to the antidote, bodhisattvas have eliminated the notion of self and have seen that they are the same as others, there is nothing at all surprising in their benefiting sentient beings as much as themselves. (3) When the greatest of ordinary beings—Brahmā, Indra, and the like—are benefited by bodhisattvas and offer gifts and respect in return, those bodhisattvas do not accept them, for they are free of attachment and think as much of those offerings as of a gob of spit. So how could they hope that ordinary beings would do anything in return for their benefiting them? Bodhisattvas benefit sentient beings with tender affection, so there is nothing extraordinary in the fact that they do not have the slightest expectation of reward. (4) There is nothing extraordinary either in their not hoping for a ripened karmic result. Bodhisattvas have no desire for mundane karmic results because they are sure to attain the three buddha bodies and untainted bliss that transcend the mundane.

> **Impartiality toward sentient beings,**
> **Being seen as a great being,**
> **Hoping for the recompense of good qualities in others,**
> **A threefold aspiration, and continuity; (XII, 69)**

"Impartiality toward beings" refers to keeping impartiality in mind—being even-minded with regard to sentient beings, without any notion of close or distant, and introducing them to the transcendent perfections. This is indicated by "In their impartiality to all in need . . ." and so on.[70]

"Being seen as a great being" refers to keeping in mind being considered as a great being. When bodhisattvas practice the six transcendent perfections, their practice will lead exclusively to happiness and benefit and not to the slightest harm. They are therefore seen as great beings who benefit all sentient beings in six ways, bringing them nothing but benefit and happiness. This is indicated by the verse on bringing benefit ("Making beings fit vessels, . . .") in the Qualities chapter,[71] and the seven similes for how bodhisattvas benefit—like mothers, fathers, kinsfolk, and so forth.[72]

"Hoping for the recompense of good qualities in others." When other beings, having been induced to practice the transcendent perfections,

---

70. Ch. 20, v. 6.
71. Ch. 20, v. 8.
72. Ch. 20, vv. 10–23.

acquire the excellent qualities of the six transcendent perfections, the bodhisattvas' wishes are fulfilled and they feel that those sentient beings have benefited them. All they hope for in return for their help is that others should gain the corresponding good qualities; they wish for no other reward. For it is by thinking, "If only sentient beings could have the excellent qualities of the transcendent perfections," that they bring beings to maturity, and when those sentient beings become mature, they completely fulfill the bodhisattvas' hopes. This is what we call "keeping in mind the desire for recompense." There is nothing greater in repayment of the bodhisattvas' kindness than that the sentient beings whom they have introduced to the transcendent perfections should acquire the qualities of the transcendent perfections. No other recompense can ever repay that kindness, because there is nothing else that bodhisattvas might wish for in return. This is described in verses 24 and 25 of chapter 20 from "Because they are not attached to wealth . . ." to "Similarly benefit bodhisattvas in return."

"A threefold aspiration" refers to keeping hopes in mind or keeping wishes in mind. What do bodhisattvas wish for? They hope and wish for three things: that all sentient beings will complete the bodhisattva levels, that they will finally achieve the level of buddhahood, and that they will benefit beings. With regard to the first of these, bodhisattvas want beings to reach the culmination of the ten bodhisattva levels, from the ultimate reach of generosity which is the completion of transcendent generosity on the first level through to the completion of transcendent gnosis on the tenth level. Second, they want them to go beyond the ten levels and attain the ultimate result, buddhahood. Third, they want them to bring benefit and happiness to all sentient beings, both while they are bodhisattvas and once they have attained buddhahood. In the root text this is indicated by the verse, "For beings and themselves . . . ."[73]

"Continuity" refers to what we call "keeping continuity in mind"—that is, practicing the transcendent perfections uninterruptedly, like the flow of a river, rather than practicing sometimes and not at other times. This means actually putting the instructions and follow-up teachings into practice and not letting them go to waste. It is indicated by "In their absence of fear . . . the buddhas' heirs are never wasteful."[74]

---

73. Ch. 20, v. 26.
74. Ch. 20, v. 27.

> In order to accomplish the Buddha's teaching,
> The intention to not fall short;
> Sadness with regard to beings who fail in that,
> And delight with regard to those who flourish; (XII, 70)

"In order to accomplish the Buddha's teaching, the intention to not fall short." To accomplish the transcendent perfections authentically as taught by the Buddha, from the moment one first arouses bodhicitta and then listens and reflects, and until one finally attains buddhahood, one must be diligent in unrelentingly practicing the transcendent perfections. This constitutes keeping in mind perfect application, which in the root text is indicated by "Generosity without expectation, ... are applying them authentically."[75] In order to do that, one must have "the intention to not fall short," that is, the intention that in one's practice of generosity and the rest, one will not fall short and remain mundane in one's scope, with a desire for the samsaric riches and so on that will result from that practice. This line is not explained in the commentary, but I think it should be linked to the previous line, which is not linked to anything; this is a point that should be checked.

"Sadness with regard to beings who fail in that, and delight with regard to those who flourish." When bodhisattvas see beings who are deficient in terms of the transcendent perfections—in other words, whose practice of the transcendent perfections has deteriorated—they lose interest in them. This constitutes keeping sadness in mind. When they see beings whose practice of generosity and the rest is increasing and progressing, they feel pleased with them. This constitutes keeping delight in mind. These two are described in the root text in the two verses beginning "Attachment to pleasure...."[76]

> Not having faith in fake meditation
> And having faith in the authentic;
> Attentiveness to refusal,
> Pleasure from predictions and certainty; (XII, 71)

Similarly, there is "Not having faith in fake meditation and having faith in the authentic." Not having faith in practicing a fake version or effigy of

---

75. Ch. 20, vv. 28–29.
76. Ch. 20, vv. 30–31.

the six transcendent perfections constitutes keeping disinterest in mind. "Fake" here refers to impure generosity (or a semblance of generosity) and other impure perfections through to impure wisdom.[77] Having faith in the practice of genuine transcendent perfections constitutes keeping interest in mind. These two are indicated by the two verses beginning with "Making a show...."[78]

"Attentiveness to refusal" refers to keeping in mind the refusal to accept stinginess and other traits running counter to the transcendent perfections, should they occur in one's own or others' mind streams, and correcting them with the antidotes, in association with wisdom. This is indicated by the verse "The wise, on all the levels, ..."[79]

"Predictions" refers to the wish for predictions—the pleasure in receiving or desire to receive predictions from the tathāgatas: "Fortunate child, one day, when you have completed the transcendent perfections, you will attain buddhahood in unsurpassable enlightenment." Alternatively, since bodhisattvas receive predictions at the time of the eighth level, it is the desire to attain the eighth level. The different kinds of predictions are indicated by the three verses beginning with "Specifying the individual and the time...."[80]

"Pleasure from . . . certainty" refers to keeping in mind the desire to attain the level of certainty. This has two aspects: wishing for certainty with regard to wealth and wishing for certainty with regard to birth. Concerning the first of these, when one attains the first level, the level on which transcendent generosity is completed, in one instant one can see one hundred buddhas, shake one hundred worlds, and so on—in all, twelve sets of one hundred extraordinary qualities. From that level, one progresses from one level to the next until at the time of the tenth level, on which transcendent gnosis is completed, one obtains qualities equal in number to the atoms in the universe, beyond the scope of words or thought. To wish for the wealth of all these inconceivable powers and the wealth of expertise in the five sciences constitutes the wish for certainty with regard to wealth. Wishing for certainty with regard to birth is the desire to reach the level of a bodhisattva

---

77. "Impure" in this context can refer to practice that is not free of the concepts of subject, object, and action. Sthiramati describes a "semblance" of generosity as, for example, the giving of weapons, poison, and so forth; a "semblance" of wisdom would be knowledge of incorrect views concerning a self, permanence, and so on.

78. Ch. 20, vv. 32–33.

79. Ch. 20, v. 34.

80. Ch. 20, vv. 35–37.

who has attained the tenth level and has only one more rebirth to go. This point is indicated by six lines beginning "For the wise, at all times, abundance, birth...."[81]

> The intention to practice with a view to future lives,
> Looking to equality,
> And, on account of engagement in the highest Dharma,
> The conviction of one's own greatness— (XII, 72)
>
> Keeping in mind the virtue that results
> From the ten transcendent perfections
> Makes the potential within a bodhisattva
> Constantly unfold and grow. (XII, 73)

"The intention to practice with a view to future lives" refers to keeping one's practice in mind with a view to future lives. Once one has aroused the mind intent on enlightenment, if one wants to attain unsurpassable enlightenment, wherever one is reborn in one's future lives one will have to practice the causal factors that lead to enlightenment—the transcendent perfections. Having seen this, one then sees that if one practices the six transcendent perfections with this intention or attentiveness while constantly practicing them in this life, the resulting effect similar to the cause will be that one will also practice the transcendent perfections in one's future lives. This, then, is the attitude with which a bodhisattva practices the transcendent perfections.

"Looking to equality" refers to keeping in mind the thought of equality— that is, the thought, "By training constantly in the transcendent perfections, I will be the same, physically, verbally, and mentally, as other bodhisattvas."

"On account of engagement in the highest Dharma, the conviction of one's own greatness" refers to keeping one's own greatness in mind. By practicing the six transcendent perfections, which constitute the highest path, one attains its result, the bodhisattva levels and buddha level. So because one is engaged in the highest Dharma, both as path and as result, one considers that one is definitely far superior to the highest of beings, including the listeners and solitary realizers.

Thinking of the ten transcendent perfections like this, or keeping in

---

81. Ch. 20, v. 38.

mind the virtue that stems from the causal factors that they embody, makes the potential for the ten transcendent perfections in a bodhisattva's mind constantly grow.

These last three kinds of attentiveness correspond to the four verses that indicate definite duties, perpetual duties, and the paramount activities of the transcendent perfections.[82]

After that, there are a number of factors to be kept in mind that are not mentioned here because the four sections that present the teachings, the truth, rational application, and vehicles in the Qualities chapter have already been included in investigating the Dharma, and so on; and because the subsequent sections are a praise of the bodhisattva, and those in the Conduct chapter from the signs of a bodhisattva to the levels deal with just the temporary qualities of the path, while the verses on the resultant qualities deal with the qualities of enlightenment, for all of which it is not necessary to ascribe specific factors to be kept in mind as they are included in the above.

In general, not counting any of the subdivisions, there are about fifty-one kinds of attentiveness, from keeping in mind joy from considering the cause (verse 61) to keeping one's own greatness in mind (verse 72). All these kinds of attentiveness, it is taught, make the potential for transcendent perfection grow. I see that they also, as it were, summarize the earlier and later chapters in this text, for the seven lines beginning "Joy from considering the cause..."[83] are also a general summary of the meaning of the chapters from "Refuge" up to "Enlightenment." "Joy from considering the cause" summarizes the chapter on the potential. "Mindfulness of the support," summarizes the chapters on the spiritual intent, the inner support, which is the foundation of the path, and the refuge, in that the outer support or object from whom one receives the vow of bodhicitta is the Three Jewels. "A yearning for a similar enlightenment" refers to the chapters on thatness and enlightenment. The remaining four lines implicitly cover the chapters on powers, full maturation, and practice. Thus, although they do not follow the order of the chapters, their import appears to be complete. The different kinds of attentiveness that are mentioned after that correspond to the

---

82. Ch. 20, vv. 39–42. Although the Tibetan speaks of "five quatrains," two of them contain six lines each, making four numbered verses. We have followed here the widely accepted numbering in Vasubandhu's commentary.

83. Ch. 12, v. 61.

correct order of the chapters, beginning with the chapter on interest, as has already been explained above.

3. Specific Kinds of Thorough Investigation

The investigation of the Dharma of transmission that is to be explained and the Dharma of realization that is to be mastered can be divided into thirteen categories.

> **Developing, possessed of superior mentality, and great—**
> **Such is held to be the thorough investigation of the steadfast.**
> **Their investigation is accompanied by factors to be eliminated,**
> **Is free of such factors, and is mastered. (XII, 74)**

At the stage of an ordinary being on the level of earnest aspiration, beginning by listening to the sacred teachings and reflecting on them, and up to the supreme mundane level, investigating the Dharma is referred to as "developing," since it makes the seed of liberation grow. From the moment someone on the path of earnest aspiration acquires the concentration of the stream of the door of Dharma at the time of the supreme mundane level, and then from the first bodhisattva level up to the seventh, investigation is referred to as "possessed of superior mentality" because one has acquired realization of the two kinds of no-self and of the sameness of oneself and others. From the eighth level up to the tenth, one's realization of the Dharma is called "great," because one acquires spontaneous nonconceptual gnosis. These three categories of realization are held to correspond to the thorough investigation of the Dharma by steadfast bodhisattvas.

Again, on the level of earnest aspiration up to the supreme mundane level, those bodhisattvas' investigation is accompanied by obstacles that have to be eliminated: their intention is unstable; they are influenced by the company they keep (virtuous or evil); and they have not eliminated the two kinds of obscurations. From the first level up to the seventh, their investigation does not have those obstructing factors to be eliminated and is therefore unhindered. Similarly, from the eighth up to the tenth, their realization of the Dharma is known as "mastered," because they have spontaneously mastered nonconceptuality, preternatural knowledge, and complete purification of realms as buddha fields. These make three categories in terms of elimination.

> Bodhisattvas' investigation is said to be
> Lacking the buddha body, body-associated, body-attained,
> And body-complete; and also with much pride,
> With subtle pride, and without pride. (XII, 75)

Furthermore, bodhisattvas' investigation of the Dharma can be divided into four categories in terms of their attainment. Ordinary beings on the path of accumulation and up to the stage of acceptance on the path of joining have not acquired nonconceptuality, which is the cause of, and analogous to, the body of truth, so their investigation is said to be lacking the body of truth. At the stage of the supreme mundane level, by eliminating the concepts of subject and object, they acquire one aspect of the body of truth, and their investigation is therefore said to be associated with the buddha body, as is explained in the *Great Commentary*. (Some authorities use the term "lacking the buddha body" to refer to the path of earnest aspiration until the middle path of accumulation, and "body-associated" to cover the attainment of the concentration of the stream of Dharma on the greater path of accumulation and the subsequent gradual acquisition of the emulative nonconceptual gnosis that is the cause of dharmakāya on the four stages of the path of joining.) The investigation of bodhisattvas from the first level up to the seventh who have acquired the effortful nonconceptual gnosis that directly sees the truth is "body-attained." And from the eighth level up to the tenth, since the effortless nonconceptual gnosis is spontaneously accomplished, it is "body-complete."

Finally, there are three categories distinguished by the presence or absence of pride. At the stage of ordinary beings up to the supreme mundane level, there is a predominance of pride. From the first level up to the seventh, there is subtle pride, because imputation has been eliminated, and from the second level onward the respective innate obscurations are also eliminated. From the eighth level up to the tenth, it is said, nonconceptual gnosis is fully matured and there is therefore no pride.

4. The Results of Investigating the Dharma

There are two categories of results: (1) the accomplishment of good qualities and (2) riddance of concepts that have to be eliminated.

a. The Accomplishment of Good Qualities

> The Dharma of the steadfast is the source
> Of qualities material and immaterial—
> The marks, and likewise freedom from disease—
> Of mastery in preternatural knowledge, and
>   inexhaustibility. (XII, 76)

The results of steadfast bodhisattvas' full investigation of the Dharma are physical or material, and mental or immaterial. Taken in order, the physical qualities that will be accomplished are the thirty-two major marks and, related to these, the eighty minor marks. These are accomplished by listening to, reflecting on, and meditating on the Dharma. Similarly, the causal factor that abolishes the disease of the defilements of attachment, aversion, and the rest in the four immaterial aggregates (feeling, perception, conditioning factors, and consciousness) is the Dharma, for by knowing the Dharma and putting it into practice, one removes forever all the defilements that have to be eliminated on the paths of seeing and meditation. Attainment of mastery in preternatural knowledge also depends on the Dharma. And even the inexhaustible qualities of the nirvāṇa without residue—the ten strengths and so on—arise through diligence in the Dharma. So it is by investigating the Dharma and putting it into practice that one obtains these four kinds of qualities—physical marks, immaterial virtues (the curing of the disease of defilements), mastery, and inexhaustibility. As we read in the *Sūtra of the Questions of Brahmaviśeṣacintin*:

> If they possess four notions, bodhisattvas will investigate the Dharma. These four are to consider that the Dharma is very rare and therefore precious; to consider it as medicine, for it results in freedom from disease; to consider it as riches on account of its wealth of preternatural knowledge; and to consider it as nirvāṇa, for it results in inexhaustibility.

Apart from occasionally, it is difficult to come across the Dharma, and to meet with it is of great significance, for it fulfills all one's wishes like a precious gem. In this context, it is because of the rarity in this world of the major and minor marks—as rare as a beautiful, pure jewel—that the Dharma is to be considered so precious. Like medicine curing an illness, the nectar of the Dharma is to be considered as a great medicine that cures the disease of the defilements, which no other medicine can treat. With the sacred Dharma, one obtains the great mastery of abundant, inexhaustible powers such as preternatural knowledge, so it should be considered as riches, worldly riches being meager and volatile. The sacred Dharma is the remedy that brings to an end forever all the sufferings of birth, aging, and so on, so it should be considered as being like everlasting bliss or nirvāṇa—peace, coolth, happiness, the nature of perfection, which once obtained is never exhausted.

b. Riddance of Concepts That Have to Be Eliminated

> Children of the buddhas should completely abandon
> The concepts of existence and nonexistence, of
>   superimposition and negation,
> The concepts of unity and multiplicity, of intrinsic nature
>   and particularity,
> And the concepts of clinging to names and objects as real. (XII, 77)

By thoroughly investigating the Dharma, bodhisattvas get rid of ten objects of elimination. These are the ten distracting concepts mentioned in the Perfection of Wisdom that conflict with the realization of thatness. By knowing the meaning of the teachings, children of the buddhas who investigate the Dharma should completely abandon these ten concepts: the four concepts of existence, nonexistence, superimposition, and negation and similarly, the concept of unity, the concept of multiplicity or of distinct entities, the concept of phenomena as intrinsic entities, the concept of their particularities, the concept of objects as names, and the conceptual clinging to names as objects.

It is said in the *Perfection of Wisdom in One Hundred Thousand Lines*: "[Seeing] a bodhisattva as existing is not seeing the bodhisattva correctly." The belief that "emptiness" means that phenomena do not exist conventionally is a nihilistic emptiness, and it is therefore to be dispelled. The dependent reality exists as dependently arising appearances, and in ultimate truth the fully present reality exists as ultimate reality. It is correct to think this, that what exists does exist, and this is therefore not an extreme. To dispel the extreme of nonexistence, "a bodhisattva as existing" indicates that conventionally this interdependent appearance as a bodhisattva exists—there *is* an individual there. However, when immature, ordinary beings take it as existing as an individual self in the same way that it is imputed, this is the extreme of existence, and the antidote that dispels it is the statement, "not seeing the bodhisattva correctly." There is an individual that appears, but there is nothing that is a "self," for the self and the aggregates are not one and the same, nor are they observed to be different and distinct.

The above demonstrates that there is no self to the individual. We shall now proceed to show that there is no self in phenomena. The antidote that dispels the extremes of superimposition and nihilistic negation is to be found in "Form is devoid of intrinsic nature, but not of emptiness." Although phenomena such as form appear, they do not exist as the nature of this or that, and for this reason they are said to be "devoid of intrinsic nature," showing that form is a mere imputation and thus dispelling the superimposition of ultimate existence. Subsequently, with "but not [devoid] of emptiness," we dispel the nihilistic negation to the effect that the empty fully present reality does not exist—the negationist view being the belief that everything is completely nonexistent, without making a clear distinction between existence and nonexistence. With these two approaches in mind, the Buddha refuted them both: "Neither do things exist, nor do they not exist." But he did so without making any assertions, refuting all incompatible views as and when they were presented. This system is held to be specifically for refuting the above positions.

The antidote to the concept of unity is "The emptiness of form is not form; form is not emptiness"—referring to phenomena such as form that have attributes and to their true nature, which is emptiness. The imputed reality and fully present reality are not one and the same. The former does not stand up to analysis and is the object of the deluded mind; the latter withstands analysis and is the object of the undeluded mind.

As the antidote to the concept that things are distinct and different, it is said, "Form is emptiness; emptiness is form. Emptiness is no other than form; form is no other than emptiness." Phenomena with attributes, or dualistic appearances as subject and object, are themselves empty, and there is no so-called emptiness apart from that. Just as heat is the nature of fire, the nature of those phenomena is emptiness. This is also stated in *Unraveling the Intent*:

> Compounded phenomena and the ultimate truth are not the same,
>   nor are they different.
> Those who think of them as being identical or different are
>   mistaken.

And for each of these two beliefs, that they are the same or different, it points out four unwanted consequences.[84]

As the antidote to both the concept of intrinsic reality (that of a vase, for example), and the concept of particularities (for example, that a vase is impermanent), it is said, "Form is merely a name. . . ." Apart from their merely being designated by names and their expressions,[85] there is in objects nothing intrinsic whatsoever that exists—no nature or essence or essential attribute such as functionality in form, experience in feeling, solidity in earth, or wetness in water.

The antidote to the concept of particularity is that form has no production, it has no cessation, neither is it defilement, nor is it purity, and so on, and this applies to all phenomena, as has been taught in the Perfection of Wisdom. In ultimate truth, there are no phenomena that exist intrinsically, nor are there any particularities such as production that exist.

When one utters a name such as "vase," one associates the name and the object and thinks of the object as if it were the name, and of the name as if it were the object—the vase, for example. The antidote to this is "Name is a counterfeit, a lie." Although there is no intrinsic connection between the name and the object, human beings, in order to make themselves understood, have adventitiously created expressions and symbols. But immature beings apprehend the object as if it were the name, and when they see an object, they refer to it by its name as if the name were the object. This kind of apprehension is a superimposition on names and objects by the immature mind. In fact, since the object referred to does not exist in any way, neither does the name that refers to it. All phenomena are inexpressible by name; they are devoid of name, so even mere names cannot be observed.

5. Concluding Summary Stating the Importance of Thoroughly Investigating the Dharma

> **Those who are thus intelligent and virtuous, relying on intense diligence,**
> **Correctly investigate the nature of the two truths.**

---

84. For these two sets of four unwanted consequences that result from considering that the two truths are identical or different, see *Treasury of Precious Qualities*, 400–401 and Kunzang Palden, *Nectar of Manjushri's Speech*, 457n188.

85. Expressions—as symbols or as spoken words, etc.

> Thereby, they will forever become the teachers of beings
> And like an ocean be filled with good qualities. (XII, 78)

As explained in this chapter, bodhisattvas possess the intelligence to consider all the profound and extensive teachings as well as the vast virtue of skillful means, their possession of the transcendent perfections. Relying on intense diligence in investigating the teachings, without becoming lazy, discouraged, or confused, they gain certainty as to what is not mistaken, or correct realization, and by this means thoroughly investigate the nature of the two truths comprising relative and ultimate truth. (The translation of this second line in Sthiramati's commentary reads, "Possessed of the two truths, they see their true nature.")

As a result of investigating the Dharma in this way, they will always be the teachers of sentient beings, explaining the Excellent Dharma to others without error. Like the ocean full of water and precious things, those bodhisattvas will be filled with all the extraordinary qualities of the path and result.

This completes the explanation of the twelfth chapter of *Ornament of the Mahāyāna Sūtras*, the chapter on thorough investigation.

13

Teaching the Dharma

This chapter is divided into five sections: (1) showing why it is worth teaching others the Dharma unstintingly; (2) the reason for teaching the Dharma; (3) how to teach the Dharma; (4) the nature of the Dharma that is taught; and (5) a summary in praise of the virtues of teaching the Dharma.

1. Showing Why It Is Worth Teaching Others the Dharma Unstintingly

When bodhisattvas thoroughly investigating the Dharma have received the teachings and gained unmistaken realization of them, they explain them unstintingly to sentient beings and thereby complete their own transcendent perfections and bring other sentient beings to maturity. There is no better means for doing so than this, and one should therefore do whatever one can to teach.

> If steadfast bodhisattvas joyously and forever give away
>   immense gifts to beings who suffer—
> The lives and riches they have won with such great difficulty
>   and yet devoid of essence—
> Need one mention their unstintingly giving of the vast
>   Dharma that benefits beings in every way,
> That is found with no great difficulty, and even when given
>   away entirely grows inexhaustibly? (XIII, 1)

Steadfast bodhisattvas have realized that even though their bodies or lives, won with great difficulty by accumulating virtue in the past, and their wealth, acquired through great hardships such as journeying overseas,[1]

---

1. This is a reference to a traditional notion that the acquisition of wealth, particularly by merchants, involved long and dangerous journeys, often by sea.

belong to them, these finally come to an end and are meaningless and unreliable. So it is with sheer delight in practicing generosity that they are forever giving away material gifts to suffering beings—vast riches or dominions that can completely fulfill others' wishes. If they can do this, then need one mention their giving away—and not just once—the vast and sacred Dharma, which will never be exhausted? Of course bodhisattvas will teach others, once they have investigated the teachings, for the Dharma benefits beings in every kind of way in both this and other lives and therefore, unlike material gifts, is utterly reliable and worthwhile. At a time when the Buddha has appeared in the world and his doctrine endures, anyone seeking the teachings can receive them quite easily without going through the enormous difficulties—setting out to sea, and so on—involved in the acquisition of material riches. And the gift of Dharma, even if given away completely, not only never runs out in the bodhisattva's mind stream but will grow more and more, spreading from one person to the next.[2] (The Tibetan syllable *lta* in the last line has no significance other than completing the meter.)

2. THE REASON FOR TEACHING THE DHARMA

> Because it is to be known by oneself, Lord Buddha did not
>   teach the Dharma;
> Yet with the breath of his teachings, rationally explained,
>   the embodiment of compassion, like a python,
> Draws beings onto the path, setting them perfectly in the
>   mouth of total peace,
> Utterly pure, vast, common, and inexhaustible. (XIII, 2)
>
> Consequently, no practitioner's meditation is pointless,
> And thus neither are the teachings of the sugatas pointless.
> If one could see the meaning simply by listening, there
>   would be no point in meditating,
> And if one could practice meditation without having
>   listened, there would be no point in teaching. (XIII, 3)

Although the ultimate realization that the noble beings are to know by their own individual experience is beyond the realm of words and letters,

---

2. Sthiramati gives the example of a candle whose flame can be used to light many other candles without going out itself.

it is impossible to ever attain it without listening to and reflecting on the Dharma of transmission that is indicated by words and letters. This is why Lord Buddha taught the Dharma of transmission, which can be heard and reflected upon, as the means for realizing that personally experienced wisdom. It is impossible to show the Dharma of realization, the individually experienced wisdom present in the minds of noble beings, directly to beings who have not realized it personally. So because that Dharma of realization can only be known by actual personal experience, the buddha bhagavāns have not taught such a Dharma in the form of words and letters. They cannot demonstrate how it is with words and letters, saying, "This is the point that has to be realized individually." It is beyond the expressions, concepts, analogies, and reasoning of ordinary people, which is why we say that it can only be known personally. It is not like the mundane knowledge of compounded phenomena such as vases and uncompounded phenomena such as space: suchness is something that is realized personally by those who have the gnosis of the noble beings. If the object of experience of those who have attained mundane dhyāna cannot be imagined by beings who have not attained it, then it goes without saying that the object of experience of supramundane gnosis is not something that can be conceived of by an ordinary person listening and reflecting.

How is it, then, that the profound sūtras are said to explain the certain meaning—the Buddha's realization, the point that can only be realized personally? This is explained by a metaphor comparing Lord Buddha, who is the embodiment of compassion for sentient beings, to a giant snake. There is a giant snake, a python, that leaves behind it a furrow the size of a river, filled with the saliva flowing from its mouth, so that from a distance it looks like a huge river. The deer, thinking that it is a river, go to drink from it, whereupon they are killed by the poisonous saliva and sucked into the python's mouth as it breathes in. Thus it is that the Buddha (illustrated by the python) draws potential disciples (analogous to the herds of deer) onto the correct path to buddhahood by means of the Twelve Branches of Excellent Speech, which are capable of drawing in others (like the python's breath)—the Excellent Words that he expounds perfectly logically and reasonably, that is, with no mistake in any points, for they possess the four kinds of rational application.[3] Drawing them in, he finally places them in buddhahood (the snake's mouth)—the body of truth, nirvāṇa, in which suffering and the origin of

---

3. The four kinds of rational application (Tib. *rigs pa bzhi*) are described on page 763 below.

suffering are completely pacified; the transcendent state[4] of sublime purity (in which the two obscurations have been purified), of sublime bliss (which is endowed with the vast qualities of the ten strengths and so forth), of the sublime "self" of a great being (for it is common to all the buddhas), and of the sublime eternity (for it will never know an end).

This is the truth-body buddha, the culmination of personal realization, and there are no sentient beings who have ever attained buddhahood through its being directly indicated by words and then realized accordingly. Nevertheless, the causal factor that leads one to attain that ultimate truth body is the Dharma of transmission that indicates, without any error, profound thatness and skillful means. By means of the path—that is, by correctly listening to, reflecting on, and meditating on the Dharma of transmission—one unfailingly acquires the personally experienced gnosis of the noble beings. With that gnosis, one unerringly realizes thatness, the inconceivable object of personally experienced wisdom, and finally one realizes the Buddha's gnosis, the body of truth. Thus, the object of personally experienced wisdom, while not being indicated directly by words, is based on, and indirectly indicated by, the Dharma of transmission.

Consequently, the meditation of a practitioner who possesses sustained calm and profound insight is not pointless, for it is in dependence on such meditation that the personally realized gnosis will arise. Meditation is indeed worthwhile, and thus the sūtras and other teachings, which the sugatas have given in order to enable one to meditate correctly, are not pointless either. For in contrast to non-Buddhist practices such as meditation on the self that are not related to the path of meditation on thatness and which are no way to attain liberation, the Dharma unmistakenly teaches the thatness of things, meditation on no-self, and so forth; and through one's hearing it, reflecting on its meaning, and meditating in accordance with the certainty one has thereby acquired, the personally experienced vision of thatness will occur.

If it were otherwise and one could directly see that very meaning simply by hearing the teachings on no-self and so forth, one would be liberated there and then, and there would be no point in meditating on the meaning of those teachings. And if one could practice meditation on no-self without listening to the relevant teachings, there would be no point either in teaching the Buddha's Excellent Words. But it is impossible that the Bud-

---

4. "Transcendent" in that it transcends the four ordinary concepts of purity, happiness, self, and permanence.

dha would have taught without reason. To acquire the gnosis of the noble beings, the personally experienced wisdom that realizes ultimate reality as it is, one must first listen to the sacred Dharma, then reflect on its meaning so that one acquires certainty, and subsequently meditate one-pointedly on that meaning. First of all, therefore, it is necessary to give rise to the wisdom that comes from listening, and it is for this reason that the Dharma of transmission, which involves listening to the teachings and explaining them, is very worthwhile and very necessary.

3. How to Teach the Dharma

This topic is divided into (1) the manner in which bodhisattvas teach the Dharma and (2) the manner in which the buddhas teach the Dharma. The first of these two is further divided into three sections: (1) different ways of teaching; (2) the excellence of the import; and (3) the excellence of the words.

a. The Manner in Which Bodhisattvas Teach the Dharma
i. Different Ways of Teaching

> The teaching of sublime bodhisattvas
> Occurs through transmission, realization, and mastery:
> From the mouth, from form of every kind,
> And from space it issues forth. (XIII, 4)

On the level of earnest aspiration, bodhisattvas explain the Dharma as they have heard it from other spiritual masters—buddhas and bodhisattvas. In other words, they teach by relying on the transmission. From the first bodhisattva level up to the seventh, they teach through the power of their realization of the expanse of reality. On the three pure levels, they explain the Dharma through their spontaneous mastery of nonconceptual gnosis and preternatural knowledge. This makes three categories.

Furthermore, on the eighth and higher levels, through the blessing of their mastery, the sound of Dharma teachings issues forth as melodious song from their own and other people's mouths, from the sounds of musical instruments, and so forth. From all kinds of form—walls, musical instruments, and other forms—come the sounds of the Dharma. And from the sky, too, comes the sound of the Dharma being taught.

ii. The Excellence of the Import

> Extensive, doubt-dispelling,
> Acceptable, and indicative of both natures—
> This, a bodhisattva's teaching,
> Is said to be perfect. (XIII, 5)

As a result of their having heard a lot of teachings, bodhisattvas' own teaching reveals or elucidates the extensive topics of the Dharma and their meanings connectedly. Since they are themselves free of doubts with regard to the teachings, it dispels others' doubts. Since they live the Dharma themselves, their words are acceptable to others—what they say is worth listening to and is also termed "pleasing." And they explain both the nature of defilement and that of purity. It is in possessing these four qualities that the Dharma teaching of a bodhisattva is said to be perfect. This is as stated in the *Sūtra of the Questions of Brahmaviśeṣacintin*. Having received numerous teachings, bodhisattvas explain the extensive Dharma so that the sacred doctrine may endure in the world for a long time. Through their explaining the teachings and training in them, their own wisdom becomes increasingly sharper, and they can remove others' doubts. Because they abide by the Dharma themselves and thus perform the activities of holy beings, others value their words. And since they teach both ultimate and relative truths, or the defilement aspect and the purity aspect, embodied in the four noble truths, their teaching is of great import.

> The Dharma teaching of a sublime bodhisattva
> Is gentle, free of conceit, tireless,
> Clear, diversified, rational,
> Intelligible, disinterested, and universal. (XIII, 6)

Furthermore, there are nine features in their perfect Dharma teaching. In teaching the Dharma, sublime bodhisattvas are gentle, since they never utter harsh words even when others argue with them. Even if they receive praise and veneration, they are free of conceit. In teaching the Dharma, they are never discouraged by difficulties. Their teachings are clear, for they teach unstintingly and explain the topics in full. They teach a wide variety of subjects without repeating themselves. They teach rationally, never contradicting valid cognition. They express themselves with words and letters that are perfectly familiar to ordinary people, so that others understand them well. Since they have given up any desire for gain and honor, they are not motivated by material offerings. Learned in all spiritual means, they expound the subjects of all three vehicles, and in this respect their teaching is universal. It is on account of its having these qualities, and of the excellent import revealed thereby, that it is termed "perfect teaching."

iii. The Excellence of the Words

> The bodhisattvas' words are not faint,
> They are pleasing, well expounded, and conventional;
> They are appropriate, free of material motives,
> Moderate, and likewise abundant. (XIII, 7)

The words that bodhisattvas use to teach the Dharma are not soft or feeble. Their voices are not faint, so that some people hear them and others do not—they are audible to their entire following. Their words are pleasant; they are gentle and good—pleasing to both ear and intellect. They are excellently or beautifully expounded—clear sentences whose meaning can be understood. If bodhisattvas were to express themselves with unconventional words, nobody else would understand them, but by using words and language that are familiar to everyone, they make them aware of the meaning—hence, their words are "conventional." Expounded in a way suited to their disciples' minds, their words are "appropriate," and their teaching in this way will be to their disciples' liking.[5] As bodhisattvas are not seeking riches and reverence, their words are disinterested or independent of material gain. A surfeit of words makes people bored, so bodhisattvas adapt their words to just the right amount that is easily retained. Similarly, their words are abundant, meaning that when bodhisattvas give detailed explanations, they are able to do so without ever running out of things to say.

It should be understood that the above are related to the eight qualities of bodhisattvas' words described in the sūtras, which speak of them being pervasive, good, clear, intelligible, pleasing to the ear, disinterested, adapted, and inexhaustible.

Being disinterested in people's offerings and reverence is, of course, a mental quality, but here it is a question of not, for example, praising and

---

5. Tib. *rna bar 'ong ba,* lit. "pleasing to the ear."

teaching people who offer riches and reverence while reproaching and refusing to teach those who do not, so I feel that perhaps this quality should be explained in terms of its being a *causal factor* that prevents faults from being introduced into a bodhisattva's words.

> Because they indicate, and likewise explain,
> Correspond to the vehicle, are pleasurable,
> Conventional, and appropriate,
> Lead to certain deliverance, and are concordant— (XIII, 8)
>
> The syllables uttered by the sublime bodhisattvas
> Are described, in short, as perfect. (XIII, 9ab)

There are also eight good qualities with regard to the manner in which bodhisattvas deliver their teachings: (1) Because they indicate topics in a condensed form, the essential meaning is easily grasped. (2) Similarly, as a result of their explaining those topics in great detail, certainty as to the meaning is acquired. (3) Whichever of the three kinds of potential their disciples have, in teaching each individual their respective vehicle, bodhisattvas give explanations that correspond to the vehicle. (4) Since they teach without mixing up the order of the words, syllables, and topics, their teachings are a pleasure to listen to. (5) They teach using familiar phrases and spellings. (6) They teach appropriately in a way suited to their disciples' minds. (7) They teach the noble path that gives certain deliverance from the three worlds. And (8) they give teachings concordant with the eightfold noble path. On account of these qualities, the syllables of these sublime bodhisattvas, in short, are said to be "perfect."

The sūtras speak of eight qualities for syllables: logical validity in the words and syllables, incorporation, conformity, harmony, acceptability, suitability, concordance, and completion of the accumulations of the wise. The *Great Commentary* explains how these correspond to the above qualities as follows: (1) Bodhisattvas' teachings supply brief explanations using words and syllables that comprise the reasoning of the three kinds of valid cognition. (2) They incorporate detailed explanations of the subjects that have been briefly introduced. (3) They conform or correspond to the vehicle. (4) They are gentle, in harmony with the mind, for they are truthful and they do not grate on the ear as a result of the words and syllables being taught in a disordered fashion. (5) The words being familiar to everyone, they are acceptable and accordingly intelligible. (6) They are appropriate, suited to the listener. (7) They indicate the noble path and are therefore concordant with nirvāṇa. And (8) corresponding to "concordant" (in the root verse), they complete the accumulations of the wise. "The wise" refers to the seven kinds of noble beings, from stream enterers to candidates for arhatship.[6] Their paths of seeing and meditation are referred to as "the completion of the accumulations," which are concordant with the eightfold noble path.

b. The Manner in Which the Buddhas Teach the Dharma

The speech of the sugatas is infinite;
With sixty qualities, it is inconceivable. (XIII, 9cd)

The words with which the sugatas teach the Dharma comprise infinite, inconceivable expressive elements, but these can all be condensed into the sixty expressive qualities of buddha speech, as taught in the *Sūtra of the Inconceivable Secrets*. And since in each of these qualities there are again infinite expressive forms of speech, their speech is inconceivable. What are these sixty?

(1) The Buddha's speech is *mollifying* or *softening*, for just as water, for example, makes the grass, trees, and so forth sprout and grow, the Buddha's speech enables sentient beings to give rise to sources of good and to develop them.

(2) It is *gentle*, for like the gods' soft clothes, whose contact with the body is so blissful, the mere sound of the Buddha's voice makes one happy in this life.

(3) It is likewise *beautiful*, for it indicates the meaning of the two truths, dependent arising, the elements that lead to enlightenment, and so on.

(4) What the Buddha says is *appealing*, for he does not speak with the language of common folk such as cowherds, but speaks in the language of the gods and noble beings.

(5) It is *perfectly pure*, for it ensues from the great supramundane gnosis, the nonconceptual gnosis in which the two obscurations have been eliminated.

---

6. These refer to the first seven of the eight kinds of noble beings in the Listeners' Vehicle: the two kinds of stream enterer (candidate [Tib. *zhugs pa*] and graduate [*'bras la gnas pa*, those who are established or abide in the result]), two kinds of once-returner (candidate and graduate), two kinds of nonreturner (candidate and graduate), and arhat candidate. See *Treasury of Precious Qualities*, 230–31.

(6) It is *immaculate*, being free of latent defilements.

(7) It is *very clear*, since he teaches with language that is known to everyone.

(8) It is *sonorous* or *powerful* and has the power to dispel unwholesome views such as those of the tīrthikas.

(9) It is *worth listening to*, for by practicing in accordance with his teaching, one is certain to be delivered from the three worlds.

(10) It is *unassailable*, for what he says cannot be refuted by his opponents.

(11) It is *well-sounding*, in that it delights the listener.

(12) It is *calming*, for it completely subdues all the defilements—attachment and the rest.

(13) It is *without harshness*, in that the precepts the Buddha ordained are easy to follow, unlike the mortification by five fires[7] and other rigorous austerities that the tīrthikas practice.

(14) It is *kindly*, in that since the Buddha teaches the methods for perfect deliverance from downfalls (by confessing them, vowing not to repeat them, and so on), such downfalls are not irremediable.

(15) In teaching the three vehicles, the Buddha's speech *fully trains* those with the corresponding potentials.

(16) It is *sweet to the ear*, for what he says is so melodious and gentle that one cannot bring oneself to leave; one feels like giving all one's attention and does not get distracted.

(17) It *brings about physical ease*, for reliance on the Buddha's teaching gives rise to concentration, resulting in suppleness.

(18) It similarly *brings about mental contentment*, on account of the profound insight it inspires.

(19) It *gladdens the heart*, for it clears away all the torment of doubt.

(20) It is *joyous* and *blissful*, for it gets rid of ignorance and misunderstanding respectively.

(21) It is *undisappointing*, in that one will never have any regrets and think that there was no point in listening to his teaching, because if one practices what the Buddha says, one will inevitably attain the result.

(22) It is *a source of comprehensive knowledge*, the source of the perfect wisdom that comes from listening.

(23) It is *a source of discerning knowledge*, the source that gives rise to the perfect wisdom that comes from reflecting.

---

7. Some non-Buddhist ascetics purify themselves by enduring the heat of four fires placed around them at the four cardinal points and of the sun above them.

(24) It is *fully illuminating*, in that the Buddha teaches without holding back on his knowledge.

(25) It is *a source of delight*, for when those who have attained their goals—that is, the eight kinds of noble beings (stream enterer and the others), the bodhisattvas on the tenth level, and the tathāgatas—see that they have done so by means of the Tathāgata's teachings, and when the noble listeners and bodhisattvas realize that by means of the Tathāgata's teachings they too will achieve their respective goals, they rejoice at the Buddha's word.

(26) It is *inspiring*, on account of the wish it inspires in ordinary beings who have not achieved their goals to practice the Tathāgata's teaching in order to achieve their goals.[8]

(27) It is the *bestower of all knowledge*, in that the Buddha's word perfectly indicates such inconceivable topics as the profound expanse of reality that is to be known personally, the nonconceptual gnosis, and the elements that lead to enlightenment. Another explanation is that the karmic actions that produce the whole variety of the external material world, the objects of a yogi's concentration, those that are the domain of the Tathāgata's gnosis, and the magical powers of medicine and mantra are all inconceivable to the ordinary mind and are therefore taught as being not to be reflected upon.

(28) It is the *bestower of discerning knowledge*, for it teaches a vast range of topics that are to be reflected upon—the aggregates, sense spheres, and senses-and-fields; the levels; the transcendent perfections; and so forth.

(29) It is *rational*, for it expresses things in association with the three kinds of valid cognition.

(30) It is *appropriate*, in that the Buddha teaches in a manner suited to the disciple; what he says is consistent with the disciple's mind stream.

(31) It is *not redundant*—referring, for example, to the different enumerations in the sūtras—because although the Buddha used many different terms to teach a single point, each term has a deliberate implication.

(32) It is *similar in force to the lion's roar*, for the Buddha's word frightens opponents and those with tīrthika views. Like the lion's roar, which terrifies all the deer and antelope, the force of the teachings on no-self and similar topics is overwhelming.

(33) It is *like the elephant's trumpeting*, reaching the entire retinue. This refers not to the elephants of the human realm but to celestial elephants like

---

8. Sthiramati refers to this quality as "truly desirous" or "truly desirable" (Tib. *mngon par 'dod pa*). "Ordinary beings" here includes practitioners on the level of earnest aspiration, as opposed to the noble beings mentioned in the previous quality.

Airāvata. Its trumpeting is not muffled or hoarse, and neither is the sound of the Tathāgata's words.

(34) It is *like the deep rumbling of thunder.*[9] The commentary explains that the thunder of the Buddha's word sounds no louder in his presence and no softer when heard from far away: it is the same irrespective of distance, "like the voice in the clouds, the roar of the dragon."

(35) It is *like the voice of the nāga king,* for just as in the nāga realm all the nāgas cannot but listen to the beautiful, noble words of the nāga king, the Buddha's word is obeyed by everyone—gods, demigods, human beings, and the like.

(36) It is as sweet *as the song of the gandharvas* or of the kiṃnaras,[10] whose voices, of all the voices of sentient beings, are the softest.

(37) *Like the song of the kalaviṅka,*[11] which sings uninterruptedly, forever changing the melody, the Buddha's teaching is uninterrupted and ever-changing. Some authorities say that the kalaviṅka's beautiful song so delights beings that no matter how long they listen to it, when it stops, they want to hear its sweet notes again; and that in the same way, once one has heard the Buddha's voice, one longs to hear it again.

(38) *Like the voice of Brahmā,* which is long and regular, not fragmented, the Buddha's voice is not marred by shortness of breath and is therefore drawn out, or far-sounding.

(39) It is *auspicious, like the call of the jīvajīvaka,*[12] which, when someone undertaking an important task hears it, is a sign that all their goals will surely be accomplished. Similarly, the sound of the Buddha's voice is an auspicious sign that all supramundane goals will be achieved, for it is through listening to the Buddha's teachings that one will subsequently accomplish all one's goals.

(40) It is *like the voice of Indra,* whose noble words everyone obeys and no one transgresses: no one can go against anything the Buddha has said.

(41) It is *like the beat of the great celestial drum* that heralds the demigods' defeat at the hands of the gods and at whose sound the demigods naturally

---

9. Tib. *'brug gi sgra dbyangs,* lit. "the dragon's roar." This is the Tibetan expression for thunder, stemming from the traditional belief that thunder was the voice of a dragon roaring in the clouds.

10. Kiṃnaras (Tib. *mi'am ci*) are a class of celestial beings, half human, half bird.

11. A human-headed mythical bird, but also identified as a cuckoo or a nightingale.

12. The jīvajīvaka (Tib. *shang shang te'u*) is a fabulous bird, half human (the head and torso), half bird, also described as a pheasant.

scatter, for the Buddha similarly routs demons and opponents, turning the wheel of the Dharma for the first time and overcoming negative attitudes in those who hear it.

(42) It is *without show or conceit*, for even when the Buddha is praised by the gods and everyone else, he has no pride.[13]

(43) It is *not timid*, in that if demons and tīrthikas criticize the Buddha's teachings saying that they are no good, he is not discouraged.

(44) It is *fully imbued with all manner of expression*, in that the Buddha's words communicate or convey (the Sanskrit term is *vyākaraṇa*), meaning in this context that everything the Buddha declares[14] concerning the past, present, and future is certain to be exactly as he has said; or that his words definitively communicate all branches of knowledge; or that they follow the rules of grammar and communicate effectively.

(45) It is *uncorrupted*, because, the Buddha's memory being unimpaired, he never omits any subjects or fails to complete the form of the words. Another explanation is that he never forgets any points that need teaching.

(46) It is *never incomplete*, in that he teaches all the actions without exception that benefit beings—actions that give rise to sources of good, make them grow, and perfect them.

(47) It is *without attachment*, for the Buddha does not hanker after honors and riches. Some editions list this quality as "undaunted."

(48) It is *not feeble* (or, as certain editions say for this, *undaunted*), for in teaching the Dharma to his followers, the Buddha has no fear of opposition from demons and the like.

(49) It is *extremely joyous*, in that when he teaches the Dharma, the Buddha does not become mentally discouraged or physically worn out by illness.

(50) It is *extensive* or *fully comprehensive*, in that he teaches all subjects extensively, or teaches pervasively: through his complete mastery of all branches of knowledge, he explains without impediment everything he is asked.

---

13. According to Sthiramati's commentary, this quality and the next one, while not referring directly to the qualities of the Buddha's speech, describe the Buddha's absence of defilements in response to those qualities being praised or criticized.

14. Tib. *lung ston pa*, meaning "to predict" when it concerns future events, but this term also includes the Buddha's explanations of current situations by relating past events (for example, explaining the karmic effects of their actions in previous lives on his disciples' present lives).

(51) It is *soothing*, for it benefits angry sentient beings who have not given rise to sources of good, and it leads all gentle beings to realize the truth.

(52) It is *continuous* or *uninterrupted*, for the Buddha is always teaching the Dharma, without interruption.

(53) It is described as magnificent, elaborate, or *rich*, in that he speaks richly or elaborately, using a wide variety of names, phrases, and letters.

(54) It *incorporates all languages*, even in a single voice, for gods, nāgas, humans, animals, hungry spirits, and other sentient beings each hear it in their respective language.

(55) It *delights or satisfies all the different intellectual capacities* of beings, for the same voice leads to each being understanding whichever meaning he or she wishes to know.

(56) It is *beyond reproach*, in that once he has made a promise, the Buddha always fulfills it; he never lets it drop or cannot be bothered. This can also be understood to mean that when the Buddha says, "If you practice this path, you will achieve this result," it will definitely happen like that, so beings cannot criticize what he says as untrue.

(57) It *never wavers or deviates* from the Buddha's unfailing mindfulness of beings' welfare and from his actually benefiting others: the Buddha's instructions are always perfectly timed for the particular beings that need training.

(58) It is *steady or unhurried*: the Buddha never teaches irrationally or badly, speaking too fast or nervously.

(59) What he says is *spoken to all his disciples* or *resounds throughout his following*, for while those in his presence hear his voice perfectly clearly, without it being too loud or too soft, those who are far away and even other beings to be trained who are many myriads of world systems distant hear it just as well as those who are near him.

(60) His speech is *most excellent in every respect*: there is nothing that impedes his teaching the Dharma, and he can take anything as an example, using it to teach every kind of subject perfectly.

These, then, are the sixty expressive qualities of buddha speech.[15]

As for the manner in which the Buddha uses his speech to teach the Dharma, this has eight aspects.

---

15. Some texts speak of sixty-four qualities or branches, with four additional qualities. These are listed in the *Sūtra of the Inconceivable Secrets* between the fifty-ninth branch and the last one. They refer to the ability of the Buddha's speech to still attachment, subdue hatred, dispel ignorance, and destroy negative forces.

With words, solid reasoning,
Brief introductions, detailed explanations,
The clearing of doubts, and much repetition,
For those who understand when merely told the title or else
    from detailed presentations, (XIII, 10)

The buddhas teach, and their teaching
Is pure, free of the three spheres;
Know that it is devoid
Of eight faults: (XIII, 11)

(1) He explains things using names and expressions such as "pillar" to indicate the essence of an object, and phrases such as "Pillars are impermanent" to indicate its particular characteristics. (2) Using valid cognition to teach, he explains things logically, fully incorporating the meaning or main point. (3) He explains things with brief presentations and (4) with detailed explanations or analyses. (5) Using logic, he removes doubts. (6) He repeats the teachings many times, making use of proofs. (7) He gives explanations for those who can understand merely from being told the title. (8) He gives explanations for those who can understand only from being given detailed presentations.

These eight are mentioned in the sūtras, which state that the Buddha expresses, designates, defines, analyzes, comments, clarifies, indicates, and gives complete instruction. (1) By expressing the essence of a thing with its name and indicating its particular characteristics with phrases, the Buddha explains things to individuals who follow him on the basis of faith with the phrase "All that is compounded is impermanent." (2) To those who follow him on the basis of reasoning, he establishes impermanence by means of reasoning—associating things with the main point or meaning, or "designating" things by means of valid cognition. (3) He defines the main body of the subject with just a brief presentation. (4) He gives a thorough, detailed analysis of its meaning. (5) He subsequently resolves uncertainties by giving a full commentary. (6) In order that the meaning be understood correctly, he expands upon the subject with numerous different explanations, repeating the teaching many times to make the meaning quite clear. (7) To those who understand simply from the title being mentioned he briefly indicates the key points. (8) To those who understand only from details he gives elaborate and detailed explanations, giving complete instructions or "fully proclaiming."

The first two of these refer to what the buddhas use to give an explanation; the next four (brief presentation and so on) refer to how they explain things; and the last two refer to the persons to whom they give explanations. The buddhas' teaching of the Dharma, with these eight aspects, is perfectly pure in terms of the three spheres—namely, who is teaching, the manner in which they teach, and whom they teach. The buddhas have perfected nonconceptual gnosis, so in their teaching of the Dharma too they have no concepts of these three spheres, and their teaching is therefore utterly, perfectly pure.

Moreover, the buddhas' teaching the Dharma should be understood as being free of eight faults in discourse.

> Laziness, incomprehensibility,
> Failure to set a time, lack of certainty,
> Failure to resolve doubts,
> Failure to stabilize freedom from doubt, (XIII, 12)
>
> Discouragement, and stinginess—
> These are held to be faults in discourse.
> Because it is free of these,
> The buddhas' teaching is unexcelled. (XIII, 13)

What are these eight? (1) A disinclination to expound the Dharma on account of a penchant for sleeping, lounging, and so on, constitutes laziness. (2) Even if one does teach the Dharma, because one does not understand it oneself, or because one fails to set forth the words or meanings clearly, the subject to be understood is not comprehended. (3) Since one does not want to teach the Dharma, one does not set a time to do so. (4) One teaches "without certainty" or without the ultimate meaning, giving the expedient teachings rather than explaining the ultimate teachings; or, alternatively, not giving detailed explanations, so that others are uncertain as to their meaning.[16] (5) Even if one does teach, one fails to clear up disciples' doubts. (6) While freeing them of their doubts, one fails to use a wide range of different explanations, repeatedly, to help them gain a definitive understanding

---

16. The double meaning of the Tibetan word *nges pa* here is lost in translation. While its literal meaning is "certainty," it is also interpreted by Sthiramati as meaning *nges don*, the certain or ultimate meaning or teachings.

and render it stable. (7) One is discouraged by the thought of how difficult it is to teach the Dharma. (8) One is miserly with the teachings and keeps them to oneself.

These are held to be faults in the context of giving discourses. Because it is completely free of these eight faults, the buddhas' exposition of the Dharma is described as unsurpassable. From the point of view of these eight incompatible traits having been abandoned, there is a correlation with the above eight aspects of the buddhas' teaching the Dharma, as follows: teaching without laziness; making the meaning understood by associating it with reasoning; choosing the right moment and giving brief presentations; getting rid of uncertainty by giving detailed explanations; actually resolving doubts; bringing about stability by repeated teaching; not getting fed up with those who need elaborate explanations to understand the subject; and unstintingly teaching those for whom the mere mention of the title affords comprehension. This correlation is not mentioned in Sthiramati's *Great Commentary*.

4. The Nature of the Dharma That Is Taught

This section comprises (1) the general characteristics of the Dharma and (2) a specific explanation of the implied and indirect teachings.

a. The General Characteristics of the Dharma

> Because it engenders faith, joy, and understanding,
> This Dharma is virtuous;
> Having twofold meaning and easy to retain,
> It teaches pure activity with four good qualities. (XIII, 14)

> Having nothing in common with others,
> Completing the elimination of the defilements of the three worlds,
> Naturally pure, and decontaminating—
> Such is held to be pure activity with four good qualities. (XIII, 15)

What constitutes the "sacred Dharma"? That which is triply virtuous, doubly excellent, and possessed of four good qualities is what we call the "sacred Dharma," the Excellent Words of the Tathāgata. What do these refer to?

Because the sacred Dharma makes us feel confident faith when we listen to it, it is virtuous in the beginning. Because it causes us to gain certainty and to feel joyful when we reflect on it, it is virtuous in the middle. And because it leads to correct understanding when we meditate, it is virtuous in the end. Thus the sacred Dharma is nothing but virtuous and wholesome, in the beginning, the middle, and the end.

Its double excellence refers to (1) excellent meaning, in that the sacred Dharma correctly and unmistakenly teaches the twofold meaning that is to be known—that of relative truth and of ultimate truth, and (2) excellent words, in that it is taught using all the right words and letters in accordance with the etymological definitions of universally accepted language, and it is therefore easy to understand or retain.

The four good qualities are properties of pure activity, the noble path, which is shown by the Dharma of transmission. "Pure," in this context, refers to nirvāṇa—as we read in the sūtras, "It is pure, it is cool, it is beyond suffering." The noble path that leads us to attain nirvāṇa is what we call "pure activity." This noble path has the following four good qualities: (1) The noble path itself is only to be found in the Buddha's teachings: it is quite distinct from other, non-Buddhist traditions such as those of the tīrthikas and has nothing in common with them. (2) The noble path brings to perfect completion the elimination of all the defilements related to the three worlds, so it is perfectly complete. Mundane paths may lead to the peak of existence, but since they subsequently involve returning, they are not complete paths that eliminate all the defilements related to the three worlds forever. (3) The noble path is completely pure, for it is untainted by nature, naturally pure like space or a crystal. (4) That path is completely purifying, for it renders the mind free of taint, removing adventitious contaminants so that they never occur again. The Dharma is thus said to have the four good qualities of pure activity.

b. A Specific Explanation of the Implied and Indirect Teachings

The tathāgatas teach the Dharma in accord with the dispositions, faculties, and aspirations of the beings to be trained, and there are therefore numerous teachings that take the form of implied teachings and indirect teachings and depend on the tathāgatas' intentions. If one takes the teachings literally without having properly understood their intention, one will not realize the correct, definitive meaning, and one will mistakenly take the intended meaning to be an expedient meaning or to be the literal meaning. Since it is extremely important to distinguish between these, there now follow explanations of (1) the four indirect teachings; (2) the four implied teachings; and (3) eight sayings intended as antidotes, together with their benefits.

i. An Explanation of the Four Indirect Teachings

> Indirect teachings given for the purpose of introducing,
> Indirect teachings on reality,
> Indirect teachings connected with remedial methods,
> And indirect teachings expressed through metaphors— (XIII, 16)

> These are the four kinds of indirect teachings,
> Given when the buddhas have in mind the listeners, reality,
> And likewise the suppression of faults
> And the expression of the profound. (XIII, 17)

The four indirect teachings are indirect teachings aimed at introducing people to the path; indirect teachings on the nature of reality; indirect teachings connected with remedial methods for overcoming faults in beings' mind streams; and indirect teachings in which the accepted, conventional meanings shown by the words and letters are given a different, metaphoric sense. These will be discussed in turn.

With the intention of introducing listeners, who are unable to approach the no-self of phenomena, to the path of liberation, the Buddha taught the existence of phenomena such as the aggregates of the nonexisting individual self. What he had in mind was that the imputed individual does not exist and that the interdependent phenomena of the dependent nature merely exist conventionally.

When the Buddha declared that phenomena are devoid of essence, are unborn, and so on, he was not saying that phenomena that exist on the conventional level do not exist at all and that there is no apparent arising and ceasing. Rather, he was indirectly teaching the ultimate reality or essential nature. Take, for example, his teaching on the three natures—namely, the imputed reality, the dependent reality, and the fully present reality. Since the imputed nature or reality does not exist at all, he spoke of the absence of characteristics. For the dependent reality, although the environment, sense objects, and body do appear to arise and cease from the mind and mental factors, apart from their appearing like that as a result of the interdependence of causes and conditions, they have no intrinsic production and cessation, and he spoke of them being unborn, devoid of essence. And for the fully present reality, he taught that it is by nature beyond suffering, peaceful, empty, ultimate, and devoid of essence.

With regard to indirect teachings connected with remedial methods, as with the previous cases, in order to overcome faults in people's minds, the Buddha said things like "In the past, I was the Buddha Vipaśyin." There are eight such examples, which will be explained below.

Indirect teachings expressed in metaphors use expressions that are not as they sound, in order to imply profound truths. Take the following verse, for example:

> In what is without essence, know the essence;
> Abide fully in what is mistaken;
> Afflict yourself with afflictive states;
> That way you will attain supreme enlightenment.

These lines, if taken at face value, seemingly show us how *not* to attain enlightenment. However, the Sanskrit word *sāra* can signify both "distraction" and "essence," so by adding the negative short "a" at the beginning of the word to make *asāra*, we get this line to mean, "In the training in superior concentration *without distraction*, know or realize the essence." To think of things as pure, happiness, permanent, and a self is to apprehend things the wrong way around. But to get *that* the wrong way around is to fully practice the training in superior wisdom that knows things to be impermanent, suffering, impure, and devoid of self. And if one afflicts oneself with the afflictions of austerities over a long period for the sake of sentient beings, one will attain supreme enlightenment. The *Great Commentary* associates the first three lines with the paths of earnest aspiration, seeing, and meditation, but they do not correspond individually, and it is sufficient to associate them with concentration, wisdom, and diligence.

These, then, are the four kinds of indirect teaching.

ii. An Explanation of the Four Implied Teachings

> Know that implied teachings are of four kinds,
> Implying sameness, another sense,
> And similarly another time,
> And with people's attitudes in mind. (XIII, 18)

Having in mind the fact that all the buddhas are identical in the body of truth, our teacher, the King of the Śākyas, said, "At that time, I was the Buddha Vipaśyin."

With another sense, that of ultimate truth, in mind, he declared that all phenomena are devoid of inherent identity, that they are unborn and unceasing, primordial peace, by nature nirvāṇa.

Similarly, with another time in mind, he told lazy people unable to perform a few positive actions that simply by reciting the prayer to be reborn in the tathāgata Amitābha's buddha field, they would be born there—implying that one day, in some future life, they would be reborn there.

Having in mind different people's attitudes, he spoke in praise of generosity to those who were able to practice generosity and the like on a vast scale. To some who were content with just a little generosity or another of the transcendent perfections, he scorned their practice or assumed a look of not being greatly impressed. To those who were satisfied with a single practice like generosity, and those who considered that there was no better practice than generosity, he compared it unfavorably to discipline and praised discipline as being better.

These, then, are examples of the four kinds of implied teaching that one should know. There are an enormous number of these implied teachings, as described in the *Compendium of the Great Vehicle*.

iii. EIGHT SAYINGS INTENDED AS ANTIDOTES, TOGETHER WITH THEIR BENEFITS

The Teachings of the Supreme Vehicle as Antidotes to Eight Obscurations

> Contempt for the Buddha and for the Dharma,
> Laziness, complacency,
> Indulgence in pride and in attachment,
> Remorse, and rejection by those of unfixed potential—
>   (XIII, 19)

> As the remedy to these obscurations in beings,
> The Buddha taught the Supreme Vehicle.
> With it, all the faults obstructing them
> Will be removed. (XIII, 20)

There were some who thought that our teacher was inferior to sublime buddhas like the Buddha Vipaśyin, who came at an auspicious time, during the age of perfect endowment.[17] The King of the Śākyas, who appeared at a time when human life span was one hundred years, was small in stature, and his life span was no longer than eighty years. His world was impure, and the beings he came to benefit were subject to the five degenerations.[18] With such thoughts, they disparaged the Buddha. To correct such attitudes, the Buddha said, "At that time, I was the Buddha Vipaśyin." What he had in mind was the fact that all the buddhas are identical in the body of truth and that consequently there are no such things as good buddhas and bad buddhas. But his disciples thought, "Vipaśyin is the Teacher himself," and they abandoned their notions of superiority or inferiority.

"Contempt for the Dharma" concerned high castes such as the priestly and warrior castes who were segregated by their brahmanical traditions and culture—which were certainly not for the likes of untouchables and other low castes. Since the Buddha's teachings could be practiced by anyone, even by low-caste untouchables, the higher castes held them in contempt, thinking, "Such teachings must be easily acquired." To remedy such attitudes, the Buddha said, "It is from having worshipped buddhas as numerous as the grains of sand in the Ganges that one will subsequently master the teachings of the Great Vehicle," indicating how difficult it is to realize the Mahāyāna teachings unless one has accumulated similar merit. In this way he made those who thought that the Dharma is easily accessible give up their disrespectful attitudes.

For lazy people who are unable to give rise to even a little virtue, the Buddha said such things as, "If you say the prayer of aspiration to attain the Blissful Realm, you will be reborn there" and "Simply by reciting the name of the tathāgata Vimalacandra, you will attain unsurpassable enlightenment." He also declared that the mere recitation of a dhāraṇī would purify negative actions like the five crimes with immediate retribution. Accordingly, by saying such prayers, reciting the buddhas' names, and chanting dhāraṇīs, even lazy people will accumulate virtue. As a result, they will definitely, one

17. An age of perfect endowment (Skt. *kritayuga*) is the first of four periods in a great kalpa when humans' Dharma, wealth, desires, and happiness are complete. Human life at this time is immeasurably long. See also *Treasury of Precious Qualities*, 484n256.

18. The five degenerations (Tib. *snyigs ma lnga*) are characteristic of the kaliyuga, or age of evil, the final of the four periods in a great kalpa. They correspond to short life span, gross defilements, physical and mental degeneration, times of war and famine, and wrong views.

day, be reborn in the Blissful Realm, attain buddhahood, and so on, as he declared. And simply by using those practices, they will also become more and more diligent and thus get rid of their laziness.

To remedy being content with just a little virtue, the Buddha instructed those who were satisfied with practicing only generosity, for instance, by praising discipline and disparaging generosity (in the sense of it being inferior to discipline). And he praised untainted virtue as being superior to the tainted virtue of mundane paths.

Some beings are infatuated with their bodies and possessions and thus indulge in pride. To remedy this, the Buddha spoke in praise of the buddhas' and bodhisattvas' immense bodies and wealth, so that when those beings heard this, they would think, "Worldly bodies and possessions, however good or great, are nothing much at all."

As a remedy against indulging in attachment to the five sense pleasures, the base enjoyments of the worldly, the Buddha gave glowing descriptions of the boundless riches and happiness to be had in the perfectly pure buddha fields. In this way he led beings full of attachment to regard samsaric sense pleasures, which are inherently tainted and associated with suffering, as if they were vomit, and to develop the determination to be free.

Some beings, in ignorance, might injure a buddha or bodhisattva, and later, when they think about it and realize that what they have done is extremely wrong and that they will go to the lower realms, they feel such remorse that they become mentally disturbed. This can prevent them from properly engaging in positive activities. So to remedy this, the Buddha said that even if one has harmed a buddha or bodhisattva, one will go to the higher realms. As a result, those beings stop feeling so remorseful, and they gain faith and think, "If I'll be reborn in the higher realms despite having hurt them, no need to mention what will come from helping them!" In the process, their virtuous activities will gradually increase. Of course, the result of inflicting injury on a buddha or bodhisattva is that one will experience suffering, but by the power of the buddhas' and bodhisattvas' aspirations, one will one day meet with happiness in the higher realms and so on, so it was with this in mind that the Buddha gave this remedial instruction.

Certain beings of unfixed bodhisattva potential begin by practicing the activities of a bodhisattva but are subsequently induced to practice the Listeners' Vehicle by a teacher such as a listener, so that they give up the bodhisattva way. In doing so, they are rejecting the Great Vehicle, so to remedy this sort of inclination, the Buddha said, "Even the listeners will ultimately attain buddhahood." By thus indicating a single vehicle, he induced those who wished to attain nirvāṇa by means of the Listeners' Vehicle to dedicate themselves to the Great Vehicle.

These eight cases, beginning with contempt for the Buddha and Dharma, all constitute obscurations for beings, and it was to remedy these obscurations that the Buddha taught the supreme Great Vehicle. The above-mentioned eight remedies from the Supreme Vehicle will remove all those people's obscurations or faults that prevent them from following the Great Vehicle.

Ten Benefits

> The best of wise beings who apply themselves
> To holding the *Two Stanzas*,
> By means of the words or meaning,
> Will acquire ten kinds of good qualities: (XIII, 21)

As to the words or points that indicate the eight remedies that eliminate the eight obscurations, they are enunciated in two verses in the *Two Stanza Incantation*: "Disparaging the Buddha, and the Dharma...," and so on. The best of wise beings who apply themselves to retaining its words and keeping in mind their distinct meanings will acquire ten kinds of excellent qualities. What are these ten?

> The fullest increase of their potential,
> The greatest happiness at the moment of death,
> Rebirth wherever they wish,
> And in all their lives, recollection of their past lives, (XIII, 22)

> Meetings with the buddhas,
> Hearing the Supreme Vehicle from them,
> Endowment with interest and understanding,
> Acquisition of the two doors, and swift attainment of
>   enlightenment. (XIII, 23)

As a result of interest and faith in all the Mahāyāna teachings, their Mahāyāna potential or buddha nature will grow to its fullest extent, and at the time of death, they will be utterly happy. These two are qualities that will occur in this present life. The next eight will occur in subsequent lives. After death, they will take birth wherever they wish. In all their lives, wherever they are reborn, they will remember their past lives; encounter their teachers, the buddhas; and hear the teachings of the Supreme Vehicle from those buddhas. They will have an interest in the Great Vehicle and gain a definitive understanding as to its meaning. They will acquire both the door of concentration (concentrations such as the Concentration of Brave Progression) and the door of retention (Inexhaustible Caskets and others). And finally, they will swiftly attain unsurpassable enlightenment.

5. A Summary in Praise of the Virtues of Teaching the Dharma

> Thus, bodhisattvas with good intellects, who are tireless,
> Loving, renowned, and expert in the right procedures,
> Are excellent exponents. In teaching,
> They are brightly shining suns in the midst of humankind.
>   (XIII, 24)

Thus, bodhisattvas who have excellent intellects and are able to explain the teachings correctly; who never lose heart in constantly explaining the Dharma; who truly love sentient beings and have no interest in honors or riches; who practice the six transcendent perfections and are universally renowned for their goodness and learning; who know the best procedure or way for teaching the Dharma (knowing, for example, which teachings to give which kinds of beings)—such bodhisattvas are excellent exponents of the sacred Dharma. In explaining the sacred Dharma, they shine as brightly as the sun among the hosts of human beings, benefiting them like the sun warming the earth and ripening the crops.

This completes the explanation of the thirteenth chapter of *Ornament of the Mahāyāna Sūtras*, the chapter on teaching.

14
Practicing the Dharma

Someone who has investigated the Dharma and thereby received a lot of teachings needs to practice those teachings, so there now follows the chapter on practice, which is divided into three sections: (1) a general presentation; (2) a detailed explanation; and (3) a summary.

1. General Presentation

In the sūtras, the practice is divided into five categories: (1) full knowledge of meanings; (2) knowledge of the way; (3) practicing the way consistent with realization; (4) entrance into conformity; and (5) cultivation of consistent realization.

a. Full Knowledge of Meanings

> The wise, neither wrong
> Nor right with regard to the two,
> Fully know, by means of the three,
> The two kinds of no-self, individual and phenomenal. (XIV, 1)

Wise beings, bodhisattvas on the level of earnest aspiration, are "neither wrong nor right" with regard to the two truths or, alternatively, with regard to the imputed reality, which does not exist, and the dependent and fully present realities, which do exist. Their understanding, on the level of earnest aspiration, of the two kinds of no-self is consistent with thatness, and so, compared to other ordinary beings' minds, they are not mistaken and they are therefore not wrong. But, compared to supramundane beings' minds, they are not right either, for they are still ordinary beings. They are therefore, by nature, not either of these two. Thus, with the three concentrations of emptiness, absence of expectancy, and absence of attributes, bodhisattvas on the level of earnest aspiration are said to have a full knowledge of the two kinds of no-self: the individual no-self and the phenomenal no-self.

With the concentration of emptiness, they understand that individuals and phenomena are merely labeled as such with names, attributes, words, and conventional designations, and know emptiness as the absence of any entity in the imputed reality. And since neither the individual self nor the phenomenal self (in form, sound, and so on) exists as an objective or subjective entity, they know fully that both kinds of self have in fact never existed since the very beginning, like the horns of a rabbit.

The incorrect mental processes of false imagination—in other words, the mind and mental factors that constitute the dependent nature, which is the basis of the dualistic appearances of subject and object—exist on the conventional level, for the process of defilement and the various sufferings of saṃsāra surely and undeniably exist, and no one can say that they do not. If they did not exist, it would be impossible, from the start, to present things in terms of defilement and purity. But there *is* saṃsāra and there *is* nirvāṇa, and no one can dispute that. Despite the dependent reality existing in this way, it is flawed by the false imagination that is the source of suffering and by defilements such as attachment, so it is not something to be hoped for or aspired to. Realizing this, bodhisattvas come to know the nature of the dependent reality through the concentration of absence of expectancy.

The fully present reality is the nature of emptiness devoid of the two kinds of self and of duality. From the beginning, it is present in all phenomena as their true nature, like the heat in fire or the wetness in water. If there were no fully present reality, subject and object and the two kinds of self would exist. Although this true nature, the fully present reality, exists, it is entirely devoid of attributes, of the conceptual elaborations of subject and object, and it is therefore a state in which all concepts that can be expressed or conceived have completely subsided. This is known with the concentration of absence of attributes.

It is thus that bodhisattvas have a full knowledge of the meanings[1] of existence and nonexistence or, put another way, that they have a full knowledge of the meanings of nonexistence and existence in relation to the two truths—relative truth (the imputed reality and dependent reality) and ultimate truth (the fully present reality).

---

1. Tib. *don kun shes pa*.

b. Knowledge of the Way

> Then, those who know the meaning
> Realize that all teachings are like a boat
> And give up being content with listening.
> Thus they are said to know the way. (XIV, 2)

What is knowledge of the way? Bodhisattvas who in this manner know the meanings of the points taught in the sūtras realize that all the teachings that express those points in the form of the names, phrases, and letters in texts such as the sūtras are dispensable. Just as a boat's usefulness comes to an end once one has crossed a river (indispensable though it has been for doing so), and one then no longer needs to rely exclusively on the boat, so too the teachings, in the form of the names, phrases, and letters used to communicate the subject they express so that one can know and understand it, are, like the boat, dispensable. Having realized this, bodhisattvas give up being content with merely hearing the words, and they put the emphasis on developing the wisdom that comes from reflecting on the words and their meanings. This is what we call "knowing the way."[2]

c. Practicing the Way Consistent with Realization

> With the knowledge of an ordinary person,
> They thus realize the two,
> And then, in order to perfect that knowledge,
> They practice the consistent way. (XIV, 3)

As ordinary beings at the stage of earnest aspiration, on the basis of the wisdom that comes from listening and reflection, bodhisattvas have knowledge of meanings and of the way. In doing so, they are neither mistaken nor correct, as explained above, and in this way they realize a general notion or reflection of the two kinds of no-self. Subsequently, in order to perfect and purify that knowledge and transform it into supramundane gnosis, they meditate on it further and further, from the stage of warmth up to that of the supreme mundane level. This is practicing the way consistent with realization.[3]

---

2. Tib. *chos shes pa*.
3. Tib. *chos la chos kyi rjes su mthun par sgrub pa*.

d. Entrance into Conformity

> After that, on the first level,
> As the equals of all bodhisattvas in that state,
> They acquire the supramundane,
> Unsurpassable gnosis. (XIV, 4)

After that, on the first bodhisattva level, Perfect Joy, those bodhisattvas become identical to all the bodhisattvas who have attained the essence of the path of seeing—that is, they acquire the unsurpassable supramundane nonconceptual gnosis, superior to that of the listeners and solitary realizers. Since they have realized the ultimate reality directly, they are referred to as practicing by having entered into conformity[4] with all those who have penetrated the faultless level of the bodhisattva.

e. Cultivation of Consistent Realization

> Having fully extinguished
> All the defilements that need to be eliminated by seeing,
> In order to eliminate cognitive obscurations,
> They apply themselves to meditation. (XIV, 5)

> By the combined practice of gnosis,
> Conceptual and nonconceptual,
> On the remaining levels they continue
> To cultivate consistent realization. (XIV, 6)

Cultivating consistent realization[5] refers to practice on the path of meditation. Earlier, with the attainment of the path of seeing, all the defilements to be eliminated on the path of seeing have been completely extinguished. Subsequently, in order to eliminate cognitive obscurations, from the second to tenth levels bodhisattvas apply themselves to meditation.

As to the kind of gnosis that eliminates the obscurations, with the pure mundane gnosis that determines knowable phenomena in the postmeditation, bodhisattvas know phenomena in their multiplicity; and with

---

4. Tib. *mthun par zhugs pa*.
5. Tib. *mthun pa'i chos la spyod pa*.

the nonconceptual gnosis of formal meditation, they know the space-like ultimate reality as it is. Practicing these two kinds of knowledge together, in alternation one after the other, they continue in the same order on the remaining levels (the second level and higher levels), cultivating the realization consistent with the insight they have already had.

The above is a general account of how one practices according to the five-fold division of the practice described in the sūtras, from the stage of earnest aspiration up to the tenth level on the path of meditation. It is now followed by a detailed explanation.

2. Detailed Explanation

The detailed explanation has three parts: (1) the conditions for practicing; (2) the essence of the practice; and (3) similes for how bodhisattvas practice.

a. The Conditions for Practicing

The conditions favorable to practice are the four great wheels—namely, staying in a suitable location, relying on a holy being, spiritual ambition,[6] and having enduring merit from deeds performed in the past. If one has these four, one will be able to practice perfectly. Therefore, these will now be explained.

The Place

> The place in which the wise practice
> Is full of virtues—well supplied,
> A good place, a healthy place,
> With good company, and comfortable for yoga. (XIV, 7)

The place in which wise bodhisattvas practice is one in which they can come by everything they need to live on, with little difficulty. It is a good place, without uncivilized people, dangerous wild animals, and so forth. There, the soil and water agree with one, and one will not fall ill; it is a pleasant and healthy place, where there is no risk of skin diseases, leprosy, and the like. It

---

6. Tib. *bdag nyid legs par smon pa*, also translated as "perfect aspiration" or "wishing the best for oneself."

is a place in which there are good, virtuous companions who share the same discipline and view; a place that feels comfortable, in which there is nothing to prick one's concentration—people going to and fro during the day, people making a lot of noise at night, and other things that act as obstacles for anyone practicing concentration. If one stays somewhere with qualities like these, one's practice will flourish. On the other hand, the opposite characteristics will hinder practice. So you should be careful to check the place first and avoid beginning your practice in any old place that is available.

Relying on a Holy Spiritual Companion

Relying on a holy spiritual companion is the most important condition for acquiring any good qualities, so what are the characteristics of holy beings?

> **Recognize that learned bodhisattvas**
> **Who have seen the truth, who are skilled in discourse,**
> **Full of love, and never tire**
> **Are great and holy beings. (XIV, 8)**

They are bodhisattvas who have entered the Great Vehicle and are extremely learned in the scriptures that constitute the Dharma of transmission. They have mastered the truths that constitute the Dharma of realization and have thus seen its meaning. They are expert at relating or explaining the Dharma to others. Full of love for others, they never tire of working for others' benefit. You should know that such holy beings are to be relied upon: they are great spiritual masters.

Spiritual Ambition

> **Excellent aim, excellent reliance,**
> **Excellent method, determination to be free,**
> **And excellent application—with these,**
> **One is said to have the right orientation. (XIV, 9)**

Spiritual ambition concerns the practitioners themselves, who are pursuing the Mahāyāna path and considering it with the three kinds of wisdom, so their aim is excellent. Not content with a few sources of good, they have accumulated as much merit and wisdom as they can, and so their reliance is excellent.[7] When their minds become wild and distracted, they reflect on the fault in this and abandon distraction by keeping in mind the special point of sustained calm. When their minds are low-spirited and dull, they encourage themselves, reflecting on the excellent qualities of the buddhas and bodhisattvas, on the benefits of concentration, and on the general and specific characteristics of the teachings; by meditating on the special point of profound insight in this way, they abandon their low spirits. When they are neither low-spirited nor wildly distracted, in that state they apply the special point of equanimity and maintain that very state without moving. These special points of sustained calm, profound insight, and equanimity constitute the meditators' excellent method. Not content with the level they are on, they are determined to gain freedom on (or are fully committed to) ever higher levels and paths, so their determination to be free is excellent. And their constant engagement on the path, using sustained calm and profound insight, constitutes excellent application. To genuinely and single-mindedly focus on having these five excellent principles—in other words, to have the armor of aspiration—constitutes spiritual ambition.

Having Merit from the Past

> A happy mind, and birth in freedom,
> Absence of disease, a capacity for concentration,
> And thorough discernment—
> All these result from merit gathered in past lives. (XIV, 10)

Because of the meritorious deeds they have performed in the past, bodhisattvas live in correspondingly pleasant places, meet with spiritual masters and the teachings, and so on, as a result of which they acquire a happy mind. They are born in freedom, rid of the eight states lacking opportunity.[8] They are physically healthy and can therefore apply themselves to the practice. They have workable minds, fit for concentration. And they possess the

---

7. Tib. *rton pa bzang po*. In some texts, for example, Jigme Lingpa's *Treasury of Precious Qualities*, and notably in Kawa Peltsek's translation of the root text, this second "excellence" is given as the "excellent teacher" (Tib. *ston pa bzang po*).

8. These are the eight conditions in which beings have no opportunity to encounter or practice the Dharma: rebirth in the hells, as a hungry spirit, as an animal, as a long-lived god, at times when there is no buddha, in regions where there is no access to the teachings, among people who have wrong views, or as someone who is mentally and physically dumb.

wisdom that distinguishes the two truths. The causal factor that produces these five advantages is their having created merit in their former lives, the results of which are now visible, and as surely indicative of past merit as smoke is indicative of fire.

b. The Essence of the Practice

The essence of the practice in the Great Vehicle is nonconceptual wisdom and the great compassion that never, ever abandons sentient beings. This is indicated in a brief synopsis and then explained again in greater detail.

i. Brief Synopsis

The first three verses indicate the nonconceptual wisdom in which there is no regarding saṃsāra as harmful and deliberately getting rid of defilements. The two verses that follow those (verses 14 and 15) show that abandoning sentient beings and entering the peaceful state of nirvāṇa alone is contrary to the practice of the Great Vehicle. I will now go straight through these.

(1) Nonconceptual Wisdom

> Besides the expanse of reality,
> There is nothing that exists.
> For this reason, the buddhas have it in mind
> That certain deliverance is attachment and the like. (XIV, 11)

Those on lower paths consider that the defilements exist inherently and that once these are eliminated or brought to an end by means of the path, they will attain nirvāṇa. Obsessed with the defects of saṃsāra and the good qualities of nirvāṇa, they abandon saṃsāra and enter peace. For bodhisattvas, on the other hand, defilements have no intrinsic existence: because they possess nonconceptual gnosis, which is a skillful means that brings liberation *by means of* the defilements themselves, they do not completely reject saṃsāra but practice the bodhisattva activities without being affected by the defects of saṃsāra. Ultimately they attain nirvāṇa, dwelling in neither existence nor peace: with the nonconceptual wisdom free of references, they realize the sameness of saṃsāra and nirvāṇa.

How they do so is described in the *Perfection of Wisdom in One Hundred*

Thousand Lines: "I do not speak of any deliverance from attachment other than by attachment." And it is similar for aversion and bewilderment. What the Buddha had in mind was that it is attachment itself, and not some other deliverance, that gives certain deliverance from attachment. Apart from the expanse of reality, there is no other entity. The very essence or mode of being or nature of all phenomena is nothing but the expanse of reality, suchness, and there is not so much as an atom's worth of phenomena that is other than that. For this reason, the buddhas had it in mind, and taught, that what gives deliverance from attachment and the other defilements is attachment and the others. If one recognizes that the nature of defilements is primordial purity and one realizes that defilements are naturally liberated by the defilements themselves, there is no need to look for other antidotes. On the other hand, if there were such a thing as a defilement that was not liberated by its very nature, no one would be able to liberate it and there would be no getting rid of it. For this reason, in the Vehicle of Characteristics, the sūtras of the ultimate teachings indicate that all phenomena are from the very beginning not bound and not liberated. And similarly, in the Resultant Vehicle of the Mantras, we read in the Purity chapter of the *Two Segments*:[9]

> Ultimately the purity of all things
> Is expressed as suchness. . . .

and,

> The pure, self-cognizant nature
> Is not liberated with any other purity. . . .

The intended essential point in these quotations is the same.

> **Besides the expanse of reality,**
> **There is nothing that exists.**
> **So this, the wise accept, was the intended implication**
> **Of the teaching on defilement. (XIV, 12)**

---

9. Tib. *brtags gnyis*. The *Two Segments* is the condensed version (the shortest of three versions) of the *Hevajra Tantra*. These two quotations are from the ninth chapter of the first section.

Similarly, when the Buddha said that ignorance and enlightenment are the same, he was indicating that apart from the expanse of reality, there are no phenomena that are other than it, and therefore that defilement is naturally the essence of enlightenment. Wise bodhisattvas know that this is what the Buddha had in mind and accept it to be thus, as we find in the sūtras, which declare that defilements are the ground of the vajra awakening, and so on.

> **Because they properly approach**
> **Attachment and the like as suchness,**
> **They will be completely free from them:**
> **Thus they are delivered from them by means of them. (XIV, 13)**

Why, then, if certain deliverance from defilements is achieved by means of the defilements themselves, have all sentient beings who indulge in defilements not achieved certain deliverance? People who ask such a question have not properly understood the intended meaning of such teachings. Beings do not know the thatness of attachment and the other defilements, and they are bound by their clinging to their attributes. Bodhisattvas, on the other hand, have realized the thatness of attachment and so forth, which is the nature of the expanse of reality, and they approach them properly, so they will be completely freed from ordinary, independently existing defilements. This is why they achieve certain deliverance from defilements by means of the defilements. Since they have no concepts of defilements such as attachment and of their attributes, attachment and aversion simply do not occur.

Subsequently, having realized the nature of attachment and the other defilements, they will attain the great enlightenment, the gnosis of exhaustion and nonarising that realizes the meaning of defilements being exhausted from the beginning and nonarisen from the beginning. But for the listeners, it is as if these defilements (which for bodhisattvas lead to great enlightenment) actually exist but will one day be exhausted and will never arise again in their streams of being. Their enlightenment is bewilderment with regard to thatness, as is stated in the *Ornament of True Realization*:

> When others say that things exist
> But that our teacher has brought to an end
> The obscurations related to the knowable,
> I am much surprised.[10]

---

10. *Ornament of True Realization*, V, 20.

Similarly, Ārya Asaṅga has written in the *Compendium of the Great Vehicle* in the verse on the profundity of the body of truth:

> For those who possess great means,
> Defilements will be branches of enlightenment,
> And saṃsāra is the nature of peace.
> For this reason, the Tathāgata is inconceivable.

This sort of pronouncement—that saṃsāra is nirvāṇa and that defilements, as elements of enlightenment, become the path—is clearly made not only in the Vehicle of Characteristics (for without realizing this with wisdom, it is not possible to attain the great enlightenment that does not dwell in either extreme of existence or peace) but also in the Resultant Vehicle, which shows in an unconcealed manner the extraordinary methods that lead to such realization. This is therefore the swift path to enlightenment.

(2) The Skillful Means of Never Abandoning Sentient Beings

The skillful means of never abandoning sentient beings is shown as being the method for attaining great enlightenment.

> Even the most terrible sufferings of dwelling in the hell realms
> For beings' sake do not harm the buddhas' heirs at all.
> The various good thoughts of those who follow lower vehicles,
> Thinking of the defects and virtues of existence and peace,
>   are harmful to the wise. (XIV, 14)

> For the wise, staying in the hells does not forever
> Prevent their vast and uncontaminated enlightenment.
> Thinking of the complete coolth of benefiting oneself in the
>   other vehicles
> Brings great happiness, but it is an obstacle. (XIV, 15)

Even the most terrible sufferings from being burned, boiled, and so forth when they stay in the hell realms for the sake of sentient beings do not in any way harm the bodies or minds of the Buddha's children or obstruct them on the Mahāyāna path. Indeed, because of those sufferings, they understand that everything is illusory and don the armor of deep compassion for beings.

What does harm the wise, acting as an obstacle on the bodhisattva path, is the various, apparently virtuous, thoughts of those who follow the lower vehicles and consider that there are good qualities in the peaceful state of nirvāṇa and defects in saṃsāra.

Why is that? When wise bodhisattvas stay in the hells, they only suffer for the time they are there, but this is not a permanent or lasting obstacle to their gaining the ten strengths and the rest of the vast and abundant qualities of great enlightenment, uncontaminated by the two obscurations—as we know from the story of Daughter the son of Vallabha and that of the strong man Bakshita.[11] Those in other vehicles who aspire to the paths and results of the listeners and solitary realizers, who think of cooling the defilements and sufferings for their own good and who strive to benefit only themselves, may be extremely happy in that situation, but it is an obstacle to great enlightenment. The same is true for those who have entered the Great Vehicle but who, because of others' ingratitude, give up their intention to attain unsurpassable enlightenment and instead realize the listeners' or solitary realizers' nirvāṇa.

ii. Further Detailed Explanations of Nonconceptual Wisdom and Great Love
(1) Nonconceptual Wisdom

> Phenomena do not exist yet are perceived;
> Defilement does not exist and yet is purified;
> Know that they are like magical illusions and so forth,
> And likewise that they are like space. (XIV, 16)

In considering that there is a contradiction between the fact that in ultimate truth phenomena do not exist and the fact that they are perceived as mere appearances, immature beings fail to understand this point and find it frightening. Furthermore, they think that there is a contradiction between defilement being intrinsically nonexistent and adventitious contaminants being purified: they grow afraid and lose interest in the Great Vehicle. This is because they do not understand the profundity of its intended meaning. If one does understand it, however, these points do not contradict each other. Why? Although phenomena exist as mere appearances, they do not truly

---

11. See ch. 4, note 11.

exist in the way they appear. They are like magical illusions, dreams, and so forth, so they *do* exist conventionally as perceptions. And similarly, in the ultimate truth, they do not exist as things conceptualized with attributes: they are to be understood as being like space. There is therefore no contradiction between perception and nonconceptuality.

> Just as on a well-drawn picture
> There are no different planes, yet there seem to be,
> To the false imagination, duality,
> Though never there, appears in different ways. (XIV, 17)

Here is an analogy, that of a clever artist skillfully painting a variety of forms on a canvas, using different colors according to the traditions or procedures of their craft. Although the surface of the painting is actually perfectly flat, the hands and feet, faces, and so forth in the painting appear to the eye to be on different planes, behind or in front of the canvas. In the same way, to the false imagination that has not realized how things truly are, subject and object, while not existent as different aspects, will appear as if they were. The way things are and the way they appear being incompatible, there *are* appearances, so there is no contradiction in things appearing as they do without ultimately existing.

> When muddy water becomes clear,
> Its clarity is not something produced from the muddy state,
> But rather the removal of the dirt contaminating it.
> So it is with the purity of one's own mind. (XIV, 18)

Neither is there any contradiction between things' being naturally pure and their appearing to be pure when they are later freed of contaminants. In its natural state, water is not mixed with bits of earth: it is quite clear. But when it is mixed with mud, it becomes turbid. When this happens, it is not that the nature of the water blends with the particles of earth and is indistinguishable from them. Rather, the water remains itself but appears to be dirty. On the other hand, when it subsequently becomes clear and its former nature becomes manifest, it is not that its clarity has been newly produced from the dirty state and was not present before. Rather, that clarity has been rid of the adventitious contaminants of mud dirtying the water. It is the same for the sky, which is naturally pure but may be cloudy or cloudless. And in the case of gold cleared of mud, there was no dirt there in the beginning, yet there appear to be two conditions, one with contaminants and one free of contaminants. Analogous to these examples are our own minds, which are similarly pure while appearing to be impure.

> The mind is held to be eternally natural clear light;
> It is coarsened by adventitious faults.
> The mind is ultimate reality, and there is no other mind but
>   clear light.
> We speak of this as the nature of mind. (XIV, 19)

In this regard, the mind's fundamental state or mode of being is held to be clear light, naturally always immaculate. That mind is contaminated and coarsened by adventitious blemishes on its own basic nature—attachment and other defilements due to improper thinking—that are not indelible. No other mind, comprising concepts or incorrect mental processes and different from the clear-light mind, the ultimate reality for which there is no contamination, is clear light. The mind that is the uncontaminated ultimate reality, or the gnosis of clear light, is termed the nature or fundamental state of the mind, the union of clarity and emptiness.

(2) The Love and Compassion That Never Forsakes Sentient Beings

> Bodhisattvas feel for sentient beings
> A heartfelt love as great as that
> Felt for an only child—
> Their constant wish is to bring them help. (XIV, 20)

Bodhisattvas have the same affection for sentient beings as a mother has for her only beloved child—an immense, unfeigned love, from the depth of the heart. Such an attitude leads to their always wanting to benefit beings and never abandoning them.

> Because it brings benefit to sentient beings,
> The fondness bodhisattvas feel does not become a downfall.
> But hatred in them will always violate
> And act against all beings. (XIV, 21)

Because it benefits sentient beings, the fondness bodhisattvas feel for them does not become a fault or downfall, for with that "attachment," they never give up feeling responsible for beings. On the other hand, hatred for sentient beings in bodhisattvas—who are individuals who live by such love and who are intent on enlightenment—is totally incompatible with their responsibility for all beings, for if they start to feel hateful, it will induce them to abandon beings and to do them harm. This is why it is said in the sūtras that it is a much greater fault for a bodhisattva to give rise to a single instant's hateful thought than to feel attachment over numerous kalpas. "Attachment to beings" here is used to mean lovingly caring for them: it does not mean having the defilement of attachment. Lay bodhisattvas' fondness for their spouses and children, for example, does not conflict with their loving-kindness, so this kind of "attachment" does not give rise to any transgression of the bodhisattva precepts.[12]

> Like doves who love their young the most,
> Staying with them and holding them close,
> With not the slightest place for anger,
> Are those whose hearts are full of love for beings, their children. (XIV, 22)

> Because they love, there's never room for rage.
> Because they pacify, malice is out of place.
> Because they benefit, they never think deceitfully.
> Because they comfort, they'll never terrify. (XIV, 23)

Of all birds, doves have the greatest attachment and are thus the most affectionate and loving with their young. From the moment they lay their eggs until the young are fully fledged, they hold them close, covering and snuggling them with their wings and body. They never get angry with the little birds, for to do so would be totally out of place with that kind of love. Kindhearted bodhisattvas feel just the same toward other living creatures or sentient beings, who are like their children. They are full of love and want beings to be happy, so it is out of the question for them to feel angry, which would lead to their wanting to harm others. They want beings' defilements

---

12. The terms "attachment" and "fondness" in this paragraph both translate the Tibetan word *chags pa*.

and sufferings to be eased, so it is out of the question for them to give rise to malice, which would create suffering. They want to use their bodies and possessions to benefit beings, so it is counterproductive for them to have deceitful thoughts and to want to cheat them. A bodhisattva is someone who comforts beings, bringing them happiness and joy, and even seeing a bodhisattva or hearing their name protects beings from fear, so it is out of the question for bodhisattvas to frighten beings by beating them up and so on.

Thus, on account of their attitude of love and great compassion, which is completely sincere and unfeigned, with no dishonesty or pretension, bodhisattvas never abandon beings. And on account of their nonconceptual wisdom, they have eliminated the notion of existence and peace as being different. It is for all these reasons that their practice is sublime.

c. Similes for How Bodhisattvas Practice

> Like the sick taking efficacious medicine,
> They enter saṃsāra.
> Like doctors for those who are ill,
> Bodhisattvas practice for sentient beings. (XIV, 24)

Bodhisattvas, in order to attain unsurpassable enlightenment, deliberately take birth in saṃsāra and, without being attached to saṃsāra, dispel the sufferings of sentient beings and bring them benefit and happiness. So, like sick people conscientiously taking the right medicine that will get rid of their disease, bodhisattvas, despite their knowing the misery that is saṃsāra, willingly accept it. Patients conscientiously rely on the medicine, even though they know it is pungent and bitter, because it will cure their disease. Similarly, because, by deliberately accepting saṃsāra, they will cure the diseases of the two obscurations, spontaneously accomplish the two goals, and attain the great enlightenment, bodhisattvas enter saṃsāra and never abandon it.

Like good, kindhearted doctors giving sick people, weakened and in pain, the medicine that matches the underlying cause of their illness, bodhisattvas give sentient beings the medicine of the sacred Dharma to cure the disease of the defilements and bring them all kinds of benefit.

> As with servants who will not work,
> Likewise do they treat themselves.
> As with merchants and their wares,
> Likewise do they use their pleasures. (XIV, 25)

When unruly servants do not do their job or anything else one wants them to do, they can be made to work by beating them, and so on. Similarly, when their minds are influenced by defilements and become unruly, or when they feel fed up with benefiting beings, bodhisattvas punish and subdue their wicked minds by being properly attentive. This is similar to the simile of breaking a horse given in the *Heap of Jewels*.

Like merchants who, in order to provide for their children and household, transform a few items of merchandise into a large profit, bodhisattvas make use of the desirable possessions they own and, with these wares of generosity, produce abundant riches and things to delight the five senses, which they then give away to all sentient beings, accomplishing their benefit and happiness. This refers to the practice of generosity.

> **As with dyers and their cloth,**
> **Likewise do they work on karmic acts.**
> **As with fathers and their infant sons,**
> **Likewise do they never injure beings. (XIV, 26)**

Just as dyers energetically wash the cloth and repeatedly apply the dye to make it fast, bodhisattvas purify their ten physical, verbal, and mental negative actions and intensively practice the ten positive actions. This refers to discipline.

Even though very young children, who are not old enough to know better, may be unrestrained in their behavior and get up to all sorts of mischief, their parents never get angry but feel all the more loving. Similarly, even when beings in the grip of ignorance commit all kinds of negative actions, bodhisattvas, on account of their patience, not only never retaliate or get angry but also manage to develop their compassion.

> **As when one rubs two sticks to make a fire,**
> **Likewise do they practice hard and all the time.**
> **Like a trustworthy person,**
> **They practice their incomplete superior concentration. (XIV, 27)**

Just as someone trying to light a fire by rubbing pieces of wood together perseveres energetically without stopping until the fire is lit, bodhisattvas never lose interest or give up but practice constantly, with great diligence, until they have perfected all virtue.

When one entrusts all one's store of valuables and belongings to trustworthy people, they will not take the smallest thing for themselves even though they could if they wanted. It is the same with regard to bodhisattvas' incomplete concentrations in the training in superior concentration: even while they are in the process of completing them, bodhisattvas do not relish the taste of concentration.

> In the same way as magicians,
> They practice with wisdom regarding phenomena.
> All these are held to show the how and the what
> Of the practice of the bodhisattvas. (XIV, 28)

In a show of magic, magicians use a combination of spells and props to make things like horses and elephants actually appear, yet they know that these are just illusory appearances and that they do not really exist. In the same way, even while they are practicing the transcendent perfections, bodhisattvas practice them as the union of the two truths, with the wisdom that comprises complete knowledge of the nature of all phenomena.

These explanations, associated with similes, are held to refer to the manner in which bodhisattvas practice and the points on which they practice.

3. Summary

> Thus, armed with constant diligence on a vast scale,
> They make the greatest efforts to bring about a twofold maturation.
> Gradually, with supreme, nonconceptual intelligence devoid
>   of contaminants,
> They proceed to the unsurpassable accomplishment. (XIV, 29)

Thus, as explained above, armed with immense diligence in constantly practicing the transcendent perfections on an infinite scale, bodhisattvas apply themselves with great effort to achieving double maturation—maturation of the two accumulations, or of themselves and others. With the highest intelligence that is uncontaminated by defilement-related and cognitive obscurations and free of the concepts of the three spheres, they gradually, starting from the path of accumulation, accomplish the ten levels to the end. This is the process by which they attain unsurpassable enlightenment.

This completes the explanation of the fourteenth chapter of *Ornament of the Mahāyāna Sūtras*, the chapter on practice.

15

Instructions and Follow-Up Teachings[1]

The means by which the practice is enhanced are the instructions and follow-up teachings, so these will be explained next. There are four parts: (1) how the instructions are acquired; (2) keeping the meanings of the instructions properly in mind; (3) how bodhisattvas progress further along the path; and (4) a description of the great benefits of the instructions and follow-up teachings.

1. How the Instructions Are Acquired

> After a measureless kalpa, there is certain deliverance,
> And faith grows ever greater.
> Like rivers flowing into the ocean,
> Virtuous activities lead to true completion. (XV, 1)

The accumulation of merit on the level of earnest aspiration over one measureless kalpa leads to certain deliverance on the first supramundane level and makes one's faith in the Mahāyāna path grow greater and greater. Like the rivers that flow into the ocean from the four directions, all the positive practices comprised in the accumulation of merit and wisdom bring the excellent qualities in one's mind stream to true completion, and at the end of the supreme mundane level one will reach the flawless level of the noble ones.

> The conquerors' heirs who have thus gathered the accumulations
> Are pure from the outset.
> They have perfect understanding and a virtuous mind;
> They apply themselves to meditation. (XV, 2)

---

1. Tib. *gdams ngag rjes su bstan pa*. Mipham gives a definition of this term below in his commentary on verse 49.

Bodhisattvas who have accumulated merit and wisdom as just mentioned have, from the beginning (that is, for many previous kalpas), purified their streams of being and observed perfect discipline. They have listened repeatedly to the extensive and profound teachings of the Great Vehicle and have perfectly understood their meaning. And they have virtuous minds, workable and free of the five hindrances.[2] Such bodhisattvas apply themselves to meditation on the path of joining.

> At that time, bodhisattvas in the stream of Dharma
> Will receive from the buddhas
> Extensive oral instructions
> For achieving a vast degree of sustained calm and gnosis. (XV, 3)

From having completed the accumulation of merit and wisdom in the past, they possess the good fortune to master the gnosis of the first bodhisattva level, so at that time they will acquire the concentration of the door-like stream of Dharma. Why is it called the "concentration of the stream of Dharma"? Because by remaining in equanimity in that concentration, bodhisattvas receive countless instructions on the sacred Dharma from innumerable buddhas and are able to continuously retain the words and meanings. While there are bodhisattvas with sharp faculties who acquire such concentration on the greater path of accumulation, some authorities say that it is acquired at the stage of the supreme mundane level. Once they have acquired it, the distinctive qualities of that concentration will grow more and more. Thus, from remaining in the concentration of the stream of Dharma, they will receive from the buddha bhagavāns, the greatest of spiritual teachers, countless oral instructions on achieving the utterly vast sustained calm and utterly vast gnosis of profound insight that will enable them to acquire the gnosis of the noble beings on the first bodhisattva level—extensive instructions that contain the teachings of many hundreds of thousands of sūtras.

2. Keeping the Meanings of the Instructions Properly in Mind

This section is divided into (1) keeping the instructions in mind by reflecting and (2) keeping the instructions in mind by meditating.

---

2. Tib. *sgrib pa lnga*, the five hindrances to meditation: wildness and remorse, malice, dullness-somnolence, desire, and indecision.

a. Keeping the Instructions in Mind by Reflecting

**Next, those who are diligent in the precepts begin by
Contemplating just the names of the sūtras
And other scriptures
That clearly explain nonduality. (XV, 4)**

Having received the instructions, bodhisattvas diligent in the precepts[3] begin by contemplating just the names of the sūtras and other scriptures of the Twelve Branches of Excellent Speech that provide clear and detailed explanations of nondual thatness (nondual in being devoid of subject and object, or in being free of the two extremes of existence and nonexistence). They simply consider their respective titles—names like the *Sūtra of the Ten Levels*, *Sūtra on the Descent into Laṅka*, and *Moon Lamp Sūtra*. This is the basic reflection.

**After that, step by step,
They classify and analyze the contents.
In each, they properly
Examine their meaning. (XV, 5)**

After that, those bodhisattvas diligent in the precepts step by step "classify and analyze the contents" of each of those sūtras. Starting with "Thus I have heard..."[4] and continuing through to the end, they examine every single phrase, classifying the sūtra by the number of chapters, verses, and letters. This is what we call the "reflection of subsequent analysis or subsequent reflection."

For the lines "In each, they properly examine their meaning," it is acceptable to add the word "sūtra" (to read: "In each sūtra, ..."), while according to Sthiramati's commentary, it is necessary to add "their own understanding" (to read: "In each, with their own understanding, they properly ..."). What this means is that after analyzing the elements in a sūtra, bodhisattvas learn the meaning of each phrase and consider both the point that is being expressed and the letters that express it. There are four processes involved

---

3. Tib. *sdom brtson*. The term "diligent in the precepts" is used to refer to a bodhisattva on the paths of accumulation and joining.

4. "Thus I have heard..." is the familiar opening of many sūtras, as recited at the First Council when Ānanda and other arhats related from memory all the sūtras and other teachings that they had heard from the Buddha.

here: enumerating those points, evaluating them, examining them, and discerning them. First, they consider and enumerate, for example, the five aggregates, eighteen sense spheres, and twelve senses-and-fields; the ten senses-and-fields relating to the aggregate of form, together with imperceptible form (which constitutes one part of the sense sphere of mental objects), making eleven; the six aspects of feeling, from feeling resulting from contact with the eye to that resulting from contact with the mind, and so on. Evaluation involves ascertaining that their numbers are not overestimated or underestimated and considering and reflecting on their characteristics individually. Examination involves considering and analyzing with valid logic the reasons for classifying the phenomena that have thus been enumerated as form and so on. Discernment refers to distinguishing the general and specific characteristics of the subjects of the above three. In short, bodhisattvas reflect on how many categories of subjects there are, check that the numbers are exact, rationally analyze the reasons for their definitive enumeration, and distinguish the general and specific characteristics of each of those subjects enumerated. Although the individual syllables—the letter *a*, for example—of an expression may not signify anything, combining several letters to form a word, and words to form a phrase, and many phrases to form a text does indicate a meaning. So bodhisattvas have to examine whether the letters mean anything or not. All this is what we call "analytic reflection."

> **Having become certain of the meaning,**
> **They summarize all the teachings.**
> **In order to achieve the point of those teachings,**
> **They then proceed to form an aspiration. (XV, 6)**

"Having become certain of the meaning" refers to what we call the "reflection of certainty," which is to be unmistakenly certain, with wisdom, of the attributes of the subjects expressed by the words, the numbers of subjects and so forth, their categories, and the attributes that define them.

With these four kinds of reflection, bodhisattvas establish definitively, in great detail and not just approximately, the words and meanings in the sūtras and other scriptures. After that, they "summarize all the teachings." When they have condensed the points taught in a particular sūtra from the beginning to the end into a single point, they understand, "It is just this." And by condensing the points in all the sūtras, they arrive at the essential point: "The essential point that is being indicated is just this." For example, in the *Sūtra of the Ten Levels*, the classification of the ten levels is taught in great detail, and everything is included in the explanations of the ten levels. So while to think, "It is all included in the meaning of the name 'The Ten Levels'" is part of the basic reflection, to condense everything into a single point is the "reflection of condensation." In short, the sūtras contain extensive and detailed explanations, some in terms of the qualities of the path, some in terms of the order, some in terms of the result, some in terms of the obscurations that have to be eliminated, and so on. And although it is important to know all these, they should be condensed into the essential point of practice: "The heart of the subject, which I now have to practice, is just this."

When they have thus become free of doubts with regard to the points taught in the sūtras, in order to actually achieve themselves those elements taught in the sūtras—the ten levels, for example—practitioners then give rise to the intense, hopeful aspiration "I will achieve this goal." This is the "reflection of aspiration."

By means of these six reflections, bodhisattvas properly keep in mind the meaning of the sacred Dharma—that is, of the sūtras and other branches of the Excellent Speech. There are eleven ways of doing so, and these are indicated in the next four verses.

> Continuously, with mental expressions,
> They should research and examine the teachings
> And analyze them with the attentiveness of the single taste
> In which expression is absent. (XV, 7)

"Mental expressions" refers to the thoughts in the mind. The use of the mind consciousness to associate names and objects and the knowledge that a given name indicates such and such a thing involves the conceptual mind, and it is this that continuously seeks out and examines the words and meanings of the Excellent Words. The latter are analyzed with gross and subtle discursiveness, that is, by the minds of those who have attained the all-sufficing preparation of the first dhyāna and the rudimentary stage of the first dhyāna, and with the subtle discursiveness (gross discursiveness being absent) in the minds of those who have attained the extraordinary stage of the actual first dhyāna, the so-called intermediate dhyāna, and the second dhyāna. When the actual concentrations of the third and fourth dhyānas are attained, both gross and subtle discursiveness are absent, so things are analyzed with the attentiveness of the single taste in concentration, where there is no expression involving gross or subtle discursiveness. These three kinds of attentiveness (that with gross and subtle discursiveness, and so on) correspond to three categories of mental state. Of the six reflections, these three kinds of attentiveness incorporate concentrating on just the names of the teachings and concentrating on the words.

> The summarization of the scriptures in their titles
> Should be understood as being the path of sustained calm.
> The path of profound insight
> Should be understood as the analysis of their meaning. (XV, 8)

Where the root verse says that in just the title all the points taught in a sūtra are summarized, the meanings of the many subjects and words (the *One Hundred Thousand Lines*, for example) that teach transcendent wisdom are included in the meaning of the title "Perfection of Wisdom." Concentration on this is to be understood as being the path of sustained calm. The path of profound insight is to be understood as analyzing the points in that sūtra with enumeration, evaluation, examination, and discernment.

> Know that the path of their union
> Is a combination of these.
> A dull mind has to be kept focused,
> And wildness must be subdued. (XV, 9)

The path of the union of sustained calm and profound insight is to be understood as combining both names and meanings. When sustained calm and profound insight are not combined, one focuses on the names and words with sustained calm and considers their meanings with profound insight. When sustained calm and profound insight are united, names and meanings are not considered separately but are combined, and one focuses on them with sustained calm and profound insight equally. These three—attentiveness related to sustained calm, attentiveness related to profound insight, and attentiveness related to their union—make three categories in terms of the path.

These are also classified into three in terms of their object, as three special points—the special points of sustained calm, maintaining one's concentration, and equanimity. If thoughts proliferate and the mind becomes wild, then by reflecting on the defects of distraction and saṃsāra, one settles the mind inward in meditation, without letting it proceed outward again. This is to keep in mind the special point of sustained calm. If the mind becomes dull and low-spirited, one keeps in mind the special point of profound insight: it is necessary to rouse the mind out of its low spirits and to encourage oneself by thinking of the general and particular qualities or attributes of buddhahood and of concentration. Wildness is analogous to profound insight and cannot, therefore, be dispelled by profound insight, so it is sustained calm that needs to be kept in mind. Dullness and low spirits and somnolence are analogous to sustained calm, so they have to be cleared with profound insight.[5] Thus the low-spirited mind is kept roused by keeping in mind the special point of profound insight. And wildness is to be subdued by keeping in mind the special point of sustained calm.

> Then, when there is evenness with regard to the object,
> Bodhisattvas settle in equanimity.
> In all this, constancy
> And devotion are to be applied. (XV, 10)

When the mind is even, with neither low spirits nor wildness, one should settle evenly in that very state, without moving, keeping in mind the special point of equanimity.

All these meditational processes have to be practiced without interruption, with two kinds of attentiveness related to devoted application and constant application. Thus, on the path one should apply to the above-mentioned kinds of attentiveness the attentiveness related to constancy (not merely keeping them in mind from time to time) and enthusiasm and respect for those different kinds of attentiveness.

b. Keeping the Instructions in Mind by Meditating

The qualities of the path will not be actualized just with the wisdom that comes from reflecting; it is necessary to meditate one-pointedly. In the

---

5. Profound insight is similar to wildness in that it is outgoing and analytic, like ordinary thoughts, so it cannot be used to subdue thoughts. In sustained calm, the mind is quiet and withdrawn, so it cannot be used to rouse the meditator out of a similar dull and drowsy state.

beginning, the mind of someone in the world of desire, not being inwardly settled in meditation, never stays still for a second. It moves like lightning, like the wind, like clouds. And like the waves in the ocean, it is difficult to stop. Yet if one uses the nine methods for settling the mind,[6] thoughts are gradually brought under control and the mind is correctly brought inward to meditation. How to accomplish such concentration is the subject of the following verses.

> Once they direct the mind at the object,
> They should not be distracted from the continuity of that.
> They should quickly realize when they are distracted
> And draw the mind back onto the object. (XV, 11)

(1) Directing the mind one-pointedly at a suitable object of concentration, one should let it rest on it.

(2) Even though it settles in this way, it may move toward other mental images without staying still for a second. If this happens, one should not be distracted from the continuity of the original object of concentration: one should use mindfulness to preserve the continuity and settle as long as possible.

(3) It may be that, despite doing so, one is unable to stay like that for any length of time and becomes distracted by other things. In that case, one should quickly realize that one is distracted by other objects and summon the mind back, settling it on the original object.

> The wise should gather
> The mind inward more and more.
> Then, because they see the virtues of this,
> They tame the mind in concentration. (XV, 12)

(4) By getting used to that again and again, one is able to maintain the continuity and thence to remain in meditation continuously for a short while. At this point, the wise should be extremely attentive and gather the mind in onto the original mental object more and more. This is known as "firmly settling."

(5) Then, when one is able to settle the mind a bit better than before, one sees for oneself the virtues of settling the mind in concentration and con-

---

6. Tib. *sems gnas pa'i thabs dgu*, also known as the nine stages of settling the mind.

sequently thinks, "Wouldn't it be good if I could achieve the concentration of mental stillness." One feels pleased and enthusiastic about concentration, and this leads to one's bringing the mind under control. It is the pleasure the distracted, untamed mind derives from concentration that acts to subdue it.

> Because they see the fault in distraction,
> They should pacify the disinclination to concentrate.
> Similarly, they should pacify covetousness
> And unhappiness, if these arise. (XV, 13)

(6) Even though one's pleasure and keenness in concentration may result in the mind settling on the object to a certain extent, the force of one's previous habituation to distraction may result in one's becoming distracted. When this happens, one should see the defect of such distraction—that it is extremely deleterious to concentration, running off with it like a robber. So thinking, "Rather than being carried away by distraction, I must make an effort to concentrate, for concentration is the root of all good qualities," one should counteract one's disinclination to concentrate (which is caused by distraction). This is the sixth method for settling the mind, "pacifying."

(7) With this sort of effort, the mind will settle much better than before. Nevertheless, from time to time covetousness, unhappiness, and so forth, and lesser defilements like agitation and sinking may come up. As in the previous case, if one is influenced by these, one will not manage to concentrate, and they are therefore very damaging. On the other hand, if one does not fall prey to these, one will achieve meditative concentration, which is the basis of extraordinary qualities such as preternatural knowledge. So, thinking, "I must on no account keep these bad thoughts in mind!"[7] one should counteract covetousness and the like by means of analysis, or by applying an antidote, or alternatively by thinking nothing of them. This is "firmly pacifying."

> Then, those who are diligent in the precepts,
> By deliberately acting on their states of mind,
> Achieve natural concentration.
> From getting used to that, they no longer make deliberate
>   effort. (XV, 14)

---

7. "Thoughts" (Tib. *rnam rtog*) here refers not only to negative thoughts and other distracting thoughts but also to mental experiences such as dullness that can hinder meditation.

(8) Subsequently, bodhisattvas diligent in the precepts settle the mind deliberately, with effort. This is the eighth method, and from habituation to this, they arrive at a point where it happens naturally. If one makes an effort to be attentive, the mind settles on the object of concentration without other thoughts being able to interrupt it. This is what we call "deliberate concentration."

(9) By getting used over a long period to deliberately settling the mind, one no longer needs to make an effort to concentrate, and the mind settles automatically on the object of concentration. Concentration becomes spontaneous, and one reaches the stage of settling the mind without deliberate application. This is the last of the nine methods of settling the mind and is what we call "mental one-pointedness that is accepted as being consistent with concentration."[8]

These nine methods of settling the mind are described in the sūtras as settling, correctly settling, withdrawing and settling, firmly settling, taming, pacifying, firmly pacifying, maintaining continuous one-pointedness, and concentrating or settling in evenness.

> **Then, they gain great fitness**
> **Of the body and mind,**
> **And are known to have attentiveness.**
> **Having fostered it, (XV, 15)**
>
> **By progressing further,**
> **They attain the states of the actual concentrations. (XV, 16ab)**

When practitioners have reached the stage where the mind settles by itself, without deliberate effort, and get used to that state, they acquire trained, fit bodies and fully trained minds. Their bodies become light and perfectly healthy, and thus fit for practicing virtue. And their minds feel lucid and clear and filled with joy, fit for conceiving virtue. After achieving this trained, workable state to a lesser and medium extent, they attain a vast degree of fitness, their bodies and minds being as subtle and limpid as shadows. It should be understood that they then keep in mind peaceful and gross states, enabling them to attain the first dhyāna.[9]

---

8. This is not yet the true concentration of higher levels.
9. It is the notion that lower states (in this case, the desire realm) are gross and higher

That attentiveness successively eliminates the lesser, middling, and greater defilements of the world of desire, and by that means meditative concentration grows, progressing from the lower level so that practitioners attain the actual concentration of the first dhyāna. You should understood that by similarly keeping in mind peaceful and gross states progressively, they accomplish the concentrations up to the actual concentration of the fourth dhyāna.

Up to this point we have explained how concentration is accomplished. There now follows a description of the virtues of achieving meditative concentration.

> From striving for preternatural knowledge,
> They are purified and become supremely fit. (XV, 16cd)

> By using the preternatural powers
> Gained through concentration,
> In order to venerate and listen to
> Countless buddhas
> They travel to different worlds. (XV, 17)

> Thus they venerate infinite buddhas
> For infinite kalpas.
> And because they have venerated them,
> Their minds become supremely fit. (XV, 18)

When bodhisattvas attain the actual concentrations of the four dhyānas, as a result of their keenness to acquire preternatural knowledge such practitioners attaining the actual concentration are purified of the impurities caused by the predominant defilements on their respective levels—craving, view, and doubt—and they become supremely fit. Through the concentration of that pure, fit state, they acquire the five kinds of preternatural knowledge (the knowledge and ability to perform miracles, for instance), and by making full use of these, they travel to different world systems in the ten directions in order to make offerings to infinite buddhas and to listen to the sacred Dharma. It is in this way that they serve and venerate infinite

---

states (the concentrations of the higher worlds) are peaceful that enables the meditator to progress.

buddhas for infinite kalpas. "Infinite kalpas" in this context does not refer to the "three measureless kalpas"[10] but rather to infinite kalpas beyond counting—infinite on account of the mental power of the concentration these bodhisattvas have attained. Because they have made boundless offerings to those sublime objects of reverence, the buddhas of the ten directions, the minds of these purely motivated practitioners become sublimely fit, and they are able to use them just as they wish.

> And so they will obtain
> Five prelusive benefits.
> For those who are to become unsurpassable,
> Perfectly pure vessels, (XV, 19)
>
> All the negative tendencies of the body
> Will be exhausted in each instant.
> And all the time, the mind and body
> Will throughout be perfectly fit. (XV, 20)

Thus, prior to attaining the first bodhisattva level, those bodhisattvas will obtain five benefits, which are signs that they are going to attain the bodhisattva levels. What are these benefits? Because their fit minds are to be the unsurpassable vessels in which the unsurpassable gnosis of the first level (far superior to that of the listeners and solitary realizers) can take birth, in order for that to happen, all the negative tendencies in those bodhisattvas' bodies—that is, of their unrestrained minds leaping about like monkeys and their heavy, unhealthy bodies, which they are unable to put to virtuous use—will, in each instant, be exhausted. This is the first good quality, that of the habitual negative tendencies of unfit body and mind present in the ground of all being purified.

All the time, their bodies and minds will be impregnated with fitness.[11] This is the second good quality. Like a launderer using water to rinse soap

---

10. "Measureless" (Tib. *grangs med*, lit. "uncountable") is in fact the highest number in the Indian system of decimal arithmetic and said to be ten to the power of sixty. Three "measureless" kalpas (traditionally the length of time it takes a bodhisattva to complete the path and attain enlightenment) therefore represents an immensely long, but not infinite, period of time.

11. Tib. *shin sbyangs*, the suppleness and mastery that comes with thorough training and which is the opposite of the unfitness of negative tendencies (Tib. *gnas ngan len*).

out of cotton or other fabrics, these two qualities purify the unfit body with the water of sustained calm and fill the mind and body with the bliss of fitness.

> **They will realize uninterruptedly**
> **The whole light of the Dharma.**
> **The signs of perfect purity**
> **Will be clearly seen without checking. (XV, 21)**

The third special quality is that at all times, uninterruptedly, the light of knowledge of the whole of the sacred Dharma will be realized. It is not as if these bodhisattvas will know some of the sacred sūtras and not others.

The signs of attaining the perfectly pure levels of the noble beings include, in real life, the absence of parasites in one's body, and, in dreams, washing one's body, receiving predictions from the buddhas, and the other signs of attaining the ten levels that one gets in dreams as described in the *Sūtra of the Ten Levels*. To clearly see these and other such signs of attaining the bodhisattva levels, even without specially checking for them, is the fourth quality. These last two qualities are indications that come through practicing profound insight.

> **Similarly, in order to perfect the body of truth**
> **And attain perfect purity,**
> **The wise take hold of their causes,**
> **Constantly and in all situations. (XV, 22)**

In this way, in order to perfect ultimate realization—the body of truth—and to purify the two obscurations that have to be eliminated, wise bodhisattvas grasp those same causes[12] of ultimate elimination and realization all the time, in both meditation and postmeditation. This is the fifth quality, which involves both sustained calm and profound insight.

Sthiramati's commentary explains the five benefits as the exhaustion of physical and mental negative tendencies, the body being filled with the bliss of fitness, the mind being filled with the bliss of fitness (in other words, he counts these two separately), the uninterrupted light of the Dharma, and seeing the signs of purity. And he refers to grasping the causes of perfecting

---

12. I.e., sustained calm and profound insight.

the body of truth and attaining perfect purity as "fully grasping" them. The above explanation of the five benefits follows the description in the *Compendium of the Great Vehicle*.

All the above, from the beginning of this Instructions chapter down to the description of the five good qualities, is an exposition of how a bodhisattva who is an ordinary being on the level of earnest aspiration obtains the teachings and good qualities.

3. How Bodhisattvas Progress Further along the Path

> Next, bodhisattvas like these
> Remain in evenness, and by doing so,
> No longer see any objects
> As anything other than mental expressions. (XV, 23)

After that, bodhisattvas who have become like that and acquired extraordinary sustained calm and profound insight on the path of accumulation rest in evenness in one-pointed concentration. As a result, they no longer see external objects as existing outside the mind—as anything more than mind-talk or thoughts. It is at this time that they gain the vision of the stage of warmth.[13]

> In order to enhance the light of Dharma,
> The steadfast apply themselves fully with diligence.
> The light of Dharma grows greater
> And they will remain in the state of mind-only. (XV, 24)

In order to greatly enhance the light of Dharma[14] that they have gained, steadfast bodhisattvas apply themselves fully, with diligence. This corresponds to the peak stage, where their vision unfolds or increases. As a result of their practicing diligently in this way, the light of Dharma grows ever greater, and they will remain in the state of mind-only, free from the perception of specifically characterized external objects and suchlike.

---

13. The stage of warmth is the first stage of the path of joining.

14. Tib. *chos kyi snang ba*, alternatively translated as "vision of reality." This is not yet the direct vision of emptiness gained on the path of vision but is analogous to seeing a reflection of the moon prior to seeing the moon itself.

> Then, everything that appears as a sense object
> Will clearly appear as the mind.
> At that time, the distracting apprehension
> Of those things will be eliminated. (XV, 25)

In what way will they remain in the state of mind-only? All forms and suchlike that appear as objects of the senses will then be clearly perceived as not existing as specifically characterized external objects—as nothing other than just the appearances of one's own mind, like the appearances in a dream when one recognizes them as such. At that time, the distracting objective apprehension of those forms and other external objects will be eliminated and will no longer appear.

> After that, only the distractions
> In the form of an apprehending subject are left.
> At that time, they quickly reach
> The concentration "with no obstruction." (XV, 26)

Subsequently, for such practitioners, there is left, uneliminated, only the subjective thought or distraction "There is a mind." This corresponds to the stage of acceptance, with the concentration that partly penetrates thatness. At this time they ask themselves, "If there is no apprehended object, how can there be a mind apprehending it?" And having rapidly come to the realization that the mode of existence of both subject and object is the same, they have no difficulty in swiftly reaching the "immediately preceding concentration"[15] for which there is nothing barring the way to the path of seeing. So this is the stage of the immediately preceding concentration of the supreme mundane level.

> Immediately after that,
> Distractions in the form of a subject are eliminated.
> The above are to be understood as being
> The successive stages of warmth and so forth. (XV, 27)

What is meant by "immediately preceding" here? Immediately after the acceptance of this realization that there is no apprehended object, the dis-

---

15. See ch. 11, note 4.

traction of an apprehending subject is also eliminated, and immediately after that bodhisattvas enter the first level, which is why the supreme mundane level is referred to as "immediately preceding."

These stages that have just been explained are to be understood as being the four successive stages—warmth, and so on—of the path of joining.[16]

> **Subsequently they acquire**
> **Unsurpassable supramundane gnosis,**
> **Nonconceptual, uncontaminated,**
> **And free of the two kinds of grasping. (XV, 28)**

There now follows a description of how the path of seeing is attained in the instant after the supreme mundane level. Bodhisattvas who have attained the supreme mundane level then acquire the supramundane gnosis that is unsurpassable (for it is superior to that of the listeners and solitary realizers), devoid of the concepts of the three spheres, uncontaminated (being free of the defilements to be eliminated by the path of seeing), and free of the two kinds of grasping (for they have eliminated the duality of grasping to subject and object). As we read in the sūtras, "They acquire the eye of Dharma with regard to the nature of phenomena, free of dust, devoid of contaminants." Because they have eliminated subject and object, it is free of dust. And because they are free of the factors that have to be eliminated by the path of seeing, it is devoid of contaminants. Or, alternatively, it is "free of dust" in terms of acceptance,[17] this being the unobstructed path, the antidote to defilement-related and cognitive obscurations; and it is "devoid of contaminants" in terms of gnosis, this being the path of perfect liberation. "With regard to the nature of phenomena" refers to the fact that it is the eye of gnosis or eye that sees suchness as it is, the true nature of phenomena.

> **This, their transformation,**
> **Is held to be the first level.**
> **Over a measureless kalpa**
> **They have become utterly pure. (XV, 29)**

---

16. The four stages of the path of joining are warmth, peak, acceptance, and the supreme mundane level.

17. "Acceptance" (Tib. *bzod pa*) here refers to the eight instants of acceptance (*bzod pa brgyad*) on the path of seeing, which also comprises eight instants of knowing (*shes pa brgyad*), together making sixteen instants of gnosis on the path of seeing (*mthong lam gyi ye shes skad cig bcu drug*).

This birth of nonconceptual gnosis, the transformation in these bodhisattvas of the ground of all, is held to be the first of the noble levels. How long does it take to attain this first level? Those who dwell in this state of transformation on the first level have practiced the boundless activities of the bodhisattvas on the level of earnest aspiration for one measureless kalpa and by doing so have attained the noble levels. From then on, they never have any of the faults of saṃsāra, and they have therefore become utterly pure.

Specific Qualities of Attaining the Bodhisattva Levels

> Having gained perfect realization
> Of the expanse of reality, sameness,
> At that time they acquire the awareness
> That all beings are the same as themselves, all the time. (XV, 30)

> With regard to sentient beings, they are even-minded
> Concerning their lack of self, their suffering, their goal,
> And in not hoping for reward;
> With regard to other bodhisattvas, they are alike. (XV, 31)

The expanse of reality is the nature of ordinary beings and the nature of noble beings: it is the same in everything, and there is no difference between them. When one gains full, direct realization of this and attains the levels, one will acquire the awareness that one is oneself the same as or equal to all sentient beings, and not the slightest bit different from them, all the time.

As a result, one realizes five aspects of sameness: (1) One realizes that one is the same as beings in being devoid of self. (2) One is the same in that the sufferings of all sentient beings, who are experiencing suffering on account of ignorance, have to be eliminated. (3) One is the same in the goal to be achieved, that is, the elimination of the origin of beings' suffering, our karmic actions and defilements. (4) As a child of the buddhas, one is even-minded in the sense that just as one would not expect to be rewarded for benefiting oneself by following the path and attaining the truth of cessation, one has the same absence of expectation that other beings will reward one for benefiting them by bringing them to the path and cessation—that being, after all, one's own goal. And (5) in one's elimination and realization, one is similar or equal to other children of the buddhas who have attained the noble levels.

> All things compounded in the three worlds
> Are false imagination.
> This they see by dint of gnosis,
> Utterly pure and free of duality. (XV, 32)

The above describes the manner in which bodhisattvas engage in benefiting others. As for their specific realization with wisdom, bodhisattvas who have attained the first level see that all the compounded phenomena of the three worlds—the five aggregates of the worlds of desire and form, the four aggregates of the formless world, and so on—are the false imagination in beings' mind streams; they are simply the mind and mental factors. With the pure mundane gnosis of postmeditation they see that there are no phenomena apart from the mind and mental factors—they are merely the mind. As we read in the *Sūtra of the Ten Levels*:

O bodhisattvas, these three worlds are merely the mind.

With what kind of gnosis do they see this? They see it by dint of nonconceptual gnosis, perfectly pure and free of obscuration, and devoid of the duality of subject and object. The nonconceptual gnosis of meditation does not perceive self and others or even "mind-only": it is as pure as space, with no subject or object. However, "by dint of" such realization, the gnosis of postmeditation, despite there being no phenomena other than just the mind, sees that same mind appearing as all kinds of different phenomena, like the appearances in a dream or in a magical illusion.

> By seeing the nature of nonexistence,
> Bodhisattvas are freed from the obscurations to be
>   eliminated.
> Consequently, at that time they are said
> To have attained the path of seeing. (XV, 33)

Those bodhisattvas who have attained the path of seeing have directly seen the fully present reality devoid of subject and object and so are freed from the obscurations to be eliminated by the path of seeing. Consequently, they are described at that time as having attained the path of seeing.

> Because they know the emptiness of what does not exist,
> And likewise the emptiness of what does exist,

> And they know the natural emptiness,
> They are described as knowing emptiness. (XV, 34)

Furthermore, those who have attained the path of seeing are described as knowing three kinds of emptiness: (1) With the postmeditational pure mundane gnosis, or the gnosis that discerns knowable phenomena, they know the emptiness of what does not exist, that of the imputed reality, which is imagined, for example, when a piece of rope is mistaken for a snake. (2) Similarly, they know the emptiness of what does exist, that of the dependent reality, which although it has nothing like the objective characteristics imputed by immature beings, is the basis of appearance. (3) And they know the natural emptiness of the fully present reality, for it is primordially free from the duality of subject and object. Thus, bodhisattvas on the path of seeing are described as "knowing emptiness." This explains the concentration of emptiness, one of three concentrations.

> The basis of absence of attributes
> Is said to be the complete exhaustion of concepts;
> The basis of absence of expectancy
> Is false imagination. (XV, 35)

Next, there is the concentration of the absence of attributes. Its basis or object is said to be the truth of cessation, the complete exhaustion of all concepts of phenomena (from form to nirvāṇa) as having attributes, as is described in a treatise that summarizes the Abhidharma:[18]

> To define the truth of cessation—
> Where does cessation occur? In suchness.
> What causes cessation? The truth of the path.
> And what ceases? Conceptual thoughts.

The basis or object of the concentration of the absence of expectancy is the impure dependent nature, false imagination. False imagination is the support of the seeds of defilement-related and cognitive obscurations, and it is the cause of all the various sufferings of birth, aging, and so forth. It is therefore seen as being an improper object of expectation.

---

18. We have been unable to identify this text with certainty.

> For the buddhas' children
> All the various elements leading to enlightenment
> Are said to be acquired forever
> Simultaneously with the path of seeing. (XV, 36)

At the same time as attaining the path of seeing, which comprises the sixteen instants of acceptance and knowing, bodhisattvas are also said to acquire forever, without losing them, all the different elements of the path that leads to enlightenment, like the thirty-seven elements that lead to enlightenment (the four close mindfulnesses and the rest). This is because at the time they first attain the untainted supramundane path, they acquire full maturity and purity in everything they have trained in earlier on the path of earnest aspiration—the four close mindfulnesses, the four genuine restraints, and so forth—and they gain all the potential to also bring to realization the higher paths that they will later train in.

The five verses that follow praise the marvelous qualities of those on the first bodhisattva level.

> Knowing with wisdom that beings are simply compounded,
> And that the nonexistent self is simply the unfolding of suffering,
> They have eliminated the view of a useless self
> And acquire the view of the "great self," which is highly useful.
> (XV, 37)

By the power of their wisdom, bodhisattvas know that all these beings, though devoid of the two kinds of self, are simply the subordinate products of dependent arising—of conditioning factors arising through ignorance, and so on. They also know that the self that experiences things is simply the unfolding of the three kinds of suffering ripening because of karmic actions and defilements. Consequently they abandon the view of a self, which is by nature a useless delusion, and acquire the view of the "great self," of the sameness of oneself and others, which is immensely useful in that it benefits infinite sentient beings.[19]

> Such bodhisattvas, while not believing in a self, know that belief;
> While not suffering, they suffer terribly.

---

19. Alternative translation: one acquires the view of the great nature (Tib. *bdag nyid chen po*), the equality of oneself and others, the great goal of benefiting infinite sentient beings.

> They never hope for anything in return for all the benefit
> they bring,
> Any more than they would seek a recompense for doing
> themselves some good. (XV, 38)

Such bodhisattvas, while not having the belief in a self, take responsibility for the view of a self in other beings—that is, for sentient beings who have not realized, as they themselves have, that the two kinds of self do not exist, and who experience all kinds of suffering on account of their deluded projections, as if the two kinds of self did exist. Until the end of time, they never give up their efforts in the different methods for dispelling the dreamlike hallucinations that beings suffer. Thus, without suffering themselves (for they have been freed of tainted ways), they will nevertheless suffer terribly on account of other beings' sufferings, like a mother whose child is sick, taking on the burden of personally getting rid of the sufferings of the infinity of sentient beings.

Having attained the first level themselves, they are free of the five kinds of fear and therefore will never be discouraged by others' sufferings that they have willingly taken on. The five kinds of fear, which they have transcended, are fear of having nothing to live on, fear of not being made famous in poems and the like, fear of their followers being ungrateful, fear of being born in the lower realms, and fear of death. Just as they would not expect any reward for themselves for having benefited themselves, they accomplish the whole benefit of other beings without expecting anything in return.

> Through supreme liberation, their minds are free,
> Yet they are bound for ages by unending chains.
> Even if they see no end to suffering,
> They apply themselves and truly set to work. (XV, 39)

> The worldly cannot bear the pains they have in just one life,
> Let alone the sum of others' sufferings for the duration of
> the world—
> Never could they imagine such a thing.
> Bodhisattvas are quite the opposite of them. (XV, 40)

With the gnosis of the first bodhisattva level, the extraordinary kind of realization of the Great Vehicle, which is supreme liberation, bodhisattvas' minds are freed from the obscurations that are to be eliminated by the path of seeing, yet their bonds, the load of promises they have made to benefit others, are unending, being as infinite as sentient beings in number. Moreover, since they never cast off the burden of their promises until the end of time, these have no expiration date, so they are bound for a long, long time. Thus, even though they will never see the end when all sentient beings' suffering is exhausted, for as long as there is suffering, they apply themselves completely or strive diligently from the depth of their hearts to dispel beings' suffering. In order to do that, they take birth in saṃsāra and diligently practice the transcendent perfections themselves and induce others to practice them. The fact that they actually do this is something truly extraordinary and wonderful.

Ordinary beings are quite unable to willingly accept and bear the burden of their own sufferings in that way, not even those that befall them in one lifetime, let alone in infinite rebirths. They do not have the strength to bear even their own troubles, so one need hardly mention their not being able to actually shoulder the whole sum of others' sufferings without expectation for as long as the world endures. Not for a single instant could they even imagine doing so. Bodhisattvas are quite the opposite of them. Even though they do not need to accept suffering for their own good, they have the strength to willingly take on boundless sufferings for the sake of sentient beings.

> The joy and love those bodhisattvas feel for beings,
> Their application, their never losing heart—
> These are the greatest wonders in all worlds;
> And yet, since bodhisattvas and beings are the same, there's
> not so much to marvel at. (XV, 41)

It is for these reasons that the deeply felt joy and love bodhisattvas feel for infinite sentient beings, their diligence or application with regard to beings' welfare, and the fact that they are never discouraged by such things as others' ingratitude are the greatest wonders in all worlds. And yet they are not as amazing as all that, for bodhisattvas have acquired the attitude of sameness, thinking of themselves and beings as the same, so it is as if they were working for their own benefit, and there is nothing extraordinary in that.

The next five verses describe the path of meditation and the path of consummation.

> Next, bodhisattvas
> Meditate on the two kinds of gnosis
> On the remaining levels, the path of meditation,
> And thereby fully purify themselves. (XV, 42)

Having attained the first bodhisattva level, bodhisattvas proceed to the remaining nine levels, from the second to the tenth. These comprise the path of meditation, on which they train in the two kinds of gnosis—the nonconceptual gnosis in formal meditation and the pure mundane gnosis in postmeditation. By doing so, they purify the defilement-related and cognitive obscurations.

> Nonconceptual gnosis
> Refines the qualities of buddhahood;
> The other, distinguishing gnosis,
> Brings sentient beings to maturity. (XV, 43)

That nonconceptual gnosis refines the qualities of buddhahood—the ten strengths, four fearlessnesses, and the rest—thereby bringing the bodhisattvas themselves to full maturation. The other gnosis, that of the postmeditation, establishes, as it is, the presentation of all the characteristics and good qualities of the ten levels and so forth, thereby bringing sentient beings to full maturation—that is, by demonstrating the attainment of full enlightenment and teaching beings the Dharma.

> By completing two measureless kalpas
> They reach the end of the path of meditation;
> Having attained the final stage of meditation,
> Bodhisattvas receive empowerment. (XV, 44)

By completing the practice over two measureless kalpas, bodhisattvas will finish or reach the end of the path of meditation, the last of the ten levels being the culmination of the path of meditation. From the second level up to the seventh, we speak of "meditation with deliberate effort," and that takes one measureless kalpa. From the eighth up to the tenth level, we speak of "meditation without deliberate effort," which takes another measureless kalpa. Once a bodhisattva has attained the state of abiding on the tenth level, the end of the path of meditation, the buddhas of the ten directions empower him or her with great rays of light as the buddhas' regent.

> Having gained the vajra-like concentration
> That no concept can destroy,
> They attain the ultimate transformation,
> The unsurpassable level— (XV, 45)
>
> The absence of all contaminating obscurations,
> The perfect accomplishment, from that abode,
> Of deeds to benefit all beings,
> And the perfect knowledge of all things. (XV, 46)

On the basis of that empowerment, they acquire the vajra-like concentration that cannot be destroyed by the conceptual thoughts of apprehension of attributes.[20] And by completely eradicating even the most subtle habitual tendencies to the dualistic perception of subject and object, they attain the ultimate transformation free of the two obscurations and habitual tendencies, the unsurpassable state endowed with triple greatness—the *great elimination* free of all contaminating obscurations; the *great activity* of one dwelling on the eleventh level, the level of no more learning, that fully accomplishes all kinds of deeds in order to benefit all beings for as long as space endures (alternatively, the *great compassion* of the highest of beings); and the *great realization* that knows everything there is to know at the same time, directly and unobstructedly.

4. A Description of the Great Benefits of the Instructions and Follow-Up Teachings

> Thus, from their always beholding the capable ones, who are
>   difficult to see,
> And from their unequaled listening, clear faith arises, and
>   by dint of this,
> Their minds will always be utterly content.
> How could this not be highly beneficial? (XV, 47)

---

20. Tib. *mtshan 'dzin gyi rtog pa*.

As explained in this chapter on the instructions, by dint of the clear faith that comes from their constantly seeing the buddhas (the capable ones who are very rarely visible to beings who have not accumulated merit and to those who have impure mind streams), and from their incomparable listening (that is, their properly listening to those buddhas' instructions on the incomparable teachings of the Great Vehicle), the bodhisattvas' minds will constantly be satisfied. How could the instructions and follow-up teachings not be of the greatest benefit for them? There is no doubt that through those instructions, they will easily attain the great enlightenment, and nothing could be more beneficial than that.

> To those who dwell at the door of the Dharma
> The tathāgatas are always present, giving advice.
> As if pulled by the hair, they are forcefully dragged
> From the thicket of evil and brought to enlightenment.
> (XV, 48)

To a bodhisattva remaining in this kind of concentration, which is the door to the Dharma, the tathāgatas constantly appear and give instructions. And just as someone sinking in a river or swamp and unable to get out on their own can easily be pulled out onto dry land by someone strong seizing them by the hair, on account of the tathāgatas' blessings and instructions the bodhisattva is dragged by the force of compassion out of the dense thicket of samsaric evils and brought to unsurpassable enlightenment.

> The buddhas praise those who constantly apply themselves
>   to their own fulfillment
> And rebuke those who act wrongly. To the best of beings
>   who devote themselves to stability and discernment,
> The victors at this time properly explain all that hinders
>   or favors progress in the practice of this, the sugatas'
>   doctrine—
> Things to be avoided and those to be embraced. (XV, 49)

What is the difference between "instructions" and "follow-up teachings"? Instructions refer to teaching for the first time the specific essential instructions on the means for eliminating factors that have to be eliminated and obtaining qualities that have to be obtained. In this regard, because the

Buddha knows the characters, intellectual faculties, and aspirations of his disciples and teaches them accordingly, his teaching is bound to be effective. Follow-up teachings are further instructions, treating the subject in detail, that are subsequently given to those who have already received the instructions, in order to repeatedly drive in the meaning.

To that end, the buddhas, by praising bodhisattvas and pointing out their good qualities, saying, "Fortunate child, well done!" encourage them to constantly apply themselves correctly to the training in superior discipline (in other words, to refrain from negative actions, gather positive actions, and work for the benefit of sentient beings), which is the goal they have to accomplish for themselves. To those who have broken the rules of discipline and practice incorrectly, they point out the negative consequences of doing so and reproach them. And to those best of beings, bodhisattvas on the path of earnest aspiration who devote themselves to the training in superior concentration (which is to rest without the mind moving) and to the training in superior wisdom (which is to perfectly discern phenomena), the victorious ones, at this time of giving the instructions, properly explain all the different factors that hinder or favor the practice of sustained calm and profound insight in this, the sugatas' doctrine. That practice will grow vaster through the avoidance of faults that hinder concentration and wisdom and through reliance on good qualities that favor these.

> Purified by their vision, awakened with nonconceptuality,
> They outshine the whole world,
> Perpetually dispelling the greatest darkness
> And shining on beings like huge suns rising. (XV, 50)

With these instructions and follow-up teachings that unmistakenly indicate the essence of the trainings in superior discipline, concentration, and wisdom, and the factors that hinder or favor them, these bodhisattvas engage in the three trainings and, by avoiding factors inconsistent with them and relying on elements consistent with them, they gain immense experience in the practice of sustained calm and profound insight and attain the bodhisattva levels. Their gnostic vision completely purifies them of the defilement-related obscurations, and their nonconceptuality acts as the antidote to cognitive obscurations, those of the concepts of the three spheres. With this supramundane path to supreme enlightenment they outshine the whole world, including the listeners and solitary realizers, and they gain the power to perpetually dispel even the great darkness of both defilement-related and cognitive obscurations, shining on beings like huge suns rising. In our world, the sun cannot light up cavities obscured by other things. But bodhisattvas, by teaching the Dharma, can dispel the darkness of everyone's ignorance, vividly and brightly lighting up the world like huge unprecedented suns—great suns rising and shining throughout the universes of the ten directions.

> Thus forever filled with the good that they have gathered,
> And having constantly received extensive instructions from
>   the buddhas,
> Supreme bodhisattvas will acquire immense concentration
>   of mind
> And travel to the far shore of the ocean of virtues. (XV, 51)

Thus, their mind streams forever filled with the accumulated virtue of merit and wisdom, like the ocean filled by all the rivers, these supreme bodhisattvas, who have constantly received extensive instructions from the perfect buddhas, the capable ones, in person, will acquire an extremely vast and extensive concentration of mind[21] endowed with profound insight and proceed from the first level up to the level of buddhahood, to reach the other shore of the ocean of boundless good qualities.

This completes the explanation of the fifteenth chapter of *Ornament of the Mahāyāna Sūtras*, the chapter on instructions and follow-up teachings.

---

21. Tib. *sems kyi ting nge 'dzin*, concentration focused on the mind, referring here to sustained calm.

Intermediate Summary

In summary, bodhisattvas have much interest,
Investigate the teachings, explain them,
Practice accordingly, and receive
The perfect instructions and follow-up teachings. (XVI, 1)

The fifth of the five metaphors indicates the approach to enlightenment, and for this we have seen the five chapters on how to reach the noble levels—first of all, giving rise to vast interest, then investigating the words of the extensive and profound teachings of the Excellent Speech and the meaning of what they teach, explaining to others the teachings that have thus been acquired, putting into practice and accomplishing the point of the teachings, and receiving the instructions and follow-up teachings that serve to enhance the practice. These constitute a sort of brief outline of the chapters that follow on the elements leading to enlightenment (Skillful Activity; Transcendent Perfections; Offering, Reliance, and Boundless Attitudes; and Elements Leading to Enlightenment), so they are grouped together here in an intermediate summary.

The main explanation of the approach to enlightenment consists of six chapters: a chapter (16) on the skillful means that embraces the practice; three chapters (17, 18, and 19) on the transcendent perfections and ways of attracting disciples; on offering, reliance, and boundless attitudes; and on elements leading to enlightenment—which are all embraced by that skillful means; a chapter (20) on the qualities that come from relying on the above; and a chapter (21) presenting the activities and the temporary and ultimate levels.

MAIN EXPLANATION

16

Skillful Activity

This chapter has two sections: (1) the activities that are to be embraced by skillful means and (2) the three aspects of skillful means that embrace those activities.

1. The Activities That Are to Be Embraced by Skillful Means

> Just as the base upon which the forests, beings,
> Mountains, and rivers rest is always the earth,
> So too the base for generosity and other forms of virtue
> Is said to always be the three activities of the wise. (XVI, 2)

The support of the forests, of living creatures, and of the mountains and rivers is, at all times and in all respects, the great earth. That is to say, all the mountains, forests, rivers, and so forth that make up the outer, inanimate world, and the beings of the inner, animate world, depend on the earth. Similarly, there is not a single virtuous activity—no act of generosity or any of the other transcendent perfections, and not one of the thirty-seven elements leading to enlightenment—that does not always depend on the physical, verbal, and mental activities of wise bodhisattvas. The basis for all virtuous deeds, therefore, is described as being the activities of the three doors.

2. The Three Aspects of Skillful Means That Embrace Those Activities

The three aspects of skillful means are indefatigability, abandoning attentiveness to lower paths, and nonconceptual gnosis. They are explained in one verse each.

Indefatigability

> Bodhisattvas, whose very nature is great diligence
> In all kinds of arduous deeds, which take many kalpas to complete,
> Will never be dispirited by their tasks here,
> Their physical, verbal, and mental activities. (XVI, 3)

The variety and nature of the activities of benefiting beings and putting up with their ingratitude, giving away one's body and possessions, and other extremely difficult deeds, are boundless. Moreover, they take many kalpas to complete, necessitating practice over three measureless kalpas. So it is in the nature of bodhisattvas to don the great armor of intense diligence sustained over a long period of time. They will never grow weary of their physical, verbal, and mental activities here in saṃsāra. Because of the power of their potential and their habituation to positive activities, not only do they never get depressed or discouraged, but also, like fire to which firewood has been added, they naturally engage their three doors in the virtuous accumulation of merit and wisdom and will never have enough of doing so. This verse shows how they rise above ever losing heart.

Abandoning Attentiveness to Lower Paths

> Just as those who wish themselves good physically avoid
> Poison, weapons, thunderbolts, and enemies,
> Bodhisattvas direct their three kinds of activities
> Away from the two lower vehicles. (XVI, 4)

Just as people who wish good for themselves physically avoid deadly poison, weapons, bolts of lightning, and enemies, doing their best not to encounter them, bodhisattvas direct their physical, verbal, and mental activities away from the lower vehicles, the two vehicles of the listeners and solitary realizers. They do not engage in any actions of their three doors for the purpose of attaining the result of the lower vehicles. Why is that? Followers of the lower vehicles, on account of their obsession with their own good, have cast aside compassion. And the lower paths, with their incomplete knowledge of the nature of knowable phenomena, which is the realization of the two kinds of no-self, are inconsistent with the path to the great enlightenment. So to engage in such paths is a terrible pitfall for followers of the Great Vehicle.

Nonconceptual Gnosis

> Continually free of concepts, they do not look at the three aspects
> Of the doer, the object, and the doing.
> So, because they are fully imbued with such skillful means,
> Their deeds are pure and transcend the infinitely good.
> (XVI, 5)

Because bodhisattvas always know the nature of knowable phenomena with the wisdom of realization of the two kinds of no-self, they have no concepts with regard to anything whatsoever. In what way? They have no concept with regard to the person performing positive actions, nor of the object (the gift or whatever), nor of the action (that of performing generosity or any other transcendent perfection) and the effort they put into it. They do not look at this or that attribute in these three, because they are naturally habituated to the wisdom free of the concepts of the three spheres. If one has this nonconceptual gnosis, one never feels discouraged by such things as beings' sufferings, their ingratitude, or long periods of time. Once one has realized sameness, the attributes of evils and virtues in existence and peace and the ordinary notions of self and others as independently existing never arise as they do in ordinary beings' minds. And since one's sources of good are not tainted by the ignorance of clinging to attributes, they become perfectly pure. For this reason, of all the infinite skillful means there are in the path of the Great Vehicle, this nonconceptual gnosis is the best and most important. So, because these bodhisattvas are fully imbued with nonconceptual gnosis, which is *the* skillful means for this practice of generosity and all the other elements of the path, all the generosity and other virtuous activities that they perform with their body, speech, and mind will be perfectly pure. They will enable them to perfect the infinity of boundless good qualities and attain buddhahood.

What makes boundless good qualities such as generosity pure and vast and profound is nonconceptual gnosis, transcendent wisdom. Practices such as generosity that are imbued with this wisdom receive the name "supramundane transcendent perfection"—which is not something the listeners and solitary realizers have, let alone ordinary beings. In an essential pith instruction, Gyalwa Longchenpa summarizes this chapter on skillful activity as follows: "If we back all our sources of good with the three supreme methods, they will constitute the path of the Great Vehicle."

Everything is included in this. If we have these three supreme methods—the supreme preparation of arousing the bodhicitta, the supreme main practice without concepts, and the supreme conclusion of dedication—we will not become discouraged on the Mahāyāna path, we will give up attentiveness related to lower paths, and we will be imbued with nonconceptual gnosis. The three supreme methods include all this, so if a bodhisattva's whole path, comprising all the virtuous activities of generosity and the other transcendent perfections performed with the three doors, is imbued with this essential point, it will indeed be the path of the Great Vehicle.

This completes the explanation of the sixteenth chapter of *Ornament of the Mahāyāna Sūtras*, the chapter on skillful activity.

17

Transcendent Perfections and Ways of Attracting Disciples

This chapter is divided into three sections: (1) the six transcendent perfections that enable one to complete the buddha qualities oneself; (2) an explanation of the four ways of attracting disciples that bring other sentient beings to maturation; and (3) a concluding summary of these two.

1. The Six Transcendent Perfections That Enable One to Complete the Buddha Qualities Oneself

This section has two parts: (1) a brief outline and (2) a detailed explanation of its topics.

a. Brief Outline

> One should know the number of perfections, their characteristics, order,
> Etymology, aspects of the training,
> Their classifications, their all-inclusiveness, the factors incompatible with them,
> Their good qualities, and how their interrelationships are determined. (XVII, 1)

If we summarize the practice of all the Mahāyāna teachings, it boils down to the six transcendent perfections, so the main practice of the path is just these. Since they translate as boundless approaches to the Dharma with different aspects and names for the practice in the different contexts of attracting disciples, making offerings, following a teacher, the boundless attitudes, and the elements leading to enlightenment,[1] it is the presentation of the six transcendent perfections that is explained first. This is to be understood as being divided into ten headings: the number of the six transcendent perfections; their individual defining characteristics; their order; the individual etymological definitions of generosity and the others; how to train in the qualities of the transcendent perfections; the detailed classifications within each of the six transcendent perfections; how all virtuous practice is included in the six transcendent perfections; how factors that are incompatible with the transcendent perfections are avoided; the excellent qualities of the transcendent perfections; and how their interrelationship is determined from the way in which each perfection is included in the others. The detailed explanation that follows contains the same ten headings.

b. Detailed Explanation
i. Establishing the Definitive Number of the Transcendent Perfections

There are four reasons that are taught for the number of the transcendent perfections. First, it is shown that there are six transcendent perfections with regard to their accomplishing the qualities of both higher rebirth and ultimate excellence.

> The transcendent perfections result in higher rebirths
> With abundant wealth, a perfect body, a perfect entourage,
>   and perfect achievement;
> And also perpetual immunity to defilements
> And absence of error in everything one does. (XVII, 2)

Four transcendent perfections are associated with higher rebirth. With generosity, one obtains abundant wealth in all one's succession of lives in saṃsāra. Discipline results in a perfect body as a human or celestial being, patience in a perfect entourage, and diligence in the perfect completion of everything one undertakes. Then, concentration subdues one's mind, constantly suppressing the defilements, so that one is no longer a slave to them. And with wisdom, one knows what to avoid and adopt in general, as well

---

1. All these are the subjects, discussed in detail, of the second half of this chapter and the two chapters that follow.

as the four truths and the factors that counter the transcendent perfections and their antidotes. This knowledge is applied without error with regard to samsaric and nirvanic activities. These two transcendent perfections are associated with ultimate excellence. In this respect, there is no need for more than six transcendent perfections, while fewer than six would not include everything, and it is for this reason that they are established as six in number.

Second, there are six transcendent perfections in terms of their accomplishing the two goals, one's own and others'.

> **Applying themselves assiduously to the welfare of beings,**
> **Bodhisattvas give, refrain from harm, and act patiently.**
> **With concentration, liberation, and the basis of these,**
> **They entirely achieve their own good. (XVII, 3)**
>
> **They relieve the destitute, avoid all forms of harm,**
> **Bear injury, are not discouraged by their task,**
> **Make others happy, and give clear explanations.**
> **Thus they fulfill the aims of others, and this is their own aim.**
> **(XVII, 4)**

In the first place, from the point of view of their own good, bodhisattvas apply themselves assiduously to the welfare of sentient beings. At such times, by giving to others, they benefit them; in observing discipline, they do not harm others by killing them, taking what is not given, and so on; and by being patient instead of retaliating even when others harm them, they help them—so they are actually working mainly for others' good. With the remaining three transcendent perfections, they are practicing entirely for their own good. With the concentration that focuses on liberation, when they settle their minds in evenness, they definitely see the true meaning. Wisdom is what makes them actually achieve liberation. "And the basis of these" refers to diligence, which is the foundation of these two, for by applying diligence one settles the mind evenly and accomplishes profound insight. Thus, with three transcendent perfections that accomplish others' welfare and three that accomplish one's own welfare, there are six transcendent perfections in all.

Furthermore, since bodhisattvas act mainly for others' sake with no regard for their own welfare, they employ the six transcendent perfections to accomplish others' good. By generously giving the poor whatever they wish for, they ensure that sentient beings do not want for possessions. By observing discipline, they do not harm beings in any way. With patience, they bear the harm other beings do them without getting angry. On account of their diligence, they never tire of working for others' welfare. As a result of their concentration, they can know hidden phenomena and display miracles, thus inspiring sentient beings and making them happy. And by means of their wisdom, they give clear explanations of the sacred Dharma. They thereby accomplish others' goals—and to accomplish others' goals is, in the very best way, to accomplish one's own goal. For however diligently one may persevere only for one's own benefit, one will never be able to attain the great enlightenment. On the other hand, by putting one's efforts into others' welfare, even on the temporary level one will automatically achieve one's own goals, and ultimately one will oneself attain unsurpassable enlightenment. For this reason, it is by means of the six transcendent perfections that the two goals are spontaneously accomplished.

Third, they are numbered for the fact that all the Mahāyāna bodhisattva's activities are included in the six transcendent perfections.

> **Bodhisattvas take no pleasure in possessions,**
> **Have deep respect, are indefatigable in two respects,**
> **Train spiritually, and are free of concepts—**
> **The entire Great Vehicle amounts to this. (XVII, 5)**

Without taking pleasure in—that is, being attached to—the objects of the five senses, their outer and inner possessions, bodhisattvas give to others without the slightest holding back. Because of their total respect for the precepts of discipline, they are unsullied by even the most minor misdeeds. Their never getting discouraged either by the harm beings do them or by hardships in the practice constitutes their patience and diligence. Patience enables them to be extremely forbearing in the face of all the troubles sentient beings cause them and of different kinds of hardship, and diligence enables them to put unbounded efforts into working for the benefit of sentient beings and undergoing great difficulties for long periods without ever losing heart. (An alternative explanation is that their never tiring of accumulating merit and wisdom constitutes patience and diligence—patience in eliminating all incompatible traits, and diligence in applying antidotes.) In concentration, they possess the supreme yoga of remaining one-pointed, and in wisdom, the absence of concepts of any attributes whatsoever. These last two transcendent perfections represent sustained calm and profound insight. So if we were to summarize the whole of the Great Vehicle, it would amount to nothing more than these six transcendent perfections. There is nothing that they do not include.

Fourth, their number in terms of the three superior trainings:

> The path of nonattachment to sense objects,
> The path of restraint from the distraction of acquiring them,
> And the paths of never abandoning beings, of increasing,
> And again, of purifying obscurations— (XVII, 6)

> These six transcendent perfections
> The Buddha has clearly explained in terms of the three trainings:
> Three perfections in the first, two in the last two,
> And one included in all three. (XVII, 7)

The path of nonattachment to the pleasures of the five senses is generosity—freely giving everything away. As well as this, there is the path of restraining the distracted mind from wanting to obtain those sensual pleasures, which is transcendent discipline—it prevents one from indulging in numerous distracting, mundane activities. The path of never abandoning sentient beings even though they are ungrateful and do one all kinds of harm is patience. The path of increasing one's accumulation of virtue more and more is diligence. Finally, concentration and wisdom constitute another path, which purifies obscurations: concentration purifies the obscurations deriving from the defilements, and wisdom purifies mainly the cognitive obscurations. (Alternatively, concentration is the path for suppressing and breaking up the two obscurations, and wisdom is the path for completely eradicating them.)

These six paths the Buddha clearly explained in terms of the three trainings immediately after explaining the six transcendent perfections, as follows. First, generosity, discipline, and patience constitute the superior training in discipline. The path of generosity without attachment is the cause of discipline. The essence of superior discipline is the path of restraint, discipline itself. And its ally is patience, the path of never abandoning sentient beings. If one has these three, one can preserve discipline correctly. The last two, concentration and wisdom, indicate the last two trainings: concentration is the superior training of the mind, and wisdom is the superior training in wisdom. One transcendent perfection, diligence, belongs to all three trainings: since the other five transcendent perfections have to be practiced with the diligence of devoted and constant application, diligence in those transcendent perfections is included in all three trainings.

It is in all these ways that the transcendent perfections are established as being six in number.

ii. The Defining Characteristics of the Transcendent Perfections

The defining characteristics of the six transcendent perfections are indicated by a verse each, beginning with generosity. Each of them has four defining characteristics, as follows.

> Generosity counters its opposite,
> Is endowed with nonconceptual gnosis,
> Fulfills all wishes,
> And ripens beings in three ways. (XVII, 8)

Generosity destroys its opposite, stinginess, for it is motivated by absence of stinginess. It is supported by nonconceptuality, freedom from the concepts of the three spheres, for bodhisattvas have realized the no-self of the individual and of phenomena and they have no concept of any intrinsic nature in the giver, the gift, or the recipient. Generosity is performed in such a way as to fulfill all the recipients' desires. The effect of generosity is to attract beings with gifts and then to bring them to maturity on the listeners', solitary realizers', or Mahāyāna path, according to their individual potential, ultimately bringing them in these three ways to the respective results of those paths. These, then, are the four defining characteristics of generosity.

> Discipline counters its opposite,
> Is endowed with nonconceptual gnosis,
> Fulfills all wishes,
> And ripens beings in three ways. (XVII, 9)

In a similar manner, discipline counters its opposite, lax discipline. It is supported and permeated by nonconceptual gnosis, with no concept of there being someone who is observing discipline, of discipline itself, or of an action that accomplishes it. By observing discipline, one does not deliberately harm other sentient beings and thus fulfills their wishes. And on account of discipline, one delights other beings and attracts them, subsequently introducing them to discipline and bringing them to the three kinds of maturity in the three vehicles.

> Patience counters its opposite,
> Is endowed with nonconceptual gnosis,
> Fulfills all wishes,
> And ripens beings in three ways. (XVII, 10)

Patience counters its opposite, anger. It is endowed with the gnosis free of the concepts of the three spheres—namely, someone who is being patient, patience, and the practice of patience. By never retaliating, one fulfills all others' wishes. And patience enables one to introduce beings to the three vehicles, so it brings them to the three kinds of maturity.

> Diligence counters its opposite,
> Is endowed with nonconceptual gnosis,
> Fulfills all wishes,
> And ripens beings in three ways. (XVII, 11)

Diligence counters its opposite, laziness. It is endowed with the gnosis free of the concepts of the three spheres—namely, someone being diligent, diligence, and the application of diligence. By benefiting beings—for instance, by helping them with any tasks they have to carry out—one fulfills all their wishes. And by means of diligence, one brings beings to the three kinds of maturity in the three vehicles.

> Concentration counters its opposite,
> Is endowed with nonconceptual gnosis,
> Fulfills all wishes,
> And ripens beings in three ways. (XVII, 12)

Concentration counters its opposite, distraction. It is endowed with the gnosis free of the concepts of the three spheres—namely, a meditator, concentration as something to train in, and the action of training in concentration. Miraculous displays and preternatural powers enable one to fulfill beings' wishes. And by means of concentration, one brings beings to the three kinds of maturity.

> **Wisdom counters its opposite,**
> **Is endowed with nonconceptual gnosis,**
> **Fulfills all wishes,**
> **And ripens beings in three ways. (XVII, 13)**

Wisdom counters its opposite, aberrant understanding such as the belief in a self. It is endowed with the gnosis free of the concepts of the three spheres—namely, an individual, wisdom, and its accomplishment. By clearing away doubts, it enables one to fulfill all others' wishes. And it serves to bring beings to the three kinds of maturity through the three vehicles.

iii. THE ORDER OF THE SIX TRANSCENDENT PERFECTIONS

> **Because the next one arises in dependence on the preceding one,**
> **And each is superior to the former one,**
> **And because each is more subtle than the former one,**
> **They are taught one after the other. (XVII, 14)**

There are three reasons for the six transcendent perfections' being in the order they are. First of all, there is the order in which each transcendent perfection comes into play in dependence on the one that precedes it. If one is attached to all kinds of possessions, one will not be able to give up the life of a layperson and take vows, whereas if one is free of attachment, one can. So generosity, whereby one is free from attachment to possessions, is explained as being the causal basis of discipline and therefore as preceding it. People with bad characters cannot bear to be criticized or otherwise abused, while those who have their bad ways under control can put up with criticism. For this reason, discipline is described as being the necessary causal basis for patience and is taught next, after generosity. Unless one is able to put up with anything unpleasant such as heat and cold or hunger and thirst, one cannot do things diligently, but anyone who is forbearing can undertake everything diligently. This is why patience is taught next, after discipline. If one is constantly diligent in practicing virtue, one is able to accomplish concentration and settle the mind in evenness, so after patience, it is diligence that is explained next. Once one possesses the concentration of settling the mind in evenness, there arises the wisdom that correctly knows the noble truths. So concentration is the next to be explained, after diligence. Concentration, then, is the causal basis of the wisdom that sees the truth, and this is why wisdom, the result of concentration, is taught last of all. This explains the order in which the transcendent perfections come into play as a process of cause and result.

Next, because the earlier transcendent perfections are inferior compared to the ones that follow, and the later ones superior to those that precede them, the inferior ones are mentioned first and the superior ones last. There may be people in the world who generously give things away, but much more rare are those who avoid negative actions physically, verbally, and mentally. So in this respect, generosity is inferior, and discipline superior. Similarly, compared to avoiding negative actions, it is much harder to patiently put up with harm from others. And compared to being patient, it is more difficult to be constantly diligent in performing positive actions. However much diligence one may have, taming the mind with concentration is much more rare. And even if one accomplishes the mental concentrations of the world of form and of the formless world, it is much harder and rarer to have the wisdom that sees the truth. So because the earlier transcendent perfections are easier and are for those who have more defilements, and the later ones are comparatively more difficult and are for those who have fewer defilements and more good qualities, they are presented in that order, from generosity to wisdom.

Again, because they are respectively more gross and more subtle, the gross transcendent perfections are taught first and the more subtle ones afterward. The gross ones are easy to engage in and continue practicing, while the subtler ones are comparatively difficult. Generosity is something that anyone, from kings and ministers down to servants and outcastes, can engage in: it is easy to understand and is an obvious action that is easy to do. Compared to that, discipline, patience, and the rest through to wisdom are increasingly subtle, the later ones being by their very nature more subtle than the earlier ones. It is in these terms that they are presented in order from generosity, which is the most gross and the easiest to begin and continue practicing, to wisdom, which is the most subtle and the hardest to practice.

iv. THE ETYMOLOGICAL DEFINITIONS OF EACH OF THE SIX TRANSCENDENT PERFECTIONS

> **One perfection banishes poverty,**
> **One obtains coolth, one puts an end to anger,**

One connects one to what is supreme, one keeps the mind
focused,
And one knows the ultimate—thus are they explained. (XVII, 15)

Why is generosity so called? The Sanskrit term for generosity is *dāna*, *dā* meaning "poverty" and *na* meaning "to throw out," so what we call generosity is that which banishes poverty. For the recipients, the gift of one's possessions removes their poverty in this life. And for the givers, it removes poverty in their other lives, for they will lack for nothing and always be wealthy.

Similarly, the Sanskrit equivalent of discipline is *śīla*, where *śī* signifies "coolth" and *la* means "to obtain" or "to receive"—hence, to obtain coolth. If one observes discipline, in this life one will not suffer the heat of the various misfortunes that result from attachment to sense objects—criminal punishment, for example—and in future lives one will avoid rebirth in the lower realms and obtain the coolth of happy rebirth as a god or human and ultimately of the bliss of nirvāṇa.

Patience is *kṣānti* in Sanskrit. *Kṣān* signifies "finished," while *ti* has the sense of "making," so what we call patience is that which puts an end to anger in one's own mind stream.

(The use of the conjunction "and" (*dang*) in this verse is self-evident, so here and in other sections I have not followed the root text to the letter.)[2]

Diligence is *vīrya*. *Vi* means "supreme" or "sublime," and *rya* means "to connect"—it is what connects one to sublime, supramundane virtue, and thus diligence is also called "connector to what is supreme."[3]

Concentration is *dhyāna* in Sanskrit, or *dhārana*, the subjoined *ya* being equivalent to a *ra*, and it means "to hold." What it holds is the mind, holding it in on the object of meditation and not letting it be distracted outwardly.

Wisdom is *prajñā*. *Pra* is a prefix meaning "superior" and is a contraction of the word *paramārtha* meaning "ultimate," so in these terms *prajña* is explained as "that which knows (*jñā*) the ultimate (*pra*)."

It should be noted that these explanations constitute a particular way of explaining the meanings of the Sanskrit terms by contracting or adding to the syllables in their linguistic elements. The translation of these Sanskrit terms into Tibetan was made directly into currently used Tibetan words

---

2. See Translator's Introduction, page xxiv.
3. Tib. *mchog sbyor*, an alternative for the usual Tibetan term *brtson 'grus*.

such as *sbyin pa* (generosity), for which such a way of explaining the etymological definitions was also applied.[4]

v. How the Transcendent Perfections Are Practiced

> For all of them the training is described
> As relying on the substance,
> And similarly on attentiveness,
> On one's attitude, pure method, and mastery. (XVII, 16)

How does one train in the transcendent perfections, from generosity through to wisdom? This verse describes five aspects of how to train in or accustom oneself to each and every one of the six transcendent perfections: (1) to train by relying on or abiding in the substance; similarly, (2) to train by relying on attentiveness; (3) to train by relying on one's attitude; (4) to train by relying on pure skillful means; and (5) to train by relying on mastery. What are all these?

(1) "Substance" refers to the object or thing. Abiding in or training in the substance of a transcendent perfection such as generosity has four aspects: abiding in the cause, abiding in the fully ripened effect, abiding in aspiration, and abiding in the power of analysis.

First, by the power of one's bodhisattva potential, acting as a cause, wherever one is reborn, even if others do not induce one to do so, one takes pleasure in practicing and training in generosity and the other five transcendent perfections, and on that basis one will accomplish the relevant transcendent perfections.

Second, as a result of habituation to practicing the transcendent perfections in previous lives, in subsequent lives one obtains a physical support that naturally engages in practicing them.

Third, the power of the prayers of aspiration one has made to continue practicing the six transcendent perfections—of the kind, "Wherever I am reborn, may I give generously without being attached to my body and possessions"—enables one to practice the transcendent perfections.

---

4. In other words, the Sanskrit term for "giving," *dāna*, whose linguistic elements imply "that which removes poverty," was translated into the commonly used Tibetan word *sbyin pa*, meaning "giving" or "gift." English translations of the transcendent perfections have often again adopted this compromise between literal or etymological meanings and words in current use.

Fourth, after analyzing things with wisdom and recognizing that possessions are transitory and devoid of essence, one engages in generosity and so on. Thus, by recognizing the excellent qualities of this and the other transcendent perfections, one can practice them properly.

(2) For relying on and training in attentiveness, there are four kinds of attentiveness.

Attentiveness related to interest: through confidence and interest in the six transcendent perfections as they are taught in the relevant Mahāyāna sūtras, the potential for transcendent perfection grows.

Attentiveness related to savoring, which is to see the good qualities in one's past practice of generosity and the other transcendent perfections, thinking of it as very good, and to feel very happy at the memory of one's past deeds.

Attentiveness related to rejoicing, which is to rejoice at all those in the universes of the ten directions who have practiced generosity and the other transcendent perfections, feeling as delighted as if one had done so oneself.

Attentiveness related to delight, which is to take pleasure in practicing the transcendent perfections, thinking, "In the future, wherever we are reborn, may I and others practice the transcendent perfections."

(3) Relying on or accomplishing one's attitude has six aspects: a never-satisfied or insatiable attitude, vast attitude, joyful attitude, attitude regarding help, untainted attitude, and virtuous attitude.

The first, the insatiable attitude, again has four aspects, which we shall illustrate with the example of generosity:

Never having enough of material generosity. In order to benefit a single sentient being and bring them to full maturation, even if a bodhisattva were to give that single being as many worlds as there are grains of sand in the River Ganges, all filled with the seven kinds of jewels,[5] it would never occur to that bodhisattva to think, "I have given them so much, now that's enough."

Never having enough of giving away one's body. Even though bodhisattvas might every instant, for the sake of a single being, give away as many of their own bodies as there are grains of sand in the River Ganges, they train their minds in never being satisfied—in never thinking, "Now I have given away this many bodies, that will do."

---

5. Tib. *rin po che sna bdun*, namely, rubies, sapphires, beryls, emeralds, diamonds, pearls, corals; or alternatively seven precious substances: beryl, gold, silver, crystal, an Indian gem called *spug* in Tibetan, red pearls, and emeralds.

Never being satisfied with the time. Even though bodhisattvas give away their bodies and possessions in this way for the sake of a single being for as many kalpas as there are grains of sand in the River Ganges without stopping for a single moment, they develop an insatiable attitude, never thinking, "I've given all these outer and inner gifts for so many kalpas, now that's long enough."

Never having enough of beings. Giving one being, in this way, as many worlds as there are grains of sand in the River Ganges, all filled with the seven kinds of jewels, and as many bodies, for as many kalpas, and bringing that one being to maturity by establishing them in unsurpassable enlightenment; and similarly establishing a second being, and a third, and finally the very entirety of sentient beings in unsurpassable enlightenment, bodhisattvas train their minds up to the point of developing the insatiable attitude that even if, hypothetically, they were to bring all those beings to buddhahood, they would never think, "Now I'm satisfied," and they thus develop an attitude of never being satisfied.

Second, the vast attitude is the attitude of wishing to practice generosity and so forth in that way continuously until one dwells in the heart of enlightenment, without a single moment when one is not doing so.

Third, the joyful attitude consists in giving rise to the happy thought that the beings whom one has attracted with generosity and the other transcendent perfections and brought to maturity are helping one to attain unsurpassable enlightenment, and to rejoice and be extremely grateful to those beings whom one has thus benefited, without their necessarily delighting in it themselves.

Fourth, the attitude regarding help. Bodhisattvas do not think, with regard to these beings they have benefited, "I have helped them." Instead, they have the attitude, "These beings who are the object of benefit have helped me." For they think, "If there were no beings to benefit, I would not complete the accumulations necessary for unsurpassable enlightenment. But by benefiting them, I will attain unsurpassable enlightenment, so they are helping me enormously."

Fifth, the untainted attitude. Even if bodhisattvas benefit others with their generosity and so forth, they do not hope for anything in return or for rebirth in the higher realms as the fully ripened result. Rather, they perform such deeds for the sake of sentient beings, without being attached to their own welfare.

Sixth, the virtuous attitude. Bodhisattvas do not wish to taste the fruit of their extensive practice of generosity and the other transcendent perfections on their own. Rather, they dedicate their sources of good so that all sentient beings may attain the result, unsurpassable enlightenment.

These six attitudes to generosity apply equally to the other transcendent perfections, from discipline through to wisdom. One might remain in the cosmos of a billion worlds completely filled with fire, forever deprived of anything that could bring relief (such as water to quench the fire), enduring not just the suffering of one of one's bodies, but of bodies equal in number to the grains of sand in the River Ganges, and not for a period of a limited number of kalpas such as a hundred or a thousand but for lifetimes lasting as many kalpas as there are grains of sand in the River Ganges. And even though, throughout all this time, one were to practice discipline in one's performance of not just a single kind of conduct but in every instant of the four kinds of conduct (moving around, lying down, sitting, and walking), and one were finally to complete the aggregate of discipline, achieving buddhahood in unsurpassable enlightenment, one would never think, "Now the aggregate of discipline is complete, that will do." The same applies to wisdom: the above attitudes—the insatiable attitude, vast attitude, and so forth—are explained as being common to all the transcendent perfections.

(4) Relying on and training in skillful means. Although this is explained as three skillful methods in terms of freedom from the concepts of the three spheres in whichever of the transcendent perfections one is practicing, in fact it refers to their being imbued with nonconceptual gnosis. It is because this enables one to accomplish all the different factors that are kept in mind[6] and all the Buddha's teachings, rendering them pure, that it is referred to as "skillful means."

(5) Relying on mastery. When bodhisattvas attain mastery on the three pure levels, the transcendent perfections are practiced spontaneously, without effort. By relying on such mastery, they ultimately obtain the perfect buddha body, buddha speech, and buddha mind on the level of buddhahood and spontaneously engage in the six transcendent perfections for the benefit of sentient beings. In this regard, there are three masteries, of body, activity, and teaching. The first refers to mastery of the body of truth and body of perfect enjoyment, the second to mastery of the manifestation body, and the third to mastery in verbally teaching the Dharma.

---

6. Tib. *yid la byed pa thams cad*, referring to the different kinds of attentiveness mentioned above (Sthiramati).

vi. Detailed Classifications

Although there are infinite classifications within the transcendent perfections, in brief, each of the transcendent perfections can be divided into six headings, beginning with their nature. These are indicated in the next twelve verses, with two verses for each transcendent perfection.

> It is the giving-away of gifts,
> Springs from reliance on a rooted attitude,
> Results in a perfect body and riches,
> Cares for both oneself and others, leads to completion, (XVII, 17)
>
> Is endowed with freedom from stinginess,
> And comprises the gifts of Dharma, of material gifts, and of
>   freedom from fear:
> Knowing that such is generosity,
> The wise accomplish it perfectly. (XVII, 18)

The subdivisions of transcendent generosity are as follows. The nature or essence of generosity is to give away outer and inner objects[7] or possessions to different fields—those with excellent qualities, those who help one, and those who are suffering.[8] Its cause or source is reliance on a mind that has the three roots of virtue—freedom from attachment, and so on.[9] The result is the attainment of a perfect body and possessions. Its function is to take care of both oneself and others, since through generosity one helps others and one obtains great riches for oneself in other lives, and material giving and giving Dharma enable one to complete the accumulations of merit and wisdom. The property of generosity is that it is endowed with and indistinguishable from the absence of stinginess. There are three categories of generosity: giving the Dharma by expounding the words and meanings of the Buddha's teaching without mistake; material generosity in giving away

---

7. Inner objects refer to such things as one's head, limbs, and so forth, while outer objects are those external to one's body.

8. The fields (Tib. *zhing*), or recipients, of generosity are the field of excellent qualities (the Three Jewels, monks and nuns, etc.), the field of benefit (friends and others who help one), and the field of suffering (the poor, the sick, etc.). A fourth, the field of offering or veneration (spiritual teachers, parents) is sometimes listed and is here included in the first.

9. See "three roots of virtue" in the glossary.

outer and inner objects; and giving or bestowing freedom from fear by protecting beings from the fear of rulers, robbers, fire, water, and so forth. Having fully understood that such are the nature, cause, and other subdivisions of generosity, wise bodhisattvas practice it correctly.

> It has six branches, springs from one's being imbued with
>   the wish for ultimate peace,
> Bestows happy states and a stable mind,
> Supports, stills, and frees from fear,
> Brings about the accumulation of merit, (XVII, 19)
>
> Is symbolically designated or naturally acquired,
> And is present in those who keep vows:
> Knowing that such is discipline,
> The wise accomplish it perfectly. (XVII, 20)

The essence of discipline is to possess its six branches—namely, abiding by discipline, perfect observance, perfect environment, being bound by the prātimokṣa vows, regarding fearfully even the most subtle shameful deed, and correctly receiving and training in the precepts. The first of these is to observe discipline correctly. The second is to use the Dharma robes and so forth[10] according to the Vinaya texts and thus be beyond reproach by holy beings. The third is to avoid entering the five improper places—brothels, slaughterhouses, bars, and the like. The fourth is related to the discipline of certain deliverance.[11] The fifth is to not be tainted by even the slightest fault. The sixth is to train completely in all the precepts.

The cause of discipline is to be imbued with the intention of certain release, that is, of nirvāṇa. The result is that one will attain the higher realms and, with a mind free of regret, one will be happy in this life, on account of which one will be granted a stable mind and accomplish concentration. Its functions are to act as the basis for all virtuous practices (in the same way that the earth supports all kinds of crops); to still the torments of the defilements; and to free one from the fear in this life of shameful deeds, of blood feuds, and so forth, and from the fear in other lives of the lower

---

10. Sthiramati refers here to "perfect rituals" (Tib. *cho ga phun sum tshogs pa*).
11. Tib. *nges par 'byung ba'i tshul khrims*. This refers to the discipline for attaining liberation and therefore particularly to the prātimokṣa vows.

realms. The property of discipline is the possession of the accumulation of merit from practicing positive actions with the body, speech, and mind. As for its manifestations or categories, there is the symbolically designated discipline, which refers to receiving the prātimokṣa vows from a preceptor by requesting and receiving them, and the discipline that is acquired naturally, referring to the dhyāna vow and the untainted vow.[12] All these aspects of discipline are present in those individuals who observe the vows and not in others. Having fully understood that discipline is like this, the wise practice it correctly.

> **It endures, ignores, and understands,**
> **Springs from compassion and dependence on the Dharma,**
> **Is described as having five benefits,**
> **Brings benefit to both oneself and others, (XVII, 21)**
>
> **Is fully endowed as the greatest of austerities,**
> **And is held to be of the above three kinds:**
> **Knowing that such is patience,**
> **The wise accomplish it perfectly. (XVII, 22)**

The essence of patience is threefold: forbearance in the face of harm done to one by sentient beings; the patience of thinking nothing of suffering; and the patience of not being scared by the meaning of the profound teachings. Its causes are compassion for sentient beings, so that one is tolerant of injury or unaffected by it; and the observance of discipline and listening to the teachings, in dependence on which the other two kinds of patience come about.

Its result has been perfectly explained in terms of five benefits. Since one will have no disputes, one will not have many grudges. Because of having many friends, one will have few differences with people. In this life one will be physically well and mentally happy. One will die joyfully. And after death, one will go to the higher realms. These are its five benefits.

---

12. The dhyāna vow (*bsam gtan gyi sdom pa*) is the discipline that those in the world of form observe naturally. The untainted vow (*zag med kyi sdom pa*) is that of those who have attained the path of seeing. The former lacks profound insight, while the latter includes it. "Acquired naturally" (*chos nyid kyis thob pa*) implies that these two kinds of discipline are acquired through meditation.

Since patience keeps one happy and does not cause others any pain, it benefits both oneself and others—this is its function. It is fully endowed with the qualities of being the greatest of all austerities. Patience is held to be of three kinds, as already explained in the above description of its essence. Having fully understood that patience is like this, the wise practice it correctly.

> It is the true delight in virtue,
> Springs from interest and determination,
> Increases qualities such as mindfulness,
> Is the antidote to defilement, (XVII, 23)
>
> Is possessed of qualities such as the absence of attachment,
> And is of seven kinds:
> Knowing that such is diligence,
> The wise accomplish it perfectly. (XVII, 24)

The essence of diligence is a true enthusiasm for virtuous activities. Its cause is interest and confidence in virtuous ways, and it is based on a determination to accomplish the latter. Its result is to make all good qualities such as mindfulness grow greater and greater. Its function is to act as the antidote to defilement. Its property is that it has all the pure qualities such as absence of attachment and so forth. Such diligence has seven categories: three for its object—namely, the three trainings; two for its essence—diligence of body and mind; and two for its application—devoted application and constant application. Another classification also lists seven categories: five kinds of physical diligence in the training in superior discipline, these being mental factors arising in association with the five sense consciousnesses, and two kinds of mental diligence in the training in superior concentration and superior wisdom, which occur in association with the mind consciousness. Having fully understood that diligence is like this, the wise practice it correctly.

> It is the settling of the mind within,
> Springs from mindfulness and diligence,
> Gives rise to bliss,
> Brings mastery of preternatural powers and the ways of
>   abiding, (XVII, 25)
>
> Is the foremost of all practices,
> And is threefold for those who have it:

> Knowing that such is concentration,
> The wise accomplish it perfectly. (XVII, 26)

The essence of concentration is that the mind rests inwardly focused and one-pointed, rather than being distracted toward objects outside. Its cause is unforgetting mindfulness of the object of meditation, and it depends on constant diligence in meditating. Its result is that it gives rise to the happiness of a trained, fit body and mind and to the bliss of rebirth in the world of form, a higher world free of the suffering of the world of desire. Its function is to lead to mastery of preternatural powers such as performing miracles, and to mastery over the ways of abiding of the beings in the celestial realms, the ways of abiding of those in the Brahmā realms, and the ways of abiding of the noble beings. The ways of abiding of the gods refer to the four dhyānas and to the four absorptions of the formless world. The ways of abiding of those in the Brahmā realms refer to the four boundless states.[13] The ways of abiding of the noble beings are the three doors of perfect liberation and so forth. The property of concentration is that it possesses the quality of being the foremost of all virtuous practices,[14] because it is in dependence on one's mastering the mind that one accomplishes extraordinary qualities and becomes a suitable support for perfect liberation and the gnosis of perfect liberation. There are three categories, which are present in individuals who train in concentration and not present in other individuals. When classified in terms of the antidote branch, the three categories are concentration with both gross and subtle discursiveness, concentration without gross discursiveness and with subtle discursiveness, and concentration without either gross or subtle discursiveness, as has been explained above. If classified in terms of the qualities branch, the three categories are as follows: up to the second dhyāna, concentration endowed with joy; on the third, concentration endowed with bliss; and from the fourth onward, concentration endowed with evenness. Having fully understood that concentration is like this, the wise practice it correctly.

> It correctly discerns knowable phenomena,
> Depends on concentration,

---

13. Tib. *tshad med bzhi*. These states of love, compassion, joy, and impartiality, though called "boundless," are not the genuinely boundless attitudes of the bodhisattvas, though they are similar to them (*rjes mthun pa*).

14. Sthiramati comments that "foremost" (Tib. *gtso bo*) in this context means that concentration is a prerequisite (*sngon du 'gro ba*) for virtue.

> Gives complete freedom from defilement,
> Provides sustenance through superior knowledge and
>   perfect explanations, (XVII, 27)
>
> Is highest of all the teachings,
> And is threefold for those who have it:
> Knowing that such is wisdom,
> The wise accomplish it perfectly. (XVII, 28)

The essence of wisdom is to perfectly and unmistakenly discern all knowable phenomena, as they are and as many as there are. The cause of such wisdom that sees the truth is meditative concentration, on which it depends. Its result is that it leads to liberation from all defilement: mundane wisdom temporarily quenches defilements; the supramundane wisdom of the listeners and solitary realizers eliminates the latent obscurations related to the defilements; and the wisdom of the Great Vehicle, the realization of both kinds of no-self, eliminates the latent tendencies of both obscurations. As for its function, the mundane wisdom that knows how to make a living by commerce, agriculture, and so forth merely sustains life temporarily, but transcendent wisdom is far superior, for with the sustenance of the profound and extensive teachings, the very life of virtuous activities continues uninterrupted, and ultimately the eternal level of great enlightenment is accomplished. Thus it is with the sublime nourishment of wisdom and with excellent discourses to others that virtue is sustained. The property of wisdom is that it possesses the qualities of transcendent wisdom, the supreme vessel of all the teachings, as is stated in the *Perfection of Wisdom*:

> Transcendent wisdom is the sublime transcendent perfection,
>   the foremost, the most outstanding.

The categories of wisdom, which are specific to individuals who have wisdom but are not present in others, are three in number, classified in this context in terms of wisdom itself: the wisdom of mundane beings up to those on the supreme mundane level; the wisdom of lesser supramundane beings, that is, listeners and solitary realizers; and the wisdom of greater supramundane beings, that is, noble bodhisattvas. Having fully understood that wisdom is like this, the wise practice it correctly.

vii. All Positive Practices Are Included in the Six Transcendent Perfections

> All virtuous practices are to be understood
> As distracted, meditational, or both.
> These three each include
> Two transcendent perfections. (XVII, 29)

The whole of the Dharma—the levels, transcendent perfections, elements leading to enlightenment, ten positive actions, and the rest—is included in the six transcendent perfections. In what way? All positive activities can be grouped into three aspects—namely, positive actions associated with circumstances in which one is distracted and not meditating; positive actions associated with the meditative mind; and those such as patience and diligence that are to be understood as being both, since they are both meditational and nonmeditational.

Of these, nonmeditational positive actions or virtuous practices are included in the first two transcendent perfections, generosity and discipline. Generosity is essentially nonmeditational since it involves physically giving things away. As for discipline, it is nonmeditational in that, of the three kinds of vow—prātimokṣa, dhyāna, and untainted—it involves the prātimokṣa avoidance of the seven physical and verbal negative actions and is not mental. Concentration and wisdom are associated with meditational positive activities. Concentration is explicitly meditational. It includes the dhyāna vow and untainted vow. Wisdom is nonmeditational as regards the wisdom of listening and that of reflecting, and meditational as regards the wisdom of meditation, for it constitutes profound insight. Patience and diligence are classified as nonmeditational when one is practicing generosity and discipline, which are nonmeditational, and classified as meditational when one is practicing sustained calm and profound insight, so these are included in both.

viii. Avoiding Factors That Are Incompatible with the Transcendent Perfections

This topic is covered by one verse for each of the six transcendent perfections.

> In their generosity, bodhisattvas are
> Unattached, unattached, unattached,

> Quite without attachment,
> Unattached, unattached, and unattached.[15] (XVII, 30)

A bodhisattva's generosity is free from seven opposing factors, as follows. Inability to give away one's possessions on account of one's attachment to them is an opposing factor, so bodhisattvas have given up such hesitation and are not attached to possessions. They have given up procrastination, that is, putting the time off and not giving immediately when a beggar arrives, and so they are not attached to postponement. They are never complacent, with biased, partial thoughts like "Giving just this much of a gift will do" or "I'll give only to this many people" or "I will give in this area; I will give for just so long." Rather, they act impartially with regard to the gift, the place, the duration, and the individual, and so they are free of attachment to any sense of satisfaction. They are also free of attachment in the form of hoping to receive something in return for their generosity. They are not attached to any wish that their acts of generosity will ripen as great wealth in the future. They are not attached to any latent tendency to the opposing factors of stinginess and attachment, and they give without being in the slightest way tainted by miserliness. They have no attachment to distracting forms of attentiveness and concepts, for they have eliminated attentiveness related to dedicating their generosity and other deeds to the listeners' and solitary realizers' enlightenment, and they are rid of the concepts of the three spheres.

> In their discipline, bodhisattvas are
> Unattached, unattached, unattached,
> Quite without attachment,
> Unattached, unattached, and unattached. (XVII, 31)

Similarly, bodhisattvas, in their discipline, are not attached to lax ways, are not attached to postponement, and are free of attachment to a biased sense of satisfaction. Neither are they attached to hoping for a reward in return for their discipline of not harming others and so on. They are not attached to any tainted ripened effect, are not attached to latent defilements, and are free of attachment to keeping lower paths in mind and to concepts of the three spheres as having any substantial reality.

---

15. Although the Tibetan translation of these six verses of the root text makes use of different forms of the word *chags pa*, we have followed the Sanskrit, which appears to employ the same form throughout.

> In their patience, bodhisattvas are
> Unattached, unattached, unattached,
> Quite without attachment,
> Unattached, unattached, and unattached. (XVII, 32)

Bodhisattvas, in their patience, have no attachment to states of mind disturbed by hatred and thus to harming others. They are not attached to postponement, that is, to not acting patiently right away. And they are free of attachment to being content with just a little, limited patience. Neither are they attached to receiving help themselves in return for their patience with someone. They do not think, "If I train in patience, in future lives I will have a beautiful face and physique and numerous attendants" but are unattached to the fully ripened effect of their patience. They are not attached to any latent tendency to hatred, which is the opposite of patience. And they are without attachment to distracting forms of attentiveness and concepts.

> In their diligence, bodhisattvas are
> Unattached, unattached, unattached,
> Quite without attachment,
> Unattached, unattached, and unattached. (XVII, 33)

Bodhisattvas, in their diligence, are not attached to the opposing factor of manifest laziness. They are not attached to postponement, on account of which they would not engage rapidly in virtuous activities. They are not attached to being content with making limited efforts. Neither are they attached to being benefited in return for their efforts in helping others. They are not attached to the ripened effect—the fact that in the future they will be able to complete everything they undertake, and so on. They are not attached to a latent tendency to laziness, the opposite of diligence. And they are free from attachment to keeping lower paths in mind and to the concepts of the three spheres.

> In their concentration, bodhisattvas are
> Unattached, unattached, unattached,
> Quite without attachment,
> Unattached, unattached, and unattached. (XVII, 34)

In their concentration, bodhisattvas are not attached to the opposing factor of manifest distraction. They are not attached to postponement, thinking,

"One day I'll meditate." They are not attached to being content with just a limited concentration. Neither are they attached to receiving anything in return for helping others through their powers of concentration. They are not attached to the ripened effect—freedom from physical ailments and rebirth in the higher worlds.[16] They have no attachment to any latent tendency to distraction, which opposes concentration. And they are free from attachment to keeping lower paths in mind and to the concepts of the three spheres.

> In their wisdom, bodhisattvas are
> Unattached, unattached, unattached,
> Quite without attachment,
> Unattached, unattached, and unattached. (XVII, 35)

In their wisdom, bodhisattvas are not attached to manifestly aberrant understanding such as eternalistic or nihilistic views. They are not attached to postponing such activities as serving a spiritual teacher and listening and reflecting. They are not attached to being content with just limited understanding. Neither are they attached to any reward, with the expectation that when they explain the teachings, others will help them. They have no attachment to the ripened effect, thinking, "If I train in wisdom, in the future I will become very learned." They have no attachment to any latent tendency to aberrant understanding. And they are free from attachment to the distractions of dedication to the nirvāṇa of lower paths and of concepts of the three spheres as having substantial reality.

ix. The Excellent Qualities of the Six Transcendent Perfections

Of the twenty-three verses that describe the qualities of the six transcendent perfections, the first ones show how each of the six transcendent perfections is endowed with four qualities: vastness, disinterestedness, immense benefit, and inexhaustibility.

> The buddhas' children, when meeting those in need, will
>   always give them something, even their own lives.
> They do so out of compassion, with no hope of reward from
>   others, and no interest in any desired result.

---

16. The world of form and the formless world.

With that same generosity, they bring all beings to the three
    levels of enlightenment.
Since their generosity is imbued with gnosis, it remains
    unspent throughout all worlds. (XVII, 36)

When they meet someone in need, bodhisattvas, the buddhas' children, will even give their own lives, not to mention other things. And they do so not just once in a while but all the time, until the very end of saṃsāra. This is the vastness of their generosity. Motivated by compassion, they give only out of a desire to help others: they do not expect to receive anything in return for benefiting others and are not after a desired result in their future lives, the pleasant ripened effect of their generosity—they are quite disinterested. Having attracted beings with such generosity, they bring them all to whichever of the three kinds of enlightenment they aspire to—this is the immense benefit of their generosity. That very generosity is imbued with the gnosis free from the concepts of the three spheres, and so, unlike the generosity of mundane beings, which is spent once its result has ripened in saṃsāra, and unlike that of listeners and solitary realizers, which comes to an end once they have attained nirvāṇa, it leads to the attainment of the great nirvāṇa that does not dwell in the extremes of saṃsāra and nirvāṇa, and remains unspent in all worlds until the end of time. This is the quality of its inexhaustibility.

The buddhas' children constantly undertake the three kinds
    of discipline whose nature is restraint and diligence.
They do not crave the higher realms and, even if they actually
    attain them, are not attached to such states.
With that discipline, they bring all beings to the three levels
    of enlightenment.
Since their discipline is imbued with gnosis, it remains
    unspent throughout all worlds. (XVII, 37)

Bodhisattvas constantly, until they attain the great enlightenment, undertake all three forms of discipline correctly—that is, they refrain from negative actions and are diligent in undertaking positive actions and benefiting others. This is the vast quality of their discipline, which is lacking in listeners and the like. They do not crave higher rebirth, which is the result of that discipline, and even if they gain a perfect rebirth in the higher realms, they do not develop attachment to the happiness there. This is the quality of disinterestedness. By means of that discipline, they bring all beings to the three kinds of enlightenment, which is the quality of its immense benefit. And since their discipline is imbued with nonconceptual gnosis, it remains in all worlds as a never-depleted treasure, which is the quality of its inexhaustibility.

> The buddhas' children endure the most arduous tasks and all the harm that people do to them.
> This is not because they seek the higher realms or are powerless, nor out of fear, nor with an eye for their own benefit.
> With their unexcelled patience, they bring all beings to the three levels of enlightenment.
> Since their patience is imbued with gnosis, it remains unspent throughout all worlds. (XVII, 38)

Bodhisattvas, in order to carry out the extremely arduous tasks of bringing sentient beings to maturity and completing the Buddha's path themselves, intentionally take birth in saṃsāra for long periods of time, thinking nothing of the sufferings they undergo—heat and cold, hunger and thirst, and so on—and similarly putting up with all the harm that people do to them. Hence the vastness of their patience. Their practice of patience is not aimed at their achieving happiness for themselves in the higher realms. Nor is it that they are incapable of retaliating when others wrong them, for they possess preternatural powers. Nor do they act patiently because they are afraid of those beings, for they are free of the five kinds of fear.[17] Nor are they patient because they are seeking to benefit themselves. So in all these respects their patience is disinterested. On account of their unexcelled patience, they bring all beings to the three kinds of enlightenment, so it is immensely beneficial. And since their patience is imbued with nonconceptual gnosis, it remains in all worlds unspent, which is the quality of its inexhaustibility.

> The buddhas' children do things with incomparable diligence, armor-like and applied,
> Destroying their own and others' defilements and causing them to attain supreme enlightenment.

---

17. For the five kinds of fear, see the commentary on ch. 15, v. 38.

> Through that very diligence, they bring all beings to the
> three levels of enlightenment.
> Since their diligence is imbued with gnosis, it remains
> unspent throughout all worlds. (XVII, 39)

Bodhisattvas set about things with unparalleled diligence—diligence both in its armor-like intention and in the application of its subsequent accomplishment.[18] Unadulterated by defilements, it is superior to ordinary people's diligence. On account of bodhisattvas' having realized the two kinds of no-self and accomplished both their own and others' goals, it is superior to the listeners' and solitary realizers' diligence. And it is hard to gauge in terms of space and time—hence its vastness. It is disinterested in its destroying all one's own and others' defilements and enabling everyone to attain supreme enlightenment. Such diligence also brings all beings to the three kinds of enlightenment, this being the quality of its immense benefit. And because bodhisattvas' diligence is imbued with nonconceptual gnosis, it remains in all worlds unspent, which is the quality of its inexhaustibility.

> The buddhas' children, endowed with concentration, have
> accomplished all kinds of concentrative states.
> They who have attained the highest bliss of concentration
> compassionately take lower births.
> Through that very concentration, they bring all beings to the
> three levels of enlightenment.
> Since their concentration is imbued with gnosis, it remains
> unspent throughout all worlds. (XVII, 40)

Bodhisattvas have a great many different kinds of concentration, such as the concentration of Brave Progression, and are omnifariously accomplished—in the four dhyānas and so on, in perfect freedom, in the powers of perceptual limitlessness, the different kinds of perceptual domination, and so forth—hence the vastness of their concentration. They who possess the highest degree of bliss in concentration sustain it and, rather than savoring that bliss, compassionately take lower births, being reborn in the world of desire[19]—hence their disinterestedness. By means of such

---

18. In other words, as Vasubandhu makes clear in his commentary, armor-like diligence (*go cha'i btson 'grus*) and diligence in application (*sbyor ba'i brtson 'grus*).

19. Instead of remaining in the world of form enjoying the blissful states there, they take birth in the different realms of the world of desire to benefit beings.

concentration, they bring all beings to the three kinds of enlightenment, so it is immensely beneficial. And since their concentration is imbued with nonconceptual gnosis, it remains in all worlds unspent, which is the quality of its inexhaustibility.

> The buddhas' children have complete knowledge of
> everything there is to know and of its nature.
> They feel no attachment to nirvāṇa, not to mention to saṃsāra.
> With that very gnosis they bring all beings to the three levels
> of enlightenment.
> Since their gnosis envelops all beings, it remains unspent
> throughout all worlds. (XVII, 41)

Bodhisattvas have complete knowledge of everything—in its nature (thatness) and in its multiplicity (everything there is to know). This is the vast quality of their wisdom. In their minds, they feel no attachment at all to nirvāṇa, let alone to saṃsāra, for they have realized that all the appearances of saṃsāra and nirvāṇa, in relative truth, are like magical illusions and, in ultimate truth, are evenness. This is its disinterested quality. By means of such gnosis they bring all beings to the three kinds of enlightenment, this being the quality of its immense benefit. Because that gnosis does not dwell in the extremes of existence and peace, it is naturally inseparable from compassion, and therefore, since it envelops all beings, it remains in all worlds without ever being spent. This is the quality of its inexhaustibility, for it is unchanging and all-pervading.

> Vast, disinterested,
> Immensely beneficial, and inexhaustible—
> Such are the four qualities that should be known
> Of all the perfections such as generosity. (XVII, 42)

Thus, vastness, disinterestedness, immense benefit, and inexhaustibility are to be understood as the four excellent qualities of all the transcendent perfections, beginning with generosity.

Furthermore, the excellent qualities of the six transcendent perfections are described from four points of view: their superiority on account of their purity; their supremacy; their qualities exemplified by a praise of generosity; and a specific explanation of the qualities of diligence. Of these four, the first is indicated in the next nine verses.

First, the Superiority of the Six Transcendent Perfections on Account of Their Purity

Perfectly Pure Generosity

> In seeing and being fulfilled, beggars
> Are delighted, sad, and full of hope.
> But even more so are the loving ones who give,
> So they will always outshine those who beg. (XVII, 43)

This verse is a praise of perfectly pure generosity. When beggars see a charitable person, they feel happy and subsequently, in the event that their desires are fulfilled by a gift, are delighted. Should they not see someone charitable and not receive a gift, they get depressed. They are always hoping that they will see a charitable person and that the latter's generosity will fulfill their wishes. In the same way, when charitable bodhisattvas, full of love for sentient beings, see some beggars and satisfy them with their generosity, they feel joyful. And when neither of these happens, they feel sad, and they hope and pray that they will see some beggars and be able to give them what they want. Their joy, sadness, and hopes are greater than those of the beggars, and they therefore always outshine the beggars in this respect. Compared to the beggars' delight at seeing a donor, the bodhisattvas' joy on seeing the beggars is much greater. And compared to the beggars' happiness at receiving a gift and having their hopes fulfilled, the bodhisattvas' joy at being able to give them what they want is much greater, and so on. For these reasons, bodhisattvas' pure generosity is particularly sublime.

Perfectly Pure Discipline

> Out of love, they constantly give to sentient beings
> Their lives, possessions, and spouses,
> And are overjoyed to do so.
> How would they not maintain abstinence with regard to these?
>   (XVII, 44)

The qualities of perfectly pure discipline are explained next. Bodhisattvas, out of love, are not in the slightest bit unhappy about constantly giving sentient beings their own lives, possessions, and spouses. They are, rather, overjoyed to do so. So how would they not maintain the discipline of avoiding selfishly taking others' lives, appropriating their possessions, and committing adultery with their partners? It is because of this that they possess the perfectly pure discipline of avoiding the three physical negative actions.

> Noble beings have no regard for themselves, are impartial,
> Fearless, and full of love,
> So how could they, who give everything away,
> Do others harm and tell them lies? (XVII, 45)

Noble bodhisattvas have no regard for their own bodies and lives. They are impartial with regard to sentient beings. They are free from the five fears and therefore not afraid of such things as punishment by the authorities. And they are full of love for all living beings. So how could they, who give away everything they own, deceive and harm others, telling them lies? People tell lies in order to save themselves from death or injury; or they lie out of partiality, for the sake of a friend or relative they love or in order to harm someone like an enemy; or out of fear of the authorities, robbers, and so forth; or because they are afraid of losing their spouse, riches, and so on. But bodhisattvas have none of these reasons for lying, so it is impossible for them to tell lies.

> Those with love who wish to help impartially,
> Who greatly fear that others might have pain,
> Who apply their minds to taming sentient beings,
> Have cast afar the three misdeeds of speech. (XVII, 46)

Similarly, since they are full of love and want to help all other sentient beings equally, they do not sow discord, driven by a lack of impartiality with regard to who are friends and who are not. Since they are extremely afraid of suffering happening to other people and want them not to suffer, they refrain from harsh speech, which comes from wanting others to suffer. And since they strive with one-pointed minds to subdue beings' defilements, they avoid worthless chatter, which makes defilements grow. They are thus a very long way from committing these three kinds of verbal negative actions.

> Those who've given everything away, who are compassionate
> And know full well that things arise dependently—

> How could they indulge
> In all the mind's defilements? (XVII, 47)

Bodhisattvas give away all their possessions, they have great compassion for others, and they are extremely knowledgeable about the doctrine of dependent arising. So how is it possible that they would indulge in all the mental negative actions, such as covetousness, evil intent, and wrong views, which arise through attachment, aversion, and bewilderment? It makes no sense that those who give others all their possessions would covet others' possessions. This same principle should be understood as applying to the other mental negative actions.[20]

Perfectly Pure Patience

> When those with love are harmed
> Or suffer helping others,
> They always find delight, thinking of the benefit.
> What, then, is there for them to bear? (XVII, 48)

When loving bodhisattvas are harmed by others or suffer in order to help others, they think, "This is the way for me to complete the practice of patience, which is a factor that leads to supreme enlightenment." The idea that someone is harming them or that they are suffering does not occur to them. Rather, they are delighted, recognizing the situation as supremely beneficial and fortunate. For such bodhisattvas, what is there to bear that is so terrible and difficult to endure? They simply do not have the notion of these things being unbearable. They are like fish swimming in water or fire salamanders entering fire[21]—for them such things are not in any way unendurable.

---

20. I.e., it makes no sense that a compassionate person would want to harm others, or that someone who understands dependent arising would have wrong views.

21. Tib. *ri dvags me'i gtsang sgra can*. This appears to be a mythological creature that bathes or cleanses itself in fire. We have been unable to identify it with an Indian equivalent and have tentatively offered as a translation the fire salamander, which in medieval Europe was reputed to live in fire.

Perfectly Pure Diligence

> They have no notion of other beings as others,
> And constant love for others more than for themselves;
> For beings, they undertake austerities, and so for those with loving tenderness
> Diligence is not hard, even if extremely difficult. (XVII, 49)

Bodhisattvas do not think of others as others. That is to say, they have realized the sameness of themselves and others. And although they have realized for themselves the meaning of the sameness of oneself and others, when they see other sentient beings who have not realized that, they always feel more love for the other beings than for themselves, and they undertake countless difficulties for beings' sake. So for them, whose love is so great, the immense efforts they make for others' sake are not in the least difficult. On the other hand, these hardships they undergo for others' benefit, thinking of others as more important than themselves, are extremely difficult for anyone else to do—that is, for ordinary beings and listeners and solitary realizers.

Perfectly Pure Concentration

> The concentration of three kinds of beings is held to have but little bliss:
> It is selfish bliss, with clinging, that loses its strength,
> Or is exhausted, and is associated with ignorance.
> A bodhisattva's concentration is just the opposite. (XVII, 50)

The concentration of mundane meditators, listeners, and solitary realizers, compared to that of bodhisattvas, leads to minor bliss, because the tainted bliss of mundane beings and the untainted concentration of the listeners and solitary realizers bring contentment only to their own minds and do not satisfy others. Mundane meditators, on account of their belief in a self, want samsaric happiness; the listeners and solitary realizers desire the bliss of nirvāṇa for themselves alone. Mundane beings cling to saṃsāra; listeners and solitary realizers cling to peaceful nirvāṇa. The bliss of mundane beings' concentration loses its strength completely. The listeners' and solitary realizers' concentration will come to an end in the state of nirvāṇa with no residual aggregates. Mundane meditators have not eliminated either of the two kinds of obscurations, while listeners and solitary realizers have not eliminated the cognitive obscurations; their concentration is therefore held to be associated with ignorance.

The bodhisattva's concentration, on the other hand, is the opposite of these, differing from them in six respects, as follows. The boundless concentrations of the Great Vehicle lead to vast happiness. Bodhisattvas enter into concentration for others' benefit. On account of their nonconceptual gnosis, it is free of clinging to existence and peace. It occurs throughout the bodhisattva's series of lives and so does not lose its strength. It is never exhausted even in the expanse of nirvāṇa without residual aggregates. And since bodhisattvas have eliminated both kinds of obscurations, it is free of ignorance.

Perfectly Pure Wisdom

> There is wisdom like one who fumbles in the dark,
> And wisdom like a light that has been concealed.
> These bear no comparison with the knowledge of the
>   compassionate ones,
> The third wisdom, which is like the rays of the sun.
>   (XVII, 51)

To explain the qualities of perfectly pure wisdom, this verse uses an analogy. The wisdom that mundane beings acquire through listening, reflecting, and meditating is analogous to looking for something at night, in the dark, feeling for things with one's hands. They can only judge the nature of things—impermanence, suffering, and so forth—by inference, without knowing it directly. The listeners' and solitary realizers' wisdom is like a concealed lamp. If a candle is placed inside a box or recess, it lights only the inside. Similarly, having realized merely the absence of an individual self in their own five aggregates, they have only the wisdom that comes from the removal of the defilements. By the same analogy, the third wisdom, the knowledge of the compassionate bodhisattvas, is like the rays of the sun, shining in all directions. It is without compare, for it has perfectly realized the nature of phenomena, the absence of the two kinds of self, and it knows clearly and distinctly all the phenomena of defilement and purity in their multiplicity. It has thereby eliminated the two kinds of obscurations and realized the two truths.

Second, the Supremacy of Generosity and the Other Transcendent Perfections

As shown in the following six verses, the supremacy of generosity and the other five transcendent perfections is comprised in their each having eight supreme aspects. These eight supreme aspects are supreme individual,[22] supreme substance or object, supreme reason, supreme dedication, supreme cause, supreme gnosis, supreme field, and supreme reliance. Because they have these eight, they possess the qualities of being transcendent, sublime, and supreme.

> In terms of the individual, substance,
> Reason, dedication,
> Cause, gnosis, fields,
> And reliance, their generosity is supreme. (XVII, 52)

(1) As far as generosity is concerned, the giver is not like an ordinary person or a listener or solitary realizer, but is a bodhisattva—a supreme individual.

(2) As for the substance or object, the thing that is given, it is far superior to what listeners give, for example. The latter give a few material gifts such as food and clothing; their gift of Dharma is the listeners' scriptural collection; and they give protection from harm in this life. But bodhisattvas make boundless gifts of things that are extremely difficult to give away (possessions on a vast scale, their heads and limbs, and so forth), of the Mahāyāna teachings, and of the refuge that, above all, brings one to the great enlightenment beyond the extremes of existence and peace.

(3) The reason is their motivation: bodhisattvas give not out of yearning faith, as do the listeners, but chiefly out of compassion from seeing sentient beings suffering.

(4) With regard to the supreme dedication, bodhisattvas dedicate the result of their acts of generosity not to any happiness in the celestial and human realms that might result, nor to the listeners' and solitary realizers' enlightenment, but to the attainment of perfect, unsurpassable enlightenment for the benefit of all sentient beings.

(5) The cause is the habitual tendency present in the ground of all that comes from their having thoroughly accustomed themselves in previous

---

22. Tib. *rten*, lit. "support."

lives to the practice of generosity imbued with the three roots of virtue (freedom from attachment, and so on), as a result of which, wherever they are reborn, they continue to engage in the practice of transcendent generosity. This is the original cause, which is like a seed, while the reason or motivation—compassion—is the cooperative condition, helping the seed to grow, like earth and water.

(6) Supreme gnosis refers to generosity being imbued with nonconceptual gnosis, free of the three concepts of giver, recipient, and gift.

(7) There are five kinds of fields: Those who beg—anyone who asks, even if they are brahmins, shopkeepers, and so on, who have a little money. Those who are suffering, such as sick people. Those who have no protector, who have no food or clothes. Those who lead immoral lives, indulging in negative actions for material gain. And those with excellent qualities, who possess qualities such as discipline and wisdom. For listeners and those who follow mundane ways, fields with excellent qualities are the most important, but bodhisattvas, on account of their compassion, esteem fields of suffering the most. They give in order to dispel their suffering and especially to turn them away from the cause of suffering, while also giving to fields of excellent qualities and the other fields when appropriate. The more lowly the fields of suffering, and the greater their suffering, the better they are as objects of generosity. It is better to give to a poor person than to any number of wealthy people, even better to give to the most destitute, and even better to give to hungry spirits, while the benefits of giving to hungry spirits with constricted throats are greatest of all. As for fields with excellent qualities, the more exalted they are, the greater the benefits of giving to them. Far better to give to one who keeps pure discipline than to countless ordinary people, and the most exalted fields are listeners, solitary realizers, bodhisattvas, and, most of all, buddhas. Thus, bodhisattvas, who consider others' welfare far above their own, give especially to those fields of generosity who manifest suffering and its cause; in terms of the fields, their generosity is particularly supreme.

(8) The "reliance" of giving (that is, what bodhisattvas rely on when they give) refers to relying on interest in generosity, relying on attentiveness, and relying on concentration, which are similar to these three as mentioned in the chapter on investigating the Dharma above. Keeping interest in mind is a corresponding confidence in the Mahāyāna teachings on the transcendent perfections. Attentiveness refers to savoring one's past generosity (or other transcendent perfection), thinking, "That was very good"; to rejoicing in

others' generosity; and to delighting in one's own and others' future generosity. Concentration refers to practicing generosity by mastering concentrations such as the Sky Treasury, and, having attained the three buddha bodies on the level of buddhahood, mastering generosity for the benefit of others.

Thus, by means of these eight aspects, the individual and the rest, a bodhisattva's generosity is held to be supreme compared to that of mundane beings and listeners and solitary realizers. The same should be understood for the other transcendent perfections, from discipline through to wisdom. Apart from the substance (which is distinguished in each case) and the field (which is the Great Vehicle and which, unlike the listeners' and solitary realizers' vehicles, is the supreme field to focus on and to set beings in), the other six aspects are no different, as we shall now see.

> In terms of the individual, substance,
> Reason, dedication,
> Cause, gnosis, field,
> And reliance, their discipline is supreme. (XVII, 53)

The individual who maintains discipline is a bodhisattva. The substance or object comprises the three aspects of a bodhisattva's discipline—refraining from negative actions, gathering positive actions, and working for the benefit of sentient beings. The reason is compassion for sentient beings. The dedication is made to unsurpassable enlightenment. The cause is habituation to discipline in previous lives. It is imbued with nonconceptual gnosis. The field, on which bodhisattvas focus and in which they set sentient beings, is the Great Vehicle. And the reliance is the three kinds of reliance on interest, attentiveness, and concentration. It is by means of these that discipline is preserved.

> In terms of the individual, substance,
> Reason, dedication,
> Cause, gnosis, field,
> And reliance, their patience is supreme. (XVII, 54)

The substance of patience comprises patience in taking harm as the practice, patience in thinking nothing of suffering, and patience in aspiring to a true knowledge of reality. The other aspects of patience are to be understood as being the same as those of the previous transcendent perfection. Hence, in terms of the individual, substance, reason, dedication, cause, gnosis, field, and reliance, patience is held to be supreme.

> In terms of the individual, substance,
> Reason, dedication,
> Cause, gnosis, field,
> And reliance, their diligence is supreme. (XVII, 55)

The substance of diligence comprises armor-like diligence, diligence in application, and diligence in benefiting sentient beings. In terms of the individual, substance, reason, dedication, cause, gnosis, field, and reliance, diligence is held to be supreme.

> In terms of the individual, substance,
> Reason, dedication,
> Cause, gnosis, field,
> And reliance, their concentration is supreme. (XVII, 56)

The substance of concentration comprises the concentration that procures a feeling of well-being in this life, the concentration that accomplishes preternatural knowledge, and the concentration that brings about the benefit of sentient beings. In terms of the individual, substance, reason, dedication, cause, gnosis, field, and reliance, concentration is held to be supreme.

> In terms of the individual, substance,
> Reason, dedication,
> Cause, gnosis, field,
> And reliance, their wisdom is supreme. (XVII, 57)

The substance of wisdom comprises the wisdom of knowing the relative truth, the wisdom of knowing the ultimate truth, and the wisdom of knowing how to accomplish the welfare of sentient beings. In terms of the individual, substance, reason, dedication, cause, gnosis, field, and reliance, their wisdom is held to be supreme.

It should also be understood that the substance or object in each case is divided into modest, middling, and greatest, and that the "supreme substance" is the best of these.

Third, the Qualities of Generosity

> Bodhisattvas feel the greatest joy
> When their generosity makes a single being happy,
> Even if it has brought them many kalpas of difficulty.
> No need is there to mention what they feel when this is not the case. (XVII, 58)

In giving generously, bodhisattvas never get depressed, even if by giving away everything they own in order to make a single sentient being happy they inflict upon themselves many kalpas of constant toil and deprivation. Rather, it brings them the greatest joy. So one need hardly mention their delight in the opposite situation, where, by bestowing the gift of Dharma and material gifts, they bring benefit and happiness not only to numerous beings but also, in the long term, to themselves. That this should be so can be put down to their heartfelt love for sentient beings.

> Because living beings desire wealth,
> The steadfast give them the very things they want.
> While humans seek riches for the sake of their bodies,
> Those very bodies the steadfast give away a hundred times.
> (XVII, 59)

Because living beings desire riches—the things they treasure and cannot bear to part with, which they seek and carefully look after—steadfast bodhisattvas give beings those very things that are prized and cherished and do not keep anything for themselves. This is the quality of their lack of attachment.

People desire wealth for the sake of their bodies and lives, and so they seek and hoard it. Steadfast bodhisattvas give away their bodies hundreds of times to others.

> When even giving their bodies brings them no mental pain,
> What need is there to mention lesser gifts?
> In this they are beyond the world, and from it they derive the greatest joy—
> The highest of all the joys experienced by those beyond the world. (XVII, 60)

Even though they give away their own bodies and lives, bodhisattvas do not suffer mentally. At such times, there is no need to mention their never getting discouraged in giving away outer things that, compared to their bodies, are inferior things that are easy to give away. This is the indefatigable quality of their generosity.

This ability to give their bodies and lives without getting discouraged and to derive great pleasure from doing so is these bodhisattvas' quality of being beyond the domain of any mundane beings. And the supreme joy that bodhisattvas derive from giving away their bodies is the highest of the joys of supramundane beings, greater even than those of the noble listeners and solitary realizers, for the listeners and solitary realizers have nothing like the joy that the bodhisattvas have. Not only do those bodhisattvas delight in such sacrifice and thus never tire of continuously practicing generosity, but they also derive the greatest joy from doing so.

> The wise, by giving all, derive delight
> From the pleasure of those who were longing for those gifts.
> The beggars feel no similar delight
> When they receive the alms they begged. (XVII, 61)

Wise bodhisattvas give away everything—their bodies and possessions—and when they see that the people who long for those things are delighted to receive such gifts and that they have helped them, the bodhisattvas feel delighted themselves. The beggars do not derive anything like such great joy when they receive the things they have begged from those bodhisattvas—such is the bodhisattvas' love for those fields.

> The wise, impoverished by giving all they own,
> Think themselves enriched.
> The beggars, now the owners of all that wealth,
> Have no such feeling that they're rich. (XVII, 62)

By giving away everything they own, these immensely wise bodhisattvas become momentarily penniless. Yet despite this, they consider themselves wealthy, thinking, "I have turned my wealth into the treasure of generosity." On the other hand, the beggars, who now possess all the abundant wealth that they have obtained from the bodhisattvas, do not think of themselves as wealthy in quite the same way as the bodhisattvas do, and they still maintain a miserly, avaricious disposition with regard to possessions. This is the bodhisattvas' quality of considering their result of generosity as much greater.

> **The wise, when properly satisfying the needy with excellent gifts,**
> **Think of them as great benefactors.**
> **The beggars, once they have received great quantities of wealth,**
> **Have no such gratitude to the giver for what they've gained.**
>   **(XVII, 63)**

The wise satisfy those who hanker after their bodies and possessions according to their desires, properly, with excellent gifts that combine respect, the fulfillment of wishes, and a lack of arrogance. In doing so, those bodhisattvas think of the beings they have satisfied as greatly benefiting them: "These people are friends helping me to complete the transcendent perfections and attain unsurpassable enlightenment." Unlike them, the beggars, having received immense quantities of riches, feel nothing like the same sort of gratitude to their benefactor for what they have acquired—they do not think, "They have given me all this."

> **Just as they enjoy delicious fruit from a tree along the road,**
> **Beings partake greatly of a bodhisattva's riches,**
> **Using them unhesitatingly as they please.**
> **Yet no one but a bodhisattva has such wealth—the joy of**
>   **generosity. (XVII, 64)**

From a great tree laden with the most sublime fruit along a well-traveled road, people partake of the fruit as they wish, without hesitation or fear. In the same way, living beings liberally and unhesitatingly take for themselves a bodhisattva's possessions, and, thinking of such bodhisattvas, "There is no one they will not give to," they use those very things as they please, without hesitation. Yet in taking pleasure from giving everything away, pleasing beings and never displeasing them by holding back any possessions, no one but a bodhisattva has such inexhaustible wealth. These last two verses refer to the quality of certainty.

From these particular ways in which bodhisattvas practice generosity with compassion, for the benefit of others, we can understand implicitly how they also accomplish discipline and the other transcendent perfections, undertaking them in the same way, with great compassion, principally for others' benefit.

Fourth, a Specific Explanation of the Qualities of Transcendent Diligence

Brief Introduction

> Diligence, it has been well taught, should be known
> For its importance, the reason for its importance, its different functions,
> Different aspects, categories in terms of individuals,
> And categories as the antidote to the four kinds of obstacles.
> (XVII, 65)

The tathāgatas have fully explained that diligence is to be understood in terms of its paramount importance among the transcendent perfections, the reasons for this, its different functions, different aspects, classification in terms of individuals, and classification as the antidote to the four kinds of obstacles.

Detailed Explanation

First: Its Paramount Importance

> Of all the host of virtues, diligence is the best. (XVII, 66a)

Of all virtuous, meritorious qualities, diligence is the greatest.

Second: Establishing the Reasons for That

> When one relies on it, virtue is subsequently achieved. (XVII, 66b)

Why is diligence the most important? Because by relying on diligence, one will subsequently achieve those virtuous activities. Unless one makes the effort, one can never achieve any good qualities or virtuous practices. The extent of one's positive activities depends on the extent of one's diligence, because they are achieved through the latter. One might wonder whether concentration and wisdom are not the most important, since they destroy defilements. Indeed they are, but they do not happen without the application of diligence. So in terms of being the cause of all virtuous activities, it is diligence that is the most important.

Third: Its Different Functions

> Through diligence, one instantly achieves the greatest happiness
> And all the qualities of this world and beyond. (XVII, 66cd)

> Through diligence, one obtains the enjoyments one desires in saṃsāra.
> Through diligence, one gains changeable pure states.
> Through diligence, one transcends the transitory composite and is freed.
> Through diligence, one attains supreme enlightenment and buddhahood. (XVII, 67)

By applying diligence, one will immediately accomplish the highest state of happiness in this life. Even ordinary, mundane people who work hard at treating sickness, overcoming poverty, and so on, see the results of their efforts in this life. And by practicing sustained calm and profound insight assiduously, they visibly acquire the good qualities of concentration and profound insight in this life. By means of diligence, one will accomplish all supramundane and mundane qualities in one's present and future lives.

By being diligent in practicing the ten mundane positive actions, one will obtain, as the result, the pleasurable states that one wishes to enjoy in saṃsāra—the happiness of gods and humans. By applying diligence in the concentrations of form and formlessness, one will obtain rebirth in the realms of the four concentrations and the four formless realms, endowed with the changeable (since it does not last forever) purity of freedom from the defilements of the lower, desire realm. Through diligence in meditating on the four truths and dependent arising, one will transcend the view of the transitory composite and attain perfect liberation in nirvāṇa as a listener or solitary realizer. Through diligence in practicing the teachings of the Great Vehicle, one will attain the supreme enlightenment of buddhahood.

Fourth: Different Aspects of Diligence

> Furthermore, there is one diligence that leads to decrease
>   and increase,
> One that has power over liberation, another that eliminates
>   counteragents,
> One that realizes thatness, one that completely transforms,
> And diligence of great significance, which is variously
>   defined. (XVII, 68)

Furthermore, there is diligence associated with the four genuine restraints, which refers to diligence that weakens one's faults by quelling negative actions that have arisen and preventing those that have not arisen from arising; and diligence that gives rise to positive states that are not yet present and augments positive states that have already arisen. Diligence associated with the five powers is "power over liberation"—the diligence that masters liberation. Diligence in the five irresistible forces is another kind of diligence, which gets rid of countering factors. At the stage of the elements leading to perfect enlightenment, there is the diligence of full engagement with thatness. At the stage of the eightfold noble path, on the noble path of right effort, there is the diligence that creates the cause of complete transformation. And there is the diligence of effort in transcendent activity, which is held to be variously defined as the "diligence of the great goal," the attainment of buddhahood, and as the "great import," since it is far superior to the listeners' and solitary realizers' diligence.

> First comes the diligence of virtue,
> Then the diligence of proper application,
> And the diligence of not being disheartened, overpowered,
>   or content.
> All these aspects the buddhas have explained. (XVII, 69)

Moreover, to begin with there is the diligence of a positive attitude, which is the diligence of devoted application. This is followed by the diligence of properly applying oneself to virtue, as one had pledged, which is the diligence of constant application. These two are distinguished in terms of their essence. There are also the diligence of not losing heart in accomplishing the extensive path and result, the diligence of not being overpowered by countering factors, and the diligence of not being satisfied with the antidotes. All these various categories of diligence have been fully described by the buddhas.

Fifth: Categories in terms of Different Individuals

> As for those people diligent in the three vehicles,
> Their attitudes and wisdom vary from limited through to vast,
> So there are further forms of diligence—lesser, middling,
>   and best—
> These are applied to the lesser goal and the greater goal.
>   (XVII, 70)

With regard to the persons exerting themselves on the paths of the three vehicles—namely, listeners, solitary realizers, and bodhisattvas—their attitudes and wisdom are respectively limited, middling, and vast. Diligence, therefore, has three further categories in terms of these individuals: least, middling, and greatest. Since the first two of these three are applied only to one's own goal, they are referred to as diligence for the lesser goal, while the last, being applied to accomplishing both one's own and others' goals, is held to be diligence for the greater goal.

Sixth: Categories in terms of Antidotes to the Four Kinds of Obstacles

> Those with diligence are never short of possessions.
> Those with diligence are not overwhelmed by defilements.
> Those with diligence are not overcome by loss of heart.
> Those with diligence are never short of attainments. (XVII, 71)

Four kinds of obstacles are shown to be avoided through diligence: obstacles from lack of wealth, obstacles due to defilements, obstacles from getting discouraged, and obstacles that prevent one from acquiring good qualities. For people who have diligence, wealth will never be a problem, because they are accomplishing the cause of wealth.[23] Those who are diligent are not over-

---

23. Lit. "will not be defeated by wealth" or "will not be the loser to wealth." The reward for being diligent in practicing generosity, for example, is riches in future lives.

whelmed by defilements, because they can give rise to their antidotes. Those who have diligence are not overcome by discouragement in actively practicing generosity and so forth, because they possess the diligence of never being satisfied. And those who are diligent have no obstacles to acquiring any good qualities,[24] because by the force of their diligence they will continue to accomplish such qualities until they reach buddhahood.

x. Determining the Interrelationships of the Six Transcendent Perfections

Since within a single one of the transcendent perfections all the others are also included, they are determined as being interrelated, as shown in the following verse.

> **Because they are mutually inclusive, because of their subdivisions,**
> **Because of their very nature, and because they are causal,**
> **You should know that the six transcendent perfections**
> **Are determined as being in every way interrelated. (XVII, 72)**

Although each transcendent perfection is distinct as an isolate, in fact the others are all complete within the same entity, and they are therefore mutually inclusive. Each one is divided into six aspects. By their very nature, if one of the transcendent perfections such as generosity is present, all the others, whichever they may be, are present in it too. And generosity and so forth is the causal factor of, or creates the cause for, the other transcendent perfections. So for these four reasons it should be understood that the six transcendent perfections are determined as being in every way interrelated.

In what way are they mutually inclusive? In generosity, discipline is also complete—discipline in giving up stinginess, in the wholehearted act of generosity itself, and in benefiting others. When one is generous, one puts up with ingratitude and accepts the loss of one's possessions—these constitute the patience aspect. In one's aspiring to give and constantly striving to do so, diligence is present. From the point of view of engaging in generosity with one-pointed mind and not falling prey to distractions that counter generosity, one is practicing concentration. And understanding the defining

---

24. Lit. "will not be defeated by any good qualities."

characteristics of the practice of generosity—pure generosity, impure generosity, and so forth—is wisdom. Also, when one has acquired the Sky Treasury concentration, one's generosity *is* concentration; when, by that means, one has gathered disciples, one's giving the gift of Dharma is wisdom. Furthermore, since a bodhisattva's generosity is permeated by nonconceptual gnosis, it is endowed with the wisdom that is the realization of thatness. It should be understood that this also holds for all the remaining transcendent perfections.

Discipline includes all the transcendent perfections within the discipline of undertaking positive actions; it is what accomplishes them all. Keeping one's vows for the sake of other beings is also, in fact, generosity. If one has discipline, one is also naturally patient with others who harm one. And in that one makes an effort to keep one's vows, diligence is naturally fully present. Focusing one's mind one-pointedly on discipline is the concentration aspect. A thorough understanding of the different categories of discipline—of what constitutes a downfall, what does not, and so forth—corresponds to the wisdom concerning the multiplicity of phenomena, and freedom from the concepts of the three spheres with regard to discipline constitutes the wisdom that realizes the nature of phenomena.

In patience, generosity is also fully present, for patience itself benefits others, one resorts to patience in the process of helping others, and one accepts giving one's things away. Patience is itself the avoidance of the negative act of anger and the undertaking of the positive action, in particular, of enduring hardship. The effort one puts into patience is diligence. All the other transcendent perfections are included in the willing acceptance of difficulties when one is practicing the transcendent perfections: from the point of view of keeping the mind one-pointed and imperturbable, there is concentration, and from the point of view of having certainty in the teachings, knowing how to train in patience, and realizing that phenomena are devoid of intrinsic nature, there is wisdom.

Diligence is applied concurrently with all the others, and so aspects of all of them are present.

The act of concentrating includes all the other transcendent perfections in its accomplishment. Benefiting others with concentration is the generosity aspect. Then there is discipline in the obtainment of the dhyāna vow, patience in not being ravished away by distractions, and diligence in the devoted and constant application to concentration. Analysis (one of the four bases of miraculous powers) corresponds to wisdom, and concentration moreover includes the wisdom that knows the nature and the multiplicity of phenomena, as above.

Wisdom includes all the other transcendent perfections within the wisdom of skill in means. It is through wisdom that generosity, discipline, patience, diligence, and concentration are accomplished. Without it, nothing will be accomplished.

With regard to their subdivisions, the way in which each of the transcendent perfections is divided into six (the generosity of generosity, and so forth), making thirty-six subdivisions in all, has been described above in the chapter on investigating the Dharma.[25] To practice the six transcendent perfections oneself and then establish others in them gives six subdivisions that constitute generosity. Being free of the six countering factors (stinginess and the others) constitutes discipline. Putting up with difficulties in applying the six perfections constitutes patience. Enthusiasm in each of the six constitutes diligence. Not being distracted from whichever of the six perfections one is practicing constitutes concentration. And being free of the concepts of the three spheres with regard to each of the six constitutes wisdom. Put differently, in a single thought of giving generously there are also the aspects of avoiding countering factors, applying the antidote, enthusiasm, lack of distraction, and discernment, so all six perfections are complete and inseparable from it. And in discipline and the others too, all the other aspects, beginning with the thought of giving for others' benefit, are complete.

For "Because of their very nature," there is an explanation that the teachings of the Excellent Words that teach the transcendent perfections include all the transcendent perfections as their subjects, and those subjects, the transcendent perfections, include all the Excellent Words of the Great Vehicle that express them.[26] But here we shall explain how they are mutually inclusive *by their very nature* in relative truth: just as in a single lump of composite matter the four individual elements are all present, if any one of the six transcendent perfections is present, then by its very nature aspects of all the others are also present. And, in ultimate truth, when a transcendent

---

25. See ch. 12, v. 64.
26. This explanation appears in Vasubandhu's commentary, which interprets the word *dharma* (Tib. *chos*) as the Buddha's teachings. In the sentences that follow, Mipham interprets the Tibetan word *chos nyid* in the root text in a wider sense as "the nature of things" or "the very nature."

perfection is imbued with nonconceptual gnosis, all the other transcendent perfections are naturally included, since they form a single taste as the emptiness supreme in all respects, as we find in the *Verses Summarizing the Precious Qualities*, which makes an analogy with the shade of a hundred billion trees in Jambudvīpa to show how everything appears to transcendent wisdom as the same taste.[27]

"Because they are causal" refers to the Buddha's teaching that when one is not attached to possessions, one is able to maintain discipline. When one has discipline, one is able to patiently accept the harm others do one. If one is patient, one undertakes things with diligence. Because of that, one settles the mind in evenness, and once settled in evenness, one sees things correctly, as they are. Furthermore, even though one may be engaged in a single transcendent perfection—generosity, for example—it will definitely help in accomplishing all the others, and there is not a single one that will not help.

2. An Explanation of the Four Ways of Attracting Disciples That Bring Other Sentient Beings to Maturation

This section is divided into five parts.

a. Definitions

> **Generosity is considered to be the same.**
> **Teaching them, encouraging others to practice them,**
> **And practicing them oneself are termed**
> **Agreeable speech, helpful activity, and consistent behavior.**
> (XVII, 73)

The definitions of the four ways of attracting disciples are held to be as follows. Generosity as a way of attracting disciples is the same as and nothing other than transcendent generosity, described earlier. To explain to others and teach the general and particular characteristics of the six transcendent perfections is "agreeable speech." To thus encourage other beings to practice the six transcendent perfections and establish them as practitioners is

---

27. Stated briefly, wherever there are trees, there is shade; wherever there is wisdom, there is emptiness.

"helpful activity." And to oneself fully engage in and practice those same transcendent perfections that one has encouraged other sentient beings to practice is "consistent behavior." Thus, teaching them, encouraging others to practice them, and practicing them oneself indicate the last three ways of attracting disciples—agreeable speech, and so on.[28]

b. THE DEFINITIVE NUMBER OF THE WAYS OF ATTRACTING DISCIPLES

> Since they are the methods for bringing beings benefit,
> For making them comprehend, for making them engage,
> And similarly for making them continue the practice,
> Know that there are four ways of attracting disciples.
> (XVII, 74)

The first way of attracting disciples, generosity, is the skillful way to benefit others physically by ridding them of such things as heat and cold, and hunger and thirst. Agreeable speech is the skillful way to clear away their ignorance, incorrect understanding, or doubts with regard to the characteristics of the transcendent perfections and to make them understand the transcendent perfections without error. Helpful activity is the skillful way to induce them to practice the transcendent perfections. And similarly, consistent behavior is the skillful way to make them pursue their practice of the transcendent perfections: if the persons teaching the Dharma practice those teachings themselves, it makes the other people too, whom they have established as practitioners, practice those teachings earnestly. So it should be understood that the method for attracting beings into one's following and bringing them to maturity comprises four ways of attracting disciples— there is no need for more than four, but fewer would not include everything.

c. THE FUNCTIONS OF THE FOUR WAYS OF ATTRACTING DISCIPLES

> The first turns beings into proper receptacles,
> The second makes them interested,
> The third makes them practice,
> And the fourth helps them train and purify themselves. (XVII, 75)

---

28. These last three are sometimes also translated as "speaking pleasantly," "giving appropriate advice," and "acting accordingly."

The first way of attracting disciples makes beings proper receptacles for the teachings. Sentient beings whom bodhisattvas have helped with material gifts feel happy with them and become suitable receptacles for listening to what they say. The second, agreeable speech, makes beings interested in the teachings that possess the riches of the transcendent perfections. The third, helpful activity, induces them to practice the transcendent perfections. And the fourth, consistent behavior, makes them practice the transcendent perfections repeatedly and train in purifying contaminants.

d. Categories of the Four Ways of Attracting Disciples

The four ways of attracting disciples can be classified into (1) two groups or (2) three categories.

i. Classification into Two Groups

> The four ways of attracting disciples
> Comprise two groups—
> Material and Dharma,
> Of which the latter includes the reference Dharma.
>   (XVII, 76)

There are two groups: attracting with material gifts and attracting with the Dharma, of which the latter has three aspects—the reference Dharma and so on. Generosity is the material way of attracting disciples. The other three are the Dharma way. From these two ways of attracting disciples, with the Dharma way subdivided into three, there are held to be a total of four ways of attracting disciples. With regard to the Dharma way, there are the reference Dharma, the practice Dharma, and the purification Dharma. The first of these comprises the sūtras and other teachings that contain the six transcendent perfections, and these are explained by means agreeable speech. The practice Dharma, by means of helpful activity, makes disciples practice. As for the purification Dharma, consistent behavior induces disciples to train in freeing themselves of contamination by stinginess and other factors that counter the transcendent perfections.

ii. Classification into Three Categories

> Know that they are categorized
> Into lesser, middling, and best ways of attracting,
> And the mostly unsuccessful, mostly successful,
> And entirely successful. (XVII, 77)

When they are classified into different categories, there are the listeners' four ways of attracting disciples, which are inferior ways because they do not benefit others; the solitary realizers' ways, which are middling, in that their faculties are superior to the listeners' but inferior to the bodhisattvas'; and the bodhisattvas' four ways of attracting disciples, which are referred to as the best because they are applied for their own and others' welfare. Bodhisattvas may also establish beings in the vehicles of the listeners, solitary realizers, or bodhisattvas, and in these three cases their attracting disciples will be inferior, middling, or best.

Furthermore, the ways of attracting disciples can be categorized in terms of the individual who is attracting them. Bodhisattvas on the level of earnest aspiration may attract sentient beings and bring them to maturation with the four ways of attracting disciples, but, apart from bringing a few beings to maturity, for the most part they will not be successful because they have not seen the thatness of phenomena and do not know beings' intentions and so forth. Bodhisattvas on the first level up to the seventh who use the four ways of attracting disciples to mature sentient beings are mostly successful in this, though there are still a few whom they will not bring to maturity. Bodhisattvas on the eighth, ninth, and tenth levels who use the four ways of attracting disciples to attract sentient beings and bring them to maturity will bring them all to maturity, without a single one being lost, and they are therefore entirely successful.

e. The Benefits of the Four Ways of Attracting Disciples

> Those who are attracting a following
> Properly depend on these methods.
> This accomplishes all the goals of everyone
> And is highly praised as the best of means. (XVII, 78)

Bodhisattvas who are gathering around them an entourage of disciples place proper reliance on methods such as these. This accomplishes all the goals of all sentient beings. There is no better means for doing so than this, and it is praised as such by all the buddhas.

> Attracting disciples in the past,
> In the future, and in the present
> Are all by these same means, which therefore constitute
> The path for ripening sentient beings. (XVII, 79)

For that reason, the past buddhas and bodhisattvas have attracted sentient beings in the past, and will similarly attract them in the future, and are attracting them at present, all by means of these same four ways of attracting disciples. It is certain, therefore, that these four ways of attracting disciples constitute the one route to bringing all sentient beings to maturity.

3. Concluding Summary of the Six Transcendent Perfections and the Four Ways of Attracting Disciples

> Thus those whose minds are ever unattached to wealth,
> Who are peaceful, restrained, perfectly diligent, settled,
> And are free of concepts with regard to existence and objects
> Are they who gather a host of sentient beings. (XVII, 80)

Thus, bodhisattvas engage in generosity with minds perpetually free of attachment to possessions. They are disciplined, their vows counteracting the definite negative actions[29] that result from attachment and so forth. Their mind streams are restrained by patience and so undisturbed by aversion. They possess transcendent diligence. Their minds rest in inner concentration, undistracted outwardly. And on account of their wisdom, they have no concepts of the attributes of existence (the five internal aggregates) or of objects (external phenomena such as forms) or of both. It is these bodhi-

---

29. "Definite negative actions" (Tib. *las lam*) refer to complete actions with a definite result that define the vows one takes. In taking a vow not to kill, for example, one promises to avoid actions that result in the victim's death. Stabbing someone, although obviously a negative action, is not the definite action of killing if it does not result in death.

sattvas who, having thus ripened themselves, use the four ways of attracting disciples to gather hosts of sentient beings and bring them to maturity.

This completes the explanation of the seventeenth chapter of *Ornament of the Mahāyāna Sūtras*, the chapter on the transcendent perfections and attracting disciples.

18

Offering, Reliance, and Boundless Attitudes

This chapter has four parts: (1) making offerings to the buddhas; (2) relying on a spiritual master; (3) meditating on the four boundless attitudes; and (4) a concluding summary.

1. Making Offerings to the Buddhas

> **In order to complete the two accumulations,**
> **Those whose minds are full of faith**
> **Offer to the buddhas robes and so forth,**
> **In both real and imagined ways. (XVIII, 1)**

The attitude with which offerings are made is one of very clear faith. The purpose is to complete the two accumulations. The field to which offerings are made is the buddhas. The offerings are Dharma robes, alms bowls, parasols, victory banners, flowers, and so forth ("and so forth" also includes such things as serving the buddhas and listening to the teachings)—in short, all kinds of things that can be offered. As to how these are offered, there are two ways. If it is at a time when a buddha's supreme nirmāṇakāya manifestation has appeared in the world, one makes the offering to the Buddha in person. At times when the Buddha is not present in the world, one imagines the tathāgatas before one, and in front of a statue, painting, or stūpa one makes the offerings to them in one's imagination.

> **The offering of one who has made the prayer**
> **That the coming of the Buddha be beneficial,**
> **Offered without conceptualizing the three spheres,**
> **Is a complete offering to the Buddha. (XVIII, 2)**

The offering of someone who has made the prayer that the Buddha will appear in the world; that one will meet him, make offerings to him, and please him; and that doing so will be meaningful for oneself and sentient beings, and all this without conceptualizing the field (the Buddha), the offerer (oneself), or the things being offered as having attributes, is a perfect and complete offering to the Buddha. If one makes an offering having prayed that one may always make boundless offerings directly to the buddhas of the ten directions in order to complete the two accumulations for oneself and all sentient beings, and in the state of mind that in ultimate truth is free of the concepts of the three spheres of offering, that offering is properly termed "complete."

> The different kinds of offerings include
> Bringing to maturity limitless sentient beings,
> Offering material things, and making offerings with the mind:
> Devotion, aspiration, (XVIII, 3)
>
> Compassion, patient forbearance,
> Correct practice,
> Focusing on the basics, realization,
> Liberation, and also suchness. (XVIII, 4)

With regard to the different categories of offering, one kind of offering to the buddhas is to bring infinite sentient beings to full maturation. To benefit sentient beings in this way is the best kind of offering that pleases the tathāgatas. In this case, one imagines that giving beings teachings particularly to arouse in their minds the wish to make offerings to the buddhas and induce them to do so, thus bringing them to maturity, is an offering that pleases the tathāgatas, and one offers it as such.

Another two categories, in terms of what is offered, comprise on the one hand offerings of a variety of material offerings such as Dharma robes and flowers, and on the other hand immaterial, mental offerings. Mental offerings are of nine kinds, from devotion to suchness, as follows:

(1) Devotion.[1] Although devotion—that is, thinking of the buddhas,

---

1. Tib. *mos pa*. This is a term with a variety of meanings, translated in its widest sense as "interest" in chapter 11. In the different contexts shown in this section, we have translated it as "devotion," "imagining," and "interest."

developing clear faith, and imagining that one is offering every kind of offering (those that are owned, those with no owner, mundane, and supramundane)—is a mental offering, it is taught in this context as being three things: interest, mental state, and mastery. Interest refers to interest in the Mahāyāna sūtras that show how to make offerings to the tathāgatas. This is also a mental offering.

Mental state has nine aspects: appreciation, rejoicing, delight, absence of complacency, vastness, joy, beneficence, freedom from defilements, and virtuous attitude. All these are also mental offerings. They are to savor the offerings one remembers having made in the past and those one is making at present, thinking how good they are; to rejoice in the offerings others make; to feel delighted at the offerings that both oneself and others will make in the future; to never be satisfied, even with unlimited offerings made to infinite objects over infinite periods of time; the vast, ceaseless attitude of the desire to make offerings uninterruptedly until one reaches the heart of enlightenment; love and joy with regard to all sentient beings, who are the field to be brought to maturity by making offerings; a desire to benefit all beings with one's offerings; freedom from defilements in being without attachment, pride, and so on, and not wishing for a tainted result;[2] and a virtuous attitude, which is to dedicate the offering so that all sentient beings attain the result, unsurpassable enlightenment.

Third, mastery is to make offerings to the tathāgatas making use of such means as the Sky Treasury concentration. This too is an offering made with the mind.

(2) Aspiration refers to arousing the mind intent on unsurpassable enlightenment and praying that in all one's lives, wherever one is reborn, one will benefit oneself and others and make infinite offerings to the tathāgatas. This too is a mental offering. It is also referred to as "dependence."[3]

(3) Compassion for sentient beings, that is, wanting to remove their sufferings, also becomes an offering to the tathāgatas.

(4) Forbearance in willingly accepting difficulties such as heat and cold, hunger and thirst, and fatigue in order to bring oneself and beings to maturity is also an offering to the tathāgatas.

---

2. Tib. *zag bcas kyi 'bras bu*, referring to a samsaric result such as mundane happiness and higher rebirth.

3. "Dependence" (Tib. *brten pa*) here refers to the fact that achieving benefit and making offerings depends on the aspiration to do so.

(5) Correctly practicing the six transcendent perfections is a means for making offerings to the buddhas.

(6) Focusing on impermanence, suffering, emptiness, and no-self, which are the basic points to be properly kept in mind, and analyzing things is also an offering to the buddhas.

(7) Once one has attained the first bodhisattva level, understanding the true nature of phenomena and giving rise to the correct view, which is the direct realization of the two kinds of no-self, is also an offering to the buddhas.

(8) Listeners are completely freed of the obscurations of defilements, and that liberation is the listeners' offering to the buddhas.

(9) After making offerings to the buddhas by gradually accomplishing the levels and transcendent perfections, bodhisattvas finally attain suchness, the elimination of both kinds of obscurations, and thereby attain unsurpassable enlightenment. This too is an offering to the buddhas.

These, then, are nine different kinds of mental offerings. Next, there are eight different points that apply to making offerings:

> **Offering has been explained**
> **In terms of the reason, dedication,**
> **Support, substance, cause,**
> **Gnosis, fields, and location. (XVIII, 5)**

(1) The reason one makes offerings is perfectly clear faith—that one considers that the Buddha, who is the consummation of all excellent qualities, is the supreme field of offering. (2) The fully ripened effect of making offerings is the completion of the two accumulations, that is, the attainment of unsurpassable enlightenment, to which one's offerings are entirely dedicated. (3) The support or basis is the buddhas, who are the object of offering. (4) The things offered are the various kinds of material and mental offerings. (5) The cause that leads one to make offerings is that one has prayed that one will coincide with the coming of a buddha and be able to make offerings to him. (6) Gnosis refers to the absence of concepts of the three spheres of offering. (7) The fields are sentient beings, for one makes the offering in order to bring countless sentient beings to maturity. (8) The location refers to both the material location and the location in the mind. If you were to ask what is the difference between the thing and its location, I think the difference is that it implicitly also indicates

the individual who possesses devotion and so forth, which is located in the mind.[4]

These eight points encompass the subjects of the four previous verses, in which the eight aspects have been explained.

> **Offerings are described in terms of**
> **Cause and result; self and others;**
> **Lesser and greater offerings,**
> **Which are two categories related to things acquired, (XVIII, 6)**
>
> **Veneration, and practice;**
> **Offerings made with pride and those without;**
> **And they are classified in terms of application,**
> **Transmigration, and aspiration. (XVIII, 7)**

There are a number of other ways of classifying offerings. In terms of the effect similar to the cause (the offerings one has made in the past being the cause that has resulted in one's making offerings now, and the offerings one is making at present being the cause that will result in one's making offerings in the future), such causal and resultant offerings are classified as past, present, and future offerings.

Offering one's own body and limbs, and listening to the teachings, reflecting on them, and so on, constitute the offering of oneself, or internal offerings. Inducing others to make offerings and offering one's own material belongings such as Dharma robes constitute the offering of others, or external offerings.

Offerings of things one has acquired (Dharma robes, alms, bedding, and so forth) and offerings of veneration (prostrations, folding one's hands in prayer, welcoming one's teacher, standing up in the teacher's presence, singing praises, and so on) are both lesser or gross offerings, while the offerings of practicing the sacred Dharma by listening, reflecting, and meditating are termed greater or subtle offerings, thus making two categories. Practice is again twofold: practice in the Lesser Vehicle, which is a lesser or inferior offering, and practice of the Great Vehicle, which is a greater or superior

---

4. "Location" or "state" here translates the Tibetan *gnas*, which can refer to the fact that a material or mental offering, at the very moment it is offered, is possessed as an offering by the person offering it, whether or not it is actually owned by them.

offering. Apart from the fact that this line is associated with the previous line, there does not appear to be a specific explanation for it.

Offerings that are not imbued with the gnosis free from the concepts of the three spheres of offering are offerings with pride. Those that are imbued with nonconceptual gnosis are free of pride. These two are also termed least and best offerings.

"Application" refers to the actual deed of offering, for which there are two kinds: offerings that are actually made at some other, later time, which are distant offerings, and offerings that are carried out at that very moment or when one thinks of doing so, which are proximate offerings. Similarly, offerings made in terms of transmigration are also of two kinds, distant and proximate—that is, offerings that are made at a later time, having been interrupted by two or many more lives after one has died, and offerings that are made immediately wherever one is reborn. Offerings are also held to be of two kinds, proximate and distant, in terms of aspiration: one can aspire to make offerings in this life or aspire to do so throughout one's series of lives.

> **Offerings made to the buddhas mentally are best,**
> **That is, with interest in the Dharma, the right mental state,**
>   **and mastery,**
> **Supported by nonconceptual means,**
> **And in a single identity with all. (XVIII, 8)**

The best kinds of offering are distinguished by the following features: devoted interest, whose object is the teachings of the Great Vehicle; the nine aspects of the mental state that is maintained, from savoring and rejoicing through to the virtuous attitude; mastery in making offerings through having attained concentrations such as the Sky Treasury concentration; the fully embraced skillful means of remaining free of the concepts of the three spheres; and the fact that from the eighth level onward, because of their spontaneous, effortless nonconceptual gnosis, the offerings made at that time by a single bodhisattva are offered in the same manner, indistinguishable from those of all the bodhisattvas on that level, and are equivalent to those of all bodhisattvas. It is on account of these features that bodhisattvas' offerings are the best compared to the offerings of mundane beings and listeners and solitary realizers.

2. Reliance on a Spiritual Master

Reliance on a spiritual master comprises three parts: (1) how to follow a spiritual master; (2) categories of doing so; and (3) the best way to follow a spiritual master. The first of these is divided into a brief introduction and a detailed explanation.

a. How to Follow a Spiritual Master[5]
i. Brief Introduction

> Reliance has been taught in terms of
> The support, basics, specific points,
> Dedication, cause, gnosis,
> Fields, and state. (XVIII, 9)

Following a spiritual master has been described in terms of eight aspects: the characteristics of the support, a spiritual master; the basic principles for following spiritual masters; specific points in relying on them; to what goal this is dedicated; the cause, which is to practice the spiritual master's instructions; the gnosis and learning one gains from a spiritual master; the fields, the container and contents that are to be purified; and the state from which one follows a spiritual master.

ii. Detailed Explanation

> Take as a teacher someone disciplined, peaceful, totally at peace,
> Possessed of superior qualities, diligence, and knowledge of the texts;
> Who has full realization, is skilled in explanation,
> Full of love, and indefatigable. (XVIII, 10)

(1) Because spiritual masters, the supports on which one relies, have bound their mind streams with the training in superior discipline, their senses are controlled. They have pacified defilements and distractions with the train-

---

5. The Tibetan term *bsten pa* has been translated in this section by both "rely" and "follow."

ing in superior concentration. They have completely pacified defilements and concepts with the training in superior wisdom. Their qualities such as discipline and learning are greater than one's own (that is, the disciple's), and if one relies on them, one will progress in virtue. (If, on the other hand, their qualities were the same as one's own or even less, there would be little point in following them.) These spiritual masters are also diligent in such things as teaching others the Dharma, and, since they have heard many teachings on the sacred Dharma, they are richly endowed with the transmissions. As for their qualities of realization, they have conclusively ascertained and realized thatness in relation to the four truths, dependent arising, emptiness, and so on. They are skilled in teaching the Dharma, clearly and relevantly. They are loving toward their disciples and never tire of teaching—they avoid such faults as being disinclined to teach the Dharma, not teaching properly, and teaching a little but not always carefully. These are the kinds of spiritual masters one should rely on.

> Follow the spiritual master with respect,
> With belongings, service, and practice.
> In accordance with those principles, the wise approach the spiritual master
> With a wish to know the Dharma, from time to time, respectfully. (XVIII, 11)

(2) Having found such spiritual masters, what are the basic principles for following them? Physical respect—prostrating to them, going to meet them or seeing them off, rising from one's seat, looking at them smilingly, with joyful eyes, and so on. Verbal respect, which includes praising them, speaking in accordance with whatever they say, and expressing oneself lovingly and respectfully. And mentally, having completely clear devotion toward them. By respecting them with one's body, speech, and mind in this way, one will follow them properly.

"Belongings" refers to following them by offering them whatever things they need, like Dharma robes and bedding. "Service" refers to serving them by attending to them (washing them, massaging them, and so forth) and carrying out any tasks that are appropriate. These ways of following them[6] constitute the outer way of doing so. The inner way of following them is

---

6. I.e., with respect, belongings, and service.

to do so through practice: practicing the Dharma correctly by listening, reflecting, and meditating in accordance with the teachings the spiritual masters have given. These outer and inner ways in which one should follow the spiritual master are what we call the "basic principles of reliance."

(3) Specific points. Knowing the specific points[7] and relying on a spiritual master with devotion, wise disciples should accordingly give up negative attitudes with regard to the teachings they are to receive—contempt, wanting to misappropriate the Dharma,[8] or seeking to criticize them—and they should adopt the attitude of wanting to really learn the Dharma. From time to time, they should go before the spiritual master and listen to the teachings, but not at inappropriate times such as when the spiritual master is meditating or taking a meal. When the moment is right, however, they should go into the master's presence, conducting themselves in a subdued manner, physically and mentally, and bowing down respectfully. They should never behave disrespectfully or arrogantly.

> **With no desire for veneration and wealth,**
> **They dedicate their reliance for the sake of accomplishment.**
> **The steadfast practice all that they've been taught,**
> **And that is what makes the master truly pleased. (XVIII, 12)**

(4) Dedication. To what goal is following a spiritual master dedicated, or for what purpose does one think of following a master and actually do so? One's following a spiritual master as described above should be free from desire—from being fixed on the idea that if one follows this person who is learned or famous, one will also become learned and famous oneself and be venerated by others and grow rich, or from the desire to dedicate one's following the spiritual master to that goal. Rather, one should follow one's spiritual masters in order to sincerely practice the three trainings in accordance with their instructions. With the determined wish, "May I follow them and, by listening to their teachings, reflecting on them, and meditating, may I accomplish the path of the noble beings and realize the meaning of ultimate reality," one dedicates one's reliance to that goal.

(5) Cause. The fact of the spiritual masters' being pleased is the causal

---

7. These specific points (Tib. *rgyu mtshan*) comprise the three points that follow: a proper attitude to the teachings, timely attendance, and respectful conduct.
8. I.e., to receive the teachings in order to become rich or famous.

factor that leads them to teach the Dharma and makes relying on them worthwhile. For this reason, a good disciple of stable character puts all the spiritual master's instructions into practice and accomplishes them. This is what truly delights the spiritual masters.

> Having become learned in the three vehicles and having realized them,
> They strive hard to accomplish their own vehicle.
> The purpose is to ripen countless beings,
> And as well to train in pure fields. (XVIII, 13)

(6) Gnosis. By hearing the Dharma from a spiritual master, one becomes learned in the three vehicles of the listeners, solitary realizers, and bodhisattvas and gains realization of the three vehicles oneself. This is the gnosis one acquires in dependence on the spiritual master. Having thus become learned in the three vehicles, bodhisattvas practice not the listeners' and solitary realizers' vehicles but their own vehicle, the Great Vehicle, exerting themselves in order to achieve their own and others' goals and to accomplish the result, the attainment of great enlightenment.

(7) Pure fields. It is from relying on a spiritual master that, in order to purify the beings or inner contents, one brings to full maturity limitless numbers of sentient beings by such means as listening to the Dharma; and that, in order to purify the universe or outer container, one trains in pure fields—buddha fields endowed with the ground of jewels, wish-fulfilling trees, rivers of nectar, and similar features of eternal perfection. It is for these purposes that one follows spiritual masters and listens to their teachings.

> They should rely fully on a spiritual master in order to possess the qualities
> For enjoying their share of the Dharma and not material gain. (XVIII, 14ab)

(8) "State" refers to the bodhisattvas' state of mind—what they keep in mind. Like people who each take what they most need as their share when their parent's or other relative's wealth is distributed, bodhisattvas have the qualities for enjoying their share of the sacred Dharma, and in order to do so they have to rely completely on a spiritual master. This is not so that they can enjoy their *material* share: they may have been attracted to the teacher

by material gifts, but they are not like some people who, instead of giving preeminence to the Dharma, listen to the teachings with material motives. This is on account of their state.

b. Categories

> The wise follow a spiritual master by cause and effect,
> In progressing from the door of Dharma and outwardly,
>   (XVIII, 14cd)
>
> By listening and with the yoga of mind,
> And with pride and without.
> The wise follow a spiritual master in terms of
>   transmigration,
> Application, and aspiration. (XVIII, 15)

Reliance on a spiritual master by the wise is classified in terms of cause and effect as follows. Following a spiritual master in previous lives is the cause, of which doing so at present is the result. Following a teacher at present is the cause, of which doing so in future lives will be the result. These, then, are three categories of following a spiritual master: past, present, and future.

By following spiritual masters and practicing their instructions and follow-up teachings, one acquires the concentration of the door of Dharma. Subsequently, one relies on a buddha or bodhisattva as a spiritual master to progress in that or to emulate those who have realized that. This is the inner aspect of reliance. Following a spiritual master with "belongings"[9] and so forth is the outer aspect of reliance.

Following spiritual masters simply by listening to the teachings—that is, hearing the sound of the Dharma from them—is gross or coarse reliance, because the mind is being distracted by just another sound. Doing the mental practice of reflection and meditation is fine or subtle reliance, because the mind is inwardly focused on the meaning.

Again, to cling to the concept that one is a real person following a real spiritual master by offering real service and so forth involves reliance with pride, which is the inferior kind of reliance. To be free of the concepts of attributes in oneself, a spiritual master, and the act of reliance is what we

9. See v. 11 above.

call "relying on a spiritual master with a mind free of pride," which is the best kind of reliance.

When the wise follow spiritual masters, there are two categories related to distance in terms of transmigration, two in terms of application, and two in terms of aspiration, making six categories of reliance on spiritual masters. What are these? Following spiritual masters in this life is proximate reliance. Following them after an interruption of many successive lives is distant reliance. In terms of application, when one follows a spiritual master in this life but at another, later time, or when one does so in other lives but not immediately, after an interruption of several successive lives, one's application in following the spiritual master is distant. On the other hand, application in following the master now, in this life, and in the very next life, is proximate. The same holds true for one's aspiration: reliance with the prayer that one will follow a master in this very life is proximate, while the prayer that one will follow a master in future lives is distant. These three pairs of categories are simply classifications of the strength or weakness of one's rebirth,[10] of one's application or practice, and of one's aspiration or intention.

c. The Best Way to Follow a Spiritual Master

> Following the sublime spiritual master mentally is best—
> That is, with interest in the Dharma, the right mental state,
>   and mastery,
> Supported by nonconceptual means,
> And in a single identity with all. (XVIII, 16)

The best way to rely on one's spiritual masters is mentally, and for this there are five aspects: following them with interest in the teachings of the Great Vehicle; following them with the nine kinds of mental state explained above, which you should know and adapt accordingly;[11] following them with mastery, that is, by having attained mastery in concentration and offering limitless riches with the Sky Treasury concentration, and by unforgettingly retaining the words and their meanings through the power

---

10. Tib. *rten*, lit. "support," i.e., the body or form one takes in a particular life.
11. See the section on mental offerings in verse 3 above. These nine mental states should be adapted to the context of following a teacher.

of memory; being completely imbued with nonconceptual methods; and, from the eighth level onward, engaging in following one's masters in a manner indistinguishable from and equivalent to that of all the bodhisattvas. Whichever of these five aspects one possesses, it will be superior to other ways of following a spiritual master.

3. Meditating on the Four Boundless Attitudes

Meditating on the four boundless attitudes is divided into two parts: (1) an explanation of the four boundless attitudes and (2) a specific explanation of compassion. The first of these is divided into six: (1) essence; (2) objects; (3) categories; (4) result; (5) countering factors; and (6) good qualities.

a. Explanation of the Four Boundless Attitudes
i. Essence

> **The pure states of the steadfast have abandoned countering agents,**
> **Are endowed with nonconceptual gnosis,**
> **Are applied to three kinds of objects,**
> **And bring sentient beings to maturity. (XVIII, 17)**

A bodhisattva's four boundless attitudes have four defining characteristics. The four pure states in the mind stream of a steadfast bodhisattva—love, compassion, joy, and impartiality—comprise the elimination of their four counteragents: respectively, malice, cruelty, displeasure, and a biased mind swayed by attachment and aversion. They are imbued with and accompanied by nonconceptual gnosis. They are practiced in three ways: with reference to sentient beings, with reference to phenomena, and with no reference. And their function is to bring sentient beings to full maturity without ever abandoning them. These are the four defining characteristics.

In this regard, to rid oneself of malice with a loving attitude and to wish that beings meet with happiness is the first distinguishing quality. To be free of the concepts of the three spheres—concepts, for instance, of someone who is meditating on love, of beings as the object, and of the love one is meditating on—is the second distinguishing quality. Applying love to three objects as follows is the third distinguishing quality. Love in ordinary beings and tīrthikas focuses on sentient beings, considering that oneself and sentient beings exist. As for listeners' and solitary realizers' love, for them there is no such thing as a so-called self and sentient beings, but they focus on these as merely multiple phenomena, that is, on the five aggregates, whose nature is multiplicity, impermanence, and suffering, and they thence give rise to love. The love of bodhisattvas who have reached the bodhisattva levels and of the buddhas has no concept of beings and phenomena existing in ultimate truth. It is from the state of their realization that sentient beings are devoid of essence (and that despite everything being, by nature, emptiness, they are experiencing the illusion-like sufferings that are their own deluded perceptions) that they perform infinite benefit for beings nonconceptually. Of these different approaches, the four boundless attitudes[12] focused on just sentient beings are common to all five—ordinary people and tīrthikas, listeners, solitary realizers, bodhisattvas, and buddhas. Love and so forth focused on phenomena are common to four: listeners, solitary realizers, bodhisattvas, and buddhas. Nonconceptual love is the uncommon love of the buddhas and bodhisattvas. This is explained in *Stages of Yogic Practice*. In the *Sūtra of the Teaching of Akṣayamati* we read:

> The love of bodhisattvas who have first aroused bodhicitta focuses on sentient beings, because these bodhisattvas have not directly realized either of the two kinds of no-self. The love of bodhisattvas who are engaged in the activities of the first to seventh levels focuses on phenomena, because they have directly realized the perfectly pure expanse of reality. The love of those on the eighth level up, who have attained the acceptance that phenomena are unborn, is nonconceptual, because love arises effortlessly, without thought.

ii. THE OBJECTS OF THE FOUR BOUNDLESS ATTITUDES

These attitudes of the steadfast are applied to
Those who wish for happiness, those tormented by suffering,

---

12. It should be noted throughout this section that although the four boundless attitudes are only truly "boundless" (Tib. *tshad med*) in the case of buddhas and bodhisattvas, they are used to denote love, compassion, joy, and impartiality in other beings as well, in much the same way as the term "enlightenment" (Tib. *byang chub*) is applied to listeners and solitary realizers who have purified the obscurations and attained the highest realization related to their respective paths even though theirs is not the perfect enlightenment of a buddha.

Those who are happy, and those with defilements,
And to the treatises on these, and to their suchness. (XVIII, 18)

The objects on which steadfast bodhisattvas focus with the four boundless attitudes are as follows. Focusing on sentient beings who want to be happy, their love takes the form of wishing that beings will meet with happiness. Their compassion focuses on beings tormented by suffering and takes the form of wishing that they will be free from suffering. Their joy focuses on sentient beings who are happy, and it takes the form of wishing that they will never separate from their happiness. And their impartiality focuses on sentient beings with defilements who, when they encounter pleasant feelings or friends, give rise to attachment, and when they encounter painful feelings or enemies, give rise to aversion; it takes the form of wishing that they may become even-minded, without attachment or aversion: "May attachment and aversion not arise in them." These lines indicate the different kinds of beings on which bodhisattvas focus.

Love focused on phenomena focuses on the sūtras of the Great Vehicle, which are the authentic scriptures that teach the four boundless attitudes, and thinks of those objects as simply productive entities.[13]

Nonconceptual love focuses on and is applied to the suchness (that is, the emptiness devoid of the duality of subject and object) of its object—the above four kinds of beings and the Mahāyāna teachings.

It is because of suchness that love is nonconceptual,
And because of its purity through attaining peace,
Because of the two kinds of action,
And because defilements have been exhausted. (XVIII, 19)

Nonconceptual love and so on can mean four different things. Because it focuses on the suchness of sentient beings and the teachings, it is referred to as "nonconceptual love," for it does not conceptualize them as self and phenomena or as outer and inner.

On the eighth level, at the stage of attaining the acceptance that phenomena are unborn, bodhisattvas have obtained the complete pacifica-

---

13. This interpretation of the Sanskrit word *dharma* (Tib. *chos*) as "teachings" (rather than "phenomena") appears to be peculiar to the *Sūtrālaṁkāra* and indeed has given rise to some debate. Here, the teachings are seen as entities that produce or create understanding of the four boundless attitudes and ultimately realization.

tion of conceptual thoughts and deliberate effort so that the seed of the four boundless attitudes has grown to its fullest extent and they happen spontaneously without effort or gross or subtle analysis. Because they have thus become perfectly pure, they are classified as nonconceptual boundless attitudes.

Loving physical and verbal actions both originate from love, with which they are causally consistent, but because they are included in the aggregate of form,[14] they are devoid of thought, so they are classified as nonconceptual love.

Because their attachment, aversion, and other defilements have been exhausted, the noble beings' love is referred to as nonconceptual. Defilements are termed mental concepts because they focus excessively on their object and fixate on it. As it is said in the sūtras, "Because the knots in their minds have been eliminated, concepts have been annihilated." So because they are devoid of such concepts, their love and other attitudes are nonconceptual.

It is for these four reasons that love is nonconceptual.

iii. Categories

> These attitudes are termed wavering, unwavering,
> Savored with attachment, and not savored.
> The attitudes of bodhisattvas remain
> Unwavering and free of attachment. (XVIII, 20)

The four boundless attitudes are of four kinds: Those whose aspects subsequently decline or deteriorate, which are termed "wavering." Those whose aspects are maintained and enhanced, which are "unwavering" and will not decline. Those that are said to be with defilements, where the concentration of the four boundless attitudes is attained but, because of attachment to it, is savored and considered sufficient, so that one does not seek more advanced qualities. And those that are said to be without defilements, which are not savored and do not give rise to a sense of satisfaction. Of these four categories, the four boundless attitudes of bodhisattvas remain unwavering and free of the attachment associated with relish and satisfaction: they are neither wavering nor defiled by defilements.

---

14. See *Treasury of Precious Qualities*, 377.

> In those who are, by nature, not concentrated,
> Who are lesser, middling, or on inferior levels,
> Whose motivation is inferior, or who have pride,
> Their love and so forth is inferior; in others it is superior.
>   (XVIII, 21)

Further categories of the four boundless attitudes are as follows. The four boundless attitudes based on the minds of beings in the world of desire, which are not concentrated by nature,[15] are lesser.

As to the worlds of form and formlessness, which are termed "concentrated," there are three realms related to the first dhyāna (the Pure, Gods Close to Brahmā or Priests of Brahmā, and Great Pure Ones), three realms related to the second dhyāna (Dim Light, and so on), and three related to the third dhyāna (Lesser Virtue, and so on); and there are three realms (Cloudless Light and the others) related to the fourth dhyāna, and the five pure abodes (Not Greater, and so on), making another eight realms in all. Of these, the four boundless attitudes of those in the realm of the Pure are lesser, the four of those in Gods Close to Brahmā are middling, and the four boundless attitudes of those in Great Pure Ones are greater. Of these three classifications of the boundless attitudes as lesser, middling, and greater on the "concentrated" levels, the lesser and middling are included in the lesser,[16] making, with the greater, two categories.

Again, "on inferior levels" refers to the fact that the boundless attitudes of those on respectively lower levels are inferior, and those in the minds of beings on higher levels are superior. The meditation on the four boundless attitudes of someone on the level of earnest aspiration is inferior and lesser compared to that of someone on the first bodhisattva level, which is superior and greater; and the meditation of someone on the first level is inferior to that of someone on the second level, which is superior—in this way they are classified as greater and lesser depending on the respective levels.

"Inferior motivation" refers to the four boundless attitudes of the listeners and solitary realizers, which, since they are not applied to the benefit of others, are lesser.

From the first level up to the seventh, they are accompanied by pride—that is, they are associated with conceptual thoughts and effort, and so are lesser.

---

15. Tib. *mnyam par bzhag pa'i ngo bo min*, not settled in evenness, or not meditational.
16. "Lesser" here refers to the general category "inferior" mentioned in the last line of the root verse.

Thus the four boundless attitudes of beings in nonconcentrated states, of those in the lesser and middling concentrated levels, those on respectively inferior levels, those with inferior motivation, and those with pride are all inferior and therefore lesser. Besides these, the four boundless attitudes of others are to be understood as superior or great—that is, the boundless attitudes of those who are great in the context of meditative concentration; those who are on respectively higher levels and not on the inferior levels; bodhisattvas and tathāgatas, whose motivation is not inferior; and those on the three pure levels, beginning with the eighth, who do not have conceptual thoughts and effort and are therefore free of pride.

iv. Result

> The wise who abide forever in these pure states
> Are born in the world of desire.
> By means of them, they complete the accumulations
> And bring beings to maturity. (XVIII, 22)

> In all their lives, they will never part from pure states
> And will be free from their counteragents.
> Even when they are not paying heed,
> They will never be overwhelmed by circumstances. (XVIII, 23)

In general, the result of training in the four boundless attitudes is rebirth in the world of form. However, wise bodhisattvas who constantly abide in these pure states—love and the others—have perfectly fit minds and inconceivable powers of concentration, and they therefore take rebirth in the world of desire in order to constantly benefit beings. This is the fully ripened effect. By training in the four boundless attitudes, bodhisattvas complete the accumulations of merit and wisdom, this being the conditioning or environmental effect. Bodhisattvas who possess the four boundless attitudes introduce beings who have not yet entered the doctrine to the teachings, and bring those who have already done so to ever-increasing stages of maturity. This comes about on account of their diligence as the proliferating effect. As a result of training in this life, in all their future lives they will never separate from the pure states, which is the effect similar to the cause. And the fact that they are free from malice and the other three factors that counter the four pure states is the separational effect.

The Sign of the Extent to Which One Has Trained in the Pure States

The sign or mark that bodhisattvas have trained in the pure states and are free of their countering factors is that although they may not be meditating specifically on love and the other boundless attitudes as the antidote to malice and so forth, but are rather conducting themselves casually or not particularly attentively, even in the face of overwhelming circumstances that would give rise to malice, their love and so forth will never degenerate. These two lines may be considered either as a digression within, and forming part of, this subsection on the result or as a separate, fifth subsection, in which case there would be a total of seven subsections in this section on the four boundless attitudes.

v. Countering Factors

> Bodhisattvas who have the wish to harm,
> Who are cruel, unappreciative,
> And full of malice, attachment, and desire,
> Are affected by many kinds of negative consequences.
> (XVIII, 24)

The defects of bodhisattvas who fail to keep the four boundless attitudes are as follows. Their thoughts are on preventing sentient beings from being happy by killing, beating, or otherwise harming them so as to make them suffer, which runs counter to love. They act cruelly, physically beating them up and so on, which runs counter to compassion, the wish that they be free from suffering. As a result of jealousy, they feel unappreciative and displeased when they see beings who are happy, which runs counter to joy. They give rise to malice when they have painful feelings or see enemies and other such beings, and they give rise to attachment and desire when they have pleasant feelings or see friends and the like, and that runs counter to impartiality. Those who possess these counteragents to the four boundless attitudes will be affected by a great many negative consequences in the form of all kinds of physical and mental suffering. What are these negative consequences?

> Because of defilements, they destroy themselves,
> Destroy sentient beings, and destroy their discipline.

> These degenerate beings have few resources
> And are disparaged by protectors and the Teacher alike.
> (XVIII, 25)
>
> Subject to arguments and unpleasant gossip,
> In other lives they will be born deprived of freedom;
> Since they will lose what they have acquired and what they have not,
> They will suffer greatly in their minds. (XVIII, 26)

On account of defilements like malice and cruelty, they will commit negative actions like taking life, as a result of which they will be crushed by suffering—in this life, they will be killed, imprisoned, and so forth; and in other lives, they will be reborn in the hells and other such realms. On account of the same defilements, they will destroy sentient beings by doing violence to others' lives, property, spouses, and so forth. And since acting in that way will violate the vows they have properly taken, they will also destroy their discipline.

Those who have deteriorated their discipline like this will think, "I have abandoned the path praised by the noble beings that leads to rebirth in the higher realms, and I have set out on the path followed by wicked, ordinary beings, the path to the lower realms. I am ruined!" Their minds thus tormented or full of remorse, they will feel daunted and downcast. Moreover, those who formerly were their benefactors will think of these monks who have deteriorated their discipline, "These people are evildoers—they are not worth supporting" and will cease to offer them anything. Likewise, others will treat them with contempt and not consider them to be worthy of offerings, so they will receive less of robes, food and drink, and anything else they need. Even the gods and similar beings who protected them in the past, when they observed proper discipline, will now disparage them and will henceforth cease to protect them. Similarly, they will also receive reproaches such as our teacher, the Buddha, made on numerous occasions, according to the Vinaya and other texts, when he said, "This monk is not fit to be a monk. He has fallen back from the principles of a śramaṇa. He is behaving like an ass. He's no better than a corpse."

Furthermore, those degenerate monks' colleagues will naturally censure them and object to them, saying, "It is not right for us to stay with him," for it is their duty to punish such monks, expel them, and so on. People will say unpleasant things about them everywhere: "He has broken his vows and committed such and such evil deeds." These individuals who have destroyed their discipline will gain much suffering not only in this life but also in other lives, being reborn in the hells and other states where there is no opportunity to practice the Dharma. The learning, discipline, four boundless attitudes, and so forth that they had previously acquired in their mind streams will fade away, and since they will subsequently be unable to acquire any as yet unacquired enlightened attributes, the qualities they have not yet acquired will be lost too. As a result, they will suffer unbearably, their minds filled with anguish and regret.

These, then, are the grave consequences of letting the countering factors, defilements, proliferate through not having their antidotes, love and the others.

vi. Good Qualities

> All these faults never occur
> In those who abide properly in love and the other attitudes.
> Free of defilements, for the sake of sentient beings,
> They never abandon saṃsāra. (XVIII, 27)

All these defects just described never occur in those who abide properly in love and the other three boundless attitudes, because, on account of their wisdom, their having the four boundless attitudes is not tainted by defilements like attachment. And although they are without defilements, through compassion, for the sake of other sentient beings, they do not abandon saṃsāra but take birth in saṃsāra and bring beings to maturity.

> The thoughts of love and so forth
> That the Buddha's children have for sentient beings
> No being can feel, even for
> Their one and only perfect child. (XVIII, 28)

Even in the entirety of ordinary beings there is nothing like the bodhisattvas' thoughts of love and the other three boundless attitudes with which they bring benefit and happiness to all sentient beings. No father or mother can give rise to anything like the love bodhisattvas have, even for an only, beloved, adorable child full of virtues.

b. A Specific Explanation of Compassion

The specific explanation covers nine topics.

i. The Objects of Bodhisattvas' Compassion

> Their compassion touches sentient beings
> Who are ablaze, who are overpowered by enemies,
> Who are oppressed by suffering or obscured by darkness,
> Who tread the hardest path, (XVIII, 29)
>
> Who are weighed down by great chains,
> Who are addicted to poisoned food,
> Who have completely lost the way,
> Who are following mistaken paths, and who are weak. (XVIII, 30)

There are ten objects of a bodhisattva's compassion. As they consider the beings in the world of desire, who are blazing with attachment to the five sense pleasures, bodhisattvas give rise to intense compassion, thinking, "Alas! Without ever satisfying their desires, these beings are rendered helpless by the fiercely blazing fire of attachment."

In the same way, they give rise to compassion for those who, even if they have begun performing positive actions, have fallen under the influence of obstacles created by enemies and demons and have given up their practice of virtue.

They give rise to intense compassion when they think of sentient beings who, born in the three lower realms, are going through the most terrible experiences or who, even in the higher realms, are oppressed by the sufferings of birth, aging, sickness, death, and so on.

They feel compassion for beings who commit negative actions—butchers, hunters, robbers, and the like—who, obscured by the gloom of ignorance, do not know that, from engaging in killing and other negative physical, verbal, and mental activities that are the cause of suffering, they will consequently suffer in the hells and other realms.

They give rise to compassion for beings without potential[17] who never give a thought to liberation. They have wandered for endless lifetimes in saṃsāra and are thus fully engaged on the hardest path of all.

---

17. Tib. *rigs chad pa*. See ch. 4.

They give rise to compassion for non-Buddhist tīrthikas, who are completely fettered by the view of "I" and "mine" and all kinds of other wrong views.

They give rise to compassion for beings in the world of form and the formless world. Such beings consider that just their meditative absorption amounts to liberation and bliss, and so they savor it and are attached to it, just as one might be attached to good, delicious food mixed with poison. But even though that absorption, like the food, is blissful at the time, its very nature in the end is to fade away, and it does not, therefore, go beyond saṃsāra.

They feel intense compassion when they consider tīrthikas who mistakenly perceive their discipline and ascetic practices—being scorched by five fires,[18] throwing themselves to their death off cliffs, and so forth—as the path and who use this to seek liberation. They have strayed completely from the true path.

They give rise to compassion for listeners and for bodhisattvas of unfixed potential who have set out on the path of the listeners or solitary realizers, for even though they have begun the path to liberation, they have strayed from the path of the Great Vehicle that accomplishes both one's own and others' goals, and they are completely involved in inferior paths.

And they feel compassion for enfeebled beings who, even though they have set out on the Mahāyāna path, have not completed the accumulations that act as favorable conditions and have been seized by adverse circumstances, so that they are unable to practice the path properly.

On the basis of these ten objects, we can therefore distinguish ten categories of compassion that bodhisattvas give rise to.

ii. The Results of Considering Sentient Beings with Compassion

> The rejection of harm, the seeds of supreme enlightenment,
> The creation of happiness and acceptance of pain,
> The cause for everything they desire, and the yielding of compassion itself—
> For the Buddha's children who rely on these qualities,
> enlightenment is not far off. (XVIII, 31)

---

18. See ch. 13, note 7.

What are the results that one obtains from considering sentient beings with compassion? Those who are endowed with compassion have completely given up anything that harms sentient beings, such as beating them up. This is the separational effect of compassion. The conditioning effect is that they gather the two accumulations that are seeds of supreme enlightenment. The proliferating effect is that they make other beings happy and remove their sufferings, and that they willingly accept all sorts of discomforts such as heat, cold, and fatigue in order to achieve that. The fully ripened effect is that those with compassion will be reborn wherever they wish to be reborn; their compassion creates the cause for anything they wish. As for the effect similar to the cause, by training in compassion in their previous lives, in their future lives too their compassion will grow continuously more and more; in other words, it will yield compassion itself. For bodhisattvas who rely on these five qualities of compassion, unsurpassable enlightenment is not far away and will be swiftly attained.

iii. The Function of Compassion Associated with Wisdom

> **Those with compassion and the highest intelligence,**
> **Knowing that everything in saṃsāra is suffering**
> **And devoid of self, will never be discouraged,**
> **Nor will they be much troubled by its faults. (XVIII, 32)**

Because of their supreme intelligence, that is, wisdom, bodhisattvas who possess great compassion know that all the external and internal phenomena included in the three worlds of saṃsāra are by nature impermanent and unsatisfactory, with the three kinds of suffering that can be subdivided further into many, many different kinds of suffering, and they know that these phenomena are empty and devoid of self. So they never get discouraged by the sufferings of saṃsāra, and they work compassionately for others' benefit. With their wisdom, they know that saṃsāra is without intrinsic existence, so they will never be greatly troubled by the ills of saṃsāra—sufferings such as birth, aging, sickness, and death—and by defilements such as attachment and aversion.

> **Those with tenderness, seeing the world's pain as their own,**
> **Know just what suffering is**
> **And the means for eliminating it.**
> **Though pained by it, they will never be discouraged. (XVIII, 33)**

Those with tenderness for others, regarding the three sufferings of all worlds as if it were their own suffering, fully realize just what that suffering is and the way to eliminate it—namely, to know the origin or cause of suffering as well as its antidote, the path, and the cessation. As a result, even though they cannot remain indifferent to others' suffering but are pained[19] by it, since they know the method for dispelling it, they never become discouraged by such suffering.

iv. Categories of Compassion

> This tenderness of those whose nature is compassion
> Is fourfold: natural, analytic,
> Related to former training,
> And acquired with the purity that weakens its
>   counteragents. (XVIII, 34)

This tenderness[20] of bodhisattvas who are the embodiment of compassion is of four kinds: (1) Natural, meaning that bodhisattvas are naturally compassionate on account of their potential. (2) Analytic, in that as methods for training the mind in compassion, bodhisattvas examine such things as the good qualities of compassion, the disadvantages of not having compassion, the way in which sentient beings helplessly wander amid the three kinds of suffering, how they have been one's relatives and friends countless times, and how, despite their all being the same in wanting to be happy and not wanting to suffer, their behavior runs counter to what they most wish for. (3) The tenderness of one who has trained in compassion in the past. And (4) the tenderness of one who has acquired the perfectly pure compassion that weakens countering factors such as malice and cruelty. This last refers to acquiring compassion free of attachment, whereby one does not give rise to attachment or aversion to anything or anyone at all.

There are thus four categories: natural, analytical, trained, and attained with freedom from attachment.

---

19. Vasubandhu points out in his commentary that "pained" (Tib. *nyam nga ba*) here means "compassionate" (*snying rje*).

20. It should be noted that throughout this section on compassion (Tib. *snying rje*) we have used "tenderness" or "tender love" to translate the Tibetan word *brtse ba* (which has a wide range of meanings, including love, compassion, tenderness, and affection), reserving the word "love" for the Tibetan term *byams pa*, the first of the four boundless attitudes.

v. The Particular Qualities of Great Compassion

This topic is divided into (1) the main explanation and (2) the greatness of great compassion indicated by the use of analogies.

(1) Main Explanation

> **That which is not uniform or constant, which is without superior intention,**
> **Which lacks the means for accomplishment, and is neither free from attachment**
> **Nor nonconceptual is not tenderness.**
> **Those who thus have no tender love are not bodhisattvas.**
>   (XVIII, 35)

Unless one's compassion is uniform, it is not great compassion. It is no different from ordinary beings' compassion or that of listeners and solitary realizers. In what way? Even though they may feel compassion for beings who are experiencing the suffering upon suffering, they do not give rise to compassion for those who feel happy or those with neutral feelings. Theirs is unequal compassion, and therefore not great compassion. Bodhisattvas, on the other hand, see that none of the tainted feelings that beings experience, whether happy, painful, or neutral, are anything other than the three kinds of suffering, and they therefore feel the same compassion, equally—as much for the beings in the Hell of Torment Unsurpassed as for those at the Peak of Existence. This is why it is referred to as "the great compassion of sameness."

Ordinary beings' compassion, which they feel intermittently, and that of listeners and solitary realizers, whose compassion for beings, however deep, is spent once they become arhats with no residual aggregates,[21] are interrupted and inconstant, and they cannot therefore be called "great compassion." The compassion of bodhisattvas arises continuously, at all stages of the path of learning, and is never spent even when they enter the expanse of nirvāṇa without residual aggregates. It is constant compassion, and therefore great compassion.

Compassion that lacks the superior intention of shouldering responsibility for others' welfare refers to ordinary beings' compassion, which is mixed

---

21. Lit. "at the time of nirvāṇa without residual aggregates."

with their own self-interest, and is merely felt for friends and relatives and other beings whom they consider as "mine" and for those who help them. It also refers to the compassion of listeners and solitary realizers, who have not realized the sameness of themselves and others and therefore do not have the motivation of taking responsibility for others' welfare. These beings' compassion cannot be called "great compassion." Bodhisattvas, on the other hand, once they have attained the first level, have directly realized the ultimate reality, the sameness of themselves and others, and because of their motivation they make no distinction between their own and others' goals. Their compassion, which is coupled with the superior intention of taking responsibility for others' welfare, is great compassion.

Certain people may feel some compassion when they see sentient beings suffering, but they do not have the means to actually accomplish protecting them from suffering. That tenderheartedness is not great compassion. The listeners and solitary realizers similarly have a certain compassion for all suffering beings, but it does not enable them to protect them from suffering. Bodhisattvas work to accomplish the benefit and happiness of sentient beings until the end of saṃsāra, so theirs is great compassion.

Ordinary beings may have compassion for those dear to them, but not all the time, and sometimes they get angry with them, and they feel hatred for their enemies, so they are not free of defilements. The noble listeners and solitary realizers do not actually have aversion, but they have not eliminated the subtle habitual tendencies to aversion. So in neither of these two cases can their compassion be called "great compassion." Bodhisattvas are free of attachment, that is, of the latent tendencies to aversion and violence, which are the counteragents of compassion, so theirs is great compassion.

Even if one has compassion, if it is not free of the conceptual attributes of the three spheres of compassion, it is not great compassion. But compassion endowed with nonconceptual gnosis is great compassion. Although this is held to be the case for bodhisattvas from the eighth level onward—when nonconceptuality is fully ripened—it is not inappropriate to apply it also to noble bodhisattvas in general.

The culmination of the bodhisattvas' compassion as described here is the spontaneous nonconceptual compassion that on the buddha level is called "Great Compassion."[22] Whether or not one associates great compassion

---

22. Tib. *thugs rje*, the honorific of *snying rje*, both terms bearing the etymological meaning of "heart lord." At the buddha level, *thugs rje* can refer more to the Buddha's

and Great Compassion with the same original Sanskrit term, they mean the same, and the important thing to understand in this context is why they are distinguished as "great," which is what has just been explained. Any tender love that is described with these six aspects—unequal, inconstant, devoid of superior intention, lacking the means for accomplishment, not free from attachment, and not nonconceptual—is not the tenderness that is great compassion. But if it has the six opposite qualities, it is great compassion. Without this great tender love, as has just been explained, one cannot be referred to as a "bodhisattva with great compassion."

(2) The Greatness of Great Compassion Indicated by the Use of Analogies

> **That which possesses compassion, forbearance, intention,**
> **Aspiration, taking birth, and the maturation of sentient beings—**
> **The first being the root; the last, the sublime fruit—**
> **Is the great tree of compassion. (XVIII, 36)**

Just as a fine fruit tree, for example, has six aspects—a root, trunk, branches, leaves, flowers, and fruit—in great compassion too (the subject of this analogy) there are the following aspects: (1) the great compassion that is the wish to protect all sentient beings from suffering; (2) arising from that, the patience to go through all kinds of difficulties for others' sake; (3) the intention to realize the various means for benefiting beings; (4) the aspiration that in all one's future lives, one may be reborn in a perfect situation, with a perfect body and abundant riches and entourage, by means of which one may benefit beings; (5) the taking of numerous births in which, by the power of one's prayers, wherever one is reborn in one's series of lives, one benefits oneself and others; and (6) the bringing, by the above means, of all sentient beings to full maturation.

The first of these, great compassion, is, as it were, the root of the other five; it is the rootlike prerequisite for all the bodhisattva qualities, as is stated in the *Sūtra of the Teaching of Akṣayamati*:

> Venerable Śāriputra, it is thus. Let us use an analogy. Exhaling

---

all-pervading activity for sentient beings than simply compassion understood in a limited sense as a mental function.

and inhaling in order to breathe is prerequisite to a person's ability to live. Similarly, in order to accomplish the Great Vehicle properly, a bodhisattva's great compassion must come first.

And in the *Sūtra on the Mountain Gayāśīrṣa* we read:

> The root of a bodhisattva's bodhicitta is great compassion. Sentient beings are its object.

The last of the above aspects, bringing sentient beings to maturity, is the sublime, fully ripened fruit from the tree. That which possesses all these "is the great tree of compassion." In other words, on the basis of the root, great compassion, the trunk appears—that is, the patience to put up with all kinds of suffering for the sake of sentient beings. Then from the trunk, forbearance, there grow the bough-like intentions regarding the means for liberating beings from suffering. From the boughs of these intentions, aspirations sprout like leaves—aspirations that, since it is impossible to benefit the infinity of sentient beings in just one lifetime, one will gradually, in all one's rebirths, take birth as limitless sentient beings. From the leaves of those aspirations, the flowers of taking birth wherever one wishes for the sake of sentient beings blossom. And from the flowers of rebirth there comes the fruit—the bringing of sentient beings to maturity. In this way, great compassion is praised as if it were an excellent fruit tree.

There now follows a detailed explanation of this. First, it is shown that without the root, the rest are prevented from occurring.

> **If the root, compassion, is absent,**
> **There will not be the forbearance to put up with hardship.**
> **If the wise cannot endure suffering,**
> **They will not have the intention to help beings. (XVIII, 37)**
>
> **Their minds devoid of that intention,**
> **They will not pray for positive and pure rebirths.**
> **And if they do not achieve a good rebirth,**
> **They will never bring sentient beings to maturity. (XVIII, 38)**

Just as without a tree's roots nothing, from the trunk to the fruit, will grow, if the rootlike great compassion is absent, one will have not the mental forbearance to willingly accept going through difficult practices for the sake of beings. One will be like ordinary beings, who feel tender love toward their relatives and exert themselves for their sake even if it is difficult but make no effort for anyone else's welfare. Or they will be like listeners and solitary realizers, who do not undergo hardships for the sake of sentient beings. Bodhisattvas, on account of their great compassion, never turn away from undergoing hardships for beings' sake.

If the wise cannot put up with suffering themselves for the sake of others, they will not have the intention "I must use this or that means to help sentient beings," for even if there exists such a means, they will be unable to accomplish it by themselves and so neither will they think of doing so.

Those whose minds lack the intention to work for the welfare of sentient beings will never make prayers of aspiration to be reborn in such a way as to benefit sentient beings—rebirths that are positive in not being adulterated by negative actions, and perfectly pure in not being sullied by self-interest. Bodhisattvas' aspirations amount to a wish to work for the welfare of sentient beings, and thus to taking rebirth in saṃsāra—not like mundane beings, who perform positive actions with the intention or wish to gain happiness in the higher realms, nor like listeners and solitary realizers, who have abandoned rebirth in saṃsāra.

If they do not, by the power of their aspirations, obtain a good rebirth that will bring benefit to sentient beings here in existence, they will not thereby bring beings to full maturation. Either, like ordinary beings, they will obtain a birth that is the fully ripened effect of their karmic actions, in which they are unable to mature beings, or, like listeners and solitary realizers, they will have cut the stream of rebirths and will therefore not work for the good of beings.

Thus, without the root, great compassion, it is impossible for the other five to appear, from the trunk of forbearance through to the fruit, the maturation of sentient beings. If the root is present, all the rest will follow, and how this happens is explained next.

> Know that with love watering their compassion,
> From their happiness when they suffer,
> It expands and grows; and from proper attentiveness,
> The great boughs grow and spread. (XVIII, 39)

> The unbroken stream of their aspirations,
> Like leaves that are cast off and renewed,

> Is fulfilled by two causes, as a result of which
> The flowers and fruit bring benefit. (XVIII, 40)

When one waters the root of a tree, it becomes robust and grows, and then from it everything from the trunk to the fruit appears and develops on a magnificent scale. So it is with the watering or irrigation or moistening of compassion, the root, with love—as explained in Sthiramati's commentary.[23] Some commentaries appear to explain the Tibetan word *'chu ba*[24] as if it were the root of the root, referring to the tiny rootlets of a tree by which it draws up the water from the earth, as in the popular expression that a fully grown tree is "that which drinks with its feet." However, such rootlets are part of the root itself, which would mean in this context explaining *'chu ba* as the root itself, compassion—for love and compassion would naturally go together, and instead of just compassion being the root, one would have to distinguish love as still another root. Rather, it would seem better to understand love as being the watering or moistening of the root itself, helping it to grow, as explained in the commentary. "With love watering their compassion" occurs in the root text and is explained like that in the commentary, so *'chu ba* must be used in the sense of the verb with the meaning of watering or wetting, the rootlets drinking or drawing up water or the root being sprinkled or drenched with water.

So, in order to make the root, compassion, grow, it is irrigated with love, so to speak. If compassion, the root, is moistened by the water of loving thoughts, compassion will increase. When bodhisattvas consider beings who are suffering, they have compassion (the wish to free them of suffering), and through that, with love (the wish that they be happy) and the consequent desire to accomplish their benefit and happiness, they see all beings as their beautiful and greatly beloved child. When a child falls sick, it does not occur to the parents that the difficulties they go through as they strive to rid the child of disease and restore him or her to good health are making them suffer. Thinking, "This medicine, this treatment, is what will help my child," they feel nothing but joy in making every effort with that treatment. In the same way, bodhisattvas full of love for sentient beings go through the experience of physical and mental suffering for the sake of others, but because of their loving wish to help beings, they perceive it as

---

23. "Love" in the commentary on these two verses translates the Tibetan *byams pa*, the first of the four boundless attitudes. See note 20.

24. *'chu ba*, translated here as "watering."

blissful, thinking, "Since it is for their sake, this is not painful but the most sublime thing, to be willingly accepted." Thus, the trunk of forbearance, for which there is nothing that cannot be borne, will expand and grow. As a result of their forbearance increasing extensively, bodhisattvas are properly attentive to the means for benefiting others—the two kinds of no-self, preternatural knowledge, form and the other phenomena included in the two truths, and the infinite different kinds of skillful means—and thus the great manifold boughs of their altruistic intention grow and spread. As a result of that, bodhisattvas unceasingly, throughout countless lives, make great prayers of aspiration to continuously bring about benefit and happiness for the sake of sentient beings. Thus they shed the small, old leaves of their previous aspirations and increasingly assume the new leaves of ever-greater aspirations. These aspirations are fulfilled by the two causes for producing the flowers of their taking birth and the fruit of their bringing others to maturity, as a result of which the flowers of rebirth materialize and produce the fruit, the maturation of countless sentient beings by the individuals in which the bodhisattvas have taken birth. It is thus that both flowers and fruit are to be understood as taking substance,[25] or appearing. Just as the direct cause of the fruit tree itself and the cooperative conditions of the soil, water, and so forth bring about the appearance of the flowers and fruit, bodhisattvas' taking birth and bringing others to maturity are brought about on account of both their own aspirations and their object, sentient beings.[26]

vi. In Praise of the Qualities of Compassion

This topic comprises two parts: (1) a general exposition in three parts and (2) a specific explanation of points that are difficult to understand.

---

25. Tib. *don yod pa*. Although the meaning here seems to be that the flowers and fruit appear, the Tibetan term usually also carries the meaning, which we have employed for the translation of the root text, of being beneficial or worthwhile.

26. In other words, their aspirations are fulfilled by the primary cause (or internal condition) of the aspirations themselves (just as the flowers and fruit are produced from the development of the tree itself) and the secondary (or external) condition of the presence of sentient beings whom they will bring to maturity (like the conditions of suitable soil, rainfall, etc., that cause the tree to blossom and bear fruit).

(1) A General Exposition in Three Parts

(a) The Emergence of Great Qualities

> Since great compassion is the source of qualities,
> Who would not have compassion for sentient beings?
> Even though they thus feel pain for them,
> Aroused through tenderness, it produces immeasurable bliss. (XVIII, 41)

Since great compassion is the source of the ten strengths, the four fearlessnesses, and the other infinite qualities of buddhahood, which is the final result, what intelligent persons would not consider sentient beings compassionately? It is entirely appropriate to do so. One might think, "If I have compassion for beings, for their sake I myself will suffer, and that will be difficult to bear." But it is not like that. "Even though they thus feel pain for those beings"—even though in this way those bodhisattvas are pained on account of their compassion for beings, their pain is not like other suffering, because through that suffering or product of their tenderness, all suffering gradually comes to end, and there arises an immeasurable happiness greater than any mundane bliss or indeed that of the listeners and solitary realizers.

(b) The Quality of Nonattachment

> Those with tenderness, who are imbued with compassion,
> Do not even set their minds on peace,
> Let alone become attached
> To mundane bliss or their own lives. (XVIII, 42)

"If I give rise to compassion," one might wonder, "will it not become a fetter, holding me down through attachment to sentient beings?" No. Unlike the listeners and solitary realizers, tender bodhisattvas, whose mind streams are completely imbued with compassion, do not even have attachment to and set their minds on the nirvāṇa in which suffering has been completely pacified, so what need is there to mention their becoming attached, like ordinary beings, to tainted, mundane happiness and to their own bodies and lives? They are not attached to anything in saṃsāra or nirvāṇa.

(c) The Quality of Sublimity

> Ordinary love is not beyond reproach,
> Nor is it supramundane.
> The love the wise feel in their tenderness
> Is irreproachable and has gone beyond the world. (XVIII, 43)

Among ordinary people, the love such as a mother has for her children is not beyond reproach,[27] nor is it supramundane. Through attachment to children and the like, one performs negative actions for their sake, and one feels aversion to those who do not get on with them, so because such love is mixed with defilements it is not in any way free of shameful deeds. And because it is associated with bewilderment, the belief in the phenomenal and individual kinds of self, it is not supramundane. The love that arises because of the tenderness that wise bodhisattvas feel for sentient beings is free of shameful deeds and is supramundane. In what way is it free of shameful deeds?

> It is the means for leading ordinary beings
> Dwelling in the gloom of ignorance
> And on the flooding waves of suffering.
> How could it not be free of fault? (XVIII, 44)

As a result of their relying on the great darkness that is ignorance of the four noble truths, ordinary beings drift on the great river of saṃsāra, violently buffeted about on the flooding waves of the three kinds of suffering. If the cause that sets up the great means for leading them to liberation is the bodhisattva's compassion and love, how could it not be irreproachable? One can be absolutely confident that it is free of shameful deeds.

> If in this world, enlightened by themselves,
> The arhats do not have such love,
> What need to speak of anybody else?
> How could it not be supramundane? (XVIII, 45)

---

27. Tib. *kha na ma tho ba med pa*, also translated in this section as "free of shameful deeds," "shameful" meaning "that which cannot be mentioned" or "that which cannot be praised," and referring to any kinds of physical, verbal, or mental action that produces suffering.

In what way is their love supramundane? In this world, even the solitary-realizer arhats, who have the sharpest faculties and have awakened themselves to, or realized by themselves, the enlightened gnosis of exhaustion and nonarising, do not have this kind of love, let alone others like listeners and mundane beings. So how could the bodhisattva's love and tenderness not be supramundane? If it transcends even that of the listeners and solitary realizers, who are supramundane beings, one need hardly mention its being beyond the world.

(2) A Specific Explanation of Points That Are Difficult to Understand

Earlier we mentioned that although bodhisattvas suffer for others' sake, that produces happiness. This will now be explained in detail.

> **Bodhisattvas do not suffer,**
> **Yet any pain they feel through tender love**
> **At first makes them afraid,**
> **But once they have arrived, it gives them the greatest joy.**
>   (XVIII, 46)

> **The pain that comes through tenderness**
> **Will outshine every mundane happiness,**
> **And even those who've reached their goal don't have it.**
> **What could be more wonderful that?** (XVIII, 47)

Although bodhisattvas in that situation do not suffer themselves (or alternatively, according to the commentary, in order that others do not suffer), because of their tenderness they experience mental suffering on behalf of others. This verse shows that however great that suffering is, it is not something to be afraid of. Less courageous people, when they reflect on the sufferings of sentient beings in detail, might consider them extremely intense and difficult to bear. They are as infinite as sentient beings. "Who," they might wonder, "would be able to dispel those sufferings? Giving away our head and limbs and putting up with the ingratitude of beings who wrongly acknowledge what we have done for them must be difficult to bear. If we take birth in saṃsāra, we will have to go through the experiences of birth, aging, sickness, and death, as well as all kinds of sufferings in that situation.

Sentient beings who suffer are so numerous, and if we take the burden of their suffering on ourselves, how will we ourselves ever be free from suffering?" But we should not think like this and feel disheartened. Why? On the level of earnest aspiration, any pain we feel on account of our tender love for sentient beings, as has just been mentioned, does make us thoroughly afraid, because we have not acquired the attitude of the sameness of ourselves and others and have not realized that saṃsāra and all its suffering are emptiness. For that reason, as is mentioned in the sūtras, one should not at first put the emphasis on giving those who have the bodhisattva potential only the teachings that deal predominantly with the sufferings of saṃsāra and disenchantment, but rather give teachings on compassion and illusion-like phenomena, and ones that praise the qualities of the buddhas and bodhisattvas.

"Once they have arrived," meaning once bodhisattvas have reached the first of the noble levels, they have realized the nature of the universal expanse of reality and therefore acquired the attitude of the sameness of oneself and others. Consequently, on account of their tender love, even if, in order to protect other sentient beings from suffering, they appear to willingly and actually accept the sufferings of the hells, it is in order to protect others, and that is what gives bodhisattvas nothing but the greatest happiness.

Neither mundane celestial beings and humans nor listeners and solitary realizers have such happiness, and it is thus the greatest and most perfect of all happiness. So the suffering produced by tenderness in this way will outshine all the happiness of mundane beings such as gods and humans. Even the listener and solitary-realizer arhats, who have achieved their own goal, do not have such bliss. What could be more marvelous than that?

Thus, from the moment one attains the bodhisattva levels onward, there is no fear of the sufferings of saṃsāra. At the same time, although bodhisattvas on the level of earnest aspiration, reflecting only on the nature of saṃsāra, recognize it as enormous suffering, even when they are at the stage of ordinary beings, on account of their potential, aspirations, and so forth they do not become discouraged by reflecting on the inconceivable state of saṃsāra—its beginning, its end, and so forth. In the past, since time without beginning until now, we and others have all experienced every kind of suffering in this existence, and each one has also experienced every kind of happiness. And yet none of all those sufferings and happiness is harming or benefiting us now. Neither is there any end to the future, and equally no time when the realms of sentient beings will ever be exhausted. On the other hand, neither will there be a time when the ever-renewed appearance of buddhas and bodhisattvas comes to an end. The end of time, the end of space, the end of sentient beings, the end of suffering—all these are inconceivable. Yet there is nothing that exists intrinsically; it is all like a magical illusion. It is in this light that we should arouse the armor-like spiritual intent: "As endless as are the realms of sentient beings, in time and space, to that extent I too will train, following the examples of the buddhas and bodhisattvas of the three times, and practice the infinite bodhisattva activities." If we pray to all the buddhas and bodhisattvas that we may accomplish this and dedicate all our sources of good for that purpose, we will never turn back from the path of the Great Vehicle and will speedily find relief in fearlessness.

> **The steadfast, with their tender gifts,**
> **Create the bliss of generosity;**
> **The happiness of those who find enjoyment in the three worlds**
> **Cannot compare to even a fraction of that. (XVIII, 48)**

When steadfast bodhisattvas, with loving tenderness, give to others, they have no expectation of getting something in return or of karmic recompense: they practice generosity solely in order to help others. By doing so, when they give things away instead of keeping them for themselves, they complete their acts of generosity that benefit others. As for the happiness they derive from doing so, beings in the three worlds might enjoy some happiness, but their pleasure does not compare to a hundredth, a thousandth, or even the tiniest fraction of the bliss that develops in bodhisattvas' minds from giving generously.

Therefore, even though bodhisattvas appear to suffer for the sake of others, in their own minds there is no suffering. Moreover, because of the joy they feel at giving away their bodies and possessions, which no mundane happiness can ever illustrate, any discomfort bodhisattvas have in willingly accepting the sufferings of saṃsāra must be understood as not being in any way suffering.

> **If, out of tenderness, for beings' sake**
> **They do not leave saṃsāra, suffering itself,**
> **What suffering will the compassionate ones**
> **Not accept in order to benefit others? (XVIII, 49)**

If, out of tender love, for the benefit of sentient beings, they do not completely abandon all that is saṃsāra, whose very nature is suffering, then which sufferings of other beings will the compassionate ones not willingly take on or accept in order to help them? They happily take on all others' sufferings.

> From the compassion, generosity,
> And wealth of those with tender hearts,
> The happiness that grows from love, from caring,
> And from their power to help will constantly increase.
> (XVIII, 50)

The compassion, generosity, and possessions of a tenderhearted bodhisattva constitute three causes that grow. Here the Tibetan word *ni* clarifies the end of the clause "will constantly increase," which therefore applies to each of the three preceding words in turn: from making gifts with tender love, compassion increases, generosity increases, and wealth increases. Out of compassion, bodhisattvas give generously, so that in all their lives their compassion grows more and more. Because of their compassion, in all their lives their generosity will grow greater and greater, uninterruptedly. And because of their generosity, in all their lives their wealth will increase more and more.

The result of these is that three kinds of happiness will increase. From the compassionate intention "I will dispel the suffering of sentient beings," there arises the loving thought "I will establish sentient beings in happiness," which leads to an act of generosity. At that time, the happiness that comes from the loving intention in that bodhisattva's mind grows, like the delight a mother feels because of her love when she gives her children food and money. Then, that generosity increases the happiness that is produced by caring for sentient beings: when bodhisattvas see that their generosity is helping beings, an extraordinary happiness grows in their hearts. And the happiness that is produced by the power of that generosity grows: because of their generosity, bodhisattvas never lack wealth and consequently have the power to help sentient beings, so that the happiness produced by that power will grow in the bodhisattvas. If they had no possessions, even if they wanted to give, they would be unable to fulfill others' hopes. But because they are wealthy, they can fulfill beings' expectations, and when they see this, the most extraordinary joy grows in them.

Thus, the more bodhisattvas help others, the more joy and happiness it will give them. Because of that, they willingly undertake to dispel others' suffering and therefore become happy themselves, and for this reason, even though they give away their bodies and possessions, it is happiness, not pain, that they experience.

> This is like an exhortation to the weak:
> "With compassion you must expand and make it grow;
> By giving, you must ripen and bring happiness;
> You must lead them perfectly and guide." (XVIII, 51)

So the way in which bodhisattvas give generously is like a good friend advising someone who is lazy, saying, "Don't be so lazy! Do it like this." When bodhisattvas practice generosity with compassion, it is as if compassion is urging and encouraging those who are but feebly accustomed to giving to beings: "With compassion, you must swell the great waves of different forms of generosity and thus make wealth, its fully ripened effect, grow too. With generosity, you must bring sentient beings to full maturity and thus make both yourself and others happy, for the recipients will be happy, their minds content, and you who give will also be happy because of the completion of generosity. You must perfectly lead other sentient beings to accumulate merit and wisdom, and you must gradually guide them to the level of unsurpassable enlightenment."

> Because of their compassion, suffering makes them suffer.
> Without creating happiness, how could they be happy?
> It is because of this that those with tender love,
> By making others happy, bring happiness upon themselves.
> (XVIII, 52)

When jealous beings see others who are happy, they feel displeased, and when they see others suffering, they are delighted. Bodhisattvas are quite the opposite of them. Because of their compassion, others' suffering makes them suffer. So unless they dispel the suffering of those who suffer and make them happy, how will they be happy themselves? They are like the mother of a beloved child who is seriously ill. For this reason, once those with tender love have themselves made other sentient beings happy, that very happiness that they have created is what makes them happy—just as when the mother has found some medicine and given it to the child. Once the child is cured of the illness and is happy and well, the mother herself feels happy. Indeed, the bodhisattva Vimalakīrti said, "As long as all sentient beings are ill, my own illness too will not be cured."

There now follows a more detailed explanation of the quality of nonattachment mentioned above.

> The compassionate always, as it were, instruct their
>   generosity:
> "Do not desire happiness for yourself;
> Make others happy with gifts of your possessions.
> Otherwise, since I make no distinctions, happiness is also
>   not for me." (XVIII, 53)

Compassionate bodhisattvas constantly take on the role of compassion as a master instructing their own generosity, telling it what to give and how: "Do not wish for happiness by keeping things for yourself. Make others happy with your possessions." (In this context, the commentary says that it is as if compassion, the master, were instructing generosity, its pupil, but since it is easy to understand it as meaning the same thing, I consider it is also satisfactory to explain it like this.) Even when they make others happy with gifts of their possessions, it is not in character for bodhisattvas to give with the hope of obtaining the resulting happiness for themselves alone. Bodhisattvas do not consider their own welfare and others' welfare as any different. They suffer in response to others' suffering and feel happy when others are happy. So they give to others, thinking, "May even the result of my giving away my possessions ripen on sentient beings and bring them happiness." On the other hand, if it were not to ripen on others, since their own and beings' welfare are no different, they would never want that resulting happiness to come even to themselves.

> "Their happiness makes me happy,
> So give beings gifts along with the result.
> If there is something you should do for me,
> Make the result wholly theirs." (XVIII, 54)

"It is because sentient beings' happiness makes me happy that I have followed the example of bodhisattvas who have abandoned their self-cherishing like poison and cherish others even more. Therefore, give sentient beings gifts along with the results of generosity." Thus does compassion instruct generosity. "If there is something you should do for me, Generosity, like bringing me riches, you must arrange that it fully becomes the result for other beings themselves, and that will benefit me." It is in this manner that bodhisattvas proceed to give others gifts along with the results.

> "Even though those who give have no desire for wealth,
> They gain abundant riches and good things.
> It's not that I want such happiness,
> But like that I can continue to give." (XVIII, 55)

In sincerely giving the result of generosity as well to sentient beings, the givers, bodhisattvas, who are not attached to their own welfare, have no desire for riches. But it is in the nature of the interdependence of cause and effect that they happen upon a great deal of wealth and things of good quality. "Even when this happens, it is not that I have any desire for the happiness of tainted wealth. I want merely to continue like that, from one life to the next, making gifts that will benefit sentient beings by using the wealth I have acquired."[28]

> "Constantly observe me
> Fully giving all I own with tender love.
> Thus you should know that the result
> Does not interest me at all." (XVIII, 56)

"Constantly examine me: instead of using everything I have for my own pleasure, I am giving it all away, with tender love, to others. That way you should understand, Generosity, that I am not interested in the result of those gifts."

> "If you do not let go of the resulting benefits you will obtain,
> There'll never be any delight in giving gifts.
> If, for a single instant, you fail to give like that,
> Then there will be no true joy in generosity." (XVIII, 57)

"If you give others only your actual wealth but do not give the riches that you, Generosity, will gain as a result, you will not be a bodhisattva who delights in the unattached generosity of giving away all the riches of future

---

28. Throughout this section, the use of the personal pronoun (*bdag*) indicates that it is compassion that is exhorting generosity.

lives; because if you are not interested in that sort of generosity in this life, even for an instant, and have no wish to give, there will not be the joy of giving compassionately for others' benefit."

> "You do not reward those who are not generous,
> But it is not like me to look for recompense like that.
> I do not have your hopes for something in return,
> And so I give the resulting benefits entirely to others." (XVIII, 58)

"Generosity, since you do not reward those who are not generous, are you not, it seems, looking for a reward? But this interest in a reward—a result from giving generously—is not a part of me or worthy of me," declares compassion for others. "Since I am free of your looking for recompense, Generosity, I completely give away even your fully ripened effect, without considering it as mine."

This way in which compassion speaks to generosity indicates how to train the mind in giving all of one's body, possessions, and sources of good completely to others without being attached to one's own welfare.

There now follows a praise summarizing the qualities of giving with compassion.

> The tender generosity of bodhisattvas
> Is free of shameful deeds, is based on purity,
> Leads to happiness, and is protective,
> Unquestioning, and without stain. (XVIII, 59)

The generosity of the buddhas' children, made with loving tenderness, has six aspects. It is free of shameful deeds, meaning that they give without harming others. They do not give things that they have stolen from someone else, or give the meat of beings that have been killed, or give to beggars while making them unhappy by belittling and humiliating them by calling them poor, starving beggars, and so on. Instead of this sort of generosity that involves harming others, bodhisattvas give properly and correctly.

They give things whose state or basis is pure. Rather than giving things that they have not examined, impure things like poisonous substances or weapons, they give pure, clean things that they have checked first.

Their gifts are beneficial, for having attracted beings with their generosity, bodhisattvas introduce them to virtue and thus lead these beings, the objects of their generosity, to its happy results in their future rebirths, that is, to the higher realms and liberation.

Bodhisattvas give protectively, that is, their generosity does not involve harming members of their entourage for whom they are responsible. They do not, for instance, treat their family, attendants, and so on wrongfully by giving everything away and leaving them with nothing. And even if they give away their spouse and children to others, they do so knowing that it is not against their will or that they will not greatly suffer in the end, but never if it would cause them intense suffering. Nor would they ever give them away to ferocious beings like yakṣa spirits and rākṣasa ogres.

They give unquestioningly, that is, equally and impartially. Once they have realized that beings are in need, even if the latter are not begging expressly, they give them things from their own hands in order to help them. They never go looking for other worthy causes or give selectively, choosing the field of merit and thinking, "I'll give this one something, but I won't give that one anything."

Their generosity is untainted or unattached, for they give without hoping for anything in return or for karmic recompense.

These six aspects are described from the point of view of purifying possible faults in practicing generosity. From the point of view of good qualities, there are nine aspects, beginning with giving away everything.

> **With tender love, bodhisattvas give everything**
> **On a vast scale and of the best quality, constantly,**
> **With joy, an absence of materialism, and purity,**
> **Dedicating their generosity to enlightenment and to virtue.**
> **(XVIII, 60)**

Bodhisattvas give away everything: there is nothing, external or internal, that they do not give. They give extensively or on a vast scale—that is, they give many vast gifts, not just a few small things. They give the best, meaning that rather than giving things that are deteriorated or rotten or unfit for use, they give the very best things that are abundant and perfect in their color, shape, and fragrance. Their generosity is constant, for rather than giving sometimes and not at other times, they give all the time, continuously. They give joyfully, taking pleasure in giving, without stingy thoughts or wondering which beggars they will give to and which not. They give without materialistic attitudes—that is, without hoping for anything in return or for karmic recompense. Their generosity is pure, in that they make pure gifts, which means the same as giving things whose basis is pure as mentioned above. It is dedicated to enlightenment: rather than dedicate their acts of generosity to happiness in the higher realms or to the listeners' and solitary realizers' nirvāṇa, they dedicate them in order to attain unsurpassable enlightenment for the sake of all sentient beings, thus devoting those acts of generosity to unsurpassable enlightenment. And their generosity is dedicated to virtue, which means the same as their gifts being beneficial as explained above: having attracted sentient beings with their gifts, they apply those beings to, or establish them in, the practice of virtue.

The manner in which practicing generosity in this way brings about happiness is as follows.

> **While those with tender love, their minds sated with joy on three accounts,**
> **Find great delight in giving everything away,**
> **No similar delight will those who revel in those gifts**
> **Derive from using all those things. (XVIII, 61)**

Tender bodhisattvas, whose minds are satiated with three kinds of happiness (those of the joy of giving, the joy of helping others, and the joy of completing the accumulations related to enlightenment) are delighted to give away everything they own. For those who receive all those pleasurable gifts, using them will never procure the same sort of delight. "Those who revel" in this context are the objects of the bodhisattvas' generosity, who obtain all they could wish for. As the commentary explains, they are incapable of deriving the same delight as the givers. They can also be explained as being those in general who enjoy the abundant pleasures of the higher realms and who never experience anything like the pleasure a bodhisattva has in being generous, as the *Verses Summarizing the Precious Qualities* states: "To give away the four continents, so beautifully adorned, as if they were drops of spit brings great delight. But there is no such delight for those who receive those continents."

vii. An Explanation of the Causal Factors That Give Rise to Compassion

> **Tender love for the stingy, tender love for the unruly,**
> **Tender love for those in turmoil, tender love for the careless,**

Compassion for those beguiled by objects,
And compassion for those who mistakenly cling— (XVIII, 62)

Compassion arises for sentient beings who lack the practice of the six transcendent perfections. With tenderness[29] in their hearts for those who, on account of stinginess, have become miserly and avaricious and are unable to give away the smallest thing, bodhisattvas tell them about the defects of stinginess and the qualities of generosity, and thus set them to practicing generosity. With tender love for those unruly beings of evil character who habitually commit negative actions such as taking life, they teach the qualities of keeping discipline and establish them in the practice of discipline. With tender love for those who minds are in a complete turmoil because of anger, they teach the defects of hatred and the good qualities of patience, and establish them in the practice of patience. With tender love for those who, on account of their laziness, delight in ordinary tasks but are careless about performing positive actions, they teach the qualities of having diligence and giving up laziness, and thus establish them in the practice of diligence. With compassion for those whose minds are constantly distracted by their being spellbound by the pleasures of the five senses, they teach the qualities of concentration and establish them in the practice of concentration. And with compassion for those who believe that there is permanence, a self, purity, and happiness in the tainted aggregates, and who are mistakenly attached to them, they teach the defects of incorrect understanding and establish them in true wisdom.

A bodhisattva's compassion
Comes from happiness and suffering and their cause;
A bodhisattva's compassion
Comes from its cause, the teacher, and its nature. (XVIII, 63)

Moreover, there are four contributory conditions that give rise to a bodhisattva's compassion. The objective condition through which compassion arises consists in considering the fact that there are no feelings whatsoever that transcend suffering. For the three worlds are pervaded by the suffering of change, comprising all tainted pleasant feelings; they are pervaded

---

29. Although Kawa Peltsek's translation of the root verse has *brtse ba* (tender love), the translation of this verse in Sthiramati's commentary has only *snying rje* (compassion) throughout.

by the suffering of suffering, comprising all painful feelings; and they are pervaded by the suffering of everything composite, comprising neutral feelings. "Their cause" is explained in the commentary as referring to the latent tendencies for pleasant, painful, and neutral feelings, and since these are by nature habitual tendencies, they are neutral feelings. Until these latent tendencies have been eliminated, happiness and suffering occur again and again, so they also constitute the subtle suffering of the suffering of everything composite. "Their cause" may also be explained as the cause of the tainted aggregates, along with pleasant and painful feelings, which refers to the suffering of everything composite. Whichever the case, the point being made here is that it is from considering sentient beings who have the three kinds of suffering that a bodhisattva's compassion arises.

The storing in the ground of all of the habitual tendency to tenderhearted compassion from training in compassion in other lives is the causal condition for compassion. Giving rise to compassion through hearing the sacred Dharma from a spiritual master is the dominant condition. And the arising of each instant of compassionate mind from the nature of the previous one is the immediately preceding condition. It is from these three conditions (causal, dominant, and immediately preceding) that a bodhisattva's compassion arises.

viii. The Superiority of a Bodhisattva's Compassion in Terms of Its Being Equal

> A bodhisattva's compassion
> Is to be understood as equal on account of its attitude,
> Its accomplishment, its absence of attachment,
> Its nonconceptuality, and its purity. (XVIII, 64)

Bodhisattvas' compassion should be understood as being equal. In what way? Although ordinary beings have compassion for their friends and relations, they do not feel compassion for their enemies, nor for those who are neither friend nor enemy. Listeners and solitary realizers have compassion for those who suffer, but they do not develop the same compassion for everybody, and their compassion is therefore unequal. Bodhisattvas' compassion, on the other hand, as explained earlier, arises in the state of sameness, the great compassion that makes no distinction between beings who have the three kinds of suffering, from the peak of existence right down to the Hell of Torment Unsurpassed. It is because of this attitude toward all sentient beings that their compassion is equal—because that attitude is equal.

Since bodhisattvas protect all beings—protecting those suffering in the hells and so forth as much as those at the peak of existence—their accomplishment is equal, so it is on account of this that their compassion is equal. They have no attachment or aversion to any class of beings, and therefore their compassion is equal on account of its absence of attachment. Their compassion is equal because they have realized that everything is one taste in emptiness, without any concepts of themselves, sentient beings, and compassion as having specific attributes. And it is equal because from the moment they attain the eighth level, in which the wisdom free of the concepts of the three spheres is purified of the movements of effort and of attributes, they have attained perfect purity.

ix. The Best Compassion

> The bodhisattvas' mental training in the four boundless attitudes
> Is the best by virtue of their interest in the Dharma,
> Their specific mental states, mastery,
> Nonconceptuality, and oneness. (XVIII, 65)

From a general point of view, simple meditation on love and the other three boundless attitudes is something the gods of the world of form and the listeners and solitary realizers also have. But the bodhisattvas' practice of the four boundless attitudes is the greatest. How? The bodhisattvas' mental training in love and the other boundless attitudes grows especially greater in their present and future lives on account of their habitual tendencies from having trained in the four boundless attitudes in their previous lives. As a result, this kind of practice is superior to that of others. Bodhisattvas have great interest and faith in the sūtras related to the four boundless attitudes. Their boundless attitudes are distinctly superior in that they are associated with the nine specific mental states described above.[30] They have mastery in concentration, or especially mastery on account of the fact that their love and other boundless attitudes arise effortlessly and spontaneously on the eighth and higher levels. Bodhisattvas' practice of the four boundless attitudes is imbued with the gnosis that has no concept of attributes in a

---

30. See the section on mental offerings above, ch. 18, v. 3.

meditator (themselves), of an object (sentient beings), and of four boundless attitudes to be practiced. And, beginning from their attainment of the eighth level, the deeds of the bodhisattvas on those levels are completely mingled and equivalent. It is on account of all this that bodhisattvas' practice of the four boundless attitudes is the best.

4. Conclusion to the Chapter on Offering, Reliance, and Boundless Attitudes

> Thus, by developing deep faith in the bhagavāns
> And making constant, extraordinary offerings—material
>   things as well as great veneration—
> By always following the beneficial friend who is possessed of
>   many qualities,
> And through tender love for beings, they will gain every
>   accomplishment. (XVIII, 66)

Thus, as described above, by developing extremely clear faith and confidence in the buddha bhagavāns as the embodiment of inconceivable qualities; by making material offerings of Dharma robes, garments, flowers, incense, and suchlike; by performing prostrations, reciting praises, circumambulating, and so on; by making the extraordinary offering of great veneration together with respectfully practicing the teachings; and by making those offerings not merely occasionally but constantly, one will obtain all mundane and supramundane accomplishments, benefiting both oneself and others.

Similarly, it has been taught that if one relies on a teacher who possesses qualities such as the qualities of a spiritual master explained above and also the other relevant qualities described in the sūtras and sacred texts, one will gain many of those boundless good qualities. By possessing such qualities one will, in this life and in all one's other lives, always follow a spiritual master who will benefit one, and one will thereby also obtain all the accomplishments.

And by means of the four boundless attitudes—love, compassion, joy, and impartiality—whose nature is a tender affection for all beings, one will benefit beings and again, on account of this, obtain all the accomplishments.

According to the commentary, by making offerings and following a spiritual master one mainly accomplishes one's own goal, while with the four boundless attitudes one mainly accomplishes others' goals. In general, any of these will lead to one's accomplishing both.

This completes the explanation of the eighteenth chapter of *Ornament of the Mahāyāna Sūtras*, the chapter on offerings, reliance, and boundless attitudes.

19
Elements Leading to Enlightenment

This chapter deals mainly with meditation, and for this there are three parts: (1) prerequisites; (2) the essence of the path or training; and (3) branches that enhance the practice.

1. Prerequisites

This section explains different prerequisites, from the observance of the discipline to which one is pledged, through listening and reflection, up to the gathering of the accumulations. Bodhisattvas have to make efforts in not transgressing the precepts by relying on (1) a sense of shame, (2) steadfastness, and (3) indefatigability; in having the perfectly pure wisdom that comes from listening through (4) knowledge of the treatises and (5) knowledge of the world, and from reflecting by way of (6) the four reliances and (7) the four kinds of perfect knowledge; and thence (8) in gathering the two accumulations. These will now be explained in order.

a. A Sense of Shame

A sense of shame is covered by the first sixteen verses and is divided into eight topics: (1) the specific characteristics of a sense of shame; (2) shameful ways; (3) categories of a sense of shame, superior and inferior; (4) the disadvantages of not having a sense of shame and decency; (5) the benefits of having a sense of shame and decency; (6) in praise of those who have a sense of shame and decency; (7) the signs of having a sense of shame and decency; and (8) the best sense of shame and decency.

i. The Specific Characteristics of a Sense of Shame

> A sense of shame has eliminated its opposite,
> Is coupled with nonconceptual gnosis,

> Has as its object lower paths that are merely free of
>   wrongdoing,
> Matures sentient beings, and belongs to the steadfast. (XIX, 1)

A sense of shame and a sense of decency consist in the elimination of their counteragents—shamelessness and a lack of consideration. One speaks of a sense of shame with regard to oneself, and of a sense of decency with regard to others. If bodhisattvas were to give up their own training, that is, the path of the Great Vehicle, and train in the practices of the listeners and solitary realizers, they would feel ashamed, thinking, "This is not for me, a bodhisattva." And their sense of decency would tell them, "Other bodhisattvas will criticize you." This, then, is the nature of a sense of shame and decency. Its ally, supporting it, is nonconceptual gnosis, which does not conceptualize any attributes in oneself, in other sentient beings, or in the sense of shame and decency.

Its objects are the paths of the lower vehicles, for bodhisattvas would feel ashamed of engaging in them. Although those who have entered the listeners' and solitary realizers' vehicles are free of any wrongdoing associated with defilements, they are engaged only in their own welfare, so their motivation, wisdom, accomplishment, and result all constitute objects that are far inferior to those of the Great Vehicle. So when they consider those objects, bodhisattvas are ashamed to engage in them. The function of a sense of shame and decency is to enable bodhisattvas to bring sentient beings to maturity.

This kind of sense of shame and decency is that of a steadfast bodhisattva. But listeners and solitary realizers, with no regard for sentient beings, who are their own kin, reject them and strive for their own peace and happiness alone, so compared to bodhisattvas, they have little sense of shame and decency, as we read in a tantra:

> Unfortunate are the listeners,
> Who have no affection even for their own children.
> Fortunate is Vajrapāṇi,
> Who makes all sentient beings happy.

ii. Shameful Ways

> When the counteragents
> Of the six perfections increase in them

And the antidotes decrease,
Bodhisattvas feel unbearably ashamed. (XIX, 2)

The steadfast are ashamed of being lazy
About training in the six perfections,
And also of indulging in activities
Related to the defilements. (XIX, 3)

One might wonder what sorts of ways bodhisattvas would be ashamed of. When stinginess and the other counteragents of generosity and the other five transcendent perfections increase in their mind streams, and their antidotes, generosity and the others, diminish, bodhisattvas are overcome with shame. They are ashamed of stinginess increasing and utterly ashamed of their generosity diminishing—even more ashamed than are worldly aristocrats of behaving like plebeians. This is known as a sense of shame with regard to increase and diminution.

Similarly, there is shame with regard to application and nonapplication. Steadfast bodhisattvas are ashamed of lazing about and not applying themselves to training their mind streams in the six transcendent perfections. They are also ashamed of not restraining the doors of their six sense organs that correspond to and give rise to attachment, aversion, and other defilements, and of indulging in their objects, the five pleasures of the senses.

iii. Categories of a Sense of Shame, Superior and Inferior

In those who are, by nature, not concentrated,
Who are lesser, middling, or on inferior levels,
Whose motivation is inferior, or who have a sense of "I,"
Their sense of shame is inferior; in others it is superior. (XIX, 4)

The sense of shame and decency of those on the level of the world of desire, who are not concentrated by nature,[1] is lesser or inferior. Similarly, the sense of shame and decency of those in the worlds of form and formlessness, who are concentrated, is divided into lesser, middling, and greater, of which the lesser and middling can be classified as lesser. On the various levels—the level of earnest aspiration, the first bodhisattva level, and so forth—

---

1. Tib. *mnyam par bzhag pa'i ngo bo min*, not settled in evenness, or not meditational. The terminology in this section is identical to that used in ch. 18, v. 21.

the sense of shame and decency on each level is categorized as lesser compared to that on the levels above it, and as greater compared to the levels below it.

The sense of shame and decency of the listeners and solitary realizers, whose motivation is inferior, is lesser, since they accomplish only their own welfare. The sense of shame of bodhisattvas on the first to seventh levels is referred to as "self-interested" because it is accompanied by pride related to its being characterized by effort.

The sense of shame of all these beings is referred to as inferior or lesser from a relative point of view. Compared to them, other degrees of sense of shame are classified as superior or greater—that is, the sense of shame of those on the level of meditative concentration; that of those in the greater category of beings on the level of meditative concentration; that of bodhisattvas on the higher levels, which is greater compared to the lower levels; the shame and decency of beings in the Great Vehicle; and the shame and decency of those on the three levels starting with the eighth who are free of any concept of self and whose nonconceptual gnosis is spontaneous, which is greater or superior because it is effortless and spontaneous.

iv. The Disadvantages of Not Having a Sense of Shame and Decency

> From a lack of decency and improper ways, the wise
> Indulge in defilements, get angry,
> Forsake what is good, and become proud, as a result of which
> They oppress sentient beings and destroy their discipline. (XIX, 5)

Bodhisattvas who have no sense of shame and decency and who engage in improper ways consequently indulge in developing defilements such as attachment. On account of their getting angry, they engage in negative actions like killing, thereby degenerating their discipline. In this way, they harm themselves in this and future lives, and they harm other beings. Similarly, they become lazy and careless, disregarding positive actions and anything that benefits sentient beings. Because of these faults, and that of pride, they oppress sentient beings and destroy their own discipline.

> They will be stricken with remorse,
> And will receive almost no respect.

> The hosts of faithful nonhumans
> And even the Teacher will ignore them. (XIX, 6)

Because of this, they will be stricken with remorse and grow sad. Others too, seeing that they have no good qualities, will afford them scant respect and give them fewer offerings. And as a result of their lack of shame and decency, the assemblies of nonhuman protectors of virtue who have faith in the teachings, and even our teacher, the Buddha, will ignore those bodhisattvas, who will no longer be objects of their special consideration.

> Their fellow bodhisattvas will condemn them,
> And in this life the world will speak unpleasantly of them,
> While in other lives to come.
> They'll be reborn in realms devoid of leisure. (XIX, 7)

Their fellow bodhisattvas will speak disparagingly of them, saying, "So-and-so is acting unworthily like this." Even from ordinary people, in this present life, they will receive insults. And later, in other lives, they will be reborn in the lower realms and other states devoid of leisure.[2]

> So all the good they have acquired
> And all that they have not yet gained
> Will fade away. Because of this they'll suffer,
> And their minds will never find true rest. (XIX, 8)

Thus, the good qualities they have already acquired in their mind streams will diminish, and they will fail to obtain those that they have hitherto not acquired. As a result, their bodies lodged in suffering and their minds pervaded by unhappiness, they will never abide in natural ease.

v. The Benefits of Having a Sense of Shame and Decency

> None of these misfortunes can occur
> For the buddhas' heirs who have a sense of shame.
> The skillful always take the best rebirth
> As human beings or as gods. (XIX, 9)

2. See ch. 14, note 8.

> Wise beings with a sense of shame swiftly complete
> The accumulations that lead to perfect enlightenment.
> The buddhas' children will never grow weary
> Of bringing beings to maturity. (XIX, 10)
>
> They will be forever free of shamelessness
> And never separate from the antidote.
> Such are the benefits
> Bodhisattvas with a sense of shame will gain. (XIX, 11)

None of these misfortunes that have just been described can ever occur in bodhisattvas who have a sense of shame and decency. These skillful beings always take the most excellent births as celestial beings and humans. This is the fully ripened effect of having a sense of shame and decency. The conditioning effect is that wise beings with a sense of shame and decency swiftly complete the accumulations that bring unsurpassable perfect enlightenment. The proliferating effect is that bodhisattvas with a sense of shame and decency bring sentient beings to maturity and will never tire of doing so. The separational effect is that they are always free of the counteragents—shamelessness and a lack of consideration. And the effect similar to the cause is that they will never separate from the antidote, a sense of shame and decency. These, then, are the benefits that bodhisattvas with a sense of shame and decency will gain.

vi. In Praise of Those Who Have a Sense of Shame and Decency

> The immature, though adorned in gorgeous clothes,
> Have no consideration and so are stained by faults.
> The buddhas' children clothed in a sense of shame,
> Though uncovered, are unstained by faults. (XIX, 12)
>
> The buddhas' children, with their sense of decency,
> Are, like the sky, never tainted by ordinary concerns.
> Counted among the assembly of buddhas' children,
> Those who are adorned with a sense of shame are the loveliest.
> (XIX, 13)

> With their sense of shame, bodhisattvas
> Love beings like a mother would her children.
> It is their sense of shame as well that constantly
> Protects them in saṃsāra from all kinds of faults. (XIX, 14)

Although immature, ordinary beings wash their bodies and wear beautiful, well-cut clothes in fine, colorful materials, their minds are devoid of a sense of shame and decency and are therefore, by nature, stained with faults such as attachment, which is something they cannot conceal under their clothes. The buddhas' children, on the other hand, are clothed with a sense of shame and decency, and even if they have no clothes to cover them outwardly, they are naturally free of contamination by faults. This verse shows that when they are resting in the natural state of union, inwardly settled in evenness, their sense of shame and decency acts as the antidote to the arising of defilements.

The buddhas' children, who have a sense of shame and decency, are like the sky unobscured by clouds or mist. Their sense of shame and decency is such that when they go somewhere like a town, they are never tainted by the eight ordinary preoccupations. Even when they are gathered among their fellow bodhisattvas who share the same view and conduct, those who are adorned with the ornaments of a sense of shame and decency are the most strikingly beautiful and well behaved. No jeweled ornaments can compare to that.

Bodhisattvas would be ashamed of themselves and of what others might think if they were to forsake the welfare of others. And so it is, with a motherly love for their disciples, that they bring sentient beings to maturity, for it would be shameful for those who love and cherish all sentient beings as if they were their only child to abandon beings and fail to protect them. Like a kingdom and its regions protected by an army of four divisions (cavalry, elephants, chariots, and infantry), when bodhisattvas work for the benefit of sentient beings here in saṃsāra, their sense of shame and decency always protects them from hostile forces—attachment and all other such faults. For when one has a sense of shame and decency, one does not indulge in the faults of defilements.

vii. The Signs of Having a Sense of Shame and Decency

> Acceptance of everything,
> Refusal of everything,
> Nonengagement, and engagement
> Are the signs of decency in an upright individual. (XIX, 15)

There are four signs of having a sense of shame and decency. In terms of their attitude, bodhisattvas happily accept everything to do with good qualities—generosity, discipline, and the like—and they do not willingly accept anything to do with negative qualities of any kind: shamelessness, a lack of consideration, attachment, aversion, and all the other defilements. In terms of their application, they do not engage in negative actions of any kind, and they engage in every kind of good quality. The appearance of any of these four signs is the mark of a sense of shame and decency in a conscientious and considerate person.

viii. The Best Sense of Shame and Decency

> The bodhisattvas' mental training in decency
> Is the best by virtue of their interest in the teachings,
> Their specific mental states, mastery,
> Nonconceptuality, and oneness. (XIX, 16)

The best sense of shame and decency is shame and decency that one trains in with one's own mind. As the commentary says, rather than thinking, "I would be ashamed if others were to know about this fault," it is much better to train in being ashamed of oneself for committing a negative action, whether or not anybody else knows about it. Training in a sense of decency like this is to be understood as best on account of the following five factors: interest in the Mahāyāna teachings that teach a sense of shame and decency; the nine mental states described earlier;[3] mastery of the mind through concentration or, from the eighth level up, effortlessness and spontaneity; freedom from the concepts of the three spheres (of oneself, others, and a sense of shame); and the fact that the activities of bodhisattvas on the pure levels

---

3. See the section on mental offerings above, ch. 18, v. 3.

are equivalent. It is on account of these that a bodhisattva's sense of shame and decency is the most important or the best.

b. Steadfastness

Steadfastness is divided into (1) a brief introduction and (2) a detailed explanation.

i. Brief Introduction

> A bodhisattva's steadfastness is far superior
> To that of those who are not bodhisattvas
> By virtue of its specific characteristics,
> Its categories, and its immutability. (XIX, 17)

A bodhisattva's steadfastness and strength of mind is far superior to that of those who are not bodhisattvas, that is, all the hosts of mundane beings and listeners and solitary realizers. This is on account of its specific characteristics, its categories, and its immutability.

ii. Detailed Explanation of Three Particular Features of Steadfastness
(1) Specific Characteristics of Steadfastness

> Their diligence, concentration, and wisdom
> Correspond to strength of mind, endurance, and stability.
> On account of these three, bodhisattvas
> Apply themselves without fear. (XIX, 18)

> Through a lack of courage, wavering, and ignorance
> There is fear of all there is to do.
> So know that the three innate states
> Are included in the word "steadfastness." (XIX, 19)

The specific characteristics of steadfastness are asserted to be diligence, concentration, and wisdom, which correspond respectively to the strength of mind not to get discouraged, the endurance not to waver elsewhere, and stability in their object from correctly knowing it and not moving from that knowledge.[4] It is on account of these three factors that bodhisattvas engage in practicing the path without fear.

What kind of fear might they feel? Those who do not have diligence feel disheartened and afraid, thinking, "I will not be able to accomplish the activities of a bodhisattva." Those who do not have concentration are unable to settle their minds one-pointedly, and they are therefore apprehensive of the movements of discursive thoughts. Those without wisdom are afraid because, being ignorant as to what the activities of a bodhisattva are, they are not certain how to carry them out. As a result of these three (being disheartened and so on), they are afraid of everything a bodhisattva has to accomplish and think, "That is not in my power. I cannot do it." So the antidotes to these three fears are diligence, concentration, and wisdom, which are accomplished naturally or spontaneously. These three innate states are to be understood as bearing the name "steadfastness" because they cannot be ravished away by their counteragents. When these innate or permanent states—spontaneous diligence, spontaneous concentration, and spontaneous wisdom—are present, and there is no need for analysis or effort, steadfastness is at its greatest, and the three kinds of fear (feeling disheartened and so on) are absent.

These are the specific characteristics of steadfastness. Even beginners may have a natural disposition to not being easily discouraged and therefore able to throw themselves into whatever they are doing. In such cases, it should be understood that strictly in those terms they may be referred to as having innate diligence and so forth.

(2) Categories of Steadfastness

> The steadfastness of the steady arises
> Naturally, through their aspirations,
> In their lack of concern,
> In the face of sentient beings' ingratitude, (XIX, 20)
>
> In their hearing of the profound and of the extensive,
> With regard to beings who are hard to train,
> And with regard to the inconceivable buddha bodies.
> It arises in the face of their different austerities, (XIX, 21)

---

4. According to Vasubandhu, diligence, concentration, and wisdom are the characteristics of steadfastness, while strength of mind, endurance, and stability are its synonyms.

> In their not abandoning saṃsāra,
> And in their freedom from defilements there.
> It is unequaled by other beings,
> So bodhisattvas are considered the greatest of steadfast
>   beings. (XIX, 22)

To begin with, there are eight categories:

(1) Natural steadfastness. Because of bodhisattvas' capacity for diligence, concentration, and wisdom, which depends on the strength of their potential, they have no fear from losing heart and so on with regard to the bodhisattva activities and the like.

(2) Steadfastness through aspiration. As a result of their arousing the mind intent on unsurpassable enlightenment and making the prayer, "May I never turn back or waver from attaining the great enlightenment and bringing all sentient beings to full liberation," wherever they are reborn, they will be unwavering and steadfast. The root of all the boundless prayers of aspiration that bodhisattvas make until they reach buddhahood is their first arousing bodhicitta. It is on the basis of this initial aspiration to attain enlightenment that all their subsequent aspirations are made, as a result of which they become more and more steadfast.

(3) "Freedom from attachment" refers to steadfastness in one's own goal. This is to be fearless and unattached, or to have no regard[5] for one's body and life, in accomplishing one's own goal.

(4) Steadfastness with regard to others' goals. This is to remain steadfast without ever getting discouraged by sentient beings' ingratitude, in all its various forms.

(5) "Profound" indicates steadfastness with regard to the meaning of thatness. It refers to a firm interest and lack of apprehension with regard to the profound meaning of emptiness, from the very beginning unborn and unceasing.

(6) Steadfastness with regard to powers. This denotes a determination to accomplish the extensive qualities (the preternatural powers, strengths, fearlessnesses, and so forth) without ever losing heart.

(7) Steadfastness in bringing sentient beings to full maturity, that is, in training those beings who, because of their rampant defilements, are

---

5. Different versions of the root text here give "freedom from attachment" (Tib. *chags pa med pa*) and "having no regard" (*lta ba med pa*).

difficult for anyone to train—training them for great lengths of time, by all kinds of means, without ever abandoning them.

(8) Steadfastness with regard to supreme enlightenment. Bodhisattvas never change their minds about their vow to accomplish by themselves the inconceivable qualities of the buddhas' three bodies—the body of truth, body of perfect enjoyment, and manifestation body.

In addition to these eight kinds of steadfastness, there are the following three categories:

(1) Steadfastness in practicing austerities. Bodhisattvas practice boundless different kinds of austerities in order to attain unsurpassable enlightenment.

(2) Steadfastness in taking birth in existence intentionally. Instead of completely abandoning saṃsāra, they fully take birth in the various kinds of existence, through compassion, for the benefit of others.

(3) Steadfastness in being free of defilements. When they take those births in saṃsāra, they are never tainted by the faults of saṃsāra, defilements.

This steadfastness that takes birth in the mind streams of steadfast bodhisattvas is unequaled by the steadfastness of nonbodhisattvas—mundane beings and listeners and solitary realizers. Thus bodhisattvas are held to be the greatest of all steadfast beings.

(3) Immutability

> Like the king of mountains assailed by butterflies,
> Garuḍas, and the ocean,
> The steadfast are not shaken by evil company,
> By suffering, or by hearing the profound. (XIX, 23)

Steadfast bodhisattvas are like Mount Meru, which cannot be shaken by butterflies, by the power of the garuḍa's wings, or by the waves of the ocean. These three similes indicate respectively that they are not perturbed or shaken by evil, nonvirtuous companions, by the different kinds of suffering, or by hearing the profound teachings on emptiness and no-self.

c. Indefatigability

> Bodhisattvas' indefatigability is incomparable
> And based on three things: their insatiable thirst for listening,
> Their great diligence, and their suffering.
> Relying on their sense of shame and their steadfastness, (XIX, 24)

> The indefatigability of the wise—
> Those who yearn for the great enlightenment—
> Is held to be, on the different levels,
> Imperfect, perfect, and utterly perfect. (XIX, 25)

Bodhisattvas' indefatigability[6] is incomparable with regard to that of others—listeners and solitary realizers. Their indefatigability is based on three things that they never tire of. In that they never have enough of listening to the teachings of the sublime spiritual master, they never tire of listening to the Dharma or of seeking the teachings. For three measureless kalpas they set about things with enormous diligence, like someone trying to light a fire by rubbing pieces of wood together,[7] and never tire of greatly persevering. And they never tire of accepting all kinds of sufferings for the sake of sentient beings; they are never discouraged by suffering. These indicate the three objects of their indefatigability.

Its cause or source or support is reliance on their sense of shame and their steadfastness, described above, which prevents them from getting discouraged. The essence or nature of their indefatigability is their determination to reach the great enlightenment. As for the categories of the indefatigability that results from this, the wise are held to have three kinds, depending on which stage of the path they are on. On the level of earnest aspiration, since they have not acquired the attitude of the sameness of themselves and others, from time to time they do get discouraged, so their indefatigability is held to be imperfect. On the first seven bodhisattva levels, they never become discouraged, and their indefatigability is therefore perfect. On the three pure levels it is absolutely perfect, being effortless and spontaneous.

d. Knowledge of the Treatises

> Because of its basis, its purpose,
> Effects, specific characteristics,
> Inexhaustibility, and perfectly accomplished result,
> Steadfast bodhisattvas' knowledge of the treatises (XIX, 26)

---

6. Tib. *mi skyo ba*. Its opposite in Tibetan (*skyo ba*) carries not only the meaning of physical tiredness but also weariness, feeling fed up and discouraged, and it has generally been translated elsewhere in this book with that nuance in mind.

7. I.e., they do not stop until they achieve the desired result.

> Is far superior.
> Contained in their concentration and their powers of retention,
> It brings sentient beings to maturity
> And serves to hold the sacred Dharma. (XIX, 27)

Steadfast bodhisattvas' knowledge of the treatises is described as knowledge of the five sciences and also spoken of as knowledge of the texts. As already explained, the five sciences comprise the inner science of the Buddhist teachings, the science of *tarka* or dialectics (including logic with reasons or proofs), grammar, the arts, and medicine. Having properly heard them from a spiritual master who is learned and skilled in giving instruction, and having reflected on their meaning so as to achieve certainty in them, bodhisattvas then teach them to others, for everything that is worth knowing is included in these five sciences. Because bodhisattvas want to become learned in all there is to know and thereby gain omniscient gnosis, they apply themselves to knowing the treatises. Although mundane beings and listeners and solitary realizers do have a certain knowledge of the five sciences, bodhisattvas' knowledge of the treatises on the five sciences is far superior, in terms of six aspects, beginning with the basis. What are these six?

First, the basis or object is the five sciences themselves. The listeners, in order to attain liberation for themselves, mainly seek just the individual no-self, which is only one part of the inner science, but they go no further into the points taught in the Mahāyāna scriptures, let alone the other sciences. Bodhisattvas seek omniscient gnosis and accomplish the welfare of the whole infinity of sentient beings, and for that, they learn and teach others all the traditions of extensive knowledge. Their inner science is the path of the three vehicles. Through their expertise in effortlessly applying the methods for combining the natural forms of the names and phrases that express ideas with the grammatical cases, condensing the words or expanding on them, and so forth, as is taught in the texts on grammar, they use the right definitions and thus make the meanings intelligible without any corrupt language forms. Establishing those meanings in accordance with direct, inferential, and scriptural valid cognition, they refute positions that are not valid and prove those that are, using these methods to develop unassailable certainty as to the meaning. With the science of medicine, they practice techniques for removing all the illnesses that afflict beings, restoring them to good health, and nurturing good health in the long term. And they practice the different kinds of arts that can benefit beings. By practicing all these themselves, they benefit others and also instruct others in these same traditions. In short, in order to accomplish their own and others' goals, bodhisattvas begin by listening to the textual traditions of the treatises or literature on the five sciences for themselves, memorizing what they have heard, training in learning them through repetition, investigating their meaning, and assimilating the meaning without any error. They thus distinguish between what is correctly taught and what is not, and by this means they teach these five sciences to others. This is how, in terms of the basis or object, their knowledge is superior.

Second, their purpose. However much the listeners and solitary realizers learn, it is mainly for their own benefit. Anything bodhisattvas learn is principally for the benefit of others. So their knowledge is superior in its purpose.

Third, the effects. Knowing the inner science of only the listeners' scriptures serves to accomplish one's own goal. For bodhisattvas, on the other hand, becoming learned in the inner science of the three vehicles enables them to practice the Great Vehicle themselves and teach it to others who have the Mahāyāna potential, and also to teach their respective vehicles to others who have the listener or solitary-realizer potential. Similarly, by means of the other four sciences (the science of logic and the rest), they benefit others and teach them the relevant treatises. So their knowledge is superior on account of its effects.

Fourth, the specific characteristics. Whereas the listeners study a few treatises that teach the individual no-self, which is only one part of the Buddhist teachings, and memorize the words and so forth, bodhisattvas listen insatiably to all the treatises, however limitless—those of the inner science, including all three vehicles, and those on grammar, logic, arts, and medicine—and retain them, learn them thoroughly, examine them, and assimilate them. So in terms of its having these five specific characteristics,[8] their knowledge is superior.

As for the fifth, its inexhaustibility, the listeners' knowledge of the treatises will come to an end in the state of nirvāṇa with no residual aggregates, whereas the bodhisattvas' knowledge of the treatises on the five sciences is never exhausted even in the expanse without residual aggregates, and in this respect it is again superior.

---

8. I.e., the fact that the treatises are heard, retained, learned, examined, and assimilated.

The sixth, the result, in being accomplished perfectly, is superior because listeners do not attain omniscience through their knowledge of the treatises, while bodhisattvas, by the power of their learning in the five sciences and their dedicating it entirely to omniscience, perfectly accomplish the result, which is the gnosis of knowing everything there is to be known.

What sorts of states of mind contain a bodhisattva's knowledge of the treatises on the five sciences? It is their doors of concentration and powers of retention. In some cases, where learning in the five sciences involves concentration, it is held by concentration and associated with it. In other cases, where it involves memory, it is held by memory and associated with it. Thus, based on whether it is contained in concentration or in the power of memory, knowledge of the treatises can also be divided into two kinds. By virtue of the concentration of Brave Progression and other kinds of concentration that they have attained, bodhisattvas settled in meditation have unobstructed knowledge of all the treatises on the five sciences and can thereby bring sentient beings to maturation. And by virtue of their natural powers of retention, whereby they remember perfectly the words and meanings of all the treatises on the five sciences that they have heard in innumerable lives in the past, they hold the whole of the sacred Dharma, the Excellent Words contained in the five sciences.

Thus, bodhisattvas' knowledge of the treatises based on concentration enables them to bring beings to maturity on account of their possessing three kinds of miraculous ability—the ability of magical transformation, the ability to tell all, and the power of instruction. And by means of their powers of retention, they hold the four branch sciences (grammar and the others) and above all the whole of the sacred Dharma, the inner science of the Buddhist teachings, so that it will never disappear from the world. These last two lines refer to the function of knowledge of the treatises.

e. Knowledge of the World

> **Steadfast bodhisattvas' knowledge of the world—**
> **Of physical and verbal conventions,**
> **And, mentally, of the truth—is without equal.**
> **It is superior to that of other beings. (XIX, 28)**

Steadfast bodhisattvas' knowledge of the world, which consists of knowledge of physical behavior, knowledge of verbal conventions, and mental knowledge of the four truths, is unequaled by other beings (mundane beings and listeners and solitary realizers). It is therefore far superior to that of those beings, who are not bodhisattvas. How, other people might wonder, can a bodhisattva's mundane knowledge be superior when ordinary people have as much conventional mundane knowledge of the world regarding ways of behaving and speaking that are acceptable to others, and listeners and solitary realizers have knowledge of the four truths? Their knowledge, unlike the bodhisattva's knowledge, does not bring other beings to maturity—hence the huge difference.

> The steadfast are always smiling;
> They always speak straightforwardly.
> This is in order to make beings fit vessels
> So that they accomplish the sacred Dharma. (XIX, 29)

Knowledge of the world has three aspects: conventional mundane knowledge, knowledge of the origin of the world, and knowledge of the cessation of the world. Conventional mundane knowledge comprises knowledge of both conventional modes of behavior and conventional ways of speaking that are accepted by everyone. What exactly do these refer to? Steadfast bodhisattvas, in their manner of conducting themselves physically, never frown at anyone, whatever their status, but always have a happy, smiling face and a respectful, joyous demeanor. In this way they make others happy. The things they say are never inappropriate but gentle and pleasing, and they speak straightforwardly, gently, and sincerely, asking such questions as, "Did your journey go well?" What is the purpose of these two? By conducting themselves in a congenial manner, they make others suitable vessels for understanding the truth. And with the words they use to teach the sacred Dharma, they help others to practice it. This is why bodhisattvas have to know these sorts of conventional ways of behaving and speaking.

> Because two truths state
> How worlds continuously come into being,
> And two how they will disappear,
> Such knowledge is known as knowledge of the world. (XIX, 30)

Mental knowledge as to what these worlds originate from and what makes them disappear is knowledge of the world. The two truths of the origin and of suffering state how the external world and its inhabitants continuously come into being. What we are calling "world" here is the production of the truth of suffering from its cause, the truth of the origin. With the two truths of cessation and of the path, the world disappears or comes to cessation. When the origin of suffering is eliminated by the truth of the path, its result, the world whose nature is the truth of suffering, ceases to be. So where it ceases to be is the truth of cessation, and what makes it cease is the truth of the path. Because of this, such knowledge is what we call "knowledge of the world." To know the origin of the world is to know the impure dependent reality; to know its disappearance is to know the pure dependent reality. And to know the three doors of perfect liberation, whose nature is the sixteen aspects of the truths, is to know all three of the three realities.

> In order to dispel the former and achieve the latter,
> The wise apply these truths.
> Because the wise know all truths,
> They are described as "knowers of the world." (XIX, 31)

When wise bodhisattvas apply themselves to these four truths and connect others to them in order to pacify the truths of suffering and of the origin and to achieve the truths of cessation and of the path, they do so through their knowledge of the world. Because wise bodhisattvas know both truths—the truth related to conventional knowledge of the world and the truth related to ultimate knowledge of the four truths—they are described as "knowers of the world." To know about the different world realms that comprise the three kinds of suffering, and the duration of life there, the happiness and suffering, prosperity and decline, and so on, along with the whole variety of worldly traditions beginning with the accepted conventions of physical behavior and ways of speaking shown in this section, and the origin or cause through which those worlds come into being—all this is relative truth, while to know the path and cessation is ultimate truth. It is by means of these two truths that bodhisattvas know everything in the world without exception.

Some authorities explain that knowledge of the four truths is authentic knowledge with regard to the world and that because knowledge of mundane behavior and ways of speaking arises from the bodhisattva's own knowledge of the world,[9] it is a result that is named after the cause; or alter-

---

9. I.e., the knowledge of the four truths.

natively that, as a cause that gives rise to knowledge of the world in others, it is named after the result. However, since this is the section on knowledge of the world, it is acceptable to hold that mundane knowledge of conventions of behavior and ways of speaking is also authentic knowledge of the world.

f. Knowledge of the Four Reliances

> The teachings taught in the scriptures,
> The meaning they imply,
> The authoritative ultimate meaning,
> And its inexpressible attainment— (XIX, 32)
>
> These are taught here to prevent
> Rejection, literal understanding,
> Understanding the truth incorrectly,
> And attaining something expressible. (XIX, 33)

It was in order to avoid faults such as relying on the individual and taking the words of the scriptures literally that the four reliances were taught.

(1) Rely on the teachings expounded by Lord Buddha in the scriptures, but do not rely just on the words of the individual person: rely on the teaching, not on the individual.

(2) With regard to those teachings, the Buddha's Excellent Words, one should not take the implied teachings literally—those that say, for example, "Slay your father and mother" but were spoken by the Buddha with another meaning in mind. Instead, rely on the meaning, not on the words.

(3) As to the meaning, there are two kinds, ultimate and expedient. Of these, one should rely on the ultimate meaning that possesses the validity of ultimate analysis. Expedient teachings are those, for example, in which the Buddha said that phenomena such as individuals and aggregates exist, while the ultimate teachings show that such phenomena have no essential existence. So, as explained in the profound sūtras expounded by the Tathāgata and in the explanations on the profound nondual nature that disclose their intended meaning by the regent Maitreya and by the great charioteers like Nāgārjuna and Asaṅga who were predicted by the Buddha, do not rely on the expedient meaning; rely on the ultimate meaning.

(4) With regard to those sūtras of the ultimate teachings, do not rely on conceptualized images that are the objects of the conceptual mind, or on

the dualistic aspects that are the objects of the eight consciousnesses. Rely instead on the inexpressible meaning devoid of subject-object duality, the domain of those who have acquired nonconceptual gnosis, which is to be realized personally. In other words, do not rely on consciousness; rely on gnosis.

Furthermore, the *Sūtra of the Teaching of Akṣayamati* states that to view the individual and the teaching as intrinsically existent is to rely on the individual. To realize that both are devoid of intrinsic existence is to rely on the teaching itself.[10] Similarly, the words refer to mundane teachings, and the meanings to supramundane teachings. Again, relative teachings are referred to as the words or teachings, while all ultimate teachings are referred to as the meaning. In the same vein, the sūtras that were taught as applying to the path are sūtras of the expedient meaning, while those that were taught as applying to the result are sūtras of the ultimate meaning. Again, those that teach the relative truth are sūtras of the expedient meaning, and those that teach the ultimate truth are sūtras of the ultimate meaning. As for what is meant by "consciousness," it refers to the consciousness of sentient beings in the world of desire, which uses as a support the aggregate of form, and similarly to the consciousness of those in the world of form, which uses the aggregate of feeling as a support; the consciousness of those in the three lower realms of the formless world, using perception as a support; and the consciousness of those at the peak of existence, which uses the aggregate of conditioning factors as a support. Thus this sūtra refers to the dwelling consciousnesses that are associated with and dwell on the four locations (the aggregates of form and so on) as "consciousness." And it refers to the knowledge that all these consciousnesses that dwell on the four aggregates are emptiness and the subsequent absence of any concept of them as consciousness as "gnosis."

The reason for teaching the four reliances is as follows. The first reliance was taught in order to prevent certain individuals, following their own opinions, from rejecting or criticizing even the true Dharma spoken by the Buddha, saying, "This is not the Buddha's word; it is not the true Dharma." The purpose of the second reliance was to prevent people from taking literally such phrases as "Slay your father and mother."

The Buddha sometimes spoke of ordinary individuals, and likewise of individual arhats and solitary realizers, and said things like, "When a cer-

---

10. Tib. *chos nyid*, also translatable as "ultimate teaching."

tain individual appears in the world, he will bring benefit and happiness to the whole world. Who is it? It is the Tathāgata." Unless one knows that he said such things from the point of view of the relative, expedient meaning, one will mistakenly think, "Individuals exist substantially," and one will take the expedient meaning to be the true meaning, so it was in order to prevent this that the third reliance was taught. Finally, although the profound nondual meaning, which is the domain of self-cognizant gnosis, is inexpressible, it might be considered as something expressible, as the domain of the consciousness, which is tainted by the various habitual tendencies to apprehending subject and object. So it was in order to refute such attainment that the fourth reliance was taught. Here, in the context of explaining the four reliances, they are being taught in order to prevent four mistaken kinds of reliance.

> Through their interest, thorough analysis,
> Learning how things are from others,
> And inexpressible gnosis,
> The steadfast will never fail. (XIX, 34)

The functions or qualities of the four reliances are as follows. If they have the first reliance, bodhisattvas will never lose interest in the teachings of the Buddha's Excellent Words. Similarly, with the second, they will never fail to thoroughly analyze the meaning of the words. With the third, they will not fail to learn from other spiritual masters exactly what has been taught in the sūtras of the ultimate meaning, as distinct from the sūtras of the expedient meaning. And with the fourth, steadfast bodhisattvas will never fail in their inexpressible gnosis that transcends any object of conceptual thought.

g. The Four Kinds of Perfect Knowledge

> On account of their knowledge of classifications,
> Characteristics, phrasing, and gnosis,
> The bodhisattvas' four kinds of perfect knowledge
> Are considered to be without equal. (XIX, 35)

(1) Perfect knowledge of phenomena. There are many different kinds of phenomena—virtuous and nonvirtuous, tainted and untainted, and so on. And for a single kind of phenomenon, there are also many different names. For

ignorance, for example, there are other terms like bewilderment, stupidity, unknowing, obscurity, and darkness. And for gnosis, there are gnosis, wisdom, awareness, intelligence, illumination, and so forth. This is perfect knowledge of the classification of names and phenomena.

(2) Unmistaken knowledge of the meanings of those names, of their general and specific characteristics, is perfect knowledge of the meanings.

(3) Those names are not expressed only in the language of one country but in the languages of every country—the particular speech of the gods, nāgas, humans, gandharvas, and demigods. Such unmistaken knowledge of the rules for combining letters to make names, and combining names to make phrases, and joining phrases with grammatical particles to make the sense clear is perfect knowledge of languages.

(4) Perfect knowledge through inner confidence and eloquence refers to the attainment of unobstructed authority in answering all kinds of questions, of the ability to reply to all objections, and of the gnosis that, starting from the meaning of a single topic, can explain it for an entire kalpa without ever coming to an end.

Because these four kinds of perfect knowledge enable bodhisattvas to know the nature of things as they are, a bodhisattva's four kinds of perfect knowledge cannot be equaled by those of the listeners and solitary realizers. This one verse indicates the defining characteristics of the four kinds of perfect knowledge. Why there are four of them is explained in the next two verses.

> The teaching and the means for teaching it
> By those who diligently teach
> Are shown by just the topics and their meanings,
> The languages, and their knowledge of these. (XIX, 36)

> Because they indicate the topics, because they explain
>   them,
> Because they bring about the complete acquisition of both,
> And because they reply to objections,
> There are four kinds of perfect knowledge. (XIX, 37)

When bodhisattvas are diligently engaged in teaching others the Dharma, this is done only in terms of what is being taught and the means for teaching it—that is, the topics and their meanings (these two being what are taught), and the languages and the inner confidence and eloquence inherent to knowledge (these being the means for teaching them).

With regard to these, the topics are indicated by names, and their meanings are explained as this or that (or, according to Sthiramati's explanation in the *Great Commentary*, it is the perfect knowledge of the meanings that summarizes and indicates the topics, and the perfect knowledge of phenomena that subsequently classifies them in detail and explains them). Perfect knowledge of languages enables the listeners to acquire a complete knowledge in both the topics and their meanings, for it is by communicating in the respective language of each country that bodhisattvas enable the listener to assimilate both the terms and their meanings. And with inner confidence and eloquence, they ask their opponents' opinions and reply in debate as to what is logically acceptable and unacceptable. For these four reasons, there are four kinds of perfect knowledge, and not three or five.

> This is complete knowledge
> Consequent on the direct cognition of sameness;
> Clearing away every kind of doubt,
> It is termed "perfect knowledge." (XIX, 38)

The causal factor of the four kinds of perfect knowledge is meditation: having settled in evenness in the self-cognizant realization of the sameness of all phenomena, bodhisattvas subsequently, with the gnosis of postmeditation, have this complete fourfold knowledge—of phenomena and so forth. These first two lines provide an etymological explanation of the Sanskrit term for the four kinds of perfect knowledge, *pratisaṃvidyā*. *Prati* means "individual" and refers to the individually realized self-cognizant nonconceptual gnosis. *Saṃ* means "perfect" or "evenness" and refers to suchness. *Vid* means "knowledge." For it is with the postmeditational pure mundane gnosis that follows the direct realization of nonconceptual gnosis that bodhisattvas teach others the topics, meanings, and so forth, and enable them to understand and know them.

The function of the four kinds of perfect knowledge is to remove all uncertainties with regard to the definitions of all the meanings of the extensive teachings (those on the aggregates, sense spheres, senses-and-fields, and so forth) and of the profound teachings (those on emptiness and suchlike). It is for this reason that they are termed "perfect knowledge."

h. The Two Accumulations

> The bodhisattvas' accumulations
> Of merit and wisdom are without equal.
> With the one, they attain the highest states in saṃsāra;
> With the other, they circle without defilements. (XIX, 39)

Bodhisattvas' accumulations, the two accumulations of merit and wisdom, are unmatched by those of the listeners and solitary realizers. As we read in the *Heap of Jewels*:

> Regard the bodhisattvas' accumulation of wisdom as like the whole of space stretching in the ten directions.
> Regard the listeners' accumulation of wisdom as no bigger than the space a worm can hollow out inside a mustard seed.
> Regard the bodhisattvas' accumulation of merit as like the water in the ocean stretching in the four directions.
> Regard the listeners' accumulation of merit as like the water in a cow's hoofprint.

Because of these two accumulations, when bodhisattvas take birth in saṃsāra, one of the accumulations, that of merit, results in their acquiring the perfect and abundant riches of the most exalted and noble beings in saṃsāra—beings like Indra, Brahmā, and the universal emperor. And the other, the accumulation of wisdom, enables them to enter the circle of existence without being obscured by the defects of saṃsāra, karma and defilements, even while remaining in saṃsāra.

> Generosity and discipline are the accumulation of merit;
> Wisdom is that of wisdom;
> The other three are both;
> Five, in part, are wisdom too. (XIX, 40)

What are the two accumulations? The two accumulations and the six transcendent perfections are mutually inclusive. Generosity, which leads to perfect and abundant wealth, and discipline, which enables one to win a perfect physical support in a celestial or human birth, both correspond to the accumulation of merit. The last transcendent perfection, that of wisdom, corresponds to the accumulation of wisdom, for through it one realizes all phenomena as emptiness and one is not obscured by defilements. The other three, patience, diligence, and concentration, belong to both merit and wisdom. Two kinds of patience—thinking nothing of being harmed and willingly accepting suffering—are included in the accumulation of merit, while patience in aspiring to a true knowledge of reality is included in the accumulation of wisdom. Diligence in helping other beings in their activities such as plowing the fields and doing business is included in the accumulation of merit, while diligence in following a spiritual master, listening to the sacred Dharma, reflecting on it, meditating, and so forth, is included in the accumulation of wisdom. As for concentration, engaging in activities for the good of sentient beings by means of the mundane concentrations of the worlds of form and formlessness and the untainted concentration is included in the accumulation of merit; the practice of nonconceptual concentration relying on the dhyānas is included in the accumulation of wisdom. The first five transcendent perfections all partly concern the accumulation of wisdom in that they are dedicated to attaining omniscient gnosis and are imbued with the wisdom free from the concepts of the three spheres.

Furthermore, confessing negative actions, rejoicing in merit, and praying with the request to turn the wheel of the Dharma correspond to the accumulation of merit. And the three meritorious activities of generosity, discipline, and meditation also belong to the accumulation of merit. Any causes and conditions that lead to the realization of gnosis, such as following spiritual masters, accompanying them, serving them, and listening to the teachings, are included in the accumulation of wisdom.

> **When continuity in the practice is achieved,**
> **Virtue is repeatedly accomplished.**
> **The accumulations of the steadfast**
> **Serve to accomplish all goals. (XIX, 41)**

The etymological definition of "accumulation" is the repeated performance of positive activities from having attained continuity in the practice. The Sanskrit word is *sambhāra*. *Sam* is derived from *samtatyā*, meaning "continuously." *Bhā* stands for *bhāvanam*, meaning "meditation," and *ra*, standing for *āhara*, means "complete accomplishment." Repeatedly practicing positive actions—generosity and the other five transcendent perfections—

enables one to accomplish the three bodies of the Buddha, and this we call "accumulation."

The two accumulations of steadfast bodhisattvas accomplish all their own and others' goals. This is their function.

> In order to enter, to be free from characteristics,
> To act spontaneously,
> To be empowered, and to reach the ultimate,
> The steadfast accomplish the accumulations. (XIX, 42)

As for the categories of accumulation, the merit and wisdom accumulated on the level of earnest aspiration—that is, from when one is an ordinary person up until the supreme mundane level—are accumulated in order to enter and attain the first bodhisattva level. The accumulations gathered from the second up to the sixth level are gathered in order to enter and attain absence of characteristics on the seventh level. When bodhisattvas attain the seventh level, they no longer keep in mind or conceive of all the various teachings in the sūtras and so on as separate points, and so we speak of being "free of characteristics." The accumulations of merit and wisdom of a bodhisattva on the seventh level are gathered in order that the two accumulations on the eighth and ninth levels occur spontaneously. The two accumulations gathered on the eighth and ninth levels are gathered in order to attain the tenth level, on which the bodhisattva is empowered by the buddhas as their Dharma regent. And the two accumulations gathered on the tenth level are gathered in order to attain ultimate buddhahood. It is for these reasons that steadfast bodhisattvas accomplish the accumulation of merit and wisdom in this way.

2. The Essence of the Path or Training

The essence of the path comprises two parts: (1) a detailed explanation of the thirty-seven elements leading to enlightenment and (2), in summary, an analysis of sustained calm and profound insight. In the first, the thirty-seven elements leading to enlightenment are divided into seven groups.

a. A Detailed Explanation of the Thirty-Seven Elements Leading to Enlightenment
i. The Four Close Mindfulnesses

> The meditation of the wise
> On close mindfulness
> Is unequaled in fourteen respects,
> And therefore far superior to that of nonbodhisattvas.
> (XIX, 43)
>
> On account of the support, the antidotes,
> And likewise the introduction,
> Object, attentiveness,
> And attainment, their practice is superior; (XIX, 44)
>
> It is so on account of its compatibility,
> Full engagement, complete knowledge, birth,
> Greatness, culmination,
> Practice, and perfect accomplishment. (XIX, 45)

Wise bodhisattvas meditate on four close mindfulnesses: mindfulness of the body, of feelings, of consciousness, and of mental objects. Their meditation is unmatched by the listeners' and solitary realizers' meditation in fourteen respects, and for this reason the bodhisattvas' meditation on close mindfulness is far superior to that of those who are other than them—listeners and solitary realizers. What are these fourteen? Superiority of the support, superiority of the antidotes, and similarly superiority of introduction, and superiority of object, of attentiveness, and of attainment, in which respects the bodhisattvas' meditation is superior. Similarly also, there are superiority of compatibility, of full engagement, of complete knowledge, and of birth, and superiority of degree or greatness, superiority of its culmination, and likewise superiority of practice and of the result obtained, or perfect accomplishment. These comprise a different enumeration from the previous verse.[11] In these fourteen respects their close mindfulness is superior. What do all these mean?

(1) The support. The listeners' practice of close mindfulness is to listen

---

11. The last Tibetan word in the root text is *gzhan*, meaning "another" or "different." This

to, reflect, and meditate on the three scriptural collections of the Listeners' Vehicle. Bodhisattvas' practice of close mindfulness, on the other hand, is based on listening, reflecting, and meditating on the scriptural collections of the Great Vehicle, so in terms of its support it is superior.

(2) Similarly, with regard to antidotes, listeners meditate on the impurity of the body, the suffering in feelings, the impermanence of consciousness, and the absence of an individual self in all phenomena, these four being the antidotes to the four misconceptions that the body is pure, and so forth. In contrast, bodhisattvas, realizing the absence of a phenomenal self in the body, feelings, consciousness, and phenomena, meditate on suchness devoid of all attributes such as purity and impurity, happiness and unhappiness. This knowledge that the nature of the body and so forth is empty is applied respectively to the truths of suffering, of the origin, of the cessation, and of the path, as is stated in *Distinguishing the Middle from Extremes*.[12]

(3) Superior introduction. Listeners practice the four close mindfulnesses in order to access the four truths. Bodhisattvas practice in order to introduce both themselves and others, and so their introduction is different.

(4) The difference in their object. Listeners meditate by considering mainly their own bodies, while bodhisattvas do so by considering the bodies of themselves and all beings, so the object is different.

(5) The difference in their attentiveness. The listeners' attentiveness to the impure nature of the body takes the form of an antidote with attributes. Bodhisattvas' attentiveness is without any reference to attributes in anything to be eliminated or its antidote, so this again is different.

(6) The difference in their attainment. Listeners practice in order to separate from the impure body, painful feelings, and so forth, and they obtain, as the result, merely the interruption of the aggregates. Bodhisattvas do so neither because they wish to separate from these nor in order to not separate. Since the body and so forth are devoid of intrinsic existence, they meditate without any concept of separation or nonseparation. When they attain the result, therefore, they attain inseparability from the perfectly pure triple body of the Buddha[13] and separation from the impure body produced by karmic actions and defilements. Thus their attainment is different.

---

would appear to refer mainly to the repetition of the Tibetan term *rjes su 'jug pa*, which we have translated as "introduction" in verse 44 and "full engagement" in verse 45.

12. *Mādhyantavibhaga*, ch. 4, v. 1.

13. Tib. *sku gsum*, the Buddha's three kāyas or bodies.

(7) The difference in their compatibility. Bodhisattvas' practice of the four close mindfulnesses is compatible with that of the six transcendent perfections. Since they have realized that the body and the other three objects of their mindfulness, while appearing like magical illusions, are devoid of intrinsic existence, they have no attachment to anything, external or internal, neither to their bodies nor to their possessions. Their practice is therefore compatible with their generously giving things away. As a result of their not being attached to their bodies and possessions, they take and keep their vows perfectly, and such pure discipline enables them to practice patience, observing the four principles of a śramaṇa—not to retaliate when someone strikes one, and so on.[14] On account of their patience, they are diligent in practicing the transcendent perfections and working untiringly for the welfare of sentient beings. Their perseverance enables them to practice concentration without being distracted mentally. And, by relying on meditative equipoise, they accomplish the wisdom of profound insight, the realization of the general and specific characteristics of all phenomena. In this way, their practice is compatible with the six transcendent perfections. The listeners, on the other hand, meditate singly and exclusively on the elements that lead to enlightenment, and they do not have the capacity to train in the six transcendent perfections like that for long periods of time.

(8) The difference in their full engagement. Even mundane beings, as well as listeners and solitary realizers, meditate on close mindfulness of the body and so forth, but compared to them, bodhisattvas' practice is superior in that it fully engages all beings to be trained, because bodhisattvas, dwelling in the four mindfulnesses themselves, then teach others (mundane beings and listeners and solitary realizers), teaching them their respective ways to meditate on close mindfulness in accord with each one's mental capacity.

(9) The difference in their complete knowledge. Bodhisattvas perceive the body as if it were an appearance in a magical illusion. For them it does not exist in the way it appears. They experience feelings as if they were pleasant or painful experiences in a dream, but these have no independent substantial existence whatsoever. They have realized that the fully present, true nature of the mind is, by nature, space-like clear light. And they know that all the phenomena of defilement and purity are like the transient clouds

---

14. The four principles of a śramaṇa are not to return abuse with abuse, not to get angry even if someone is angry with one, not to strike anyone even if one has been struck oneself, and, even if one's faults are exposed, not to find fault in return.

and mist that appear in the sky, which itself is clear. These are not the basic nature of the mind but appear adventitiously because of conditions, like reflections. So it is in these ways that bodhisattvas' complete knowledge of the nature of the body and so forth is superior.

(10) The difference in their taking birth. Listeners train in close mindfulness in order to stop rebirth in saṃsāra. Although bodhisattvas are not reborn in saṃsāra as a result of karmic actions and defilements related to attachment, they assume the perfect bodies and riches of Indra, Brahmā, universal emperors, and the like intentionally to benefit sentient beings, and they subsequently act to benefit others, but defilements such as attachment do not arise. And even when they take birth as lowly, ordinary people, as animals, and so forth, they do so without getting discouraged, or being weakened, or giving rise to defilements. So their taking birth is superior.

(11) The difference in their greatness. Bodhisattvas naturally have sharp faculties, and even when they are practicing close mindfulness, they are doing so in order to achieve both their own and others' goals and are meditating on the no-self of the individual and that of phenomena. For these reasons, even though their meditation may not count for much when they are ordinary beings (because they practice for short periods of time and have not attained the noble levels), it is still better and greater than the listeners' and solitary realizers' practice of close mindfulness.

(12) The difference in their culmination. Once bodhisattvas have reached the eighth level, their practice of the four close mindfulnesses is fully complete. When it becomes effortless and spontaneous, their meditation is mingled and amalgamated with that of other bodhisattvas, and in this respect has reached its culmination. When one bodhisattva on the eighth level practices the four close mindfulnesses, the other bodhisattvas on the pure levels also do so, and when others are practicing them, that bodhisattva is practicing them too. So it is in this respect that their meditation is referred to as "mingled and amalgamated," because it is mingled and equivalent. Another explanation in the commentary is that the meditation is termed "mingled" in the first instant when a bodhisattva attains the eighth level from the seventh level and "amalgamated" from the second instant until the ninth level is entered.

(13) The difference in their practice. Because bodhisattvas' practice of close mindfulness is completely imbued with the great compassion that does not forsake sentient beings and with the great wisdom that is the realization of the two kinds of no-self, it surpasses the listeners' and solitary realizers' practice of close mindfulness.

(14) The difference in their perfect accomplishment of the result. By meditating on close mindfulness, the listeners attain the level of stream enterer and their other three resultant levels. Bodhisattvas, by meditating on the four close mindfulnesses, attain the ten levels and the resultant level of buddhahood, so their attainment is far superior.

ii. The Four Genuine Restraints

> The genuine restraints of the steadfast
> Are unmatched by beings.
> They are practiced as the remedies for
> Faults in the practice of close mindfulness. (XIX, 46)

Bodhisattvas' four genuine restraints are unmatched by those of other beings, that is, of listeners and solitary realizers, because they are practiced for the benefit of all sentient beings and because the essence of what they are practicing, close mindfulness, is different. The four genuine restraints are the avoidance of nonvirtuous factors that have not yet occurred, the elimination of nonvirtuous factors that have occurred, the production of virtuous factors that have not yet arisen, and the development of virtuous factors that have already been produced.

What does the practice of the four genuine restraints remedy? It remedies the faults that counteract close mindfulness, for the four genuine restraints eliminate the faults that counteract the fourteen aspects of a bodhisattva's mindfulness (the support and so on that have just been explained). These faults are to be understood as follows. Not listening, not reflecting, and not meditating on the Mahāyāna teachings runs counter to the support—that is, listening, reflecting, and meditating on the Mahāyāna teachings. Similarly, practicing with the attributes of purity, happiness, permanence, and self, as do the listeners and solitary realizers, runs counter to the bodhisattvas' antidotes. And likewise for the other aspects, through to the fault of not attaining the ten levels and buddhahood, which runs counter to perfect accomplishment. This, then, is a summary of the meaning of the four genuine restraints.

> In order to make use of saṃsāra,
> Get rid of hindrances,
> Discard misplaced attentiveness,
> Enter the levels, (XIX, 47)

> Dwell in the absence of attributes,
> Receive predictions,
> Bring sentient beings to maturity,
> Receive empowerment, (XIX, 48)
>
> Purify the universe,
> And reach the ultimate,
> Wise bodhisattvas practice these genuine restraints
> As the antidotes to counteragents. (XIX, 49)

There now follows a detailed classification of these genuine restraints. Once bodhisattvas have taken birth as Brahmā, Indra, a universal emperor, and so on, here in saṃsāra for beings' benefit, in order not to be influenced and obscured by defilements such as attachment at the time they are making use of their abundant riches, they practice the four genuine restraints. They practice them, similarly, in order to get rid of the five hindrances—namely, an inclination for pleasure, malice, dullness and somnolence, wildness and remorse, and indecision. They practice the four genuine restraints in order to get rid of attentiveness to the lower vehicles and the listeners' and solitary realizers' result instead of attentiveness to the goal of the Great Vehicle; in order to eliminate factors that will become hindrances to their entering the first noble level from the level of earnest aspiration, and so on; and in order to eliminate faults on the second to sixth levels that will act as obstacles to attaining the way of abiding without attributes on the seventh level. They practice the four restraints in order to eliminate faults that will prevent them from receiving predictions on the eighth level. They practice them in order to eliminate obscurations that will obstruct their acquiring the four kinds of perfect knowledge and thereby teaching sentient beings the Dharma and bringing them to maturity on the ninth level. And they practice them in order to remove hindrances to the tathāgatas' empowering them as Dharma regent on the tenth level. They practice the four restraints in order to eliminate obscurations that interrupt their achieving the purification of their environment as a buddha field on the three pure levels—the eighth, ninth, and tenth. And they practice the four genuine restraints in order to attain the eleventh and ultimate level, the level of buddhahood—in other words, in order to eliminate obscurations that will counter that attainment. Thus, wise bodhisattvas practice the four genuine restraints from the level of earnest aspiration up to the final stage of the tenth level as the antidotes to factors that act counter to the path.

On the basis of keenness,
They practice the yoga with special points,
Described as the antidote
In all the practices of genuine restraint. (XIX, 50)

As for how the four genuine restraints are practiced, this is indicated by five expressions in the sūtras: giving rise to keenness, making effort, applying diligence, keeping the mind focused, and letting the mind rest correctly.

Keenness is the basis of diligence. The other four refer to diligence itself. On the basis of keen interest to avoid nonvirtuous factors that have not yet occurred, to eliminate those that have occurred, to give rise to virtuous factors that have not yet arisen, and to increase those that have, bodhisattvas make efforts or strive to train in the yoga of sustained calm and profound insight, which is what is referred to as "making effort" (or "striving").

When one is practicing sustained calm and profound insight like this, it sometimes happens that one feels low-spirited and dull, which is a negative tendency related to sustained calm; sometimes the mind becomes wild and distracted, which is a negative tendency related to profound insight; sometimes neither tendency is present, and one rests naturally. One therefore has to use mindfulness and vigilance to be aware of whichever of these tendencies occurs and to be attentive to the three special points of sustained calm, self-encouragement, and equanimity, as appropriate. This is what is referred to as "practicing the yoga with the three special points." The application of the three special points is what is meant by "applying diligence."

By means of the three special points, one keeps the mind focused, and when one is resting naturally without low spirits or wildness, one lets the mind rest correctly in that state without moving. In this regard, if the mind becomes introverted and low-spirited, or sleepy and dull, one should concentrate on the special point of self-encouragement, thinking of the excellent qualities of the tathāgatas and bodhisattvas or the virtues of concentration, and lift one's spirits. If the mind becomes occupied with the pleasures of the senses or with external objects and grows wild and distracted, one should calm the mind's involvement with objects by reflecting on the defects of saṃsāra and the drawbacks of distraction and by banishing wild thoughts, concentrating inwardly on the special point of sustained calm. Then, when the mind is freed in this manner from low spirits and wildness, rest in equanimity in that state by keeping in mind the special point of equanimity, and do not apply any other remedy. This is how one keeps the mind focused with the three special points, using the special point of sustained calm to keep it from wildness, the special point of self-encouragement or profound insight to keep it from low spirits and dullness, and the special point of equanimity to hold the mind in that very state free of dullness and wildness. Here, diligence refers to diligence in employing the three special points, and the three special points are the means for keeping the mind focused. With the use of these same means to keep the mind focused again and again, it becomes fit and rests naturally with effort, and this is "letting the mind rest correctly," which is, as it were, the result.

Although there appear to be other ways of explaining these five expressions in the sūtras, we have explained them in this context according to Sthiramati's commentary. Thus these five aspects are described in this context as the antidotes that eliminate the respective counteragents for all the genuine restraints.

iii. The Four Bases of Miraculous Powers

> Steadfast bodhisattvas' four bases of miraculous powers,
> Endowed with superior characteristics,
> Are brought into play in order to accomplish
> All their own and others' aims. (XIX, 51)

The specific characteristic of steadfast bodhisattvas' four bases of miraculous powers is that they have greater qualities than those of the listeners and solitary realizers. These four are keenness as a basis for miraculous powers, and likewise diligence, attention, and analysis as bases of miraculous powers. They are so called because if one possesses these four, one gains mastery in such miraculous powers as traveling through space. Since they are brought into play in order to accomplish all the goals, mundane and supramundane, of oneself and other sentient beings, they are superior to the four bases of miraculous powers of the listeners and solitary realizers.

> With the support, detailed classification,
> Means, and full accomplishment,
> The bases of miraculous powers of the steadfast
> Are fully presented. (XIX, 52)

> They are described as being
> Based on transcendent concentration,

> With four categories and means,
> And six kinds of full accomplishment. (XIX, 53)

With regard to the presentation of the bases of miraculous powers, wise bodhisattvas' four bases of miraculous powers are presented in full with four points: support, classification, means, and full accomplishment.

The four bases of miraculous powers arise on the basis of the support—namely, transcendent concentration. It is in dependence on their training in the four boundless attitudes and thereby gaining a fit, workable mind and attaining perfect purity in the first, second, third, and fourth dhyānas that bodhisattvas acquire preternatural knowledge.

The classification and the means are both fourfold. Keenness, diligence, attention, and analysis make up the four categories, based on their nature. On the basis of their conviction that all phenomena are empty and devoid of self, bodhisattvas undertake the practice with diligence, enthusiastically and respectfully, and through this they acquire one-pointed concentration—concentration based on keenness. Alternatively, they acquire one-pointed concentration through the diligence of devoted application on account of their keenness in the four genuine restraints. Or again, they acquire one-pointed concentration through the diligence of constant application in the four genuine restraints. This is diligence as a basis of miraculous powers. In short, keenness is the causal factor that leads to concentration, and from it comes diligent undertaking, which is the actual means for accomplishing concentration.

Attention is actually sustained calm. Relying on their habitual tendency to sustained calm from having trained in it in previous lives, in this life, with little effort, bodhisattvas gain a state of mental one-pointedness, that is, mental concentration.

Analysis refers to profound insight. Following the instructions they have received on concentration, bodhisattvas use the thorough discernment of wisdom to clear away all doubts and acquire one-pointed concentration. To sum up, in one-pointed concentration on the object, all four—keenness, diligence, attention, and analysis—are equivalent and complete.

> One of these means is the application of effort,
> The second acts as an aid,
> The third directs the mind,
> And the fourth is an antidote. (XIX, 54)

This verse indicates the four kinds of means. There are eight types of mental application that eliminate the five faults that prevent one from accomplishing concentration, and in this context they are condensed into four means for accomplishing concentration. The eight eliminatory types of mental application are faith, keenness, effort, fitness, mindfulness, vigilance, mental exertion, and equanimity. First of all, through faith that one will achieve concentration, one is keen to accomplish it, so one gives rise to effort. If effort is present, therefore, it has obviously been preceded by faith and keenness, so these three are included in effort, which is the first means, enthusiasm or "the application of effort." The second means is fitness, whose nature is to help accomplish concentration by means of a workable body and mind. Mindfulness and vigilance have the same function and are therefore condensed into one to constitute the third means, directing the mind undistractedly onto the object. Mental exertion and equanimity together constitute the fourth means, which is the antidote to discursive thoughts and defilements.

> These result in the accomplishment of powers of vision,
> And of instructions, different displays,
> Aspirations, powers,
> And the acquisition of qualities. (XIX, 55)

The six kinds of full accomplishment are as follows. By relying on the bases of miraculous powers, bodhisattvas fully accomplish the power of vision, that is, the five kinds of eye. Through the full ripening of their training in the bases of miraculous powers, they see with the eye of flesh all the gross and subtle forms that exist in the various worlds of a great universal system of one thousand million worlds. The miraculous eye, or divine eye, results from practicing the four concentrations, from the first up to the fourth; it is superior to the flesh eye in that it knows every kind of form, large and small, in the ten directions and the three times. The wisdom eye of the noble beings sees ultimate reality, thatness, with nonconceptual gnosis. The eye of Dharma constitutes unobstructed knowledge of the words and meanings of all the sūtras and other scriptures. And the buddha eye directly sees all knowable phenomena of the past, present, and future, in their nature and in their multiplicity.

The flesh eye ranges in power from seeing for one yojana, through a hundred yojanas, to the length and breadth of Jambudvīpa, up to knowing the gross and subtle forms in all the realms of a great thousandfold universe. The Buddha's flesh eye sees all present forms in all the universes of the ten directions. As for the divine eye, there are two kinds: the divine eye that is produced by karmic actions and the one that is the result of meditation. The first is that of celestial beings, who have gained extremely clear faculties resulting from their karmic actions and can therefore clearly see all forms, near and far. The divine eye that results from meditation is that of practitioners who, by the power of their concentration, gain exceptionally clear faculties made from the elements in their particular worlds of concentration, and with it they see from where sentient beings have previously died and transmigrated, where they will be born in the future, and all past, present, and future forms. Those with the Dharma eye behold the general and specific characteristics of phenomena and see whether individuals' mental level is equal to or less than their own. The buddha eye sees all phenomena unobstructedly. Different explanations of the five eyes are also given in the commentary.

Full accomplishment of instructions refers to the six kinds of preternatural knowledge. Relying on the bases of miraculous powers, bodhisattvas receive instructions from the tathāgatas and give instructions to other sentient beings. The cause for their being able to do so is their accomplishing the six kinds of preternatural knowledge, on the basis of concentration. With the preternatural knowledge and ability to perform miracles, they travel unhindered to the realms of the buddhas and to the abodes of sentient beings. With the divine eye they can see the bodies of the buddhas and those of beings. With the divine ear they can hear the teachings[15] of the tathāgatas and the voices of sentient beings. By knowing others' minds, they know what beings are thinking. From their memory of former lives, they know where they and others took birth in the past. Through their knowledge of death and transmigration, they know where they will be reborn in the future. And through their knowledge of the exhaustion of taints, they bring to an end the defilements present in their own and others' minds. It is because of all these that they can receive instructions from the tathāgatas and teach and transmit them to other beings.

Displaying different ways of abiding means that through their preternatural knowledge of miracles, they display all sorts of miracles and manifestations in the maṇḍala of the Tathāgata's retinue and so on.

---

15. Tib. *gsung*, lit. "speech" or "voice."

"Aspirations" refers to the full accomplishment of their prayers of aspiration. Through the power of their gnosis, which is born through the force of their aspirations, they take birth in accordance with the prayers they have made in whichever states they wish (as gods, humans, and so on) and display the deeds of benefiting sentient beings in all kinds of ways. As it is said in the *Sūtra of the Ten Levels*, the physical qualities of these bodhisattvas who have taken birth through the power of their prayers, the qualities of their mental powers, the qualities of their melodious voices, and so forth, are not easy to describe.

The full accomplishment of acquiring powers refers to acquiring the ten powers. Because of their training in the four bases of miraculous powers, the conditioning factor of their vital energy[16] is blessed and they can live for as long as they wish. This is (1) power over life. Similarly, they have (2) power over mind: they can enter the infinite meditative absorptions of the Great Vehicle just as they wish; (3) power over material things: they rain down from the sky whatever kinds of material things are desired and thus benefit sentient beings; (4) power over activities: they manifest all kinds of physical and verbal activities, or they bless[17] their activities for taking birth in other worlds and realms in which beings are born and thus travel to different worlds and realms; (5) power over birth: while remaining in the concentrations of the world of form, without their concentration declining, they take birth in the world of desire to benefit sentient beings; (6) power over aspirations: whatever beings might aspire to (that the ground be of gold, the water be nectar, and so forth), it comes true; (7) power over prayers: they fully accomplish countless great prayers to completely fulfill their own and others' goals, beginning with the ten great prayers of aspiration that they make on the first level; (8) power of miracles: in order to inspire faith in sentient beings, they exhibit infinite miracles and magical displays such as blazing with fire, flying through the sky, radiating light, and so on; (9) power over gnosis: they have reached the summit of the four kinds of knowledge related to phenomena, meanings, language, and inner confidence and eloquence; and (10) power over the Dharma: they teach beings all the sūtras and other forms of the Dharma, using a wide variety of names, words, and letters, and thus make them content.

---

16. This is one of the nonassociated conditioning factors included in the fourth of the five aggregates. See *Treasury of Precious Qualities*, appendix 4.
17. "Bless" in this context means to enhance or bring into play.

The causes that produce these ten powers are as follows. The first three are gained through perfecting transcendent generosity: by giving protection from fear, bodhisattvas acquire power over life; with the gift of Dharma, power over the mind; and with material generosity, power over material things. Power over activities and power over birth are gained from perfecting transcendent discipline: by purifying their physical activities, they can send forth all kinds of bodily manifestations; by purifying their verbal activities, they can send forth many different manifestations of speech; and by maintaining perfectly pure discipline, they can take birth wherever they wish. By perfecting transcendent patience, they cease to disturb beings' minds and can act in accordance with those beings' wishes, so that they can accomplish whatever aspirations they make, thus obtaining power over aspirations. By perfecting transcendent diligence, they gain power over prayers, because as a result of their former efforts for their own and others' welfare, they subsequently accomplish the prayers they have made for their own and others' good. By perfecting transcendent concentration and gaining power over the mind, they gain the power to perform any miracles they wish. Power over gnosis and power over the Dharma are achieved by means of perfecting transcendent wisdom.

"The acquisition of qualities" refers to full accomplishment of the acquisition of qualities, that is, to achieving the ultimate excellent qualities such as the Buddha's ten strengths, four fearlessnesses, and eighteen distinctive qualities.

Thus, by relying on the four bases of miraculous powers, bodhisattvas accomplish the six kinds of full accomplishment.

iv. THE FIVE POWERS

The five powers comprise the powers of faith, diligence, mindfulness, concentration, and wisdom. Of these, faith is of three kinds: confidence in existent realities—the fact, for example, that actions infallibly give rise to their effects; the vivid faith and clear state of mind that is experienced when thinking of the qualities of the Three Jewels; and the yearning faith experienced on seeing that it is possible to achieve nirvāṇa and to accomplish the noble path. Another explanation of the power of faith is given in the *Sūtra of the Teaching of Akṣayamati*, which speaks of having faith in four things, which are as follows. Through having confidence in the reality of karmic cause and effect, one avoids negative actions even if one's life is at risk. From having faith in the bodhisattva activities, one has no interest in other vehicles. Faith in profound emptiness—the absence of self in phenomena (which arise interdependently), the nature of the three doors of perfect liberation—destroys the latent tendencies of all kinds of wrong views. And through faith in all the extensive qualities of the Buddha—the strengths, fearlessnesses, and so forth—one will, without any doubts or uncertainties, accomplish them.

It is the power of diligence that enables one to accomplish the teachings in which one has faith. This implies the four genuine restraints.

The power of mindfulness consists of being perfectly mindful of the teachings that are to be accomplished with diligence; this involves achieving the four close mindfulnesses.

The power of concentration consists of achieving the absorptions of the four dhyānas and four formless states and using the power of mindfulness to settle the mind one-pointedly and continuously on the teachings without letting them go to waste.

And the power of wisdom consists of knowing the general and specific characteristics of the objects on which one has focused one-pointedly with the power of concentration, or of knowing the four noble truths.

The above is a general explanation, but the text at this point describes the bases or grounds or objects of the five powers.

> Enlightenment, activities, supreme learning,
> Sustained calm, and profound insight
> Should be known as being the objects of faith and the others
> In the sense of these bringing the accomplishment of those
>   goals. (XIX, 56)

The object or basis of the power of faith is enlightenment. When bodhisattvas consider enlightenment, referring to the inexhaustible gnosis that is the result of the Great Vehicle or to the nondual gnosis of the first level, they have faith in it and think, "I will attain that!" With the power of diligence, they consider the bodhisattva activities contained in the trainings in superior discipline and wisdom and characterized by the levels and transcendent perfections, and they use diligence to accomplish those activities. With the power of mindfulness, they retain their supreme learning, without ever forgetting the teachings of the Great Vehicle that they have heard, remembered, and thus extensively ascertained with words. With the power of concentration—that of bodhisattvas on the level of earnest aspiration—they consider how to attain the extraordinary sustained calm of the first level. And with the power of wisdom, they consider how to attain the nonconceptual gnosis, the profound insight, of the first level. Enlightenment and so forth are therefore to be understood as being the bases or objects of faith and the other powers.

Why are these five described as powers? They are termed "powers" in the sense that they control the accomplishment of everything related to the process of purification. Faith enables bodhisattvas to master enlightenment, diligence to master the bodhisattva activities. Mindfulness enables them to master the Mahāyāna teachings, concentration the attainment of sustained calm, and wisdom the attainment of profound insight. Alternatively, it can be said that the five powers enable them to accomplish their own and others' goals.

v. The Five Irresistible Forces

> **Faith and the others lead to the bodhisattva levels**
> **But are considered to be associated with defilement.**
> **Because they weaken their counteragents,**
> **They are termed irresistible forces. (XIX, 57)**

The five irresistible forces comprise the forces of faith, diligence, mindfulness, concentration, and wisdom—described as irresistible forces when they can no longer be quashed by their respective counteragents. It is because of the irresistible force of faith and the other four at the stage of earnest aspiration that bodhisattvas enter the first of the noble levels. As these forces grow stronger and stronger, they lead directly to the noble levels, but since they do not free one from the obscurations to be eliminated on the path of seeing, they belong to the level of ordinary beings, associated with defilement.

What, then, is the difference between powers and irresistible forces? The five irresistible forces belong to the mundane level, but as long as they can be suppressed and obstructed by lack of faith, laziness, forgetfulness, distraction, and the ignorance of aberrant understanding, they are termed "powers." When these countering factors are weakened and cannot adversely affect or suppress faith and the other four antidotes, that faith and the others are termed "irresistible forces."

vi. The Seven Branches of Enlightenment

The seven branches of enlightenment are those of mindfulness, perfect discernment, diligence, joy, fitness, concentration, and evenness. Mindfulness, on account of its relationship to sustained calm, makes the thirty-seven elements leading to enlightenment that are realized through practice and experience appear clearly to the mind, without being forgotten. Perfect discernment of phenomena refers to wisdom and is related to profound insight; on the path of seeing, it is that which knows clearly and distinctly the specific characteristics of factors related to defilement (to be rejected) and factors related to purity (to be adopted). Diligence serves to take up the extraordinary qualities of higher levels and to eliminate the faults that prevent one from gaining such qualities. Joy is the sublime physical ease and mental happiness that occur when bodhisattvas on the first level gain direct realization of the universal expanse of reality and are thereby rid of the obscurations to be eliminated on the path of seeing (and it is for this reason that this level is called Perfect Joy). Fitness refers to being free of the negative tendencies that render the body and mind unworkable, resulting in a workable body, resplendent and healthy, and a workable mind that is unimpeded in engaging its object. Concentration refers to the one-pointed mind that considers suchness, the expanse of reality. Evenness refers to remaining naturally without movement, like a clear lake without waves or muddiness, once all faults—that is, low spirits and wildness—have been eliminated.

Of these seven, perfect discernment, diligence, and joy are related to profound insight. Fitness, concentration, and evenness are related to sustained calm. Mindfulness is related to both and is universal.

The classification of these seven branches of enlightenment has four aspects: their classification in terms of time, their classification in terms of what bodhisattvas know, their classification as seven branches, and the classification of these seven as five branches.

> The branches of enlightenment are classified as such
> For those who have entered the levels.
> This is because they have realized sameness
> With regard to phenomena and all beings. (XIX, 58)

(1) Classification in Terms of Time

Although bodhisattvas already have mindfulness, wisdom, and so forth on the level of earnest aspiration, these do not bear the name "branches of enlightenment." On the other hand, the mindfulness and so forth present in the mind streams of those who have entered the noble levels—the levels without fault—and attained the first level are held to be classified as "branches of enlightenment."

(2) Classification in Terms of Bodhisattvas' Knowledge: The Meaning of These Being Described as Branches of Enlightenment

Why are they described as branches of enlightenment? Bodhisattvas have acquired direct knowledge of the nature of the arborescent state of evenness that is enlightenment, so for that reason mindfulness and the others are classified as its branches. Bodhisattvas have realized that all the phenomena of the origin of suffering and all sentient beings are sameness, being enlightened from the beginning, the perfectly pure ultimate reality that is primordially and naturally unborn. At that time, therefore, the supramundane, ultimate bodhicitta actually takes birth. Moreover, by realizing that phenomena are devoid of self, bodhisattvas directly realize the sameness of phenomena, and by realizing that beings or individuals are devoid of self, they directly realize the sameness of sentient beings. Alternatively, by fully understanding in formal meditation that phenomena and individuals are devoid of self, like the midst of space, they know the sameness of phenomena; and by fully understanding in postmeditation the absence of any difference between themselves and others—that all sentient beings are the same as oneself, that one is the same as all sentient beings, and that as much as one removes one's own suffering, one must remove all beings' suffering too—they know the sameness of all sentient beings.

(3) Classification as Seven

In the same way that, for example, the universal emperor possesses the seven precious attributes of his royal state, for a bodhisattva who has directly realized the primordially unborn enlightened state there are seven branches of enlightenment.

When a universal emperor appears in the world, by the force of his merit there appears a precious wheel made of celestial materials and fashioned by divine artisans, with a thousand spokes and a multicolored rim. Like a second sun, it rises high in the sky, followed by the universal emperor and his troops traveling through the sky. As soon as it arrives in the regions of the minor kings living in the forts and castles in the lands around, the latter receive the emperor and become his subjects, and the wheel confers absolute victory over all those lands that have not already fallen under its dominion and been conquered. This is what we call the precious wheel.

Similarly, the precious elephant is like a snow mountain traveling through the sky. With its perfect, powerful body, all its limbs perfectly set, it befits the greatest of monarchs. It is perfectly tame and overcomes all hostile forces.

The precious horse is pure blue in color, as beautiful as the feathers on a peacock's neck, and of perfect build. All-knowing, in just the time it takes to eat breakfast it can easily go around the lands at the farthest reaches of the ocean and come back again, and it has all the qualities of the perfect steed.

The precious jewel is the source of everything one could need or desire, made of beryl, dark blue in color and beautifully shaped. Even at night, it can light up everything for a yojana around as brightly as the sun. In hot weather it provides coolth; in cold weather it gives warmth. Its mere contact cures all kinds of illness, and even in arid, bleak plains it is the source of clear streams. In this and other ways it has the abundant power to fulfill every purpose.

The precious queen is the height of physical beauty; the mere sight of her brings delight. Never indulging in adultery, she has few defilements and has the deepest respect for her husband. Her beautiful manners enchant everyone. From her mouth and body comes the fragrance of divine perfumes. Her sublime touch, cool or warm,[18] delights, and she possesses all kinds of other extraordinary qualities.

The precious steward is as wealthy as Vaiśravaṇa,[19] for simply stretching out his hand produces all the precious things one could wish for. He carries out all the emperor's commands perfectly and possesses all the finest qualities of the highest of all the emperor's closest commissioners.

The precious lord chancellor or minister or general outshines all others

---

18. Her touch feels cool when it is hot and warm when it is cold.
19. Vaiśravaṇa, one of the four great kings and guardian of the north, renowned for his enormous wealth.

with his unparalleled courage, steadfastness, and strength. In disposing his troops, he is skillful in advance and retreat alike, cares for those who act correctly, subjugates those who do wrong, fulfills the emperor's wishes, and vanquishes his enemies. He is able to accomplish all this without delay and acts in accordance with the emperor's orders.

All these can be used as analogies for what follows.

> In order to conquer unconquered knowledge,
> They specifically practice mindfulness.
> Their perfect discernment destroys
> Every conceptualized attribute. (XIX, 59)

When bodhisattvas attain the first level, there are knowable phenomena that they did not directly know previously on the level of earnest aspiration, or obscurations to direct knowledge that they have not previously overcome. So in order to have direct knowledge at the time of the first level and to overcome the obscurations to that direct knowledge that are to be eliminated on the path of seeing, they specifically practice unforgetting mindfulness of the elements in which they have previously trained on the path of earnest aspiration. Such mindfulness is like the precious wheel that enables the universal emperor to be victorious over the whole earth.

The wisdom of perfect discernment of these first-level bodhisattvas destroys all dualistic concepts of the phenomenal and individual self, like the precious elephant routing all the enemy's troops.

> They apply their diligence
> In order to realize everything swiftly.
> As the light of Dharma grows,
> They are forever filled with joy. (XIX, 60)

The diligence of bodhisattvas on the first level is applied in order to swiftly realize and accomplish every one of the extraordinary qualities such as the different kinds of preternatural knowledge, like the precious horse, which swiftly reaches its desired destination. When they attain the first level, they realize thatness directly, so that the great supramundane light of the Dharma[20] shines brighter and brighter and their bodies and minds are

---

20. Tib. *chos kyi snang ba*, also translatable as "vision of reality."

constantly filled with joy. Joy, therefore, is likened to the light of the precious jewel dispelling the darkness.

> **Because they are free of all obscurations,**
> **They are fully fit and thus accomplish bliss.**
> **Their concentration gives rise**
> **To all the wealth they could desire. (XIX, 61)**

On the path of perfect liberation at the first level, they are freed or liberated from all the obscurations to be eliminated by the path of seeing, and the resulting fitness and absolute workability of body and mind leads to their attaining bliss, like the precious queen's touch that so delights the universal emperor. Through the branch of enlightenment that is genuine concentration, they come to acquire all the qualities such as preternatural knowledge and to reach all their intended goals according to their wishes, so concentration is likened to the precious steward, who produces all the precious things that the emperor wishes for in abundance.

> **With evenness, they abide**
> **At all times as they wish;**
> **In their postmeditation and nonconceptual states,**
> **They remain constantly sublime. (XIX, 62)**

With the branch of enlightenment that is genuine evenness, the minds of bodhisattvas on the first level are at all times free of defilements and lesser defilements, such as attachment and aversion, and low spirits and wildness, as a result of which they rest naturally, just as they wish. In the postmeditation, the pure mundane gnosis enables them to act for beings' benefit, to acquire the qualities of the higher levels that they have not yet obtained, and to eliminate the faults that they have not yet eliminated and leave the lower levels behind. And in formal meditation, with nonconceptual gnosis, the supreme bodhisattvas constantly remain in the state of dwelling without dwelling anywhere. Alternatively, it can be said that they remain constantly in the way of abiding of the greatest noble beings, Sthiramati's commentary quoting this line of the verse as "In dwelling, they are forever sublime."

Evenness is thus like the precious general marshaling his four divisions, using them to put to flight those who have to be defeated and driven out, and withdrawing troops that need to be assembled and protected, placing them in a position where they will not be endangered or harmed. Similarly, as if assembling troops and banishing enemy forces, the pure mundane gnosis takes up those factors that have to be adopted and eliminates factors that must be abandoned. And as if letting the troops rest where they will not be in danger, the nonconceptual gnosis settles in the state where all concepts are completely stilled.

> **Courageous beings with such qualities**
> **Are compared to the universal emperor;**
> **They are constantly surrounded by the branches of enlightenment**
> **As if by his seven precious attributes. (XIX, 63)**

Like the universal emperor and his seven precious attributes of royalty, bodhisattvas who possess the above qualities are the masters or employers of those qualities, and as such are always surrounded by and endowed with the seven branches of enlightenment.

(4) Classification of the Seven Branches as Five

> **These are the nature branch and the source branch,**
> **Third, the branch of certain deliverance,**
> **Fourth, the branch of benefit,**
> **And the threefold branch of absence of defilements. (XIX, 64)**

This condensation of the seven branches into five also explains the meaning of the term "branches." Perfect discernment of phenomena is the nature branch, because it is, by nature, the realization of the essence of enlightenment. Mindfulness is the branch that is the source, because it is through the mindfulness at the time of the great supreme mundane level, which is the culmination of repeated training and unforgetting mindfulness of the elements of the practice at the stage of earnest aspiration, that perfect discernment and the other branches arise. Third, diligence is the branch of certain deliverance, because it is by the force of diligence that bodhisattvas pass beyond the level of earnest aspiration and attain certain deliverance on the first level. The specific mindfulness and diligence at the time of the first level are the resultant mindfulness and diligence, the culmination of the mindfulness and diligence employed on the path of earnest aspiration. Fourth, joy is the benefit branch—the benefit of realizing the expanse of reality when the first level is attained, for because of that realization, extraordinary joy arises in the mind. Fitness, concentration, and evenness together constitute the branch of absence of defilements. Physical and mental fitness frees bodhisattvas from the negative tendencies of the defilement-related and cognitive obscurations—it is what leads to absence of defilements or is the source of absence of defilements. Concentration is the ground on which they dwell, thus leading to absence of defilements, because when one rests in concentration, the lesser defilements such as drowsiness and excitement are dispelled. And evenness is the very essence of absence of defilements, for there can be no defilements when one is resting evenly in the natural state.

vii. The Eightfold Noble Path

The eightfold noble path comprises the noble paths of right view, right thought, right speech, right conduct, right livelihood, right effort, right mindfulness, and right concentration. Right view involves contemplating and training in the direct realization—gained on the path of seeing with the wisdom of perfect discernment—of evenness, the expanse of reality, devoid of individual and phenomenal self. Right view leads to right thought—that is, the thought of or desire for superior discipline, superior concentration, and superior wisdom, which together constitute the cause for certain deliverance from the three worlds; and thoughts free of defilements such as hedonism and malice. Right speech involves teaching right view and right thought as one has understood them oneself to other beings in order to benefit them, and completely avoiding the negative verbal actions of lying, harsh words, sowing discord, and worthless chatter. Right conduct involves avoiding the three negative physical acts (taking life and so on) and engaging in the path to perfect liberation. Right livelihood implies the avoidance of all forms of wrong livelihood involving flattery, hypocrisy, and so forth. Right effort applies to training continuously on the noble path, relying on right view, thought, conduct, and livelihood, in order to eliminate the two obscurations to be eliminated on the path through meditation. With right mindfulness, the points of the teachings that one has understood are not forgotten and appear clearly to the mind. And with right concentration, the mind is settled evenly and one-pointedly on suchness, the expanse of reality.

Of these eight, right speech, right conduct, and right livelihood are to be observed during one's daily activities, whereas when one is practicing inner concentration one should train in sustained calm and profound insight.

In the latter case, right view, right thought, and right effort are related to profound insight: right view is profound insight itself, while right thought and effort are accessories of profound insight. And right concentration and mindfulness are related to sustained calm: right concentration is sustained calm, and mindfulness is accessory to it.

These eight branches of the path are indicated in the next two verses.

> After that, bodhisattvas follow up
> Their realization of the nature as it is,
> They realize its presentation
> And apply that presentation, (XIX, 65)

> They purify the three acts,
> And they cultivate the antidotes
> To factors that obscure knowledge,
> The path, and extraordinary qualities. (XIX, 66)

After attaining the first level, from the second level onward bodhisattvas train in the eight branches of the noble path. By following up the realization (through the perfect discernment branch of enlightenment) of the nature as it is, the absence of the two kinds of self, they realize and meditate on that expanse of reality. This is right view, with which bodhisattvas master their understanding of thatness. What establishes that understanding as being like this or like that is right thought. How does it establish that? The sūtras and other scriptures that indicate by means of names, phrases, and letters that thatness is like this or like that are referred to as "teachings of presentation" because they indicate and present the meaning of thatness. Consequently, to realize oneself the meaning of that presentation as it is, to explain it like that to others, and to apply it by unmistakenly discerning the intended meaning of that scriptural presentation is right thought.

The three kinds of acts[21] are purified by means of right speech, conduct, and livelihood. Relying on right effort for two measureless kalpas, bodhisattvas cultivate the antidotes to cognitive obscurations. Similarly, with right mindfulness they cultivate the antidotes to the factors that obscure

---

21. According to Sthiramati, the three kinds of acts are verbal acts, physical acts, and acts that involve both speech and body (in this context, flattery, hypocritical behavior, and so on).

the path—that is to say, when they are practicing the paths of sustained calm and profound insight, if sinking or wildness occur, obscuring that path, these obscurations are cleared by mindfulness of the three special points (the special point of sustained calm, the special point of maintaining one's concentration, and the special point of equanimity, as has already been explained).[22] With right concentration they cultivate the antidotes to the factors that obscure extraordinary qualities such as the six kinds of preternatural knowledge described in the Powers chapter.

b. SUMMARY, AN ANALYSIS OF SUSTAINED CALM AND PROFOUND INSIGHT

> Because, on the basis of right abiding,
> The mind settles on the mind,
> And because phenomena are perfectly discerned,
> There is sustained calm and profound insight. (XIX, 67)

By relying on right abiding,[23] that is, on the four concentrations of the world of form, untainted by defilements, the mind settles one-pointedly on the mind alone (there being no phenomena apart from the mind), resulting in sustained calm. And on the basis of that sustained calm, the unmistaken knowledge of the meaning of the thatness of all phenomena perfectly discerns phenomena, resulting in nonconceptuality, that is, profound insight. This is a brief presentation of the defining characteristics of sustained calm and profound insight according to the Great Vehicle. There now follows a detailed treatment of sustained calm and profound insight.

> These are held to be universal, partial,
> Not partial, and causal.
> Related to realization and to certain deliverance,
> Devoid of attributes, not deliberate, (XIX, 68)

> Completely purifying, and perfectly pure—
> The yoga of sustained calm and profound insight of the steadfast

---

22. See page 376.
23. Tib. *yang dag par gnas pa*. According to Sthiramati, this is a synonym for right concentration.

Is universal for all levels;
It is this that accomplishes everything. (XIX, 69)

Sustained calm and profound insight are both universal for the whole training and accomplishment of good qualities—"universal" because they are indispensable for all who are training toward enlightenment, who wish to acquire the dhyānas and concentration, and who want to gain preternatural knowledge and other qualities. The main body of all meditation is these two.

"Partial" refers to the fact that the meditation of the four formless absorptions is predominantly sustained calm, with little profound insight, and therefore partial, and that the first, second, and third concentrations of the world of form consist predominantly of profound insight, with a little sustained calm, and they are therefore also one-sided or partial. "Not partial" refers to the fact that sustained calm and profound insight are combined, with neither being predominant, and they are therefore not partial or one-sided—this being the case during the meditation of the fourth concentration of the world of form.

The practice of sustained calm and profound insight on the level of earnest aspiration is held to be the cause for attaining the first bodhisattva level. The sustained calm and profound insight practiced at the time of the first level are termed "sustained calm and profound insight of perfect realization," because at that time bodhisattvas realize the all-pervading expanse of reality. From the second level up to the sixth, sustained calm and profound insight are termed "sustained calm and profound insight of certain deliverance" because they successively eliminate all conceptual attributes and lead to certain deliverance on the seventh level, devoid of attributes. The sustained calm and profound insight on the seventh level are known as "sustained calm and profound insight without attributes" because at that stage bodhisattvas no longer distinguish different attributes in the various teachings such as the sūtras, and everything is meditated as a single taste without any attributes. On the eighth, ninth, and tenth levels, the practice of sustained calm and profound insight is termed "nondeliberate sustained calm and profound insight" because bodhisattvas remain in sustained calm and profound insight effortlessly and spontaneously. The practice of sustained calm and profound insight on these three pure levels leads to their "completely purifying" buddha fields. And because they enable the bodhisattva to attain buddhahood, in which the two obscurations together with habitual tendencies have been totally purified, they are referred to as "perfectly pure."

Thus the yoga of sustained calm and profound insight of the steadfast on these different levels is universal to all the levels, from that of earnest aspiration up to the tenth level. It is this that enables bodhisattvas to accomplish all their own and others' goals and to accomplish all the excellent qualities from each level to the next.

3. Branches That Enhance the Practice

The branches are explained in four parts: (1) skill in the means that enable one to accomplish the great meaning unfailingly and with little difficulty; (2) the power of memory that never forgets teachings previously received; (3) prayers of aspiration that enable one to acquire good qualities in the future; and (4) an explanation of concentration and the four summaries of the Dharma that make the path completely pure.

a. Skill in the Means That Enable One to Accomplish the Great Meaning Unfailingly and with Little Difficulty

> Skill in completing the Buddha Dharma,
> In bringing sentient beings to full maturation,
> In swift attainment, in accomplishing activities,
> And in not interrupting the path—(XIX, 70)

> The means employed by bodhisattvas
> On all levels are without equal:
> By relying on such skill in means,
> They accomplish every kind of goal. (XIX, 71)

The means for completing the whole of the Buddha Dharma, from the qualities of the path such as the levels, transcendent perfections, and elements leading to enlightenment through to the resultant qualities of the strengths, fearlessnesses, omniscience, and so forth, is nonconceptual gnosis. It is through the absence of concepts with regard to attributes that every one of the qualities of the path and its result will be completed and perfected. For as we find in the *Perfection of Wisdom in One Hundred Thousand*

Lines, "If one wishes to complete transcendent generosity, one must train in transcendent wisdom," and so on, through to "Those who wish to acquire omniscient gnosis should train in transcendent wisdom."

The means for bringing sentient beings to full maturation are the four ways of attracting disciples, because these extract beings from nonvirtuous modes of conduct and set them in virtuous practices.

The means for rapidly acquiring preternatural powers and swiftly attaining buddhahood is to confess, rejoice, pray, and dedicate, as is shown in the sūtras:

> I shall confess all negative actions.
> I shall rejoice in all merit.
> I shall pray to all the buddhas.
> May I attain supreme enlightenment, unsurpassable gnosis.

The means for accomplishing activities are the two doors of the power of memory and concentration. By using the power of memory to retain the words and meanings, bodhisattvas accomplish their own good; by using concentration to display all kinds of miraculous activities, they accomplish others' good.

Skill in not interrupting the path refers to not interrupting the lineage or family line of the tathāgatas, the path that accomplishes the nondwelling nirvāṇa, combining wisdom and compassion—for with wisdom one does not dwell in the extreme of saṃsāra, and with compassion one does not dwell in the extreme of peace. Here, in developing the two aspects of bodhicitta (relative and ultimate) together, these two means being complete, the others are also implicitly included in it, so this is the supreme skillful means, sufficient on its own.

These five aspects of skill in means apply to bodhisattvas on all levels, from the level of earnest aspiration to the ten noble levels. Such skillful means, which are used not for following the lower vehicles but for accomplishing the path and result of the Great Vehicle, are without equal compared to the methods of mundane beings and listeners and solitary realizers, and it is by relying on such skill in means that bodhisattvas easily accomplish all their own and others' goals.

b. The Power of Memory That Never Forgets Teachings Previously Received

> The powers of memory that come through maturation,
> Habitual listening, and concentration
> Are respectively lesser and greater,
> The greater itself being threefold. (XIX, 72)
>
> That of the wise who have not yet entered
> And that of those who have entered, albeit on impure levels,
> Are lesser and middling.
> The power of memory of those on pure levels is greater. (XIX, 73)

The power of memory consists of extraordinary memory and wisdom. By this means, bodhisattvas perfectly retain every single one of the words and meanings of the Buddha's teachings. Even teachings and topics they have not previously heard manifest in their minds. And they gain all the qualities that lead to enlightenment.

As to how the power of memory is gained, by asking questions on the sacred Dharma, making offerings, memorizing the teachings, reading them, and so on in other lives and thereby accumulating the merit for acquiring the power of memory, bodhisattvas are able to perfectly retain the words and meanings of any subject from a single explanation. This is the power of memory that comes through maturation. Through habituation to hearing a lot of teachings from numerous spiritual masters in the present life, they retain, without forgetting them, the words and meanings of the subjects explained by the buddhas, bodhisattvas, preceptors, and instructors; this is the power of memory through habituation to listening. And as a result of training in the appropriate concentration—that of emptiness, absence of attributes, or absence of expectancy, for example—they are able to retain any teaching they have heard once, which is the power of memory through concentration.

The powers of memory that come through maturation and listening are termed lesser, while the power of memory that comes through concentration is greater. The greater power of memory itself is of three kinds: lesser, in the case of the power of memory that arises through the practice of concentration by bodhisattvas on the level of earnest aspiration, who have not entered the noble levels; middling, for those who have reached the noble levels but are still on the seven impure levels; and greater in the case of those dwelling on the three pure levels. All these are categories of the power of memory.

> **Bodhisattvas who repeatedly**
> **Rely correctly on these**
> **Constantly teach others the sacred Dharma**
> **And retain it themselves. (XIX, 74)**

As for the function of the power of memory, it is by relying correctly on the three powers of memory that come through maturation and so on, continuously, again and again, that bodhisattvas constantly teach others the sacred Dharma and retain its words and meanings themselves.

c. Prayers of Aspiration That Enable One to Acquire Good Qualities in the Future

> **The prayers of the steadfast**
> **Are accompanied by a yearning intention,**
> **Aroused by gnosis,**
> **And on all levels they have no equal. (XIX, 75)**

The prayers[24] of steadfast bodhisattvas are accompanied by the intention and earnest aspiration to achieve the great enlightenment and any other result they may wish for. The prayers are initiated by the gnosis that knows that the object that is aspired to is a proper one: it is not as if bodhisattvas pray for tainted things for their own benefit. So having aroused their intention with extraordinary gnosis, they make their prayers by mentally wishing them and also putting them into words. This is the cause or essence of their prayers of aspiration. The *Great Commentary* explains that the fact that they arise from gnosis as their cause (gnosis in this context being nonconceptual gnosis), or alternatively that they are dedicated to gaining that gnosis, is what is termed "aroused by gnosis."

"On all levels they have no equal" indicates the level of the aspirations. The prayers that bodhisattvas make at different times on all the levels—the

---

24. The Tibetan term *smon lam* has been translated throughout this section interchangeably as "prayer" or "aspiration."

level of earnest aspiration and the ten noble levels—are never equaled by the prayers of mundane beings, nor by the prayers of the listeners and solitary realizers.

> **They are to be known as the cause,**
> **Bringing accomplishment through their mere intent;**
> **They thus bear fruit the moment they are conceived**
> **And in the future are fulfilled. (XIX, 76)**

The virtues of bodhisattvas' aspirations are as follows. Bodhisattvas' aspirations are to be understood as being the causal factors that enable them to accomplish their own and others' goals, both in this life and in other lives. Even if they do not do anything else for that purpose physically or verbally, the mere intent of whatever aspirations they make ensures their being accomplished accordingly. For that reason, the very instant they wish and pray for something in their minds, it starts to yield results in this present life, and in the future that prayer will accomplish all goals.

> **They are diverse, great, and, on ever higher levels**
> **Until enlightenment, pure;**
> **Thus it is that bodhisattvas' goals,**
> **Their own as well as others', are fully accomplished. (XIX, 77)**

The different categories of aspirations are described next. The prayers of bodhisattvas who are at the stage of earnest aspiration are of all different kinds. At that time they have not yet realized the nature of the universal expanse of reality: they see the dangers of saṃsāra and want a means for finding peace from them, and they consider good qualities and want to accomplish them. So the prayers they make—"In the future, may I become like this or that to benefit sentient beings," and so on—are of all different kinds. Once they have reached the first level, because they are fully accomplishing the ten great aspirations,[25] their prayers are made on a vast scale. From then on until they attain ultimate great enlightenment, as they progress further through the second and other remaining levels, their aspirations become more and more vast and exalted and more and more pure.

As for the function of their aspirations, it should be understood that it is

---

25. The ten great prayers or aspirations are listed on page 204.

on the basis of their prayers of aspiration that bodhisattvas' goals, both their own and those of others, are achieved, as is indicated in the sūtras, which state that it is not easy to describe in words how the power of bodhisattvas' aspirations, charged with the force of their merit, brings about their own and others' benefit by means of infinite bodily manifestations, infinite rays of light, and infinite miraculous activities.

d. An Explanation of Concentration and the Four Summaries of the Dharma That Make the Path Completely Pure

This section consists of (1) an explanation of the three kinds of concentration (the subject)[26] and (2) an explanation of the four summaries of the Dharma (the object to be understood through concentration).

i. An Explanation of the Three Kinds of Concentration

> The domains of the three kinds of concentration are
> The two kinds of no-self,
> The support of belief in a self,
> And the permanent elimination of the latter. (XIX, 78)

The three kinds of concentration—concentration related to emptiness, to absence of expectancy, and to absence of attributes—constitute the most important aspect of the path, so they will now be explained. The domains or objects of these three kinds of concentration are as follows. The two aspects of absence of an imputed self—in the individual and in phenomena—constitute the domain of the concentration related to emptiness. The domain of the concentration related to absence of expectancy comprises the five perpetuating aggregates, which are the tainted support for the interdependent appearances of the dependent reality that constitute the belief in the two kinds of self. The domain of the concentration related to absence of attributes is the fully present reality in which all attributes have been completely eliminated, the very basis or support for the exaggerated misconceptions of

---

26. Mipham Rinpoche qualifies these three concentrations as "the subject" (Tib. *yul can*), whose object is the four summaries.

the two kinds of self having always been, by its very nature, devoid of the two kinds of self.

> From the very nature of subjects and objects,
> You should know these concentrations are of three kinds.
> They take the form of nonconceptuality,
> Rejection, and perfect joy. (XIX, 79)

Because these three concentrations focus on the above three objects and are thus, by their very nature, their subjects, inasmuch as the objects are different, their subjects the concentrations are also to be understood as being of three kinds.

Now to explain the aspects of the three kinds of concentrations, the concentration of emptiness takes the form of nonconceptuality—the absence of concepts of the two kinds of self. The concentration of absence of expectancy takes the form of nonattachment, rejection,[27] and absence of expectancy with regard to the five causal aggregates, for they are impermanent and are the seat of all kinds of suffering. The concentration of absence of attributes takes the form of intense joy and confidence in the ultimate truth, the expanse in which all attributes and sufferings have been completely extinguished.

> In order to completely know,
> To eliminate, and to realize,
> The concentrations such as emptiness
> Are declared to be three. (XIX, 80)

The reasons for there being three concentrations are as follows. In order to know completely that from the very beginning the two kinds of imputed self do not exist, there is the concentration of emptiness. In order to eliminate the dependent, impure support for the belief in the two kinds of self, there is the concentration of absence of expectancy. And in order to realize the fully present truth of cessation, there is the concentration of absence of attributes. Thus three kinds of concentration, beginning with the concentration of emptiness, are proclaimed for the three purposes just mentioned.

---

27. Tib. *rgyab kyis phyogs*, literally "turning one's back on."

ii. An Explanation of the Four Summaries of the Dharma

With the wish to benefit beings,
The four summaries of the Dharma
Were taught to bodhisattvas
As the causal basis for concentration. (XIX, 81)

Our incomparable teachers, the buddhas, wishing to bring the greatest possible benefit to sentient beings, taught the bodhisattvas four summaries or epitomes that include the whole meaning of the Dharma, these being the causal bases of the three concentrations on emptiness, and so on. They are as follows: "All that is compounded is impermanent. All that is tainted is suffering. All phenomena are devoid of self. Nirvāṇa is peace."

In what way are these four the causal bases of concentration? Two summaries—"All that is compounded is impermanent" and "All that is tainted is suffering"—are explained as the causal basis for realizing the concentration of absence of expectancy. Once one realizes that compounded phenomena are by nature impermanence and suffering, one has no attachment or expectancy with regard to compounded phenomena, which are like the teeth of a saw, or like poisoned food, and one thus realizes the concentration of absence of expectancy. The summary that teaches "All phenomena are devoid of self" is the causal basis for realizing the concentration of emptiness, for if one knows that the individual self and phenomenal self are merely imputed to all phenomena and do not in fact exist, one realizes the concentration of emptiness. The summary that says "Nirvāṇa is peace" is the causal basis of the concentration of absence of attributes, because by settling in evenness in the fully present reality, which is peace from the very beginning and can only be known personally, one realizes the truth of cessation, nirvāṇa in which all conceptual constructions have been extinguished.

For the steadfast, these four signify
Nonexistence, conceptualization,
Simple imputation,
And the complete extinction of concepts. (XIX, 82)

What do these four terms—impermanence, suffering, no-self, and peace—mean? For steadfast bodhisattvas, these four summaries have the following significance.

Once compounded phenomena have come into being, they do not remain for a second instant: they do not exist permanently, and this is what is meant by impermanence. The Sanskrit word for "impermanence" is *anityatā*: *nityatā* means "eternal," and *a* is a negative particle, giving "not eternal" or "impermanent." The *Great Commentary* states that it is not merely the coming into being and disintegration of phenomena that bodhisattvas should understand as impermanence but rather that things do not last forever in the way that the two kinds of self are imagined as doing. Although they appear to arise and then disintegrate, in ultimate truth, they do not even arise, so how can they disintegrate? They do not. Thus there is no basis at all for considering that what is not permanent is permanent, so neither is there anything to be expected. This is evident from the point of view of ultimate truth.

Mere conceptualization refers to suffering. Bodhisattvas know that as long as one mistakenly imputes a subject and object that do not exist, one will suffer in saṃsāra, and this is the meaning of suffering.

The meaning of absence of self is that within the dependent reality that appears as subject and object, apart from subject and object merely being imputed as individual and phenomenon, there is nothing that exists in that way.

The meaning of peace is that once the nature of the fully present reality has been recognized, when one reaches the ultimate point of training in this, all concepts of attributes are completely extinguished.

We shall now establish, using reasoning, the meanings of (1) impermanence and (2) absence of self. The first of these, establishing that everything that is compounded is impermanent, is indicated in the next ten verses. It is divided into a general exposition and a detailed explanation.

(1) Establishing Impermanence
(a) General Exposition

From the basic premise that all outer and inner compounded phenomena are impermanent from one moment to the next, there are fourteen arguments in the next two verses that establish it.

> **Impermanence is established because of an impossibility,
> because things arise from causes,
> Because of a contradiction, because things do not last by
> themselves,**

> Because of an absence, because the nature of things has been determined,
> Because of their succession, and because of cessation; (XIX, 83)

(1) In saying, "because of an impossibility," what is it that is impossible? All compounded things arise from causes and conditions, and their ceasing in the previous instant and arising in the next instant occurs continuously and uninterruptedly, just as a river continues to flow for as long as the flow is not obstructed. But if they were not momentary, it would be illogical or impossible for those things, once having arisen, to continue to occur for variously greater or shorter lengths of time.

Our opponents might say,[28] "It is not impossible. Because of the coming together of causes and conditions, things are produced in the first instant and then do not cease immediately but continue for as long as they do not encounter the condition for their disintegration, which may be for days or months or years." If that were the case, although we can see the thing in the first instant, there is no causal factor to give rise to a second and subsequent instants, and therefore the thing would not continue but would cease to exist immediately after the first instant had occurred. You would have to tell us what are the causes that make it persist for a second instant and so on, and what is the cause for it finally ceasing. In fact the cause that has produced the first instant cannot give rise to a nonmomentary entity that continues to exist for days and months like that, because both cause and result are momentary.

Let us take the example of a flowing river. Its flow is constantly renewed without being interrupted. But if one were to block the water upstream, the flow would be cut. The flame of a lamp too burns continuously: from the causal factors of the cotton wick and the oil, the oil is transformed into a flame until the lamp runs out of oil. The flame is continuously renewed, but when the causal oil is exhausted, the resultant flame too ceases to continue. However, the flame that was there in that first instant does not last for a moment without there being more oil as the causal factor.

Some authorities pad this out by saying that if a thing were not destroyed by momentariness, it would be impossible for it to ever disintegrate (at the end of its continuity), which comes to the same thing as saying that something that does not disintegrate in the beginning will not do so at the end.

---

28. Tib. *gzhan dag*, lit. "others" or "the other side," our opponents in any debate on impermanence.

Although this is not incorrect, it is better to understand this point according to the above explanation from the commentary.

Again, our opponents might think that for a thing to continue as long as it does, no other cause is necessary; the cause that produced its first instant propels it into persisting like that. But this is not the case. Once the cause that produces the first instant has produced it, that cause has ceased, and for that reason it is impossible for it to drive the thing's persisting for a greater number of instants. A thing that is not momentary is impossible: one might as well speak of the son of a barren woman being born. If a nonmomentary thing could be produced by a cause, it would also follow that a permanent thing could arise, which is utterly illogical and impossible.

The same holds for those who think that the first instant of a thing is created by a cause and that after lasting for as long as it does the thing then disintegrates by itself without any other cause—that it is all done by just the initial cause. If they claim that there are no other causes for the thing enduring as long as it does and finally disintegrating, in that case why do they not claim that there is no cause for the first instant either? That a first instant could occur without a cause contradicts direct valid cognition, so we cannot accept their assertions, and this brings us to the next argument.

(2) "Because things arise from causes." We have established that having been produced in that way,[29] a thing's continuity too is produced from the causes of the succeeding instants, and no other causes than those can be observed. Our opponents might say that once the cause that makes things arise has produced them, they have finished arising, and they do not need to arise again and again but remain in that situation of having arisen for as long as they last; and until then, there is no succession of other instants of creation and disintegration, and no need for other causes to bring them about.

Let us look at the illogicality and contradiction in this. If things do not disintegrate immediately after arising but are destroyed at a later time, is it that the things are not destroyed by momentariness but persist and are then destroyed later? Or is it that they are destroyed by momentariness and then later cease? To answer the first question, if a thing persists without being destroyed by momentariness, it must be persistent by nature and it cannot be perishable by nature, so that thing will not disintegrate even later—it will last forever. While if it is something that is perishable by nature, then in its

---

29. I.e., that a first instant arises from a cause, for we have just agreed that it cannot arise without a cause.

perishable nature there cannot be a permanent or long-lasting nature, so the thing will disintegrate from the very first instant and it will be impossible for it to last any length of time without ceasing—hence the contradiction. Furthermore, if a thing were to come into being, endure for a while, and then finally cease, you would have to tell us what the cause for its ceasing would be. If you say that it is the cause that created the thing, you are contradicting yourself: if creation, whereby a thing exists, and cessation, whereby it no longer exists, are brought about by one and the same cause, there is a contradiction between that cause making the thing exist and making it not exist—it cannot possibly do both, just as it is impossible for a single cause to produce both light and darkness, or cold and warmth.

(3) "Because of a contradiction." If things were produced by themselves and, instead of being perishable by nature and not remaining for a second instant, they were to come into being and then last forever, they would contradict both scriptural authority and reason. Where is the contradiction? Such a thesis would contradict Lord Buddha's own words, for he said, "Compounded phenomena are like magical illusions, which come into being through causes and conditions. Being born, it is their nature to cease, and therefore they disintegrate. Having arisen, they do not remain longer than a single instant, and they are therefore temporary. They disintegrate as soon as they are produced, and so they last a very short time."

And from the point of view of reason, it would contradict the direct experience of practitioners. Practitioners who meditate on or keep in mind the four noble truths see that all compounded phenomena are characterized by arising and ceasing through momentariness; disenchantment grows in them, and they become free from attachment and attain liberation and nirvāṇa. But if they were to see things as lasting forever, they would not become disenchanted, nor would they attain freedom from attachment or perfect liberation. They would be like ordinary people: even if they recognize cessation and impermanence when people are dying and they then feel sad, up until that point they never feel disenchanted but think they will go on living. That way, no one would ever become disenchanted with compounded phenomena and be free of attachment.

(4) "Because things do not last by themselves" refers to a contradiction by inference. If compounded phenomena were not to disintegrate as soon as they came into being and were to last for as long as they do, would it be that they last because of something intrinsic to themselves, or that they endure because of other, extrinsic causes and conditions? If the first case were true,

they would have to last forever, but there are no compounded phenomena that can last until the very end of time, because it is their very nature to be destroyed by momentariness; even their continuity is destroyed when they encounter the relevant conditions.[30] As for their enduring because of other causes and conditions, we cannot, with valid cognition, observe any other causes and say, "The cause is this." Once a thing has been produced, it does not last for a second instant.

(5) "Because of an absence."[31] Our opponents say, "Things do not need another cause for them to remain for as long as they do. Once they themselves have come into being, as long as they do not encounter the cause for their disintegrating, they persist; and subsequently, when they encounter a cause for their disintegrating, they disintegrate. Take the case of an iron, which stays blue and without heat for a while; then, when it is brought into contact with fire, it ceases to be blue and cool and becomes red and hot.[32] And an earthenware pot, for example, persists until it encounters a hammer; then, when it comes into contact with a hammer, the pot is smashed to pieces." This is not correct, because things disintegrate by themselves, and there are no other causes for their disintegration. How? For example, when a stone is thrown into the air, there is a cause (one's hand, for example) that projects it into the air, but it does not need another cause to make it fall to the ground—it falls of its own accord. Similarly, as soon as things are brought into being by the respective causes that create them, they disintegrate of their own accord: they do not need another cause for that. The iron's blueness and the pot's shape disintegrate naturally from one instant to the next even before they come in contact with the fire and the hammer, so it is not that the fire and hammer destroy them. Rather, the final instants of the iron and the pot constitute the direct cause of their destruction, and the fire and hammer constitute the cooperating condition, and these produce the situation of their redness and fragments, at which point we consider that the iron is red and the pot has been smashed. Until then, our impression that the iron and pot are lasting is an illusion of homogeneity and continuity, but it is not correct.

You might argue that a figure painted on the iron or pot is not a cause for

---

30. The apparent continuity that we call a vase, for example, is brought to an end by its being struck with a hammer.
31. I.e., an absence of any cause of disintegration.
32. Lit. "its blueness and coolth cease and redness and heat arise or are produced."

its disintegration. But in fact one state (the unpainted iron or pot) has ceased and another state (the painted iron or pot) has been obtained. The iron and the pot are by nature impermanent, as the wise know. That being so, from the fact of their causes being different, things take on a variety of different aspects, while from the fact of the causes being the same, they arise as a homogeneous, unbroken continuum. However, both of these situations are momentary: there is not the slightest difference between them. In a nonmomentary thing it would be impossible to ever see different, dissimilar states.

Similarly, it might be asserted that boiling water over a fire and evaporating it, smashing a pot and reducing it to powder, and other such cases constitute the causes for their destruction. If we examine such assertions properly, we will see that things are changed into different states like that by momentariness and contact with other conditions, but otherwise, there is absolutely nothing that is destroyed by any cause other than momentariness. We can compare this to the creation of a pot from clay by means of the potter's hands, tools, and so on.[33] When the pot is created, the clay's own condition has not been destroyed, while the fashioning of the pot by the hand and so forth has "disintegrated" and ceases to be.

Furthermore, with regard to anything that is to be destroyed by a destructive cause, is it that thing's own nature to disintegrate or not? If its nature is not to disintegrate, the destructive cause could never make it disintegrate. And if its nature is to disintegrate, then it would not need a destructive cause to make it disintegrate. Again, when the destructive cause is bringing about a thing's disintegration, is it making the thing itself or something else? If it is making the thing itself, then it is creating and not destroying. And if it is making something other than the thing, it is not affecting the thing in any way, just as making woolen cloth does not destroy a pillar.

(6) "Because the nature of things has been determined." The nature of all compounded phenomena has been unequivocally determined as impermanent. It is not as if there are different possibilities—that some compounded phenomena, for example, are permanent and some are impermanent, while some are both permanent and impermanent, and others are neither permanent nor impermanent. And Lord Buddha was unequivocal in affirming that all compounded phenomena are impermanent. If things were to be permanent for a while and then impermanent, they would be both permanent

---

33. Just as a pot's nature is clay, the nature of things is momentariness. The factors that appear to create a pot or destroy things are merely conditions.

and impermanent, and that is impossible, so all compounded phenomena cannot be anything other than naturally subject to destruction by momentariness—just as it is the nature of fire to be hot.

(7) "Because of their succession." Our opponents might argue, "If all things are impermanent and momentary and therefore a thing is a new, different thing from one moment to the next, how is it that later, when one sees the things one saw earlier, one recognizes them and says, 'This is what I saw before'? Surely, the thing one saw earlier did not disintegrate but has persisted." Your earlier and later things are not the same thing but similar things that succeed each other in an unbroken sequence. Their being one and the same thing is simply an illusion. It is like when an illusionist throws several balls rapidly into the air and catches them again continuously, and one thinks that he is repeatedly throwing and catching the same ball. A river too is an unceasing flow of preceding instances of water going by followed by new instances of water; yet, because of their similarity, we think, "I have already crossed this river many times, and now I am crossing it again" and "Later I will again have to cross it."

(8) "Because of cessation." According to our direct experience, we do not think that the first thing we saw and the one we see later are different, and we might ask, "How can you say that the former and the latter are not the same?" It is the nature of things that every instant ceases before the next, so for that reason they are not the same. If the thing that was there in the first instant did not cease but remained as it was, it could never cease later. The thing one saw earlier would still be there in the present instant, and it would likewise still be there in the subsequent instants: the thing would be a nonmomentary thing, and it could never have different aspects.

> **Because of visible transformation,**
> **Because of cause and result,**
> **Because of being seized, because of ownership,**
> **And because of following purity and beings. (XIX, 84)**

(9) "Because of visible transformation." If things were not momentary and their nature did not change over time, one would never see any change from how they were in the beginning. And yet we do notice that, on the inner level, people's bodies change from childhood to youth, through early adulthood and the prime of life to old age, when they become decrepit, white-haired, and wrinkled. And on the outer level too we notice places

changing, articles changing from fresh to old, and the time changing from before to after. Beginning from the first instant when things first come into being, they definitely gradually change. If they did not change from the first instant onward, it would be impossible for them to change in subsequent instants. But because we actually see them transforming, we can be sure that they are changing from moment to moment. Even if people who look at the body of a young child and watch undistractedly cannot distinguish the aging of its body from moment to moment and day to day, they can infer it in seeing the gross changes that have taken place when the "child" becomes white-haired. As years and months go by, months and days, days and hours, hours and minutes, the child is gradually changing. But it is not that it remains without changing for a while and then becomes white-haired all of a sudden. The same is true for external things, which also change like that, subtly with every instant. For example, when milk turns into yogurt, with each instant it gradually becomes sourer—we never see any other way of changing that is not from moment to moment. Ordinary people, who fail to notice subtle, moment-to-moment change and take what is merely the same continuum to be a single thing, mistake it as one and the same thing. Thinking, "This is the thing I saw before," they are deluded into thinking that things are permanent.

(10) "Because of cause and result." The eternalists say, "However much we examine things, we cannot directly distinguish subtle change, while we can decide, 'That thing is this,' so how can we believe in momentary change?" The fact that those things are results that have arisen from causes, and the fact that causes come before and results come after, prove that those things are momentary. Since the cause is momentary, the result is momentary, and since the result is momentary, its cause too must be momentary. Permanent causes cannot give rise to results, just as flowers and pots cannot appear from space. Permanent results cannot be the products of anything, as is the case with space. So causes and results are by nature momentary. If they were nonmomentary, nothing would change, so cause and result would be impossible.

This is a general overview. Now, to examine this point in detail, because all the different consciousnesses, starting with the eye consciousness, arise from four conditions, they occur momentarily in rapid succession—Buddhists and tīrthikas both acknowledge this, and neither claim that the mind exists permanently, without changing. The cause of that consciousness is the sense organ and its object (form, for example), as is explained in the sūtras: "In dependence on the eye and form, the eye consciousness arises..." and so on. Therefore, since the mind, which is the result of compounded phenomena, has been established as being momentary, the compounded phenomena that cause and produce it must be momentary too. Our opponents might claim that compounded phenomena are permanent and that they give rise to an impermanent, momentary mind. But it is a logical impossibility for something momentary to arise from something nonmomentary, for that would mean that something impermanent like a pot could arise from something permanent like space. So the causes of the mind too are established as being momentary, in the same way that the mind is.

Again, all compounded phenomena are the result of the mind: there are no external objects that are other than those that appear on account of the habitual tendencies present in the mind, and there are no such things as independent external objects that do not originate from the karmic actions accumulated by the mind. Thus, the causal mind being momentary, the resultant compounded phenomena are shown to be momentary.

One might wonder how we know that compounded phenomena are the result of the mind and how we know that since the mind is momentary, compounded phenomena are also momentary. The answer to this is indicated in the last four arguments—"because of being seized, because of ownership, and because of following purity and beings."

(11) "Because of being seized." The fact that the five sense organs and their location, the body that supports the sense organs together with the innards, arise through being seized by the consciousness proves that they are the result of the mind. In what way are they seized? When the consciousness enters the mother's womb and blacks out, it takes hold of it, then, beginning with the different stages of the embryo formed from the father's semen and mother's ovum,[34] the body together with the sense organs becomes fully formed. But if the consciousness, having infiltrated the semen and ovum, did not combine with them and black out, the various stages of embryonic development would never occur. So the body follows the mind and is seized by the mind, as is stated in a sūtra: "Nanda, if the consciousness does not black out in the womb, no embryo will develop from the parents' fluids." Furthermore, if the mind is hurt, the body too will be hurt; when the mind is happy, the body too will feel perfectly at ease. It follows the mind.

---

34. Traditional Indian and Tibetan medicine speaks here of the mother's blood rather than ovum.

Without the mind, the body becomes devoid of feeling and decomposes. So because they are seized by the mind, compounded phenomena are the results of the mind.

(12) "Because of ownership." Because the mind has mastery over compounded phenomena or is their owner, they are the results of the mind. In what way is it the owner? Lord Buddha said, "This world is conducted by the mind; it is led by the mind." Whatever the mind intends, the body follows—it is conducted and led by the mind. If attachment arises in the mind, the body too follows it and one behaves excitedly, laughing and smiling and so on. When aversion arises in the mind, one's behavior is transformed accordingly—angry looks, a scowling face, clenched fists, and so forth. So the mind is the owner or master of compounded phenomena.

There is a second scriptural argument, given by the Tathāgata when he said, "Because of consciousness, there is name-and-form." Without consciousness, the stage of name-and-form will not occur, and without name-and-form, the six sense powers and the rest will not arise.

(13) "Because of following purity" refers to things following the pure mind. By the power of their pure minds, yogis can transform things through concentration into whatever they like. For example, if they want the ground to be gold, it appears as gold. The sūtras too speak at length of the attainments of monks' meditative concentration and so on. So for this reason, compounded phenomena are said to result from the mind.

(14) "Because of following beings." In that it is the positive and negative karmic actions accumulated by sentient beings' minds that bring into existence the various worlds, compounded phenomena follow beings' minds. The crops harvested by beings who have committed negative actions are of inferior color, smell, taste, and so forth, and even things made of gold appear to them as charcoal and the like. On the other hand, for those who have performed meritorious actions, because of their minds, the grains and so forth are fully and perfectly colored, fragrant, and flavorsome, and even unpleasant things appear to them as precious substances and the like. From this, it is evident that compounded phenomena are the result of the mind.

For all these reasons, since the cause, mind, is momentary, its results, compounded phenomena, cannot possibly be permanent, and we should therefore understand that they too are momentary by nature. Up until this point, outer and inner things have been treated together and not separately, with these two verses showing that compounded phenomena in general are momentary and impermanent.

(b) Detailed Explanation

The detailed explanation is divided into (1) the impermanence of inner compounded phenomena and (2) the impermanence of outer compounded phenomena.

(i) The Impermanence of Inner Compounded Phenomena

The next five verses establish that all inner compounded phenomena—the mind and mental factors together with the body—are momentary and impermanent. They indicate fourteen instances of life (life in its initial phase, life in subsequent growth, and so on),[35] for which there are fourteen arguments or logical reasons, from causes and measurable differences through to following the mind, that show these to be momentary, thus establishing that all inner compounded phenomena are momentary.

> Life at the beginning, during growth,
> During development, related to the substantial supports,
> During change, and during maturation,
> Likewise inferior and superior lives, (XIX, 85)

> Lives with light and without light,
> In the process of migration to other places,
> With seeds, and without seeds,
> And in manifestations— (XIX, 86)

(1) Life in its initial phase refers to the first instant of reconnection with a new birth when, after the consciousness associated with the death process has ceased, the consciousness enters the mother's womb and blacks out as it joins the sperm and ovum. Because the consciousness associated with the death process and the consciousness associated with the birth process occur like the swing of a balance arm, they must be momentary.

(2) Life in the phase of growth. In the first instant, the consciousness enters the womb, after which, in the second and subsequent instants, the

---

35. "Life" here translates the Tibetan term *skye ba*, whose many meanings include birth, arising, production, and coming into being. In this particular context of the impermanence of the mind and body, "life" more or less fits all of the fourteen cases described in this section, but it is important to understand that the basic meaning is that of "arising."

different stages of the embryo gradually grow bigger. As it abandons the previous stage and takes on a different form, it gradually changes from one instant to the next.

(3) "Development" refers to life in the phase of development. There are four causes for the development of the body: food, sleep, wholesome activities, and concentration. In the world of desire it is the first three, and in the world of form it is concentration, that make the body grow from something fragile into its developed form. (Instead of mentioning "wholesome activities" such as massage that enable the body to develop, the commentary speaks of "pure conduct"[36] here.) Since the body develops like this through these developmental causes, it is momentary, for if it were permanent, it would be impossible for it to grow bigger.

(4) "Substantial supports" refers to life related to the substantial supports. The locations or supports of the eye consciousness and the other five sense consciousnesses are the substantial eye organ and the other five sense organs. These too are momentary, for, as their own results, they give rise to momentary consciousnesses. As long as they constitute cause and result, they will be momentary, and if there were no change from one instant to the next, cause and result would be impossible, as has already been explained above.

(5) "Change" refers to life related to change. When desire and so on arise in the mind, the body's appearance changes accordingly, so this proves it to be momentary.

(6) "Maturation" refers to life related to maturation. Since the body will gradually mature through its different stages—from newborn infant, through childhood and first steps, through youth and an aptitude for sports, through the prime of life when one's physical and mental powers are complete, and past that to middle age when one's youth begins to fade, and to old age when one becomes white-haired, wrinkled, and decrepit—you should understood that it comprises an unbroken succession of instants.

"Likewise inferior and superior" refers to (7) inferior life and (8) superior or supreme life, of which inferior life is rebirth in the three lower realms, and life superior to that, or supreme life, is birth as a god or human being. These vary unpredictably as one takes birth from lower realms to higher, from higher realms to lower, and in similar classes of being (a human reborn as a

---

36. Tib. *tshangs par spyod pa* ("pure conduct") in the place of *legs par bya ba* ("wholesome activities").

human, for example) or in different classes of being. One is therefore impermanent, taking birth in this manner through a succession of instants. If one were everlasting, it would be impossible to take a variety of different forms.

(9) "With light" refers to radiant life. The gods in Enjoying Magical Creations and Mastery over Others' Creations (of the six gods' realms in the world of desire), and the gods of the world of form and the formless world are what are here termed "radiant," because their enjoyments and their meditative absorptions depend solely on their minds; they can experience them just as they wish. In what way do they experience them? When the gods in Enjoying Magical Creations want a celestial maiden with a particular color, shape, dress, ornaments, and so forth, they manifest her just by thinking of her, and they delight in her. Similarly, the goddesses too manifest and delight in the male gods just as they wish. The gods in Mastery over Others' Creations, in order to experience the pleasures of the desire realm with other gods, mentally manifest whatever they wish for and enjoy them. And the gods in the form and formless worlds who wish to enter into the different concentrations of meditative absorption accomplish and actualize these by means of their own minds. Such things would be impossible for permanent phenomena: you should understand that they arise through the power of the momentary mind.

(10) "Without light" refers to nonradiant life; that is, the remainder of beings other than those just described—all the beings in the world of desire from the gods of the Joyous Realm down to the hells. They cannot accomplish all their goals merely by thinking of them with their minds, so they are termed "nonradiant." These beings' minds and experiences also represent a whole variety of different states, so they are to be understood as being momentary and impermanent. The beings of the three worlds generally change from realms of light to realms of no light, and from those of no light to those of light, without any definite certainty as to which realm they will be reborn in, and within these they take all sorts of specific rebirths. So you should understand that they are impermanent and their succession of lives is momentary.

(11) "Migration to other places" refers to life in proceeding to other places. A person in one place, having died and transmigrated, ceases to be and proceeds to take birth in another place. Or, from the world of form upward, the body travels to another abode not on the same level. In either case, it enters or proceeds in a succession of instants. But if it were permanent, such a process would be impossible.

(12) "With seeds" refers to life with seeds, that is, being born with the

habitual tendencies or seeds of the defilements that lead to rebirth in the three worlds. Apart from arhats with residual aggregates who have exhausted the defilements to be eliminated on the paths of seeing and meditation, and the instants of their final aggregates, all others—candidates for arhatship, nonreturners, once-returners, stream enterers, and the ordinary beings of the three worlds—possess the seeds of defilements, so life as the continuity of the five aggregates is life with seeds. Their lives are thus phenomena associated with cause and result, which have been shown to be momentary.

(13) "Without seeds" is life without seeds, referring to the nature of those who do not have the seeds of rebirth in saṃsāra. Their aggregates, however, arise through the process of former causes and subsequent results. Apart from the final instants of the aggregates of arhats with residual aggregates who are on the point of entering the state with no residual aggregates, arhats with residual aggregates, despite not having the seeds for further birth in existence, possess residual aggregates propelled by their previous karmic actions, and until they enter the state without residual aggregates, they have life through the continuity of instants. On the other hand, the final instant of their residual aggregates from then on does not have life through continuity, and they enter the expanse without residual aggregates. So as long as their aggregates arise, they are momentary. And since they change from formerly having seeds to subsequently not having them, it is definite that they are impermanent and comprise a continuity of instants.

(14) "Manifestations." Through the power of the concentration of an individual who is practicing the eight perfect freedoms and so forth, manifestations appearing in different shapes and colors—blue, yellow, white, and red—actually appear as objects of the mind. Such manifestations that appear to the mind through proficiency in concentration are not there one moment and then appear in the next, so they are impermanent. Furthermore, they result from gradual habituation, a stream of mental instants, which therefore proves that they are momentary. From this we should understand that even dreams and visions resulting from meditating on repulsiveness and so on are all just mental appearances and are impermanent.

Thus, the fourteen instances of life, from life in its initial phase through to life in manifestations, are to be understood as being devoid of permanence and momentary—for the reasons that will now be given.

> **These are the fourteen aspects of life.**
> **Considering these, because of causes and measurable differences,**

> The unreasonableness of there being no point in development,
> The impossibility of a support, (XIX, 87)
>
> The impossibility of things persisting,
> The final immutability of things that do not disintegrate in
>   the beginning,
> And the impossibility, likewise, of inferior and superior births
> And of radiant and nonradiant lives, (XIX, 88)
>
> Because of the absence of migration, the impossibility of
>   persistence,
> And the impossibility of final aggregates,
> And because they follow the mind—for all these reasons,
> All compounded phenomena are momentary. (XIX, 89)

(1) Because life in its initial phase is the cause that leads to the other stages of embryonic development, it is established as momentary. If there were not other causes for its gradual change into the later stages, such change would be impossible—because it would be causeless. That being the case, beginning with the initial phase of life, the stage of the first-week embryo, that of the second-week embryo, and all the other stages occur in a succession of instants, coming into being and ceasing as is their nature as preceding causes and subsequent results, and occurring in an unbroken continuity. (The Tibetan words *dang* in this verse connect each argument to the next, so they do not need to be specifically explained.)[37]

(2) The growth aspect of life involves change from one instant to the next in terms of measurable differences such as size, shape, and form.

(3) Similarly, if the body were permanent, there could be no change from its initial state, so there would be no point in making the body develop by feeding it and so forth. But this is not the case: it is undeniable that food and so forth help the body to develop, which proves that it is impermanent from one instant to the next.

(4) The coming into being of the eye consciousness and other consciousnesses in dependence on their respective supports (their sense organs) is logically, because of the nature of momentariness, impermanent. If the sup-

---

37. The Tibetan word *dang* is either translated into English as "and" or indicated by a comma.

ports were permanent, it would be impossible for them to be supports for the consciousnesses, because being permanent they would be unnecessary as supports—as causes—and it is illogical for permanent things to give rise to anything else, that is, to results. Also, if that were the case, the six consciousnesses could not arise in dependence on the sense organs, which proves that both the sense organs that are the supports and the supported consciousnesses must be momentary and impermanent. Where is the contradiction in a permanent support, the sense organ, giving rise to an impermanent consciousness that is supported? In the same way that without a horse as a mount, there cannot be a rider, if the support remains permanent without changing into anything else, it is impossible for the supported consciousness to change into something else and to not remain. As when one burns some cloth (the support), the blue color supported on it is also burned, the support and the supported entity are indistinguishable in both being impermanent.

(5) Whereas the production of changes in physical expression through desire and so forth and (6) of maturation through the different stages of childhood, youth, and so on can be demonstrated indisputably, it is impossible to see such changes and maturation in things that persist forever, for it would be illogical for any other aspects to occur that are different from those things' substantial condition, whatever it is. This proves that the body is momentary.

What, you might ask, is the contradiction in something persisting permanently for a while without changing from one instant to the next? There is an enormous contradiction. If something were to persist like that without disintegrating in the first instant, its initial condition would remain forever exactly as it is, and in the end it would never change. All things for which there were no different condition in their first instant, and similarly no difference either in all their subsequent instants, could only be everlasting. Such a thing is completely illogical, because we never see anything that is all the time, by its very nature, permanent.

You might think that things stay without changing and last for as long as they do, and then they cease to exist. But if things were to persist for a second, or a little while, a day, a month, a year, or a kalpa without changing and were to cease at the end of that time, they would have long or short durations of cessation, which is logically inadmissible. Everything would persist as it was in the instant immediately after it first came into existence, and it could never change in the instant immediately preceding its disintegration. If the thing that had just come into being and the thing just about to disintegrate were one and the same, why would the thing that has just come into being not disintegrate as soon as it arose, as it were, in the instant immediately preceding disintegration; or why would the thing about to disintegrate not still remain as it was in the instant immediately succeeding its coming into being? For you are asserting they are both the same. By inference it can be established that for as long as something exists, from its initial creation until the instant of its disintegration, there must be a series of different instants.

"The final immutability of things that do not disintegrate in the beginning" is the main logical argument, and it is on this that the key points of all these arguments depend. The commentary classifies "the impossibility of persistence" as a proof related to both life in change and life related to maturation, and "the final immutability of things that do not disintegrate in the beginning" as another proof. Indeed, changes in the body on account of desire and so on would be impossible if it were not momentary but remained as it was in the first place, and the process of maturation through the stages of childhood, youth, and so forth accords with cessation in the first instant followed by production in another. But even if one makes the argument in a different order—"If it did not disintegrate in the beginning, it would not do so at the end either; its initial condition would persist forever without its ever disintegrating"—I see no difference in the meaning.

Similarly, when we consider (7) inferior and (8) superior births and assert that these too are momentary and impermanent, this is correct. But if they were not impermanent and momentary, it would be illogical for them to finally change, and inferior and superior birth would be impossible. Similarly, (9) beings with light and (10) those without light would be impossible. This can be understood from the previous arguments, so we will not go into repetitious detail on these points.

(11) "The absence of migration" to other places implies simply that if there were no succession of instants, there would be no going from one place to another. This is further explained in the commentaries, from which I have made the following summary. When fire spreads through grass, although it appears to have traveled from one hillside to the next, apart from the formation of an unbroken succession of instants of fire that arise from each blade of grass, there is no permanent, singular entity that we call "fire" going from one place to another. In the same way, an individual who migrates through all kinds of rebirths in saṃsāra, moving from one place to another and taking birth as a continuum of aggregates, is simply an unbroken succession of

instants of aggregates that has gone to another place. But there is absolutely no permanent entity, a "being," migrating from one place to another.

One might think, "The migrating being causes their bodily constituents to go to another place. Thinking, 'I will go over there,' that agent moves the constituents of their body and goes in that direction. If there were no goer, there would be no act of going either; an action cannot happen without an agent." If the cause of the action of the bodily constituents going to another place is the agent that makes them go, does it make the constituents go elsewhere after it has come into being, or does it make them go without coming into being? In the first case, at the moment the phenomenon we call "the goer" has come into being, the bodily constituents have not gone anywhere, so how could it have made them go somewhere else? To assert this is not logical. "The bodily constituents do not remain; it is their nature to go to another place," you might say. Apart from the bodily constituents that have gone elsewhere, is there another entity that makes them go? We have never seen one. If the goer has not yet come into being, how can it make the constituents go elsewhere? At that time there is no going.

There are a number of other arguments on this point. Does the one who makes them go transfer the bodily constituents to another place while itself remaining stationary? Or does it transfer them to the other place while dwelling in the other place? If it is the first case, then if it stays here and does not go to the other place, how does it make the bodily constituents arrive at the other place? When a horse enables a person to travel to another place, it is impossible for the person to be transported to the other place without the horse moving from the starting point. On the other hand, if the goer is dwelling in the other place, then it has already gone there, while the bodily constituents staying here have not yet gone, so how, with the goer and the transporter being in different places, can it make them go to another place? It would be like a horse in the east carrying a person in the west somewhere else.

Again, of the bodily constituents and the agent that causes them to go, (a) is it the mover that comes into being first and then moves the bodily constituents; or (b) is it the bodily constituents that come into being first and are then moved by a mover that comes into being afterward; or (c) do both of them come into being simultaneously and then move to the other place? If the first of these three possibilities is true, then at the time the mover has come into being, the bodily constituents that are to be moved have not come into being, so what can it move? One cannot feed a baby that has not yet been born. For the second case, at the time the bodily constituents have come into being, the mover has not yet come into being, so it cannot move them, just as a horse that has not been born cannot move or carry a person to another place. If the third case is true, then since they both come into being simultaneously, like the left and right horns of an ox, neither could provide the cause for moving the other. Both would reach the other place at the same time, so the mover would not have moved the compounded phenomena in the slightest. This being the case, from giving the label "going" to the movement in a succession of instants of five aggregates to another place, and calling the five aggregates themselves the "goer," the bodily constituents themselves appear to go in a continuity. But apart from that, it should be understood that there is nothing that makes them go anywhere. The limbs and the entity that possesses limbs do not exist separately: they merely exist as a result of imputations.

The above has been summarized and arranged according to the commentaries by Vasubandhu and Sthiramati. Thus apart from a thing migrating through a succession of instants, there is absolutely no other so-called migrator and migration. For this reason, migration is to be understood as momentary.

In general, there are many different kinds of movement to other places. There is movement by the power of the mind: once the cause—the thought—has been created, the compounded phenomena move to another place, as when, for example, the thought of walking results in the body taking a number of steps and proceeding to another place. There is movement through the power of previous actions, as when beings in the intermediate state enter the womb and so on. Movement by propulsion is like that of a shot arrow flying through the air. Movement by connection is like that of a person mounted on a horse and both of them proceeding to another place, or like the connection of a river and boat resulting in the boat going wherever the river takes it. Movement by being moved is like that of grass and leaves being carried by the wind and going in different directions. Natural movement is exemplified by the wind going directly from one place to another, fire rising into the air, water going downhill so that it flows into the valleys, and suchlike. Movement by magical powers is like that of mantra adepts who travel from place to place through the power of mantras; or of beings who travel to other places through the power of special substances that they drink as medicine or anoint on their bodies; or of iron moved by a magnet and being drawn directly upward; or those who use miraculous powers to go from one place to another. All these comings and goings must be understood as being momentary.

(12) With regard to possession of the seed of saṃsāra, it is logical to assert that although the previous instant in the succession of instants ceases, the next arises with the same way of being, and it is therefore momentary and impermanent. But a seed in something that persists without coming into being and ceasing is implausible, or, put another way, a seed that does not arise or cease but stays as before is impossible. So all phenomena that possess the seed of existence are also established as momentary.

(13) Even when the seed of saṃsāra previously present in the mind stream has been destroyed by means of the path and the mind remains, by nature, devoid of seeds, it is correct to say that the mind is momentary. But if that mind were nonmomentary and permanent by nature, the final aggregates of an arhat with residual aggregates would be impossible, because it would be impossible for it to have seeds one minute and no seeds the next, to be subject to birth one minute and then free from rebirth. So the arising of a succession of aggregates without the seeds of saṃsāra is also shown to be momentary.

(14) The manifestations that appear as the object of concentration follow the mind, so they too are shown to be momentary.

In this way all inner compounded phenomena are none other than an unbroken succession of instants.

(ii) The Impermanence of Outer Compounded Phenomena

> The elements and the six objects
> Are described as being momentary
> Because water dries up and its level rises;
> Because wind, by nature, moves, rises, and drops; (XIX, 90)

The four elements (earth, water, fire, and wind) and the six sense objects (forms, sounds, smells, tastes, and physical sensations, along with imperceptible forms belonging to the sphere of mental objects) are also described as being momentary. Different forms of water—streams, rivers, puddles, lakes, pools, and so forth—gradually become smaller and dry up in winter and spring because of the dry weather and so forth, and they slowly rise and increase as a result of conditions such as the summer rains. For this to happen, they must be momentary, for there is increase and decrease. If they were permanent and nonmomentary by nature, they could not increase or decrease.

Wind, too, by nature never stays in one place without moving. It moves and travels in different directions, so it must be momentary. And because it rises and drops, grows stronger and weaker, it must be momentary. If it were permanent, it would be impossible for it to move and to increase and decrease.

> Because earth is related to those elements;
> And because it undergoes four kinds of transformation.
> Colors, smells, tastes, and physical sensations are similar,
> And so, like them, they are momentary. (XIX, 91)

As for earth, its dependence on and connection with the elements wind and water, and the four transformations in its nature, prove that it is impermanent on account of its momentary character. In what way does earth arise from water and wind? When the universe was first formed, the movement of energy in space led to the formation of the wind element. From the wind element, water appeared, the element or maṇḍala of water being formed by a fall of raindrops the size of cartwheels. From the foam created by the water being whipped up by the wind, the ground, Mount Meru, and the four continents were formed, and thus it was that the earth element arose from water and wind. Thus indirectly, in terms of both the causes that give rise to earth and their result, earth is momentary.[38]

If we consider the four kinds of transformation in earth, there is first of all its transformation through specific deeds. The gods, who are beings who have accumulated virtuous deeds, perceive the ground as soft and springy like cotton. For hell beings, who have committed negative actions, it appears in a variety of forms as the basis of their suffering—the ground of red-hot iron, ravines, thorns, and the like. In the lands of humans, earth remains barren and devoid of crops when left unplowed and untended but yields good harvests when it is tended. The second transformation is the appearance of holes and pits from the earth's being struck with cudgels, pickaxes, and other tools. The third transformation is that wrought by the elements—

---

38. In that it is a result, earth must logically be momentary. And because its causes have already been shown to be momentary, their result too must be momentary. The argument here is based on the theories of ancient Indian cosmology.

it is elevated or flattened through being burned by fire or driven by the wind and washed away by water. The fourth transformation is transformation with time, referring to the differences in the earth's appearance at earlier and later times. During periods of prosperity, the earth is the source of crops growing well; in bad times, it produces poor growth. In summer the grass grows green, while in winter it turns yellow and the ground freezes. Some places, originally lonely and isolated, later become noisy, crowded cities, and places that were cities in the past are now deserted.

These four transformations come about through a succession of instants. Although the earth may not have a different aspect in each instant that passes, if it were a permanent, nonmomentary entity, it would be impossible to ever perceive any changes in it. It is because of its appearance in the above ways through its arising with different aspects at earlier and later times that the element earth too is shown to be momentary.

Colors, smells, tastes, and physical sensations are the same in resulting from the four elements. So, being similar to the elements, these four are shown to be momentary by means of the logical arguments that establish the elements as being momentary.

> **Because fire burns in dependence on fuel,**
> **Because sound is observed to grow louder,**
> **Because imperceptible forms follow the mind, and because**
>   **of the answers to questions—**
> **For these reasons, external phenomena too are momentary.**
>   (XIX, 92)

Fire is shown to be momentary because its functioning depends on fuel. If fuel is present, the fire burns; if there is none, it does not burn. If there is a lot of fuel, the fire too will be big; if there is little fuel, the fire will be small. Just as fire is momentary, so too is the firewood: from the gradual burning of the wood, the fire is produced. But if the fire were to occur with the wood remaining as it was before, how would both the fire and the firewood ever come to an end? The fire does not continue when the fuel is used up, so the two constitute a sequence of causal instants and resultant instants, and as long as the cause is present, the fire, its result, is produced. But when the cause is no more, its result, fire, does not appear. In this way, all things appear as the uninterrupted arising and cessation of causes and results.

One might think that it would be logical to have mentioned fire in the context of explaining the four elements, and then to mention color and so forth afterward, and that the order by which fire is explained after color and the others is somewhat awkward. Whichever way it is taught, there is no contradiction in the meaning, and it has been said that it was taught like this for the sake of ease in the arrangement of the verse composition. Furthermore, it was also in order to show, by means of the fire and firewood example, that all the elements and things derived from the elements arise and cease from one instant to the next in the succession of their corresponding causes and results.

Some people say that sound is permanent, unlike color and the other sense objects; they say that as long as any sound resounds, it is permanent and nonmomentary. This is not so. The fact that we can perceive a continuous sound getting louder with the effort produced by the person making it, and that the sound of a bell or similar instrument gets softer and softer, proves that sound is momentary. If sounds did not fade and in a single sound there were no instants, sound could not grow louder or softer, so sound must be momentary. Take, for example, the words that people deliberately utter—their breath makes the words successively come into being and cease.

Imperceptible forms belonging to the sphere of mental objects—the prātimokṣa, dhyāna, and untainted vows, for example, which are imperceptible in physical or verbal form, follow after the mind. They never come into being independently of the mind, which is their cause. So since the cause, mind, is impermanent, the results, imperceptible forms, must also be momentary.

"Because of the answers to questions." Although ordinary people and tīrthikas accept that compounded phenomena are impermanent insofar as they finally perish, as long they do not actually see things perishing—someone dying or a pot breaking, for example—they claim that a thing's own nature is not momentary but persists. Let us ask them then, "You accept that compounded phenomena are impermanent in the end, but why do you not accept that they are impermanent and momentary until then?" They will reply, "We can see compounded phenomena finally perishing, but until they have perished, we do not see them being destroyed by momentariness, so we do not accept this idea of destruction with each instant."

To this we would ask them the following question: "The flame of a lamp and the flow of a mountain torrent, for example, are renewed from one instant to the next, as their preceding instants cease. Both Buddhists and tīrthikas accept this. And yet, when you do not directly see with your own eyes momentary destruction in a river viewed from a distance or in a lamp with no wind to stir it, why do you then not accept them as being momentary?"

"We do not *always* see that things are the same later as they were formerly. Although a mountain torrent seen from afar is as if it were the same thing, if we approach and look more closely, we can actually see from the constant renewal of water that it is not the same. And in a lamp too, we can see that the preceding instances of flame are successively burned out at the tip and disappear, and that the flame is successively renewed from the base; and in the end when it runs out of oil, the flame grows smaller and smaller and goes out. So we cannot say that things are not momentary. On the other hand, pillars, pots, houses, people, rocks, and so on can be left for months and years without growing bigger or smaller, and they remain just as they were when we saw them before: in such cases, we do not see them disintegrating with each instant."

We would therefore ask them again, "Is it not so that even things like pillars change their color, shape, and so on from their initial, former appearance, on account of circumstances intervening in the meanwhile; and in the end, they meet with the appropriate circumstances and are actually destroyed? Why, then, are these things any different from lamps in being momentary?"

"Lamps and things like pillars and pots are different: they do not have the same characteristics," they will say. "We can see that it is characteristic of a lamp to be hot, to shine, and to be unstable, arising and ceasing from moment to moment. But things like pillars and pots are different. We can see that once they have been produced, and for as long as they last, they are characteristically solid and stable, fulfilling their functions in supporting beams, pouring water, and so forth. Lamps and pillars are just not the same."

To this we must give the following explanation. "Of course, simple differences in the characteristics of compounded things show that they are different from one another, but that does not mean that they do not share the characteristic of compounded phenomena being impermanent and momentary. The reason is that there are two kinds of differences in characteristics: differences in nature and differences in presentation. Differences in nature are, for example, the fact that the nature of fire is to be hot while that of water is to be wet. As for differences in presentation, lamps and so forth come into being and disintegrate in each instant, while other compounded phenomena like pots come into being, persist for as long as they do, and are then destroyed, so these are different in the way they present. Obviously it is this difference that you are insisting upon. But while lamps and pots are indeed different in nature, that does not prove that they are different in their presentation of momentariness. Moreover, by taking the example of a lamp to demonstrate momentariness to you, we can prove that other compounded phenomena such as pots are momentary. It is unacceptable to take things of the same nature as examples—like a lamp as an example to prove a lamp, or an ox to prove an ox. But we can use other things that are not of the same nature to prove the same point, saying, 'The sun and lamps are similar in being hot; oxen and wild oxen are similar.' Thus, although pots and lamps differ in the aspects of their specific characteristics, we can prove that there is no difference in their general characteristic, the fact that they are impermanent and momentary. For this reason, it is not possible that simply because of their different aspects, some things disintegrate from one instant to the next while others persist for a while and disintegrate later. All compounded phenomena are no different in disintegrating from one instant to the next.

"Furthermore, according to your viewpoint, the heart of the candle flame is not momentary but persists, and it is this that produces the flame as a succession of instants; pillars, pots, and so forth are not momentary but persist as themselves. If this is the case, you must think that last year, this year, next year, and so on, they do not at those times give rise to different results such as pouring water and supporting beams. So we ask you this: When a person mounts a horse and goes to another place, does that person get to the other place while the horse stays put without going anywhere? If you were to reply, 'No one on earth would say that, because it is impossible; the person and horse go to the other place together,' we would say, 'If you accept that, then it is equally illogical for the heart of a candle flame to be nonmomentary and persist while giving rise to a momentary flame, for a pot or the like to remain without moving while carrying out its function of pouring water and so forth, for the eye (or other sense organ) to stay without moving from its previous state while giving rise to its respective consciousness—in other words, for an unmoving cause to create a constantly renewed, moving result. In what way is your assertion that the causes of those results do not move any different from the horse staying here while the person riding it goes somewhere else? The heart of the lamp is repeatedly soaked with oil, which is consumed by the flame and gradually runs out, so that when the oil is exhausted, the lamp goes out. The wick too burns out. But if the wick were to give rise to the flame without arising and ceasing, the wick would never cease and the flame would never cease either. That does not happen, however, so both cause and result must be momentary. In the same way, you should understand that the example of the lamp also applies to pillars, pots, and the like performing their functions and to the arising of the sense consciousnesses from the sense organs—in all these cases, both cause and result are momentary.'"

One might argue, "If all compounded phenomena are momentary, why is ordinary people's vision incapable of determining that they are impermanent in the same way that lamps are?" The inability of ordinary people to see and determine that things are momentary is not because compounded phenomena have different characteristics—momentary and nonmomentary. Lightning, bubbles, clouds, candles, and mountain torrents come to an end in a short time, and because they have different aspects that appear even as they are perceived, it is easy to understand that they are impermanent from one instant to the next. On the other hand, although pillars, pots, rocks, diamonds, and the like are momentary, they give rise to the illusion of the same kind of thing appearing uninterruptedly, and as long as they do so, there occurs the mistaken notion that they are permanent. But that things could be nonmomentary and last forever is quite impossible. Sentient beings of feeble intelligence, gripped by delusion, are mistaken in their thinking, which is incompatible with how things actually are, and they conceive purity, happiness, permanence, and a self with regard to compounded phenomena, just as when someone with jaundice sees a conch shell as yellow, or a whirling firebrand at night looks like a wheel, or a rope seen unclearly in the half-darkness is taken to be a snake. It is because we have this mistaken thinking that we create saṃsāra, and it is by getting rid of that mistaken thinking through wisdom associated with valid cognition that we will inevitably achieve purity. On the other hand, if ordinary people's way of seeing things were always the correct way, and there were no mistaken thinking, then everyone would be free from the very beginning, or, put another way, there would never be liberation. But this is not the case: unquestionably, there *is* the defilement aspect and there *is* the purity aspect, so if perfectly ordinary beings cease to take as valid simply what they see or do not see and rely instead on the path of correct reasoning associated with valid cognition, their intelligence and vision will be very greatly enlarged.

Thus it is for the reasons just mentioned, from "water dries up and its level rises" to "answers to questions," that one should understand that outer compounded phenomena are also momentary. The above is a clearly ordered summary, complete in its meaning, of Ācārya Sthiramati's detailed elucidation of the ideas in Vasubandhu's commentary.

(2) Establishing the Individual No-Self

In this specific explanation of those of the four summaries of the Dharma that are difficult to understand, impermanence is taught in two ways: impermanence in the sense of existing no longer[39] and impermanence in the sense of disintegration from one instant to the next. Of these two, to establish impermanence from one instant to another, there are fourteen kinds of reasoning that establish it in general, fourteen kinds of reasoning that specifically establish that inner compounded phenomena are momentary, and about ten explicitly stated arguments establishing that outer phenomena are momentary. These are now followed by a section establishing the individual no-self.

The above proof that the five aggregates are impermanent from one instant to another also naturally establishes the nonexistence of a single individual self. Nevertheless, mundane beings and tīrthikas assert the existence of an independent agent that carries the aggregates as a burden, which they call the "self," the "life force," the "individual," the "creator." In the same manner, they speak of "forceful ones" (since they continuously nourish the aggregates and enable them to have different kinds of creative force), "owners of force," "those born from force" and "children of force" (since they are born from what they call "the Powerful Creator, Lord of Beings"),[40] and other synonymous terms.[41] For them, this self exists and is the basis for being bound and for being liberated. Some Buddhist schools, the Vātsīputrīyas, for example, also accept the existence of a self. And even Lord Buddha taught about ordinary individuals, individuals who are stream enterers, and so forth, and he spoke of individuals called tathāgatas, whose appearance in the world brings benefit and happiness to the whole world. So all sentient beings have a self. If there were no self, who would be bound in saṃsāra? Who could be liberated? Who could accomplish their own and

---

39. Tib. *med pa*, lit. "nonexistence." This is the gross level of impermanence, that of a person dying or a pot breaking and therefore becoming nonexistent.

40. Tib. *skye dgu'i bdag po shed byed*, a powerful creator such as Brahmā.

41. These are all synonyms of sentient beings or humans.

others' goals? Who could set out on the path? It is for these reasons that people assert that there is a self. The tīrthikas say that the size of the self is proportionate to the body; some people say the self is inanimate, some that it is the consciousness, others that it has physical form, and yet others that it has no physical form, and so on—there are numerous points of view, but they all assert a universal self that is permanent and single, and also speak of it as independent, a creator, and so on, imputing a variety of properties to it according to their views. The Vātsīputrīyas hold that there is a substantial self, but since it is neither the same as the aggregates nor distinct from them, it cannot be spoken of as being permanent, impermanent, or whatever. We shall now, therefore, show that things are not as they all claim them to be.

> **An individual is to be expressed**
> **As existing as a designation; it is not substantial.**
> **It cannot be perceived, is a mistaken notion,**
> **And is the cause of the defilement process and the**
>   **defilements. (XIX, 93)**

What we call the individual or the self is an expression for something that, taking the support of the five aggregates, exists only as a conventional designation. With this in mind, the Buddha too, conforming with ordinary people's ideas, taught in conventional terms, designating everyone, from ordinary beings to buddhas, as individuals. But it is not that there is a self or individual that exists substantially or ultimately or intrinsically. His showing that it exists as a designation but does not exist substantially avoids the errors of two parties—those who hold that the self as a mere conventional designation is unacceptable and those who hold that the self exists intrinsically.

How can it be shown that the self does not exist substantially? If there were a substantial self, one should be able to perceive it with direct valid cognition or with inferential valid cognition. The fact that we cannot perceive it with valid cognition proves that it does not exist substantially. How is that? It is because it is impossible that one would not perceive it with the eye and eye consciousness or any other of the six sense organs and sense consciousnesses.

Others might argue, "Even though we cannot perceive the self with the eye and eye consciousness or any other of the five sense organs and five consciousnesses, that alone does not prove that it does not exist. The mind and mental factors that are not perceived by the five sense organs and consciousnesses *are* perceived by the mind consciousness and are therefore accepted as existing. In the same way, those who posit an existent self perceive it with the mind, so the self must exist. Even the Buddha spoke of perceiving the self, saying, 'In this life, people perceive and designate a self.'" Those who posit an existent self are mistaken in perceiving a self. Their imagining that something nonexistent exists is a delusion, like imagining a rope to be a snake. But it is not the case that they see and perceive it as existing directly with the mind consciousness. Lord Buddha was not saying that there is a substantially existent self and that it can be perceived by a valid cognizer, but that while there is no existent self, people believe in a self, and, having perceived it mentally, they then verbalize it and give it the name "self."

Those who speak of an existent self might say, "It would indeed be impossible for even the mind to perceive a self that from the start had never existed. But all sentient beings mentally perceive a self, so how can you say that they are mistaken in their notion of a self?" If the notion of a self were not a mistake, there would necessarily be no fault in that. But the belief in a self is by nature an error; it is the essence of the defilement process and the cause of all other defilements, so it is obvious that it is mistaken. Furthermore, this notion of a self is the view of the transitory composite, which is a specific instance of defiled view, one of the six root defilements. From it all the defilements such as attachment develop, and because of that, saṃsāra, whose nature is the different kinds of suffering, comes about. This is what is wrong with it. It is a mistaken notion.

To our opponents who say, "Even though this belief in a self is characterized by defilement, it is not mistaken," we would give the following answer. If it were not mistaken, it would be impossible for it to lead to defilement. Anything to do with defilement—for example, the belief that things are permanent or pure—is mistaken. Anything that is not to do with defilement—for example, the view that things are impermanent and impure—is not mistaken. So it is that by clearing away the mistaken concepts of purity, happiness, permanence, and a self by means of the path—on which one realizes that things are impure, suffering, impermanent, and devoid of self—one attains purity, perfectly purified of faults. It is like gaining clear eyesight, wherein there are no longer the mistaken perceptions seen with faulty, blurred vision.

Again, the proponents of a self might say, "It is impossible even for you, who say that the individual exists as a designation, to designate something without a basis for designation, so on what basis are you designating the individual?" When we designate something as an individual, we are not designating a so-called individual on the basis of a substantially existing individual. We are simply putting the label "individual" on the five perpetuating aggregates. In the sūtras too we read, "Designating anyone—a śrāmaṇera, a brahmin, or whoever—as 'I' or 'mine' is simply ascribing the name 'I' or 'mine' to the five perpetuating aggregates."

Is this saying, then, that the designation "individual" and the five aggregates that are the basis for designation are the same or different? The answer to this question is given in the following verse.

> **On account of two faults, it cannot be described**
> **As identical to or different from the aggregates,**
> **For they would then be the self**
> **Or it would be a substantial thing. (XIX, 94)**

If we take the viewpoint of those who posit a substantially existent individual, they have to accept that the individual and the aggregates are either the same or different. Something that exists substantially will be distinct from other things and not anything else than itself—just as a pot is different in substance from woolen cloth and is the same as its own pot-substance. The designation "individual" has no substance other than the aggregates, and since they are different in terms of being the basis of designation and the designation, they are also not the same. As will be explained in a moment, because of two faults, the self cannot be described as being the same as or different from the aggregates: the individual or self is not the same as the aggregates, nor is it different or distinct from them. The two faults are as follows. If the self were the same as the aggregates, the five aggregates would be the self, and if the self were different from the aggregates, that self would have to be a substance quite distinct from the aggregates. "What," you might ask, "is the problem with these?" If the aggregates were the self, the self would, like the aggregates, be multiple and impermanent. Alternatively, the five aggregates would, like the self, be single and permanent. And if the aggregates were distinct from the self, we would perceive it as different from the aggregates and the experiences of happiness and suffering resulting from the accumulation of karmic actions by the five aggregates would have no relationship with the self.

> If it exists substantially, it is necessary to provide
> The reason why it cannot be described.
> To say that it cannot be described as being the same or different
> Without giving a reason is inadmissible. (XIX, 95)

Among the proponents of a self are the Vātsīputrīyas, who, although they consider the Buddha as their teacher, ignore the Teacher's instructions on no-self and hold that the self exists substantially. We would dispute this as follows: "If there is a substantially existent self, which cannot be said to be the same as or different from the five aggregates, nor permanent or impermanent, you have to tell us the reason or need for establishing this point of view. You cannot establish your own tenet system without a reason or purpose simply with words, saying 'It can't be described.'"

To this objection, they might reply, "The self and aggregates are not the same, because it has to be accepted that even when the previous aggregates have ceased, the self still remains in saṃsāra. The self and the aggregates are not different either, because one never sees an entity accumulating karmic actions and experiencing the ripened effects that is other than the aggregates. Nor is it permanent, because it changes from one life to the next. And the self is not impermanent either, because since time without beginning and until the end of time, there is only one self: there are not multiple selves that arise and cease. Consequently, you have to accept that a self that exists substantially as the support for actions and their results cannot be spoken of as being identical to or distinct from the aggregates, and so on. For example, fire and firewood are not the same, because firewood alone does not perform the function of burning, and fire does not function as firewood. Nor are they distinct, because apart from fuel being transformed into fire, one never sees fire as a separate thing."

Having claimed that both the self and the aggregates exist substantially, you say that it is not possible to speak of them both as being the same or distinct and different. This is nothing but nonsense—just words, without the slightest purpose or reason that serves to prove your viewpoint. It is unacceptable. Why is it unacceptable? Because once you have asserted that pillars and pots exist as separate substances, if you then say that a pillar and a pot are not identical, those very words prove that they are different, so it is quite redundant to again say that a pillar and a pot are different. In the same way, once you assert that the self and the aggregates are both substantially existent, it is logical to accept that the self and the aggregates are not the same. But saying that they are not distinct or different not only serves no purpose, it also completely contradicts your own viewpoint, as if you were saying that a pillar and a pot are not distinct. When you assert that they are distinct, that undermines your saying that one never sees a self performing karmic actions and experiencing the ripened effects that is other than the aggregates, so with this misgiving you accept that they are also not different. If you think in this way, then you have not got any further than the fault mentioned above in holding the substantial self and substantial aggregates to be not different but the same. If you say that, out of fear of such a fault, you also do not accept that they are the same, you are asserting that they are distinct, so your claim that they are the same immediately falls to pieces. Thus, your saying things that directly contradict your position not only serves no purpose but also has extremely grave consequences. If you must assert that the self exists substantially, you should then assert that it is either identical or distinct. Substantial things that are not either the same or distinct are impossible conventionally; neither are they mentioned in the scriptures, nor can they be demonstrated by reasoning. Any faults that occur in asserting that the self and the aggregates are the same or distinct are due to the fact that the self is a mere imputation and does not exist substantially, as has been stated above. Instead of understanding that it is because the self is held to be a mere imputation that it is impossible to say that it is the same or different, you hold that the self is substantial and in doing so declare that it cannot be described as the same or different and that it cannot be described as permanent or impermanent. Not only are these mere words that are completely contradictory, but they do not in the slightest prove the purpose of the self in acting as the support of cause and effect.

> In considering what are their defining characteristics,
> What ordinary people can see, and what is written in the treatises,
> It is incorrect to compare the self and aggregates to fire and firewood,
> Saying that they are both and inexpressible, for they are two.
> (XIX, 96)

As for your giving the example of fire and firewood being neither the same nor different, that does not hold, for in terms of the defining characteristics of fire and firewood, they are distinct. The characteristic of fire is to burn and be hot, while that of firewood is not to be hot and make things burn but to be hard and usable for different purposes, so they are quite distinct in their characteristics. Even ordinary people see them as different: firewood can exist on its own without fire; flames can be blown a long way by the wind, even if no fuel is present; and fire can appear from striking steel on flint. Furthermore, according to the academic treatises, fire is one of the four elements, and firewood is a compound of the elements, being produced principally from water (which holds it together), earth (which gives its solidity), and wind (which makes it supple). Thus to say that the self and aggregates, like fire and firewood, are inexpressible in being both the same and different, is not valid, for they are two distinct things.

> Because consciousness comes into being when the two conditions are present,
> Anything that is not those conditions serves no purpose.
> For that reason, the self will never be anything—
> From that which looks to that which is liberated. (XIX, 97)

There now follows a refutation of the self that constitutes the view of the non-Buddhist tīrthikas. The tīrthikas say, "There *is* a self: it is what looks at forms. Likewise, that which hears sounds, smells odors, tastes flavors, feels physical sensations, and knows mental phenomena is the self. It is that which performs positive and negative actions, which experiences their ripened effects or experiences objects, and which is liberated from sentient beings' three bonds (*sattva*, *rajas*, and *tamas*). How can there not be such a self?" It is not like that. Even without a self it is possible for there to be something that looks, something that hears, and all these things that you say it is, through to something that is liberated. But the self does not perform any functions at all such as looking. You might wonder how it is that it does not perform these functions. So let us ask you, is the self a contributory condition supporting the sense organs and their objects, and without which looking and so on cannot occur? Or is it that by the power of the self, the organs and other conditions are activated, and that the self is the owner or ruler that thus makes looking and so on happen? The first of these cannot be the case. If the two conditions—the eye or other sense organ, and form or other sense object—are present, in dependence on them the eye consciousness and the other five sense consciousnesses arise. There is no need for any other condition. One does not see the sense consciousnesses being produced by any conditions other than these two, so the self cannot be a contributory condition for the arising of consciousness. Just these two can give rise to unimpaired, mentally active consciousness, and there is no need for the self-acting as another cause: such a cause would serve no purpose. To take an example, fire is produced by firewood; it does not need water as well. For this reason, what looks at forms is the eye consciousness, and similarly what is liberated is the consciousness, and we refer to the consciousnesses as that which looks, that which hears, and so forth. Thus the self will never be that which looks, nor that which is liberated, for one never observes a self—that is, anything that is not a consciousness—that looks and is liberated.

> If the self were a ruler,
> It would never let impermanence or unwanted things occur.
> You have to establish its functions and attributes.
> And it would invalidate the three aspects of perfect awakening. (XIX, 98)

As for the second hypothesis, you might say that seeing and any other sense occurs from the coming together of the object, sense organ, and sense consciousness, which itself comes about by the power of the self, and that without the self it would not occur. If the self were an independent ruler that had the power to control everything it wished in that way, then it would arrange for beings to be happy, and to be happy forever without impermanence changing things. But it does not. Furthermore, it would never let unwanted suffering occur, but again, there are no sentient beings who are unfailingly happy and who never suffer. You should thus understand that the self is not independent. The contact of sense organ and object occurs in the form of a variety of wanted or unwanted events because of karmic actions, and the different forms of happiness and suffering arise through the coming together of conditions. You must get it into your heads that it is not at all because of the wishes or blessings of the self. The self can never be that which looks or that which is liberated.

There is another problem with those who say that the self exists, which is that if the self exists substantially, you have to establish what that self's functions and characteristics are like. For example, we say that the function of the eye organ and eye consciousness is that they enable one to see forms, and that the eye organ consists of very refined matter and the eye consciousness is that which knows an object is blue and so forth. In the same way, you have to say what the self's functions and characteristics are. Now since the self does not exist substantially, it is impossible to perceive it with valid cognition, like the child of a barren woman or the horn of a rabbit, and so you cannot properly talk about its functions and attributes. And to speak of the aggregates' functions and attributes as attributes of the self is an inferior, mistaken philosophy. It is the target of hundreds of logical invalidations, with the consequence that you are inviting trouble for yourselves.

There is yet another problem. If there is an individual self, the Buddha should see it, for the Buddha has understood everything there is to know. You might think that the Buddha sees the individual self because he spoke of ordinary individuals and noble individuals. But this has already been explained above, and if you say that that means that the individual self exists substantially, this would invalidate the three aspects of perfect enlightenment. The three aspects of perfect enlightenment are profound true and perfect enlightenment, uncommon true and perfect enlightenment, and supramundane true and perfect enlightenment. The first of these is the realization that there is no self in phenomena. The second is the realization that there is no self in the individual, and it is so called because it has nothing in common with the tīrthikas' realization. And since mundane beings have no such realization of these two kinds of no-self, we speak of supramundane true enlightenment. Alternatively, the three aspects of true enlightenment (profound, uncommon, and supramundane) can be associated respectively with the realization that the imputed reality does not exist, that the dependent reality exists conventionally, and that the fully present reality is, by nature, peace. In fact, the absence of existence of the two kinds of self cannot be realized by the minds of mundane beings with limited vision; it was realized by the Buddha, who then taught it to his disciples. However, if the Buddha were to see a self as existing, his vision would be no superior to the vision of mundane beings and it would not be in any way profound, uncommon, or supramundane, so the three aspects of enlightenment would be invalidated.

> **Because of three faults,**
> **Its activity in looking and so forth is not spontaneous,**
> **Nor is it a contributory condition of these functions;**
> **It has no activity in looking and the like. (XIX, 99)**

A further problem arises in positing a substantially existent self. If the self exists substantially and it is the one that looks, listens, and so forth, then when it wants to look, does that self look without making the effort of opening the eyes and so on, or does it look by making an effort? On examining this point, we will see that neither of these two possibilities is feasible, because there are three faults, which will be explained below. It is not the case that in looking and so on, the self's activity is effortless and spontaneous. Nor is it that these functions have the self as a contributory condition, making the effort of opening the eyes and looking, directing the ears and listening, and so on; for looking is produced by the consciousness in dependence on the sense organ and the object, and the self does not play any part in seeing, listening, and so forth. The meaning of these lines is explained in the following verses.

> Because it is not the agent, because they are impermanent,
> And because they would operate all at once or constantly,
> The functions of looking and so forth
> Could never occur spontaneously. (XIX, 100)

If the function of looking and so on is spontaneous without the self doing anything, the self cannot be the agent, for the very reason that the looking is spontaneous without the self doing anything.

Since the functions of looking and so on occur from time to time, they are impermanent and therefore must have a cause, which does not tally with their being spontaneous and causeless. If they were spontaneous and causeless, these functions would be permanent, but this is negated by direct valid cognition.

If the functions of seeing and so on occurred without a cause, their results, arising without a cause, would occur without depending on a cause, so all these functions would have to occur all at once or operate continuously, all the time.

For these reasons, it is impossible for functions such as looking to occur spontaneously, without effort.

> Similarly, because its activity would continue as it was before,
> Or would dissolve and be impermanent,
> And no third alternative is possible,
> It cannot be a contributory condition. (XIX, 101)

The self is also not a contributory condition for looking, listening, and so forth. Why not? Let us examine whether a permanent activity of the self could be the contributory condition of looking, listening, and so on; or whether an impermanent activity of the self could be the contributory condition; or whether an activity that is neither permanent nor impermanent could be the contributory condition.

The first possibility is not feasible. If a permanent activity of the self were the contributory condition of looking and so forth, that permanent activity of the self would remain exactly as it was before, all the time, and it would forever serve as the contributory condition for looking and so forth, so that the agent of looking would necessarily be present even before the sense organ and the object came together and the eye did its looking (and so on). However, because there is no looking, listening, or whatever before anything has been looked at or listened to, such a permanent activity of the self could never be the contributory condition for looking and so on.

If, as in the second hypothesis, an impermanent activity of the self served as the contributory condition of looking, and so on, that activity would not last forever and would cease to be from one moment to the next; because of its impermanence, the agent (the self) would also be impermanent, and there would be a difference between its states of activity and inactivity.

Nor could there ever be a third or alternative hypothesis, that of the self's activity being neither permanent nor impermanent. Permanence and impermanence are direct opposites, so if it is not one, it must be the other, and any third alternative between these two is impossible.

Although there exists an analysis of the self as permanent or impermanent, in this case it seems more convenient to investigate a permanent and impermanent activity of a self.

> **Thus all phenomena are devoid of a self,**
> **And ultimately are emptiness.**
> **To conceive of a self**
> **Is explained as a fault and nothing else. (XIX, 102)**

Having, up to this point, established no-self by means of reasoning involving direct and inferential valid cognition, we now establish it by the valid cognition of scriptural authority, and this is addressed to the Buddhist exponents of a self. Lord Buddha taught that all phenomena are devoid of a self. Where did he say this? In his teaching on the four summaries of the Dharma, where he said, "All phenomena are devoid of self." Similarly, in the listeners' sūtra *Ultimate Emptiness* he also declared, "In ultimate truth, or ultimately, all phenomena are emptiness." Again, in the listeners' *Long Scriptures*, which presents things starting from one, two, three, four, or five aspects, in the last section explaining groups of five he said, "If one believes in a self, five kinds of fault occur," and declared, "Where there are positive and negative actions, there are the experiences of the ripened effects, happiness and suffering. But apart from being a conventional designation for something that is born in and enters saṃsāra through the workings of the twelve links of dependent arising, there is no individual who abandons the aggregates of this life and seizes the aggregates of another life." Therefore, to conceive of a substantially existing self is explained as being a fault and simply goes against what the Buddha taught.

The five faults are as follows. "One believes in a self and a life force"—that is, if one holds that the individual exists substantially, where in fact there is no "I" or "mine," then one will have the view of a self and of a life force. This is the first fault.

"One is no different from the tīrthikas"—that is, there is no difference between the tīrthikas' assertion that the self exists and this view that the individual exists substantially, which is the second fault.

"One has entered the wrong path." The path to nirvāṇa and liberation consists of meditation on impermanence, suffering, emptiness, and no-self. The belief in a self and in an individual is not the path to liberation; it is the entrance to the wrong path, for it introduces one to the path of rebirth in saṃsāra and the lower realms. This is the third fault.

"One's mind does not incline to emptiness." Emptiness is the absence of "I" and "mine," which is incompatible with the view of a substantially existent individual, so one's mind does not incline to emptiness. As it is said in this regard, "One does not listen, reflect, or meditate, and thus one does not have faith, dwell, or take an interest." This is the fourth fault.

"One's noble qualities will not be perfected"[42]—that is, someone with the view of a substantially existent individual will not eliminate the defilements and truly attain nirvāṇa by relying on the practices of the noble ones (the paths of seeing and meditation). This is the fifth fault.

**The specific distinctions between the stages
Of defilement and purification,**

---

42. Alternative translation: "One's noble practices will not lead to purity."

**And the particular differences between their beginning and
continuing,
Were taught in terms of individuals. (XIX, 103)**

The proponents of a substantially existing individual might say, "In the sūtras, Lord Buddha spoke of a great many kinds of individual—those with full knowledge, those with newly found knowledge, those who have laid down their burden, those individuals who follow out of faith, those individuals who follow with wisdom, and so on.[43] If there is no substantially existent individual, why did he speak of so many individuals like that? If he spoke in that way, it must be that there are substantially existent individuals." His mentioning different kinds of individuals does not mean that such individuals exist substantially. It was in order to easily understand the specific details in distinguishing or demarcating the stages of the defilement process and those of the purification process and the specific differences between those who first engage in the defilement process or the purification process and their continuity that he taught those subjects using names or designations as individuals. But it was not that those individuals existed substantially in any other way than as designations. How were the names given in terms of individuals? When a continuum of five aggregates possesses the qualities of the defilement aspect, it is called "an individual with defilements," a name by which one can easily gain an idea of all the characteristics that make up the condition of that continuum, but that is all. Apart from the qualities of a continuum of aggregates that is associated with defilement, the Buddha was not describing some separate, substantially existent individual that possesses defilements. In the same way, he spoke of continua of aggregates possessing the qualities of the purity aspect as awakened individuals. With regard to those who abide in the stream of defilement there are also many different kinds—those who abide to a small degree in defilement, those who abide to a medium degree, and those who abide to a great degree—of which he spoke using designations, saying things such as, "This person has little attachment," or similarly medium attachment, or great attachment. And in the same way he indicated different "individuals" in terms of their particular defilements, such as aversion. Likewise, because

---

43. These refer to specific terms for practitioners on different stages of the path: those on the path of meditation, those on the path of seeing, arhats, and stream enterers. (Vasubandhu also mentions those on the path of no more learning.)

there are those who abide in purity to a lesser, medium, or greater degree, he spoke of individuals who have attained the lesser path, and so on. He categorized those who consistently practice positive or negative actions as virtuous or nonvirtuous individuals, and likewise spoke of individuals who are entering the process of defilement or the process of purification, individuals who possess defilement or purity, individuals who do not possess those, individuals with sharp or dull faculties, individuals burdened by suffering and its cause, individuals who have attained cessation by means of the path and have thereby laid down their burden, individuals abiding on the path of accumulation and so on, those on the level of earnest aspiration, ordinary beings, listeners, solitary realizers, bodhisattvas, and buddhas, and their different categories—those who have entered the four results, those who have attained the first level, and so on. It should be understood that if he had not taught in terms of all these different kinds of individuals, one would not be able to distinguish their different states, so he taught using the names of individuals in relationship to the names of the factors that distinguish specific continua of the five aggregates, in particular their consciousness.

> No need is there to develop the belief in a self—
> We have been accustomed to it from time without
>   beginning.
> If individuals existed, everyone would be effortlessly
>   liberated,
> Or there would be no liberation. (XIX, 104)

If the names with which Lord Buddha indicated different kinds of individuals were showing that individuals exist substantially, those words would be giving rise to the belief in a self. But there is no need to give rise to the belief in a self—sentient beings have all had that belief in a self since the very beginning. It is not that he taught that there is a substantially existent self in order for us to get accustomed to the self (even though we have had the belief in a self since time without beginning), considering and meditating on the so-called self in order to purify that self and thus see the self and be liberated. The habit of a self has been present since time without beginning, and beings in saṃsāra have accustomed themselves to it for that duration, yet because of it, not only will they not be liberated, but it is the very root that binds them in saṃsāra. Consequently, the Buddha's teaching by using the term "individual" could not possibly have been in order to teach the view of a substantially existing self and meditation on the self, so why would he speak of an individual existing substantially? There would be no purpose in doing so. Either that belief in a self would be something that the Buddha had to arouse in sentient beings, in which case everyone would be effortlessly liberated by the belief in a self, or it would not be something that the Buddha had to arouse and he would refute it, and in that case there would be no liberation for those who have the belief in a self. There cannot be any possibility other than these two. So if there definitely were a substantially existing "individual" or "self," all sentient beings with such a view would be undeluded, and it would follow that they would be liberated from the very beginning without having to make any effort on the path. But in fact, as long as they have not realized the absence of self, no one will attain liberation. This view of a substantially existing self is a mistake that fetters us and therefore has to be refuted; it is not something to be accomplished and developed.

If there were an intrinsically existent self, no one would be able to refute it by means of reasoning, and with such an irrefutable self, it would be impossible for anyone to turn away from grasping at a self. And as long as there were grasping at a self, there would be attachment to anything to do with "I" and "mine," aversion to anything to do with others, and all the other defilements. There would be no way to turn away from them. Because of defilements, we would accumulate karma and go around and around in the three worlds of saṃsāra like a waterwheel, forever, and never be liberated. Thus, it is utterly impossible that the Tathāgata's teaching would indicate a substantially existing individual. We should understand that the fundamental view that distinguishes the Buddha's doctrine and makes it superior to all the views of mundane traditions and of the tīrthikas in indicating the means for liberation from saṃsāra is this teaching on the two kinds of noself, and there is absolutely nothing in all the teachings he gave that points to a substantially existent individual or self.

Conclusion to the Chapter

> Thus bodhisattvas who constantly possess
> All these excellent qualities
> Not only do not forsake their own goal
> But they also accomplish the goals of others. (XIX, 105)

Thus bodhisattvas who constantly possess the excellent qualities of having trained in the elements that lead to enlightenment, from a sense of shame to the explanation on the individual no-self, not only do not abandon their own goal, perfect elimination and realization, but also, by setting sentient beings in similar elimination and realization and so on, accomplish others' goals.

This completes the explanation of the nineteenth chapter of *Ornament of the Mahāyāna Sūtras*, the chapter on the elements leading to enlightenment.

20

Qualities

The exposition of the excellent qualities of bodhisattvas who have put into practice the points set forth in the chapters explained above, from Interest through to Elements Leading to Enlightenment, consists of two parts: (1) qualities that are accomplished and (2) qualities that are highly praised.

1. The Qualities That Are Accomplished

The qualities that are accomplished comprise three sections: (1) a general presentation of three groups of qualities; (2) a detailed explanation of qualities related to the practice of the transcendent perfections and twelve categories from reciprocal benefit to paramount duties; and (3) an exposition of the qualities of learning in terms of how their teaching the Dharma is presented.[1]

a. A General Presentation of Three Groups of Qualities

There are three groups of qualities: qualities that correspond to the cause, resultant qualities, and qualities manifestly related to sentient beings.

With regard to the first of these, by long habituation on the paths of training, bodhisattvas' mind streams take on the nature of the path. The qualities that have appeared on earlier stages of the path become stable, and those that have not appeared appear and increase. This is indicated in the first two verses, beginning, "Their own bodies they give away." The resultant qualities are indicated by the verse "To be born in the tathāgata family..." (verse 3). These three verses together refer to the wondrous qualities. They are followed by one verse on what is not so wondrous, showing that there is

---

1. The last of these three sections is actually included in the second section as its seventeenth subsection.

nothing amazing in a perfect result coming about through having a perfect cause, and it is thus a praise of the cause of accomplishment. This is also a quality. The qualities that are manifestly related to sentient beings comprise a causal quality (the attainment of the attitude of sameness), indicated by the three verses beginning, "With regard to themselves . . ." (verses 5 to 7); and a resultant quality (bringing benefit), indicated by the sixteen verses beginning, "Making beings fit vessels . . ." (verses 8 to 23).

Here, to begin the explanation, we shall explain all this in the same order as the root text, with seventeen sections: (1) wondrous qualities; (2) the not so wondrous; (3) the attitude of sameness; (4) bringing benefit; (5) reciprocal benefit; (6) hope; (7) nonwastefulness; (8) authentic application; (9) diminution and enhancement; (10) the imitative and the authentic; (11) correction; (12) predictions; (13) certainty; (14) definite duties; (15) perpetual duties; (16) paramount duties; and (17) how the Dharma is taught.

b. Detailed Explanation
i. Wondrous Qualities

> Their own bodies they give away,
> And relinquish their abundant wealth to keep the vows of
>   discipline;
> They're patient with those who are downcast,
> And, with no regard for their bodies or their lives, (XX, 1)
>
> They diligently strive;
> They do not savor the bliss of concentration,
> And, in their wisdom, have no concepts—
> Such are considered the wonders of the wise. (XX, 2)

These refer to the wonder of accomplishing the six transcendent perfections. In what way is this wondrous? It is wondrous because ordinary beings and listeners and solitary realizers do not have such accomplishment, which is impossible for others to have. What is that accomplishment? Even ordinary people and listeners and solitary realizers possess material generosity in giving away food, clothing, and so on. But giving away one's own body many, many times is something no one but a bodhisattva can do. Even though they may have acquired the perfect and abundant wealth of a universal emperor or similar being, in order to keep their vows and discipline, bodhisattvas give it all up, rejecting it like a gob of spit and renouncing worldly life. Unlike powerful, influential kings, ministers, and so forth, bodhisattvas are undisturbed by any trouble that beggars, outcastes, and others who are weaker than themselves may cause them, and they are lovingly patient with them. Without any regard for their own bodies and lives, they practice diligently. They may have attained the supreme bliss of the first dhyāna and other three dhyānas, but they never savor it and so take birth again in the world of desire, even in the three lower realms. And though they have acquired the wisdom that discerns the nature of all phenomena, they have no concepts of attributes related to wisdom and phenomena. Such are the wondrous qualities of wise bodhisattvas.

> To be born in the tathāgata family,
> Receive predictions and empowerment,
> And fully attain enlightenment too—
> These are held to be most marvelous. (XX, 3)

The results of this extraordinary accomplishment of the transcendent perfections are as follows. When they first acquire nonconceptual supramundane gnosis on the first level, bodhisattvas are born in the family of the tathāgatas. By spontaneously acquiring the effortless nonconceptual gnosis on the eighth level, they receive predictions from the buddhas. And on the tenth level, they are empowered by the buddhas as their Dharma regents. These three comprise the results of the stages of training. On the level of buddhahood, they fully attain unsurpassable enlightenment. Since no one else in this world, not even the listeners and solitary realizers, has these qualities, they too are held to be a source of great wonder.

ii. THE NOT SO WONDROUS

> In view of their freedom from attachment, their compassion,
> And likewise their attainment of the highest meditation
> And their attitude of sameness,
> Their dedication to those perfections is not so very
>   wondrous. (XX, 4)

This verse shows that there is nothing to wonder at, pointing out that even if the above qualities are certainly extraordinary from the point of view of mundane beings and listeners and solitary realizers, as far as bodhisattvas are concerned, whose attitude and activities are so vast, why would they not obtain them? Bodhisattvas have seen that even the wealth of a universal emperor is like a cesspool, and they are free of attachment to any compounded phenomenon. So there is nothing at all amazing in their giving away gifts on outer and inner levels. In the same way, there is nothing particularly wondrous in their dedication to keeping the discipline of refraining from taking others' lives (for they have great compassion and want to dispel the sufferings of all sentient beings), to being patient with other beings (for they have trained in cherishing others more than themselves), likewise, to undertaking everything with diligence (for they have attained supreme meditation and can engage in things effortlessly and naturally, like firewood catching fire), to tirelessly working for others' welfare (for they have acquired the attitude of the sameness of themselves and all sentient beings and phenomena), to experiencing concentration, and to nonconceptuality through wisdom. And there is nothing so very amazing either in what they attain on account of all that, from being born in the tathāgata family through to unsurpassable enlightenment. If they have those qualities, why would they not obtain such effects and results? It is perfectly natural.

iii. The Attitude of Sameness

> With regard to themselves, their wives,
> Their children, and their companions,
> Sentient beings are nothing like the wise,
> Whose love for all that lives is so immense. (XX, 5)
>
> In their impartiality to all in need,
> Their faultless discipline,
> Patience in all respects,
> Great diligence for the sake of all, (XX, 6)
>
> Their constant virtuous concentration,
> And nonconceptual wisdom—
> In all these the bodhisattvas' attitude of sameness
> Should thus be known. (XX, 7)

Whereas wise bodhisattvas, with their deep love for all sentient beings, hold them in affection and esteem, sentient beings have no such love for themselves. Sometimes, their minds disturbed, they kill themselves, swallow poison, and so on. They get angry too with their spouses, children, and relatives and friends, beating them and so forth. Never abandoning love throughout their whole series of lives is not for them, so they do not have a bodhisattva's sort of love.

Since bodhisattvas have acquired this loving attitude that considers all sentient beings the same, they practice generosity impartially, without any bias such as giving to their own relatives and not giving to others, or distinguishing between friends and enemies, or poor and not poor, when someone in need appears. They observe all the rules of discipline, gross and subtle, without distinction, all the time, without breaking them, guarding against naturally shameful deeds and those that violate edicts. They are patient in every way—in all places, at all times, with all sentient beings. For the benefit of all beings they incessantly apply great diligence. They dwell constantly in virtuous (that is, pure and untainted) concentration[2] and never fail in this. And by means of their wisdom, they discern all phenomena distinctly, and yet they never lose nonconceptuality, completely purified of the concepts of the three spheres. From this, the bodhisattvas' application in deed,[3] their faultless and impartial practice of these six transcendent perfections, we should understand their attitude of sameness.

iv. Bringing Benefit

Bringing benefit is divided into (1) benefiting by means of the six transcendent perfections and (2) seven similes for how bodhisattvas bring benefit.

(1) Benefiting by Means of the Six Transcendent Perfections

> Making beings fit vessels,
> Establishing them in discipline,
> Patiently enduring harm,
> Traveling in order to benefit, (XX, 8)

---

2. Sthiramati mentions three kinds of concentration: with defilements (attachment to the bliss of concentration), pure (without attachment), and untainted. Bodhisattvas practice only the last two kinds of concentration.

3. Tib. *sbyor ba*, the application of the bodhisattvas' intention or attitude (*bsam pa*); the deed as opposed to the thought.

> Introducing them to this doctrine,
> Removing their doubts—
> All this is held to be the benefit
> The wise bring to sentient beings. (XX, 9)

With generosity, bodhisattvas make sentient beings into fit vessels for practicing virtue. To those who cannot practice the Dharma because they lack for food, clothes, and so forth, they give whatever things they want and make them happy and content, subsequently setting them on the path. They bring benefit by observing discipline themselves and then introducing others to discipline. Whatever harm others may do them, they patiently put up with it. To perform actions that will benefit others, they travel everywhere without difficulty. By the power of their concentration, they display miraculous feats and so on, and thereby introduce beings to this, the perfect doctrine. And by the power of their wisdom they remove all beings' doubts and teach them the paths of the three vehicles. All this is held to constitute the benefit that the wise bring to all beings.

(2) Seven Similes for How Bodhisattvas Bring Benefit

These seven similes are clearly indicated by the respective words of the root text.

> Constantly caring for sentient beings
> With an attitude that considers them all the same,
> They give birth to the noble levels,
> Cause virtue to grow, (XX, 10)
>
> Protect from wrongdoing,
> And help them train in what they have heard.
> With these five activities, the buddhas' heirs
> Are like mothers to beings. (XX, 11)

Bodhisattvas always consider sentient beings with the same attitude of love and compassion that makes no distinctions, caring for them until the very end of saṃsāra without abandoning them, like a mother carrying her child in her womb. They give birth to the noble levels—that is, from the path of seeing of the Great and Lesser Vehicles up to the stage of no more learning—like a mother giving birth to her child from the womb. They make sentient beings develop mundane and supramundane virtue like a mother bringing up her child by giving it milk and food, bathing it, massaging it, and so on. They protect sentient beings from all the sufferings of the three lower realms and their causes, the negative actions that accumulate bad karma, like a mother protecting her child from falling into ravines, abysses, and the like. And they teach beings the Dharma and make them train in what they have heard, like a mother teaching her child names and phrases, signs, and expressions. With these five activities, the buddhas' heirs are like mothers to beings.

> Constantly causing faith to be born
> In all sentient beings,
> They teach them superior discipline and the like,
> Connect them to perfect liberation, (XX, 12)
>
> Pray to the buddhas on their behalf,
> And eliminate their obscurations.
> So with these five activities, the buddhas' heirs
> Are like fathers to beings. (XX, 13)

Similarly, bodhisattvas constantly cause faith in the Three Jewels to be born in all sentient beings, like a father engendering children from his seed, for this is the cause for obtaining the body of the three vehicles. They instruct them in the three superior trainings (the training in superior discipline, and so on), like a father teaching his son the crafts and traditions corresponding to his own caste. Because they connect them to perfect liberation from the sufferings of saṃsāra, they are like a father summoning his son, taking a wife for him, and joining them in joy and happiness. For the sake of sentient beings, they pray to the buddhas to not pass into nirvāṇa, to turn the wheel of the Dharma, and so on, like a father who, in order to help his son in his life and worldly affairs, entrusts him to a master, a friend, or someone similar. And because they act to eliminate the defilement-related and cognitive obscurations in the minds of those beings, they are like a father clearing or annulling any debts his children may have contracted that will be a burden for them. Thus, with these five activities, bodhisattvas are like fathers to beings.

> They keep secret those teachings
> That are unsuitable for beings,

> Reproach them for lapses in the training,
> Praise them for excellence, (XX, 14)
>
> Give them instructions,
> And warn them of demons.
> With these five activities, the buddhas' heirs
> Are like kinsfolk to beings. (XX, 15)

If bodhisattvas were to show small-minded beings the profound and extensive teachings and inconceivable subjects of the Great Vehicle, which ought not to be taught to such persons, the latter would be afraid and reject them. So they keep those teachings secret and do not teach them to those beings, like relatives or kinsfolk in ordinary life who keep secret any talk that would be injurious to their other relatives' lives and worldly affairs. Bodhisattvas reproach others who are failing in the three trainings, saying, "What you are doing is wrong," and show them the negative consequences of their acts, like relatives who reproach their kin for acting improperly and stop them from doing so. When they see sentient beings who have all the sublime qualities of the three trainings, they praise them accordingly, which pleases them so that they do not give up those good qualities, like relatives delighting in their kin's good deeds and praising them. In order to make sentient beings master the noble path, bodhisattvas give them teachings on the essential instructions, which comprise the methods for doing so, like relatives giving one another advice and assistance with internal and external affairs. They warn of the deceptive seductions of the sense pleasures, evil company, and so on that act as obstacles on the path for sentient beings, saying, "This is a demon, these are the work of demons," like relations who protect one another from making enemies and being imprisoned, and from being harmed by robbers, fire, floods, and so on. With these five activities, bodhisattvas are like kinsfolk for beings.

> Having no confusion in their own minds
> Concerning defilement and purity,
> They give all that is abundant and perfect,
> Both mundane and beyond; (XX, 16)
>
> Never discouraged and unwavering,
> They always wish beings' benefit and happiness.

> With these five activities, the buddhas' heirs
> Are like friends to beings. (XX, 17)

Bodhisattvas know exactly what is useful for bringing sentient beings benefit and happiness and what is not. Having understood both aspects—that of defilement, which includes suffering and the origin of suffering, and that of purity, which includes the path and cessation—unmistakenly, without any confusion in their own minds, they instruct beings accordingly, just as like-minded friends in ordinary life know what to do to help their other friends and what not to do, and teach them what they know. Bodhisattvas give beings all mundane perfections (the happiness of Brahmā, Indra, the universal emperor, and the rest) and supramundane perfections (the bliss of buddhahood and the levels leading to it). They are like friends who provide their other friends with the things that will benefit their lives and worldly affairs immediately and in the long term. They constantly benefit beings without ever getting discouraged, like friends who never get fed up with helping their fellows. In working for the welfare of sentient beings, bodhisattvas are never put off or affected by such things as negative forces and hardships, like trustworthy companions who cannot be split by divisive talk and will always remain unwaveringly loyal friends. Bodhisattvas never waver from their desire that all sentient beings be constantly benefited with supramundane qualities and made happy with mundane qualities, like friends who never give up wishing long-term benefit and immediate happiness for their other friends. With these five activities, bodhisattvas are like close friends for all beings.

> Forever diligent in the task
> Of bringing beings to maturity,
> They speak of perfect deliverance,
> Patiently bear all kinds of ingratitude, (XX, 18)
>
> Bestow the two kinds of excellence,
> And are expert in the means for achieving these.
> With these five activities, the buddhas' heirs
> Are like servants for beings. (XX, 19)

Bodhisattvas are constantly diligent, and never neglectful, in their work of bringing sentient beings to maturity, like servants in ordinary life who are properly heedful of their masters' commands and carry out their duties enthusiastically, without being lazy. They speak without error to sentient beings of the path that gives perfect deliverance from all suffering, like good servants who undeceitfully tell their master whatever they have seen or heard. They patiently put up with all kinds of harm that beings may inflict on them and with the ingratitude of those whom they have helped but who have hurt them in return, like servants who even put up with their master's beatings and harsh rebukes and willingly accept what they say. They give sentient beings everything that is excellent, both mundane and supramundane, like servants producing and providing everything their masters wish, whenever they are ordered. They are expert at helping other sentient beings perfect the accumulations of merit and wisdom, which constitute the means for attaining all that is excellent, mundane and supramundane, like good servants who are proficient in the means for swiftly carrying out the various tasks their masters command them to do. With these five activities, bodhisattvas are like servants for all beings.

> They wish that others may acquire
> The acceptance that phenomena are unborn,
> They teach all vehicles,
> Prepare them for the accomplishment of yoga, (XX, 20)
>
> Maintain a lovely countenance, and never look for
> Reciprocal help or karmic recompense.
> With these five activities, the buddhas' heirs
> Are like teachers for beings. (XX, 21)

Having naturally, on the eighth level, acquired the acceptance that phenomena are unborn, bodhisattvas wish that all beings will acquire the acceptance that phenomena are unborn; they are like professors, who themselves have received much instruction and are extremely learned, looking after their students. They teach the whole Dharma of the three vehicles to suit beings' mind streams, like learned teachers teaching the subjects their pupils want to learn. They prepare them for accomplishing the yoga of sustained calm and profound insight, like good teachers who teach their pupils quickly without filling up the time.[4] In teaching all beings, they always have a smil-

---

4. According to Sthiramati, bad teachers teach their pupils slowly in order to hold them under sway.

ing, lovely expression, and they never act angrily or threateningly; they are like teachers who, out of love for their pupils, always have a smiling face and speak gently. And whatever they have done for beings' welfare, it is never with an eye for any benefit they might want for themselves in return, or for the effects of their having helped beings ripening on themselves; they are like teachers who teach their subjects out of love for their pupils, and without any thought of material recompense. Thus, with these five activities, bodhisattvas are like teachers for all beings.

> **Those who are extremely diligent in benefiting beings**
> **Help them complete the accumulations,**
> **Swiftly bring those who have accumulated merit to**
>   **liberation,**
> **Make them eliminate incompatible factors, (XX, 22)**
>
> **And connect them to all excellence,**
> **Mundane and supramundane.**
> **With these five activities, the buddhas' heirs**
> **Are like preceptors for beings. (XX, 23)**

Bodhisattvas are extremely diligent in working for the benefit of all sentient beings, and so they help those beings who have not completed the two accumulations to fully complete them, like a preceptor giving ordination to disciples, making them give up worldly life for that of a homeless renunciant and giving them the monastic precepts. They cause those who have gathered the accumulations to swiftly be liberated on the resultant level, like a preceptor who gives disciples who have renounced worldly life full ordination with the complete vows. They train beings, inducing them to get rid of factors incompatible with the six transcendent perfections that constitute the path for attaining perfect liberation and nirvāṇa, just as a preceptor teaches disciples the radical defeats, residual faults, downfalls, and the other faults that go against the precepts and induces them to avoid wrongdoing. And they provide beings with everything that is excellent, mundane and supramundane, like a preceptor who helps disciples materially and spiritually. Thus, bodhisattvas, who benefit all sentient beings with five activities like the five functions of a preceptor,[5] are like preceptors for all sentient beings.

---

5. The last of what appear to be only four functions mentioned here is double: as explained

v. Reciprocal Benefit

> Because they are not attached to wealth,
> Keep faultless discipline,
> Are full of gratitude,
> And apply themselves to the practice, (XX, 24)
>
> Beings who in that way undertake
> The six transcendent perfections
> Similarly benefit
> Bodhisattvas in return. (XX, 25)

When bodhisattvas benefit sentient beings by introducing them to the transcendent perfections, those beings' faultless practice of the transcendent perfections is of reciprocal benefit to the bodhisattvas. In what way? When bodhisattvas give things, the beings whom they have enriched with those things are grateful to the bodhisattvas. Similarly, when those beings who have become wealthy give generously without attachment to their wealth, the bodhisattvas are grateful to them, thinking, "They have benefited sentient beings." The same applies when beings whom bodhisattvas have introduced to discipline do not let their discipline deteriorate. Furthermore, bodhisattvas on whom all kinds of harm have been inflicted, instead of feeling any ill will, remain patient, gratefully acknowledging, "These people are being instrumental in my giving rise to patience, so they are helping me." Similarly, the beings whom they have introduced to patience likewise also practice patience. And just as when bodhisattvas introduce beings to the practice of diligence, concentration, and wisdom, those beings are grateful to the bodhisattvas, likewise, because the beings whom the bodhisattvas have introduced to those three practices apply themselves to the practice accordingly, the bodhisattvas are grateful to them. This is explained in the commentary.

In fact, the beings who engage in the six transcendent perfections in this way are helping the bodhisattvas in return, just as they were themselves helped by the bodhisattvas. Their practicing the transcendent perfections like that makes the bodhisattvas very joyful at heart, but bodhisattvas do

---

by Sthiramati, the fourth and fifth of a preceptor's or abbot's functions are to help monks and nuns materially and to help them spiritually.

not wish for anything else such as a material reward. So on the one hand, sentient beings, their minds full of gratitude to those bodhisattvas, practice the transcendent perfections accordingly; and on the other hand, bodhisattvas gratefully acknowledge them, thinking, "They are helping me." This too constitutes an extraordinary quality of bodhisattvas, namely, nonmaterialistic hope.

vi. Different Forms of Hope

> For beings and themselves, bodhisattvas always wish
> For increase, decrease,
> Maturation, progress on the levels,
> And unsurpassable enlightenment. (XX, 26)

Bodhisattvas' hope takes five forms. Constantly, they hope and wish that the six transcendent perfections in their own and others' mind streams will increase. They hope and wish that everything incompatible with the six transcendent perfections will decline and decrease. They hope and wish that sentient beings who have not developed faith will develop it, that those who have developed faith will be set in virtuous ways, and that those who are practicing virtue will be brought to maturity. They hope and wish that they will progress higher and higher through the ten levels, from attaining the first level to attaining the second level, and similarly all the way up to the tenth level. And they hope and wish that they will go beyond the tenth level and attain unsurpassable enlightenment. Apart from these five forms of hope, bodhisattvas do not give rise to the slightest hope for other, mundane perfections or for the listeners' and solitary realizers' paths and results. This is the quality of their wishes and hopes.

vii. The Quality of Their Practice Never Going to Waste

> In their absence of fear, their correct intent,
> The removal of doubts,
> And their use of the instructions on practice,
> The buddhas' heirs are never wasteful. (XX, 27)

Listeners and solitary realizers engage in their own welfare alone and therefore do not benefit others, so their practice is wasted. The practice that mundane beings hopefully undertake is, for the most part, fruitless, and it is therefore also wasted. On the other hand, bodhisattvas, with their perfect, correctly conceived hope, accomplish everything accordingly, whatever they do, and it is thus not wasted. This quality of their practice not being wasted takes four forms: (1) Were they to be afraid of the profound and extensive teachings of the Great Vehicle, bodhisattvas would be wasting their practice in the Great Vehicle. But they are free of fear with regard to the Great Vehicle's profound and extensive teachings and have also dispelled others' fears, so their practice in the Great Vehicle is not wasted. (2) If their spiritual intent were motivated by a desire for mundane perfections or for the paths and results of the listeners and solitary realizers, their practice of the Great Vehicle would be wasted. But bodhisattvas never give rise to such an intent; they have the correct spiritual intent, arousing the mind set on unsurpassable enlightenment for themselves and all sentient beings. So because they never fail in correctly arousing the mind intent on enlightenment, their practice is not wasted. (3) Even having aroused the mind intent on enlightenment, if they were to have doubts from not knowing the methods for accomplishing enlightenment, they might turn back from their spiritual intent and let it go to waste. But bodhisattvas clear away their doubts concerning the path and result of the Great Vehicle, so their practice is not wasted. (4) Were they not themselves to accomplish the instructions on the levels, the transcendent perfections, and the yoga of sustained calm and profound insight that the buddhas and bodhisattvas have taught and to teach them to others, they would be wasting them. But when bodhisattvas receive the instructions on accomplishment, they put them into practice themselves and teach them to others, so their practice is never wasted. These four qualities constitute the bodhisattvas' constant nonwastefulness.

viii. Authentic Application

> Generosity without expectation,
> Discipline with no desire for higher rebirth,
> Patience with all in every respect,
> Diligence in gathering all good qualities, (XX, 28)
>
> Likewise, concentration that is not intended for the formless world,
> And wisdom possessed of skillful means—

> Those who are steadfast in these six perfections
> Are applying them authentically. (XX, 29)

Bodhisattvas who perform their physical, verbal, and mental activities while remaining unwasteful in this way are applying themselves unmistakenly, properly, authentically. Although they give completely to the poor and destitute whatever of the three kinds of gift they wish for, they give without hoping for any benefit to themselves in this life nor for great personal wealth in other lives. Their generosity is the authentic application of transcendent generosity. In the same way, they observe discipline in order to attain unsurpassable enlightenment, with no wish for higher rebirth in saṃsāra. With regard to those who harm them, they practice patience with all three doors, not only in not retaliating physically and verbally but also in never giving rise to anger mentally; and regardless of how good or bad the beings are who harm them, and of how much harm they inflict, they are patient with all of them. It is not that they are diligent in just a few transcendent perfections or just a few vehicles: in exerting themselves in all the transcendent perfections and in the Great Vehicle, in which the qualities of the paths and results of all vehicles are complete, they are applying the diligence that is the source of all virtue or good qualities. Similarly, although they have attained the concentration of the four dhyānas and of the four formless states, they do not take birth in the formless world. Since they are unable to complete the path to buddhahood and bring sentient beings to maturation in the formless world, they take birth in the worlds of form and desire; in particular, having taken birth in the world of desire, they perform the infinite deeds of completion and maturation. And since bodhisattvas who lack either wisdom or skillful means are fettered, their wisdom is endowed with skillful means, combining the wisdom that knows all phenomena to be emptiness and great compassion, by means of which they bring sentient beings to maturation through the four ways of attracting disciples. Such bodhisattvas who are steadfast in the practice of the six transcendent perfections are applying them properly and authentically. This is further stated in the *Heap of Jewels Sūtra*:

> Generosity without hope of karmic recompense, discipline that is not observed for any rebirth in existence, patience devoid of anger for any sentient being, diligence that perfectly gathers all sources of good, concentration untainted by the formless world,

and wisdom that brings to maturation through means endowed with the four ways by which the skilled attract disciples, ...

ix. Diminution and Enhancement

The two categories of diminution and enhancement refer to factors that diminish whichever of the six transcendent perfections one is practicing and factors that enhance whichever of the transcendent perfections one is practicing, making them grow and progress. Factors that counteract the six transcendent perfections weaken and diminish bodhisattvas' authentic practice of the six transcendent perfections, while remedial factors make it grow like the moon waxing. This section indicates these categories of diminution and increase.

Diminution

> Attachment to pleasure, violations,
> Pride, indulging in pleasure,
> Savoring, and concepts
> Result in diminution for the steadfast. (XX, 30)

If one is attached to the enjoyment of sensual pleasures, one is unable to give things away, and this diminishes transcendent generosity. Similarly, if one rends and deteriorates the most subtle injunctions of the precepts, this diminishes transcendent discipline. Pride, with a lack of deference physically, verbally, and mentally for preceptors, instructors, and beings with good qualities, and an inability, due to such pride, to respect them, diminishes patience. Craving for and indulgence in the extreme of merit-sapping pleasures[6] diminishes transcendent diligence. Savoring the taste of concentration diminishes transcendent concentration. And conceptualizing things as substantially real diminishes the wisdom in which there is no conceptualization of attributes. These six are the causes that diminish the transcendent perfections of a steadfast bodhisattva.

---

6. Tib. *'dod pa bsod nyams kyi mtha'*, attachment to pleasure as a result of which one's merit declines.

Enhancing Qualities

> The antidotes to these,
> For bodhisattvas who use them,
> Are to be understood as their opposites,
> And therefore as favorable, enhancing qualities. (XX, 31)

The antidotes for the above are to have no attachment to sensual pleasures, to not deteriorate one's discipline, to be free of pride, to have no craving for pleasurable indulgence, to not savor concentration, and to have no concepts of substantial attributes. They are to be understood as being the favorable qualities of enhancement that make the six transcendent perfections grow in bodhisattvas who use these antidotes, for they are the opposite of those diminishing factors.

x. Distinctions between the Imitative and the Authentic

> Making a show, pretense,
> Putting on a serene face,
> Likewise applying oneself from time to time,
> Remaining calm in body and speech,
> And being superbly eloquent—
> All these are divorced from accomplishment: (XX, 32)

> They are explained as not being
> The authentic practices of the bodhisattvas.
> The practices of those who apply themselves to their opposites
> Are explained as being authentic. (XX, 33)

The following practices fall short of the true six transcendent perfections and are mere effigies of them. Making a show of giving or pretending to give—for example, not making gifts on outer and inner levels after saying that one will, or giving openly and then secretly taking—is a mere effigy of transcendent generosity. Similar to that is continuously indulging in the faults one should be guarding against, but in front of others, pretending to observe discipline. Though full of hatred and unable to tolerate others, one puts on an appearance of patience, physically by looking serene and verbally by speaking gently. Similarly, one is forever lacking in diligence and only applies oneself to making effort occasionally, for example, when there are a lot of people around. One may appear to be in a state of calm, physically staying in a solitary place and looking peaceful, and verbally keeping silent, but rather than remaining in concentration, one's mind is wandering about in a state of distraction. Similarly, though one lacks the wisdom that comes from a proper knowledge of the meanings of the teachings of the three vehicles, one gives credence to words from having learned a certain amount of grammar or logic and, as if one were a brilliant scholar and the author of numerous philosophical-sounding discourses, one teaches crowds of fools. This is an effigy of wisdom. These interpretations of the six transcendent perfections, which are divorced from proper accomplishment, are explained as being mere effigies, inauthentic versions of the bodhisattvas' six transcendent perfections.

Authentic transcendent perfections are the opposite of these six inauthentic, imitative practices. The transcendent perfections of those who apply themselves to authentic generosity and the others through to the wisdom that unmistakenly knows the nature of phenomena are explained as being uncontrived and authentic. For this reason, bodhisattvas do not practice contrived transcendent perfections that are a pretense, a mere appearance. Rather, they practice the authentic transcendent perfections without pretense, undeceitfully, and this quality of theirs is like untarnished gold. We should therefore understand that this has been presented in terms of both faults and qualities so as to show up the qualities of the antidotes, which are unadulterated by such faults.

xi. CORRECTION

> The wise, on all the levels,
> Practice generosity and the others
> And thereby correct
> The six counteragents in beings. (XX, 34)

Bodhisattvas whose quality it is to practice the transcendent perfections authentically are able to correct factors that counteract the six transcendent perfections and that are present in the mind streams of other sentient beings. The individuals who are performing this correction are wise bodhisattvas. The stages on which they dwell and correct beings are all the stages of the ten levels. The means by which they correct them are the practices of the six transcendent perfections—generosity and the rest. Those whom they correct are sentient beings, and what they are correcting in them are factors such as stinginess that counteract the six transcendent perfections, factors that diminish them, and their contrived forms.

xii. Different Kinds of Personal Prediction

> Specifying the individual and the time,
> The predictions the wise receive are twofold.
> There are predictions of enlightenment, of predictions,
> And also ones that are described as "great," (XX, 35)
>
> Which are for those who have gained acceptance of the
>   unborn,
> Who have abandoned pride and effort,
> And are of the same nature
> As the buddhas and their children. (XX, 36)
>
> Again, it is in terms of their buddha field, name,
> Time, the name of the kalpa,
> Their following, and the duration of their doctrine
> That predictions are said to be made. (XX, 37)

Because they possess the quality of utterly pure transcendent perfections, wise bodhisattvas receive predictions concerning their attaining unsurpassable enlightenment, and these have two aspects: predictions that specify individuals and predictions that specify times.

Predictions that specify individuals are of four kinds: predictions concerning individuals who possess the potential; predictions concerning individuals who have aroused the mind intent on enlightenment; predictions concerning individuals who are actually present; and predictions concerning individuals who are not present. The first of these four kinds is a prediction that someone who has not aroused bodhicitta but dwells in the family and has the potential and seed of the six transcendent perfections will attain buddhahood in unsurpassable enlightenment. The second is a prediction given once the mind intent on unsurpassable enlightenment has been aroused. The third is a prediction concerning an individual actually present in that Buddha's entourage: "So-and-so will in the future become the Buddha known as X." The fourth is a prediction about someone who is not actually present in the entourage: "The bodhisattva X who is present in another buddha field...." It was with predictions such as "In the future, the individual called X will appear and will attain unsurpassable enlightenment" that Nāgārjuna, Asaṅga, and others were predicted.

Predictions that specify times are of two kinds: predictions with a defined timescale (it will take so many kalpas or lifetimes to attain unsurpassable enlightenment) and predictions in which the timescale is indefinite (one day, sometime in the future, one will attain buddhahood).

Predictions are categorized into two further groups: those in which the Buddha himself predicts that a particular individual will attain great enlightenment and those that predict, "In the future, such and such a buddha will give you a prediction"—these are called "predictions of predictions."

Furthermore, there are predictions that are described as "great." These concern bodhisattvas on the eighth level who have acquired the acceptance that phenomena are unborn. They have abandoned conceit, have given up all effort associated with attributes, and are of the same nature or essence as all the buddhas and bodhisattvas on the pure levels, without any notion of distinct streams of being. For this reason, predictions concerning them are termed "great predictions." Since those who have attained the eighth level realize that they will without any doubt attain buddhahood and they then make their own prediction, "I myself will attain buddhahood," and the tathāgatas also make predictions concerning them, these are termed "great predictions" or "greatly predicted."

Predictions are further classified as follows. Bodhisattvas are said to be predicted by the name of their buddha field, their name at the time of attaining buddhahood, the time when they will attain buddhahood, the name of the kalpa in which they will attain buddhahood, the size of that buddha's following, and how long that buddha's sacred teachings will endure.

xiii. Certainty

> For the wise, at all times,
> Abundance, birth, indefatigability,
> Perpetual training, unimpaired concentration,
> The accomplishment of their deeds,

And spontaneous acceptance
Will certainly be obtained. (XX, 38)

Apart from their yearning to achieve unsurpassable enlightenment, bodhisattvas have no desire for any riches they might gain in the meantime. However, up until their attainment of ultimate great enlightenment, in all their intervening lives they will certainly, beyond any doubt, also obtain the six respective results of the transcendent perfections. What are these? Wherever they are reborn, wise bodhisattvas who genuinely practice the six transcendent perfections will be certain to always obtain the results of generosity—namely, the abundant and perfect riches of Brahmā, Indra, the universal emperor, and others. As a result of discipline, they are certain to obtain rebirth wherever they wish, among gods, humans, and the like. As a result of patience, it is certain they will never be discouraged by suffering for the sake of others. The result of their diligence is that they will certainly always cultivate or train in virtuous activities. As a result of their concentration, it is certain they will never wane in the meditative absorption they have acquired, and by the power of their concentration, they will gain preternatural powers such as that of performing miracles and be certain to benefit beings. And the result of their wisdom is that they will certainly acquire acceptance, the spontaneous nonconceptual gnosis; that is to say, it is certain, beyond any doubt, that on the lower paths they will acquire a semblance of effortless nonconceptual gnosis and that on the eighth level they will acquire the real thing.

xiv. Different Kinds of Definite Duties

Making offerings, taking the precepts properly,
Compassion, cultivating virtue,
Likewise, carefulness in lonely places,
And insatiability in study—
These are the definite duties
Of the steadfast on all the levels. (XX, 39)

One does not attain buddhahood in unsurpassable enlightenment by doing nothing, and there are practices that are definitely indispensable. These are referred to as definite duties. What are these? It is indispensable for bodhisattvas to make offerings to the tathāgatas—actual material offerings and imagined ones. This is their duty related to generosity. It is indispensable—and thus a definite duty—to take the precepts correctly and to never fail in their discipline. So also is training in patience with a desire, out of compassion for sentient beings, to dispel their suffering; being diligent in cultivating mundane and supramundane virtue; similarly, in order to achieve concentration, staying in a lonely place with no distracting activities and maintaining carefulness; and for the sake of perfect wisdom, relying on a spiritual master and being insatiable with regard to studying the sūtras and other scriptures. These are definite and essential duties for steadfast bodhisattvas on all the levels.

xv. Perpetual Duties

> To know the defects of desire,
> Examine mistakes,
> Willingly take on suffering,
> Cultivate all forms of good, (XX, 40)
>
> Avoid savoring bliss,
> And be free of concepts
> Are the perpetual duties
> Of the steadfast on all the levels. (XX, 41)

There are six things that have to be done constantly, and not just from time to time, in order to complete the six transcendent perfections. In order to complete transcendent generosity, bodhisattvas have at all times to recognize the defects of attachment to the five sense pleasures, constantly keeping in mind the fact that samsaric sense pleasures are impermanent like clouds and lightning, and that if one is attached to them they turn into states of suffering, like poisoned food, a blazing pit of fire, the edge of a sword, or a nest of snakes, and are as undependable as a magical illusion or a dream. Similarly, for the sake of discipline, they have to examine the mistakes in their own bad conduct—physical, verbal, and mental—and act carefully. They have to reflect again and again on how sentient beings, under the control of their deeds and defilements and without the slightest control of their own, are drifting on the waves of the three kinds of suffering, and thus to be clothed in great compassion and armor, training in willingly taking on themselves all kinds of suffering for beings' sake. Lazy people do not accomplish even mundane tasks, let alone supramundane goals. If one undertakes things with diligence, one will even attain buddhahood, not to mention other goals. So bodhisattvas reflect on the fact that diligence is the indispensable root of all virtuous practice, and they constantly cultivate and accomplish both mundane and supramundane virtue. With the mind distracted, it is impossible to obtain any virtuous qualities, so concentration is indispensable. However, if one savors and clings to the bliss of concentration, that same concentration will become a fetter. So even when they are practicing concentration, bodhisattvas always avoid savoring its bliss so as not to impair their concentration. The wisdom that knows the nature and multiplicity of phenomena is the most important of the transcendent perfections and is therefore indispensable. However, since no phenomenon whatsoever, from form through to omniscience, exists naturally or inherently with attributes, if one is attached to substantiality and attributes in any phenomenon, the meaning of ultimate reality will not be realized and one will be contaminated by obscurations as to the nature of knowable phenomena. So it is by having no concepts of subject and object as attributes in any phenomenon that one will complete transcendent wisdom. These six practices, then, are the perpetual duties, on all levels alike, of a steadfast bodhisattva.

xvi. Paramount Duties

> The gift of Dharma, pure discipline,
> The attainment of acceptance that phenomena are unborn,
> Diligence in the Great Vehicle,
> Dwelling in the last of the dhyānas, endowed with compassion,
> And wisdom—these are the most important aspects
> Of the transcendent perfections for the wise. (XX, 42)

Within each of the six transcendent perfections there are items that are supreme or sublime, and because of them, bodhisattvas who possess them are also supreme or sublime. What are they? Of the three categories of generosity, the gift of Dharma is of paramount importance, or supreme. This is because material giving and protection from fear may procure mundane happiness, but the gift of Dharma enables beings to accomplish supramundane perfection. For this reason, it is taught in the *Diamond Cutter Sūtra* and other texts:

More than someone who gives a great universal system of one thousand million worlds filled with the seven precious attributes of royalty, someone who teaches and explains just one four-line verse from this sūtra will develop infinite merit.

Of the three categories of vows—prātimokṣa, dhyāna, and untainted—the untainted vow is the best or most important, because it constitutes the utterly pure discipline that pleases the noble beings. Of the three kinds of patient acceptance,[7] acquiring the acceptance that phenomena are unborn (which is included in the patient acceptance of certainty in the Dharma) is the most important. Of all the different kinds of diligence—including those of mundane beings and of the listeners and solitary realizers, the practice of diligence in listening to the teachings of the Great Vehicle, reflecting on them, and meditating on them is the best and most important. Of the four dhyānas, the last, which is the highest state in which sustained calm and profound insight are balanced, is the fourth dhyāna, and to take support of this and abide in that state endowed with boundless compassion is the best of all concentrations. Transcendent wisdom within the first five transcendent perfections is the best or most important, as is stated in the *Prajñāpāramitā*:

> If one wishes to perfectly complete transcendent generosity, one must train in transcendent wisdom....

These, then, are held to be the most important of the transcendent perfections for wise bodhisattvas.

xvii. How Teaching the Dharma Is Presented[8]

How bodhisattvas' teaching of the Dharma is presented comprises five sections: (1) how the different aspects of the Dharma that is to be taught are presented; (2) how the meaning of the Dharma that has to be completely

---

7. Sthiramati lists these three as patient acceptance in thinking nothing of suffering (Tib. *sdug bsngal ji mi snyam pa'i bzod pa*), patience in accepting harm (*gnod pa nyams su len pa'i bzod pa*), and the patient acceptance of certainty in the Dharma, or certainty with regard to reality (*chos la nges pa rtog pa'i bzod pa*).

8. This seventeenth section corresponds to the third main part of the qualities that are accomplished, which is related to the quality of learning (see the beginning of this chapter).

understood is presented; (3) how the immeasurable qualities of the bodhisattva who teaches it are presented; (4) how the result of such teaching is presented; and (5) how the features of the Great Vehicle are presented, along with a summary.[9]

(1) How the Different Aspects of the Dharma That Is to Be Taught Are Presented

Benefiting sentient beings takes many different forms, on both temporary and ultimate levels, but the most important is to liberate beings' mind streams by teaching them the Dharma, hence the following presentation of the Dharma. Bodhisattvas need to have the qualities of learning from having themselves repeatedly listened to the profound and extensive teachings of the Great Vehicle and properly developed certainty as to their meaning. Otherwise they will be unable to give teachings suited to the temperaments, faculties, and aspirations of the different kinds of beings. As the *Commentary on Valid Cognition* declares:

> Those for whom the result of means and its cause are a mystery
> Will have difficulty explaining them.

In other words, those who do not themselves know the truth of cessation that results from skillful means and the truth of the path that is its cause, and for whom these are a mystery, cannot teach the path of liberation and its result. This is why a fourfold presentation of how bodhisattvas explain the Dharma is given here. One might ask whether this has not already been explained in chapters 12 and 13 (on investigating and explaining the Dharma) and wonder why it is being explained again. In this case, we are in the chapter describing the bodhisattvas' qualities, and here it is the qualities of their skill in four aspects of teaching the Dharma that is presented. Although the points here are no different from the above explanations, they are presented differently and are indicated by means of particular enumerations that summarize the points to be understood. So not only is there no fault in repeating them, but it is also very helpful.

Those bodhisattvas who have the supreme qualities of practicing the path

---

9. The Tibetan term *rnam bzhag* used in all these headings denotes the systematic way in which things are arranged and classified and thus presented.

of the transcendent perfections, as explained above, know the methods for training sentient beings, and by knowing those methods, they will become the teachers of sentient beings. For how they become teachers and teach the Dharma, the wise explain four aspects of teaching the Dharma. What are these four? (1) Explaining how the teachings are presented; (2) explaining how the truth is presented; (3) explaining how the four kinds of rational application are presented; and (4) explaining how the three vehicles are presented.

(a) How the Teachings Are Presented

> For the steadfast on all levels,
> The presentation of the sciences
> In specific sections such as the condensed discourses
> Is what is called the presentation of the teachings. (XX, 43)

The presentation of the five sciences (the inner science of Buddhist teachings, grammar, logic, art, and medicine) in specific sections of the Twelve Branches of Excellent Speech (condensed discourses, prophecies, discourses in verse, and so forth) is to be understood as being what we call "the presentation of the teachings" for steadfast bodhisattvas on all the levels—the level of earnest aspiration and the ten levels of the noble beings. What do we mean by "presentation"? Let us take the example of the science of grammar. Just as in the past, in the texts on grammar, the buddhas, bodhisattvas, and great rishis presented the various systems in which letters are combined to form words, whose nature is then transformed by applying grammatical cases and other accessory elements, so too bodhisattvas use those systems to explain and present the science of grammar to others. In the same way, for the science of logic, they present the different ways of evaluating the three kinds of thesis (manifestly evident, occult, and extremely occult) by direct valid cognition, inference, and scriptural authority. For the science of medicine, they present the methods for maintaining good physical health and, in the event of illness, the proper ways to make use of the four remedies—diet, conduct, medicines, and treatment. And for the various arts, they present the relevant physical, verbal, and mental trainings. They also know how to present the various specific arts beginning with arithmetic, astrology, and the eight kinds of examination. They have a proper knowledge of the widely known presentations in the source texts on the branches of the science of grammar—the source texts on poetry that enable it to have the melodious styles of word and meaning highlighted by verse, prose, and the alternation of verse and prose; and source texts of the treatises on the compilation and composition of verse, with stressed and unstressed syllables, treatises on songs composed in various languages, dance steps, and drama; and treatises on synonyms, which provide knowledge on the various different words having the same meaning. And for the inner science of the Buddhist teachings, they teach and present unmistakenly all the systems of the path and result in each of the three vehicles. All this is what is referred to as the presentation of the teachings.

Now one might ask, aren't the Twelve Branches of Excellent Speech (the condensed discourses and the others) the inner science? How, by explaining them, is one explaining the presentation of the other sciences? If this is not the case, in what way does "The presentation of the sciences in specific sections such as the condensed discourses" show that the five sciences are included in the condensed discourses and the other branches?

It is true that the Twelve Branches of the Buddha's Excellent Speech are the source texts that teach mainly the inner science. But since the other four of the five sciences are also present as its branches, the extremely extensive sūtras of the Great Vehicle unmistakenly teach the condition of all phenomena, in their nature and in their multiplicity. So it is not at all the case that apart from the Mahāyāna discourses they do not teach the five sciences. One should never consider that the Buddha's teachings are limited to the Mahāyāna sūtras. Thus, the Buddha, in his teachings, presented and explained all five sciences to the bodhisattvas. The bodhisattvas have retained them accordingly and, in order to benefit sentient beings, manifest from time to time in the form of rishis and great brahmins possessing the five kinds of preternatural knowledge and give teachings, numberless times, as we read in these extracts from the *Sūtra of the Precious Lamp*:

> Appearing in the world, they soon gain knowledge.
> To all those beings who do not know how to act properly
> They describe the worldly activities of agriculture,
> Commerce, and the various arts.
> Those whose deeds are without harm or violence
> Bring happiness to beings and are praised by the wise.
> All the various castes, powers, medicines, and treatises
> Those rishis perfectly describe.
> To the worldly who believe in gods,
> Those wise beings perfectly describe

The supreme and sacred activities of the rishis,
And all the highest ascetic deeds and practices.
Those who follow the way constantly appear
As masters of the tīrthikas to tīrthikas
Who practice penance just as Gautama did, to those who never speak,
To naked ascetics without clothes, and devoted śrāmaṇeras.

and:

With all kinds of skillful means,
Wandering the world, they work for beings' good.
Unattached to the world, like a lotus in a lake,
They constantly bring joy and faith.
Masters of poetry, they compose in verse;
As dancers, drummers, athletes, musicians,
Beauteous, adorned and garlanded, they dance;
Masters of magic, they constantly display numerous forms:
As citizens, mayors, universal monarchs,
Likewise captains, merchants, and householders,
Kings, ministers, advisers, messengers,
Doctors, and masters of worldly treatises and rituals,
As great trees in the wilderness,
Inexhaustible treasures of jewels and medicines,
Wish-fulfilling jewels, wish-granting trees,
And guides for those who hesitate or have taken the wrong road.

Boundless manifestations of the buddhas and bodhisattvas, in endless, infinite buddha fields in the ten directions, explain, by the power of the buddhas and bodhisattvas, the unmistaken treatises containing the five sciences. The *Sublime Continuum* indicates the quality of the Buddha's melodious speech as follows:

In short, in all the realms of the world,
For the gods and those dwelling on the earth, the causes of happiness
Are described as entirely depending on the melodious voice
That appears throughout all worlds without exception.[10]

---

10. *Sublime Continuum*, IV, 41.

So it is extremely small-minded to consider that the sciences of grammar and so on are not present in the Buddha's teachings and are confined to non-Buddhist traditions. There are a great many source texts on grammar and other subjects that were composed by Buddhist and non-Buddhist scholars after they had been taught by the buddhas and bodhisattvas of the past, but how can one be sure that if the authors were non-Buddhist, that knowledge belongs to the non-Buddhist tradition, and that if they were Buddhist, it belongs to the Buddhist tradition? The four sciences are common sciences, so one cannot distinguish them as being Buddhist or non-Buddhist. Nevertheless, we need hardly mention that the presentations in the sūtras on logic, the *Seven Treatises on Logic*, and similar texts on how to establish the teacher and teaching as authentic are unknown to non-Buddhists and are therefore particular to the inner, Buddhist science—as also are the explanations in the mantra texts of the secret language of the tathāgatas; those in the *Tantra of the Essence of Nectar*, for example, related to maturation and liberation, with mantras that dispel obstacles related to disturbances in the elements and the body; those on the arts concerning dance and melody in Secret Mantrayāna rituals, the measurements of statues, and so on; and the presentation in the chapter on the outer universe in the *Tantra of the Wheel of Time* of the relationship between the astrological aspects of the planets and the number of breaths in the central channel.

The inner science in non-Buddhist traditions includes meditation on the concentrations of the worlds of form and formlessness, the practice of prāṇa-yoga by followers of Śiva, the Nirgrantha Jains' meditation on thatness by means of nāda, meditation on the nature of ātman, and so forth, but they do not have the realization of no-self, so although they may well accomplish a few temporary miraculous powers, these traditions are not the path to liberation. They do not in any respect include the authentic inner science and do not lead beyond the world. The Buddha's teachings, on the other hand, show the path that leads beyond the world and are therefore the genuine inner science.

Thus, since this inner science is what definitively establishes the nature and the multiplicity of all phenomena, grammar and all the other sciences, being branches that provide knowledge of phenomena in their multiplicity, are also its branches. Although the Buddha's teachings are beyond measure and limit, even among the sūtras that are available nowadays in India and Tibet, one can read various discourses on grammar and the other sciences. Where the sūtra *Unraveling the Intent* and other texts speak of the four kinds of rational application (dependency, function, and the others), they are setting forth the complete science of causes or logic. With regard to the science of grammar too, passages in the sūtras such as "Because it obstructs, it is form" or "Feeling which is the nature of experience...," reflect not only a knowledge of the etymological definitions of words and perfect knowledge of language in Sanskrit, but also a knowledge of the etymological definitions in the countless languages of all beings. And when it is said that the Tathāgata's speech is beautifully expressed, this refers to excellent etymological definitions in which the names and accessory grammatical cases are properly put together. And from each of the Buddha's declarations, which have the most ornamental poetic styles such as metaphoric ornaments, exquisite expressions, figures of speech, and so on, there are countless ones worth mentioning as examples of poetry. The *Tantra of the Wheel of Time* actually teaches astrological rituals. The various kinds of dance, song, crafts, and examination too appear incidentally in the sūtras, and the ways in which the bodhisattva perfected the arts are described in the *Play in Full*. Even the science of medicine is taught in the *Sūtra of Sublime Golden Light*.

From these examples, we should understand that it is not the case that none of the sciences apart from the inner science appear in the Buddha's Excellent Words, and that therefore within the Mahāyāna sūtras, all the sciences are included. Whatever benefit and happiness, temporary or ultimate, it will bring sentient beings, when the Buddha encounters a disciple (as the condition for teaching) and receives a request, there is nothing that he does not know and does not speak about. And the bodhisattvas too, having retained his words with their unforgetting powers of memory, teach them when the time is right. So every kind of knowledge, of both the nature and the multiplicity of phenomena, is to be found in the Buddha's Excellent Words.

(b) How the Truth Is Presented

> The truth is presented on the basis of
> Seven aspects of suchness. (XX, 44ab)

It is on the basis of seven aspects of suchness that the truth is presented. The seven aspects of suchness are as follows.

Suchness of engagement refers to continuous engagement in saṃsāra. In what way is there engagement? As a result of ignorance, conditioning factors and the other links of the twelve links of dependent arising are produced one after another, leading to continuous engagement in saṃsāra—uninterruptedly, with no beginning and no end.

Suchness of reality refers to the three realities—the imputed, dependent, and fully present realities. The dualistic imputed reality of subject and object does not exist in the way it is imputed to be. The cause or ground of the mistaken dualistic perception of subject and object exists conventionally as the dependent reality. The ultimate reality devoid of duality (in that subject and object have no existence in the dependent reality) is the fully present reality.

Suchness of cognitive awareness refers to the fact that all phenomena, compounded and uncompounded, do not exist other than as the mind, which is why the *Sūtra of the Ten Levels* says, "O bodhisattvas, these three worlds are merely mind." Thus, all phenomena amount to nothing more than appearances in the mind and exist, therefore, as cognitive awareness itself.

Suchness of abidance is that of samsaric phenomena, which abide forever in the nature of the three kinds of suffering.

Suchness of wrong practice corresponds to the truth of the origin, characterized by actions and defilements, for it wrongly produces the nature of suffering.

Suchness of perfect purity corresponds to the truth of cessation, for it is perfectly purified of faults, that is, of suffering and the origin of suffering.

Suchness of authentic practice corresponds to the truth of the path, because through it the truth of cessation is correctly accomplished.

In terms of their engagement, abidance, and wrong practice, all sentient beings are alike. In terms of those parts of the suchness of reality that are the dependent and fully present realities, all compounded and uncompounded phenomena are alike; and within the dependent reality, the suchness of cognitive awareness is also included. The sūtra *Unraveling the Intent* speaks of the suchness of reality only as the two kinds of no-self, in which case it corresponds to the fully present reality. In terms of the suchness of perfect purity, the enlightenments of the listeners, solitary realizers, and buddhas are said to be equivalent, meaning that they are alike merely in their having attained the truth of cessation. In terms of the suchness of authentic practice, all acts of listening, reflection, and meditation with regard to the teachings of the authentic meaning are equivalent. This is as stated in *Unraveling the Intent*.

Accordingly there is a correspondence with the four truths. Engagement and abidance in saṃsāra correspond to the truth of suffering, with its four aspects (impermanence, and so on). Wrong practice corresponds to the truth of the origin with its four aspects (source, intense production, and so on). The fully present nature, free of adventitious contaminants, corresponds to the truth of cessation with its four aspects (cessation, peace, and so on). And the suchness of authentic practice corresponds to the truth of the path, with its four aspects (path, pertinence, and so forth).

Cognitive awareness refers to the eight consciousnesses. For this there is the impure dependent nature (when the imputed nature is seen, giving rise to dependent arising in direct order), which belongs to the truth of suffering (the aspect of abidance in saṃsāra) and to the truth of the origin, wrong practice (the aspect of engagement). And there is the pure dependent nature (when the fully present nature is seen), the practice of the path, which belongs to authentic practice and so, as mentioned in *Distinguishing the Middle from Extremes*, is included in the fully present nature that is suchness of cognitive awareness. The fully present nature that is suchness free of adventitious contaminants corresponds to the truth of cessation.

In this context, although it is not mentioned in either the root text or any of the commentaries, the three realities can also be expanded into the five categories. The five categories are name, reason, conception, suchness, and authentic gnosis. Name refers to labeling things with names such as "pillar" or "pot" and apprehending them as this or that; it corresponds to the imputed nature. Reason refers to appearance as the apprehended-object aspect of the dependent nature, appearing as bulbous or whatever; it is what appears as the reason or attributes that give a thing its name. Conception refers to the eight consciousnesses, which appear as the apprehending-subject aspect. Suchness refers to the unchanging fully present nature. Authentic gnosis is the unmistaken fully present nature, the subject of suchness, and is called "fully present nature" (the subject being named for the object) because the way things are accords with the way they appear. Thus, as we read in the *Sūtra on the Descent into Laṅka*:

> In the five categories, three natures,
> Eight consciousnesses,
> And two kinds of no-self
> The whole of the Great Vehicle is included.

These thus constitute an important general summary of the Dharma.

Rational application and vehicles
Are presented respectively as being of four and three kinds.
    (XX, 44cd)

This verse is a brief introduction to the presentation of rational application and vehicles as being of four kinds and three kinds respectively. These will now be discussed.

(c) How the Four Kinds of Rational Application Are Presented

> Properly keeping things in mind,
> The correct view that possesses the result,
> Discernment with valid cognition, and the inconceivable
> Are to be understood as the four kinds of rational
>   application. (XX, 45)

Rational application concerning function leads to the knowledge of which causes produce which effects. Rational application concerning dependency leads to the knowledge of which results depend on which causes. Then there is that which concerns the relative nature of things (the facts, for example, that fire is hot and water is wet) and their ultimate nature, which is that all phenomena are emptiness. Rational application concerning the demonstration of correctness makes use of direct and inferential valid cognition to evaluate things as they are.

With regard to rational application concerning function and that concerning dependency, to properly keep in mind the meaning of the two kinds of no-self on the level of earnest aspiration leads to the correct view that sees the truth of ultimate reality on the path of seeing, so it is associated with the result. And the correct view of the path of seeing possesses the result, which is perfect liberation, nirvāṇa. From the point of view of those causes performing the function of producing those results, and of those results depending on their respective causes, these correspond to rational application concerning function and that concerning dependency.

This connection between cause and result constitutes the unfailing principle of dependent arising. Just as a shoot grows from a healthy seed, if there is a cause (whose function it is to produce the result of a cause), it follows that there is a result; if there is no cause for a result (which depends on a cause), then there is no result. To discern or realize this kind of correctness or logicality by valid cognition is rational application concerning the demonstration of correctness. Although things unfailingly appear like that on the relative level, in ultimate truth there are no concepts of things that are produced and things that produce them: this is the inconceivable true nature, which corresponds to rational application concerning the nature of things.

These are the four kinds of rational application as applied only to the authentic path. It should be understood that, on the same principle, all methods of evaluating the truth can be included in the four kinds of rational application.

(d) How the Three Vehicles Are Presented

> Distinguished by their attitude,
> Teachings, application,
> Accumulations, and accomplishment,
> There are held to be three vehicles. (XX, 46)

It is on the basis of distinctions between lesser, middling, and greater levels associated with five points (attitudes, and so on) that there are the three vehicles—the Listeners' Vehicle, the Solitary Realizers' Vehicle, and the Great Vehicle.

The listeners have a lesser attitude in that they wish to realize only the individual no-self and only want to gain liberation for themselves, quickly. And it is in accordance with that attitude that the Tathāgata gives them the lesser teachings on the individual no-self and the four noble truths—the sufferings of saṃsāra and so forth. The listeners train in those lesser teachings for three or seven lifetimes, and in this respect their application is lesser. Inasmuch as their application is lesser, their accumulations of merit and wisdom are also lesser. And proportional to their meager accumulations is their result, which is that they accomplish the lesser enlightenment of the listeners. It is with such distinctions that the Listeners' Vehicle is presented.

The solitary realizers are of middling faculties and are therefore able to realize one-and-a-half kinds of no-self[11] and can prolong their training for one hundred kalpas. Unlike the listeners, they have middling faculties and attitudes, and to them the Tathāgata accordingly gives teachings on dependent arising (in forward and reverse orders), the illusion-like nature of the apprehended object, and other suitable subjects. Of middling quality too are their application to these and the accumulations that they gather, being

---

11. Tib. *bdag med phyed gnyis rtogs*, in other words, they realize the individual no-self and half-realize the no-self of phenomena.

better than the listeners'. As for the result, although there is no difference in the nirvāṇa they attain, there is a difference in their preternatural powers. The miraculous eye of a listener arhat cannot see further than a million worlds distant, whereas solitary-realizer arhats, with their miraculous eyes and ears, can see forms, hear sounds, and so on, in the worlds of a great universe of a thousand million worlds. In this respect, their faculties are sharper than those of the listeners, and because of their greater realization and miraculous powers, their result is superior. Such is the presentation of the Solitary Realizers' Vehicle.

Bodhisattvas have the best faculties and are able to realize the two kinds of no-self. With such wisdom and with compassion, they consider others' welfare and are thus able to accomplish both their own and others' goals, so their attitude is vast. Accordingly, they are given the profound and extensive teachings of the Great Vehicle. In conformity with the teachings they have received, they apply themselves physically, verbally, and mentally to accomplishing the two goals. They gather a vast accumulation of merit and wisdom and finally attain the vast result, the accomplishment of unsurpassable great enlightenment. It is thus that the path and result of the Great Vehicle are presented, and that there are held to be three different vehicles. The seven features that make the Great Vehicle great, along with a summary of the Great Vehicle, will be explained below.

(2) How the Meaning of the Dharma That Has to Be Completely Understood Is Presented

> Names and objects
> Are reciprocally investigated as being adventitious;
> The two kinds of designation
> Are investigated as being no more than that. (XX, 47)

Those who are skilled in explaining the above four systems of presentation skillfully teach the Dharma to sentient beings by means of words and help them investigate and gain a knowledge of the meanings or characteristics of phenomena. It should be understood that such investigation is made at the stage of earnest aspiration by means of four kinds of investigation, on four subjects—investigating names, investigating objects or things, investigating designations of entityness, and investigating designations of specific properties.

What we call by the names "pot" and "woolen cloth" signify a bulbous vessel for pouring water and a combination of woolen threads that can be worn. With regard to these two, ordinary people take the name to be the object and the object to be the name: they apprehend them as if the name and the object were intrinsically connected. The wise, however, investigate or examine the name and the object reciprocally, analyzing how an adventitious name is conceptually ascribed to an object and an object is designated a name by an adventitious concept, as if borrowed or on loan. If the object and the name, instead of being separate (the object appearing without being adventitiously designated with a name, and the name appearing just after), were of the same nature, it would follow that when something like a pot were destroyed and ceased to be, the name "pot" would also be destroyed and cease to be. However, even after a pot is broken, there is still the name. Similarly, when a person takes monastic ordination, the name "layperson" (or whatever) becomes something else, and yet the physical person does not change. And since it is not impossible to give any name to any object, the wise know that apart from merely using adventitious labels in order to communicate, there is no intrinsic connection between names and objects. If one realizes this, one knows that designations of entityness (the understanding from the name "pot" something with an essentially bulbous pot-nature) and designations of specific properties (designations using words to indicate a pot's specific properties such as the pot being tall and the pot being impermanent) are both adventitious. Or, as Sthiramati's commentary puts it, apart from being designations by mere names, mere words, neither of the two kinds of designation—designations by intrinsic characteristics (such as the solidity of earth and the wetness of water) and classifications by specific properties, such as everything (earth, water, and so on) being impermanent, suffering, tainted, untainted, and so forth—has any intrinsic existence as this or that, and to know this is what is called investigating designations of entityness and designations of specific properties. Whichever way it is explained, these two kinds of designation too, of entityness and of specific properties, are investigated in that way as being merely adventitious designations.

The crucial point here is that names and objects are linked and designated by the mind. If one analyzes the object that has been designated, what we call a "pot" does not exist as a whole, single thing: it is designated from parts such as its base, belly, and so on. And those parts too can be broken up, eventually into the minutest particles, which, when dissected in terms of directional parts, do not exist in any distinctive way either.[12] Thus, apart from simply being designated by name, anything that is designated as an entity or as a specific property is realized as merely existing as an imputation without having any true essence.

Such investigation gives rise to four kinds of complete knowledge, and this is shown in the next eight verses.[13]

> **Because of nonconceptuality with regard to everything,**
> **There are four kinds of true gnosis.**
> **These enable the steadfast**
> **To accomplish all their goals on all levels. (XX, 48)**

From one's having investigated things with these four kinds of investigation on the level of earnest aspiration, four kinds of complete knowledge arise on the path of seeing. Because bodhisattvas have no concepts at all of name, object, entityness, and specific properties, there arise four kinds of gnosis that know things as they truly are: the knowledge of the way things truly are associated with the investigation of name; the knowledge of the way things truly are associated with the investigation of objects or things; the knowledge of the way things truly are associated with the investigation of intrinsic nature or entityness; and the knowledge of the way things truly are associated with the investigation of specific properties. These are defined as the nonconceptual knowledge that all names are devoid of thingness and, similarly, the nonconceptual knowledge that all things such as pots, all intrinsic characteristics or any essential nature intrinsic to each thing, and all their properties, such as the qualities of arising, ceasing, and so on, are devoid of intrinsic nature—making in all four kinds of complete knowledge. These enable steadfast bodhisattvas on all the ten levels to accomplish all their goals—those of eliminating factors to be eliminated and realizing factors to

---

12. This is a refutation of the substantial existence even of the most minute, supposedly indivisible particles. Because each particle logically has four sides corresponding to the four cardinal directions and a top and bottom, it can be divided into these six parts, each of which must also have six sides. Such particles can therefore be divided ad infinitum, so it is impossible for them to exist substantially as indivisible entities.

13. Mipham here follows Sthiramati in speaking of ten verses (*tshigs su bcad bcu*), which also appears to be the number mentioned in the original Sanskrit of Vasubandhu's commentary. However, the Tibetan translation of the latter speaks of eight verses (*brgyad*), which appears to match the number of quatrains in this section.

be realized, or their own and others' goals. According to the commentary, the first half of this verse indicates the definition of complete knowledge, and the last half indicates its function. Such knowledge, moreover, will give release from the bonds of karma, so this will now be explained.

> The causes of bondage—
> The support, enjoyments, and seeds—
> Here bind the mind, mental factors,
> And the body, along with the seeds. (XX, 49)

That which creates bondage comprises three causes or reasons of bondage: the support-cause or source of bondage, which is the outer universe appearing as the object perceived by the consciousness of the ground of all; the enjoyments-cause, comprising the six objects that the six consciousnesses enjoy; and the seed-cause or reason, which is the consciousness of the ground of all or consciousness of all seeds.[14] What is it that they bind? They bind the five aggregates "to this" saṃsāra, or "here" (indicating proximity)[15]—that is, they bind the mind (meaning the eight consciousnesses), the fifty-one mental factors (feeling, perception, contact, and so forth), and the support (the supporting body organ and innards, along with the others of the six sense organs from the eye to the mind, constituting the aggregate of form) that are concurrent with the three fetters. How are these bound? They are "bound along with the seeds," meaning that they are bound because they possess the seeds. As long as the habitual tendencies or seeds of the support-cause and enjoyments-cause accumulated and possessed in the ground of all have not been eliminated, we continue to be bound and not liberated.

> Conceptual structures placed before the mind
> And those that are naturally present—
> The wise destroy them all,
> Thus attaining supreme enlightenment. (XX, 50)

These bonds having thus been identified, there now follows an explanation of the method for being released from them. There are conceptual struc-

---

14. The consciousness of all seeds is explained in the commentary for ch. 12, v. 44.
15. These are two explanations of the Tibetan word *'dir* ("here") in the root verse.

tures[16] placed before one's own mind on the basis of previous application to listening, reflecting, and meditating on the teachings—decomposing corpses, skeletons, and so forth, in short, the attributes taken as objects for consideration by the mind. And there are conceptual structures that are not placed before the mind by that sort of deliberate consideration but are present on their own—that is, they exist naturally in the object of the mind; these are the attributes of the various phenomena such as pillars and pots to which sentient beings have been habituated since the beginningless beginning of saṃsāra, and on which there is therefore no need to concentrate deliberately. Once they have understood that the conceptual structures examined by the mind in that way and those that appear without being examined are both nonexistent, the wise completely destroy all conceptual structures and, having severed all bonds, attain supreme enlightenment.

As to how they destroy the two kinds of conceptual structures, they meditate as follows. First, the conceptual structures examined by the mind, the conceptual structures that appear in the form of skeletons and so on, are analyzed as being no more than appearances to the mind and as having no true essence existing as this or that. Subsequently, in the same way, they recognize that all those that are naturally present—things such as vases—are also no more than appearances to the mind and mental factors, and that they are without intrinsic or essential existence. Thus, the listeners and solitary realizers dismantle the concepts of purity, happiness, permanence, and a self with regard to the aggregates and meditate on impurity, impermanence, suffering, and the absence of an individual self, and thereby they attain their respective levels of enlightenment. Bodhisattvas, by breaking down the very nature of the individual and phenomena into nonconceptual emptiness and meditating on that, will attain unsurpassable enlightenment.

> **With the knowledge that perceives suchness,**
> **The elimination of dualism,**
> **And the direct perception of residual negative tendencies,**
> **The wise are held to bring an end to these. (XX, 51)**

---

16. Note that the Tibetan term used here is *mtshan ma* (also translated as "attribute") and that, in the translation of Sthiramati's commentary, the same term is used in the previous verse, where it is synonymous with *rgyu mtshan*, meaning "cause" or "reason." Such terms that have several different meanings in Sanskrit and Tibetan cannot be translated into English in the same manner.

The manner in which such meditation liberates and releases bodhisattvas from the fetters of conceptual structures is as follows. Complete knowledge of the nature of the three realities eliminates the habitual tendencies of defilement-related and cognitive obscurations present in the consciousness of the ground of all and brings about liberation. The knowledge or gnosis that perceives the expanse of reality, the suchness of all phenomena, makes the nature of the fully present reality directly cognizable. The elimination of the dualistic notions of subject and object, or of the belief in the two kinds of self, individual and phenomenal, leads to the nature of the imputed reality being directly cognizable. And when the nature of the consciousness of the ground of all containing the residues or accumulations of the negative tendencies of the defilement-related and cognitive obscurations is directly perceived, the dependent nature becomes directly cognizable. Once wise bodhisattvas have directly perceived the three realities in this way, all the defilement-related and cognitive obscurations present in the consciousness of the ground of all, whose nature is the dependent reality, are brought to an end, and the bodhisattvas are held to be freed from all bonds.

> **With the gnosis that perceives suchness**
> **They meditate on the absence of distinct aspects**
> **And directly perceive existence and nonexistence,**
> **This being referred to as "mastery over thought." (XX, 52)**

If even the noble listeners have the correct knowledge that destroys the attributes that constitute the four misconceptions,[17] what, you might wonder, is the difference between that and the bodhisattvas' correct knowledge that destroys the attributes perceived as the two kinds of self? Bodhisattvas' meditation without attributes is superior to the listeners' meditation without attributes in the following way. The gnosis with which bodhisattvas perceive suchness does not perceive saṃsāra and nirvāṇa as distinct attributes. Since the nature of both saṃsāra and nirvāṇa is the expanse of reality, nirvāṇa from the very beginning, bodhisattvas realize that there are not two distinct aspects—saṃsāra as something to be abandoned and nirvāṇa as something to be adopted—and they cultivate the complete knowledge that saṃsāra itself is nirvāṇa, that all phenomena are empty. Their meditation is therefore superior to the listeners' meditation without attributes. As we read in the *Sūtra of the Teachings of Akṣayamati*:

---

17. The four misconceptions are those of purity, happiness, permanence, and a self.

The expanse of reality, the realm of saṃsāra, the realm of nirvāṇa, the realm of sentient beings, and the realm of all phenomena are the same. Why are they the same? It is because they are equal in emptiness that they are the same.

The listeners perceive attributes (namely, saṃsāra) and absence of attributes (nirvāṇa) as distinct, so looking on saṃsāra as constituting unpeaceful attributes, since it is associated with the sufferings of birth, aging, illness, death, and so on, they wish to abandon it; and looking on nirvāṇa as constituting peaceful aspects, since it is devoid of all suffering and all negative attributes, they wish to realize it. Unlike them, bodhisattvas meditate on all attributes as not distinct in the expanse of reality, and when they fully accomplish that meditation, they directly see the fully present reality, the nature devoid of duality that exists from the very beginning, and they also directly perceive the nonexistence of the imputed reality of subject and object. They thus acquire the correct knowledge that directly perceives existence and nonexistence. At that time, whatever the mind may wish for,[18] it is accomplished accordingly. If they wish for a rain of provisions falling from the empty sky, those things rain down. So in this case we speak of "dominion over, or mastery of, thought."

> For the immature, the true state of things is concealed
> And everywhere the untrue state of things appears.
> For bodhisattvas, that has been dispelled,
> And everywhere the true state of things appears. (XX, 53)

> Know that what does not exist and what exists
> Does not appear and does appear.
> Such is transformation:
> Because they can act as they please, they are free. (XX, 54)

One might argue, "If saṃsāra itself is, by nature, nirvāṇa, why are all sentient beings not in nirvāṇa from the beginning?" Although the nature of saṃsāra is nirvāṇa, for immature, ordinary beings, the obscurations of the habitual tendencies of clinging to a self and phenomena conceal the true state of things—suchness, which from the very beginning is nirvāṇa. And

---

18. Tib. *sems kyi gang dang ci bsam pa*. Note that Sthiramati here reads *sems can gang dang gang bsams*, meaning "whatever sentient beings may wish for."

so for them, the untrue state of things, dualistic perception, appears everywhere as the nature of saṃsāra, in the same way as the hairlike floaters that people with certain eye conditions see,[19] or the rope that someone mistakes for a snake. Bodhisattvas do not apprehend any intrinsic nature in self and phenomena, so they have dispelled those dualistic perceptions of subject and object, and to them the true state of things, suchness devoid of duality, appears everywhere. They are like someone with completely healthy eyes whose vision is free of floaters or someone with an unconfused mental consciousness who knows that a rope is a rope.

So it should be understood that the immature are failing to see what does exist and are seeing what does not exist, and their way of seeing things does not require any special effort on their part. On the other hand, to bodhisattvas, the attributes that are subject and object, which do not exist, and suchness, which does exist, respectively do not appear and do appear, and this happens naturally, without their needing to concentrate. In other words, that which exists appears, and that which does not exist does not appear. In such a case, the consciousness of the ground of all that is by nature the dependent reality is referred to as transformed. Since this state of transformation is completely unfettered by attributes, the mind is naturally independent and can act as it wishes, so we speak of "liberation." Just as people released from their bonds are allowed to behave as they wish, the transformed mind too, like space, is no longer subject to defilements such as attachment and can therefore do whatever it wants.

The question now presents itself: "Although the mind has been released from all its bonds like this, how can one's perceptions of the vast universe, the outer container, be stopped, for this cannot bring to an end the attributes of the environment?" To answer this, the manner in which the environment is purified as a buddha field will now be explained.

> The vast object, which always appears
> To be the same in kind at different moments,
> Creates an obstacle.
> So, fully recognizing this, they eliminate it. (XX, 55)

Even the things that appear in the form of the outer world are world-related

---

19. Tib. *rib rab*, a symptom of certain eye conditions in which the shadows that deposits in the vitreous humor cast on the retina are perceived as threads and spots.

habitual tendencies present in the domain of the ground of all, the mental images of the objective aspect appearing as if they were a world. But they are perceived by the consciousness of the ground of all inside, so there is no other external object, a substantial universe, that is other than the mere appearances as subject and object. They are like the appearances of the world that arise when one is dreaming.

Thus, the vast container that appears as the object outside, appearing as if uninterruptedly, all the time, appears in this way from the continuous sequence of instants of the consciousness of the ground of all as the world itself, with its ground and other attributes. As long as there are attributes appearing like that, and attachment and clinging to them as such, the world will not appear as a pure buddha field: it will appear as ordinary, and this is an obstacle to purifying the realm.

"If the great earth and the rest of the universe is an appearance to the mind in each instant of the consciousness of the ground of all, but there is no object outside, how is it that it always remains so stable as the object of experience of its inhabitants, and that there is no difference between the world we saw before and the world we see afterward?" The answer to this objection is as follows. Although the world, with its ground and so on, is momentary, it appears to be of the same kind from one moment to the next and, on account of that similarity, is mistaken as being the same. Likewise, the beings born in this world have the habitual tendencies of similar karma, so because of those habitual tendencies, even to all those different people the world appears similar and does not appear different. On the other hand, if the mind's habitual tendencies change, the world too changes in different aspects. For example, those who carry on their lives under the earth see the earth as full of holes through which they can pass, and so on. Thus, as long as there is clinging to perceptions of an independently existent world outside, it creates an obstacle to purifying the world as a perfectly pure buddha field.

What does one have to do, then, for the world to become a pure buddha field? As long as there is in the mind the specifically characterized appearance of an outer world such as the vast earth and there is clinging to that, then this is an obstacle to purifying it as a perfectly pure buddha field. So having fully recognized that it is an obstacle, bodhisattvas eliminate the attributes of the world and the clinging to them and then abide in suchness devoid of attributes. By doing so, they accomplish the complete purification of the world as a pure buddha field, perfect and complete in the layout of its ground, ornaments, and so forth.

(3) How the Immeasurable Qualities of the Bodhisattva Who Teaches Are Presented

> The objects that are to be brought to full maturity, to be purified,
> To be attained, that are ready to be brought to maturity,
> And that are to be authentically taught
> Are the immeasurable objects of the wise. (XX, 56)

There are five categories. Bodhisattvas who, by means of authentic gnosis, have thus been freed from the bonds of attributes have to bring to full maturity sentient beings reaching to the ends of space. They have to bring to maturity beings with the three kinds of potential (listener, solitary realizer, and bodhisattva), by means of their respective vehicles. They have to bring to maturity beings of unfixed potential by means of whichever of the three vehicles is suitable. And they have to introduce beings without potential to the ten positive actions and thus bring them to maturity in the higher realms. All these beings are referred to as "immeasurable objects to be brought to full maturity."

Immeasurable objects to be purified refer to the complete purification of world systems as perfectly pure buddha fields that are beautiful and utterly pure in their layout, with the jeweled ground, rivers of nectar, wish-fulfilling trees, and the like, and in which the world's impure elements such as ravines, thorns, and dirt are completely absent. And because the whole universe is then like an all-brocade tent the size of space, these are immeasurable.

Immeasurable objects to be attained refer to the immeasurable factors that have to be achieved—with regard to nonvirtue, the elimination of all negative qualities; and with regard to virtue, the realization of untainted positive qualities such as the ten strengths, four fearlessnesses, and ten powers.

Immeasurable objects that are ready to be brought to maturity comprise the four kinds of beings (not including those without potential), who are objects ready to be brought to maturation by means of the three vehicles. These too are immeasurable. What is the difference between these and the objects to be brought to maturation? It is explained as simply being a classificatory difference between all beings, who, whether or not they have the potential, are objects to be brought to maturity, and particular beings who are ready to be brought to everlasting maturity and are being ripened into liberation.

Immeasurable objects that are to be authentically taught or explained are immeasurable because teaching the Dharma, which is the means for training the beings to be trained, comprises an inconceivable number of spiritual approaches—meditation on ugliness for those with attachment, meditation on love for those who are full of hate, and so on.

These five categories are respectively related to the beings that are considered,[20] the environment in which they live, the attainments they will have, the ones who have the potential, and the teachings that will bring them to maturity. The five objects that have been indicated like this are the wise bodhisattvas' five immeasurable objects.

(4) How the Result of Teaching the Dharma Is Presented

> The birth of bodhicitta,
> Acceptance of the unborn,
> The lesser uncontaminated eye,
> And the exhaustion of taints, (XX, 57)
>
> The long duration of the sacred Dharma,
> Detailed knowledge, resolution, and enjoyment—
> These are the results of the explanations
> Of the wise who are so engaged. (XX, 58)

There are eight aspects: As a result of bodhisattvas teaching the Great Vehicle, (1) some beings arouse the mind intent on unsurpassable enlightenment, and (2) others attain the acceptance that objects are unborn. Through the teaching of the Great Vehicle, some individuals, at the stage of earnest aspiration, acquire an indirect understanding of the acceptance that phenomena are unborn; their acceptance applies to a part of thatness—this is lesser acceptance. Having attained the first bodhisattva level, they directly realize thatness devoid of subject and object and actually attain the acceptance that objects are unborn. Compared to the eighth level, this is middling acceptance. On the eighth level, they spontaneously and nonconceptually attain the great acceptance that phenomena are unborn. This accords with the

---

20. Tib. *gang la dmigs par bya ba*. In Mipham Rinpoche's commentary, the first of these appears to be missing, no doubt due to a scribal error. We have taken the liberty of inserting it from the relevant passage in Sthiramati's commentary.

sūtras, where, in the exposition of these categories, it is said that such and such an individual has aroused the mind intent on unsurpassable enlightenment, acquired the acceptance of phenomena consistent with the Dharma, attained the noble path, and attained the acceptance that phenomena are unborn.

(3) As a result of bodhisattvas teaching the Dharma of the Listeners' Vehicle, their disciples acquire the uncontaminated eye of Dharma with regard to phenomena (which is an inferior level to the Mahāyāna path of seeing); and (4) ultimately they attain the level of arhat where all taints have been exhausted. Acquiring the eye of Dharma represents the listeners' path of seeing, on which there arises gnosis like the eye of Dharma, which sees the four truths. Since the eight instants of acceptance are antidotes, we speak of this eye being free of the dust of defilements, and for the eight instants of knowing we speak of it being uncontaminated, that is, freed of the obscurations that have to be eliminated on the path of seeing. Thus, someone who acquires the dustless, uncontaminated eye of Dharma is a stream enterer freed of the obscurations to be eliminated on the path of seeing. Such a person who has attained the listeners' path of seeing relies on the teachings to eliminate the defilements included in all the levels of the three worlds that are to be eliminated on the path of meditation, and having exhausted all taints, acquires the gnosis of exhaustion and nonarising and attains the level of arhat. Again, the sūtras, explaining these categories, say, "Some individuals give rise to the dustless, uncontaminated eye of Dharma with regard to phenomena," and, "Some individuals completely free their minds from all taints, without grasping."

Whether it is the teachings of the Great Vehicle or lesser vehicles that are taught, (5) the teachings spread from one teacher to another, so that the sacred Dharma endures for a long time here in the world. (6) Those who have no previous knowledge of the general and particular characteristics of the teachings acquire that knowledge. (7) Those who are doubtful have their doubts resolved. And (8) having become certain of the meaning of the teachings, without any gaps of knowledge or doubts, they become the enjoyers of the sacred Dharma, delighting in it unashamedly.[21]

Any of these are to be understood as being the result of the Dharma teachings of the wise, who are engaged in teaching the Dharma.

---

21. Tib. *dga' ba kha na ma tho ba med pa*, "unashamed" in the sense that their enjoyment of the Dharma is completely free from any shameful deeds (*kha na ma tho ba*) or wrongdoing.

(5) How the Features That Distinguish the Great Vehicle Are Presented, Along with a Summary

The greatness of its reference,
And likewise of its twin accomplishment,
Its gnosis, diligent application,
Its skill in means, (XX, 59)

Its great consummation,
And great buddha activities—
It is because it possesses these forms of greatness
That the Great Vehicle is so described. (XX, 60)

The Great Vehicle is superior to the Lesser Vehicle in seven respects: (1) Its great reference: compared to the listeners, who refer to the three listeners' collections, bodhisattvas refer to the infinite scriptural collections of the extensive and profound Great Vehicle. (2) Likewise, its great accomplishment: whereas listeners accomplish only their own goal, bodhisattvas have a double accomplishment—that of their own goal and that of others' goals. (3) Great gnosis: listeners realize only the no-self of the individual; bodhisattvas realize the no-self in the individual and in phenomena. (4) Listeners practice diligently for a mere three or seven lifetimes; bodhisattvas practice diligently for as long as three measureless kalpas, hence their greater application of diligence. (5) Listeners are not skilled in means, for out of fear they reject saṃsāra and strive for peace. Bodhisattvas, on the other hand, are skilled in means: they are like lotuses growing out of the mud, never abandoning saṃsāra (because of their compassion) and yet never tainted by defilements (because of their wisdom). These five distinguish the vehicles in terms of the carrier—that is, the cause or path.

(6) Once listeners have attained the result of arhat and just the various powers of perceptual limitlessness, different kinds of perceptual domination, and the six kinds of preternatural knowledge, these come to an end in the state without residual aggregates. The result of the Bodhisattva Vehicle, comprising immeasurable qualities such as the strengths and fearlessnesses, never comes to an end, hence their great consummation. And (7) even though listeners attain the level of arhat, they do not achieve full enlightenment, turn the wheel of the Dharma, or anything else like that. Bodhisattvas, on the other hand, attain true buddhahood and subsequently

display such deeds as residing in the palace of the highest heaven,[22] entering the womb, and manifesting full enlightenment, and this for as long as there are sentient beings—hence their great buddha activities. These two distinguish the vehicles in terms of where they carry one—that is, the result.

It is because it possesses these seven aspects of greatness that it is described as the "Great Vehicle."

Presentation of a Summary of the Great Vehicle

This is summarized as the potential, interest in the teachings,
And likewise arousing bodhicitta,
Practicing the transcendent perfections,
Entering the flawless levels, (XX, 61)

Bringing beings to maturity,
Purifying the universe,
Realizing the nondwelling nirvāṇa,
Attaining supreme enlightenment, and displaying enlightened activities. (XX, 62)

If we were to mention all the points in the countless Mahāyāna sūtras, such as the *Perfection of Wisdom in One Hundred Thousand Lines* and the *Sūtra of the Ornament of the Buddhas*, they would exceed all bounds. Nevertheless, if we summarize the meaning of the whole Great Vehicle, it can be condensed into the following eightfold or tenfold presentation, which we refer to as the Great Vehicle. What are these points? (1) Possession of the Mahāyāna potential or element; based on that, (2) interest in the teachings of the Great Vehicle; and similarly, because of interest, (3) the arousal of the mind intent on unsurpassable enlightenment. These three result from the condition of abiding in the Mahāyāna family.

After arousing the mind intent on enlightenment like this, (4) bodhisattvas on the level of earnest aspiration practice the six transcendent perfections—generosity and the others. As a result, (5) on the first level there arises the gnosis devoid of subject and object, and they enter the flawless, supramundane noble levels. (6) From the second level up to the seventh, they

---

22. Tib. *'og min gyi pho brang*, the realm of Akaniṣṭha.

practice the elements leading to enlightenment and the transcendent perfections, and by doing so they lead beings who do not have faith to develop faith and bring those who have faith to full maturity in virtue. This makes six points.

On the three pure levels, they accomplish the purification of the universe and beings.[23] For this they combine (7a) training in purifying them as buddha fields and (7b) realizing the nondwelling nirvāṇa as the sameness of existence and peace: because of wisdom there is no dwelling in saṃsāra, and because of compassion there is no dwelling in peace. These two are counted as one. Subsequently, (8a) they pass the tenth level and achieve supreme enlightenment, attaining the three buddha bodies on the level of buddhahood; and (8b) having attained enlightenment, for as long as there are sentient beings they display activities such as manifesting full enlightenment and the other deeds of a buddha. These two are also counted as one, making eight in all. Alternatively, if these last four are counted separately, they are presented as ten categories.

Up to here we have explained the seventeen categories of the qualities that bodhisattvas accomplish, from wondrous qualities through to how they teach the Dharma. These are now followed by the qualities that are highly praised.

2. Qualities That Are Highly Praised

This section has two parts: (1) categories of bodhisattvas as objects of praise and (2) the actual praise.

a. Categories of Bodhisattvas as Objects of Praise

> Some bodhisattvas are interested,
> Others have pure superior intention,
> Conceive attributes, are without attributes,
> And practice without deliberate effort—
> These five should be understood
> As referring to the bodhisattvas on all the levels. (XX, 63)

What we call bodhisattvas are those dwelling on the eleven levels, that is,

---

23. Tib. *snod dang bcud*, lit. "the vessel and contents."

the ten levels and the level of earnest aspiration, and these are summarized under five categories according to their situation: (1) One of these refers to those on the level of earnest aspiration. They have not directly realized the nature of the universal expanse of reality but nevertheless have confidence and faith in the expanse of reality and are therefore termed "interested."

(2) Bodhisattvas who have reached the first level are known as having "pure superior intention" because, having realized the nature of the universal expanse of reality and acquired the state of mind that realizes the sameness of oneself and others, they therefore possess the superior intention of taking responsibility for others' welfare, purified of the obscurations that are to be eliminated on the path of seeing. This one is different[24] from the previous category of bodhisattva and is the second category.

(3) Those on the second to sixth levels are called "bodhisattvas with attributes." On the second level, they use the attributes that variously distinguish the vehicles of the listeners, solitary realizers, and bodhisattvas. On the third level, they eliminate[25] the attributes of the innate view of the transitory composite. On the fourth level, they see the truths of suffering and of the origin as harmful attributes and see the truths of cessation and of the path as pacifying attributes. On the fifth level, they engage in different kinds of arts, while conceptualizing their attributes. And on the sixth level, they still have concepts with regard to dependent arising in forward and reverse orders.

(4) Bodhisattvas on the seventh level are referred to as "bodhisattvas without attributes" because they have eliminated all the attributes that occur up to the sixth level.

(5) Those on the nonreturner levels—that is, the eighth, ninth, and tenth levels—are known as "bodhisattvas who practice without deliberate effort" because they act for their own and others' welfare by means of spontaneous and effortless nonconceptual concentration.

These five instances of bodhisattvas should be understood as being the specific qualities of the bodhisattvas abiding on all the levels.

---

24. Tib. *gzhan*. This sentence comments on the significance of the Tibetan word *gzhan*, which has been translated as "others" in the root verse.

25. In the absence of a verb in Mipham's commentary here, we have inserted "eliminate" from the corresponding sentence in Sthiramati's commentary: *lhan cig skyes pa'i 'jig tshogs la lta ba'i mtshan ma spangs so*.

b. The Actual Praise: Praising the Characteristics of These Five Kinds of Bodhisattvas

The actual praise is divided into two: (1) a praise based on the significance of the word "bodhisattva" from the point of view of their irreversible strength of mind in practicing the causal factors, the transcendent perfections, and (2) the qualities that are praised in accordance with the significance of the word "bodhisattva" from the point of view of their realization of the result, enlightenment. The first of these is divided into, first, a praise in terms of nine categories beginning with delight in enlightenment and, second, an indication of the different names of a bodhisattva.

i. A Praise Based on the Significance of the Word "Bodhisattva" from the Point of View of Their Irreversible Strength of Mind in Practicing the Causal Factors, the Transcendent Perfections

(1) A Praise in Terms of Nine Categories Beginning with Delight in Enlightenment

> One who is unattached to pleasure, pure in the three deeds,
> Who overpowers anger, strives for sublime qualities,
> Never moves from the practice, and sees profound thatness
> Is a bodhisattva who delights in enlightenment. (XX, 64)

In completely giving away their outer and inner possessions without any attachment to the five sense pleasures, bodhisattvas practice transcendent generosity. Their discipline is devoid of negative actions—physical, verbal, or mental—and so it is perfectly pure. By exercising patience, they overpower anger. With their diligence, they devote themselves to sublime qualities—that is, supramundane virtue.[26] Because of their concentration, they never waver from the practice of resting one-pointedly. And with wisdom, they see profound thatness, the two kinds of no-self. Those who practice the

---

26. We have followed the Tibetan of the root verse (*yon tan mchog lhur len*) on the assumption that the commentary's *yon tan mchog gyur len pa* (lit. "seize sublime qualities") could be a scribal error.

six transcendent perfections in this way are delighted that they will attain the result, great enlightenment; they practice for that purpose and dedicate their practice to that. For this reason, it is said that they are bodhisattvas who delight in enlightenment. This verse praises the qualities of those who practice the six transcendent perfections purely.

> One who wants to help, intends no harm,
> Willingly accepts others' harm,
> Is steadfast, careful, and learned
> Is a bodhisattva who strives for others' good. (XX, 65)

Similarly, they want to help beings by means of their generosity. With discipline they look to, or wish to, do no harm whatsoever with their three doors, such as adversely affecting others' lives, possessions, and spouses, and cheating them with lies. With patience they willingly accept being harmed by others. They undertake everything with diligence, steadfast in never turning back from their efforts. Their concentration is characterized by carefulness—that is, they remain in solitary places, undistracted, and have no attachment to the taste of concentration. And they have the wisdom that comes from having listened many times to the teachings of the sacred Dharma. It is in these terms that they are bodhisattvas who exert themselves for others' welfare, for their whole practice of the transcendent perfections helps sentient beings on a temporary level and is dedicated ultimately to unsurpassable enlightenment for the sake of all beings. This verse praises them as being bodhisattvas from the point of view of their qualities in benefiting others.

> One who knows the defects of keeping things for oneself,
> Who is without attachment, and never holds a grudge,
> Practices yoga, is expert in the special points, and is without
>   wrong views
> Is a bodhisattva who is perfectly settled inwardly. (XX, 66)

Bodhisattvas know the disadvantages of keeping their possessions for themselves—namely, that they are without essence, impermanent, associated with suffering, and illusory, and that the mistake of being attached to wealth leads to rebirth in the lower realms and is an obstacle to the attainment of mundane and supramundane perfection—and so they give them away as gifts. Free of attachment to sensual pleasure, they abandon lay life to take ordination and subsequently observe discipline. Rather than harboring resentment for the harm others have done them, they are patient. They are diligent in the Mahāyāna yoga of sustained calm and profound insight. When they are training in one-pointed concentration, they are expert in the three special points—the special point of sustained calm, that of encouraging or rousing oneself, and that of equanimity. And they possess the wisdom that is free of wrong views such as the view of a self. They are bodhisattvas who are perfectly settled inwardly. In this manner, they are praised from the point of view of their abiding perfectly in true inner composure.

> One who is full of love, maintains the virtues of a sense of shame,
> Who happily accepts suffering, is unattached to personal well-being,
> Gives priority to mindfulness, and is a master of perfect equipoise
> Is a bodhisattva who is never at odds with the vehicle. (XX, 67)

Those who are full of love for all suffering sentient beings give generously. Maintaining the qualities of a sense of shame, they observe discipline. They willingly accept the harm others do them and similar sufferings, and thus are patient. Without any attachment to their own well-being, in particular the pleasures of sleep and idleness, they work diligently for the good of others. Constant mindfulness is their chief preoccupation, so they never give in to distraction. And because they constantly possess the wisdom that knows the sameness of all phenomena, free from the extremes of existence and nonexistence, they are lords of perfect meditative equipoise. They are thus bodhisattvas whose minds are never at variance with the Great Vehicle. This verse praises them from the point of view of the quality of their never being in conflict with the Mahāyāna path.

In his commentary, Sthiramati notes that in all these verses, the first three lines indicate bodhisattvas' practice of the six transcendent perfections, and the fourth line indicates the fact of their being dedicated to unsurpassable enlightenment.

> One who dispels suffering, never causes pain,
> Who accepts suffering, is unafraid of difficulties,

> Is liberated from suffering, and has no concepts of misery
> Is a bodhisattva who willingly takes on suffering. (XX, 68)

Because of bodhisattvas' generosity, other beings' sufferings due to deprivation are dispelled. On account of their discipline, they never cause sentient beings to suffer, by killing or robbing them, for instance. They patiently accept their own suffering. They have no fear of suffering in entering saṃsāra for others' sake and striving diligently for beings' welfare. Since they have acquired the concentrations of the dhyānas, they have been completely released from the pain and anguish of the world of desire. And on account of their wisdom, they do not conceptualize suffering. Such beings are bodhisattvas who willingly accept or take on suffering. This verse praises them from the point of view of their not abandoning saṃsāra, with all its suffering, and not being discouraged by suffering.

> One who gets no joy in certain ways, delights in natural ways,
> Despises other ways, and is diligent in virtue,
> Has mastered the teachings, and is not obscured with regard to phenomena
> Is a bodhisattva for whom the Dharma is the most important thing.[27] (XX, 69)

Bodhisattvas take no delight in stingy, ungenerous ways. They delight in disciplined ways, which are by nature free of faults and full of virtues. They condemn angry ways and are truly diligent in virtuous ways. By the power of the concentration of mastery of the teachings, they have acquired mastery of the mind. And they possess the wisdom that is free of the gloom of ignorance with regard to all phenomena. Thus, they are bodhisattvas who give priority to the true Dharma. This is a praise from the point of view of not giving priority to material considerations and instead making the sacred Dharma the most important thing.

> One who is careful with possessions, careful in discipline,
> Careful to remain on guard, careful in virtue,

---

27. This verse exploits the multiple meanings of the Tibetan word *chos* (Sanskrit *dharma*), which in different contexts refers to the sacred Dharma or Buddhist teachings, ways, virtue, phenomena, and so on.

Careful with bliss, and careful with regard to phenomena
Is a bodhisattva who is careful with regard to the vehicle. (XX, 70)

Those who have wealth yet hoard and guard it instead of giving it away to others are careless, for in the end, possessions go to waste. So in order to make their possessions meaningful, bodhisattvas give them away to others. This is being careful with regard to possessions. To not guard oneself from naturally shameful deeds and those that violate edicts would be careless. But those who are disciplined control their body, speech, and mind and are untainted by faults, natural and proscribed. They are termed "careful in discipline." (Some texts have "careful in certainty,"[28] but it is better to say "disciplined" as in the translation of Sthiramati's commentary. In some texts one finds "careful on the surface,"[29] which is simply a misspelling.) Failure to guard one's mind, and that of others, from retaliating instead of patiently accepting harm from others is careless. But bodhisattvas' minds are never perturbed when others harm them, and instead of retaliating, they help them. This is patience—being careful in guarding both oneself and others. Failure, due to laziness, to practice positive actions, would be careless, but instead bodhisattvas are diligent, taking care to practice mundane and supramundane virtue. Though they have gained the bliss of concentration, they never crave the experience of bliss—this is being careful with regard to bliss. To consider that phenomena are permanent, and that they are therefore associated with happiness, constitute a self, and are not empty, would be careless, but bodhisattvas have unmistakenly realized that phenomena are impermanent and so on. This is wisdom—being careful with regard to phenomena. In these respects, they are bodhisattvas who are careful in properly keeping in mind the teachings of the Great Vehicle. This is a praise from the point of view of the qualities of practicing the six transcendent perfections in someone who is careful.

One who is ashamed of showing disrespect, ashamed of the
    slightest fault,
Ashamed of not being patient, ashamed of failing,
Ashamed of distraction, and ashamed of lower views
Is a bodhisattva who is ashamed of other vehicles. (XX, 71)

---

28. Tib. *nges la bag yod*. Sthiramati's commentary has *gdul ba la bag yod*.
29. Tib. *ngos la bag yod*, for which we have given one possible translation.

Bodhisattvas would be ashamed to not give when beggars appear, or to give disrespectfully, scowling and abusing them. In ordinary life, when beggars ask rich people for alms, the latter abuse them and do not even give them anything. How shameful! But bodhisattvas, out of compassion, are committed to giving away everything for the sake of others, and so it would be shameful and out of character for them to be displeased and reproachful when they are asked for alms. Bodhisattvas view fearfully, and shy away from, the smallest shameful deeds (those that are naturally shameful and those that violate edicts), so they are ashamed of even the smallest faults occurring. They patiently put up with all harm and suffering, so they are ashamed if they fail to be patient and let their minds be perturbed when others harm them. If a bodhisattva is someone who is diligent, continuously undertaking great waves of activities, then it is shameful when they founder from their practice of virtue and succumb to laziness. Bodhisattvas are beings who gain mastery of the mind in boundless meditative absorptions and concentrations, so it is shameful for them to remain physically distracted in the midst of frivolous entertainments and to stay mentally distracted, their minds occupied with outer objects. Since bodhisattvas are beings who naturally possess wisdom and have the wisdom that has realized the two kinds of no-self taught in the teachings of the Great Vehicle, they are ashamed if they have realized only the lower view of the individual no-self and are not free of the view of attributes in phenomena. So they do not engage in other vehicles, the vehicles of the listeners and solitary realizers. They are bodhisattvas who are ashamed of practicing other vehicles. This is a praise from the point of view of their having no desire for other vehicles.

> For now and the hereafter, through equanimity,
> Application, attainment of mastery,
> Appropriate teaching, and the great result,
> Bodhisattvas engage in benefiting beings. (XX, 72)

There now follows a praise in terms of the qualities of those who benefit others by means of all these practices of the transcendent perfections, giving priority to others' welfare. By generously giving their possessions to the poor, they benefit them in this life; attracting them with gifts and the like, they introduce them to discipline, thereby benefiting them in the next world. By patiently remaining even-minded, instead of letting their minds be perturbed and retaliating when hurt, they bring benefit to sentient beings. Because of their diligence or application in helping others with their tasks, they benefit them. By acquiring mastery, through concentration, in such qualities as preternatural knowledge, they benefit others. By using their wisdom to teach the five sciences, and especially all the teachings of the three vehicles that make up the inner science of Buddhist teachings, in accordance with beings' inclinations, they benefit them. And by attaining buddhahood, which is the great result of practicing the transcendent perfections in this way, they benefit sentient beings for as long as space exists. So it is by means of these causal factors and their result that bodhisattvas engage in bringing benefit to all sentient beings. Sthiramati's commentary explains that this verse summarizes the meaning of the previous verses.

(2) An Indication of the Different Names of a Bodhisattva

These are names whose meanings correspond to bodhisattvas' qualities, so they also serve as enumerations of their qualities. This section thus proclaims sixteen different names—Hero of Enlightenment, and so on—as general names for all bodhisattvas.

> Hero of Enlightenment, Great Hero,
> Wise One, Supremely Brilliant One,
> Child of the Buddhas, Foundation of the Victorious Ones,
> Victor, Sprout of the Victors; (XX, 73)

Because they have single-minded faith in the profound knowledge of the two kinds of no-self, they are known as Heroes of Enlightenment.[30] Alternatively, it is because of their steadfast intention to accomplish unsurpassable enlightenment that they are called Heroes of Enlightenment. "Great Heroes"[31] designates those who have mastered great magical powers, such as displaying in a single pore of their bodies a kalpa of formation and destruction of a third-order great universal system of one thousand million worlds. Alternatively, because they wish to attain unsurpassable enlightenment themselves, they are called Heroes of Enlightenment, and because they wish

---

30. Tib. *byang chub sems dpa'*, Skt. *bodhisattva*. An alternative translation, which follows the Sanskrit, would be "Enlightenment Being."
31. Tib. *sems dpa' chen po*, Skt. *mahāsattva*.

to liberate all sentient beings from the sufferings of saṃsāra and set them in nirvāṇa, they are called Great Heroes. Again, from the point of view of their being, on account of their great wisdom, untainted by the faults of saṃsāra even while staying in saṃsāra, they are Heroes of Enlightenment; and because, through their great compassion, they strive endlessly for the welfare of sentient beings, they are referred to as Great Heroes. And again, those who have aroused the mind intent on accomplishing unsurpassable enlightenment are Heroes of Enlightenment, and those who possess that which has the seven forms of greatness as explained above are Great Heroes.[32] Apart from these comparative distinctions, there is no difference between a Hero of Enlightenment and a Great Hero, both being general names for a bodhisattva. From the point of view of different levels, those on the earlier levels are Heroes of Enlightenment and those on the later ones are Great Heroes. Those on the level of earnest aspiration, who have aroused the mind intent on enlightenment, are Heroes of Enlightenment, while those who have attained the noble levels are Great Heroes of Enlightenment. Those on the seven impure levels are Heroes of Enlightenment, while those dwelling on the pure levels are Great Heroes. Whichever the case, it is because they are courageous and undaunted in practicing boundless transcendent perfections, the causes of unsurpassable enlightenment that are so difficult to practice, and in attaining unsurpassable enlightenment, the result that is so difficult to attain, that they are called Heroes of Enlightenment.

Because they possess the intelligence that is the wisdom of the profound and extensive, they are called The Wise. And because they elucidate the intended meaning of the profound teachings and spread the light of the teachings in the ten directions, they are called The Supremely Brilliant or The Supremely Resplendent. Since they hold the lineage of the tathāgatas uninterruptedly and have been born in the family of the buddhas, they are known as Children of the Buddhas. Because they are the causes for becoming buddhas, they are known as The Foundations of the Victorious Ones. Similarly, they are called Victors—victorious over all the defilements present in their own and others' mind streams. And because they are the causes that grow into the qualities of the victorious buddhas—the three buddha bodies, the strengths, fearlessnesses, and so forth, which are like leaves, flowers, and fruits—they are the Sprouts of the Victorious Ones.

32. I.e., those who possess the Great Vehicle, whose seven forms of greatness are described in verses 59 and 60 of this chapter.

Powerful One, Most Exalted One,
Pilot, Supremely Famed One,
Compassionate One, One of Great Merit,
Mighty Lord, and likewise, Truthful One. (XX, 74)

Bodhisattvas are able to subdue demons and cross beyond the land of ignorance and habitual tendencies, so they are singularly courageous Powerful Ones. They are the most marvelous of beings in the world, so they are the Most Exalted Ones. They enable those who have set sail on the ocean of saṃsāra to reach the city of nirvāṇa, so they are Pilots. Because the delightful sound of their qualities resounds throughout the infinite buddha fields in the ten directions, they are Greatly Famed or Supremely Famed Ones. Having the great compassion that never abandons any beings, they are Compassionate Ones. They possess boundless sources of good from their generosity and so forth, and so are Ones of Great Merit. Since they have mastery over everything that is perfect, both mundane and supramundane, they are Mighty Lords. And similarly, being free of shameful deeds and untainted, they are called Truthful Ones.

Thus, beginning with these sixteen names, which are the main ones and the most widely known, bodhisattvas are described by all kinds of synonyms, including the fearless, heroes, the steadfast, chiefs among beings, and so on.

ii. The Qualities That Are Praised in Accordance with the Significance of the Word "Bodhisattva" from the Point of View of Their Realization of the Result, Enlightenment

This topic has two parts: (1) the actual praise and (2) categories. The former is indicated by five verses.

(1) The Actual Praise

> Because of five particularities—their excellent realization of thatness,
> Their perfect realization of the great goal, their realization of everything,
> Their constant realization, and their realization of means—
> They are called bodhisattvas. (XX, 75)

Because they realize[33] that there is no self in phenomena and individuals, they have excellent realization of thatness. Since they realize what they have to accomplish—their own and others' great goal—they have perfect realization of the great goal. They have complete realization of all knowable objects—compounded and uncompounded, tainted and untainted. Their knowledge, rather than being realized for a while and then one day being spent, does not come to an end in the expanse without residual aggregates, so their realization is constant and eternal. And they realize all the skillful means—the infinite methods for training beings, such as what manifestations to display and what teachings to give in order to train them. Because of their superiority on account of these five qualities, they are called bodhisattvas. *Bodhi* indicates complete understanding and mastery, and *sattva* means "possessing the mind," so a bodhisattva is someone who considers and realizes something. This praise of the qualities based on the etymological definition of the word "bodhisattva" is a general explanation.

There are four further aspects of their realization, as follows.

> **Because of their subsequent realization of the self,**
> **Realization of subtle views, realization of the various consciousnesses,**
> **And realization of all as being false imagination,**
> **They are called bodhisattvas. (XX, 76)**

Of the three—mind, mind faculty, and consciousness—mind refers to the consciousness of the ground of all, the one with all the seeds. To know or realize that it is from mind that the place or container, the sense objects, and the appearances of the body all arise is what we call "subsequent realization of the self." It is to know that there is no other so-called self and that the continuous flow of instants of one's own ground consciousness is merely imagined as a self by the defiled mind consciousness, looking inward.

What we call "mind faculty" is the defiled mind consciousness. Taking the ground of all as its object, it possesses the subjective apprehension of

---

33. It should be noted that throughout this section the terms "realize" and "realization" (Tib. *rtogs pa*) can equally be translated as "understand" and "understanding" or "know" and "knowledge." Indeed, the Tibetan translation of Sthiramati's commentary consistently uses the term *shes pa*, which includes all these meanings.

"I," accompanied by the five omnipresent factors[34] together with four factors—the view of a self, attachment to self, ignorance with regard to a self, and egoistic pride. To realize the nature of this omnipresent, unobscured indeterminate state of the mind, which is virtuous, nonvirtuous, or unspecified, is what we call "the realization of subtle views," because bodhisattvas have identified the view of the transitory composite, which, since it is the cause of all wrong views and defilements, is the subtle fundamental view.

"Realization of the various consciousnesses" refers to understanding the nature of the six consciousnesses. The six consciousnesses (from the eye consciousness to the mental consciousness), which arise from the object, sense organ, and attentiveness, take as their objects the six sense objects (form and the others) and are associated with the accompanying mental factors—virtuous, nonvirtuous, and unspecified—and whichever feelings may then arise. To recognize the nature of these various aspects of consciousness is what we call "realization of the various consciousnesses."

All these eight consciousnesses dualistically conceive subject and object, even though there is no dualistic existence of subject and object. Bodhisattvas realize that this false imagination is merely the nature of the dependent reality, like an illusion or dream.

Because of these four kinds of realization, they are called bodhisattvas. This is the way in which they realize the way things appear in relative truth.

> Because of their realization of the unrealized,
> Realization of the subsequent realization, realization of
>   nonsubstantiality,
> Realization of production, and realization of the unknown,
> They are called bodhisattvas. (XX, 77)

The space-like, nonreferential realization, the nonconceptual gnosis that has not been previously realized by mundane beings, is "realization of the unrealized."

The realization that realizes, with the subsequently attained gnosis, that all phenomena are the same as illusions and so forth is "realization of the subsequent realization." Alternatively, knowledge of dependent arising in

---

34. The five omnipresent factors (Tib. *kun 'gro lnga*) are the first of the fifty-one mental factors (*sems byung*) and comprise feeling, perception, intention, contact, and attentiveness or mental engagement. See also *Treasury of Precious Qualities*, appendix 4.

the forward order, starting with nonrealization or ignorance, is realizing what has not been realized; and knowledge of dependent arising in the reverse order—that if ignorance is halted, conditioning factors are halted, and so on—is what we call the realization of the subsequent realization.

Realization of the imputed reality, which is devoid of substantial specific characteristics, is "realization of nonsubstantiality."

The knowledge that everything that appears as subject and object arises momentarily from the dependent nature is "realization of production."

And to know the fully present reality, the ultimate reality devoid of duality that was previously unknown by them when they were ordinary, immature beings, is what we call "realization of the unknown (or unrealized)."

Because they realize these five objects, they are called bodhisattvas. This is in terms of the way in which they realize the two truths. There are five other ways in which they realize the two truths, as now follows.

> Because of their realization that objects do not exist,
> Realization of ultimate truth, realization of all objects,
> Realization of the totality of objects, and realization of the
>   realized, realizer, and realization,
> They are called bodhisattvas. (XX, 78)

From the dependent nature or consciousness all the subject-object appearances of the three worlds arise and, as a result of attachment to them, suffering is continuously experienced. However, bodhisattvas realize that they do not exist as subject-object objects.[35] This realization is known as "realization that objects do not exist."

Their realization of the fully present reality, the nature of emptiness that is the absence of duality,[36] is "realization of ultimate truth."

Their realization that all dualistic appearances are none other than mere imputations is the "realization of all objects" that appear as subject and object.

Their "realization of the totality" of phenomena included in the multiplicity of aggregates, sense spheres, senses-and-fields, and the rest is realization of relative truth.

---

35. Tib. *gzung ba dang 'dzin pa'i don*.
36. Tib. *gnyis stong*, lit. "empty of the two," that is, devoid of apprehending subject and apprehended object.

And their realization without concepts of the three spheres—that is, of the object that is to be realized, of the realizer (the basis of realization), and of realization—is realization of the ultimate truth.

Because they have realized these five points—the three realities and the two truths—they are called bodhisattvas.

> Because of their realization of the accomplishment,
> Realization of the abode, realization of the womb,
>   realization of the stages,
> And realization of bringing about realization and dispelling
>   doubts,
> They are called bodhisattvas. (XX, 79)

There are five more kinds of knowledge for which they are called bodhisattvas. The "realization of the accomplishment" of the unsurpassable great enlightenment refers to realization of the three buddha bodies that must be actualized in the Great Unexcelled.[37] "Realization of the abode" refers to knowing that one must dwell in the Tuṣita realm as a bodhisattva in their final existence and benefit the gods. "Realization of the womb" refers to knowing that one must enter a mother's womb in Jambudvīpa and bring beings to maturity there. "Realization of the stages" refers to knowing that one will appear from the womb, enjoy the five pleasures of the senses in the retinue of queens at the palace, leave the palace and renounce worldly life, practice austerities, and at Vajrāsana display the attainment of manifest enlightenment as a manifestation-body emanation. And there is the realization that having attained buddhahood, one will turn the wheel of the Dharma that dispels the doubts of all sentient beings. Because of these, one is called a bodhisattva. This verse indicates bodhisattvas' realization from the point of view of knowing the manner in which a bodhisattva in their final existence, taking support of the body of perfect enjoyment in the Unexcelled, realizes the great enlightenment and then, as a body of manifestation, displays the great enlightenment in Jambudvīpa.

---

37. Tib. *'og min chen po*, the highest heaven of Akaniṣṭha.

(2) Showing Them to Be Bodhisattvas in Terms of Eleven Categories of Knowledge

> For the wise, intelligence[38] is acquired, unacquired,
> Or fully present; realized or consequently realized;
> Used for teaching or beyond expression; with an "I" or with the "I" destroyed;
> And either immature or fully mature. (XX, 80)

It is also on account of their knowing and realizing eleven kinds of knowledge that they are described as bodhisattvas. The eleven categories are past, present, and future; inner and outer; gross and subtle; base and excellent; and proximate and distant.

The intelligence of wise bodhisattvas in their knowing past phenomena is referred to as "knowledge that has been obtained (or acquired)," because those past phenomena have already been obtained as such in the past. Their realization of phenomena that will appear in the future is referred to as "knowledge that has not been acquired," because at present those phenomena do not exist (or have not been obtained) as such. Their realization of present phenomena is referred to as "fully present" because they have arisen and have not yet ceased.

Bodhisattvas' own mental realization of impermanence, suffering, and so forth is inner knowledge, because they have realized it within, with their own intelligence. The knowledge that comes from the causal factor of being taught by another person, a spiritual master, is realization consequent on that outer condition. The intelligence used to teach the general and specific characteristics of phenomena is gross, in that it is dependent on names, phrases, and letters. The intelligence related to resting in inner evenness is subtle, in that it remains in a state free of thoughts without verbal expression.

Up to the seventh level, bodhisattvas have subtle movements of the belief in a self, and therefore their intelligence with an "I" is ordinary or inferior. From the eighth level onward, on account of their spontaneous nonconceptual gnosis, they are free of even the subtle movements of the belief in a self, and therefore their intelligence, in which the "I" has been destroyed, is excellent. Alternatively, "with an 'I'" can refer to the realization of those on the level of earnest aspiration, because they have not eliminated the concepts of

---

38. Tib. *blo*, referring to the rational mind.

subject and object. Those on the noble levels have eliminated the concepts of subject and object and are therefore referred to as having destroyed the "I."

Immature intelligence refers to bodhisattvas' intelligence up to the seventh level, because they have not acquired nonconceptual gnosis spontaneously, without effort. This is distant intelligence. From the eighth level onward, their intelligence is referred to as "truly mature," because their nonconceptual gnosis is spontaneous and requires no effort. This is proximate intelligence, because they are close to the level of buddhahood. Alternatively, we can speak of "immature" and "mature" for the level of earnest aspiration and the noble levels respectively.

This completes the explanation of the twentieth chapter of *Ornament of the Mahāyāna Sūtras*, the chapter on qualities.

21

Conduct and Consummation[1]

This chapter is divided into four sections: (1) the signs of a bodhisattva; (2) how bodhisattvas take birth; (3) how they attain the levels; and (4) a praise of the ultimate qualities.

1. The Signs of a Bodhisattva

> Compassionate, soft-spoken,
> Steadfast, openhanded,
> And able to comment on the profound intention—
> These are the marks of the wise. (XXI, 1)
>
> For they are caring, inspire interest,
> Are not discouraged, and attract in two ways.
> It should thus be understood there are five signs,
> Which are related to their intention and application. (XXI, 2)

Just as one knows from an indication or sign such as smoke that there is fire, there are five signs that appear in those who are bodhisattvas, consistent with their practicing the six transcendent perfections. From these signs one knows that they are bodhisattvas and can be counted as bodhisattvas. The five signs are that (1) they are full of compassion and thus care for sentient beings; (2) they speak pleasantly and well, both in ordinary conversation and when teaching the Dharma; (3) for others' sake, they are steadfast and undaunted by danger and suffering; (4) they are always unreservedly openhanded and generous, giving away all they possess; and (5) they can

---

1. "Conduct" (Tib. *spyod pa*) refers to the continued practice and activity of the bodhisattva along the entire length of the path.

comment definitively on the enlightened intention of the Buddha's Excellent Speech. These five are the marks of wise bodhisattvas.

With their compassion, they take care of beings. Their gentle speech has the effect of inspiring beings to take an interest. On account of their steadfastness, they are not discouraged by suffering. And by being openhanded and elucidating the profound intention, they attract sentient beings with material gifts and the gift of Dharma. The first of these signs relates to intention and the last four relate to application. From these we are to understand that there are five signs.

The nature of compassion is twofold, related to intention and to practice. The intention is the intention to bring benefit, raising beings out of nonvirtuous activities and introducing them to virtue, and the intention to bring happiness, dispelling the sufferings of the three lower realms and so on and setting beings in the happiness of the higher realms. In reliance on that intention to bring benefit and happiness, practical compassion consists of using one's body, speech, and mind to bring sentient beings benefit and happiness. Someone who has that is referred to as a compassionate bodhisattva.

Gentle speech is also of two kinds: ordinary, conventional conversation and explanations of the Dharma. Of these two, the first is also twofold: conversation that makes everyone happy (pleasing them by smiling, inquiring after their health, and so forth) and conversation that genuinely delights people (pleasing advice on how to make their children and relatives flourish, increase their savings, boost their crops, and so on). Talking about the Dharma involves explaining the transcendent perfections, the elements leading to enlightenment, and so forth, thus enabling sentient beings to attain the higher realms and liberation.

Steadfastness refers to having a steadfast, forbearing disposition on account of one's concentration, diligence, and wisdom, as a result of which bodhisattvas are unafraid of any suffering or danger. Undaunted and powerful, they never turn back.

Being openhanded refers to both giving on a vast scale and giving without defilements. The first involves, on the internal level, giving things such as one's head and limbs and, on the external level, giving even the regal riches of a universal emperor, not to speak of other things. It is immense, unstinting generosity. Giving without defilements means not giving things such as poison and weapons that will lead to harm in this and other lives and, instead, making pure gifts, without stinginess, and without looking for anything in return.

Commenting on the profound intention means that, because they have the four kinds of perfect knowledge, bodhisattvas have correctly understood the implied teachings, indirect teachings, and so on and can explain their profound meaning without mistake.

Compassion has five objects: those who are suffering, those who are conducting themselves wrongly (taking lives and so on), those who are careless, those who have adopted wrong views, and all ordinary beings who have not eliminated their latent defilements.

The support or object of gentle speech is also of five kinds: speaking correctly (asking after people's health, and so on), pleasing people (giving advice on increasing their circle of friends and wealth), comforting people (saying things that protect them from fear), initiating things (even without being specifically asked, promising to help with projects and tasks), and making truly authoritative statements (teaching the Dharma, which is the means for attaining the higher realms and liberation).

The support or object of steadfastness is also fivefold: the sufferings of saṃsāra, beings' ingratitude, long periods of time, opponents' attacks, and the training in the extensive precepts.

The location and support of openhandedness is again fivefold: giving gifts on a vast scale (as mentioned above), giving impartially, giving respectfully, giving without defilements, and giving without depending on a reward or on karmic recompense.

Commenting on the profound teachings also has five supports or objects: first, dependent arising in forward and reverse orders, associated with emptiness, which shows the depth of the Tathāgata's profound sūtras; second, learning in the Vinaya, with knowledge of the downfalls and the restoration of downfalls; third, the general and specific characteristics of phenomena; fourth, detailed analysis of the names and phrases in the sūtras together with their intended meanings; and fifth, distinctions of the words of the teachings.

The result of having compassion is that in this life one is happy and has no enemies, and in other lives one is born in happy states. The result of gentle speech is that by avoiding the four negative actions of speech, in all one's lives one's words will be respected and those words will be worth retaining. The result of steadfastness is that in this life one will not fail in the vows of discipline one has taken, and one will patiently care for oneself and others, and in other lives one will never turn back from seeing one's undertaking as a bodhisattva through to the end. The result of openhandedness is the benefit it brings others in this life, which in turn has the effect that in other lives one will personally obtain immense wealth and complete the accumulations that lead to enlightenment. The result of commenting on the profound teachings is that in this life, by explaining the three scriptural collections, one will clear away others' ignorance, wrong understanding, and doubts, and in other lives too one will be learned in the five sciences.

The five signs are explained in this order for the following reason. Bodhisattvas begin with compassion, because of which they speak gently. Those who, out of compassion, speak gently are not discouraged by the sufferings of saṃsāra. Because they are steadfast, they attract disciples with material gifts and subsequently teach them, explaining the intention of the teachings, and thus bring them to maturity.

In which of the transcendent perfections are these five signs included? Compassion depends on the seed of the potential—that is, it is related to habituation to the four boundless attitudes, and so it is included in transcendent concentration. Gentle speech is included in transcendent discipline (insofar as it is the avoidance of harsh speech) and wisdom (where it refers to talking about the Dharma). Steadfastness is included in the transcendent perfections of diligence, patience, and wisdom. Openhandedness is included in transcendent generosity. Commenting on the profound intention is included in the transcendent perfections of concentration and wisdom.

The five effects of these signs have already been explained, as shown in the root text. It is by having these first three (compassion, gentle speech, and steadfastness) that bodhisattvas have the superior intention toward sentient beings in the last two. The intention "I will set beings in the nirvāṇa with residues" is what we call the superior intention to bring benefit, because this comprises the benefit of not being harmed by defilements. The intention "I will set them in the nirvāṇa without residues" is the superior intention to bring happiness, because it comprises the happiness free of all the sufferings of birth, aging, and the rest. These five signs (compassion and the rest) are thus shown to be included in the superior intention to bring benefit and happiness. The categories of this superior intention are indicated below by "impure, pure . . . ," and the function of superior intention, to attract a following of disciples, is indicated by "On each and every level, the wise . . . ."[2]

---

2. See ch. 21, vv. 6–7.

2. How Bodhisattvas Take Birth as Sentient Beings

> Bodhisattvas always
> Become lay universal emperors,
> And in all those births
> They work for beings' good. (XXI, 3)

Bodhisattvas of steadfast superior intention, on account of their love and compassion for sentient beings, do not turn their backs on saṃsāra as do the listeners. Instead, without abandoning saṃsāra, they take birth again and again for the benefit of sentient beings, and thus they bring beings to maturity, displaying a variety of different births, particularly in the physical form of laypeople and ordained persons. In certain circumstances bodhisattvas always take a succession of lay rebirths as universal emperors, and in all those rebirths they work for the benefit of sentient beings, maturing them into virtuous ways.

> On all the levels, the wise
> Take ordination by receiving the vows,
> By obtaining them naturally,
> Or otherwise, by displaying ordination. (XXI, 4)

On all the bodhisattva levels too, beginning with the first level, they obtain ordination in three ways: by the four-part formal procedure including requesting the vows from a preceptor; by obtaining them naturally, possessing the untainted vow; and otherwise, by displaying the ordained state through manifested bodies.

> Those who've taken ordination
> Have boundless good qualities;
> Thus those diligent in the precepts
> Are superior to lay bodhisattvas. (XXI, 5)

While laypeople are subject to a great many distractions, sufferings, and defilements such as attachment and aversion, those who have taken ordination have boundless qualities that are the opposite of these faults, as praised by the Buddha using a variety of metaphors—they are said to have crossed over the swamp, crossed the river, and crossed over the cesspool or the pit of fire. Thus bodhisattvas who are diligent in the precepts are superior as supports[3] to bodhisattvas who are laypeople.

> On each and every level, steadfast bodhisattvas
> Wish to bring beings pleasant results in future lives,
> They wish to introduce them to virtue in this life,
> And they wish that they may attain nirvāṇa.
> These constitute their superior intention for sentient beings,
> Which is said to be impure, pure, or utterly pure. (XXI, 6)

The causal factor for a bodhisattva's taking birth in saṃsāra is the superior intention comprising the wish to bring sentient beings benefit and happiness, so this will now be explained. Steadfast bodhisattvas on all the levels (the level of earnest aspiration and the ten levels) connect sentient beings to the pleasant, agreeable result that is happiness in other worlds or subsequent lives—hence their intention to bring happiness. Their desire to introduce beings to virtue devoid of defilements in this life is the intention to bring benefit. The wish that they ultimately reach nirvāṇa, with and without residue, is the intention to bring benefit and happiness, as explained above. The wish to set them in happiness is the superior intention to bring happiness. And the wish to make them free of defilements is the superior intention to bring benefit. In short, the wish to bring all sentient beings temporary and ultimate benefit and happiness is what we call the superior intention.

As to the categories of that superior intention, on the level of earnest aspiration, bodhisattvas have not directly realized ultimate reality, so because of their dualistic clinging, which has to be eliminated on the path of seeing, their superior intention is termed "impure superior intention." From the first level to the seventh, it is pure superior intention, and on the three pure nonreturner levels, it is termed "utterly pure superior intention." These, then, are held to be bodhisattvas' superior intentions for sentient beings. The eighth level and the levels above it are termed "nonreturner levels" because once one has attained the eighth level, it is impossible to turn back to the state associated with characteristics and involving effort.

There are thus two categories as far as sentient beings are concerned (the superior intention to bring benefit and the superior intention to bring happiness) and three categories as far as one's own mind stream is concerned

---

3. Tib. *rten*, meaning rebirths or bodies, the physical supports for pursuing the path.

(impure, pure, and utterly pure), making five categories of superior intention in all.

> On each and every level, the wise
> Take care of beings through prayers of aspiration,
> By having the attitude of sameness, by becoming sovereigns,
> And by attracting a following. (XXI, 7)

Relying on that superior intention, bodhisattvas bring sentient beings into their care, and this is the function of superior intention. Bringing them together through prayers of aspiration consists of giving rise to the thought, on the level of earnest aspiration, "I will establish all sentient beings in the expanse of nirvāṇa," and receiving all beings into their care with their prayers of aspiration. Starting from when they attain the first level, they acquire the thought of oneself and all beings being equal, and thus they gather and care for them with the attitude of sameness. Bringing them together through sovereignty refers to becoming a sovereign such as a universal emperor, with power and influence, and taking care of sentient beings, benefiting them with material gifts and introducing them to the ten positive actions. And caring for them by guiding an assembly consists of becoming the instructor or preceptor of an assembly and, by teaching the Dharma, bringing together a following of disciples. It is through these four ways of bringing them into their care that bodhisattvas look after sentient beings.

> The wise are said to take birth
> Through the power of their actions,
> And also through their prayers,
> Concentration, and mastery. (XXI, 8)

There are four causes for bodhisattvas' taking birth. Of wise bodhisattvas who take birth, those who are on the level of earnest aspiration do so mainly as a result of their karmic deeds. Since they have not acquired mastery over their minds, there is no certainty that they will definitely be born wherever they have wished or aspired to be born, and although it can occasionally happen that they take birth in accordance with their aspirations, in most cases they are reborn by the karmic force of their accumulated merit in situations that will be beneficial to themselves and others.

Besides this, there are those who take birth by the force of their prayers of aspiration. These are bodhisattvas who have entered the first and second levels and who, by the power of their prayers, are reborn in the celestial, human, animal, hungry spirit, and hell realms in accordance with their aspirations to benefit the beings there. In times of great disasters, in order to dispel beings' hunger and thirst, they take the bodies of fish, elephants, and so on, and satisfy beings with their own flesh. During ages of sickness and the like, they take the form of medicinal creatures and cure the illnesses of beings who eat their flesh. And they manifest as accomplished mantra adepts and great doctors and cure the various diseases of sentient beings. Thus they take all kinds of rebirths, as is described in scriptures such as the *Sūtra That Teaches the Secret of the Tathāgata's Body*.

Bodhisattvas from the third level up to the seventh take birth by means of concentration. Although they have attained the four dhyānas by virtue of their exceptional fitness in mental concentration, instead of taking birth in the world of form, which is the result of such concentration, they are reborn in the world of desire and take birth through concentration wherever they wish.

Bodhisattvas on the eighth, ninth, and tenth levels display any kind of birth, anywhere. In this they are their own masters, and so they are said to take birth by virtue of their mastery. They also display manifestation bodies, descending from the Tuṣita heaven, entering the womb, and so forth, and manifest all kinds of births. In the *Sūtra of the Ten Levels*, in the chapter on the eighth level, it is said that bodhisattvas acquire ten powers:

> By attaining full accomplishment of the gnosis of the body, in order to bless the duration of life for inexpressibly inexpressible kalpas,[4] they acquire power over life.
> In order to access the gnosis perfectly realized by concentration, they acquire power over mind.
> In order to truly display the blessings of adorning and draping all worlds with manifold ornaments, they acquire power over material things.
> In order to manifest blessings in a timely manner on account of the ripening of deeds, they acquire power over activities.

---

4. An inexpressibly inexpressible or inexpressible squared (Tib. *brjod du med pa'i yang brjod du med pa*) is the largest number in the system of counting that Indriyeśvara taught the bodhisattva Sudhana as recounted in the *Gaṇḍavyūha-sūtra*. It represents a cosmically vast quantity.

> In order to completely display births in all worlds, they acquire power over birth.
> In order to perfectly demonstrate manifest enlightenment whenever and in whichever buddha field they like, they acquire power over prayers.
> In order to perfectly demonstrate completely filling all worlds with buddhas, they acquire power over aspirations.
> In order to perfectly demonstrate miracles and magical displays in all buddha fields, they acquire power over miracles.
> In order to perfectly demonstrate the strengths and fearlessnesses of a tathāgata, the distinctive qualities of a buddha, the major and minor marks, and manifest enlightenment, they acquire power over gnosis.
> In order to perfectly display the light of the Dharma without limit or center, they acquire power over the Dharma.

Thus, although bodhisattvas on the level of earnest aspiration may take birth through the power of their aspirations, they mainly take birth through the power of their actions. Those who have reached the first and second levels may take birth through the power of their concentration, but they are mostly born through the power of their aspirations. Those on the third to seventh levels take birth through the power of concentration, and those on the pure levels, who have acquired the ten powers, take birth by virtue of their mastery. When bodhisattvas are born like this, in various places of birth as a result of these four causes of birth, the purity of their minds is lesser, middling, or greater, and this follows the order of the levels.

3. An Explanation of the Levels on Which the Bodhisattvas Abide

The bodhisattva levels are presented in (1) a brief introduction and (2) a detailed explanation.

a. Brief Introduction

> The states of abiding and the levels themselves
> Are described in terms of characteristics, individuals, training,
> Aggregates, accomplishment, signs,
> Etymological definitions, and attainment. (XXI, 9)

The ten levels are explained under eight headings. What are they? The defining characteristics of the levels, the individuals on them, the training, the aggregates, accomplishment, marks or signs, etymological definitions, and attainment. These eight serve to describe the states of abiding on the levels, and the levels themselves. Just as the great base on which sentient beings and insentient organisms such as grass and trees come into being and dwell is referred to as the ground, the different states of bodhisattvas' minds, with their lesser, middling, or greater degrees of purity, and in which all mundane and supramundane good qualities are produced, are therefore referred to as "grounds" or "levels."[5]

b. Detailed Explanation

The detailed explanation comprises the aforementioned eight headings.

i. The Defining Characteristics of the Levels

> The sublime realization of emptiness;
> The persistence of deeds, which are never wasted;
> Rebirth in the world of desire
> After dwelling in the intense bliss of concentration; (XXI, 10)

Because, on the first level, bodhisattvas directly realize the two kinds of no-self, individual and phenomenal, that supreme realization of emptiness is the defining characteristic of the first level. Thus the *Sūtra of the Ten Levels* describes the attainment of the first level as being "firmness of intention and superior intention, analysis and discernment by the force of mind and force of intellect, and realization of the three times as evenness." Realization of the individual no-self is what is called "extreme firmness of intention." Realization of the no-self in phenomena is "extreme firmness of superior intention." Again, realization of the individual no-self is "thorough analysis by the force of mind." Possession of the wisdom that realizes the no-self

---

5. It should be noted that the same Tibetan word used here (*sa*, Skt. *bhūmi*) can be translated as "earth," "ground," "level," "position," "floor," or "story" according to the context. Some translators use the more literal translation "ground" when speaking of the ten bodhisattva bhūmis. The point of the present example is that the ten bhūmis or levels refer to the support on which the qualities of the Buddhist path appear and grow.

in phenomena is "discernment of the subtlest distinctions by the force of intellect." The realization that everything in the three times is of one taste in emptiness is "realization of the three times as evenness."

After attaining the first level in this way, bodhisattvas attain the second, at which point, having seen that the results of positive and negative actions ripening as happiness and suffering are never wasted but endure, they spend all their time practicing exclusively the path of the ten positive actions, and apart from that they never follow the path of negative actions, even in dreams. So the defining characteristic of the second level is established as being that actions are never wasted. Thus those on the second level perpetually turn away from actions such as killing and never even give rise to harmful intentions, let alone actually inflict harm physically. For all sentient beings, the whole of their falling into the lower realms comes about through the path of the ten negative actions, and therefore bodhisattvas think, "I must abide in virtue, the correct practice, and introduce others too to the correct practice," as is extensively taught in the sūtra.

The defining characteristic of the third level is that having remained in the state of intense bliss of the four dhyānas, without losing that concentration, bodhisattvas, after obtaining the concentration of dhyāna, take birth in the world of desire. The sūtra describes how when bodhisattvas authentically see the boundless qualities of the tathāgatas' gnosis and realize that compounded phenomena bring much harm, they more particularly settle on ten mental attitudes with regard to sentient beings, beginning with their thinking of sentient beings who are without protector and without support. It goes on to describe in detail how, from hearing the teachings and gaining a definite understanding of them in their own minds, bodhisattvas go alone to a secluded place, and how they accomplish the first, second, third, and fourth concentrations and give rise to concentrations, perfect freedoms, and so on.

> Then, full dedication to saṃsāra
> Of the elements conducive to enlightenment;
> With defiling factors absent from the mind,
> The full maturation of sentient beings; (XXI, 11)

Next, the defining characteristic of the fourth level is that having, with wisdom, brought to realization the elements that lead to enlightenment, bodhisattvas compassionately dedicate them all to samsaric states. Some people might argue that if the elements leading to enlightenment constitute the path for certain deliverance from saṃsāra, how can they be dedicated to saṃsāra and how can they become the cause of saṃsāra? To answer this objection, let us use an analogy. Poison that is not taken skillfully will cause death, while poison used skillfully can be medicinal. In the same way, the practice of the elements leading to enlightenment unsupported by the skillful means of great compassion is the cause for release from saṃsāra, while the practice of the elements leading to enlightenment supported by great compassion is the cause for being reborn in saṃsāra. Bodhisattvas do not turn their backs on saṃsāra, and even though they practice the elements leading to enlightenment, they practice with great compassion to benefit sentient beings, so those elements conducive to enlightenment do not make them turn away from saṃsāra. On the contrary, they become a cause for actually turning toward saṃsāra, and so they are dedicated completely to saṃsāra. This is explained in the commentary. We also read in the sūtra: "O children of the buddhas, the bodhisattvas who dwell on this bodhisattva level, the Radiant, possessed of thorough application and vigilance and mindfulness, have completely eliminated mundane mental states of attachment and unhappiness, and they abide in the examination of the body related to the inner body.... All this is because of their steadfastness in watching over all beings and accomplishing their former prayers, their practice, above all else, of great compassion, their great love...."

The defining characteristic of the fifth level is that without any defiling factors in their minds, they bring sentient beings to full maturity. On this level, without having any defilements such as attachment (as a result of meditating on the four noble truths as the antidotes to defilements), they become learned in the various arts and sciences and bring sentient beings to full maturity by means of the three vehicles. The sūtra has this to say: "Their attentiveness having become irreversible through their having developed the mental forces of mindfulness, intelligence, and realization, they know perfectly and correctly, as it is, 'This is the noble truth of suffering.'" And: "By being diligent in thoroughly investigating the extraordinary Dharma, they fully accomplish everything there is to do with languages, literature, astrology, laws, and so forth that there are in this world. They research into the causes of disease and practice surgery. They dispel negative forces that cause wasting and forgetfulness, and elemental spirits. They thwart those who prepare poisons and create zombies. And they make beings happy with mantras, dances, speeches, music, and tales..., compassionately accomplishing all these deeds that bring beings benefit and happiness in order to introduce them to the Buddha's teachings."

Protection from defilement
When taking birth through specific intention;
The path of the single certainty of the absence of attributes,
Connecting to the path of single progress; (XXI, 12)

The defining characteristic of the sixth level is that when, with sentient beings' welfare specifically in mind, they take birth in the realm of saṃsāra, as a result of their meditating on dependent arising they are protected from and untainted by defiling factors. When bodhisattvas dwelling on the sixth level take birth in the three worlds, it is not that they are born because of deeds and defilements, powerlessly. Rather, backed by their immense accumulation of merit and wisdom, without any deterioration in mindfulness and vigilance, and with the specific intention "For the sake of sentient beings, I will take birth in this or that place," they take birth as they wish. And from having meditated many times on dependent arising, they are protected from and untainted by defilements. The sūtra describes in detail how when they reflect thus on the nature of all phenomena, giving priority to ever greater compassion, they look at the origin and destruction of the world and see that by improper use of the mind, by clinging to a self, karma is produced, and so on.

The defining characteristic of the seventh level is that bodhisattvas are connected to the path of single progress and are single-mindedly certain of the absence of attributes. The path of single progress is the eighth level. Until they reach that level, the efforts and so forth in the mind streams of individual bodhisattvas are distinct, and their progress is not the same, whereas once they have attained the eighth level, nonconceptual gnosis is spontaneously accomplished in the state of evenness, so there are no concepts of distinct efforts and mind streams, and thus their progress is the same, like the single taste of the water in the ocean with all the many rivers flowing into it. Being connected to the path of single progress refers to the seventh level because the eighth level is attained immediately after it. When they attain the seventh level, bodhisattvas realize that even the meanings of the sūtras and other teachings are of a single taste, the absence of attributes; it is the path of the single certainty that they are devoid of attributes in every respect. In the sūtra we read, "O children of the buddhas, it is thus.

For example, unless they have the great strength and force of prayer, skillful means, wisdom, and preternatural knowledge, no one, on a mere whim, can cross the gap between the defiled, impure world and the perfectly pure world. O children of the buddhas, in the same way, unless they have the great strength and force of prayer, skillful means, wisdom, preternatural knowledge, and gnosis, no one, on a mere whim, can cross the gap between the mixed practices[6] of the bodhisattvas and the completely pure practices." This is what is meant by the seventh level being connected to the path of single progress. On the meaning of single certainty as to the absence of attributes, the sūtra says, "Thus, at the time of dwelling on the seventh level, the boundless activities of the body free from attributes arise completely; the boundless activities of the speech free from attributes arise completely; the boundless activities of the mind free from attributes, completely purified, manifesting infinitely with the acceptance that phenomena are unborn, arise completely."

> Spontaneous accomplishment of the absence of attributes,
> And purification of the universe;
> Subsequent accomplishment
> Of the maturation of sentient beings; (XXI, 13)

The defining characteristic of the eighth level is that the absence of attributes is spontaneously accomplished and there is no movement with effort, and that everything is purified as a buddha field. At the time of one's dwelling on the eighth level, the nonconceptual gnosis that knows absence of attributes is spontaneously and effortlessly accomplished. And the universe and beings are purified as a pure buddha field, as is explained in detail in the sūtra: "O children of the buddhas, as soon as bodhisattvas who have that kind of acceptance attain the bodhisattva level Immovable, they attain a profound bodhisattva's state of abiding that is difficult to know. It is unadulterated, free from all attributes, turned away from all conceptual grasping, limitless. Their vacuity cannot be rivaled by any of the listeners and solitary realizers. They have attained the realization of every kind of vacuity.[7] O children of

---

6. Tib. *spyod pa 'dres pa*. On the seventh level, which is one of the impure levels, the bodhisattva's practice in postmeditation is still mixed with, or adulterated by, thoughts and subtle obscurations.

7. "Vacuity" (Tib. *dben pa*) in this case refers to the total absence of concepts and so on in these bodhisattvas, the fact that they are devoid of all negative qualities.

the buddhas, it is like this. For example, a monk who possesses miraculous powers...." It goes on to explain that in the same way that the absorption of cessation is devoid of the movements of thoughts and concepts, the eighth level is free of all effortful conception and activity. When a sleeping person who dreams that they have fallen and been carried away by a great river is woken by their struggles to escape, they are immediately free from those efforts. In the same way, once sentient beings carried away by the four rivers of defilement think of being liberated, they make great efforts to be freed, but as soon as they attain the eighth level, they are free of all movements involving deliberate effort. Again, a seagoing boat has to be deliberately propelled until it reaches the open sea, but once there, it is taken up by the wind so that it can travel all over the ocean without the need for deliberate propulsion. Similarly, having reached the eighth level, bodhisattvas effortlessly enter omniscient gnosis—which could never have been accomplished by their previous, deliberate activities. So too, with regard to such activities as their effortless purification of everything as a buddha field by dint of their spontaneous nonconceptual concentration, the sūtra speaks of "Boundless manifestation of births, boundless purification as buddha fields, boundless maturation of sentient beings...."

After the eighth level is attained, there is the ninth level, whose defining characteristic is that, as a result of bodhisattvas' acquiring the four kinds of perfect knowledge, there is no obstruction to their teaching the Dharma, so that they are able to accomplish bringing sentient beings to full maturity. Again the sūtra explains this in detail: "Bodhisattvas dwelling on this bodhisattva level, Perfect Intellect, are great teachers, preserving the treasure of the tathāgatas' doctrine. Because of their boundless mastery in gnosis regarding the methods of teaching the Dharma, those bodhisattvas' utterances, being fully manifested by the four kinds of perfect knowledge, reveal the Dharma. With the perfect knowledge of each and every aspect of the Dharma, they perfectly know the specific characteristics of all things. With the perfect knowledge of all the meanings, they perfectly know the categories of the teachings. With the perfect knowledge of etymological definitions, they perfectly know how to teach the subjects without confusing them. With perfect knowledge through inner confidence and eloquence, they always perfectly know which teachings are appropriate...." And so on.

Concentrations and powers of retention;
And perfect purity, enlightenment—

> Presented thus, the defining characteristics
> Of the levels can be known. (XXI, 14)

The defining characteristic of the tenth level is established as the obtainment of boundless doors of concentration and powers of retention. When bodhisattvas attain the tenth level, they acquire boundless doors of concentration, such as the "uncontaminated concentration of a bodhisattva," and the "vision of Mahāyāna," these concentrations being "doors" that act as the cause or source for the arising of numerous qualities such as preternatural knowledge. Similarly, they acquire infinite powers of retention,[8] such as Inexhaustible Caskets and Infinite Doors, these powers of retention being termed "doors" because they are the cause of bodhisattvas' unforgetting retention of the words and meanings taught by the Buddha and of their expounding all the various teachings to sentient beings. As we read in the sūtra, "O children of the buddhas, it is said of bodhisattvas who possess that kind of gnosis and receive empowerment that they will realize the 'uncontaminated concentration of a bodhisattva.' ... It is said that they will realize the 'bodhisattva's concentration of the present Buddha being present in person.' ... Bodhisattvas dwelling on this tenth level acquire infinite countless hundreds of thousands of bodhisattvas' doors of liberation similar to these. Likewise, they acquire countless hundreds of thousands of concentrations and hundreds of thousands of powers of retention."

The eleventh level, the level of buddhahood, is presented as having the defining characteristic of extreme purity, great enlightenment endowed with the gnosis of exhaustion and nonarising, for the two obscurations together with habitual tendencies have been eliminated. As we read in *Unraveling the Intent*: "The state in which the negative tendencies present in the shell have been eliminated corresponds to the first and second levels. The state in which those present in the flesh have been eliminated corresponds to the third level onward. The state in which the negative tendencies present in the kernel have been completely eliminated and all latent tendencies are entirely absent I explain as the level of a buddha."

From these presentations, we should understand what are the defining characteristics of the levels, from the first level up to the buddha level.

---

8. Tib. *gzungs kyi sgo dpag tu med pa*, lit. "infinite doors of the power of retention," meaning the ability to remember and therefore expound an infinite variety of teachings that serve as entrances through which beings may eliminate their particular defilements.

ii. A Presentation of the Individuals Who Dwell on the Ten Levels

> The bodhisattvas on these levels are those with perfectly
>   pure view,
> Those with extremely pure discipline, those who are settled
>   in evenness,
> Those who are rid of pride with regard to the Dharma, who
>   have no pride with regard to
> Distinctions between mind streams and between defilement
>   and purity, (XXI, 15)
>
> Those who have acquired the mental capacity for
>   instantaneous realization,
> Those who dwell in equanimity and purify fields, those who
>   are skilled in ripening beings,
> And those who have great powers, have perfected the body,
> Are skilled in clear display, and receive empowerment.
>   (XXI, 16)

Individuals dwelling on the first level are called "bodhisattvas with perfectly pure view," because they have acquired the nonconceptual gnosis that is realization of the two kinds of no-self. Those dwelling on the second level are known as "individuals with extremely pure discipline," because even the subtlest faults and downfalls do not occur in them. Similarly, those dwelling on the third level are individuals who are always settled in evenness, because wherever they are reborn in their series of lives, their attainment of dhyāna and concentration never degenerates.

Bodhisattvas dwelling on the fourth level are individuals who have abandoned pride with regard to the Dharma. When they are on the third level, it is said that by virtue of their having the wisdom of thorough examination, bodhisattvas particularly venerate and investigate the teachings, night and day listening to the teachings, seeking the teachings, reflecting on the teachings, and practicing in accordance with the teachings. For the sake of the Dharma, there is nothing, not the slightest thing, external or internal, that they will not give. There is no act of veneration for the teacher that they will not carry out. They have not the slightest element of disrespect or arrogance, nothing other than the deepest respect and enthusiasm for the teachings and the teacher, recognizing how rare and difficult they are to come by. Were someone to show a third-level bodhisattva a huge fire pit, burning throughout in a single mass of fiercely blazing flames, and to say, "If you throw yourself into this fire and accept the ordeal of being horribly burned, I will teach you a verse of the Dharma the Buddha taught on how to train in the activities of a bodhisattva," it goes without saying that that bodhisattva would jump straight into the fire. For the sake of just a single verse of the teachings the Buddha gave on training in the bodhisattva activities, such bodhisattvas would gladly be thrown out of the world of Brahmā and into a great universe of a billion worlds filled with fire. They would seek the teachings even if they had to experience all the sufferings of beings in the hells, so what are the accompanying pains of being burned to them? Now, however, when they attain the fourth level, their seeking the teachings with such a strong intention would make their minds distracted and proud, so by emphasizing the meaning of the teachings, that is, the practice of the elements leading to enlightenment, they counter the pride involved in thinking, "I will earnestly seek the teachings," and it is in this sense that they are individuals who have abandoned pride with regard to the Dharma.

Bodhisattvas dwelling on the fifth level are known as "individuals without pride regarding different mind streams." At that time, they acquire ten forms of mental attitudes of sameness with regard to purity, and thus realize that there are no differences in the characteristics of purity between the streams of being of the buddhas of the three times, the qualities of the tathāgatas of the three times, and the mind streams and qualities of the bodhisattvas dwelling on the fifth level. It is in this sense that they are individuals who have no pride with regard to particularities of mind stream. The ten attitudes of sameness with regard to purity are described as follows in the explanation of the fifth level in the *Sūtra of the Ten Levels*:

> O children of the buddhas, bodhisattvas on the fourth bodhisattva level who have completed the path of that level enter the fifth level, entering it by means of ten kinds of sameness of mind with regard to perfect purity. What are these ten? (1) The attitude of sameness with regard to the purity of the qualities of the past buddhas, and likewise of (2) the qualities of the future buddhas and (3) the qualities of the present buddhas; (4) the attitude of sameness with regard to the purity of their discipline; (5) the attitude of sameness with regard to the purity of their minds; (6) the

attitude of sameness with regard to the purity of their having dispelled wrong views, doubts, and apprehension; and similarly four attitudes of sameness with regard to the purity of (7) their knowing what is and what is not the path, (8) their knowledge of scrupulous elimination, (9) their progressive practice of the elements leading to enlightenment, and (10) their bringing sentient beings to full maturity.[9]

The point of these is that just as the buddhas of the past achieved the perfectly pure qualities of buddhahood, so too, bodhisattvas who have attained the fifth level acquire the attitude, "Before too long we will, like them, achieve those pure qualities, the three trainings and other buddha qualities."

Bodhisattvas dwelling on the sixth level are known as "individuals without pride regarding any distinction between defilement and purity." While dwelling on that level, by acquiring the ten kinds of sameness of phenomena, they realize the emptiness of dependent arising. As a result, they realize that in emptiness there is neither the black aspect (the arising of conditioning factors caused by ignorance and so on) nor the white aspect (the halting of ignorance and so on), that everything is unborn, of one taste as the nature of emptiness. They thus have no pride or conceptual attitude with regard to a distinction between defilement and purity. Bodhisattvas on the sixth level are said to enter that level by virtue of ten aspects of sameness of phenomena, as follows: the sameness of all phenomena in being devoid of attributes;[10] their sameness in being devoid of characteristics; and similarly the sameness of all phenomena in being unborn,[11] unproduced,[12] devoid,[13] primordially pure, free of elaboration, and free of acceptance and rejection; in being the same as magical illusions, dreams, optical distortions, echoes,

---

9. These ten attitudes concern (1–3) the buddhas' qualities such as the ten strengths; (4) their discipline; (5) their concentration; (6–9) their wisdom; and (10) their maturation of sentient beings.

10. Tib. *mtshan ma med pa*. According to Vasubandhu's commentary on the *Sūtra of the Ten Levels*, this effectively means "devoid of essence."

11. Tib. *mi skye ba*. Vasubandhu's commentary explains this as "not coming into being from one rebirth to the next."

12. Tib. *ma byung ba*. Vasubandhu's commentary explains this as "not coming into being from one moment to the next."

13. Tib. *dben pa*, devoid, according to Vasubandhu's commentary, of all attributes of defilement.

the moon's reflection on water, images in a mirror, and manifestations; and in not being either existent or nonexistent.

Bodhisattvas dwelling on the seventh level are known as "individuals who have acquired the mind that in an instant trains in the elements leading to enlightenment," these being the causal factors that give rise to all the buddha qualities, as is explained in the sūtra: "O children of the buddhas, bodhisattvas who thus dwell on this bodhisattva level, Far Progressed, will thus complete the ten transcendent perfections and will also complete the four ways of gathering disciples. In an instant, they will complete the four pure states,[14] the thirty-seven elements leading to enlightenment, the three doors of perfect liberation—in short, all the elements of the branches of enlightenment."

Bodhisattvas dwelling on the eighth level are known as "individuals who dwell in equanimity and purify everything as a buddha field." By remaining in the spontaneous concentration that does not conceive any attributes whatsoever, they remain in effortless equanimity and purify everything as a perfectly pure buddha field, as is mentioned in the sūtra, which explains effortlessness with the analogy of the boat sailing on the ocean and describes how bodhisattvas display the blessings of fully ornamenting and adorning all worlds with every kind of ornament.

Bodhisattvas dwelling on the ninth level are known as "individuals skilled in bringing sentient beings to maturation." By acquiring the four kinds of perfect knowledge, they become great teachers for all sentient beings and are thus expert in bringing them to maturity.

Bodhisattvas dwelling on the tenth level are known as "individuals who have acquired great powers, have perfected the body, are skilled in clear display, and receive empowerment"—that is, they have acquired great powers of preternatural knowledge; they have completely perfected the body of powers of retention and concentrations, which is the cause for attaining the body of truth; they are skilled in clearly displaying the deeds of a buddha (dwelling in the Tuṣita heaven, entering the womb, attaining manifest enlightenment, and so on); and they receive the great light rays empowerment from the tathāgatas. The sūtra explains this in great detail: "By means of preternatural knowledge, they acquire hundreds of thousands of accomplishments. When they so desire, they can bestow their blessing on a world, transforming it from something small and cramped into something

---

14. Tib. *gnas bzhi*, probably the *tshangs pa'i gnas bzhi*, the four brahmavihāras.

vast and spacious, and from vast and spacious into small and cramped." And, "They acquire countless hundreds of thousands of doors of perfect liberation such as these ten doors of perfect liberation, and likewise similar numbers of doors of concentration and powers of retention." "Bodhisattvas dwelling on this Cloud of Dharma bestow their blessing in one world to display all the deeds of a tathāgata according to sentient beings' aspirations and how they are to be trained—beginning with residence in the Tuṣita heaven, transfer and descent, entrance into the womb, and so on, through to the attainment of manifest enlightenment, exhortation, the turning of the wheel of the Dharma, and the great parinirvāṇa." And, "As soon as they achieve that,[15] there appears a great jeweled king of lotuses, equal in size to a million trichiliocosms...."[16] "When the eldest son of a universal emperor, bearing the marks of his royal state, is placed on a golden throne, amid all kinds of ornamental arrays and to the accompaniment of music and song, and empowered on the crown of his head with water from a golden vase containing water from the oceans, he is counted as having been empowered, crowned as the princely future king. In the same way, as soon as those bodhisattvas are empowered by the buddha bhagavāns with the great rays of light, they are said to have been empowered with the full empowerment of gnosis. Having completely perfected the ten strengths, they are counted as truly perfect buddhas...."

iii. How Bodhisattvas Complete the Training in the Three Trainings on the Ten Levels

> After truly realizing ultimate reality,
> They train here in superior discipline,
> Superior mind, and superior wisdom.
> The object of wisdom is twofold: (XXI, 17)
>
> The suchness of phenomena, and the processes
> That operate from not knowing and knowing that suchness.

---

15. "That" here refers to the last of a series of concentrations that bodhisattvas experience before being empowered by the tathāgatas and attaining buddhahood, as detailed in the sūtra at the beginning of the chapter on the tenth level.
16. This giant lotus, forming the bodhisattva's throne, appears as the result of the bodhisattva's accumulation of supramundane merits.

These are the objects of wisdom
On which they dwell on the two levels. (XXI, 18)

Training and meditating
Leads to four further results:
Dwelling in the absence of attributes
With deliberate effort is the first result. (XXI, 19)

Doing the same without deliberate effort
And purifying everything as a buddha field
Is the second result.
Then there is the accomplishment of maturing beings, (XXI, 20)

And the accomplishment of concentrations and powers of retention,
Which constitutes the supreme result.
These four results
Are directly related to the four levels. (XXI, 21)

The direct realization on the first level of the truth of ultimate reality is the foundation for rendering all the trainings pure. After that, "here" (meaning at the time of the other levels), on the second level, bodhisattvas train in the training of superior discipline. Even in their dreams they never break their vows, so one need hardly mention their ever actually doing so. Thus their discipline is of the purest kind. Those on the third level train in the training in superior concentration, attaining the dhyānas and unfailing concentration.

On the fourth, fifth, and sixth levels, they train mainly in the training of superior wisdom. On the fourth level there is the extraordinary wisdom that comes from practicing the thirty-seven elements leading to enlightenment. The object of that wisdom that comes from practicing the elements leading to enlightenment has two aspects. The object on which bodhisattvas train on the fifth level comprises the suchness of phenomena and the four noble truths. On the sixth level, their object is the manner or process by which not knowing suchness (referring to dependent arising) results in the forward order of dependent arising, starting from ignorance, while knowing it with wisdom results in the reverse order, in which the power of gnosis brings about the halting of ignorance and leads to the halting of conditioning factors and so on. The two objects of their wisdom, then, are the four truths and the twelve links of dependent arising, so it is on these two that bodhisattvas dwell on the fifth and sixth levels.

In the postmeditation period, they train in these trainings, and during formal meditation they train in nonconceptual gnosis, and these lead to four further results. Their dwelling in the absence of attributes, albeit with deliberate effort, on the seventh level is the first result. Spontaneous absence of attributes without deliberate effort and purifying everything as a buddha field on the eighth level is held to be the second result. On the ninth level, bodhisattvas teach the Dharma by means of the four kinds of perfect knowledge and thereby accomplish bringing sentient beings to maturity, which constitutes the third result. Accomplishing the highest concentration and powers of retention corresponds to the tenth level, the fourth result. This is the supreme result, the summit of all the levels. These four results are thus directly related to four levels, from the seventh to the tenth.

iv. How the Five Untainted Aggregates Are Purified on the Levels

> Having truly realized ultimate reality,
> Here, they purify the aggregate of discipline,
> After which they purify the aggregates
> Of concentration and wisdom. (XXI, 22)
>
> On the other levels
> They purify liberation from four obscurations
> And the gnosis of liberation
> From even the impeding obscurations. (XXI, 23)

The perfect realization of ultimate reality on the first level is the support for all the untainted aggregates, so having achieved such realization, here, on the second level, bodhisattvas train in purifying the aggregate of discipline. After the second level, on the third level they train in purifying the aggregate of concentration, and on the fourth, fifth, and sixth levels they train in purifying the aggregate of wisdom, as above.

On the four further levels (namely, the seventh, eighth, ninth, and tenth levels), they purify the aggregate of perfect liberation—that is, liberation from four kinds of obscuration. On these four levels, beginning with the seventh, they obtain the four results as have just been explained—the absence of attributes, the absence of deliberate effort, the maturation of beings, and the acquisition of powers of retention and concentration. The four hindrances to their obtaining these are the arising of subtle attributes, efforts, failure to acquire the perfect knowledge for bringing sentient beings to maturity, and failure to acquire mastery in powers of retention and concentration. As they attain the four levels, beginning with the seventh, in order, they are liberated from these obscuring counteragents, so that even the most subtle attributes do not arise, and thus they purify the aggregate of perfect liberation of these four. And on the level of buddhahood, the vajra-like concentration, the path without obstacles, destroys the most subtle cognitive obscurations, the habitual tendencies of deluded dualistic perception, so that they are completely freed even from the impeding factors that obscure their knowing the totality of knowable phenomena, and they thereby purify the aggregate of the gnosis of perfect liberation. This verse thus presents the purification of the aggregate of perfect liberation on the seventh to tenth levels and the purification of the aggregate of the gnosis of perfect liberation on the level of buddhahood.

One might argue that if perfect liberation, the analytical cessation that corresponds to the elimination of obscurations, is uncompounded, how can it be classified as an aggregate? In reply to this objection, the commentary states that the Sanskrit term for perfect liberation, *vimukti*, can refer to both elimination and inclination, and that in this context it refers to inclination, so it is classified as an aggregate. Even though one is completely freed of all deliberate application, the spontaneous, effortless gnosis is present, so this is not like a nonaffirming nihilistic emptiness in which the factors to be eliminated have been exhausted. It is from the point of view of the presence of the qualities of elimination of that gnosis, freed of obscurations, that perfect liberation can be thought of as an aggregate.

v. How Qualities Are Accomplished and Not Accomplished

> All the levels should be understood
> As levels of nonaccomplishment and accomplishment.
> And those of accomplishment are again held to be
> Levels of nonaccomplishment and accomplishment. (XXI, 24)

All the eleven levels—the level of earnest aspiration and the ten levels—are to be understood as including both nonaccomplishment and accomplishment. How is that? Even though the level of earnest aspiration is called a level, it is not included in the noble levels, and so it is referred to as a level of nonaccomplishment, because bodhisattvas on that level have not realized the nature of the all-pervasive expanse of reality and have not therefore accomplished seeing the truth. The levels from the first level onward are to be understood as being levels of accomplishment, because bodhisattvas have seen the truth of ultimate reality, and they have therefore accomplished the supramundane state of noble beings and have also realized and accomplished the qualities that have to be realized on each of the respective levels. These ten levels are also held to be levels of nonaccomplishment and of accomplishment from the point of view of their greater and lesser qualities. The seven impure levels, on which the yoga of absence of attributes involves effort and is therefore not spontaneous, are levels of nonaccomplishment. And the three pure levels, on which the yoga of absence of attributes is effortless and spontaneous, are referred to as levels of accomplishment.

Their accomplishment is to be understood from
Keeping the system in mind,
From knowing that it is all thought,
And from nonconceptuality with regard to that. (XXI, 25)

What is it that enables bodhisattvas to accomplish those noble levels? It is what is known as "keeping the system in mind." In other words, the system of each level—its qualities, the faults that have to be eliminated on it, and the factors in which the bodhisattva has to train on that level—appear clearly to the mind, and the bodhisattva keeps in mind the qualities of the next level and the factors that enable one to achieve it. For example, with regard to the first level that is to be accomplished, keeping the system in mind involves keeping in mind the qualities of the first level and the factors in which one must train on that level, and keeping in mind the causal factors on that level that will lead to attaining the second level. Keeping in mind the qualities of the first level is also mentioned in the sūtra: "O children of the buddhas, beings who have practiced the intensive accumulation of sources of good, who have intensively gathered the accumulations. . . ." And with regard to how first-level bodhisattvas keep in mind the cause for attaining the second level, we read, "O children of the buddhas, a bodhisattva who has trained thoroughly on the first level and is now bent on attaining the second level has ten mental attitudes. What are these ten? They are the attitudes of straightforwardness, tenderness, workability...." Alternatively, keeping the system in mind involves reflecting on and keeping in mind the points of the respective levels as they have been described with names, phrases, and letters in order to realize them.

When bodhisattvas accomplish a level by keeping the system in mind like this, they recognize that apart from the levels and their arrangements appearing to their respective minds, there is nothing else that exists as an object, and therefore even the levels are their own conceptualized thoughts. Because of this, they understand that there is no apprehended object, and that if there is no object, the subject too must be nonexistent. Subsequently, as a result of their no longer conceptualizing an apprehending subject, they are to understand the absence of subject and object. Thus, by recognizing the mental state corresponding to each level, the fact that it is merely one's own mind, and that there is no subject or object, bodhisattvas accomplish the first level, and so on—it should be understood that for all the other levels too, each respective level is accomplished by one's training in this way.

> **Because they can only be known personally,**
> **And because they are the domain of the buddhas,**
> **The training and its accomplishment**
> **On all the levels are inconceivable. (XXI, 26)**

Training on the levels and accomplishing them in this manner are something that ordinary folk could never possibly imagine. Because the levels can only be known personally by the noble beings who attain them, and also because the arrangement of those levels is the domain of the buddhas, you should understand that on all the levels, the respective training and the accomplishment of those levels by completing the training are inconceivable to ordinary beings, listeners, and solitary realizers, as is stated in the *Sūtra of the Ornament of the Buddhas*:

> Just as the trace of a bird flying through the sky
> Is extremely hard to see, impossible to describe,
> So too, the levels of the children of the sugatas
> Cannot be known by the mind or be an object of the mind.

vi. The Signs of Attaining the Levels

The explanation of these signs is divided into (1) the actual signs and (2) the qualities of the levels that bear those signs.

(1) The Actual Signs

> They have clear vision and interest,
> Are undaunted and never weak-minded,
> Are independent of others,
> Have understood everything perfectly, (XXI, 27)
>
> Are even-minded toward all,
> Are never influenced, have no attachment,
> Know the means, and take birth within the retinue—
> These are considered the signs on all the levels. (XXI, 28)

Just as one recognizes the presence of water from seeing water birds, and fire from seeing smoke, one knows from the corresponding signs or marks that bodhisattvas have attained the levels, as will now be explained. The five signs described above[17] are the general signs of bodhisattvas who have or have not attained the levels, but here it is the ten signs of those who have attained the levels that are described.

(1) The first mark or sign is their clear vision of the factors to be eliminated, of those to be adopted, and of the elements to be cultivated on whichever level they have attained, together with an interest and desire to attain the levels above it.

(2) Bodhisattvas have seen the truth, so they are unafraid of and undaunted by the profound and extensive teachings.

(3) They never turn back and are never discouraged, on account of their irrepressible attitude in the face of such things as heat and cold, exhaustion, and austerities and painful experiences such as giving away their heads and limbs.

(4) Through the strength of their two accumulations, they have realized their own particular level, and they do not have to rely on others for whatever

---

17. See the opening verse of this chapter.

they have accomplished on their respective level. They are not dependent on others to explain the arrangement of that level and to train in its meaning.

(5) Even at the time they attain the first level, they acquire full proficiency in perfectly understanding all the systems for accomplishing all the remaining levels. On the strength of their dwelling in nonconceptual gnosis in formal meditation, in the postmeditation period they know, through their pure mundane gnosis, the methods for accomplishing the remaining levels. Thus, on all the levels, they are thoroughly proficient in the systems that constitute the means for accomplishing the higher levels, following the teachings on the methods by which each level is accomplished from the one before it—for example, the ten expedients by which first-level bodhisattvas enter the second level (straightforwardness, tenderness, and so on), and the ten expedients by which second-level bodhisattvas enter the third level (pure intention, immovable intention, and so on).

(6) Bodhisattvas have acquired the attitude of sameness, for which there is no difference between oneself and the whole infinity of sentient beings.

(7) They are never led astray. Bodhisattvas who have entered the levels possess the most perfect and abundant accumulation of merit and, in their accumulation of wisdom, have realized the emptiness of all phenomena. They therefore have no attachment or aversion to anything. So they do not swagger when they are praised or happy, and they do not get depressed or disheartened when they are not praised or are suffering. Never influenced by circumstances, they cannot be drawn or led.

(8) Those who have entered the levels possess the abundant supramundane wealth of the buddhas and bodhisattvas, so they regard even the riches of such beings as Brahmā, Indra, and the universal emperor as being like excrement and have no attachment to them. As a result, they abandon them and give them to others and renounce worldly life.

(9) They know the means for accomplishing unsurpassable enlightenment—namely, the gnosis free of the concepts of the three spheres.

(10) On account of their prayers of aspiration for the sake of sentient beings, unless they take birth in worlds in which no buddha is present, in all their lives they are born in the circle of a buddha's retinue.

These ten signs are held to be the signs common to bodhisattvas dwelling on all the ten levels. They are not the only signs. There also occur sixteen marks[18] related to achieving the ten transcendent perfections on the corresponding levels.

---

18. As Mipham notes below, the exact enumeration of these sixteen is not very clear.

> Never lacking determination, bodhisattvas have no
> attachment, no hostile feelings, no anger, no laziness,
> No intentions that are not loving and compassionate, and
> they are not carried away by wrong understanding and
> concepts.
> Their minds are not distracted; they are not carried away by
> happiness, nor affected by suffering.
> They follow spiritual masters, devote themselves to listening,
> and are diligent in making offerings to their teachers.
> (XXI, 29)
>
> They who know the supreme means share with others
> The vast entirety of the merit they have gathered and
> dedicate it daily to perfect enlightenment.
> Born in excellent places, they constantly practice virtue and
> revel in the qualities of preternatural knowledge.
> Know that they are treasuries of qualities surpassing all the
> buddhas' children. (XXI, 30)

Bodhisattvas never lack the determination to practice the ten transcendent perfections on all the levels. This is a general statement showing that they very much have determination. Specifically, on the first level, bodhisattvas achieve the completely pure transcendent perfection of generosity, so they are free of attachment to their bodies and possessions. On the second level, related to their pure discipline, they do not indulge in the ten negative actions, even in their dreams, so they are free of hostile, injurious feelings or thoughts. On the third level, on account of their completely pure transcendent patience, they never get angry. On the fourth level, their completely pure transcendent diligence results in their never being lazy. On the fifth level, because of their completely pure transcendent concentration, they possess in particular the four boundless attitudes, so they are free of intentions that are not loving and compassionate. On the sixth level, related to their completely pure transcendent wisdom, they are never carried away by wrong or inverted thoughts such as the wrong understanding of purity, happiness, permanence, and a self, or by the concepts of clinging to substantiality. This makes six marks associated with the six levels and six transcendent perfections.

On the ten levels there are certain transcendent perfections, from generosity to gnosis, that predominate, so these are mentioned in particular, but the ten transcendent perfections are practiced to some degree on all the levels. The numbering of the next six signs does not seem to be clearly explained in the *Great Commentary*, though several different ways of counting them appear in other commentaries.

On the seventh level, bodhisattvas achieve completely pure transcendent skill in means and are therefore not distracted by the listeners' and solitary realizers' ways of thinking. On the eighth level, they achieve completely pure transcendent strength, so they are not carried away by attachment to happiness, nor are they affected by suffering. Without moving from the state of evenness, of spontaneous nonconceptual gnosis, they manifest as Brahmā, Indra, universal emperors, and so on, and even though they send out bodies as numerous as the atoms in the universe, they are free of concepts. On the ninth level, through their transcendent aspirations they closely follow the buddhas and bodhisattvas as spiritual masters and devote themselves to listening to all the teachings as entrances to the Dharma. And they are diligent in venerating their teachers, the buddhas in all the buddha fields in the ten directions, with infinite kinds of offerings such as flowers and incense.

On the seventh level, those who know the supreme method that enables one to attain buddhahood dedicate all the merit accumulated by themselves and others in the past, present, and future, all perfectly gathered into one utterly vast whole, and share it with all other sentient beings, also dedicating it daily to unsurpassable perfect enlightenment. By the power of their prayers of aspiration, they are reborn in excellent places.[19] Through their transcendent strength, they overwhelm unfavorable factors and constantly perform exclusively positive actions. Although these three signs are principally associated with the seventh, ninth, and eighth levels respectively, taking birth in excellent places and constantly performing positive actions are included in one support and counted as a single sign.

On the tenth level, with their completely pure transcendent gnosis, bodhisattvas play with the qualities of preternatural knowledge. Reveling in all kinds of displays, such as demonstrating immensity by filling the vast universe with a single speck of dust and demonstrating minuteness by condensing and enclosing vast universes in a single speck of dust, the buddhas' children on the tenth level, on account of their extensive qualities (powers of retention, concentrations, and the rest), are to be known as treasuries of qualities, surpassing all other bodhisattvas.

---

19. According to Vasubandhu, "excellent places" refers to places that do not lack buddhas and bodhisattvas.

Since each level is associated with a predominant transcendent perfection, the signs that constitute the qualities of those transcendent perfections are also mainly refined on the respective levels. But you should understand that bodhisattvas also practice the ten transcendent perfections on all ten levels, so they have parts of all sixteen marks as well.

(2) The Qualities of the Levels That Bear Those Signs

> On all the levels, overall,
> There are five benefits for the wise,
> Related to sustained calm,
> To profound insight, and to both. (XXI, 31)

On all ten noble levels, overall, the benefits of those levels for wise bodhisattvas are held to be essentially five: two related to sustained calm, two related to profound insight, and one common benefit related to both sustained calm and profound insight. The two benefits that depend on sustained calm are as follows. The power of the workable mind that results from practicing sustained calm is such that all the supports of negative tendencies that become latent defilement-related and cognitive obscurations are, in each instant, destroyed and brought to an end. This is the first benefit. Even the sustained calm and profound insight of the level of earnest aspiration weaken the attributes associated with negative tendencies, but they cannot completely destroy them, while from the first level onward, in each instant those attributes are completely destroyed. Similarly, bodhisattvas are free of the various notions of distinct phenomena—those with form, those without form, compounded, uncompounded, and so on—and they experience in one-pointed concentration the joy of the quality of abiding in the absence of attributes. This is the second benefit. These two are the qualities related to sustained calm.

Of the two qualities related to profound insight, the first is the bodhisattvas' attainment of the undifferentiated light of Dharma, of the boundless presentations of the Dharma of transmission, the vision of all the knowable phenomena in the ten directions and three times, all phenomena being a single taste in the absence of attributes. The second sign is the manifest appearance, without checking for them, of the signs corresponding to the stages of purity.

The benefit that appertains to both sustained calm and profound insight is that the bodhisattva increasingly takes hold of elimination and realization, which are the causes of liberation and of the body of truth respectively.

The nature of these five has already been explained.[20] Since these five benefits have to be seen with the bodhisattvas' own inner experience, they may be treated as signs of the levels. Sthiramati's commentary explains three of these benefits and then concludes, so it is incomplete.[21]

vii. The Etymological Definitions of the Levels

> When they see they are approaching enlightenment
> And accomplishing beings' goals,
> They will feel the greatest joy.
> Because of that, it is called Perfect Joy. (XXI, 32)

When bodhisattvas see that they are approaching their own goal, the attainment of unsurpassable enlightenment (in other words, when they see that they are certain to attain it), and that they can accomplish the goals of other sentient beings, they feel extremely happy. For this reason, the first level is called Perfect Joy.

> Because they are free of the contamination of broken vows
>   and misplaced efforts,
> This level is called Immaculate.
> Because they make the great light of Dharma shine,
> It is called Luminous. (XXI, 33)

On the second level, bodhisattvas are free of contamination by breaches of discipline and by attentiveness and efforts related to the lower vehicles, so this level is called Immaculate. On the third level, by the power of their concentration, they receive infinite teachings and moreover make the great light of the Dharma shine for others, so this level is called Luminous.

> Because they have the hotly burning light,
> This Dharma leading to enlightenment,

---

20. See ch. 15, vv. 19–22.
21. The Tibetan translation of Sthiramati's commentary appears to have been made from an incomplete version of the Sanskrit.

> This level, burning up the two,
> Is known as Radiant. (XXI, 34)

On the fourth level, they thus have the teachings that lead to enlightenment, whose practice is like a light completely burning up the defilement-related and cognitive obscurations. So this level, in burning up the two obscurations, is called Radiant.

> **Because they bring sentient beings to maturity**
> **And also guard their own minds,**
> **It is difficult for the wise to train,**
> **So it is called Hard to Conquer. (XXI, 35)**

On the fifth level, through their realization of the four truths, they bring sentient beings to full maturation and, putting up with beings' ingratitude, they protect their own minds. These two are difficult to do, so because the wise take on this difficult training, this level is called Hard to Conquer.[22]

> **As bodhisattvas rely on transcendent wisdom,**
> **Both saṃsāra and nirvāṇa**
> **Become clearly manifest here,**
> **So this level is called Clearly Manifest. (XXI, 36)**

On the sixth level, bodhisattvas rely on transcendent wisdom, and on this level the nature of both saṃsāra (the result of dependent arising in the forward order) and nirvāṇa (the result of the reverse process) becomes clearly manifest, so they dwell in neither saṃsāra nor nirvāṇa. For this reason, it is called the Clearly Manifest level.

> **Because it is connected to the sole path to tread,**
> **This level is known as Far Progressed.**
> **Because it is unmoved by the two kinds of apprehension,**
> **It is called Immovable. (XXI, 37)**

Because the seventh level is connected to the eighth level, the sole path to

---

22. "Hard to Conquer" translates the Sanskrit name of this level, *sudurjayā*, translated into Tibetan as *shyang dka'*, which can also mean "difficult to train in."

tread, coming immediately before the latter, and because it is the culmination of practice with effort, it is held to be the Far Progressed level.

On the eighth level, nonconceptual gnosis is spontaneously accomplished, unmoved by either the apprehension of attributes up to the sixth level or the effortful apprehension of absence of attributes, so it is called Immovable.

> Because of their excellent intelligence, with perfect
>   knowledge,
> That level is Perfect Intellect.
> Because the immensity of their sky-like minds is filled
> With the two like clouds, it is Cloud of Dharma. (XXI, 38)

Bodhisattvas on the ninth level possess the excellent, especially sublime intelligence related to the four kinds of perfect knowledge, so for this reason that level is known as Perfect Intellect.

On the tenth level, like great clouds filling the sky, the cloud-like, boundless doors of powers of retention and concentration fill the whole immensity of the sky-like expanse of reality of the bodhisattva's mind stream, so this level is called Cloud of Dharma.

> Because they constantly and joyfully abide
> In the various practices of virtue,
> The levels of those bodhisattvas
> Are considered to be "states of abiding." (XXI, 39)

What is meant by the "states of abiding" of the bodhisattvas dwelling on these ten levels? Because bodhisattvas constantly abide with joyful minds in the boundless, multifarious practices of virtue related to the two accumulations that are included in those different levels, the bodhisattva levels are held to be "states of abiding."

> On them, the fears of countless beings are removed;
> On them, there's ever higher progress.
> For these reasons, those immeasurable states
> Are considered to be levels. (XXI, 40)

Why do we speak of "levels"? In ordinary, mundane terms, the Sanskrit word *bhūmi*, meaning "the ground," is the support for the infinite sentient beings, grasses and trees, forests, and so on. They are supported by it and thus have no fear of falling, and it is the medium on which they can travel from one place and sphere of activity to another. In the same way, the bodhisattva levels are the supports and dwelling places of infinite beings to be trained. They are the places where they are rendered fearless; they provide the medium on which they can go or progress further and further, higher and higher, on those stages associated with the infinite qualities of increasingly higher levels. It is for these two reasons that these bodhisattvas' states of abiding are held to be levels.

viii. Four Ways of Attaining the Levels

> Attainment of the levels is fourfold:
> By means of interest,
> By engagement in activities,
> By realization, and by accomplishment. (XXI, 41)

There are four ways in which bodhisattvas attain the levels: (1) by acquiring interest in the meaning of the Great Vehicle, corresponding to the level of earnest aspiration; (2) by acquiring the conduct on that same level of earnest aspiration[23]—namely, engaging in the ten Dharma activities;[24] (3) by attaining realization on the first to seventh levels, realizing the meaning of the Dharma; and (4) by acquiring accomplishment on the three pure levels, effortlessly accomplishing nonconceptual gnosis. These make four different ways of attaining the levels, by means of interest, activity, realization, and accomplishment.

> The four activities of the steadfast
> Were taught in accordance with a sūtra
> In order to inspire beings interested in the Great Vehicle,

---

23. These first two ways refer to the two components of the term "earnest aspiration" (Tib. *mos pa spyod pa*, lit. "practice with interest"): interest or faith (*mos pa*) and practice or conduct (*spyod pa*).

24. The ten Dharma activities (Tib. *chos spyod bcu*) are copying the scriptures, making offerings (i.e., venerating the Three Jewels), giving generously to others, listening to the teachings, reading them, committing them to memory, explaining them to others, performing the daily recitations of prayers and scriptures, reflecting on the meaning of the teachings, and meditating on them.

To inspire those interested in lower vehicles,
To inspire those interested in both,
And in order to subdue beings. (XXI, 42)

A detailed account of the activities that lead to enlightenment would be infinitely long, but in brief they can be summarized as follows. The activities of the six transcendent perfections were taught for those beings who are interested in the Great Vehicle. The activities of the thirty-seven elements leading to enlightenment were taught mainly for those who are interested in the lower vehicles. The activities of preternatural knowledge were taught in order to inspire both of these kinds of beings as a gateway to attaining powers. And the activities of the four ways of gathering disciples were taught in order to subdue beings and bring them to maturation. These four bodhisattva activities are explained in the *Sūtra of the Questions of Ratnacūḍa* and have been presented in this treatise too following that sūtra.

This concludes the section explaining the paths and levels that constitute the approach to enlightenment. There now follows a series of verses praising the qualities of the result, great enlightenment, which has already been explained above. These verses describe the qualities obtained as the result once the ten levels have been traversed, beginning with the qualities of the four boundless attitudes and ending with those of the six transcendent perfections. Finally, there are two verses that distinguish the characteristics of the buddha level.

4. In Praise of the Ultimate Qualities
In Praise of the Buddha's Four Boundless Attitudes

To you possessed of love for sentient beings,
Who wish them to encounter and be free,
Who wish them to never be deprived,
And who wish for their benefit and happiness, I pay homage.
(XXI, 43)

"Possessed of constant love for sentient beings"[25] is a general indication. Specifically, boundless love is the enlightened intention or wish that sentient beings encounter happiness; boundless compassion is the enlightened

---

25. The word "constant" is Mipham's own addition to this quotation from the root text.

intention that they be free from suffering; and boundless joy is the enlightened intention that they be never deprived of happiness. These three constitute the enlightened intention that beings be happy. Boundless impartiality is the enlightened intention or wish that they remain impartial, without the defilements of attachment and aversion. So, with great respect physically, verbally, and mentally, the author pays homage to the Buddha, to him[26] who has this enlightened intention to bring benefit and happiness to all sentient beings.

The Eight Perfect Freedoms, Eight Kinds of Perceptual Domination, and Ten Powers of Perceptual Limitlessness[27]

> Capable One, definitively released from all obscuration,
> Dominant over all worlds,
> Your knowledge pervades all that can be known.
> To you whose mind is free, I pay homage. (XXI, 44)

The eight perfect freedoms (from the perfect freedom of form beholding form to the perfect freedom of cessation), the eight kinds of perceptual domination related to shapes and colors (for example, perceiving oneself as physically embodied, to have power over smaller external physical forms), and the ten powers of perceptual limitlessness (which are associated with earth, water, fire, wind, space, consciousness, blue, yellow, white, and red)— all these constitute the path of training in manifestation through concentration, which is begun with the perfect freedoms, applied with perceptual domination, and accomplished with perceptual limitlessness. These three qualities of the Buddha are spontaneously accomplished within the nature of nonconceptual gnosis and are superior to the equivalent qualities that mundane beings and listeners and solitary realizers cultivate. Not only are the eight perfect freedoms present in the Buddha's (the Capable One's) mind perfectly free from their respective counteragents, but they have also been definitively and entirely released from the influence of the two obscurations

---

26. Although, throughout this section of praise, the commentary copies the root verse's "To you . . . I pay homage," we have chosen to use the third person in order to maintain consistency with the explanation in each section of the commentary.
27. For these and the other qualities described in this section, see *Treasury of Precious Qualities*, appendix 9, 431 et seq.

and habitual tendencies. Similarly, his eight kinds of perceptual domination constitute not only dominance over shape and color but also dominance over all world systems. And not only does his perceptual limitlessness fill restricted localities with the perceptions of earth and other elements, but the Victorious One's knowledge pervades all knowable phenomena. Homage is therefore paid to him whose mind is free of all obscuring factors—those that obscure meditative absorption, obscurations related to the defilements, and cognitive obscurations.

The Nonarising of Defilement

> To you who destroy every defilement
> In all sentient beings,
> Who act to overcome defilements
> And are imbued with love for those with defilements, I pay homage. (XXI, 45)

The listeners and solitary realizers, with reference to themselves, can only guard against causing defilements to arise in other sentient beings. The Tathāgata's nonarising of defilement, on the other hand, can destroy all the defilements without exception in the minds of all beings. Proceeding deliberately for the sake of those beings in whom defilements have arisen, he acts to overcome their defilements. Homage is paid to him who is imbued with love for all sentient beings with defilements.

Knowledge of Wishes and Aspirations

> Spontaneous, free of attachment,
> Without impediment, constantly in meditation—
> To you who give answers to all questions,
> I pay homage. (XXI, 46)

When other people ask listeners questions and so on, the listeners have to specially reflect and settle evenly in concentration in order to know the answer. But they do not know all knowable phenomena without impediment; neither are they constantly in equipoise, nor are they able to answer all questions. The Buddha's knowledge of wishes and aspirations is quite different and has the following five special features. It is spontaneous and effortless. It does not have the habitual tendencies of defilements (or, alternatively, it does not require reliance on meditative absorption), and it is therefore free of attachment. Because he has eliminated cognitive obscurations, it is without impediment. He never moves from constant equipoise. And he answers all the questions sentient beings may ask. So it is to him, the Buddha, that homage is paid.

The Four Kinds of Perfect Knowledge

> With regard to what is explained—the support and supported—
> And what is used to explain—your words and knowledge—
> Your mind is always unimpeded.
> To you, excellent teacher, I pay homage. (XXI, 47)

The Buddha's intellect is always unimpeded with regard to what is taught (the subjects that are the support, and the meanings they support), and what it is that is used to teach (both the Buddha's words, the expressions that are understood in the languages of all sentient beings, and the unbounded confidence and eloquence that comes from his knowledge of everything there is to be known). So homage is paid to him who, by these means, perfectly teaches the sacred Dharma.

The Six Kinds of Preternatural Knowledge

> Proceeding and knowing all activities,
> You give excellent instructions,
> In their languages, on the comings and goings of beings
> And their certain deliverance. To you, I pay homage. (XXI, 48)

With his preternatural power to perform miracles, the Buddha proceeds to wherever there are beings to be trained. Then, with his knowledge of others' minds, he knows the eighty-four thousand activities in their minds. By means of the clairaudience of the divine ear, he gives excellent instruction, in the language of each of those sentient beings, on where beings in this life have come from (through the knowledge of their previous lives), on where they will be reborn in the future (through the clairvoyance of the divine eye), and on the manner of their certain deliverance from saṃsāra (through the preternatural knowledge of the exhaustion of taints). To him who has such preternatural knowledge, homage is paid.

The Thirty-Two Major Marks and Eighty Minor Marks of Excellence

> When beings see you,
> They all know you to be a holy being.
> To you, the mere sight of whom
> Creates faith, I pay homage. (XXI, 49)

When beings of all kinds see his body, they fully acknowledge or know that he is a holy being, saying, "This is a great being." Just seeing him inspires clear faith in them, and they pay homage to him.

The Four Complete Purities

> To you who have mastery
> In assuming, abiding, and relinquishing,
> In manifestation and transformation,
> In concentration, and in gnosis, I pay homage. (XXI, 50)

Because of the complete purity of the body, or support or place, the Buddha has mastery in assuming a new support, in abiding with that support for a while, and relinquishing the conditioning factor of life as he wishes. On account of the purity of objects, he has mastery in newly manifesting things that did not previously exist and in transforming things that already exist. Through the complete purity of his mind, he has mastery in concentration. And through the complete purity of his wisdom, he has mastery in inconceivable gnosis. To him, therefore, homage is paid.

The Ten Strengths

> To you who vanquish the demons
> That utterly deceive sentient beings with regard to
> The means, refuge, purity,
> And certain deliverance by the Great Vehicle, I pay homage.
> (XXI, 51)

With the strength of the knowledge of what is correct and what is incorrect, the Buddha knows what is and what is not a causal factor, and thus he vanquishes the demon that deceives beings as to the cause or means for rebirth in the higher and lower realms—overcoming, for example, the deceptive idea that things like harmful offerings and gifts, which are not the cause of higher rebirth, constitute the way to obtain happy rebirths. With the strength of knowing the fully ripened effects of actions, he shows that apart from the power of deeds, nothing, including Īśvara and similar beings, is able to afford protection on its own, and thus he destroys deceptive notions with regard to refuge. With the strength of knowing all the concentrations related to defilement and purity, he destroys deceptive notions with regard to purity—the view that one can be purified and liberated from saṃsāra simply by attaining the world of form and formless world. And with the remaining seven strengths, he vanquishes the demon that utterly deceives sentient beings with regard to certain deliverance by means of the Great Vehicle. With the strength of knowing all beings' fundamental makeup, the strength of knowing their various interests, and the strength of knowing their various mental capacities, he knows, respectively, their potential, their faith, and the different categories of faith and so forth in the beings to be trained, and hence their particularities as potential disciples. Then, with the strength of knowing past lives and the strength of knowing deaths and transmigrations, he knows the supports for the path. With the strength of knowing all paths and where they lead, he knows the nature of the path. And with the strength of knowing the exhaustion of taints, he knows the result, certain deliverance. With such knowledge, he teaches disciples accordingly, and thus he vanquishes the demon that lures beings away from certain deliverance by the path of the Great Vehicle. Homage is therefore paid to him who possesses these qualities, the ten strengths.

The Four Fearlessnesses

> To you who, for your own and others' sake,
> Show gnosis and elimination,
> Teach certain deliverance and what hinders it,
> And will never be crushed by tīrthikas and others, I pay homage. (XXI, 52)

For his own sake, the Buddha is not afraid of proclaiming his perfect realization, for he possesses omniscient gnosis, and he is not afraid of proclaiming his perfect elimination, for he is rid of the two obscurations together with their habitual tendencies. And for others' sake, he is not afraid of teaching the path, for he shows the correct path that affords certain deliverance from saṃsāra, and he is not afraid of teaching the hindrances on the path, for he indicates the hindrances or obstacle makers that interrupt the path, with authentic words of truth, saying, "The belief in a self, and defilements such as attachment, create obstacles to being liberated from saṃsāra." He will never be crushed by attacks from others who dispute that, whether they are celestial beings, demons, Brahmā, śrāmaṇeras and brahmins, or tīrthikas. It is to him that homage is paid.

Absence of Secretiveness and the Threefold Limpidity

> Never on your guard nor forgetful,
> You speak boldly in the midst of your disciples;
> To you who have eliminated the two defilements
> And gather a following, I pay homage. (XXI, 53)

The Buddha is utterly uncontaminated by faults in body, speech, and mind, so there is nothing that he needs to keep secret or be shy about, out of fear that others might come to know of it. He therefore never hides or guards any aspect of his physical, verbal, or mental conduct. Accordingly, it is not as if he deliberately forgets and ignores any faults that might have occurred. Rather, he is fearless in the midst of his disciples and teaches the Dharma with a bold voice, like a lion.

Moreover, he possesses threefold limpidity: he never feels attached to those who listen to the teachings, hostile toward those who do not listen, or attached and hostile to both those who listen and those who do not listen. So because he has eliminated both defilements—attachment and hostility—he gathers a group of followers around him. To him homage is paid.

The Complete Destruction of Habitual Tendencies

> Omniscient One, all the time,
> Whenever you move, whenever you stay,
> You have no activities in which you are not omniscient.
> To you who truly merit that name, I pay homage. (XXI, 54)

All the time, in everything he does, whether he is moving about (for such purposes as seeking alms in the villages) or staying still, perfectly settled inwardly, the Omniscient One never does anything in which he is not omniscient. In all his activities—going, sitting, and so forth—he never falls out of the state of remaining evenly in all-seeing omniscience. So he does not have even the slightest deluded, nonomniscient behavior that could be called a defect, and thus he can truly be called omniscient. To him, then, we pay homage.

Although the listener arhats have no defilements, they have not eliminated the habitual tendencies, so when they travel, they can sometimes behave in all kinds of unconsidered ways—sometimes they meet crazed elephants, chariots, and so forth; they tread on venomous snakes, lose their way in the dark, jump like monkeys, laugh loudly like horses, and so on. But this is never the case for the Buddha.

Absence of Forgetfulness

> **In acting for the sake of all beings,**
> **You are never untimely,**
> **So your deeds are always meaningful.**
> **To you who are never forgetful, I pay homage. (XXI, 55)**

Since he never misses the right moment for benefiting all beings, all his actions are always meaningful. In this respect, he never forgets beings' welfare. To him we pay homage.

Great Compassion

> **In all worlds, six times during the night and day,**
> **You look upon each and every being,**
> **Manifesting great compassion.**
> **To you whose intention is to help, I pay homage. (XXI, 56)**

In all the worlds in the ten directions, the Buddha constantly, rousing himself six times by day and night, looks on each and every being and manifests great compassion, thinking, "Who is ailing, who is flourishing, whom should I help, and how?" This is the essence of his compassion. Its function is to bring benefit to all sentient beings. So homage is paid to him who has this intention to help.

The Eighteen Distinctive Qualities

> To you who surpass
> All the listeners and solitary realizers
> In your conduct, realization, gnosis,
> And activities, I pay homage. (XXI, 57)

Six of the eighteen distinctive qualities are included in the Buddha's conduct: physically, he is free of erroneous behavior; concerning his speech, he never speaks noisily and unrestrainedly; mentally, he never loses mindfulness; his mind is never not in meditative equipoise; he does not have different kinds of discriminatory perceptions; and his equanimity never lacks discernment. Another six are included in his realization and concern his unfailing enthusiasm, diligence, mindfulness, concentration, wisdom, and perfect freedom. (Some source texts list these six with "gnosis that sees perfect freedom" instead of "concentration." These follow the intended meanings of different sūtras.) Three concern his gnosis, which penetrates the past, and likewise the present and future, unobstructedly. And three concern his activities: all the activities of his body, which are preceded and accompanied by gnosis, and likewise the activities of his speech and mind. To him who possesses these eighteen distinctive, uncommon qualities of buddhahood, and who therefore surpasses all the listeners and solitary realizers, we pay homage.

Omniscience

> With the three buddha bodies, you have attained
> Great enlightenment, in all aspects.
> To you who remove the doubts of all beings
> On every plane, I pay homage. (XXI, 58)

With the three buddha bodies, the Buddha has attained great enlightenment supreme in all aspects, or knowledge of all aspects.[28] By attaining the body of truth, he attains the expanse of reality endowed with the two purities; this is called profound manifest enlightenment. By attaining the body

---

28. Tib. *rnam pa kun mkhyen pa*, meaning "omniscience," but translated literally here to convey Mipham's interpretation of the phrase "all aspects" (*rnam pa kun*) in the root verse.

of perfect enjoyment, he acquires the four kinds of gnosis, which is called uncommon manifest enlightenment. And by attaining the manifestation body, he acts in multifarious ways for the benefit of sentient beings for as long as space endures, which is supramundane manifest enlightenment. The two aspects of the form body together constitute vast manifest enlightenment. Homage is paid to him who has thus attained great enlightenment, whose function is to remove all sentient beings' doubts on every level.

The Consummate Qualities of the Six Transcendent Perfections

> To you who have no grasping, commit no fault,
> Are undisturbed, never stay still,
> Never stir, and are free from elaborations
> With regard to all phenomena, I pay homage. (XXI, 59)

Because he has no grasping, the Buddha has completed transcendent generosity. Similarly, he has completed the transcendent perfection of discipline, for he never commits any fault; transcendent patience, for his mind is never disturbed; transcendent diligence, for he is never indifferent to beings' welfare; transcendent concentration, for he never moves from meditative absorption; and transcendent wisdom, the absence of all mental elaborations and concepts with regard to all phenomena. So to him we pay homage.

A Concise Description of the Buddha Level, Distinguishing Its Characteristics

> He has accomplished ultimate truth,
> Having been definitively released from all the levels.
> He is the highest of all beings
> And acts to liberate all sentient beings. (XXI, 60)

> Possessing unequaled, inexhaustible qualities,
> He appears in worldly realms, and in maṇḍalas,
> But is completely invisible
> To gods and humans. (XXI, 61)

The essence of the buddha level is the accomplishment of the ultimate truth or suchness in great enlightenment, endowed with twofold purity—natural purity and the purity of freedom from adventitious contaminants. Its cause is to have been definitively released from all the levels, one after the other, and to have reached their culmination. The result is that one has become the very best of all sentient beings and is without peer. Its function is to bring all beings to perfect liberation. Its property is that it possesses inexhaustible excellent qualities such as the strengths, unequaled by the listeners' and solitary realizers' enlightenment. Its manifestations or categories are the body of manifestation, in which the buddhas appear in impure worlds; the body of enjoyment, which appears in a buddha's maṇḍala to pure disciples; and the body of truth, which, however, is invisible in any form to anyone (celestial beings or humans) but the Buddha himself.

Although this completes the original text, the following single verse was added by scholars to create auspicious conditions for increasing beings' welfare.

> **Nevertheless, through his power,**
> **In accordance with the fortunes of beings**
> **And for as long as the world endures,**
> **The stream of his deeds will never cease. (XXI, 62)**

Nevertheless, by the power of the body of truth, in accordance with the fortunes of beings to be trained, and for as long as existence—that is, the world—endures, the deeds of that truth-body buddha occur uninterruptedly. This verse indicates his uninterrupted activities.

This completes the explanation of the twenty-first chapter of *Ornament of the Mahāyāna Sūtras*, the chapter on conduct and consummation.

Conclusion

The Author's Colophon

The poem entitled *Ornament of the Mahāyāna Sūtras* was composed by Ārya Maitreya.

The poem entitled *Ornament of the Mahāyāna Sūtras* was composed by Ārya Maitreya.

The Translators' Colophon

It was translated, corrected, and finalized by the learned Indian abbot Śākyasiṃha and the great reviser and translator Venerable Peltsek and others. At a later date the paṇḍita Parahita, the great brahmin Sajjana, and the monk-translator Loden Sherab explained it with a few corrections and produced a definitive version.

It was translated, corrected, and finalized by the learned Indian abbot Śākyasiṃha (Lion of the Śākyas) and the great reviser and translator Venerable Kawa Peltsek and others. Subsequently the paṇḍita Parahita, the great brahmin Sajjana, and the translator Ngok Loden Sherab explained it with a few corrections and produced a definitive version.

Lama Mipham's Colophon

Wonder!
This treatise by the sublime regent Maitreya
Includes the whole tradition of the Great Vehicle,
Obtained but rarely through merit that takes many kalpas to gain.
To teach and study it will bring the benefits
Of explaining and receiving all the Mahāyāna teachings,
The same as teaching from the Great Charioteer's *The Stage of a Bodhisattva*.

I composed this nectarous feast of teachings from the Supreme Vehicle
In order to share it with infinite beings,
With great respect for the sublime doctrine,
And out of a desire to benefit others.

With the brilliant moonlight of the virtue gathered by my efforts in this,
May the fresh night-jasmine flowers of beings' minds open,
And may the sweet scent of the excellent teachings spread everywhere,
Clearing away the cloudiness in every being's mind.

In my whole series of lives,
With Mañjuśrī and the Invincible Regent[1]
Watching me with the blossoming utpalas of their joyful eyes,
May I engage in the infinite activities of the bodhisattvas.

May all the infinite beings filling the ends of space
Set out on the path of the Supreme Vehicle
And, reaching the end of the ocean of completion, maturation, and purification,
May they attain the level of the All-Seeing One.

During the summer months of the Iron Pig year (1911) while in strict retreat reciting the mantra of the Noble Lord of Knowledge,[2] I, Mipham Jamyang Gyatso, wrote this between sessions in about forty days, taking the commentary of Ācārya Sthiramati as a basis and clarifying and condensing the meaning. May it be auspicious. Maṅgalam.

The Publisher's Colophon

Śrī Śrī Śrī Vijayanta
Invincible lord of a hundred gods in Tuṣita,
Set on the crown of the very crown of the Capable One,
Great Love, Second Conqueror, Lord of Dharma,
I bow at the feet of the Regent, lord of the tenth level.
His Excellent Speech, the great drum of the teachings,
The Dharma tradition pervading the whole of the ten directions,

---

1. Tib. *rgyal tshab mi pham pa*, another name for the regent Maitreya.
2. Tib. *rje btsun mkhyen pa'i bdag po*, a reference to Mañjuśrī.

Decorated with canopies of jeweled clouds,
Extinguishes the flames of beings' defilements.
This necklace, a diamond *ornament*
That essentializes the extensive and profound teachings
Of the many hundreds of thousands, hard to comprehend,
Of the Buddha's extensive and profound *sūtras*,
The Noble Asaṅga tied to his crown.
Many wondrous commentaries are there by earlier masters,
But this liberating *feast of the nectar of the Supreme Vehicle*
By Lord *Mipham*, sublime scholar of unimpeded intellect,
Stands alone in the eyes of fortunate beings of the three worlds.
It is an ornament for the gods and all the world,
An elegant volume of excellent meaning, like a blossoming lotus.
Therefore, with the aspiration for those who desire liberation,
In order to fulfill the wishes of the uncontaminated mind
Of the supreme refuge, the Lord, Jamyang Lama Gyaltsab,
And to increase the mind intent on enlightenment
For beings as numerous as the sky is vast,
My nephew, the monk Gelek Gyatso
And the attendant Shingkyong, with devoted diligence,
Virtuously put together the magical woodblocks,
An ornament embellishing the treasure of the Dharma
Of the four classes and ten virtuous actions,
Thus opening the door of the unstinting gift of Dharma,
Which is never exhausted for as long as space endures.
By this merit, may I and the whole infinity of other beings
Be diligent in the infinite practices of the bodhisattvas
And, having mastered the infinite qualities of elimination and realization,
May we attain the infinite buddha bodies and qualities.

I, Jamyang Lodrö Gyatso, prayed with these verses of aspiration as a publisher's colophon. May excellence increase.

May all beings find happiness and liberation.
May the Buddha's teachings spread and grow.
May all those who make this connection be reborn in a pure buddha field.
And may auspiciousness and well-being pervade all space and time.

May the light of the sun and moon of excellent explanation
Fill the whole of Jambudvīpa, and may auspiciousness and glory blaze.
May the lotus garden of study and practice blossom
And, never diminishing, increase more and more.

This is what came immediately to mind, written on the fourth day of the ninth month of the Wood Snake year (1965). Virtue!

Appendix 1: Mipham Rinpoche's Structural Outline of the *Sūtrālaṃkāra*

I. THE TITLE

II. TRANSLATOR'S HOMAGE

III. THE ACTUAL TEXT

INTRODUCTION: How the treatise was composed

THE MAIN TEXT OF THE TREATISE

Part One: What Is to Be Established: Establishing the Great Vehicle as the Buddha's Word
    Chapter 1: Establishing the Great Vehicle as the Buddha's Word: General Presentation
    Chapter 2: Establishing the Great Vehicle as the Buddha's Word: Specific Explanations
        1. Different arguments to counteract wrong ways of thinking
        2. Instructions on getting rid of wrong beliefs regarding the Great Vehicle

Part Two: What Is to Be Specifically Known
    Chapter 3: Refuge
        1. Particular features
            a. Brief presentation of the four particular features
            b. Detailed explanation of these four points in order
                i. Universality
                ii. Commitment
                    (1) The actual commitment

                (2) Analogies indicating the virtues of that commitment
                    (a) The analogy of a prince for one who is born into the supreme Buddha family
                    (b) The analogy of a great minister
            iii. Realization
            iv. Overpowering supremacy
    2. The refuge itself that has the above particular features
    3. Concluding summary
Chapter 4: The Potential
    1. An explanation of having the potential
        a. Synoptic introduction
        b. Detailed explanation of each of the points in order
            i. The existence of different potentials
            ii. The supremacy of the Mahāyāna potential
            iii. The different categories of the nature of that potential
            iv. The marks or signs of the potential
            v. A further classification of the potential
            vi. Threats to the potential
            vii. The benefits or excellence of the Mahāyāna potential
            viii. Two analogies
                (1) Gold
                (2) Precious stones
    2. An explanation of how the potential may be lacking
    3. Concluding summary of the chapter, praising the supreme potential for the Great Vehicle
Chapter 5: The Spiritual Intent: Bodhicitta
    1. Definition
    2. Classifications
        a. Classification in terms of the different levels
        b. Classification in terms of eleven elements of these different kinds of bodhicitta, beginning with the root
        c. Classification in terms of bodhicitta acquired formally and that acquired naturally
    3. Analogies for arousing bodhicitta
    4. In praise of the benefits and advantages of bodhicitta
Chapter 6: Practice
    1. General exposition of the perfect practice for accomplishing the twofold goal

2. Specific explanations of the practice for accomplishing others' goals
      a. How bodhisattvas engage in benefiting others
      b. Categories of altruistic activity
      c. The highest altruistic activity
      d. The superiority of the bodhisattvas' practice
      e. The uninterrupted nature of the practice
      f. Not being discouraged by others' ingratitude when acting for their benefit
   3. Concluding summary showing the greatness of the practice

Part Three: What Is to Be Reflected Upon
   Chapter 7: Thatness
      1. The defining characteristics of thatness
      2. Establishing thatness: proving the two kinds of no-self by reasoning
         a. Proving the absence of self in the individual
         b. Showing the absence of self in phenomena
      3. The stages by which the ultimate, thatness, is realized
   Chapter 8: Powers
      1. The essence of the powers
      2. The causal factors that lead to preternatural knowledge
      3. The results of accomplishing preternatural knowledge
      4. The functions of preternatural knowledge
      5. The qualities of possessing preternatural knowledge
      6. Categories of preternatural knowledge or power and how they are used to benefit beings
      7. Conclusion showing the greatness of the qualities of the bodhisattvas' powers
   Chapter 9: Full Maturation
      1. Maturing oneself
         a. Brief introduction
         b. Detailed explanation
            i. Delight
            ii. Faith
            iii. Peace
            iv. Compassion
            v. Forbearance

        vi. A sharp mind
        vii. Power
        viii. Immunity to beguilement
        ix. Possession of the branches
     c. Summary
        i. Maturing oneself
        ii. An analogy for maturation
  2. Bringing others to maturity
     a. Categories
     b. The special qualities of their intention
     c. The special qualities of their application
        i. Generosity
        ii. Discipline
        iii. Patience
        iv. Diligence
        v. Concentration
        vi. Wisdom
        vii. Summary

Part Four: The Inconceivable, That Which Is beyond Reflection
  Chapter 10: Enlightenment
     1. Brief introduction in terms of enlightenment being the ultimate attainment
     2. Detailed explanation of the nature of great enlightenment
        a. A general exposition in terms of ten qualities
           i. The quality of inconceivability
           ii. The quality of fulfillment of the two goals
           iii. The quality of being the supreme refuge
               (1) The accomplishment of one's own goal
               (2) The accomplishment of others' goals
               (3) Establishing the enlightened state as the incomparable refuge, on account of its twofold accomplishment
           iv. The quality of transformation
               (1) An explanation of transformation itself
               (2) An explanation of its superiority
                   (a) How the Buddha's transformation is superior to the listeners' and solitary realizers' transformation

    (b) Ten divisions of the qualities of the Buddha's transformation
  v. The quality of all-pervasiveness
    (1) The main explanation of how the enlightened state pervades all entities of time and space
    (2) Clarification of a doubt
  vi. The quality of performing deeds spontaneously and nonconceptually
  vii. The quality of the inestimable profundity of the expanse that is the enlightened state
    (1) Profound characteristics
      (a) The characteristic of perfect purity
      (b) The characteristic of the enlightened state being the sublime "self"
      (c) The characteristic of inexpressibility
      (d) The characteristic of perfect liberation
    (2) Profound abiding
    (3) Profound activities
      (a) Activities related to enlightenment, like a mine of gems
      (b) The activity of bringing sentient beings to full maturity
      (c) The activity leading to ultimate perfection
      (d) The activity of teaching the Dharma
      (e) Activities such as manifestation
      (f) Activities of the manifestation of gnosis
      (g) Nonconceptuality in the buddhas' activities
      (h) The activity of instantly knowing multifarious aspects
      (i) The activity of gnosis being inaccessible
      (j) Differences in the activity of gnosis despite equality in terms of perfect liberation
      (k) Concluding summary of these three aspects of profundity
  viii. The quality of its unchanging essence—the changeless expanse of reality, suchness
  ix. The quality of its boundless attainments
    (1) The superiority of the Buddha's attainments

  (2) An enumeration of different categories of those attainments
 x. The quality of bringing sentient beings to maturity
  (1) How beings are brought to maturity
  (2) The individuals that are brought to maturity
  (3) The various deeds or means by which beings are brought to maturity
  (4) Nonconceptuality in maturing beings
  (5) Impartiality in maturing beings
  (6) Maturing beings in a chain reaction
  (7) How maturation continues unceasingly without ever reaching a sufficiency and without increase or diminution
b. A presentation of great enlightenment in terms of six aspects
 i. The actual presentation
 ii. A specific explanation of its manifestations
  (1) An explanation of the supports, the three buddha bodies
   (a) Brief introduction
   (b) Detailed explanation
    (i) Individual explanations of the three buddha bodies
     1. The body of perfect enjoyment
     2. The natural body or body of truth
     3. The Buddha's manifestation body
    (ii) Explanation of the inclusiveness, equality, and eternity of the buddha bodies
  (2) An explanation of the four kinds of gnosis that are supported
   (a) Brief introduction
   (b) Detailed explanation of each of the four kinds of gnosis
    (i) Mirrorlike gnosis
    (ii) The gnosis of equality
    (iii) All-discerning gnosis
    (iv) All-accomplishing gnosis
   (c) The causes for acquiring the four kinds of gnosis
    (i) The ripening causes

                1. Main explanation
                2. Additional points
            (ii) The cause for attaining complete purity
        (d) Showing that the culmination of all paths is the Buddha's gnosis
    3. Concluding summary of the chapter with a verse in praise of great enlightenment as an instruction for arousing bodhicitta

Recapitulation listing the first ten chapters

Part Five: The Approach to Enlightenment
   Preliminaries
      Chapter 11: Interest
         1. General description of the categories of interest
            a. Twenty-six categories of interest
            b. Sixteen obstacles to interest
            c. Eleven benefits of having interest
         2. Specific explanation of interest in the Great Vehicle
            a. Showing by similes the superiority of interest in the Great Vehicle
            b. Instructions on following the Great Vehicle enthusiastically without getting discouraged
                i. Following the Great Vehicle without getting discouraged
                ii. Following the Great Vehicle enthusiastically because it gives rise to immense merit
                iii. A summary on following the Great Vehicle in terms of three virtues
      Chapter 12: Thorough Investigation
         1. The Dharma that has to be investigated
            a. Investigating the Dharma of transmission that is to be expounded
                i. Thorough investigation of the subject, the Buddha's Excellent Words
                ii. Thorough investigation in discovering the point, the meaning indicated by the three scriptural collections
                iii. Thorough investigation of the investigator, attentiveness

(1) Attentiveness associated with the three families
(2) Attentiveness associated with performing activities
(3) Attentiveness associated with different kinds of support or condition
(4) Attentiveness associated with maintaining interest
(5) Attentiveness associated with enthusiasm
(6) Attentiveness associated with remaining in concentration
(7) Attentiveness associated with knowledge
(8) Attentiveness associated with considering the teachings in combination
(9) Attentiveness associated with considering things separately
(10) Attentiveness associated with the certainty of complete knowledge
(11) Attentiveness associated with the object of meditation
(12) Attentiveness associated with the nature of the two paths
(13) Attentiveness associated with excellence or benefits
(14) Attentiveness associated with correctly receiving instructions and follow-up teachings
(15) Attentiveness associated with application
(16) Attentiveness associated with mastery
(17) Attentiveness associated with the lesser vehicles, the paths of the listeners and solitary realizers
(18) Attentiveness associated with the Great Vehicle, the vast path of the bodhisattvas

b. Investigating the Dharma whose meaning is to be realized
  i. Investigating the thatness of phenomena
  ii. Investigating the illusion-like nature of phenomena
  iii. Investigating knowable phenomena
  iv. Investigating defilement and purity
  v. Investigating mere awareness
  vi. Investigating different realities

vii. Investigating perfect liberation
viii. Investigating absence of intrinsic existence
ix. Investigating the acceptance that phenomena are unborn
x. Investigating the intention in teaching a single vehicle
xi. Investigating the five sciences
2. The different forms of attentiveness used in investigation
3. Specific kinds of thorough investigation
4. The results of investigating the Dharma
   a. The accomplishment of good qualities
   b. Riddance of concepts that have to be eliminated
5. Concluding summary stating the importance of thoroughly investigating the Dharma

Chapter 13: Teaching the Dharma
1. Showing why it is worth teaching others the Dharma unstintingly
2. The reason for teaching the Dharma
3. How to teach the Dharma
   a. The manner in which bodhisattvas teach the Dharma
      i. Different ways of teaching
      ii. The excellence of the import
      iii. The excellence of the words
   b. The manner in which the buddhas teach the Dharma
4. The nature of the Dharma that is taught
   a. The general characteristics of the Dharma
   b. A specific explanation of the implied and indirect teachings
      i. An explanation of the four indirect teachings
      ii. An explanation of the four implied teachings
      iii. Eight sayings intended as antidotes, together with their benefits
5. A summary in praise of the virtues of teaching the Dharma

Chapter 14: Practicing the Dharma
1. General presentation
   a. Full knowledge of meanings
   b. Knowledge of the way
   c. Practicing the way consistent with realization
   d. Entrance into conformity

                e. Cultivation of consistent realization
            2. Detailed explanation
                a. The conditions for practicing
                b. The essence of the practice
                    i. Brief synopsis
                        (1) Nonconceptual wisdom
                        (2) The skillful means of never abandoning sentient beings
                    ii. Further detailed explanations of nonconceptual wisdom and great love
                        (1) Nonconceptual wisdom
                        (2) The love and compassion that never forsakes sentient beings
                c. Similes for how bodhisattvas practice
            3. Summary
        Chapter 15: Instructions and Follow-Up Teachings
            1. How the instructions are acquired
            2. Keeping the meanings of the instructions properly in mind
                a. Keeping the instructions in mind by reflecting
                b. Keeping the instructions in mind by meditating
            3. How bodhisattvas progress further along the path
            4. A description of the great benefits of the instructions and follow-up teachings

Intermediate Summary

Main Explanation
    Chapter 16: Skillful Activity
        1. The activities that are to be embraced by skillful means
        2. The three aspects of skillful means that embrace those activities
    Chapter 17: Transcendent Perfections and Ways of Attracting Disciples
        1. The six transcendent perfections that enable one to complete the buddha qualities oneself
            a. Brief outline
            b. Detailed explanation

i. Establishing the definitive number of the transcendent perfections
  ii. The defining characteristics of the transcendent perfections
  iii. The order of the six transcendent perfections
  iv. The etymological definitions of each of the six transcendent perfections
  v. How the transcendent perfections are practiced
  vi. Detailed classifications
  vii. All positive practices are included in the six transcendent perfections
  viii. Avoiding factors that are incompatible with the transcendent perfections
  ix. The excellent qualities of the six transcendent perfections
  x. Determining the interrelationships of the six transcendent perfections
 2. An explanation of the four ways of attracting disciples that bring other sentient beings to maturation
  a. Definitions
  b. The definitive number of the ways of attracting disciples
  c. The functions of the four ways of attracting disciples
  d. Categories of the four ways of attracting disciples
   i. Classification into two groups
   ii. Classification into three categories
  e. The benefits of the four ways of attracting disciples
 3. Concluding summary of the six transcendent perfections and the four ways of attracting disciples
Chapter 18: Offering, Reliance, and Boundless Attitudes
 1. Making offerings to the buddhas
 2. Reliance on a spiritual master
  a. How to follow a spiritual master
   i. Brief introduction
   ii. Detailed explanation
  b. Categories
  c. The best way to follow a spiritual master
 3. Meditating on the four boundless attitudes
  a. Explanation of the four boundless attitudes

i. Essence
ii. The objects of the four boundless attitudes
iii. Categories
iv. Result
v. Countering factors
vi. Good qualities
b. A specific explanation of compassion
i. The objects of bodhisattvas' compassion
ii. The results of considering sentient beings with compassion
iii. The function of compassion associated with wisdom
iv. Categories of compassion
v. The particular qualities of great compassion
(1) Main explanation
(2) The greatness of great compassion indicated by the use of analogies
vi. In praise of the qualities of compassion
(1) A general exposition in three parts
(a) The emergence of great qualities
(b) The quality of nonattachment
(c) The quality of sublimity
(2) A specific explanation of points that are difficult to understand
vii. An explanation of the causal factors that give rise to compassion
viii. The superiority of a bodhisattva's compassion in terms of its being equal
ix. The best compassion
4. Conclusion to the chapter on offering, reliance, and boundless attitudes

Chapter 19: Elements Leading to Enlightenment
1. Prerequisites
a. A sense of shame
i. The specific characteristics of a sense of shame
ii. Shameful ways
iii. Categories of a sense of shame, superior and inferior
iv. The disadvantages of not having a sense of shame and decency

              v. The benefits of having a sense of shame and decency
              vi. In praise of those who have a sense of shame and
                  decency
              vii. The signs of having a sense of shame and decency
              viii. The best sense of shame and decency
          b. Steadfastness
              i. Brief introduction
              ii. Detailed explanation of three particular features of
                  steadfastness
                  (1) Specific characteristics of steadfastness
                  (2) Categories of steadfastness
                  (3) Immutability
          c. Indefatigability
          d. Knowledge of the treatises
          e. Knowledge of the world
          f. Knowledge of the four reliances
          g. The four kinds of perfect knowledge
          h. The two accumulations
    2. The essence of the path or training
          a. A detailed explanation of the thirty-seven elements leading
              to enlightenment
              i. The four close mindfulnesses
              ii. The four genuine restraints
              iii. The four bases of miraculous powers
              iv. The five powers
              v. The five irresistible forces
              vi. The seven branches of enlightenment
                  (1) Classification in terms of time
                  (2) Classification in terms of bodhisattvas'
                      knowledge
                  (3) Classification as seven
                  (4) Classification of the seven branches as five
              vii. The eightfold noble path
          b. Summary, an analysis of sustained calm and profound
              insight
    3. Branches that enhance the practice
          a. Skill in the means that enable one to accomplish the great
              meaning unfailingly and with little difficulty

- b. The power of memory that never forgets teachings previously received
- c. Prayers of aspiration that enable one to acquire good qualities in the future
- d. An explanation of concentration and the four summaries of the Dharma that make the path completely pure
  - i. An explanation of the three kinds of concentration (the subject)
  - ii. An explanation of the four summaries of the Dharma (the object to be understood through concentration)
    - (1) Establishing impermanence
      - (a) General exposition
      - (b) Detailed explanation
        - (i) The impermanence of inner compounded phenomena
        - (ii) The impermanence of outer compounded phenomena
    - (2) Establishing the individual no-self

Conclusion to the chapter

Chapter 20: Qualities

1. The qualities that are accomplished
   - a. A general presentation of three groups of qualities
   - b. Detailed explanation
     - i. Wondrous qualities
     - ii. The not so wondrous
     - iii. The attitude of sameness
     - iv. Bringing benefit
       - (1) Benefiting by means of the six transcendent perfections
       - (2) Seven similes for how bodhisattvas bring benefit
     - v. Reciprocal benefit
     - vi. Different forms of hope
     - vii. The quality of their practice never going to waste
     - viii. Authentic application
     - ix. Diminution and enhancement
     - x. Distinctions between the imitative and the authentic
     - xi. Correction
     - xii. Different kinds of personal prediction

xiii. Certainty
xiv. Different kinds of definite duties
xv. Perpetual duties
xvi. Paramount duties
xvii. The qualities of learning: how teaching the Dharma is presented
   (1) How the different aspects of the Dharma that is to be taught are presented
      (a) How the teachings are presented
      (b) How the truth is presented
      (c) How the four kinds of rational application are presented
      (d) How the three vehicles are presented
   (2) How the meaning of the Dharma that has to be completely understood is presented
   (3) How the immeasurable qualities of the bodhisattva who teaches are presented
   (4) How the result of teaching the Dharma is presented
   (5) How the features that distinguish the Great Vehicle are presented, along with a summary
2. Qualities that are highly praised
   a. Categories of bodhisattvas as objects of praise
   b. The actual praise: praising the characteristics of these five kinds of bodhisattvas
      i. A praise based on the significance of the word "bodhisattva" from the point of view of their irreversible strength of mind in practicing the causal factors, the transcendent perfections
         (1) A praise in terms of nine categories beginning with delight in enlightenment
         (2) An indication of the different names of a bodhisattva
      ii. The qualities that are praised in accordance with the significance of the word "bodhisattva" from the point of view of their realization of the result, enlightenment
         (1) The actual praise

(2) Showing them to be bodhisattvas in terms of eleven categories of knowledge

Chapter 21: Conduct and Consummation
  1. The signs of a bodhisattva
  2. How bodhisattvas take birth as sentient beings
  3. An explanation of the levels on which the bodhisattvas abide
     a. Brief introduction
     b. Detailed explanation
        i. The defining characteristics of the levels
        ii. A presentation of the individuals who dwell on the ten levels
        iii. How bodhisattvas complete the training in the three trainings on the ten levels
        iv. How the five untainted aggregates are purified on the levels
        v. How qualities are accomplished and not accomplished
        vi. The signs of attaining the levels
            (1) The actual signs
            (2) The qualities of the levels that bear those signs
        vii. The etymological definitions of the levels
        viii. Four ways of attaining the levels
  4. In praise of the ultimate qualities

IV. CONCLUSION
  Author's colophon
  Translators' colophon
  Lama Mipham's concluding poem and colophon
  Publisher's colophon

# Appendix 2: The Five Bodhisattva Paths and the Thirty-Seven Elements Leading to Enlightenment

The Five Bodhisattva Paths

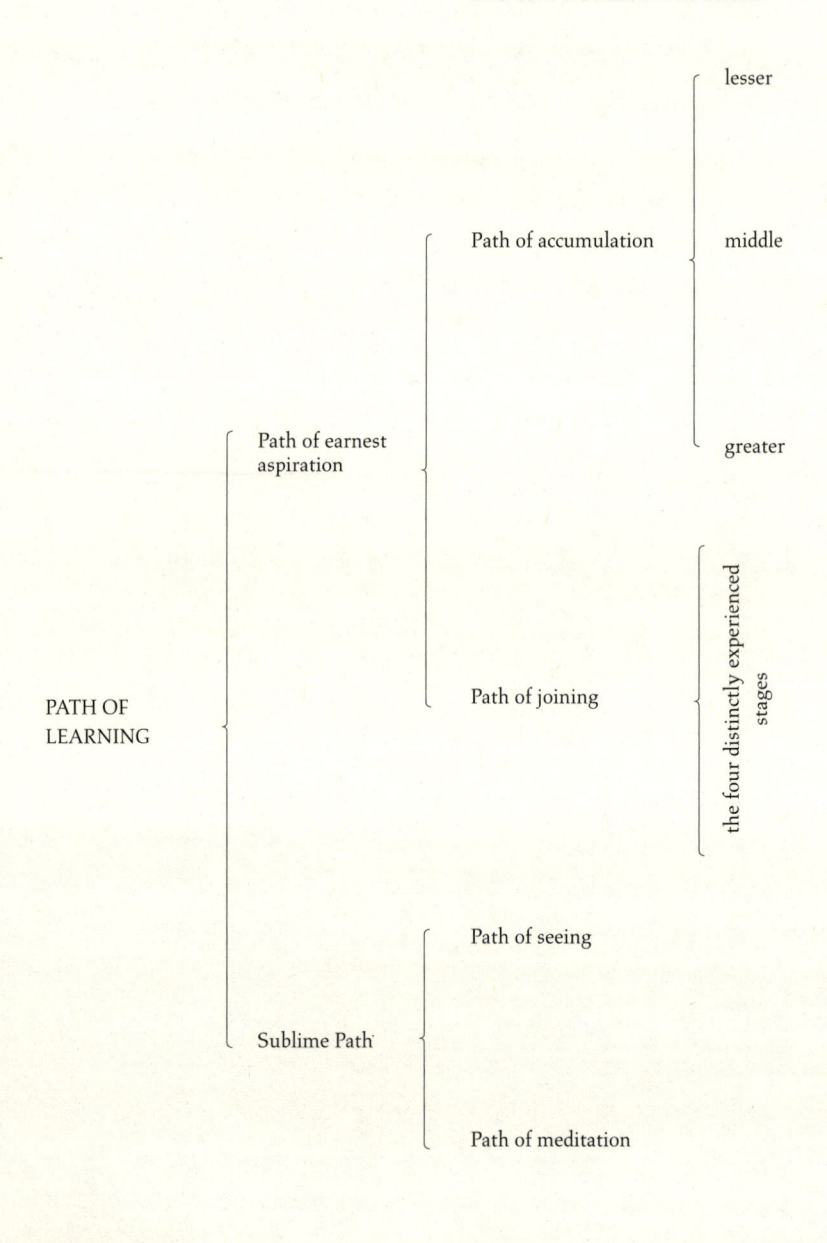

PATH OF LEARNING
- Path of earnest aspiration
  - Path of accumulation
    - lesser
    - middle
    - greater
  - Path of joining
- Sublime Path
  - Path of seeing
  - Path of meditation

the four distinctly experienced stages

PATH OF NO MORE LEARNING
- Path of no more learning

The Thirty-seven Elements Leading to Enlightenment

Four close mindfulnesses
- 1 mindfulness of the body
- 2 mindfulness of feelings
- 3 mindfulness of consciousness
- 4 mindfulness of mental objects

Four genuine restraints
- 5 avoidance of nonvirtuous factors not yet occurred
- 6 elimination of nonvirtuous factors already arisen
- 7 production of virtuous factors already arisen
- 8 development of virtuous factors already produced

Four bases of miraculous powers
- 9 keenness
- 10 diligence
- 11 attention
- 12 analysis

warmth / peak — Five powers
- 13 faith
- 14 diligence
- 15 mindfulness
- 16 concentration
- 17 wisdom

acceptance / supreme mundane level — Five irresistible forces
- 18 faith
- 19 diligence
- 20 mindfulness
- 21 concentration
- 22 wisdom

1st Bodhisattva level — Seven branches of enlightenment
- 23 mindfulness
- 24 perfect discernment
- 25 diligence
- 26 joy
- 27 fitness
- 28 concentration
- 29 evenness

2nd–10th Bodhisattva levels — Eightfold Noble Path
- 30 right view
- 31 right thought
- 32 right speech
- 33 right conduct
- 34 right livelihood
- 35 right effort
- 36 right mindfulness
- 37 right concentration

Appendix 3: The Three Worlds and Six Realms

World of formlessness		Gods of the world of formlessness
World of form	Gods	The seventeen classes of gods of the world of form
		The six classes of gods of the world of desire
	Demigods	
	Humans	
World of desire	Animals	
	Hungry spirits	
	Hells	

The four formless realms at the peak of existence		Sphere of neither existence nor nonexistence Sphere of Utter Nothingness Sphere of Infinite Consciousness Sphere of Infinite Space
The five pure abodes		Unsurpassed (Akaniṣṭha) Good Vision Manifest Richness Without Distress Not Greater
The twelve ordinary realms of the four concentrations	Fourth concentration	Great Result Merit-Born Cloudless Light
	Third concentration	Flourishing Virtue Limitless Virtue Lesser Virtue
	Second concentration	Clear Light Measureless Light Dim Light
	First concentration	Great Pure Ones Priests of Brahma The Pure
Gods of the four sky abodes		Mastery over Others' Creations Enjoying Magical Creations The Joyous Realm (Tushita) Heaven Free of Conflict (Yama)
Gods on top of Mount Meru Gods on the steps of Mt. Meru		Heaven of the Thirty-Three Four Great Kings

Demigods

Humans of the four continents

Animals living in the depths
Animals that live scattered in different places

Hungry spirits who live collectively
Hungry spirits who move through space

The eight hot hells
The neighboring hells
The eight cold hells
The ephemeral hells

Glossary

Abhidharma (Skt.), Tib. *chos mngon pa*. One of the three scriptural collections; the branch of the Buddha's teachings that deals mainly with psychology and logic.
aggregates, see five aggregates.
antidote, Tib. *gnyen po*. Also called remedy or remedial method. Any means used for eliminating defilements and other factors that hinder the attainment of happiness and enlightenment.
arhat (Skt.), Tib. *dgra bcom pa*, lit. "one who has vanquished the enemy" (the enemy being defilements). A practitioner of the Lesser Vehicle (that is, a listener or solitary realizer) who has attained the cessation of suffering, i.e., nirvāṇa, but not the perfect buddhahood of the Great Vehicle.
attentiveness, Tib. *yid la byed pa*. Deliberate mental activity directed onto a particular object or topic. In this translation we have used "to keep in mind" to convey its verbal form.
bhagavān (Skt.), Tib. *bcom ldan 'das*. An Indian term of veneration for someone of high spiritual attainment, used in Buddhism as an epithet of the Buddha. In its Tibetan translation, which might be conveyed in English as "Transcendent, Virtuous Conqueror," it is defined as "he who has overcome (*bcom*) the four demons, who possesses (*ldan*) the six excellent qualities, and who does not dwell in either of the two extremes of saṃsāra and nirvāṇa but has gone beyond them (*'das*)."
bodhicitta (Skt.), Tib. *byang chub kyi sems*. The bodhisattva's spiritual intent, the mind set on perfect enlightenment. On the relative level, it is the wish to attain buddhahood for the sake of all beings, as well as the practice of the path of love, compassion, the six transcendent perfections, and so forth, necessary for achieving that goal; on the ultimate level, it is the direct insight into the ultimate nature.
bodhisattva (Skt.), Tib. *byang chub sems dpa'*. A follower of the Great Vehicle whose aim is perfect enlightenment for all beings. One who has taken the vow of bodhicitta and practices the six transcendent perfections.
bodhisattva levels, Tib. *'phags pa'i sa*, Skt. *bhūmi*, lit. "levels of the noble ones." The ten levels of realization reached by bodhisattvas on the paths of seeing, meditation, and no more learning. In some classifications additional levels are added.
body of manifestation, Tib. *sprul sku*, Skt. *nirmāṇakāya*. The aspect of buddhahood that manifests out of compassion in all sorts of forms to help ordinary beings.

body of perfect enjoyment, Tib. *longs spyod rdzogs pa'i sku*, Skt. *saṃbhogakāya*. The spontaneously luminous aspect of buddhahood, only perceptible to highly realized beings.

body of the essential nature, Tib. *ngo bo nyid kyi sku*, Skt. *svabhāvikakāya*. Generally considered the fourth body, which is the very essence or aspect of inseparability of the body of truth, the body of perfect enjoyment, and the body of manifestation. The one mention of it in this text appears to equate it with the body of truth.

body of truth, Tib. *chos sku*, Skt. *dharmakāya*, lit. "Dharma body." Also called absolute dimension. The emptiness aspect of buddhahood.

Brahmā (Skt.), Tib. *tshangs pa*, lit. "pure." The name given to a number of gods in the world of form.

brahmin (Skt.), Tib. *bram ze*. A member of the priestly caste in Indian society.

buddha (Skt.), Tib. *sangs rgyas*. One who has dispelled (Tib. *sangs*) the darkness of the two obscurations and developed (Tib. *rgyas*) the two kinds of omniscience (knowing the nature of phenomena and knowing the multiplicity of phenomena).

buddha body, Tib. *sku*, Skt. *kāya*. An aspect or dimension of buddhahood. Generally four in number: the body of truth, body of perfect enjoyment, body of manifestation, and the body of the essential nature.

buddha field, Tib. *sangs rgyas kyi zhing khams*, also *dag pa'i zhing*. A pure land or world manifested by a buddha or great bodhisattva through the spontaneous qualities of their realization, in which beings can progress toward enlightenment without falling back into the lower realms of cyclic existence. Also, any place whatsoever, when it is perceived as a pure manifestation of spontaneous wisdom.

buddha nature, Tib. *de gshegs snying po*, Skt. *tathāgatagarbha*. Also called essence of buddhahood. The potential of buddhahood present in every sentient being.

Capable One, Tib. *thub pa*, Skt. *muni*. An epithet of the Buddha Śākyamuni, often translated as Mighty One. He was called "capable" because, when he was a bodhisattva and there was none who had the courage to tame the most unfortunate beings, with extremely gross views, defilements, and actions, he, our kind teacher, was the only one, of all the 1,002 buddhas of this Excellent Kalpa, who had the strength or capacity to vow to benefit them.

certain deliverance, Tib. *nges 'byung*, Skt. *niḥsaraṇa*. A synonym for liberation from saṃsāra.

child (of the Buddha), Tib. *rgyal sras*. An epithet for a bodhisattva.

Cittamātra (Skt.), Tib. *sems tsam*, lit. "mind-only." The teaching that the objects of the senses do not exist outside the mind and are simply projections of the mind. This doctrine was propagated in particular by the followers of the Yogācāra school. Its proponents are known as Cittamātrin (Tib. *sems tsam pa*).

collection, Tib. *sde snod*, Skt. *piṭaka*. A collection of scriptures, originally in the form of palm leaf folios stored in baskets. The Buddha's teachings are generally divided into three collections or baskets: Vinaya, Sūtra, and Abhidharma.

GLOSSARY — 873

completion, maturation, and purification, Tib. *rdzogs smin sbyang*. Three aspects of a bodhisattva's practice: completing the accumulations of merit and wisdom, bringing beings to maturity, and training in purifying the realm as a buddha field.

deeds, Tib. *las*, Skt. *karma*. Also translated in this book as "actions," or as "past deeds." Implied in the use of this term is the force created by a positive or negative action which is then stored in an individual's stream of being and persists until it is experienced as pleasure or pain (usually in another life), after which the deed is said to be exhausted or spent. Although the Sanskrit term *karma* simply means "action," it has come to be widely used to signify the result produced by past deeds (Tib. *las kyi 'bras bu*), which is sometimes wrongly equated with destiny or fate, that is, with something beyond one's control. In the Buddhist teachings, the principle of karma covers the whole process of deeds leading to results in future lives, and this is taught as being something that is very definitely within one's control.

defilement, Tib. *kun nas nyon mongs pa*, Skt. *saṃkleśa*. This term, used in apposition to purity, covers both the truth of suffering and the truth of the origin—in other words, saṃsāra and the whole process that results in saṃsāra. It is the opposite of purity.

defilement and purity, Tib. *kun nas nyon mongs pa dang rnam par byang ba*, Skt. *saṃkleśa* and *vyavadāna*. Also translated as defilement aspect and purity aspect, defilement process and purification process. The sum of defilement and purity, the two sides of the whole of phenomena seen in the context of the spiritual path. See also defilement; purity.

defilements, Tib. *nyon mongs pa*, Skt. *kleśa*. Also called afflictive emotions, negative emotions. The mental factors that influence thoughts and actions and produce suffering. The three principal defilements are bewilderment or ignorance, attachment or desire, and aversion or hatred.

demigod, Tib. *lha min*, Skt. *asura*. A class of beings whose jealous nature spoils their enjoyment of their fortunate rebirth in the higher realms and involves them in constant conflict with the gods in the god realms.

demon, Tib. *bdud*, Skt. *māra*. In the context of Buddhist meditation and practice, a demon is any factor, on the physical or mental plane, that obstructs enlightenment.

determination to be free, Tib. *nges 'byung*. Also translated as "renunciation" and, depending on context, "certain deliverance." The deeply felt wish to achieve liberation from cyclic existence. See also certain deliverance.

dhāraṇī (Skt.), Tib. *gzungs*. (1) An incantation or long mantra. (2) A bodhisattva's power of retention, often paired with eloquence, enabling them to teach the Dharma.

Dharma (Skt.), Tib. *chos*. The Buddha's doctrine; the teachings transmitted in the scriptures and the qualities of realization attained through their practice. Note that the Sanskrit word *dharma* has ten principal meanings, including "anything that can be known." Vasubandhu defines the Dharma, in its Buddhist sense, as the "protective dharma" (*chos skyobs*): "It corrects (*'chos*) every one of the enemies, the defilements; and it protects (*skyobs*) us from the lower realms: these two characteristics are absent from other spiritual traditions."

dhyāna (Skt.), Tib. *bsam gtan*. A state of concentration, especially one of the four states of concentration associated with the world of form.

downfall, Tib. *ltung ba*. A fault due to the transgression of a rule (monastic or otherwise).

eight consciousnesses, Tib. *tshogs brgyad*. The consciousnesses of the five senses, together with the mind consciousness, defiled mind consciousness, and the consciousness of the ground of all.

eight kinds of noble beings, Tib. *skye bu gang zag brgyad*. The four results of the Listeners' Vehicle—namely, stream enterer, once-returner, nonreturner, and arhat, for each of which there are two kinds: those who have entered their respective level ("candidates," Tib. *zhugs pa*) and those who are firmly established on it ("graduates," Tib. *'bras la gnas pa*), hence the alternative Tibetan term *zhugs gnas brgyad*.

eight ordinary preoccupations, Tib. *'jig rten chos brgyad*. The normal preoccupations of unrealized people without a clear spiritual perspective. They are gain and loss, pleasure and pain, praise and criticism, fame and infamy.

eloquence, Tib. *spobs pa*, Skt. *pratibhāna*. Also called brilliant eloquence, confidence and eloquence. Bodhisattvas' ability to speak from insight, realization, or the Buddha's inspiration. It implies that they are never afraid of being unable to teach. See also power of retention.

emptiness, Tib. *stong pa nyid*, Skt. *śūnyatā*. The absence of true existence (in the sense of any permanent, independent, and single entity) in all phenomena.

etymological definition, Tib. *nges tshig*. Also called literal definition, precise definition. A device used by commentators to provide a definition of a term, usually based on a breakdown of the original Sanskrit term into its component roots. This does not necessarily correspond to the way in which etymology is understood in the West.

Excellent Words, Tib. *gsung rab*, Skt. *pravacana*. Also called Excellent Speech. The words of the Buddha, the teachings that he gave.

expedient teachings, Tib. *drang don*. Teachings intended to lead unrealized beings toward the truth of the ultimate (or definitive) teachings.

extensive aspect, Tib. *rgya che ba*. Also called vast aspect. That aspect of the teachings and practice, based on the Buddha's third turning of the wheel of the Dharma and the teachings of Asaṅga and his followers, that stress the buddha nature (tathāgatagarbha) and the extensive activities, levels, and so on of the bodhisattvas.

false imagination, Tib. *yang dag pa min pa'i kun tu rtog pa*. The incorrect mental processes that lead to the imputations of subject and object and of intrinsic existence.

five aggregates, Tib. *phung po lnga*, Skt. *pañcaskandha*. The five psychophysical components into which a person can be analyzed and that together produce the illusion of a self. They are form, feeling, perception, conditioning factors, and consciousness. The term is often used to denote an individual as the basis for imputing a self.

five crimes with immediate retribution, Tib. *mtshams med lnga*, Skt. *panchanantariya*. Also called five sins with immediate effect: (1) killing one's father, (2) killing one's mother, (3) killing an arhat, (4) creating a split in the Saṅgha, and (5) malevolently causing a buddha to bleed. Someone who has committed one of these five actions takes rebirth in the Hell of Torment Unsurpassed immediately after death, without going through the intermediate state between one rebirth and the next.

five untainted aggregates, Tib. *zag med kyi phung po lnga*. Discipline, concentration, wisdom, liberation, and the aggregate of seeing the gnosis of liberation.

four noble truths, Tib. *'phags pa'i bden pa bzhi*, Skt. *caturāryasatya*. The truth of suffering, the truth of the origin of suffering, the truth of cessation, and the truth of the path. These constitute the foundation of Buddha Śākyamuni's doctrine, the first teaching that he gave (at Sarnath near Varanasi) after attaining enlightenment.

four results of the Listeners' Vehicle, Tib. *'bras bu bzhi*. Stream enterer, once-returner, nonreturner, and arhat.

four summaries of the Dharma, Tib. *chos kyi sdom bzhi*. Also called the four seals. "All that is compounded is impermanent. All that is tainted is suffering. All phenomena are devoid of self. Nirvāṇa is peace."

four kinds of gnosis, Tib. *ye shes bzhi*. Mirrorlike gnosis (*me long lta bu'i ye shes*), gnosis of equality (*mnyam pa nyid kyi ye shes*), all-discerning gnosis (*so sor kun tu rtog pa'i ye shes*), and all-accomplishing gnosis (*bya ba grub pa'i ye shes*).

gandharva (Skt.), Tib. *dri za*, lit. "one who feeds on smells." A kind of spirit that feeds on scents. Gandharvas are also classed as inhabitants of the lowest gods' realms, where they are renowned for their musical skills. The name is used as well for beings in the intermediate state: since they inhabit a mental body, they feed not on solid food but on odors.

garuḍa (Skt.), Tib. *mkha' lding*. A mythological bird, master of the skies. It traditionally preys on the nāgas.

gnosis, Tib. *ye shes*, Skt. *jñana*. Also called primal wisdom or primordial wisdom. The knowing (*shes pa*) that has always been present since the beginning (*ye nas*); awareness, clarity-emptiness, naturally dwelling in all beings.

gods, Tib. *lha*, Skt. *deva*. Also called celestial beings. A class of beings who, as a result of accumulating positive actions in previous lives, experience immense happiness and comfort and are therefore considered by non-Buddhists as the ideal state to which they should aspire. According to the Buddhist teachings, however, they have not attained freedom from cyclic existence. Those in the world of form and world of formlessness experience an extended form of the meditation they practiced (without the aim of achieving liberation from cyclic existence) in their previous life. Gods like Indra and others of the six classes of gods of the world of desire possess, as a result of their merit, a certain power to affect the lives of other beings and they are therefore worshipped, for example by Hindus. The same Tibetan and Sanskrit term is also used to refer to enlightened beings, in which case it is more usually translated as "deity."

Great Vehicle, Tib. *theg pa chen po*, Skt. *mahāyāna*. The vehicle of the bodhisattvas, referred to as great because it leads to perfect buddhahood for the sake of all beings, and because of the greatness of its object, accomplishment, gnosis, diligent application, skill in means, consummation, and activities.

ground of all, Tib. *kun gzhi* or *kun gzhi rnam par shes pa*, Skt. *ālaya*. The ground consciousness that is the basis for the other consciousnesses and in which the habitual tendencies are stored.

habitual tendencies, Tib. *bag chags*. Habitual patterns of thought, speech, or action created by one's attitudes and deeds in past lives.

heir (of the Buddha), Tib. *rgyal sras*. An epithet for a bodhisattva, also translated as "child of the Buddha."

Hell of Torment Unsurpassed, Tib. *mnar med*. The hell in which the very worst suffering is experienced, for incalculable periods of time.

hells, Tib. *dmyal ba*. One of the six realms, in which beings suffer from hallucinations of intense heat or cold, mainly as a result of violent deeds motivated by hatred.

higher realms, Tib. *mtho ris*. The gods' realms, the demigod realm, and the human realm.

immature, Tib. *byis pa*, lit. "childish." Ordinary beings who are spiritually immature.

imperceptible form, Tib. *rig byed ma yin pa'i gzugs*. An aspect of the aggregate of form asserted by certain listeners and said to comprise vows (commitment to virtue), nonvows (commitment to negative deeds), and intermediate activities (positive or negative deeds performed without conscious intention).

Indra (Skt.), Tib. *brgya byin*, "He who is honored with a hundred gifts." The ruler of the Heaven of the Thirty-Three in the realms of the gods.

intellectuals, Tib. *rtog ge ba*, Skt. *tārkika*. Also dialecticians, polemicists. A term often used pejoratively to refer to individuals who are more concerned with philosophical debate on the intellectual level than with gaining genuine spiritual realization.

Īśvara (Skt.), Tib. *dbang phyug*, lit. "Mighty Lord." A general Indian name for a creator god.

Jambudvīpa (Skt.), Tib. *dzam bu gling*, "Land of the Jambu Tree." The southern continent in the ancient Indian cosmology, the world in which we live.

kalpa (Skt.), Tib. *bskal pa*. A unit of time (of inconceivable length) used in Buddhist cosmology to describe the cycles of formation and destruction of a universe, and the ages of increase and decrease within them.

karma (Skt.), see deeds.

keep in mind, Tib. *yid la byed pa*. See attentiveness.
King of the Śākyas, Tib. *shakya'i rgyal po*. Śākyamuni, the Buddha of our era.
Lesser Vehicle, Tib. *theg pa chung* or *theg dman*, Skt. *hīnayāna*. The basic vehicle comprising the vehicles of the listeners and solitary realizers, whose ultimate result is the state of arhat. It is termed "lesser" or "lower" in comparison to the Great Vehicle.
liberation, Tib. *thar pa*. Freedom from saṃsāra, either as an arhat or as a buddha.
listener, Tib. *nyan thos*, Skt. *śrāvaka*. A follower of the Lesser Vehicle whose goal is to attain liberation for themselves as an arhat. The listeners are so called because they listen to the Buddha's teaching and then teach it to others.
lower realms, Tib. *ngan song*. The hells, the realm of hungry spirits, and the animal realm.
Mādhyamikas (Skt.), Tib. *dbu ma pa*. The followers of Nāgārjuna who adhere to the Madhyamaka, the Middle Way that avoids the extremes of existence and nonexistence.
Mahāyāna (Skt.), Tib. *theg pa chen po*. See Great Vehicle.
Maitreya (Skt.), Tib. *byams pa*, lit. "Love." One of the Buddha's eight closest bodhisattva disciples. As the future Buddha, he presently resides in the Tuṣita heaven.
major and minor marks, Tib. *mtshan dpe*. The thirty-two major marks and eighty minor marks of excellence that characterize a buddha's physical form.
Mañjuśrī (Skt.), Tib. *'jam dpal*, lit. "Gentle and Glorious." The bodhisattva who embodies the buddhas' knowledge and wisdom.
mantra (Skt.), Tib. *sngags*. In Buddhism, a manifestation of supreme enlightenment in the form of sound: a series of syllables that, especially in the sādhanas of the Secret Mantrayāna, protect the mind of the practitioner from ordinary perceptions and invoke the wisdom deities. Mantras are also used in non-Buddhist spiritual practices and as spells in black magic.
Mantrayāna. See Secret Mantrayāna.
Māra (Skt.), Tib. *bdud*. The demon, the tempter in general, that which makes obstacles to spiritual practice and enlightenment.
mental factors, Tib. *sems byung*, Skt. *caitta*. The aspects of mental function that accompany the main mind (citta), apprehending and reacting to the objects detected by consciousness.
merit, Tib. *bsod nams*, Skt. *puṇya*. The first of the two accumulations. "Merit" is also sometimes used loosely to translate the Tibetan terms *dge ba* (virtue, positive action) and *dge rtsa* (sources of good for the future).
Middle Way, Tib. *dbu ma'i lam*, Skt. *madhyamaka*. The series of teachings on emptiness based on the second turning of the wheel of the Dharma first expounded by Nāgārjuna and considered to form the basis of the Secret Mantrayāna. "Middle" in this context means that it is beyond the extremes of existence and nonexistence.
mind stream, Tib. *rgyud*, lit. "continuity" or "continuum." Also translated as

"stream of being," or simply "mind." This term denotes that aspect of an individual that continues from one moment to the next and from one lifetime to the next, and which therefore includes the individual's stock of positive and negative deeds along with their positive and negative habitual tendencies.

momentary, Tib. *skad cig ma*. This important term, also translated in its adverbial form as "from one instant to the next," does not, in the context of discussions on impermanence and emptiness, mean simply "short-lived" or "lasting only a moment." It is used in this text to denote the fact that the existence of all phenomena is made up of a succession of moments or instants that cease as soon as they arise. This succession of instants makes it possible for things to change from one moment to the next. Depending on the degree to which these changes are perceptible, things appear to last for smaller or greater lengths of time, and even to give the illusion of being permanent.

Mount Meru, Tib. *ri rgyal po ri rab*. The immense mountain, wider at the top than at the bottom, that forms the center of the universe around which the four continents of the world are disposed, according to ancient Indian cosmology.

mundane, Tib. *'jig rten pa*. The opposite of supramundane, anything that does not transcend saṃsāra. Translations of this term as "ordinary" or "worldly" can be misleading since meditators who have mastered the four dhyānas (but without being liberated from saṃsāra), and who have immense powers of concentration, magical powers, and so forth, cannot really be called "ordinary," nor are they worldly in the sense of being materialistically minded and interested only in the present world.

nāga (Skt.), Tib. *klu*. A serpent-like being (classed in the animal realm) living in the water or under the earth and endowed with magical powers and wealth. The most powerful ones have several heads. In Indian mythology they are preyed on by the garuḍas.

Nāgārjuna (Skt.), Tib. *klu sgrub*. "He whose accomplishment is related to the nāgas." The great first–second-century Indian master and father of the Profound View tradition who rediscovered the Buddha's teachings on transcendent wisdom (prajñāpāramitā) in the realm of the nāgas and composed numerous treatises that became the basic texts for the proponents of the Madhyamika or Middle Way philosophical system.

nirvāṇa (Skt.), Tib. *mya ngan las 'das pa*, lit. "beyond suffering" or "the transcendence of misery." While this can be loosely understood as the goal of Buddhist practice, the opposite of saṃsāra or cyclic existence, it is important to realize that the term is understood differently by the different vehicles. The nirvāṇa of the Lesser Vehicle, the peace of cessation that an arhat attains, is very different from a buddha's "nondwelling" nirvāṇa, the state of perfect enlightenment that transcends both saṃsāra and nirvāṇa.

nirvāṇa without residual aggregates, Tib. *phung po lhag med kyi myang 'das*. The final state of enlightenment attained when an enlightened being (an arhat or buddha) leaves their earthly body (composed of aggregates) and "passes into nirvāṇa." When listeners attain cessation in the arhat's nirvāṇa without residual aggregates, all their accumulated merit and qualities come to an end. On the other hand, the virtue and qualities that bodhisattvas accumulate never come to an end but continue to be active once they attain buddhahood.

noble being, Tib. *'phags pa*, Skt. *ārya*. Also called sublime being. An epithet applied, in the Great Vehicle, to someone who has attained the path of seeing, a bodhisattva on one of the ten bodhisattva levels. In the vehicles of the listeners and solitary realizers, it is used to refer to stream enterers, once-returners, nonreturners, and arhats.

noble levels, Tib. *'phags pa'i sa*. See bodhisattva levels.

nondwelling nirvāṇa, Tib. *mi gnas pa'i myang 'das*. The state of perfect enlightenment that transcends both saṃsāra and nirvāṇa.

nonreturner, Tib. *phyir mi 'ong ba*. In the context of the Lesser Vehicle, a state of realization where one will no longer be reborn in the desire realm. It is the stage before the attainment of the level of arhat. In the context of the Great Vehicle, a bodhisattva nonreturner is one who cannot return to a samsaric state of mind, though they may still manifest in saṃsāra to benefit beings.

no-self, Tib. *bdag med*, Skt. *anātman, nairātmya*. Also called egolessness. The absence of independent or intrinsic existence, either of oneself (Tib. *gang zag gi bdag med*) or of external phenomena (Tib. *chos kyi bdag med*).

obscurations, Tib. *sgrib pa*, Skt. *āvaraṇa*. Factors that veil one's buddha nature, maintaining one in cyclic existence and preventing one from attaining enlightenment. See also two obscurations.

parinirvāṇa (Skt.), Tib. *mya ngan 'das*. The point at which an enlightened being leaves their earthly body.

path of accumulation, Tib. *tshogs lam*. The first of the five paths, according to the Great Vehicle. On this path, one accumulates the causes that will make it possible to proceed toward enlightenment.

path of earnest aspiration, Tib. *mos spyod kyi lam*. A collective term for the paths of accumulating and joining. The level of earnest aspiration is a sort of prelevel before one reaches the first of the ten bodhisattva levels. Practitioners on the paths of accumulating and joining have not yet realized emptiness and cannot therefore practice the six transcendent perfections in a truly transcendental way. Their practice is more a question of willingness than of the genuine practice of a mature bodhisattva.

path of joining, Tib. *sbyor lam*. The second of the five paths. On this path one connects oneself to or prepares oneself for seeing the two kinds of no-self on the path of seeing.

path of meditation, Tib. *sgom lam*. The fourth of the five paths, during which a bodhisattva traverses the remaining nine of the ten levels.

path of no more learning, Tib. *mi slob pa'i lam*. The last of the five paths, the culmination of the path to perfect enlightenment—buddhahood.

path of seeing, Tib. *mthong lam*. The third of the five paths, the stage at which a bodhisattva in meditation gains a genuine experience of emptiness and attains the first of the ten levels.

peace, Tib. *zhi ba*. A synonym for the arhat's nirvāṇa, the peace of cessation.

perceptual domination, powers of, Tib. *zil gyis gnon pa'i skye mched*. Also called dominant āyatanas. The power to control and transform characteristics such as size, shape, color, and so on.

perceptual limitlessness, powers of, Tib. *zad par gyi skye mched*. Also called limitless āyatanas. The power, through concentration, to transfer the characteristics of the different elements, colors, space, and consciousness onto other elements, etc., thus enabling one to walk on water as if it were earth, for example.

perpetuating aggregates, Tib. *nyer len gyi phung po*. The five aggregates that are at the same time the result of past defilements and deeds and the causal basis of the defilements and deeds that perpetuate rebirth in saṃsāra.

power of retention, Tib. *gzungs*, Skt. *dhāraṇī*. Bodhisattvas' ability to remember unfailingly the infinite words and meanings of the Dharma, enabling them to teach for kalpas on end.

prātimokṣa (Skt.), Tib. *so sor thar pa*, lit. "individual liberation." The collective term for the different forms of Buddhist ordination and their respective vows, as laid down in the Vinaya.

profound aspect, Tib. *zab mo*. That aspect of the teachings and practice, based on the Buddha's second turning of the wheel of the Dharma and the teachings of Nāgārjuna and his followers, that stress the profound view of emptiness. See also extensive aspect.

profound insight, Tib. *lhag mthong*, Skt. *vipaśyanā*. The perception, through wisdom, of the true nature of things.

pure levels, Tib. *sa dag pa gsum*. The last three of the ten levels.

purity, Tib. *rnam par byang ba*, Skt. *vyavadāna*. Also called complete purity. This term, used in apposition to defilement, covers the truth of cessation and the truth of the path, both the purity that is nirvāṇa and the process of purification that leads to nirvāṇa. It is the opposite of defilement.

reflexive awareness, Tib. *so rang rig*. The state of nondual wisdom that, while transcending the subject-object duality, knows itself.

relative truth, Tib. *kun rdzob bden pa*, lit. "all-concealing truth." The apparent truth perceived and taken as real by the deluded mind, which conceals their true nature. See also ultimate truth.

saṃsāra (Skt.), Tib. *'khor ba*, lit. "wheel." Cyclic existence, the endless round of birth, death, and rebirth in which beings suffer as result of their actions and defilements.

scriptural collection, see collection.

Secret Mantrayāna, Tib. *gsang ngags kyi theg pa*. A branch of the Great Vehicle that uses the special techniques of the tantras to pursue the path of enlightenment for all beings more rapidly. Because these practices are based on the realization of the diamondlike nature of the mind, this vehicle is also known as the Diamond Vehicle.

self (belief in or clinging to a self), Tib. *bdag*, Skt. *ātman*. In Buddhist philosophy, the term "self" is used to denote the mistaken notion of a permanent, single, and independent entity, whether applied to a personal sense of "I" or a divine creator.

self-cognizant wisdom, Tib. *so so rang gis rig pa*. Nondual wisdom whose object is itself.

sense of decency, Tib. *khrel yod*. Also called modesty, consideration of others. To be ashamed because of what others might think if one commits negative actions. This is one of the seven noble riches.

sense of shame, Tib. *ngo tsha shes*. Also called conscientiousness, honesty. To be ashamed of oneself if one commits negative actions. This is one of the seven noble riches.

sense spheres, Tib. *khams*, Skt. *dhātu*. The collective terms for the sense objects, sense faculties, and sense consciousnesses (form, the eye, and the eye consciousness, for example). Since there are six sense organs (including the mind), there are eighteen sense spheres in all.

senses-and-fields, Tib. *skye mched*, Skt. *āyatana*. Also called sense bases, sources of perception, and so on. The twelve āyatanas comprise the six sense organs and the six sense objects. Together, they give rise to the six sense consciousnesses.

shameful deeds, Tib. *kha na ma tho ba*, lit. "that cannot be mentioned" or "cannot be praised." This term covers every kind of action that results in suffering and not only the most serious kinds of wrongdoing. Shameful deeds are divided into those that are naturally negative and those that are negative in that they involve breaches of vows.

six consciousnesses, Tib. *rnam shes tshogs drug*, lit. "six gatherings of consciousness" (signifying the gathering of a sense object, a sense organ, and a consciousness). The consciousnesses related to vision, hearing, smell, taste, touch, and mentation.

six sense organs, Tib. *dbang po drug*. The eye, ear, nose, tongue, body, and mind.

six transcendent perfections, Tib. *pha rol tu phyin pa drug*, Skt. *ṣaḍpāramitā*. Generosity, discipline, patience, diligence, concentration, and wisdom.

solitary realizer, Tib. *rang sangs rgyas*, Skt. *pratyekabuddha*. This term is applied to followers of the Lesser Vehicle who attain liberation (the cessation of suffering) on their own, without the help of a spiritual teacher. Although some solitary realizers with sharp intellects remain alone "like rhinoceroses," others with dull minds need to stay in large groups, "like flocks of parrots." Solitary realizers' practice consists, in particular, of meditation on the twelve links of dependent arising.

spiritual friend, Tib. *dge ba'i gshes gnyen*, Skt. *kalyāṇamitra*. A spiritual guide or teacher.

śramaṇa (Skt.), Tib. *dge sbyong*. An Indian term for a renunciant or mendicant, denoting anyone, Buddhist or non-Buddhist, pursuing a religious life.

steadfast, Tib. *brtan pa*, lit. "firm, stable." Used widely in the *Sūtralaṃkāra* as an epithet for a bodhisattva.

Sthiramati (Skt.), Tib. *blo gros brtan pa*. A fifth–sixth-century Indian Abhidharma scholar. He was a disciple of Vasubandhu and wrote numerous commentaries on his master's works.

stream enterer, Tib. *rgyun du zhugs pa*. The first of the four results of the listeners' path, one who has completed the listeners' path of seeing.

suchness, Tib. *de bzhin nyid*, Skt. *tathatā*. The ultimate nature of things, emptiness, the expanse of reality free from elaboration.

sugata (Skt.), Tib. *bde bar gshegs pa*, lit. "one who has gone to bliss." An epithet of a buddha.

superior intention, Tib. *lhag bsam*. Also called altruistic attitude. The good heart and unselfish attitude that is an essential aspect of a bodhisattva's spiritual intent, bodhicitta.

supramundane, Tib. *'jig rten las 'das pa*. Anything that transcends saṃsāra. The term "supramundane being" is generally applied to the noble beings of the Great Vehicle and Lesser Vehicle.

supreme mundane level, Tib. *chos mchog*. The highest possible state of worldly realization, the fourth stage of the path of joining that immediately precedes the direct realization of emptiness on the path of seeing.

sustained calm, Tib. *zhi gnas*, Skt. *śamatha*. The basis of all concentrations, a calm, undistracted state of unwavering concentration.

sūtra (Skt.), Tib. *mdo*. A scripture containing teachings given by the Buddha or by one of his disciples inspired by the Buddha.

tainted (actions, bliss, etc.), Tib. *zag bcas*. Descriptive of actions or states in which the three concepts of subject, object, and action are present, and which are therefore tainted by defilements, so that they cannot lead to liberation from saṃsāra.

tathāgata (Skt.), Tib. *de bzhin gshegs pa*, "one who has gone to thusness." A buddha; one who has reached or realized thusness, the ultimate reality. Also, one who is "thus come," a buddha in the body of manifestation (nirmaṇakāya) who has appeared in the world to benefit beings.

ten directions, Tib. *phyogs bcu*. The four cardinal points, the four intermediate directions, and the zenith and nadir.

ten levels, Tib. *sa bcu*. See bodhisattva levels.

ten negative actions, Tib. *mi dge ba bcu*. The physical acts of killing, stealing, and sexual misconduct; the verbal acts of lying, divisive speech, harsh speech, and meaningless chatter; and the mental acts of covetousness, malice, and wrong view.

ten transcendent perfections, Tib. *pha rol tu phyin pa bcu*, Skt. *dāśapāramitā*. Transcendent generosity, discipline, patience, diligence, concentration, and wisdom, together with transcendent means, aspirational prayer, strength, and gnosis. Each of these ten is practiced predominantly on one of the ten bodhisattva levels—generosity on the first level, discipline on the second, and so forth. They are termed "transcendent" because their practice involves realization of the view of emptiness.

thatness, Tib. *de kho na nyid*, Skt. *tattva*. The nondual ultimate reality that is neither existent nor nonexistent, neither the same nor different, neither produced nor destroyed, subject to neither growth nor diminution, neither pure nor impure.

three buddha bodies, Tib. *sku gsum*, Skt. *trikāya*. The three aspects of buddhahood: the body of truth, body of perfect enjoyment, and body of manifestation.

three collections, *sde snod gsum*, Skt. *tripiṭaka*. The Vinaya Collection, Sūtra Collection, and Abhidharma Collection. See also collection.

three doors, Tib. *sgo gsum*. The three means by which a person acts—namely, the body, speech, and mind.

three doors of perfect liberation, *rnam thar sgo gsum*. Emptiness, absence of attributes, and absence of expectancy.

Three Jewels, Tib. *dkon mchog gsum*, Skt. *triratna*. Collectively, the object of refuge of all Buddhists. The Buddha, Dharma, and Saṅgha.

three kinds of enlightenment, Tib. *byang chub gsum*. The enlightenment of the listeners, solitary realizers, and bodhisattvas.

three kinds of suffering, Tib. *sdug bsngal gsum*. The three fundamental types of suffering to which beings in saṃsāra are subject: the suffering of change, suffering upon suffering, and the suffering of everything composite (or all-pervading suffering in the making).

three natures, Tib. *ngo bo nyid gsum*, Skt. *trisvabhāva*. Three aspects, as presented by the Yogācāra school, of the nature of phenomena: the imputed nature, the dependent nature, and the fully present nature. Also called three realities.

three pure levels, Tib. *sa dag pa gsum*. The eighth, ninth, and tenth bodhisattva levels.

three realities, Tib. *mtshan nyid gsum*, Skt. *trisvabhāva*. Another name for the three natures. The imputed reality, the dependent reality, and the fully present reality.

three roots of virtue, Tib. *dge rtsa gsum*. Freedom from attachment, freedom from aversion, and freedom from bewilderment.

three spheres (concepts of), Tib. *'khor gsum du dmigs pa*. The concepts of subject, object, and action perceived as having a real and independent existence.

three times, Tib. *dus gsum*. In general, the past, present, and future.

three trainings, Tib. *bslabs pa gsum*, Skt. *triśikṣā*. The threefold training in discipline, concentration, and wisdom.

three vehicles, Tib. *theg pa gsum*, Skt. *triyāna*. The vehicles of the listeners, solitary realizers, and bodhisattvas.

three worlds, Tib. *khams gsum*. The world of desire, the world of form, and the world of formlessness. Alternatively (Tib. *'jig rten gsum, sa gsum, srid gsum*): the world of gods above the earth, that of humans on the earth, and that of the nāgas under the earth.

tīrthika (Skt.), Tib. *mu stegs pa*. A term generally used to denote non-Buddhist proponents of nihilistic and eternalistic philosophical views. The Tibetan term refers to the fact that they are said to stay on the steps (*stegs*) leading down to the edge (*mu*) of the river, that is, the path flowing into the ocean of nirvāṇa.

transcendent perfection, Tib. *pha rol tu phyin pa*, Skt. *pāramitā*. The principal practice of a bodhisattva, combining skillful means and wisdom, the compassionate motivation of attaining enlightenment for the sake of all beings and the view of emptiness. See six and ten transcendent perfections.

transitory composite (view of), Tib. *'jig tshogs la lta ba*. The view whereby the five aggregates, which are transitory and composite, are regarded as a permanent, independent, and single "I" and "mine." This view is the basis of all other wrong views.

treatise, Tib. *bstan bcos*, Skt. *śāstra*. In the context of Buddhist literature, a work by an Indian or Tibetan master that comments on the Buddha's teachings or presents them in condensed or more accessible form.

Twelve Branches of Excellent Speech, Tib. *gsung rab yan lag bcu gnyis*. The twelve types of teaching given by the Buddha, corresponding to twelve kinds of text: condensed (Tib. *mdo sde*, Skt. *sūtra*), melodious (*dbyangs bsnyan, geya*), prophetic (*lung bstan, vyākaraṇa*), verse (*tshigs bcad, gāthā*), spoken with a purpose (*ched brjod, udāna*), contextual (*gleng gzhi, nidāna*—questions, talks, etc.), concerning his past lives (*skyes rab, jātaka*), marvelous (*rmad byung, adbhutadharma*), establishing a truth (*gtan babs, upadeśa*), biographical or "expressing realization" (*rtogs brjod, avadāna*), historical (*de ltar byung, itivṛttaka*), and very detailed (*shin tu rgyas pa, vaipulya*).

twelve links of dependent arising, Tib. *rten 'brel bcu gnyis*. The twelve factors or stages through which the process of birth and rebirth in cyclic existence takes place. They are ignorance, conditioning factors, consciousness, name-and-form, the sense powers, contact, feeling, craving, grasping, becoming, birth, and aging-and-death.

two accumulations, Tib. *tshogs gnyis*. The accumulation of merit (Tib. *bsod nams*) and the accumulation of wisdom (Tib. *ye shes*).

two extremes, Tib. *mtha' gnyis*. Depending on context, the extreme of saṃsāra and the extreme of nirvāṇa; the extremes of existence and nonexistence; the extremes of pleasurable indulgence and excessive austerity.

two goals, Tib. *don gnyis*. One's own goal, benefit, or welfare (Tib. *rang don*) and that of others (Tib. *gzhan don*). Often understood in the ultimate sense of the goal for oneself being achieved by the realization of emptiness, the body of truth (Skt. *dharmakāya*), and the goal for others by compassion manifesting as the form body (Skt. *rūpakāya*).

two kinds of no-self, Tib. *bdag med gnyis*. The no-self of the individual (Tib. *gang zag gi bdag med*) and the no-self of phenomena (Tib. *chos kyi bdag med*). See also no-self.

two obscurations, Tib. *sgrib pa gnyis*. Obscurations related to defilements, or defilement-related obscurations (*nyon sgrib*), and those that obscure knowledge, or cognitive obscurations (*shes sgrib*).

two truths, Tib. *bden gnyis*. Relative truth and ultimate truth.

ultimate excellence, Tib. *nges legs*. The lasting happiness of liberation and omniscience, i.e., buddhahood.

ultimate reality, Tib. *chos nyid*, Skt. *dharmatā*. Also translated as "true nature." The true nature of phenomena, which is emptiness.

ultimate teachings, Tib. *nges don*. Also called definitive teachings. Teachings that, unlike the expedient teachings, comprise the direct expression of truth from the point of view of realized beings.

ultimate truth, Tib. *don dam bden pa*. The ultimate nature of the mind and the true status of phenomena, which can only be known by gnosis, beyond all conceptual constructs and duality. See also relative truth.

universal emperor, Tib. *'khor los sgyur ba'i rgyal po*, Skt. *cakravartin*. An emperor who, with his golden, silver, copper, or iron wheel, has dominion over the beings of the four continents. Universal emperors only appear in certain eras when the human life span is greater than eighty thousand years.

untainted, Tib. *zag med*. Uncontaminated by defilements, including concepts due to the defilement of ignorance.

Vasubandhu (Skt.), Tib. *dbyig gnyen*. Asaṅga's half-brother and disciple, famous in particular for his authorship of the classic text *Treasury of Abhidharma* (*Abhidharmakośa*).

Vātsīputrīya (Skt.), Tib. *gnas ma'i bu pa*. One of the eighteen original schools of the Listeners' Vehicle in India. Its followers believed in a substantially existing self.

vehicle, Tib. *theg pa*, Skt. *yāna*. The means for traveling the path to enlightenment.

victorious one, Tib. *rgyal ba*, Skt. *jina*. Also called conqueror. A general epithet for a buddha, one who has won victory over all negative forces.

Vinaya (Skt.), Tib. *'dul ba*, lit. "taming." The section of the Buddha's teaching that deals with discipline, and in particular with the vows of monastic ordination.

wisdom, Tib. *shes rab*, Skt. *prajñā*. The sixth of the six transcendent perfections. The ability to understand correctly, usually with the particular sense of understanding emptiness.

wise (person), Tib. *blo ldan*. A common epithet for a bodhisattva, with its plural ("the wise") being used to denote bodhisattvas, and in some instances translated directly as such.

world of desire, Tib. *'dod khams*, Skt. *kāmaloka* or *kāmadhātu*. The first of the three worlds, comprising the hells, and the realms of the hungry spirits, animals, humans, demigods, and the six classes of gods of the world of desire.

world of form, Tib. *gzugs khams*, Skt. *rūpadhātu*. The second of the three worlds, comprising the twelve realms of the four concentrations and the five pure abodes.

world of formlessness, Tib. *gzugs med khams*, Skt. *ārūpyadhātu*. The third of the three worlds, at the peak of existence. It comprises the spheres of infinite space, infinite consciousness, utter nothingness, and neither existence nor nonexistence.

wrong view, Tib. *log lta*, Skt. *mithyādṛṣṭi*. A false belief, particularly a view that will lead one to courses of action that bring more suffering. It includes views that deny the law of karma and the view of the transitory composite.

yoga (Skt.), Tib. *rnal 'byor*, lit. "union (*'byor*) with the natural state (*rnal ma*)." A term for spiritual practice.

Yogācāra (Skt.), Tib. *rnal 'byor spyod pa*. One of the principal schools of the Great Vehicle, based on the teachings of the third turning of the wheel of the Dharma and propagated by Asaṅga, Vasubandhu, and their followers. Its philosophical tenets included the doctrine of mind-only (cittamātra), the eight consciousnesses, the ground of all as the storehouse of karmic tendencies, and the three natures or realities.

yogi (Skt.), Tib. *rnal 'byor pa*. A person practicing a spiritual path.

yojana (Skt.), Tib. *pag tshad*. An ancient Indian measurement. Different sources describe it as between one and several miles.

Works Cited

Texts Quoted

Commentary on Valid Cognition, *Tshad ma rnam 'grel, Pramāṇavārttika*, by Dharmakīrti (Toh 4210)

Compendium of the Great Vehicle, *Theg bsdus, Mahāyānasaṃgraha*, by Asaṅga (Toh 4048)

Diamond Cutter Sūtra, *rDo rje gcod pa, Vajracchedikā* (Toh 16)

Distinguishing the Middle from Extremes, *dBus mtha' rnam 'byed, Madhyāntavibhāga*, one of the five treatises of Maitreya-Asaṅga (Toh 4021)

Heap of Jewels, *dKon mchog brtsegs pa, Ratnakūṭa*, a collection of sūtras (Toh 45–93)

Long Scriptures, *Lung ring po*, one of four categories of sūtras (mdo sde lung sde bzhi)

Ornament of True Realization, *mNgon rtogs rgyan, Abhisamayālaṃkāra*, one of the five treatises of Maitreya-Asaṅga (Toh 3786)

Perfection of Wisdom, *Sher phyin, Sher mdo, Yum*, etc., a general reference to the Prajñāpāramitā sūtras (Toh 8–30)

Perfection of Wisdom in One Hundred Thousand Lines, *Sher phyin stong phrag brgya pa, Śatasāhasrikāprajñāpāramitā* (Toh 8)

Sublime Continuum, *rGyud bla ma, Mahāyānottaratantraśāstra-ratnagotravibhāga*, one of the five treatises of Maitreya-Asaṅga (Toh 4024)

Sūtra in Repayment of Kindness, *Drin lan bsab pa'i mdo*, the teachings the Buddha gave his mother when he visited the Heaven of the Thirty-Three, where she had been reborn (Toh 353)

Sūtra Like a Saw, *Sog le lta bu'i mdo*, most probably a text from the Mūlasarvāstivādin canon, which is no longer extant

Sūtra of the Lion's Roar of Śrīmālādevī, *dPal phreng gi mdo, Śrīmālādevīsiṃhanādasūtra*, part of the Heap of Jewels (Toh 92)

Sūtra of the Myrobalan, a sūtra cited by both Sthiramati and Vasubandhu, which we have not been able to locate with certainty

Sūtra of the Ornament of the Buddhas, *Sangs rgyas phal po che, Buddhāvataṃsakasūtra*, (Toh 44)

Sūtra of the Ornament of the Light of Gnosis, *Ye shes snang ba rgyan gyi mdo, Sarvabuddhaviṣayāvatārajñānālokālaṃkāra-sūtra* (Toh 100)

Sūtra of the Precious Lamp, *dKon mchog ta la la'i mdo, Ratnolkādhāraṇī-sūtra* (Toh 145)

Sūtra of the Questions of Brahmaviśeṣacintin, *Tshangs pa khyad par sems kyis zhus pa'i mdo* (cited as *Tshangs pas zhus pa'i mdo*), *Brahmaviśeṣacintiparipṛcchā-sūtra* (Toh 160)
Sūtra of the Teaching of Akṣayamati, *'Phags pa blo gros mi zad pa'i mdo*, *Akṣayamatinirdeśa-sūtra* (Toh 175)
Sūtra of the Ten Levels, *mDo sde sa bcu pa*, *Daśabhūmika-sūtra*, the thirty-first chapter of the *Sūtra of the Ornament of the Buddhas*
Sūtra on Buddhahood, *'Phags pa sangs rgyas kyi sa*, *Buddhabhūmi-sūtra* (Toh 275)
Sūtra on the Descent into Laṅka, *Lang kar gshegs pa'i mdo*, *Laṅkāvatāra-sūtra* (Toh 107)
Sūtra on the Mountain Gayāśīrṣa, *Ga ya'i ri'i mdo*, *Gayāśīrṣa-sūtra* (Toh 109)
Two Segments, *brTag gnyis*, the condensed *Hevajra Tantra in Two Segments*
Two Stanza Incantation, *Tshigs su bcad pa gnyis pa'i gzungs*, *Gāthādvaya-dhāraṇī* (Toh 143)
Ultimate Emptiness, *Don dam par stong pa*, probably a no longer extant sūtra from the Mūlasarvāstivādin canon
Unraveling the Intent, *'Phags pa ba shes bya ba theg pa chen po'i mdo* (cited as *dGongs pa nges 'grel*), *Saṃdhinirmocanasūtra* (Toh 106)
Verses Summarizing the Precious Qualities, *Yon tan rin po che sdud pa*, another name for *Verses That Summarize the Perfection of Wisdom*, *'Phags pa shes rab kyi pha rol tu phyin pa sdud pa tshigs su bcad pa*, *Āryaprajñāpāramitā-sañcayagāthā* (Toh 13)

Texts Mentioned but Not Quoted

Jeweled Lamp of the Middle Way, *dBu ma rin po che'i sgron me'i stan bcos*, *Madhyamakaratnapradīpa*, by Bhāvaviveka (Toh 3854)
Moon Lamp Sūtra, *Zla ba sgron ma'i mdo*, apparently another name for the *Sūtra of the King of Concentrations*, *Ting 'dzin rgyal po*, *Samādhirāja-sūtra* (Toh 127)
Play in Full, *rGya cher rol pa*, *Lalitavistara* (Toh 95)
Seven Treatises on Logic, *Tshad ma sde bdun*, by Dharmakīrti
The Stage of a Bodhisattva, *Byang chub sems dpa'i sa*, *Bodhisattvabhūmi*, part of the *Stages of Yogic Practice*, *rNal 'byor spyod pa'i sa*, *Yogācārabhūmi*, by Asaṅga (Toh 4035)
Story of Daughter the son of Vallabha, *mDza' bo'i bu mo'i rnam thar*, source unidentified
Story of the Strongman Bakshita, *Gyad bakshita'i rnam thar*, source unidentified
Sūtra of Sublime Golden Light, *gSer 'od dam pa'i mdo*, *Suvarṇaprabhāsottamasūtrendrarāja* (Toh 556 or 557)
Sūtra of the Inconceivable Secrets, *gSang ba bsam gyis mi khyab pa'i mdo*, *Tathāgatācintyaguhyanirdeśa-sūtra*, part of the Heap of Jewels (Toh 47)
Sūtra of the Perfectly Pure Sphere of Activity, *sPyod yul yongs su dag pa'i mdo sde*, probably no longer extant
Sūtra of the Questions of Dhāraṇīśvararāja, *'Phags pa gzungs kyi dbang phyug chen*

po'i rgyal po'i mdo, another name for *The Sūtra Teaching the Great Compassion of the Tathāgatas, De bzhin gshegs pa'i snying rje chen po nges par bstan pa'i mdo, Tathāgatamahākaruṇānirdeśa-sūtra* (Toh 147)

Sūtra of the Questions of Ratnacūḍa, *gTsug na rin chen gyis zhus pa'i mdo, Ratnacūḍaparipṛcchā-sūtra*, part of the Heap of Jewels (Toh 91)

Sūtra that Teaches the Secret of the Tathāgata's Body, *De bzhin gshegs pa'i sku'i gsang ba bstan pa'i mdo*, a chapter from the *Sūtra of the Inconceivable Secrets, De bzhin gshegs pa'i gsang ba bstan pa'i mdo* (Toh 47)

Tantra of the Essence of Nectar, *bDud rtsi snying po'i rgyud*

Tantra of the Wheel of Time, *Dus 'khor, Kālacakra*

Tantra of Vairocana's Enlightenment, *rNam snang mngon byang, Vairocanābhisaṃbodhi* (Toh 494)

White Lotus Sūtra of the Sacred Dharma, *Dam chos pad ma dkar po, Saddharmapuṇḍarīka-sūtra* (Toh 113)

Bibliography

Tibetan Sources

Asaṅga. *rNal 'byor spyod pa'i sa las byang chub sems dpa'i sa, Yogācārabhūmau-bodhisattvabhūmiḥ (The Bodhisattva Stage)*. Translated by Prajñāvarma and Ye shes sde. Toh 4037.
Aśvabhāva. *Theg pa chen po'i mdo sde'i rgyan gyi rgya cher bshad pa, Mahāyāna-sūtrālaṃkāraṭīkā*. Translated by Śākyasiṃha and dPal brtsegs. Toh 4029.
Jñānaśrī. *mDo sde rgyan gyi don bsdus pa, Sūtrālaṃkārapiṇḍārtha (Digest of the Sūtrālaṃkāra)*. Translated by Jñānaśrī and Chos kyi brtson 'grus. Toh 4031.
Maitreya. *Theg pa chen po mdo sde'i rgyan zhes bya ba'i tshig le'ur byas pa, Mahāyāna-sūtrālaṃkārakārikā*. Translated by Śākyasiṃha and dPal brtsegs. Toh 4020.
Parahitabhadra. *mDo sde rgyan gyi tshigs su bcad pa dang po gnyis kyi bshad pa, Sūtrālaṃkārādiślokadvayavyākhyāna (A Commentary on the First Two Verses of the Sūtrālaṃkāra)*. Translated by Parahitabhadra and gZhon nu mchog. Toh 4030.
Sthiramati. *mDo sde rgyan gyi 'grel bshad, Sūtrālaṃkāravṛttibhāṣya (Detailed Commentary of the Sūtrālaṃkāra)*. Translated by Municandra and lCe bkra shis. Toh 4034.
Vasubandhu. *mDo sde'i rgyan gyi bshad pa, Sūtrālaṃkārabhāṣya*. Translated by Śākyasiṃha and dPal brtsegs. Toh 4026.

Western Language Sources

Ārya Asaṅga. *The Bodhisattva's Path to Unsurpassed Enlightenment*. Translated by Artemus B. Engle. Boulder: Snow Lion Publications, 2016.
Gampopa. *Ornament of Precious Liberation*. Translated by Ken Holmes. In *Stages of the Buddha's Teachings: Three Key Texts*. Somerville, MA: Wisdom Publications, 2015.
Kunzang Pelden. *The Nectar of Manjushri's Speech*. Translated by the Padmakara Translation Group. Boston: Shambhala Publications, 2007, 2010.
Longchen Yeshe Dorje, Kangyur Rinpoche. *Treasury of Precious Qualities, Book One*. Translated by the Padmakara Translation Group. Boston: Shambhala Publications, 2001. Revised version with root text by Jigme Lingpa, 2010.
Maitreya. *Middle Beyond Extremes: Maitreya's Madhyāntavibhāga with Commen-

taries by Khenpo Shenga and Ju Mipham. Translated by the Dharmachakra Translation Committee. Ithaca, NY: Snow Lion Publications, 2007.

——. *Ornament of the Great Vehicle Sūtras: Maitreya's Mahāyānasūtrālaṃkāra with commentaries by Khenpo Shenga and Ju Mipham*. Translated by the Dharmachakra Translation Committee. Boston: Snow Lion Publications, 2006.

——. *The Universal Vehicle Discourse Literature (Mahāyānasūtrālaṃkāra) by Maitreyanātha/Āryāsaṅga: Together with Its Commentary (Bhāṣya) by Vasubandhu*. Translated by L. Jamspal, R. Clark, J. Wilson, L. Zwilling, M. Sweet, R. Thurman. New York: Columbia University Center for Buddhist Studies and Tibet House US, 2004.

Patrul Rinpoche. *The Words of My Perfect Teacher*. Translated by the Padmakara Translation Group. Boston: Shambhala Publications, 1998.

Shantideva. *The Way of the Bodhisattva*. Translated by the Padmakara Translation Group. Boston: Shambhala Publications, 2008.

Soûtra des Dix Terres: Dashabhûmika. Translated by Patrick Carré. Paris: Librairie Arthème Fayard, 2004.

Index

Abhidharma, 360, 509
  classifications and etymologies of, 45, 363, 364
  contents of, 362
  in India, decline of, xv
  of Listeners' and Great Vehicles, lack of contradiction in, 5, 155–56, 159, 160
Abhidharmakośa (Vasubandhu), 219n17
Abhisamayālaṃkāra. See *Ornament of True Realization*
abiding
  in buddhahood, 34, 289, 298–99, 303–4
  concentration and, 80, 542, 543
  in Dharma, 376
  discipline and, 540
  displaying, 106, 665
  in mind's expanse, 49, 394
  nonabiding and, 333
  remaining in, 674
  right, as concentration, 678n23
  in suchness, 773
  on tenth level, 513–14
  in training, 535–36
abodes, 23, 50, 123, 249, 251–52, 403–4, 595, 793
acceptance
  of nonarising/unborn phenomena, 52, 115, 118, 120, 412–14, 740, 753, 754, 775–76, 810
  on path of seeing, 506
  patient, 754
Adornment of the Middle Way (Śāntarakṣita), xxi
aggregates. See five aggregates
Airāvata (celestial elephant), 458
Ajātaśatru, King, 191
Ajitanātha, Lord of the Ten Levels (Maitreya), 141–42
Akaniṣṭha, 788n22, 793n37
all-accomplishing gnosis, 39, 327–28
all-discerning gnosis, 39, 320, 326–27

all-pervading activity, 605–6n22
altruistic activity, 19, 223–27
Amitābha, 309n24, 321, 467
analogies. See metaphors, similes, analogies
analysis
  with attentiveness of single taste, 68, 495–96
  as basis of miraculous powers, 105, 662, 663
  of compassion, 603
  defilements and, 499
  habituation through, 26, 262–63, 265, 272
  of instructions, four processes of, 67, 493–94
  second reliance and, 103, 649
  in training, 536
  wisdom and, 570–71
Ānanda, 365, 493n4
anger
  compassion toward, 623
  harm due to, 167
  lack of, 129, 825
  from lack of shame, 99, 632
  transcendent patience and, 121, 531, 781
antidotes
  to discursive thoughts, 105, 663, 664
  on eightfold path, 107, 677–78
  to eight obscurations, 59–60, 467–70
  in four close mindfulnesses, 104, 655, 656
  four genuine restraints as, 105, 659, 660, 661–62
  illusory nature of, 48, 388–89
  shame and decency as, 99, 100, 631, 634, 635
  three kinds of individuals and, 224
  training in, 374
  transcendent perfections as, 53, 425

appearances
  arising of, 393–94
  and emptiness, union of, 238, 320n29, 385
  as imputed reality, 50, 398–99
  lack of ultimate existence of, 63, 485
  mental, 701
  as mind and mental factors, 144, 368, 378–79, 383, 400, 769
  threefold, of subject and object, 50, 399–400
  transformation of, 405
  See also dualistic appearances; mere appearances
application, 436
  attentiveness associated with, 46, 377–80
  of bodhisattvas, 72, 512
  in bodhisattvas' signs, 125, 798
  devoted and constant, 68, 497, 542
  diligence in, 87, 551n18, 567
  excellent, 62, 478, 479
  in following spiritual masters, 590
  in offerings, 90, 583, 584
  quality of, 122, 786–87
  shame associated with, 631
arhats, 205, 776
  behaviors of, 839
  compassion of, 604, 612–13
  gnosis of, 413
  liberation of, 404
  and ordinary people, difference between, 243
  rebirth of, 701, 707
  subtle mental body of, 243n17
arts and crafts, 421, 423, 642, 643, 756, 757, 760
Asaṅga, xv–xvii, xxii, 137, 236, 647, 750.
  See also *Compendium of the Great Vehicle* (Asaṅga)
asceticism, 270, 361. See also austerities
aspiration
  of bodhisattvas, 164, 172, 173, 179
  of great compassion, 94, 606–10
  in Listeners' and Great Vehicles, differences between, 162
  lowly, 7, 165–66
  in offerings, 89, 90, 580, 581, 583, 584
  power of, 469
  reflection of, 67, 494, 495
  of sentient beings, 252
  in single vehicle, 52, 415
  as spiritual ambition, 479
  steadfastness and, 101, 638, 639
  threefold, 54, 434, 435
  See also ten great aspirations
aspiration prayers, 468–69
  attentiveness to, 53, 426, 427, 431
  for buddhas' appearance, 89, 579–80, 582
  as cause for rebirth, 52, 126, 417, 418, 803–4, 824, 826
  for continued practice, 535
  full accomplishment of, 106, 664, 666
  great compassion and, 94, 607, 610
  implied teachings and, 467
  for nonconceptual gnosis, 681
  for others, 114, 737
  qualities due to, 108, 683–85
  root of, 639
  uninterrupted, 229
attachment, 555
  antidotes for, 59, 224, 374n22, 467, 469
  arising of, 593
  bodhisattvas' lack of, 113, 392, 528, 625, 636, 658, 733–34
  of bodhisattvas to sentient beings, 64, 486, 487–88
  buddhas' speech as lacking, 459
  compassion free from, 94, 603, 604, 605
  as countering factor of boundless attitudes, 92, 597
  deliverance from, 62, 480, 481, 482
  of desire-world beings, compassion for, 600
  Dharma in abolishing, 442
  diligence and, 80, 542
  in enlightened state, 298
  freedom from, 217, 639
  habituation to, 190
  impartiality and, 209, 429
  lack of fear of, 215
  lack of potential and, 184, 186
  manifest interest and, 349
  negative actions and, 376–77, 555, 612
  as obstacle to interest, 349
  of ordinary beings, 20, 227
  to pleasure, 361
  root of, 229
  to self, 240
  shame in giving rise to, 631

attainments
  of buddhas, superiority of, 34, 305–6
  in four close mindfulnesses, 104, 655, 656
  investigation of Dharma and, 55, 441
  of seven transformations, 34–35, 306–10
  sublime, 39, 332–33
attentiveness, 50, 401, 402, 496
  as basis of miraculous powers, 105, 662, 663
  development of, 69, 500, 501
  distracting forms of, 546, 547
  eighteen categories of, 46, 369–80
  five bases of knowable phenomena and, 397
  in four close mindfulnesses, 104, 655, 656
  great compassion and, 94, 608, 610
  in investigation, forms of, 53–54, 423–40
  to lower paths, abandoning, 75, 105, 522, 659, 660
  in *Mahāyānasūtrālaṃkāra*, corresponding sections on, 432–33, 439–40
  order of, 424
  relying on, 559–60
  of single taste, 68, 495–96
  to thatness, 407
  training in, 79, 535, 536
attributes, concentration of absence of, 71, 108, 432, 473–74, 509, 682, 685–86, 687
austerities
  diligence in, 84, 556
  improper, 285, 456
  joy in, 197
  patience as, 80, 541, 542
  perseverance in, 9, 173
  result of, 29, 279–80
  steadfastness in, 101, 638, 640
aversion, 555
  antidote to, 225, 374n22
  arising of, 593
  bodhisattvas' lack of, 392, 603, 625, 636
  Dharma in abolishing, 442
  habituation to, 190
  impartiality and, 209, 429
  liberation by means of, 481, 482
  manifest interest and, 349

  negative actions and, 376–77, 612, 666
  root of, 229
  shame in giving rise to, 631
  subtle habitual tendencies to, 605
awareness, cognitive, 761, 762. *See also* reflexive awareness

Bakshita, 191, 484
beggars, 83, 86, 553, 563–64, 620, 621, 733, 786
beguilement, matured immunity to, 25, 26, 259, 265
benefiting beings, 50, 218, 396
  analogy for, 207
  bodhicitta and, 15, 199
  bodhisattvas' attitude in, 79, 535, 536–38
  bodhisattvas' engagement in, 19, 222–23
  boundlessness of, 305–6
  branch of, 107, 675–76
  by buddhas and bodhisattvas, differences between, 335–36
  through buddhas' speech, 58, 455–60
  compassion as means for, 610
  delight in, 18, 216–17
  through Dharma teaching, importance of, 755
  diligence in, 18, 219
  disregarding, 632, 635
  on first level, 508, 510n19
  joy in, 16, 203
  love in, 63–64, 486–88
  through Mahāyāna, 9, 10, 171–72, 176
  through manifestation body, 322
  as never ceasing, 228–29
  through patience, 80, 541, 542
  potential in, 14, 192, 193
  as result of enlightenment, 318
  seven similes for, 114–16, 434, 736–41
  by six transcendent perfections, 114, 735–36
  superior intention in, 125–26, 802
  through teaching, 57, 447–48, 471
  thirteen ways of, 19, 223–27
  through transcendent perfections, 122, 425, 786–87
  See also maturation
bewilderment, 555
  antidote to, 374n22
  habituation to, 190
  liberation by means of, 481

bewilderment (*continued*)
  love and, 612
  manifest interest and, 349
  negative actions and, 376–77, 555
  root of, 229
  See also delusion
Bhāvaviveka, 237–38
birth
  aspiration and, 666
  of bodhisattvas, 18, 125–26, 129, 177, 215–16, 392, 488, 512, 550, 551, 640, 801–5, 809, 825, 826
  bodhisattvas knowledge of others', 23, 249
  buddhas' display of, 36, 313
  certainty regarding, 437–38
  concepts leading to, 49, 393–95
  four close mindfulnesses and, 104, 655, 658
  in freedom, 62, 479
  and peace, ultimately, 21, 242–43
  protection from, 30, 286
  See also rebirth
bliss
  of buddhas' speech, 456
  of concentration, 16, 35, 80, 84, 113, 204, 309–10, 542, 543, 551, 556–57, 674, 732, 734
  of Dharma, 450
  of fitness, 503
  of generosity, 95, 615
  of great compassion, 94, 611
  mental, 42, 351–52
  not savoring, 118, 752, 753
  of supreme wisdom, 10, 177
  transient, 20, 227
  See also great bliss
Blissful Realm, 309, 468–69
bodhicitta, xx, 15, 329, 330, 339, 377
  acquired formally (relative), 16, 201–2
  acquired naturally (ultimate), 16, 201, 202–6, 671
  applying, 17–18, 212–19
  arising of, four causes, 16, 203, 204
  arousing, 40, 120, 121, 336–37, 524, 775, 778
  in aspiration prayers, 639
  as basis of practice, 221
  by bodhisattva level, 198–99, 200–201
  definition of, 197–98

  as great compassion, 607
  kinds of, 199–201
  in maturing beings, 311
  potential and, 749–50
  predictions and, 414
  refuge and, 178
  relative and ultimate, union of, 201, 681
  as support for transcendent perfections, 424
  twenty-two similes for, 17, 206–12
  uninterrupted, 228–29
bodhicitta vow, 202n8, 330–31
Bodhisattvabhūmivyākhā (Sāgaramegha), 186n3
bodhisattva levels, xxi–xxii, 126, 178, 340, 490, 659, 778–79, 805–6
  acceptance on, 775–76
  accomplishment and nonaccomplishment on, 128, 820–22
  aspiration prayers on, 108, 683–84
  attracting disciples from, 575
  benefits of, 129, 827–28
  birth on, 125–26, 802–5
  bodhicitta on, 15, 198–99, 200–201
  bringing others to, 19, 226
  causes of, 164
  compassion on, 262
  eightfold noble path and, 375–76, 677
  establishing others on, 269
  factors to be eliminated on, 440, 749
  fear on, lack of, 614
  firmly engaged interest on, 348
  five irresistible forces on, 106, 669
  four genuine restraints on, 105, 659, 660
  four ways of attaining, 130, 831–32
  gnosis on, 288, 402
  hope on, 116, 743
  indefatigability on, 641
  instructions received on, 73, 514–17
  investigation on, 440, 441
  keeping the system in mind on, 16, 205–6, 821–22
  knowledge categories on, 794–95
  level, etymological definition of, 130, 806n5, 830–31
  mastery of remainder, 16, 203, 205
  meditation on, 332, 658
  objects of praise on, 121, 779–80
  obscurations destroyed on, 280–81
  offerings on, 584

ordination on, 125, 801
power of memory on, 108, 682–83
purification of untainted aggregates on, 128, 819–20
qualities on, 71–73, 113, 147, 507–14, 733
refuge and, 180
shame and decency on, 631–32
signs attainment is certain, 502–4
sixteen marks on, 129, 824, 825–27
skill in means on, 108, 680, 681
as states of abiding, 130, 830, 831
superior intention on, 125–26, 802–3
sustained calm and profound insight on, 107, 678, 679
teaching on, 57, 451
ten signs common to, 128, 823–24
three trainings on, 127–28, 817–19
two accumulations on, 654
virtue on, 10, 178–79
wishing for others to complete, 435
See also three pure levels; *individual level*
bodhisattva qualities, 121–22, 175
of benefiting others, 782
of care with Great Vehicle, 784–85
compassion as root of, 606–7
of delight in enlightenment, 781–82
eleven categories of knowledge of, 123, 794–95
increasing through practice, 20, 230
of inner composure, 782–83
of lack of desire for other vehicles, 785–86
names corresponding to, 787–89
of not being at odds with Great Vehicle, 783
of prioritizing Dharma, 784
of takes on suffering, 783–84
on ten levels, 779–80
that praise the result, 123, 789–93
bodhisattvas, 781
appearance of, 615
attainments of, 34, 305–6
attentiveness of, 370
attitudes of, 40, 79, 333–34, 535–36, 536–38, 539, 823
as audience for *Ornament of the Mahāyāna Sūtras*, 142
bondage of, 72, 511–12
and buddhas, relationship between, 9, 34, 173, 299, 305, 335–36

buddhas appearing as, 313
as children of Buddha's mind, 174n2
conceit, absence of, 49, 389–90
demeanor of, 102, 115, 645, 740–41
Dharma teaching of, 57–58, 60, 451–55, 471
etymology of, 790
five signs of, 125, 797–800
four extraordinary and four unextraordinary thoughts of, 54, 432, 433–34
as friends of beings, 26, 217–18, 266–67
giving up their intention, 484
infinite number of, 316
interest of, 42, 353–55
liberation of, 406
manifestations of, 415, 757–58
meditation of, 332, 374
realization of, 394
reverting to lower vehicles, 224n5
rewards and recompense, disinterest in, 54, 72, 97, 115, 434–35, 507, 510–12, 615, 620–22, 740–41, 745–46, 799
as spiritual masters, 589
state of mind of, 588
supremacy of, 10, 178–79
as teachers, qualities of, 19, 225–27, 446
ten categories of, 140
three types, 10, 178–79
undeluded, 47, 384
of unfixed potential, 416, 601
vow of, 15, 199 (*see also* bodhicitta vow)
bodhisattvas' collection, 360
body
appearances of, 790
bodhisattvas' offering of, 85, 113, 172, 173, 215, 217, 355, 433, 536, 558, 562, 563, 583, 732–33
bondage of, 119, 768
excellent, as support, 262, 264
fitness of, from concentration, 69, 500, 501, 502–3, 543, 664, 670, 674
four causes for development of, 699, 702
and generosity, resulting from, 79, 539
in maturing others, 27, 270
negative tendencies of, 408–9
pure maturation and, 26, 263–64
as seized by consciousness, 696–97
transformation of, 50, 51, 365–66, 405

body of essential nature (*svabhāvikakāya*), 317
body of gnosis, 304, 329
body of manifestation (*nirmāṇakāya*), 322, 793
  appearance of, 33, 253–54, 291, 297, 302
  at enlightenment, 37, 319
  as eternal, 324
  five sense consciousnesses transformed into, 320
  four types of, 38, 306, 322–23
  mastery of, 538
  offerings to, 579
body of perfect enjoyment (*sambhogakāya*), 793
  appearances of, 37, 320–21
  and body of truth, relationship between, 37, 321–22
  at enlightenment, 37, 319, 320
  as eternal, 324
  mastery of, 538
  mirrorlike gnosis as, 325
body of truth (*dharmakāya*), 317
  attaining, 816
  and buddhas, lack of distinction between, 299, 301
  causal factor of, 449–50, 828
  at enlightenment, 282, 319–20, 403–4
  as eternal, 324
  investigation and, 55, 441
  mastery of, 538
  perfecting, 70, 503–4
  profundity of, 483
  sameness of, 203, 467
  as unborn, 413
bondage, 72, 119–20, 242–43, 409, 511–12, 768–73
Brahmā, 172, 412, 430, 434, 458, 652, 658, 751, 824, 826
Brahmā realms, 543
Brave Progression concentration, 192, 253, 256, 261, 273, 318, 471, 551, 644
Buddha
  as beyond two extremes, 32, 297
  bodhisattvas lacking shame and, 99, 633
  children of, 174n2
  confidence in, 370
  contempt for, 59, 467–68
  Dharma teaching of, 57, 448–51

  epithets of, 25, 32, 92, 99, 137, 261, 296–97, 331, 598, 633
  in establishing no-self, 722
  etymology of Tibetan for, 390n37
  five sciences and, 757
  on monastic precepts, 365
  predictions by, 750
  proclaiming name of, 24, 254
  seven ways of recalling, 370
buddha activity, 31–32, 35, 293–95, 310, 778
  diversity of, 327–28
  equality of, 324
  in expanse of reality, 294–95, 303–4, 314
  ten categories of, 33–34, 299–303
  types of, 36, 313–14
  uninterrupted, 133, 842
  See also enlightened activities; teaching Dharma
buddha family, 113, 174, 224, 226, 227, 733, 734, 778, 788
buddha fields
  all-accomplishing gnosis in, 328
  deeds in, 313
  display of, 24, 254, 404
  intention in teaching, 469
  mastery over, 51, 406, 440
  predictions of, 117, 749, 750
  purification of, 35, 308–9, 660, 679, 772–73, 774, 810, 811, 816, 819
  rebirth in, 467, 468–69
  riches of, 327
  of sambhogakāya, 37, 320–21
  training in, 90, 91, 588
buddhahood, 173, 340
  accomplishment of, 659, 733
  benefiting beings through, 787
  cause of, 185n2
  through diligence, 86, 566
  gnosis that refines qualities of, 72, 513
  in Listeners' and Great Vehicles, differences between, 5, 158–59, 161–62
  of listeners with unfixed potential, 418
  three qualities of level of, 178
  time for accomplishing, 29, 156, 159, 280
  two accumulations and, 654
  wishing for others to attain, 435
  See also enlightenment
buddha level, 201, 395, 514
  attainments of, 225

bodhicitta on, 199
body, speech, mind on, 538
characteristics of, 127, 133, 812, 841–42
contentment of, 73, 514–15
five sciences and, 422
nonconceptual gnosis of, 246
purification on, 820
sameness on, 50, 403–4
spontaneous nonconceptual compassion on, 605–6
triple greatness of, 514
buddha nature, xvii, xix, 187, 303, 303n16, 304, 403, 420, 470
buddha qualities, 140, 147, 178, 179, 380, 611, 668, 816
buddhas
　appearance of, 31, 292–93, 318, 614–15
　and bodhisattvas, relationship between, 9, 34, 173, 299, 305, 335–36
　bodhisattvas' veneration of, 69, 501–2
　characteristics and aspects, lack of, 329
　constant presence of, 73, 515
　deeds of, 212, 254, 313, 320, 323, 804, 816, 817
　equality of, 323–24
　gnosis of, two kinds, 288–89
　manifestations of, 39, 328, 415
　perfect realization of, 379
　sameness of, 468
　and sentient beings, lack of difference between, 316–17
　singularity and multiplicity of, 32, 33, 39, 298–99, 300–301, 330–31
　as spiritual masters, 589
　succession of, 36, 315
　superiority of, 390
　teaching by, 58, 455–63, 758
Buddha Vipaśyin, 466, 468

Candrakīrti, 238
capacity, 4, 152–53, 156, 163, 268
carelessness, 41, 349–50, 365
caste, 468
cause and effect/result
　in establishing impermanence, 109, 694–95, 701
　faith in, 667–68
　in following spiritual masters, 91, 589
　interdependence of, 329
　offerings and, 90, 583
　rational application and, 763–64
　six transcendent perfections and, 532–33
　sublime, 312
　of wealth and generosity, interdependence of, 619
causes and conditions, 411–12
　of compassion, 610
　dependent reality and, 413
　for Dharma, 29, 283–84
　in establishing impermanence, 109, 689, 691–94
　interest arising through, 347
　leading to gnosis, 653
　of phenomena, 242
　variant views on, 410
certain deliverance
　from attachment and defilements, 62, 480–81, 482
　branch of, 107, 675
　Dharma teaching and, 58, 454
　due to bodhicitta, 16, 203–4, 206
　eightfold path and, 676
　by Great Vehicle, 132, 836–37
　from saṃsāra, 132, 808, 835, 837, 838
　of sentient beings, 131, 132
　sustained calm and profound insight in, 107, 678, 679
　time in attaining, 67, 491
　transcendent perfections and, 15, 200
　in Vinaya, 45, 364, 365–66, 540
certainty
　about thatness, 28, 273–74
　desire to attain, 54, 436, 437–38
　in Dharma, 148, 451
　generosity and, 564
　in Great Vehicle, 755
　lack of, 7, 59, 166, 462, 463
　on path of accumulation, 244
　reflection of, 67, 494
　in results of transcendent perfections, 118, 750–51
　superior, in Great Vehicle, 265
　in two truths, 446
cessation
　absence of, 52, 411–12
　absorption of, 256, 811
　analytical, 820
　in establishing impermanence, 109, 694
　truth of, 507, 509, 646, 686, 687, 755, 761–62

Che Tashi, xxiii
Cittamātra, xx–xxi, 186–87, 235–36, 236–38, 395, 395n43, 414, xviin1
clear light, 63, 187, 238, 486, 657
clear vision, 128, 823
clinging
  to appearances, 773
  defilement of, 394
  freedom from, 523
  to imputed reality, 47, 382
  to names, 55, 443
  to spiritual masters, 589
  to substantiality, 825
Commentary on Ornament of the Mahāyāna Sūtras (*Sūtrālaṃkārabhāṣya*, Vasubandhu), xxii, 603n19, 706, 714
  dharma, use of term in, 571n26
  on diligence, 551n18
  on five unexcelled metaphors, 143
  on potential, 188n9
  on steadfastness, 638n4
  on ten aspects of sameness of phenomena, 815nn10–13
Commentary on Valid Cognition, 755
common vehicle, 224
companions
  base, 7, 165–66
  conducive to practice, 62, 477–78
  evil, 6, 14, 41, 102, 162, 163, 189–90, 348–49, 640
compassion
  of Asaṅga, xvi–xvii
  bodhicitta and, 15, 16, 18, 199, 204, 214, 215
  of bodhisattvas, 20, 113, 125, 139n1, 174, 180, 191, 218, 227, 228, 229–30, 488, 489, 733–34, 797
  of bodhisattvas, superiority of, 97, 624–25
  boundless, 118, 208–9, 753, 754
  of buddhas, 5, 31, 158, 289–90, 515
  causal factors of, 97, 622–24
  as cause of patience, 80, 541
  as cause of refuge, 10, 179, 180
  as cooperative condition, 559
  definite duty of, 118, 751, 752
  discipline and, 84, 554–55
  embodying, 18, 216–17
  fourfold, 93, 603
  generosity and, 82, 96, 548, 549, 615–17
  and gnosis, inseparability of, 552
  gnosis of equality and, 38, 326
  in Great Vehicle, distinction of, 158–59
  as instructing generosity, 96–97, 618–20
  in lower vehicles, 522
  maturation of, 25, 28, 259, 262, 274
  objects of, 91, 93, 593, 600–601, 799
  offerings of, 89, 580, 581
  in *Ornament of Mahāyāna Sūtras*, composition of, 3, 142
  practice of, 62–63, 483–84
  qualities of giving with, 97, 620–21
  realization of, 237
  result of, 799
  as sign of potential, 13, 188–89
  in six perfections, 564–65
  skillful means and, 745
  of supreme refuge, 30, 286–87
  in teaching Dharma, 57, 449–50
  twofold nature of, 798
  wisdom and, 93, 602–3, 681
  See also four boundless attitudes; great compassion
Compendium of the Great Vehicle (Asaṅga), 144, 237, 247, 331, 370, 467, 483, 504
complacency, 59, 467, 469
compounded phenomena
  impermanence of, 109, 688–97
  inner, impermanence of, 109–10, 698–707
  mistaken views on, 444
  nature and presentation, differences between, 711–13
  outer, impermanence of, 110, 707–14
  three characteristics of, 410
conceit, 49, 58, 389–90, 452, 459
concentration, 471
  in accomplishing activities, 681
  all-discerning gnosis and, 39, 326–27
  attentiveness associated with remaining in, 46, 371
  as benefit of interest, 352
  bliss of, 35, 309–10
  bodhicitta and, 16, 204
  bodhisattvas instruction on, 224
  boundless, 256
  branch of enlightenment, 106, 670, 674
  buddhas' speech and, 456

as cause for bodhisattvas' birth, 126, 803, 804, 805
and discipline, relationship between, 362
on eightfold path, 376
in enlightened state, 318–19
five benefits of, 69–70, 502–4
five faults that prevent, 664
fivefold knowledge of object of, 46, 372, 373
of form and formless worlds, 227
incomplete superior, 64, 489–90
knowledge of treatises in, 102, 642, 644
matured faith and, 25, 261
natural, 68, 499–500
obstacles to, 478
power of, 667, 668–69
relying on, 559–60
as root of all good qualities, 499
savoring, 116, 118, 490, 551, 746, 752, 753, 782
sense of shame and, 632
source of, 14, 192–93
steadfastness and, 101, 637–38, 639
of stream of Dharma, 67, 377, 440, 441, 492
on tenth level, 127, 811–12, 816, 817, 819, 830
virtues of, 69, 501–2
See also nine methods for settling the mind; superior concentration; three doors of perfect liberation (three concentrations)
concentration, transcendent
bodhicitta and, 208
defining characteristics of, 78, 531–32
eight supreme aspects of, 85, 561
etymology of, 79, 533, 534
factors incompatible with, 81, 547–48
four excellent qualities of, 83, 551–52
in maturing others, 28, 273
and other perfections, relationship between, 570–71
purity of, 84, 556–57
subdivisions of, 80, 542–43, 571
as support for miraculous powers, 105, 662–63
ten powers and, 667
transcendent wisdom and, 80, 543–44
two accumulations and, 653
conception (birth), 109, 696–97, 698

concepts/conceptualization, 16, 51, 55, 205–6, 406–7, 443–45. *See also* mere concepts
conceptual elaboration, absence of, 50, 235, 304, 332, 333, 381, 401, 407
conceptual structures, 768–70
conceptual thought, 35, 309, 348, 407, 509, 514, 594, 595–96, 649
confession, 365, 426, 456, 653, 681
confidence, 346
in Buddha, 25, 261
fearlessness and, 257
inexhaustible, 211
inner, 650, 651
in meaning of teachings, 265
in Three Jewels, 370–71
in three wisdoms, 368
in transcendent perfections, 427
in ultimate truth, 686
consciousness, 111, 236, 238, 648, 695–96, 720–21. *See also* eight consciousnesses; ground of all; six consciousnesses
container world, 254, 772–73
continuity, attentiveness to, 54, 434, 435
conventional truth. *See* relative truth
creators, 242, 412, 714

Daughter, 191, 484
death
of bodhisattvas, 215–16
consciousness associated with, 698
happiness at, 60, 470–71
joyful, 541
preternatural knowledge of, 249, 256, 665, 837
protection from, 30, 284–85, 286
decency. *See* sense of decency
dedication, 524, 681, 845–46
of generosity, 97, 558, 621–22
of merit, 129, 825, 826
of offerings, 581
to spiritual masters, 90, 585
to transcendent perfections, 113, 733–34
deeds
attentiveness associated with, 46, 369, 370
of buddhas, 212, 254, 313, 320, 323, 804, 816, 817
of completion and maturation, 745
sameness of, 16, 203
See also shameful deeds

defiled mind consciousness, 308, 320, 325, 400, 406, 790–91
defilement and purity, 114–15, 452, 738
  appearances of, 388–89
  in establishing impermanence, 713
  of individuals, establishing no-self by, 112, 725–27
  investigating, 49, 367, 393–95
  lack of confusion about, 115, 738, 739
  roots of, 237
  on sixth level, 127, 815
  of suchness, 234–35
defilements, 219
  accumulation of wisdom and, 104, 652
  appearance of, 395
  of bodhisattvas, 92, 598
  conventional existence of, 474
  delusion and, 388
  Dharma for eliminating, 59, 463, 464
  diligence as antidote to, 80, 82, 542, 550–51
  dispelling, 25, 261–62
  elimination on bodhisattva levels, 126, 476, 807, 808
  exhaustion and nonarising of, 363n9
  in four boundless attitudes, 594
  freedom from, 80, 92, 101, 298, 442, 544, 581, 599, 639, 640, 838
  giving without, 798
  habituation to, 14, 189–90
  impure body and, 656
  indulging in, 99, 631, 632
  influence of, 257
  karma and, 237
  lack of fear of, 18, 215–16
  in Lesser Vehicle and Great Vehicle, different views of, 480, 482
  liberation by means of, 62, 480–83
  as mental concepts, 594
  negative actions and, 554
  nonarising of, 131, 834
  obstacles due to, 568–69
  of ordinary beings, 229–30
  protection from, 30, 126, 284–85, 286, 809
  purification of, 63, 389–90, 484–85
  rebirth and, 658
  ripening of, 510
  root of, 239, 240
  in settling mind, 499
  of spiritual masters, 585–86
  threefold absence of, 107, 675, 676
  in three vehicles, 415
  See also five branches of elimination
delight
  attentiveness and, 536
  in Dharma, 4, 152–53, 776
  in discipline, 784
  in generosity, 86, 96, 97, 563, 619–20, 622
  maturation of, 25, 259, 260–61, 267
  in objects of meditation, 53, 429–30
  in offerings, 581
  in patience, 84, 555
delusion
  dualistic, 47, 382–83, 387
  nature and cause of, 48, 386–87, 388–89
  recognizing, 46, 381–82
  suffering and, 21, 241–42
  See also bewilderment
demigods, 294, 458–59, 650
demons, 114, 155–56, 259, 265, 459, 600, 738, 789, 836–37
dependent arising, 763–64, 799
  appearances of, 443
  attentiveness to, 369–70
  of beings, 71, 510
  diligence in meditation on, 566
  discipline and, 84, 554–55
  emptiness of, 815
  in Listeners' and Great Vehicles, distinctions in view of, 156, 162
  in Madhyamaka view, 235
  of phenomena, 21, 233–34, 241–42
  realization of, 791–92
  on sixth level, 780, 809, 818–19
  three natures and, 144, 233–34
  two kinds, 237, 829
dependent reality/nature, 246
  appearances of, 144, 373, 386, 388, 401, 443, 685, 686, 688
  Cittamātra view of, 235–36
  as conventional truth, 151
  as devoid of intrinsic existence, 410, 411–12
  emptiness of, 509
  in five indicative stages of yoga, 402–3
  impure and pure, 384, 646
  and imputed nature, relationship between, 383

INDEX — 903

intention of, 465
investigating, 50, 399–400
mere appearances in, 385
no-self and, 407
perception of, 384, 394
realization of, 474
thatness and, 233–34
transformation of, 317, 772
desire, 42, 92, 118, 310, 353–55, 587, 597, 752. *See also* world of desire
despair, regarding as enemy, 53, 429, 430
Detailed Commentary of the Ornament of the Sūtras (*Sūtrālaṃkāravṛttibhāṣya*, Sthiramati), xxii–xxiv, 167n12, 339n2, 415, 463, 662, 706, 714, 787, 826, 843
on abiding/dwelling, 674
on aggregates, 239
on antidotes in mediation, 374n22
on aspiration prayers, 683
on attentiveness, 538n6
on bad teachers, 740n4
on benefiting beings, 180
on benefits of ten levels, 828
on bodhisattva qualities, 783
on bodhisattvas, 139n1, 333
on body as support, 264
on buddhas, 390
on Buddha's absence of defilements, 459n13
on buddhas' speech, 457n8
on concentration, 503–4, 543n14, 735n2
on concentration and discipline, relationship between, 362n7
on designations, 766
on Dharma teaching, simile for, 448n2
on discipline, 271, 540
on discursiveness, 371
on five branches of elimination, 266n4
on five metaphors, 143–44
on four inconceivable things, 146n12
on four seals of Dharma, 294n10
on great enlightenment, 313
on impermanence, 688
on intellectuals, 161n4
on interest, use of term, 345
on investigation and buddha bodies, 441
on joy of first level, 203n9
on Listeners' Vehicle, 416n59
on love, 609
on maturation, 311n25

on mind and mental factors, 395, 397
on mirrorlike stage of yoga, 402
on monastic downfalls, 365
on nirmāṇakāyas, 254, 324n33
on nonconceptual gnosis, object of, 317
on *Ornament of Great Vehicle*, structure of, 140
on pain, acceptance of, 217
on patient acceptance, 754
on perfect knowledge, 651
on perfect liberation, 409
on poverty, 190n10
on preceptor's functions, 741–42n5
on preternatural knowledge, 251n4, 254
on reasoned analysis, 265
on right concentration, 678n23
on right livelihood, 376n27
on semblance of perfections, 437n77
on sense consciousnesses, 309
on sense organs at transformation, 307
on shame, 636
on stream of mindfulness, 247
on three kinds of acts, 677n21
on three kinds of individuals, 144, 223n2
on three obscurations, 219n17
on three realities, 144
on three secrets, 176n5
on twofold potential, 187
on two truths, 446
on wisdom, 396n44
on words and syllables, 454–55
on yoga, nature and cause of, 46, 371
determination to be free, 62, 469, 478–79
devotion, 89, 580–81, 586, 587
dhāraṇī, 468. *See also* power of retention
Dharma
causes and conditions for, 29, 283–84
compassion from hearing, 624
confidence in, 370–71
contempt for, 59, 467–68, 587
definitive and expedient, importance of distinguishing, 464–65
delight/joy in, 3, 4, 59, 147, 148, 152–53, 211, 463–64, 776
door of, 73, 91, 515, 589
eight conditions lacking opportunity for, 479
engagement in, 54, 438
expedient and definitive/ultimate, 103, 464–65, 647–49

Dharma (*continued*)
  eye of, 664, 776
  general characteristics of, 59, 463–64
  gift of, 57, 79, 118, 447–48, 539, 558, 562, 574, 753
  holding entirety of, 102, 642, 644
  hostility toward, 7, 162, 163, 166–67
  impartiality of, 36, 314
  implied and indirect teachings, 59, 465–67
  interest in, 16, 204
  lack of contradiction in, 5, 159–60
  light of, 70, 106, 129, 504, 673–74, 827, 828
  listening, reflecting, gnosis of, 6, 164
  power over, 666
  proclaiming, 254
  rain of, 39, 327
  rarity of encountering, 442
  of realization, 449, 478
  sound of, 57, 318, 451
  as supreme refuge, 30, 286–87
  time of endurance of, 776
  of transmission, 3, 147–48, 151, 449, 450–51, 464, 478 (*see also* three collections (*tripiṭaka*))
  uninterrupted realization of, 69, 503
  See also four summaries of Dharma; teaching Dharma
dharma, uses of term, 571n26, 593n13
dharmakāya. *See* body of truth (*dharmakāya*)
Dharma Wheel, turning of, 36, 313–14
dhyāna. *See* four dhyānas
dialectics, 642. *See also* logic; reasoning
Diamond Cutter Sūtra, 282, 753–54
diligence
  armor-like, 75, 197, 273, 427n65, 522, 551n18, 561
  as basis of miraculous powers, 105, 662, 663
  in benefiting being, 18, 20, 219, 228
  branch of enlightenment, 106, 670, 673
  in five sciences, 422–23
  in four boundless attitudes, 596
  four excellent qualities of, 82, 550–51
  four obstacles and, 87, 568–69
  indefatigability in, 102, 640, 641
  interest and, 41, 348, 349, 350–51
  in investigating Dharma, 55, 445–46
  in mastering Mahāyāna, 260
  power of, 667, 668, 669
  steadfastness and, 101, 637–38, 639
  sustained, 143
  in yoga, 105, 661–62
diligence, transcendent, 489
  aspects of, 87, 567–69
  bodhicitta and, 208
  concentration and, 80, 542, 543
  constant, 65, 490
  defining characteristics of, 78, 531
  eight supreme aspects of, 85, 561
  etymology of, 79, 533, 534
  factors incompatible with, 81, 547
  functions of, 86, 566
  importance of, 86, 565–66
  in maturing others, 28, 272–73, 512
  and other perfections, relationship between, 570
  at peak stage, 70, 504
  purity of, 84, 556
  subdivisions of, 80, 542, 571
  ten powers and, 667
  of three kinds of individuals, 87, 568
  in transcendent perfections, 436
  two accumulations and, 653
discernment, perfect, 106, 673
discipline, 19, 199, 226, 227, 361. *See also* superior discipline
discipline, transcendent
  accumulation of merit and, 104, 652, 653
  benefits of, 489
  bodhicitta and, 208
  defining characteristics of, 78, 530–31
  destruction of, 92, 99, 597–99, 632
  eight supreme aspects of, 85, 560
  etymology of, 79, 533, 534
  factors incompatible with, 81, 546
  four excellent qualities of, 82, 549–50
  in maturing others, 27, 271–72
  and other perfections, relationship between, 570
  purity of, 83–84, 553–55
  subdivisions of, 79, 540–41
  ten powers and, 667
discouragement
  indefatigability and, 641
  from lacking diligence, 638
  lack of, 20, 93, 214, 221, 229–30, 426, 451, 602–3, 614, 823

obstacles due to, 87, 568, 569
in teaching Dharma, 59, 462, 463
discourse, eight faults of, 58–59, 461,
    462–63
discursiveness, 371, 495–96, 543, 638
disposition. *See* potential
Distinguishing the Middle from Extremes
    (*Madhyāntavibhāga*), xvii, 386, 656,
    762
distractions
    antidotes for, 68, 498, 499
    compassion toward, 623
    drawbacks of, 661
    manifest, 547
    on path of joining, 70, 505
    of sense objects, 78, 529
    transcendent concentration and, 531
divine ear, 209, 249, 251, 665, 835
divine eye, 165, 209, 249, 251, 252, 255,
    506, 664, 665, 835
doubt
    about enlightened state, 31, 292–93
    all-discerning gnosis and, 39, 327
    clarifying and removing others', 28, 58,
    273–74, 452, 456, 461
    dispelling, 360
    failure to resolve others', 59, 462–63
    faith and, 345
    four kinds of perfect knowledge and,
    103, 651
    freedom from, 260, 265
    in not wasting practice, 116, 743, 744
downfalls, 741
    of bodhisattvas, 64, 271, 486–87, 813
    deliverance from, 456
    denial of Three Jewels as, 156
    transcendent discipline and, 570
    in Vinaya, 45, 361, 364–66, 799
dreams
    appearances in, 387, 391, 505, 508, 773
    impermanence of, 701
    as metaphors, 240, 241, 252, 384, 400,
    811
    signs of attainment in, 503
dualism
    elimination of, at enlightenment, 119,
    282–83, 284, 769–70, 772
    elimination of, on first level, 265
    freedom from, 22, 244–45
    of subject and object, 233–34, 236

dualistic appearances
    freedom from, 49, 394, 474
    as illusory, 48–49, 385, 387–88
    as imputation, 792
    investigating, 444–45
    mind as, 49, 395–96
    as relative truth, 47, 383
    three realities and, 398–401
dullness, 68, 496, 497, 499n7
duties, types of, 118, 751–54

eight consciousnesses, 648, 762, 791
    appearances and, 395
    bondage of, 768
    as dependent reality, 144, 400
    four kinds of gnosis and, 325
    as mind basis, 396–97
    transformation of, 237, 288
eighteen distinctive qualities, 840
eightfold noble path, 58, 107, 373, 375–76,
    454, 455, 567, 676–78
eighth bodhisattva level (Immovable)
    acceptance of phenomena on, 740
    attainments of, 211–12, 224–25
    defining characteristic of, 126, 810–11
    desire to attain, 437
    etymological definition of, 130, 829–30
    mark of, 826
    mastery on, 51, 406
    nonconceptual gnosis on, 177, 178–79,
    198, 211, 414, 733, 751, 810, 811
    nonconceptual love on, 593–94
    predictions on, 105, 113, 224–25, 414,
    660, 733, 750
    types of bodhisattvas on, 127, 816
eight kinds of examination, 421
eight kinds of noble beings, 455n6, 457
eight obscurations, antidotes to, 59–60,
    467–70
eight ordinary preoccupations, 100, 634,
    635
eight perfect freedoms, 24, 256, 701, 833–34
eight states lacking opportunity, 479
eighty inexhaustible qualities, 206n10,
    207–12
eloquence, 206n10
    bodhicitta and, 209, 211
    inauthentic, 117, 747–48
    perfect knowledge of, 209, 650, 651,
    666, 811, 835

embryos, 696, 699, 702
empowerment, 113, 733
  four genuine restraints in receiving, 105, 660
  of great light rays, 10, 72, 175, 225, 226, 227, 513–14, 816, 817
emptiness, xvii, 329, 368
  and appearance, union of, 238, 320n29, 385
  black and white aspects of, 815
  and clarity, union of, 187, 486
  compassion and, 625
  concentration of, 108, 473, 474, 509, 682, 685–86, 687
  equality in, 771
  faith in, 668
  as focus in offerings, 582
  form and, 444, 445
  fully present reality and, 401
  intrinsic existence, absence of, 165
  lack of contradiction in teaching, 160n3
  misunderstanding, 151, 443
  nature of, 32, 296
  as object of right view, 164n8
  partial vision of, 504n14
  on path of seeing/first level, 71, 126, 508–9, 806–7
  of phenomena, 242, 316–17, 653, 770
  as positively established, 233–34
  realization of, xxi, 200, 792
  reason for teaching, 162
  reflecting on, 244
  in refutation of self, 725
  skillful means and, 745
  steadfast interest in, 102, 639, 640
  supreme in all respects, 572
  three kinds of, 71, 508–9
Enjoying Magical Creations (god realm), 700
enlightened activities, 51, 121, 406, 407, 778, 779
enlightened element. *See* buddha nature
enlightenment, xxi, 140, 224, 339, 340
  approach to, 146–47
  attaining, 29, 60, 121, 279–81, 470, 471, 778, 779
  bodhicitta and, 197
  cause of, 14, 37, 192–93, 317–18, 431
  as complete purity, 39–40, 331–34
  through diligence, 86, 566

displaying, 291, 793
hope for, 116, 743
and ignorance, sameness of, 482
in names for bodhisattvas, 122, 787–88
as object of faith, 106, 668
praise of, 40, 336–37
as result of transcendent perfections, 113, 733
steadfastness regarding, 640
swift path to, 483
use of term, 592n12
yearning for, 53, 423–24
See also ten qualities of enlightenment
enthusiasm/keenness, 16, 203, 204–5
  about concentration, 499
  to acquire preternatural knowledge, 501
  attentiveness associated with, 46, 53, 369, 370–71, 427–28
  as basis of miraculous powers, 105, 662, 663
  giving rise to, 105, 661
  mental application of, 664
enumeration, 494
environment, transformation of, 50, 405
equality
  attentiveness to, 54, 438
  of compassion, 97, 624–25
  in generosity, 27, 270
  mind of, 177
  of oneself and others, 19, 222, 510n19
  on path of meditation, 22, 245–46
  of three buddha bodies, 38, 323–24
equanimity, 376
  on eighth level, 816
  mental application of, 664
  quality of, 122, 786–87
  remaining in, 492
  special point of, 68, 479, 497, 661–62, 678, 783
equipoise. *See* meditative equipoise
essence of sugatas. *See* buddha nature
eternalism, 394
evenness
  branch of, 106, 670, 671, 674–75
  on path of accumulation, 70, 504
  with regard to object, 68, 497
  settling in, 651
  state of, 288, 334, 826
  subtle intelligence of, 794
  ultimate truth of, 552

evil ways, consistently following, 14, 193
Excellent Words, 7, 166–67, 347, 359–60, 450–51, 463–64, 647, 649, 760.
  See also Twelve Branches of Excellent Speech
expanse of reality, 62, 480, 481–82
  abiding in, 32, 298–99
  body of truth and, 321
  buddha activity in, 32, 34, 294–95, 303–4, 314
  buddhas as, 329
  direct realization of, 22, 177, 244, 245, 265
  as enlightened state, 37, 292, 316–19
  evenness of, 334
  fully present reality as, 401
  lack of distinction in, 331
  perception of, 770
  realization of, 71, 379, 507
  sameness of, 203, 223
  settling in, 22, 246
  as suchness, 282
expectancy, concentration of absence of, 71, 432, 473–74, 509, 682, 685–86, 687
expedient teachings, 465
  as fault in discourse, 462
  in four reliances, 103, 210, 647, 648, 649
  as hindrance to sound-produced interest, 349
  intention of, 414–15
  wisdom in understanding, 274

faith, xxi, 142, 837
  bodhicitta and, 198
  causing in others, 114, 224, 253, 254, 737
  clear, 53, 73, 98, 426–27, 514–15, 579, 581, 582, 626
  in concentration, 664
  in Dharma, 59, 463–64
  in four boundless attitudes, 625
  hope and, 743
  increasing, 67, 491
  manifestation of, 49, 395
  maturation of, 25, 259, 261
  in offerings, 89, 579, 581
  power of, 667–68, 669
  purpose of, 345–46
  teaching Dharma and, 461
  in transcendent perfections, 54, 437
  two accumulations and, 266
  in two kinds of no-self, 787
  use of term, 345n1
  See also interest
false imagination, 47, 382–83, 386
  appearances of, 63, 485
  cause of, 50, 398, 399
  as dependent reality, 50, 399–400, 401, 474
  perception of, 383–84
  realization of, 71, 123, 508, 791
fear
  five kinds, 177, 511, 550, 554
  freedom from, 79, 539, 540–41, 823
  of Great Vehicle, 6, 151–52, 162–65
  in not wasting practice, 116, 743, 744
  of ordinary beings, 20, 227
  steadfastness and, 101, 637–38
  of suffering, 95, 613, 614
fearlessness, 83, 257, 554, 615, 639. *See also* four fearlessnesses
Feast of the Nectar of the Supreme Vehicle (Mipham), xxiii–xxv, 843–44
fields (Tib. *zhing*), 89, 90, 539n8, 559, 582, 585
fifth bodhisattva level (Hard to Conquer)
  defining characteristic of, 126, 807, 808–9
  etymological definition of, 130, 829
  mark of, 825
  types of bodhisattvas on, 127, 814–15
first bodhisattva level (Perfect Joy), 137n2, 177, 394
  acquiring, 61, 476
  attainments of, 223, 224, 226, 437
  being born into tathāgata family on, 733
  branches of enlightenment on, 673–76
  cause of, 679
  defining characteristic of, 126, 806–7
  direct realization on, 236, 265, 318, 352, 367–68
  etymological definition of, 129, 828
  faith on, 261
  four boundless attitudes on, 595, 596
  gnosis of equality on, 326
  great compassion on, 605
  joy on, 113, 144, 733
  keeping the system in mind on, 821–22
  mark of, 825

first bodhisattva level (Perfect Joy)
    (*continued*)
  merit for, 370
  nonconceptual gnosis on, 332
  offerings from, 582
  omnipresence on, 292
  qualities of, 71–72, 510–12
  sameness on, 614
  superior intention on, 780
  time needed to attain, 70, 506–7
  types of bodhisattvas on, 127, 813
  ultimate bodhicitta on, 203
  See also path of seeing
First Council, 493n4
five aggregates, 374, 792
  appearance of, 241–42
  of bodhisattvas, 335–36
  bondage of, 768
  of buddhas, 329
  concentration related to absence of
    expectancy and, 685
  consciousness and, 648
  continuity of, 701, 704–5
  as defiled, 726
  extinction of, 10, 178
  as false imagination, 508
  impermanence of, 714
  intention of, 465
  interruption of, 656
  investigating, 367
  in Lesser Vehicle, 592
  of listeners, discontinuation of, 420
  in Listeners' and Great Vehicles,
    distinctions in view of, 156
  momentariness of, 707
  sameness of, 203
  as self, views on, 21, 111, 239–40, 379,
    715, 717–20
  three natures and, 404
  transformation of, 288
  See also five untainted aggregates;
    perpetuating aggregates
five branches of elimination, 25, 26, 259,
    265–66
five crimes with immediate retribution,
    190, 193, 219n17, 284, 286, 468
five degenerations, 468
five forms of hope, 116, 743
five hindrances, 105, 492, 659, 660
five improper places, 540

five irresistible forces, 106, 669
five kinds of eye, 106, 664–65
five kinds of preternatural knowledge, 18,
    69, 206n10, 209, 216–17, 501–2, 757
five paths, 22, 178, 244–46, 392–93, 394,
    396n44. *See also individual path*
five powers, 106, 567, 667–69
five pure abodes, 595
five sciences, 162, 437
  in Dharma teaching, 118, 756–60, 787
  on fifth level, 808–9
  investigating, 53, 420–23
  knowledge of, 642–43, 644
five sense consciousnesses, 35, 308–
    9, 325, 387, 400, 542. *See also* six
    consciousnesses
five sense organs, 34, 306, 307, 387, 396–
    97, 696–97, 699, 715–16
five sense pleasures, 469
  attachment to, 116, 227, 600, 623, 746,
    752
  genuine restraint of, 661
  interest and, 42, 353–55
  nonattachment to, 121, 747, 781, 783
  shame in indulging, 631
Five Treatises of Maitreya, xvii. *See
    also Distinguishing the Middle from
    Extremes; Ornament of the Mahāyāna
    Sūtras; Ornament of True Realization;
    Sublime Continuum*
five untainted aggregates, 128, 819–20
follow-up teachings, 75, 377, 435, 515–
    16, 519
forbearance, 19, 25, 26, 94, 152, 221–22,
    259, 262–63, 606–10. *See also* patience
forgetfulness, absence of, 839
form basis, 396, 397, 405
form body, 31, 292–93
four absorptions of formless world, 116,
    543, 566, 679, 744, 745
four bases of miraculous powers, 105–6,
    374, 570, 662–67
four boundless attitudes, 208–9, 340, 429,
    800, 825
  abiding properly in, 92, 599
  bases of miraculous powers and, 663
  categories of, 92, 594–96
  defects of failure in, 92, 597–99
  defining characteristics of, 91, 591–92
  objects of, 91, 592–94

praise of, 131, 832–33
result of, 92, 98, 596, 626–27
sign of, 597
superiority of, 97, 625–26
four boundless states, 543
four close mindfulnesses, 104–5, 374, 510, 655–59, 659–62, 668
four complete purities, 836
four delights, 216–17
four dhyānas, 419, 566
  abiding in, 543
  analysis in, 495–96
  attaining, 501, 745
  concentration and, 668
  first, attaining, 69, 500–501
  fourth, as supreme, 118, 753, 754
  fourth, attaining, 23, 250
  inferior and complete, 46, 371
  mundane, 449
  never savoring, 113, 732, 734
  preternatural knowledge and, 663
  realms in, 595
  rebirth from, 807
four elements, 110, 242, 707–10, 720
four extremes, freedom from, 21, 233–35
four fearlessnesses, 152, 611, 774, 837–38
four genuine restraints, 104–5, 374, 510, 567, 659–62, 663, 668
four good qualities of pure activity, 59, 463, 464
four great wheels of practice, 62, 477–80
four implied teachings, 59, 466–67
four indirect teachings, 59, 465–66
four kinds of complete knowledge, 119–20, 767–73
four kinds of conduct, 229, 295, 538
four kinds of gnosis, 38, 119, 192, 225, 316, 324–25, 767, 841
  mirrorlike gnosis as support in, 38, 325–26
  ripening causes of, 39, 328–31
  at transformation, 288
four kinds of perfect knowledge, 103, 131, 206n10, 649–51, 666, 835
  bodhicitta and, 209
  in commenting on profound intention, 799
  mastery and, 406
  on ninth level, 660, 811, 816, 819, 830
four kinds of rational application, 119, 449, 759–60, 762–63

four misconceptions, 411, 656, 659, 713, 716, 769, 770, 785, 825
four noble truths, 416n59
  attentiveness to, 369–70
  complete knowledge of, 373
  diligence in, 566
  on fifth level, 808, 818, 829
  on fourth level, 780
  ignorance of, 612
  knowledge of world and, 102, 644–47
  realizing, 603, 776
  suchness and, 761–62
  in teaching Dharma, 452
  transcendent perfections and, 527, 532–33
  wisdom and, 668
four obstacles, 87, 568–69
four powers, 53, 424–26
four principles of a śramaṇa, 657
four reliances, 103, 210, 430, 647–49
four results of the Listeners' Vehicle, 379. *See also* arhats; nonreturners; once-returners; stream enterers
four summaries of Dharma, 109, 211, 294n10, 366, 432, 687–88, 714, 724, 725
fourteen aspects of life (arising), 109–10, 698–707
fourth bodhisattva level (Radiant)
  defining characteristic of, 126, 807–8
  etymological definition of, 129, 828–29
  mark of, 825
  types of bodhisattvas on, 127, 813–14
four ways of attracting disciples, 209, 255, 426, 428, 577, 620–21, 745–46
  beings taught for, 832
  benefits of, 88, 575–76
  definitions and number of, 87, 572–73
  functions of, 87, 573–74
  seventh level and, 816
  skillful means in, 681
  ways of classifying, 88, 574–75
fully present reality/nature, 143n8
  concentration related to absence of attributes and, 685–86, 687, 688
  as devoid of intrinsic production and cessation, 412
  at enlightenment, 282
  as ground to be purified, 401
  investigating, 50, 400–401

fully present reality/nature (*continued*)
  natural emptiness of, 509
  no-self and, 407
  obscuration and purity of, 382
  perception of, 384
  phrases, names, letters and, 373
  realization of, 474, 657
  transcendent wisdom and, 39, 332
  truth of cessation and, 762
  two types, 144
  as ultimate truth, 151, 233, 383, 402–3, 443

Gaṇḍavyūha-sūtra, 804n4
gandharvas, 17, 209, 253, 458, 650
garuḍas, 102, 640
Gelek Gyatso, 845
generosity, transcendent, 666n16
  accumulation of merit and, 104, 652, 653
  in attracting disciples, 87, 572, 573, 620–21
  benefits of, 489
  bodhicitta and, 207
  compassion and, 95, 96–97, 615–17, 618–22
  defining characteristics of, 78, 530
  of Dharma, 57, 447–48
  eight supreme aspects of, 84, 558–60
  etymology of, 79, 533, 534
  factors incompatible with, 81, 545–46
  four excellent qualities of, 82, 548–49
  insatiable attitude toward, 536–38
  material, 536, 539–40, 574, 667, 732
  in maturing others, 27, 270–71
  and other perfections, relationship between, 569–70
  praise for qualities of, 85–86, 562–65
  purity of, 83, 553
  results of, 79, 539, 568n23
  subdivisions of, 79, 539–40, 571
  ten powers and, 667
gnosis, 72, 237, 513, 650
  aspiration and, 666
  in buddha activity, 33, 34, 300–302, 303
  of buddhas, 5, 158, 165, 288–89
  conceptual and nonconceptual, combined practice of, 61, 476–77
  of Dharma, 6, 164
  of exhaustion, 413
  of exhaustion and nonarising, 482, 613
  free from dualistic conceptions regarding phenomena, 16, 203
  free from two obscurations, 32, 297–98
  inaccessibility of, 33, 302
  inexpressible, 103, 649
  in Listeners' and Great Vehicles, differences between, 162
  manifestation of, 33, 301
  mastery of, 24, 51, 254, 257, 406, 407
  personal experience of, 450
  self-illuminating, 238
  source of, 14, 192
  spiritual masters, in dependence upon, 90, 588
  subsequently attained, 791
  supramundane, 70, 288, 318, 402, 449, 475, 506
  of tenth level, 175–76
  universality of, 9, 172
  untainted, 241
  See also four kinds of gnosis; nonconceptual gnosis; omniscience; pure mundane gnosis
gnosis of equality, 38, 308, 320, 326
gods, 430, 598
  abiding of, 543
  bodhicitta of, 202
  boundless attitudes of, 625
  Buddha's speech and, 455, 458–59, 460
  happiness and pleasures of, 294, 566, 614, 758
  insensate, 219n17
  language of, 650
  manifestation as, 318, 322, 328
  perception of, 133, 708, 841–42
  rebirth as, 100, 177, 215–16, 253, 419, 479n8, 534, 633–34, 699–700, 751
  refuge in, 285
grammar, 421, 423, 459, 642, 643, 748, 756–57
Great Being (epithet of Buddha), 32, 296–97
great bliss, 10, 14, 42, 175, 195, 351–52
Great Commentary. See *Detailed Commentary of the Ornament of the Sūtras* (*Sūtrālaṃkāravṛttibhāṣya*)
great compassion, 139, 216, 514, 555
  accumulation of merit and, 200
  of bodhisattvas, 787–88
  of Buddha, 289–90

force of, 356
in four close mindfulnesses, 658
gnosis of equality and, 38, 326
nonconceptual wisdom and, 480, 488
on path of meditation, 418
perfecting force of, 356
praise to, 132, 839
qualities of, 94–95, 611–13
as root of all aspects, 94, 606–10
six aspects of, 94, 604–6
wisdom and, 158–59, 287
Great Vehicle (Mahāyāna)
attentiveness of, 380
authenticity of, xviii–xix
bodhicitta in, 202, 206–7
as Buddha's word, 5, 144, 145, 155–58, 339
delight in, 25, 259, 260–61, 267
discipline of, 362
enjoyment of, 321, 404
essence of, 480, 488
examining, 164
fear of, 6, 162–65
in five categories, 143–44
five sciences and, 422
interest in, 13, 42–43, 130, 188–89, 194–95, 199, 348, 353–57, 355–56, 831–32
listeners and solitary realizers entering, 52, 415, 416–17, 420
losing interest in, 484
offering practice of, 583–84
Ornament of the Mahāyāna Sūtras, significance of, xv, xvii–xviii, 141, 142
phenomena, view of in, 243
predictions about, 5, 158
pure view of, 332
rejection of, 151–52, 469–70
rewards of, 3, 152
seven aspects of greatness of, 120–21, 138, 140, 777–78
shame and decency in, 632, 636
specific maturation in, 275
summary of, 121, 762, 778–79
superiority of, xx, xxi–xxii, 7, 11, 145–46, 166, 179–80
ten benefits of, 60, 470–71
three wisdoms and, 197, 199, 202–3, 328
and transcendent perfections, importance of in, 77, 525, 528–29, 571
as ultimate vehicle, 415

Great Vehicle Abhidharma, 160
ground, path, result, 372
ground of all
appearances arising from, 393–94, 773
body and, Asaṅga's view of, 236
bondage of, 768
defilements in, 389
habitual tendencies in, 246, 308, 624, 770
mind as, 237, 395–96, 408, 790
purification of, 502
seed of transcendent perfections in, 424
as self, view of, 400, 406, 790
six inner sense faculties and, 391
transformation of, 309, 317, 319–20, 324, 328, 384, 405–6, 507, 772
virtue in, 558–59

habitual tendencies, 624
in arhats and buddhas, differences between, 404
bodhisattvas' knowledge of others', 249
complete destruction of, 838–39
elimination of, 199, 246, 280–81
of four boundless attitudes, 625
in ground of all, 308, 393, 400, 405, 558–59, 773
imputed reality of, 50, 398–99
in mind, 696
purification of, 502
reversal of, 10, 177, 178
of subject and object, 384
subtle, eradication of, 73, 514
and supramundane qualities, realization of, 402
of sustained calm, 663
at transformation, 288
See also seeds
happiness
of bodhisattvas and other beings, differences between, 95, 615
from compassionate generosity, 96, 97, 618, 622
from compassionate suffering, 95, 96, 611, 613, 614, 616–17
delight in, 18, 214
through diligence, 86, 566
four kinds, 17, 212–14
great compassion and, 94, 608, 609–10
latent tendencies of, 624

happiness (*continued*)
  of Mahāyāna, 10, 179–80
  mundane and supramundane, 10, 177, 222
  not being carried away by, 129, 825, 826
  as obstacle, 63, 483, 484
  of ordinary beings, 20, 228
  as result of compassion, 93, 97, 601–2, 620–21
  samsaric, 194, 556
  superior intention in, 125–26, 802
  temporary and ultimate, 269–70
  wishing for others', 591, 593
Heap of Jewels Sūtra, 225, 489, 652, 745–46
Hell of Torment Unsurpassed, 18, 167, 217, 604, 624–25
hell realms/beings, 62, 63, 191, 253, 483–84, 708, 804
Hindu mythology, 242n13
homages, 3, 137, 138
hope. *See* five forms of hope
human birth, 42, 100, 355–56, 633–34
hungry spirits, 253, 460, 479n8, 559, 804

ignorance, 242
  arising of, 49, 393–95
  concentration and, 84, 556, 557
  in enlightened state, 298
  and enlightenment, sameness of, 482
  freedom from, 784
  habitual tendencies of, 281
  of ordinary beings, 95, 612
  of others, attitude toward, 269–70
  steadfastness and, 101, 637, 638
  terms for, 650
  of ultimate reality, 47, 382
Illusion-Like concentration, 253, 256
illusions, 18, 49, 215–16, 236, 241–42, 490. *See also* magical illusions
impartiality, 7, 167
  of buddhas in maturing beings, 36, 314
  in compassionate giving, 621
  of mirrorlike gnosis, 325
  objects of boundless, 593
  toward sentient beings, 54, 83–84, 113, 434, 554, 734, 735
imperceptible forms, 110, 494, 707, 709, 710
impermanence, 109, 687–88, 714, 782

of aggregates, 686
as focus in offerings, 582
fourteen ways of establishing, 109, 688–97
inner knowledge of, 794
investigating, 396n44
reflecting on, 244
of sense pleasures, 752
See also under compounded phenomena
imputed reality/nature, 144, 233–34
  confusion about, 47, 382
  and dependent reality, relationship between, 383
  as devoid of intrinsic existence, 411, 412
  emptiness of, 474, 509
  at enlightenment, 282
  and fully present reality, relationship between, 401, 444
  investigating, 50, 398–99
  nonexistence of, 403
  superimposition of, 386, 401
inconceivability, 143, 144, 148
  of all-accomplishing gnosis, 39, 327–28
  of bodhisattva levels, 128, 822
  of buddha activity, 35, 310
  of Buddha's attainments, 34, 305–6
  of Dharma, 161
  of enlightenment, 29–30, 281–84
  of four things taught by buddhas, 146n12, 260
  twofold (powers and maturation), 145
indefatigability, 53, 75, 102, 424, 426, 522, 563, 640–41
Indian Buddhism, xv–xvi, xviii, xxi
Indian cosmology, 334n37
Indra, 254, 294, 434, 458, 652, 658, 751, 824, 826
inexhaustibility, 55, 57, 102, 442, 443, 448, 641, 643
Inexhaustible Caskets, 318, 471, 812
Infinite Doors, 318–19, 812
inner science, 422, 423, 642, 643, 644, 757–60, 787
instructions, 75, 519
  acquiring, 67, 491–92
  correctly receiving, 377, 427
  and follow-up teachings, differences between, 515–16
  great benefits of, 73, 514–17
  not wasting, 116, 743, 744

putting into practice, 435
reflecting on, 67, 493–97
intellectuals, 6, 155–56, 160–61, 165
intelligence, 53, 93, 429, 430, 602
intended meaning, 62, 481–83, 484, 799.
  See also expedient teachings
intention, 464–65
  in aspiration prayers, 108, 683
  attentiveness to, 54, 436, 438
  bodhicitta and, 15, 197–98, 199
  in bodhisattvas' signs, 125, 798
  of charioteers, 236, 237
  of great compassion, 94, 606–10
  of Great Vehicle, 6, 158, 163–64, 167
  happiness from, 616
  of listeners, relinquishment of, 418
  loving, 20, 230
  in not wasting practice, 116, 743, 744
  pure, 16, 203, 205
  of single vehicle, 52–53, 414–20
  steadfast, 787
  of three buddha bodies, equality of, 323–24
  See also superior intention
interest, 75, 519
  attentiveness related to, 46, 369, 370, 536
  in attracting disciples, 87, 573–74
  benefits of, 42, 351–53
  in Dharma, 97, 625–26
  in emptiness, 639
  first reliance and, 103, 649
  in generosity, 559
  in Great Vehicle, 91, 121, 130, 590, 778, 831–32
  obstacles to, 41, 348–51
  quality of, 121, 779, 780
  as root of virtue, 345–46
  similes for, 42, 353–55
  twenty-six categories of, 41, 346–48, 351
  use of term, 345n1
intermediate state, 706
introduction
  in four close mindfulnesses, 104, 655, 656
  indirect teaching for, 59, 465
  keeping in mind, 53, 429, 430, 434–35
investigations, 75, 359, 519
  attentiveness and, 46, 369–80
  of Dharma of realization, 46–53, 381–423

of Dharma of transmission, 45–46, 359–69
four kinds, 119, 765–67
importance of, 55, 445–46
results of, 55, 441–45
through subject, qualities, means, 50, 396–401
thirteen categories of, 54–55, 440–41
Īśvara, 53, 172, 412, 430
"I," view of. *See* self

Jainism, 242n13. *See also* Nirgrantha Jains
Jambudvīpa, 313, 320, 572, 664–65, 793, 846
Jamyang Lama Gyaltsab, 845
Jamyang Lodrö Gyatso, colophon of, 844–46
Jeweled Lamp of the Middle Way (Bhāvaviveka), 237–38
Jñānaśrī, 144–45, 145n11
joy, 72, 512, 537
  attentiveness to, 53, 54, 423–24, 424–27, 431
  in benefiting others, 16, 203, 217
  in bodhisattvas' powers, 257
  branch of enlightenment, 106, 670, 673, 674
  of buddhas' speech, 456, 459
  of celestial and human existence, 214
  from compassionate suffering, 95, 613, 615–16
  from concentration, 500
  concentration of absence of attributes and, 109, 686
  in Dharma, 3, 59, 147, 148, 211, 463–64
  of first bodhisattva level, 144, 177
  in generosity, 85, 96, 97, 562–64, 619–20, 621–22
  in offerings, 581
  in practice, 221, 356
  See also four boundless attitudes

kalpas, infinite and measureless, distinctions between, 502n10
karma, 391
  accumulation of wisdom and, 652
  defilements and, 237
  delusion and, 388
  from hostility to Dharma, 6, 162, 163–65
  influence of, 257

karma (*continued*)
   not hoping for recompense, 115, 433, 434, 615, 621–22, 740, 745–46, 799
   obscuration of, 219
   release from, 768
   similar, habitual tendencies of, 773
   in three vehicles, equivalence of, 415
karmic actions
   compounded phenomena and, 696, 697
   as defilement aspect, 393
   by five aggregates, 717, 718
   impure body and, 656
   rebirth and, 608, 658, 701, 803
   ripening of, 510
   and self, view of, 240
   three kinds, 239
Kawa Peltsek, xxiii, 133, 138, 148n13, 843
keenness. *See* enthusiasm/keenness
Khyentse Wangpo, Jamyang, xv
kindness, repayment of bodhisattvas', 54, 434, 435
King of the Śākyas (Buddha), 331
knowable objects, 38, 325, 790
knowable phenomena, 753
   all-discerning gnosis and, 327
   embracing all, 172–73
   emptiness of, 316–17
   five bases of, 51, 396–98, 401, 404–5, 408
   five sciences and, 420–21
   inner science of, 422, 423, 642, 643, 644, 757
   intellectual's uncertainty in ascertaining, 161n4
   investigating, 49, 392–93
   mirrorlike gnosis and, 38, 325
   nonconceptual gnosis of, 80, 523, 543–44
   on path of seeing, 402, 673
   in postmeditation, 476
   pure mundane gnosis of, 509
   on tenth level, 820
   vision of, 827
knowledge, 73, 514
   of all aspects, 840–41
   attentiveness associated with, 46, 371
   in buddhas' speech, types of, 456–57
   fivefold complete, 46, 372, 373
   in four close mindfulnesses, 104, 655, 657–58

   superior, 80, 544
   of treatises, 102, 641–44
   of wishes and aspirations, 834–35
   of world, 102–3, 644–47
   See also four kinds of complete knowledge; four kinds of perfect knowledge
Kongtrul, Jamgön, xv

laity, 125, 370, 487, 801
language, 103, 373n20, 398, 460, 650, 651, 760
latent tendencies/propensities, 243n17, 546, 547, 548, 624, 668
laziness
   antidotes to, 59, 468–69
   compassion toward, 623
   diligence and, 531, 547
   lack of as sign of attainment, 129, 825
   from lack of shame, 632
   as obstacle to interest, 41, 348–49
   shame in, 99, 631
   in teaching Dharma, 59, 462, 463
learning, 41, 349–50, 668, 731, 755
Lesser Vehicle, 142, 156, 163, 360, 363, 583, 630, 736, 777–78
level of earnest aspiration. *See* path of earnest aspiration
liberation, 10, 177
   characteristic of, 32, 297–98
   connecting others to, 114, 737
   in establishing no-self, 112, 714–15, 727–28
   investigating, 51, 405–9
   of listeners, 243
   by means of defilements, 480–83
   non-Buddhist views on, 409
   no-self and, 240
   offerings of, 89, 580, 582
   and potential, differences in, 14, 184–85, 193–94, 403–4
   as untainted aggregate, 820
light rays
   aspiration prayers for, 685
   of bodhisattvas, 23, 253, 254
   of buddhas, 33, 285, 300–302, 420
lineage of buddhas, 9, 174, 681, 788. *See also* buddha family
listeners (śrāvakas), xviii, 236
   attainments of, 34, 195, 305–6, 312

attentiveness of, 369, 380
behaviors of, 839
bodhisattvas' superiority to, 10, 171–72,
  173, 178–79, 185, 222, 250, 251n4, 438
boundless attitudes of, 625
Buddha's compassion for, 31, 289–90
Buddha's transformation as superior
  to, 291
as children of Buddha's speech, 174n2
compassion for, 601
compassion of, 199, 418, 604–5, 608,
  613, 624
concentration of, 556
diligence of, 219, 551, 556, 566
discipline of, 549
enthusiasm of, 205
fields for, 559
with fixed potential, 186
generosity of, 549
in Great Vehicle, 187, 469–70
happiness of, 212–14, 611, 614
hardship of, lack of, 279, 280
infinite number of, 315
interest of, 42, 347, 353–55
joy of, 563
knowledge of, 363, 421, 642, 643, 645,
  650
liberation of, 403–4, 406
love in, 592
meditation of, 374, 655, 656, 657, 659,
  769
miraculous powers of, 662
motivation of, 595
offerings of, 582, 584
and phenomena, view of, 410
potential of, 190, 192
practice of, 227, 743
qualities of, 732, 733
realization of, 237, 242–43, 303, 379
rebirth of, 658
refuge of, 145, 179–80, 286
restraints of, 659
shame and decency of, 632
spiritual intent of, 204
supramundane wisdom of, 544
two accumulations of, 652
of unfixed potential, 52, 416–18, 419
ways of attracting disciples of, 88, 575
wisdom of, 557
listeners' collection, 360

Listeners' Vehicle (Śrāvakayāna)
  bodhisattvas' abandoning of, 522
  Buddha's intention and, 415
  defilements, view of in, 480, 482, 484
  eye of Dharma in, 776
  and Great Vehicle, distinctions between,
    5–7, 159, 630
  presenting, 764
  protection from, 30, 285
listening
  devotion to, 129, 825, 826
  to Dharma, 6, 164, 643
  habitual, memory from, 108, 682
  incomparable, 515
  indefatigability in, 102, 640, 641
  power of, 16, 202
Loden Sherab, 133, 843
logic, 396n44, 421, 423, 461, 642, 643,
  748, 756, 759
Longchenpa, 523–24
Long Scriptures, 725
love, 19, 222
  bodhicitta and, 18, 214
  bodhisattvas as embodying, 27, 269–70
  of bodhisattvas for sentient beings,
    63–64, 72, 83–84, 122, 486–88, 512,
    553–54, 609–10, 783
  gnosis of equality and, 38, 326
  nonconceptual, 91, 592, 593–94
  of others more than oneself, 84, 556
  from spiritual masters, 62, 90, 478, 585,
    586
  supramundane, 95, 612–13
  translation of term, 603n20
  See also four boundless attitudes

Madhyamaka. *See* Middle Way
  (Madhyamaka) school
*Madhyāntavibhāga. See Distinguishing the
  Middle from Extremes*
magical illusions, 215–16, 236, 241–42, 615
  bodhisattva practice as, 64, 490
  defilements as, 63, 484
  in four close mindfulnesses, 657
  phenomena as, 18, 47–49, 215–16, 288,
    382–92, 508, 691
  relative truth as, 552
  saṃsāra as, 356
  sense pleasures as, 752
  sentient beings as, 23, 252

Mahākāśyapa, 365
Mahāyāna family, 778. *See also* buddha family
Mahāyānasūtrālaṃkāra. See *Ornament of the Mahāyāna Sūtras*
Mahāyānottaratantraśāstra-ratnogotravibhāga. See *Sublime Continuum*
Maitreya, xvi–xvii, 133, 141–42, 236, 337, 647, 843, 844. *See also* Five Treatises of Maitreya
major and minor marks, 9, 55, 174, 175, 262, 307, 442, 836
manifestation
  activity of, 23, 253–54, 300–301
  aspiration prayers for, 685
  in establishing impermanence, 110, 701, 707
  of noble beings, 52, 53, 418, 419–20
manifestation body. *See* body of manifestation (*nirmāṇakāya*)
Mañjuśrī, 253, 844
mantras, power of, 706
Mantrayāna. *See* Secret Mantrayāna
Māra, 23, 253, 254
mastery
  attainment of, 122, 786–87
  attentiveness associated with, 46, 380
  as bodhisattva teaching method, 57, 451
  of buddhas, 459
  as cause for bodhisattvas' birth, 126, 803, 804, 805
  in following spiritual masters, 91, 590
  in four boundless attitudes, 97, 625
  four kinds, 51, 54, 406–7, 440
  of mind, 784
  in offerings, 581
  over thought, 120, 770–71
  shame and decency in, 101, 636
  in training, 79, 535, 538
Mastery over Others' Creations (god realm), 700
materialism, absence of, 97, 621–22
maturation, xx, 121, 140, 274–75, 339, 778, 779
  analogy for, 27, 267–68
  of bodhicitta, 15, 198
  bodhisattvas' power of, 9, 10, 14, 175, 178–79, 190–91, 212, 256
  by buddhas, 33, 35–36, 299–300, 311–16

defilement aspect of, 393
delight in, 146
on fifth level, 808–9
on first level, 510
through four boundless attitudes, 92, 596
four genuine restraints in, 105, 660
great compassion and, 94, 606–10
in Great Vehicle, 6, 162
through knowledge of treatises, 102, 642, 644
life related to, 109, 699, 703–4
memory through, 108, 682
on ninth level, 816
through offerings, 89, 580
of oneself, nine signs of, 25–27, 259–67
of others, categories and intentions of, 27, 268–70
on path of meditation, 72, 513
pure, 26, 263–64
qualities of, 120, 774–75
sense of shame in, 99, 100, 630, 634, 635
six perfections and, 27–28, 53, 270–74, 428
skill in, 107, 680, 681
steadfastness in, 639–40
twofold, 65, 490
worldly knowledge and, 645
medicine, 421–22, 423, 474, 642, 643, 756, 760
meditation, 629
  accumulation of merit and, 653
  attentiveness to object in, 46, 374–76
  as causal factor of four kinds of perfect knowledge, 651
  conceptual structures in, 768–70
  dwelling on nominal in, 368
  faith in, 54, 436–37
  of listeners and bodhisattvas, differences between, 120, 770–71
  as mingled and amalgamated, 658
  in non-Buddhist traditions, 759
  nonconceptual gnosis in, 211–12, 477, 513, 674–75, 819, 824
  and postmeditation, lack of difference between, 289
  realization in, 503
  on skeletons, example of, 48, 388
  sublime, 39, 332–33
  sustained calm and profound insight as body of, 679

with and without deliberate effort, 513
    See also profound insight; sustained calm
meditative absorption, 23, 250, 253, 392, 601, 666, 700, 751, 786, 841. *See also* four absorptions of formless world; four dhyānas
meditative equipoise, 122, 288–89, 317, 353, 384, 657, 783, 834–35, 840
memory, 108, 459, 591, 644, 665, 681, 682–83. *See also* power of retention
mental apprehension, 51, 407
mental consciousness, 308, 772, 791
mental expressions, 68, 70, 495, 504
mental-factor basis, 396, 397, 405
mental factors, 15, 197–98, 389, 791n34.
    See also mind and mental factors
mental states
    in offerings, nine aspects, 90, 91, 97, 101, 581, 584, 590, 625, 636
    three categories of, 496
mere appearances, 47–48, 384–86, 388–89, 398–99, 484, 773
mere awareness, 395–96
mere concepts, 22, 206, 246, 688
mere expression, 22, 244–45
mere mind, 407, 408, 508, 761
merit, accumulation of, 6, 152, 162
    of bodhisattvas, 10, 177
    diligence and, 78, 529
    from discipline, 79, 540, 541
    and interest, relationship between, 41, 42, 348, 349, 350–51, 352, 356–57
    on level of earnest aspiration, 491
    in memory, acquisition of, 682
    from past deeds, 62, 479–80
    pleasures that sap, 746
    rebirth and, 803
    severing, 193
    sharing with others, 129, 825, 826
    for understanding Dharma, 165
metaphors, similes, analogies
    antidote, universal, 22, 245–46
    army with four divisions, 635
    arrow heated in fire, 49, 394
    being pulled by hair, 73, 515
    for benefiting beings, 434
    bird in tree, 141
    blind person, 165
    boats, 61, 475, 816
    for bodhicitta, 17, 206–12
    for buddhas' speech, 457–59
    candle flame, 448n2
    chest of jewels, xxii, 3, 29, 139, 145, 147, 279, 280, 281, 340, 341
    child of barren woman, 298, 722
    clear lake, 670
    clouds, 17, 29, 30, 33, 212, 283, 284, 299–300, 302, 657–58
    for compassion (great tree), 94, 606–10
    crystal, 464
    doves, 64, 487
    dreams, 240, 241, 252, 384, 400, 811
    drums, 31, 294
    dyed cloth, 34, 303, 489
    earthenware pot, 692–93
    fathers, five activities of, 114, 737
    fire and fuel, 31, 110, 111, 292, 293, 709–10, 718, 719–20, 734
    fire and heat, 187, 235, 444, 474
    fire salamanders, 555
    fire spreading, 419, 704
    fish in water, 555
    five unexcelled, 3–4, 130–40, 143–44, 145–47, 339–40
    floaters in eye, 32, 297–98, 772
    friends, five activities of, 115, 738–39
    frog in well, 165
    gold, 46, 382, 486
    gold mine, 14, 191–92
    grains of sand in Ganges, 328, 468, 536, 537, 538
    hide, 394
    horse in east carrying person in west, 705
    horse shown straight course, 340
    of illusion, eight, 49, 390–92
    illusory king's defeat by another illusory king, 49, 389
    in indirect teachings, 59, 465, 466
    on interest in Great Vehicle, 42, 353–55
    iron's fading heat, 32, 297–98, 692–93
    jewels, 4, 14, 152–53, 192–93
    kinsfolk, five activities of, 114–15, 738
    lamp and flame, 689, 710–11, 712–13
    lamps, single and multiple, 36, 315
    lions, 257, 838
    medicine and disease, 55, 64, 442–43, 488, 617
    medicine with foul smell, 3, 151

metaphors, similes, analogies (*continued*)
  mine of jewels, 29, 33, 283, 299
  minister, great, 10, 173, 176
  mirages, 241, 252
  mirrors, 302
  molasses and sweetness, 235
  monarch, 3, 152
  moon, full, 33, 300
  moon's reflection, 31, 292, 293
  mothers, five activities of, 114, 736–37
  mothers and children, 63, 100, 218, 345, 486, 616, 617, 635
  mountain torrent, 710–11, 713
  muddy water becoming clear, 63, 485
  myrobalan fruit, 184, 250
  for natural purity, 235
  ocean, 36, 315
  for ordained bodhisattvas, 125, 801
  ores, different types of, 186, 189
  painting picture in sky, 34, 303–4
  paintings, 63, 485
  pillar and pot as same or different, 718–19
  pleasure grove, 18, 215, 216
  poisoned food, 93, 600, 601, 687, 752
  poison taken skillfully, 808
  for practice, 64, 488–90
  preceptors, five activities of, 115, 741
  Precious Gem, 32, 294
  prince, 9–10, 173, 174–76
  python, 57, 449
  rabbit's horns, 403, 413, 474, 722
  reflection in mirror, 148
  river flowing, 689
  rivers and oceans, merging of, 40, 67, 334–36, 491
  robber, 499
  rope mistaken for snake, 236, 240, 381, 383, 411, 509, 716, 772
  ruler, 111, 721
  servants, five activities of, 115, 739–40
  for settling mind, 498
  seven kinds of jewels, 536, 537
  sky, 46, 299, 382, 485, 635
  space, 413
  for steadfastness, 102, 640
  sun, 73, 471, 516–17
  sun and rays, 33, 84, 300–302, 557
  teachers, five activities of, 115, 740–41
  for three levels of wisdom, 84, 557

  treasure house, 39, 326–27
  trees, 14, 86, 94, 195, 564, 572n27, 606–10
  two moons, perception of, 378–79, 385, 391
  water, 46, 382
  white cloth, dyed, 189
method, of Listeners' and Great Vehicle, differences in, 5, 159, 161–62
middle way, 386, 407
Middle Way (Madhyamaka) school, xx–xxi, 186–87, 235, 236–38, 420, xviin1
migration, 110, 700, 704–7. *See also* rebirth
mind
  abiding in expanse of, 49, 394–95
  appearances of, 49, 395–96
  bodhisattvas' knowledge of others', 23, 209, 249, 251, 255
  conceptual, 368, 495
  content, 73, 514–15
  deluded, 388, 394, 403, 411, 444
  directed to meditation objects, 105, 663, 664
  fitness of, from concentration, 69, 500, 501, 502–3, 543, 663, 664, 670, 674
  as ground of all, 237, 395–96, 408, 790
  happy, acquisition of, 62, 479
  impermanence of, 710
  knowing others', 665
  mastery of, 28, 273
  momentariness of, 696–97
  movement by power of, 706
  natural liberation of, 772
  nature of, 63, 187, 245, 420, 486, 657–58
  negative tendencies of, 51, 408–9
  perfect liberation of, 32, 297–98
  pure and impure stages of, 298
  purity of, 63, 485–86
  resting naturally, 661, 662
  "root," 246
  settling on mind, 107
  sharp, maturation of, 25, 26, 259, 263–64
  stages of realizing, 22, 244–46
  strength of, 101, 637–38
  suppleness of, 394, 456
  transformation of, 34, 51, 308, 406
  variant views of, 237–38
  See also mere mind

INDEX — 919

mind and mental factors
   appearances of, 144, 368, 378–79, 383, 400, 769
   bondage of, 119, 768
   as illusory kings, example of, 389–90
   impermanence of, 698
   as mirage, 391
   perception of, 715–16
   phenomena and, 508
   as subject and object, 410
   two views on, 395
mind basis, 396–97, 405
mind consciousness, 309, 320, 325, 400, 542
mind faculty, 790–91. *See also* defiled mind consciousness
mindfulness
   attentiveness to, 53, 423–24
   branch of, 106, 670, 673
   diligence in, 80, 122, 542, 668, 783
   distraction and, 498
   matured peace and, 261–62
   of meditation object, 80, 542, 543
   mental application of, 664
   power of, 667, 668, 669
   stream of, 22, 246, 247
   in sustained calm and profound insight, 661
mind-only, 51, 70, 245, 395, 407, 504–5, 508. *See also* mere mind
Mind-Only school. *See* Cittamātra
Mipham, Jamgön, xv, xviiin1, xxi, xxiv, 236, 845. See also *Feast of the Nectar of the Supreme Vehicle* (Mipham)
miraculous displays
   aspiration prayers for, 685
   of bodhisattvas and buddhas, distinctions between, 257
   delight in, 18, 216
   function of, 23, 252, 254
   teaching through, 225, 255, 273
   at tenth level, 10, 175–76
   transcendent concentration and, 531–32
miraculous ear. *See* divine ear
miraculous eye. *See* divine eye
miraculous powers, xx, 146, 249, 644, 706–7, 787. *See also* four bases of miraculous powers
miraculous transformation, 209, 224, 251
mirrorlike gnosis, 39, 320, 325–26

momentariness, 410
   in establishing impermanence, 689–90, 691–97
   of inner compounded phenomena, 109–10, 698–707
   of outer compounded phenomena, 110, 707–14
   of world, 773
monastic colleges, xv, xviii, xxiii
monasticism, 125, 361, 364–66, 370, 801–2
Moon Lamp Sūtra, 493
mother of highest transcendent perfection, 16, 204
motivation, 92, 99, 558, 595, 596, 631, 632. *See also* aspiration
Mount Meru (king of mountains), 31, 102, 279, 289, 315n26, 334n37, 640, 708
movements, kinds of, 706–7
Mūlasarvāstivāda school, 167
multiplicity, eliminating concept of, 55, 443, 444
mundane beings. *See* ordinary beings
Municandra, xxiii

Nāgārjuna, xviii, xxi, 647, 750, xviin1
nāgas, xviii, 318, 458, 460, 650
name-and-form, 368, 697
names, 103, 143, 244, 649–50
   clinging to, 55, 443
   expression and, 445
   investigating, 119, 765–67
   meaning and, 378, 496, 642, 651
   on path of joining, 51, 402, 408
names, phrases, letters, 142–43, 372–73, 377–78, 421, 460, 475, 677, 794, 822
natural body, 37, 319–20, 321–22. *See also* body of truth (*dharmakāya*)
nature of phenomena, 21, 234, 241–42, 304
   complete knowledge of, 64, 490
   as expanse of reality, 62, 481–82
   as illusion-like, 47–49, 382–92, 393
   realization of, 42, 352
   suchness of, 506
negation, extreme of, 55, 443
negative actions
   attachment and, 612
   by bodhisattvas, 92, 598–99
   of body, speech, mind, 83–84, 554–55

negative actions (*continued*)
  compassion for others', 600, 623
  definite, 576
  from lack of shame, 632
  of others, attitude toward, 269–70
  protection from, 30, 284–85
  refraining from, 246, 549, 636
  restraint from committing, 18, 214
  ripening of, 190–91
  vow to avoid, 199
  See also ten negative actions
negative tendencies, 51, 408–9
  of body, 69, 502–3
  of defilements, 239
  direct perception of residual, 119, 769–70
  dispelling, 376–77
  of mind, 503
  in sustained calm and profound insight, 661
  on ten levels, 812, 827
nihilism, 394, 407, 443, 444, 548
nine methods for settling the mind, 68, 498–500
ninth bodhisattva level (Perfect Intellect)
  defining characteristic of, 811
  etymological definition of, 130, 830
  mark of, 826
  types of bodhisattvas on, 127, 816
Nirgrantha Jains, 409, 759
nirmāṇakāya. *See* body of manifestation (*nirmāṇakāya*)
nirvāṇa
  attachment to, 386
  as benefit of interest, 352
  buddhas' display of, 313
  conventional existence of, 474
  delight in, 52, 419
  dependent arising of, 829
  illusory nature of, 389
  of lesser vehicles, 214
  in Listeners' and Great Vehicles, distinctions in view of, 156, 238, 480
  mind as root of, 237
  natural, 52, 411
  nonattachment to, 83, 548, 552
  potential as basis of, 192
  as purity aspect, 393
  purity of, 464
  universality of, 9, 172–73
  See also cessation: truth of; nondwelling nirvāṇa
nirvāṇa without residual aggregates, 179, 185, 207, 238, 420, 442, 556, 604, 643
noble beings, 11, 165, 181, 457
  abiding of, 543
  and buddhas, differences between, 329
  discipline of, 271, 375
  flawless level of, 491
  merit of path of, 357
  nonconceptual love of, 594
  and ordinary beings, comparison between, 243, 307n22, 507
  potential of, 403
  See also seven kinds of noble beings
noble levels. *See* bodhisattva levels
noble path
  as cause for rebirth, variant views on, 52, 417–18
  causes of, 6, 164
  excellent body as support for, 264
  four good qualities of, 464
  as purity aspect, 393
  realization by listeners, 419
nonassociated conditioning factors, 369, 397, 405, 666n16
nonattachment
  generosity and, 96–97, 618–20
  great compassion and, 95, 97, 611, 624, 625
  to sense objects, 78, 529
  as sign of attaining levels, 128, 823, 824, 825
nonconceptual gnosis, 143, 144, 206
  aspiration prayers and, 108, 683
  as body-attained, 55, 441
  buddhas' perfection of, 462
  in buddhas' speech, 455
  as cause of preternatural knowledge, 23, 250, 251
  as chest of jewels, 144
  compassion and, 94, 604, 605
  direct realization of, 651
  on eighth level, 177, 178–79, 198, 211, 414, 733, 751, 810, 811
  on first level, 61, 245, 476, 507, 508
  five powers and, 669
  in formal meditation, 211–12, 477, 513, 674–75, 819, 824
  in four boundless attitudes, 91, 97, 591, 625–26

generosity and, 559
in Great Vehicle, 6, 162
in meditation, 393
as object of bodhicitta, 15, 199
as object of postmeditational gnosis, 37, 317
in offerings, 584
on path of meditation, 22, 72, 245–46, 513
realization of, 648, 791
ripening in others, 226
shame and, 99, 629, 630, 632
six perfections and, 78, 82, 243, 530–32, 549, 550, 551, 552, 572
skillful means of, 75, 523–24, 538, 680–81
spontaneous, 751, 780, 794, 795, 820, 826, 830
teaching through, 57, 451
on three pure levels, 831
transcendent wisdom and, 332
at transformation, 34, 288, 308
ultimate bodhicitta and, 201
wisdom eye and, 664
nonconceptuality, xxx
as antidote to cognitive obscurations, 73, 516–17
in buddha activity, 301–2, 314
of compassion, 97, 624, 625
concentration of emptiness and, 109, 686
in four kinds of complete knowledge, 119, 767
of fully present reality, 401
of Great Vehicle, 6, 161–62
investigation and, 45, 49, 367, 392–93
mastery of, 51, 406–7, 440
of profound insight, 678
in shame and decency, 101, 636
of subject and object, 49, 392, 393
at transformation, 31, 287–89
wish for, 54, 431
nondwelling nirvāṇa, 173n1, 178, 230, 681
generosity and, 549
realization of, 121, 243, 778, 779
transformation and, 35, 309
two goals and, 20, 228
nonreturner levels. *See* three pure levels
nonreturners, 52, 205, 416–17, 418, 701
nonsectarian movement, xv

nonviolence, 271
no-self, 109, 687–88
as distinction of Buddha's doctrine, 728
established by reasoning, 111–12, 715–24
established by scripture, 112, 724–28
as focus in offerings, 582
individual, proof for, 21, 239–40
individual, realization of, 52, 415
one-and-a-half kinds of, 764
steadfastness in hearing about, 102, 640
See also two kinds of no-self
Nyingma school, xv

obscurations/faults, 63, 235, 282, 292, 296, 317, 382, 401, 484–86. *See also* two obscurations
offerings, 98, 327, 626
best kinds, 90, 584
bodhisattvas' disinterest in, 58, 434, 453–54
to buddha fields, 357
to buddhas, 23, 53, 69, 251–52, 428, 501–2, 579–80
classifying, 89–90, 582–84
definite duty of, 118, 751–52
material, 579, 580, 582, 583
nine kinds of mental, 580–82
to spiritual masters, 129, 586, 825, 826
omnipresence, 31, 291–93
omniscience, 10, 161, 179, 238, 811
attaining, 29, 45, 279–81, 363
establishing in others, 226
five sciences as necessary for, 53, 420–23, 642
praise to, 132, 133, 838–39, 840–41
once-returners, 205, 416–17, 701
oneness, 97, 101, 625–26, 636–37
one taste/single taste, 301, 407, 572
attentiveness of, 68, 495–96
of Dharma, 809
in emptiness, 625, 807, 815
of enlightened state, 331, 333, 403
of saṃsāra and nirvāṇa, 9, 172–73
openhandedness, 125, 797–98, 799–800
ordinary beings, 251n4
attainments of, 305, 311–12
belief in self of, 714
compassion of, 604–5
concentration of, 556–57
delights of, 216–17

ordinary beings (*continued*)
  diligence of, 551, 556
  generosity of, 549
  goal of, 284–85
  interest of, 42, 353–55
  knowledge of, 645
  limited vision of, 722
  love in, 95, 591–92, 608, 612
  meditation of, 332n35, 658
  offerings of, 584
  practices of, 228, 743–44
  refuge in, 172, 181
  seeds of, 701
  shame and decency of, 635
ordination, 125, 801–2. *See also* monasticism
Ornament of the Mahāyāna Sūtras
  colophons of, 133, 843
  commentaries on, xxii–xxiv
  composition of, 3, 139–48
  grammatical analysis of, 141–42
  importance of, xv
  structure of, xviii–xxii, 41, 144–45, 148, 339–41, 519
  title, commentary on, 137–38
  versions of, xixn4
Ornament of True Realization (Abhisamayālaṃkāra), 482
other-production, 242
outer container. *See* container world

Parahita, 133, 843
parinirvāṇa, 36, 38, 212, 254, 291, 313–14, 322, 323, 370, 817
Parinirvāṇa-sūtra, 167n12
particles, refutation of substantial existence of, 767n12
path, 340, 409
  causal factors of, 146–47
  Dharma of transmission and, 450
  elements, imputation of, 389
  interest on, obscured and unobscured, 348
  of single certainty/progress, 126, 130, 809–10, 829–30
  skill in not interrupting, 107, 680, 681
  supramundane, 510, 516–17
path of accumulation, 490
  application on, 378
  attainments of, 244, 504

  bodhicitta on, 198
  compassion on, 262
  as foundation, 51, 402, 408
  investigation on, 441
  reflection on, 493n3
path of consummation, 512
path of earnest aspiration, 178, 473–75
  abiding in mind's own expanse on, 49, 394
  acceptance on, 775
  accomplishment and nonaccomplishment on, 128, 820–21
  all-discerning gnosis on, 329
  aspiration prayers on, 684, 803
  attainments of, 504
  attentiveness to deeds on, 370
  attracting disciples from, 575
  birth on, 803, 805
  bodhicitta on, 198, 201, 202
  bringing others to, 275
  concentration on, 377
  fear on, 614
  five sciences on, 422
  four boundless attitudes on, 595
  four genuine restraints on, 660
  indefatigability on, 641
  inspiration on, 457n8
  instructions on, 516
  interest on, 130, 348, 780, 831
  investigation on, 440
  joy on, 221
  knowable phenomena on, 392
  meditation on, 332
  merit over one measureless kalpa, 491
  mind, sharpness of on, 259
  mindfulness on, 673
  ordinary beings on, 416
  phenomena, view of on, 236
  realizations on, 408, 475, 794–95
  sameness on, 222–23
  shame and decency on, 631–32
  superior intention on, 125–26, 802
  sustained calm and profound insight on, 679, 827
  teaching on, 57, 451
  two accumulations on, 318, 654
path of joining, 137n2
  attainments of, 70, 244–45, 504–6
  attentiveness on, 402, 407
  bodhicitta on, 198, 207

body of truth on, 441
compassion on, 262
investigation of, 368
meditation on, 492
phenomena, view of on, 236
realizations on, 378–79, 408, 414, 475
reflection on, 493n3
path of learning, 147, 238
path of meditation, 22, 246, 380
  defilements eliminated on, 298, 442
  eightfold path and, 373
  in Listeners' and Great Vehicles,
    distinctions in view of, 156
  listeners of unfixed potential on, 418
  realization on, 72, 476, 513
  thatness on, 394
  time needed to attain, 72, 513
path of no more learning, 147, 238, 246,
  514
path of seeing
  application of perfect realization on, 379
  arising of, 402
  branches of enlightenment on, 670
  defilements eliminated on, 61, 298, 442,
    476, 776
  eightfold path and, 373
  four kinds of complete knowledge
    arising on, 119, 767–68
  in Listeners' and Great Vehicles,
    distinctions in view of, 156
  realizations on, xxi, 70, 245, 414,
    506–10
  sixteen instants on, 374, 506n17, 510
  time needed to attain, 70, 506–7
  untainted vow of, 541n12
  See also first bodhisattva level (Perfect
    Joy)
path of training, 201, 256
patience, 19, 89, 226, 227, 580, 581
patience, transcendent
  acceptance and, 412n53
  armor of, 427n65
  benefits of, 489
  bodhicitta and, 208
  defining characteristics of, 78, 531
  eight supreme aspects of, 85, 560–61
  etymology of, 79, 533, 534
  factors incompatible with, 81, 547
  four excellent qualities of, 82, 549
  in maturing others, 27, 272

and other perfections, relationship
  between, 570
purity of, 84, 555
subdivisions of, 80, 541–42, 571
ten powers and, 667
two accumulations and, 653
peace
  and birth, ultimately, 21, 242–43
  delight in, 20, 227
  fully present reality and, 50, 401
  maturation of, 25, 259, 261–62
  nirvāṇa as, 109, 687–88
  nonconceptual love and, 91, 593
  nondwelling, 38, 326
  primordial, 52, 411
  See also nirvāṇa
peak of existence, 464, 624–25, 648
Peak of Existence, 604
peak stage (on path of joining), 207, 278,
  504
perception
  conventional existence and, 63, 484, 485
  of duality, 48, 387–88, 393–94
  in establishing no-self, 111, 715–16
  of material and immaterial, 48, 386–87
  of momentariness, 713
  transformation of, 51, 405–6
perceptual domination, powers of, 24,
  256, 340, 777, 833, 834
perceptual limitlessness, powers of, 24,
  224, 256, 340, 777, 833, 834
Perfection of Wisdom, 318, 332, 333, 389,
  443, 445
Perfection of Wisdom, 544
*Perfection of Wisdom in One Hundred
  Thousand Lines*, 377–78, 443, 480–81,
  496, 680–81, 778
perfections, mundane and supramundane,
  739, 782–83
perfectly pure nature, 296, 403
perpetuating aggregates, 214, 373, 685, 717
phenomena
  in Abhidharma, 362, 364
  bodhisattvas' mastery of, 10, 175–76
  boundless love focused on, 592, 593
  dependent arising of, 233–34
  emptiness of, 204, 217, 602, 770
  as enlightened state, 29–30, 281–84
  as illusory, 18, 47–49, 215–16, 288, 382–
    92, 508, 691

phenomena (*continued*)
  intentions in teaching, 465–66
  knowledge of, 799
  as mere appearances, 63, 484–85
  as merely mind, 49, 395–96, 761
  nature and multiplicity of, 283–84, 288, 317, 476–77, 552, 557, 570, 753, 759, 760
  noncompounded, 396, 397, 404, 405
  perfect discernment of, 107, 678
  perfect knowledge of, 103, 649–50
  purity of, 334–36
  realization of characteristics of, 657
  sameness of, 16, 203, 815–16
  suchness of, 37, 283–84, 316–17
  totality of, 792
  as unborn, 52, 115, 118, 211, 224–25, 412–14, 740, 753, 754
  See also compounded phenomena; knowable phenomena; nature of phenomena
philosophical systems, four, xxn5
phrasing, flawless, 3, 142–43
physical behavior, knowledge of, 102, 644–45, 646
places
  five improper, 540
  offerings and, 89, 582–83
  of practice, 62, 477–78
Play in Full, 760
positive actions, 104, 193–94, 632, 653–54. *See also* ten positive actions
postmeditation, 819
  evenness in, 106, 674, 675
  nonconceptual gnosis in, 37, 211–12, 246, 317
  perception of dependent nature in, 384
  pure mundane gnosis in, 289, 393, 476, 508, 509, 513, 651, 824
  realization in, 503
  sameness in, 671
potential, xix, 13–14, 121, 183, 339, 424, 510, 778, 837
  analogies for, 14, 186, 189, 191–93
  base, 7, 165, 166
  benefits of, 190–91
  bodhicitta and, 16, 202
  bodhisattvas' knowledge of others', 223–24
  categories of, 189
  as cause, 187–88, 535

compassion and, 262, 603
developed/evolving, 54, 185, 187–88, 194–95, 438, 439
differences in, proof of, 183, 184–85
five types, 186
fixed, 369–70, 415, 420
forbearance and, 263
gotra, derivational gloss of, 188
for Great Vehicle, xx, 6, 13, 145, 157n1, 162–63, 185, 194–95, 377, 422
immeasurable objects of, 774
increasing, 60, 470–71
lack of, 193–94, 274, 600
maturation and, 268
natural interest and, 347
naturally existing, 185, 186–87, 194–95
of noble beings, 50, 403
numbers of buddhas and, 39, 330–31
predictions and, 414, 749
and refuge, relationship between, 182
rigs, meanings of, 183n1
seeds of, 800
signs of, 188–89
and single vehicle, intention of, 52, 415–17, 420
skillful according with, 306
steadfastness and, 639
threats to, 189–90
in three vehicles, 58, 454, 456
unfixed, 52, 59, 285, 415, 418, 420, 467, 469–70, 601
power of retention, 211, 318
  all-discerning gnosis and, 39, 326–27
  attentiveness to, 431
  door of, 471
  of knowledge of treatises, 102, 642, 644
  on tenth level, 127, 811–12, 816, 817, 819, 830
powers, 23–24, 140, 146, 339
  accomplishment of, 250, 251
  of enlightened state, 37, 316–17
  essence of, 249–50
  greatness of, 256–57
  maturation of, 25, 26, 259, 264
  See also preternatural powers; ten powers
practice, 75, 140, 145, 519
  in attracting disciples, 87, 573–74
  conditions for, 62, 477–80
  fivefold division of, 61, 473–77

four kinds of greatness of, 230
  as inexhaustible, 19, 226, 227
  never wasting, 116, 743–44
  offerings of, 89, 580, 582
  superiority of bodhisattvas', 20, 223, 227–28
  three great aspects of, 19, 221–22
  of three types of individuals, differences in, 104, 655, 658
  as uninterrupted, 20, 228–29
  See also altruistic activity
Prajñāpāramitā, 754. See also *Perfection of Wisdom*
Prajñāpāramitā sūtras, xvii, xviii. *See also* Perfection of Wisdom
prātimokṣa, 361–62, 365n12, 540, 541
precepts, 224
  of bodhisattvas, 487
  definite duty of, 118, 751, 752
  deteriorating, 746
  discipline and, 540
  establishing, 10, 175, 176
  of monastic ordination, 361
  not transgressing, 629
predictions, 226, 227
  of buddhas, 5, 158
  different kinds of, 117, 749–50
  on eighth level, 105, 113, 224–25, 414, 660, 733, 750
  on Great Vehicle, 5, 155, 156
  pleasure from, 54, 436, 437
preternatural knowledge. *See* five kinds of preternatural knowledge; six kinds of preternatural knowledge
preternatural powers, 69, 80, 224, 501–2, 531–32, 542, 543, 550, 681, 751
pride
  antidote to, 59, 467, 469
  on bodhisattva levels, 55, 127, 441, 813–14, 815
  of bodhisattvas, 40, 333
  buddhas' speech as lacking, 459
  in Dharma, 7, 166–67, 361
  in diminution of transcendent perfections, 116, 746
  in four boundless attitudes, 92, 595–96
  as obstacle to interest, 41, 349, 350
  offerings and, 90, 583, 584
  in one's spiritual master, 91, 589–90
  shame and, 99, 632

production, absence of, 52, 411–12
profound insight
  accomplishment of, 657
  acquisition of, 504
  analysis and, 68, 496, 663
  attentiveness and, 371, 376
  benefits of, 129, 503, 827–28
  bodhicitta and, 210–11
  branches of enlightenment and, 670
  defining characteristics of, 107, 678
  diligence in, 566
  five powers and, 669
  for listeners of unfixed potential, 418
  on path of accumulation, 244
  result of, 516
  special point of, 479, 497, 661–62, 678, 783
  transcendental wisdom and, 529
  See also under yoga
profound intention, sign of commenting on, 125, 797–98, 799, 800
Profound View tradition, xviin1
protectors of virtue, nonhuman, 99, 633
pure levels. *See* three pure levels
pure mundane gnosis, 289, 393, 476, 508, 509, 513, 651, 675, 824
purification
  in attracting disciples, 87, 573–74
  five powers and, 669
  of four dhyānas, 501
  by four genuine restraints, 105, 660
  by gnostic vision, 73, 516–17
  illusion-like defilement and, 389–90
  on path of meditation, 72, 513
  by sustained calm and profound insight, 107, 678, 679
  of universe, 121, 126, 778, 779, 810
purity, 23, 251–52
  achievement of, 24, 254
  of arhats and buddhas, differences between, 404
  of buddhas' speech, 58, 455, 461
  of compassion, 97, 624, 625
  of compassionate generosity, 97, 620–22
  complete, cause for, 39–40, 331–34
  conventional existence of, 474
  of deeds, 75, 523
  of defilements, 481
  of Dharma, 57, 448, 450
  of eleventh level, 127, 811–12

purity (*continued*)
  in establishing impermanence, 109, 697
  on first level, 70, 506-7, 508, 510
  four qualities of, 144
  of gnosis of equality, 38, 326
  imputed reality of, 411
  investigating, 49, 394-95
  of mind, 63, 485-86
  of nonconceptual love, 91, 593
  perfect, 32, 295-96
  of phenomena, 288
  signs of, 69-70, 503-4, 827
  of six perfections, 83-84, 553-57
  twofold, 321, 331, 841-42

qualities, 639
  acceptance of, 636
  eighteen distinctive, 840
  eighty inexhaustible, 206n10, 207-12
  of learning, 731, 755 (*see also* teaching Dharma)
  obstacles preventing, 568, 569
  praise of ultimate, 131, 832-41
  of realization, 10, 177-78
  of six transcendent perfections, 121-22, 781-86, 841
  three groups, 731-32
  ultimate excellent, 106, 664, 667
  wondrous, 113, 732-33
  See also bodhisattva qualities; buddha qualities

Rāhula, 174n2
realization, 9, 171
  as bodhisattva teaching method, 57, 451
  cause of, 50, 401-2
  consistent, 61, 476-77
  eight excellent qualities of, 10, 177-78
  as individual experience, 57, 448-50
  in Listeners' and Great Vehicles, differences between, 162
  offerings of, 89, 580, 582
  outer and inner, 45-46, 367-69
  perfect, eleven categories of application in, 378-80
  praising qualities of, 123, 789-93
  of spiritual masters, 586
  sustained calm and profound insight in, 107, 678, 679

reasoning, 143-44
  on absence of self in individual, 21, 239-40
  on absence of self in phenomena, 21, 241-43
  on ascertaining Great Vehicle, 151
  on impermanence, 109, 688-97
  in teaching Dharma, 58, 461
rebirth
  control over, 60, 470, 471
  fetter of, 219n17
  from four boundless attitudes, 92, 596
  great compassion and, 94, 606-10
  higher, bodhisattvas' lack of craving, 82, 549
  knowledge of, 251n3, 256
  in lower realms, bodhicitta and, 214
  in lower realms, potential and, 14, 190-91
  memory of, 665
  of noble listeners, 417-19
  in realms devoid of leisure, 100, 633
  as result of compassion, 602
  from sense of shame, 100, 633-34
  strength or weakness of, 590
  of subtle mental body, 243
  from transcendent discipline, 271-72
  from transcendent patience, 541
  transcendent perfections and, 77, 526, 751
  types of, 699-700, 704
  See also migration
recollection, 26, 60, 263-64, 470, 471
reflexive awareness, xx-xxi, 238
refuge, 339
  bodhisattvas' gift of, 558
  deceptive notions, destruction of, 132, 836, 837
  Mahāyāna, superiority of, xix, 9, 145, 171-72
  resultant, 284-87
  six aspects of, 10-11, 179-81
  in three vehicles, 181-82
refusal, attentiveness to, 54, 436, 437
rejoicing, 426, 427, 457, 536, 559-60, 581, 653, 681
relative truth, 329-31, 402-3, 791, 792. See also two truths
remedial methods, 59, 465, 466, 469. See also antidotes

remorse, 59, 99, 467, 469, 598, 632–33
repudiation, 48, 386. *See also* nihilism
restraint, 25, 259, 261–62. *See also* four genuine restraints
Resultant Vehicle of the Mantras, 481, 483
results
  of bodhisattvas' signs, 799–800
  of compassion, 93, 601–2
  of compassionate generosity, 96–97, 618–20
  of eliminating concepts, 55, 443–45
  of good qualities, 55, 442–43
  from knowing treatises, 102, 641, 643
  of Mahāyāna, qualities of, 207
  samsaric, 581n2
  of six transcendent perfections, 113, 118, 733, 750–51
  of three vehicles, 764
  wish for shared, 53, 423–24
retention. *See* power of retention
retinues, 37, 39, 128, 320–21, 322, 327, 404, 457–58, 665, 824, 825

Sāgaramegha, 186n3
Sajjana, 133, 843
Śākyasiṃha, xxiii, 133, 843
sameness, 16, 19, 202, 222–23
  on abode stage, 50, 403–4
  aspiration for, 415
  attitude of, 113–14, 126, 733, 734–35, 803, 824
  of bodhisattvas and other beings, 618
  compassion and, 624–25
  direct cognition of, 103, 651
  five aspects of, 71, 507
  of fully present reality, 401
  of great compassion, 94, 604
  in implied teachings, 59, 466–67
  omnipresence and, 292
  of oneself and others, 72, 84, 510, 512, 556, 605, 614
  in perfect liberation, 51, 407, 408
  realization of, 440, 671
  of saṃsāra and nirvāṇa, 326, 480, 483, 770–72, 779
  skillful means and, 523
Sāṃkhya school, 410
saṃsāra, 409, 602
  accumulation of merit and, 104, 652
  arising of, 394, 829

as beginningless, 52, 412
  bodhisattvas' remaining in, 18, 64, 92, 95, 101, 151, 177, 215, 228, 488, 599, 615–16, 639, 640, 784
  continuous engagement in, 760–61
  conventional existence of, 474
  disenchantment in, 41, 350–51
  enjoyments of, 86, 566
  fear of, in lesser vehicles, 354
  full dedication to, 126, 807–8
  lack of fear of, 203, 214, 386
  making use of, 105, 659–60
  mind as root of, 237
  nonattachment to, 83, 552
  and peace, one taste of, 9, 172
  reflected on defects of, 661
  and self, view of, 240
  See also under sameness
Saṅgha, 254, 371
Śāntarakṣita, xxi
Śāntideva, xviii
Sarvāstivādin tradition, 365
Sautrāntika system, xxn5
seclusion, delight in, 26, 265, 266
second bodhisattva level (Immaculate)
  defining characteristic of, 126, 807
  discipline on, 271
  etymological definition of, 129, 828
  mark of, 825
  types of bodhisattvas on, 127, 813
secretiveness, absence of, 132, 838
secrecy, 114, 737, 738
Secret Mantrayāna, 237, 238, 759
seeds
  of appearances, 393
  arhats' elimination of, 404
  bondage of, 119, 768
  of compassion, 800
  of enlightenment, 93, 601–2
  in ground of all, 559
  of liberation, 270, 440
  life with and without, 110, 700–701, 707
  of phenomena, 242
  of transcendent perfections, 749
  of transcendent virtue, 284
  at transformation, 31, 51, 287–88, 291, 307–8, 405
  of two kinds of virtue, 264
  See also habitual tendencies; potential

self
  as aggregates, views on, 111, 715, 717–20
  belief in, 51, 99, 229, 308, 325, 408–9, 532, 556, 612, 631, 632, 714–15, 794
  as contributory condition, refutation of, 112, 723–24
  as conventional designation, 111, 715–17, 725
  five faults in view of, 725
  freedom from concept of, 632, 783, 838
  ground of all mistaken as, 400, 406
  habit of, 112, 727–28
  as imputed reality, 411
  as independent, refutation of, 111, 720–22
  lack of function of, 111–12, 722–23
  sublime/great, 32, 71, 296–97, 450, 510
  subsequent realization of, 123, 790
self-cognizant wisdom, 6, 164, 245, 649
sense consciousness. *See* six consciousnesses
sense of decency, 99, 100, 101, 630, 631–32, 631–35, 636–37
sense of shame, 99–100, 122, 783
  attentiveness to, 53, 429
  benefits of, 100, 633–34
  best sense of, 636–37
  indefatigability and, 102, 640, 641
  lack of, 631–35
  praise of, 634–35
  qualities of, 122, 785–86
  signs of, 101, 636
  specific characteristics of, 629–30
  superior and inferior, 631–32
senses-and-fields, 156, 241–42, 307–8, 329, 391, 396, 792
sense spheres, 156, 241–42, 329, 792
sentient beings
  all-accomplishing gnosis and, 327–28
  as beloved children, 609
  buddha nature of, 420
  categories of wisdom of, 544
  gnosis of equality and, 38, 326
  great burden of, 18, 218–19
  infinite number of, 35, 312, 330
  ingratitude of, 101, 638, 639, 829
  innate notion of "I" of, 240
  insatiable attitude toward, 537
  inspiring, 23, 251–52
  nature of, 31, 187, 291–93
  negative actions toward, 92, 597–99
  never forsaking/abandoning, 20, 62–63, 63–64, 78, 230, 483–84, 486–88, 529, 789
  as objects of boundless love, 591–93
  as objects of compassion, 93, 600–601, 607
  obscurations of, 33, 302
  as offering field, 582
  qualities manifestly related to, 113–14, 734–35
  refuge as protection of, 30, 287
  sadness and delight in, 54, 436
  sameness of, 16, 71, 203, 222, 507, 671
  suchness of, 34, 304, 316–17
  ten mental attitudes regarding, 807
  universality in liberating, 9, 172
  See also ordinary beings
seven branches of enlightenment, 106, 670–71
  fivefold, 107, 675–76
  sevenfold, 106–7, 671–75
seven kinds of noble beings, 455
seven kinds of wrong belief, 54, 432
seventh bodhisattva level (Far Progressed)
  defining characteristic of, 126, 809–10
  etymological definition of, 130, 829–30
  mark of, 826
  postmeditation on, 810n6
  types of bodhisattvas on, 127, 816
Seven Treatises on Logic, 759
sexual activity, transformation of, 35, 309–10
shame. *See* sense of shame
shameful deeds, 97, 99, 370, 540–41, 612, 620, 630–31, 776n21, 785, 786, 789
Shingkyong (attendant), 845
similes. *See* metaphors, similes, analogies
single basis, 385
single identity, 91, 590–91
single nature, 413
single path, 211–12
single taste. *See* one taste/single taste
single vehicle, 52–53, 414–20, 470
Śiva, 759
six consciousnesses, 400, 699, 702–3
  appearance of, 397
  bondage of, 768
  diligence and, 542
  dualistic apprehension by, 387

lack of intrinsic existence of, 379
realization of, 123, 790, 791
six kinds of preternatural knowledge, 23, 24, 249–50, 257, 380, 777
   beings taught for, 832
   benefiting others through, 787
   as benefit of interest, 42, 352, 353
   causal factors of, 250–51
   concentration and, 273, 499, 561, 674, 678
   full accomplishment of, 665
   functions of, 252–54
   levels of attainment of, 305–6
   mastery of, 55, 440, 442, 443
   power of, 406
   praise to, 131, 835
   qualities and categories of, 24, 255–56
   results of, 251–52
   on tenth level, 129, 816, 825, 826
six sense faculties, 390–91
six sense fields, 367, 391
six sense objects, 791
   as appearance of one's mind, 70, 505
   bodhisattvas and, 20, 228–29
   momentariness of, 110, 707–14
   on path of joining, 379, 402
   transformation of, 405
six sense organs, 34, 306–8, 405, 631, 703, 768
six sense powers, 186, 367, 697
sixth bodhisattva level (Clearly Manifest)
   defining characteristic of, 126, 809
   etymological definition of, 130, 829
   mark of, 825
   types of bodhisattvas on, 127, 815–16
six transcendent perfections, 77, 88, 121, 525–26, 576–77, 778, 779
   attentiveness and potential for, 53, 423–24, 439
   authentic application in, 116, 744–46
   beings taught for, 832
   bodhicitta and, 15, 200, 207–8, 217
   bodhisattvas' signs in, 797, 800
   causal and resultant qualities of, 113, 732–34
   as cause of purity, 331–32
   compassion toward those lacking, 623
   constant diligence in, 65, 490
   consummate qualities of, 841
   delight in, 262
   diminution and enhancement of, 116–17, 746–47
   effects of, 425–26
   establishing number of, 77–78, 526–30
   etymologies of, 79, 533–35
   factors incompatible with, 115, 117, 425, 426, 574, 741, 748–49
   four close mindfulnesses and, 657
   four excellent qualities of, 82–83, 548–52
   gnosis on, 243
   imitative and authentic, distinctions between, 117, 747–48
   interrelationships of, 87, 569–72, 681
   introducing others to, 434–35
   maturation and, 27–28, 270–74
   meditational and nonmeditational, 81, 544
   as offerings, 582
   order of, 79, 532–33
   qualities of, 121–22, 781–86, 841
   reciprocal benefits of, 116, 742–43
   results of, 118, 750–51
   ripening from, 224
   sameness in, 113–14, 734–35
   semblances of, 437n77
   shame in, 99, 630–31
   six subdivisions of each, 428
   spontaneous practice of, 538
   as support of perfect enlightenment, 53, 188–89, 430
   as supramundane, 523
   supreme aspects of each, 118, 753–54
   ten powers and, 667
   time in attaining, 244
   types of duties of, 118, 751–54
   as uninterrupted, 229
   See also individual perfection
sixty expressive qualities of Buddha's speech, 58, 455–60
skillful means/methods
   to accomplish Great Vehicle, 107–8, 680–81
   attentiveness associated with, 427
   bodhicitta and, 212
   of bodhisattvas, 446
   of Dharma of transmission, 450
   display of, 175
   of enlightened activity, 318
   nonconceptual gnosis and, 480

skillful means/methods (*continued*)
  realization of, 790
  of rebirth in saṃsāra, 808
  three aspects of, 75, 521–24
  of three doors, 75, 521, 522, 523
  of three spheres, 584
  in training, 79, 535, 538
  of uninterrupted practice, 229
  wisdom and, 116, 744, 745
Sky Treasury concentration, 91, 192, 253, 256, 310, 318, 560, 570, 581, 584, 590–91
solitary realizers, 419, 522
  attainments of, 34, 195, 305–6, 312
  attentiveness of, 380
  bodhisattvas' superiority to, 10, 171–72, 178–79, 222, 250, 251n4, 438
  boundless attitudes of, 625
  Buddha's compassion for, 31, 289–90
  Buddha's transformation as superior to, 291
  compassion of, 604–5, 608, 613, 624
  concentration of, 556
  and defilements, view of, 484
  diligence of, 219, 551, 556, 566
  generosity of, 549
  happiness of, 212–14, 611, 614
  hardship of, lack of, 279, 280
  infinite number of, 316
  interest of, 42, 347, 353–55
  joy of, 563
  knowledge of, 643, 645, 650
  liberation of, 403–4, 406
  love in, 592
  meditation of, 655, 657, 658, 659, 769
  miraculous powers of, 662
  motivation of, 595
  offerings of, 584
  potential of, 190, 192
  practice of, 227, 743
  protection from vehicle of, 30, 285
  qualities of, 732, 733
  realization of, 237, 243, 303, 379
  refuge of, 286
  restraints of, 659
  result of, 156
  shame and decency of, 632
  supramundane wisdom of, 544
  ways of attracting disciples, 88, 575
  wisdom of, 557

Solitary Realizers' Vehicle, 764–65
sovereigns, bodhisattvas' birth as, 126, 803
space, 32, 294–95
  defilements as like, 63, 484, 485
  Dharma teaching issuing from, 57, 451
  purity of, 464
  transformation of perception of, 35, 310
speech
  of bodhisattvas, excellence of, 58, 453–55
  bodhisattvas' knowledge of others', 23, 249
  of buddhas, 58, 318, 455–60, 758, 760
  disparaging, 100, 633
  flawless, eight branches of, 3, 142
  gentle, as bodhisattva sign, 125, 797–98, 799, 800
  knowledge of conventions of, 102, 644–45
  See also Twelve Branches of Excellent Speech
spiritual ambition, 62, 478–79
spiritual friends, 16, 202
spiritual intent, xx, 144–45, 172, 197n1, 199–200, 204, 339, 615
spiritual masters, 328, 419
  best way to follow, 91, 590–91
  on bodhisattva levels, 129, 825, 826
  characteristics of, 62, 90, 478, 585–86
  enthusiasm for, 53, 428
  faith in, 25, 259
  indefatigability in listening to, 641
  and maturation, role in, 260
  nonattachment to, 548
  and potential, role in arousing, 187, 189, 193
  reliance on, 90–91, 98, 585–89, 626, 794
  third reliance and, 103, 649
  ways of following, 91, 589–90
stability, 101, 430, 637–38
Stage of a Bodhisattva, The (*Bodhisattvabhūmi*, Asaṅga), xxii, 843
stage of acceptance, 367, 379, 505
stage of warmth (on path of joining), 207, 244, 348, 378, 402, 407, 475, 504
Stages of Yogic Practice, 592
steadfastness
  categories of, 101, 638–40
  of fourth level, 808
  immutability of, 102, 640
  indefatigability and, 102, 640, 641

shame and, 99, 630
sign of, 125, 797–98, 799, 800
specific characteristics of, 101, 637–38
Sthiramati, 137, 159n2, 380. See
  also *Detailed Commentary of
  the Ornament of the Sūtras
  (Sūtrālaṃkāravṛttibhāṣya)*
stinginess, 79, 530, 539
  compassion toward, 97, 622–23
  freedom from, 574
  giving without, 798
  shame in, 631
  in teaching Dharma, 59, 462, 463
stream enterers, 205, 416–17, 418, 659,
  701, 776
study, 118, 427, 751, 752
subject and object
  appearances of, 63, 485
  arising of, 393–94
  on bodhisattva levels, 794–95, 822
  bodhisattvas' perception of, 407, 408,
    772, 791, 792
  clinging to, 47, 382
  in dependent reality, 50, 399–400, 688
  as devoid of intrinsic existence, 411
  emptiness of, 444
  freedom from, 409, 753
  fully present reality and, 401
  habitual tendencies of, 649
  as imputed reality, 411
  investigating, 45, 367–68, 383–84, 387
  nonconceptuality of, 393
  on path of joining, 70, 505
  on path of seeing, 506
  three concentrations and, 109, 686
  three natures and, 381–82, 474
  two views of, 395–96
*Sublime Continuum
  (Mahāyānottaratantraśāstra-
  ratnogotravibhāga)*, xvii, xix, 187, 420,
  758
subsequent accomplishment, 126, 551,
  810–11
subsequent realization, 123, 790, 791–92
suchness, 143, 144
  abiding in, 773
  of defilements, 63, 482–83
  as free from contamination, 32, 295–96
  as free from extremes, 234–35
  as free from two kinds of self, 282

as fully present reality, 144, 401
listening, reflecting, meditating on, 318
as nirvāṇa, 771
as object of boundless attitudes, 91, 593
offerings of, 89, 580, 582
perception of, 119, 769–72
personal realization of, 449
as present in all, 187
purifying, 334–36
realization of, 51, 367–68, 407
seven aspects of, 119, 760–61
three natures and, 404
transformation of, 37, 316–17
as unchanging essence, 34, 304
See also under phenomena
Sudinna, 366
suffering, 109, 687–88, 782
  acceptance of, 18, 19, 26, 62, 118, 122,
    173, 214–16, 217, 222, 223, 262–63,
    483–84, 488, 550, 752, 783–84
  of aggregates, 686
  bliss arising from, 94, 611
  compassion for, 188
  conventional existence of, 474
  delusion and, 21, 241–42
  from failing in boundless attitudes, 92,
    597–99
  as focus in offerings, 582
  freedom of others from, 593
  gross, freedom from, 10, 177
  from hostility toward Dharma, 167
  indefatigability in, 102, 640, 641
  inner knowledge of, 794
  lack of fear of, 257
  from lack of shame and decency, 100,
    633
  latent tendencies of, 624
  light rays in soothing, 23, 253
  of lower realms, 14, 190, 191
  not being affected by, 129, 825, 826
  of ordinary beings, 20, 95, 228, 612
  pacification of, 449–50
  patience and, 541
  reflecting on, 244
  sameness of, 71, 507
  and self, view of, 240
  of sentient beings, bodhisattvas'
    suffering for, 72, 84, 93, 95, 218, 510–
    12, 554, 602–3, 613–17
  steadfastness in face of, 102, 640

suffering (*continued*)
  subtle, 177n6
  in three vehicles, equivalence of, 415
  See also three kinds of suffering
superimposition, 48, 55, 386, 407, 443
superior concentration, 362, 489, 490, 516, 529–30, 542, 586, 676
superior discipline, 176, 361–62, 516, 529, 542, 585, 668, 676
superior intention
  bodhicitta and, 15, 198, 207
  bodhisattvas' signs and, 800
  five categories of, 126, 802–3
  function of, 803
  great compassion and, 94, 604–5
  quality of, 121, 779, 780
superior wisdom, 362, 516, 529–30, 542, 586, 668, 676
support(s)
  attentiveness associated with, 53, 370, 424
  in four close mindfulnesses, 104, 655–56, 659
  stage of indicative yoga, 50, 403–4
  two kinds, 46, 371
supreme mundane level, 178, 245
  bodhicitta on, 201, 207
  body of truth and, 441
  certain deliverance on, 67, 491
  concentration immediately preceding, 505
  concentration of, 352, 407, 440
  investigation on, 367
  phenomena, view of on, 236
  realization on, 402, 408, 475
  six consciousnesses on, 379
Supriya (gandharva), 253
sustained calm
  acquisition of, 504
  as attention, 663
  attentiveness and, 371, 376
  benefits related to, 129, 827–28
  bodhicitta and, 210–11
  branches of enlightenment and, 670
  defining characteristics of, 107, 678
  diligence in, 566
  on eightfold noble path, 676–77
  five powers and, 669
  on path of accumulation, 244
  result of, 516

as right mindfulness, 376
self-satisfaction in, 41, 349, 350
special point of, 479, 496–97, 661–62, 678, 783
summarization of scriptures as, 68, 496
transcendental concentration and, 529
  See also under yoga
Sūtra Collection, 5, 45, 155–56, 159, 160, 360, 362, 363, 364
Sūtra in Repayment of Kindness, 423
Sūtrālaṃkāra-piṇḍārtha (Jñānaśrī), 145n11
Sūtra Like a Saw, 167
Sūtra of Sublime Golden Light, 760
Sūtra of the Inconceivable Secrets, 176, 455, 460n15
Sūtra of the Lion's Roar of Śrīmālādevī, 419
Sūtra of the Myrobalan, 184
Sūtra of the Ornament of the Buddhas, 778, 822
Sūtra of the Ornament of the Light of Gnosis, 282
Sūtra of the Perfectly Pure Sphere of Activity, 229
Sūtra of the Precious Lamp, 345, 757–58
Sūtra of the Questions of Brahmaviśeṣacintin, 442, 452
Sūtra of the Questions of Dhāraṇīśvarāja, 307
Sūtra of the Questions of Ratnacūḍa, 832
Sūtra of the Teachings of Akṣayamati (*Akṣayamatinirdeśa-sūtra*), 206n10, 592, 606–7, 648, 667, 770–71
Sūtra of the Ten Levels, 372, 493, 495, 503, 508, 666, 761, 804–5, 806, 814–15
Sūtra on Buddhahood, 316
Sūtra on the Descent into Laṅka, 400, 493, 762
Sūtra on the Mountain Gayāśīṣa, 607
Sūtra That Teaches the Secret of the Tathāgata's Body, 804
syllables, 58, 454–55, 494

taints, exhaustion of, 120, 250, 251, 255, 256, 665, 775, 776, 835, 837
Tantra of the Essence of Nectar, 759
Tantra of the Wheel of Time, 759, 760
Tantra of Vairocana's Enlightenment, 237
tathāgata family. *See* buddha family
Teacher. *See* Buddha

teaching Dharma, 10, 19, 31, 175–76, 225–27, 273, 293, 294
  bodhisattvas' manner of, 57–58, 451–55
  by buddhas, 33, 58, 300, 455–60, 460–62, 463
  conventional knowledge in, 645
  eight faults in, 58–59, 461, 462–63
  five sciences in, 118, 756–60
  fourfold presentation of qualities in, 755–56
  four genuine restraints and, 660
  four perfect knowledges in, 103, 650–51
  gentle speech in, 123, 797, 798, 799
  immeasurable qualities of, 120, 774–75
  knowledge of treatises in, 643
  memory, power of in, 108, 683
  merit of, 43, 356–57
  on ninth level, 811, 819
  praise of, 60, 471
  presenting results of, 120, 775–77
  presenting truth in, 119, 760–63
  reason for, 57, 448–51
  by spiritual masters, 586
  value of, 57, 447–48
  verbally, mastery in, 538
ten aspects of sameness of phenomena, 815–16
ten attitudes of sameness, 814–15
ten benefits of Great Vehicle, 60, 470–71
ten Dharma activities, 831
ten great aspirations, 16, 204–5, 684
ten levels. *See* bodhisattva levels
ten limitless objects, 204–5
ten negative actions, 271, 284, 286, 807, 825
ten objects of elimination, 55, 443–44
ten positive actions, 274, 566, 803, 807
ten powers, 106, 252, 254, 257, 664, 666–67, 774, 804–5
ten qualities of enlightenment, 281
  all-pervasiveness, 31, 291–93
  boundless attainments, 34–35, 304–10
  deeds, 31–32, 293–95
  inconceivability, 29–30, 281–84
  maturing beings, 35–36, 311–16
  profundity, 32–34, 295–304
  supreme refuge, 30, 284–87
  transformation, 31, 287–91
  two goals, fulfillment of, 29–30, 283–84
  unchanging essence, 34, 304

ten strengths, 152, 340, 611, 774, 817, 836–37
tenth bodhisattva level (Cloud of Dharma)
  defining characteristic of, 127, 811–12
  etymological definition of, 130, 830
  great light rays empowerment on, 72, 175–76, 225, 513–14
  mark of, 826
  perfect realization on, 379
  types of bodhisattvas on, 127, 816–17
ten transcendent perfections, 10, 54, 176, 198, 201, 433, 438–39, 825–26
thatness, xx, 140, 339, 677
  on bodhisattva levels, 775–76
  certainty in, 28, 273–74
  of defilements, 482
  defining characteristics of, 21, 233–35
  diligence of engagement with, 87, 567
  five paths and, 22, 244–46
  investigating, 46, 381–82
  knowledge of, 678
  manifestation of, 49, 394–95
  meditation on, 332
  mental apprehension of, 51, 407
  partial penetration of, 505
  personal experience of, 450
  realization of, 121, 123, 781, 789–90
  reflection upon, 145, 146
  steadfastness regarding, 639
  transformation and, 288
  variant views on, 235–38
Theravāda school, xix
third bodhisattva level (Luminous)
  defining characteristic of, 126, 806, 807
  etymological definition of, 129, 828
  mark of, 825
  types of bodhisattvas on, 127, 813
thirty-seven elements that lead to enlightenment, 46, 104–7, 210, 374–76, 510, 655–78, 816, 818, 832
three buddha bodies, 403–4, 788
  attaining, 133, 560, 779, 840–41
  as enlightened state, 37, 319–20
  equality and eternity of, 38, 323–24
  inseparability from, 656
  realization of, 123, 793
  relationship between, 38, 322–23
  steadfastness in accomplishing, 101, 638, 640

three buddha bodies (*continued*)
  as supreme refuge, 30, 286–87
  two accumulations and, 654
  See also body of manifestation (*nirmāṇakāya*); body of perfect enjoyment (*sambhogakāya*); body of truth (*dharmakāya*)
three collections (*tripiṭaka*), 155–56
  classifications of, 45, 359–60, 363
  defining, reasons for, 360–62
  result of explaining, 800
  superiority of Great Vehicle's, 655–56
  three wisdoms and, 45–46, 367–69
three doors (body, speech, mind), 75, 121, 521, 522, 523, 745, 781, 782
three doors of perfect liberation (three concentrations), 543, 816
  as antidotes to three mistaken beliefs, 432
  faith in, 668
  four noble truths and, 646
  four summaries of Dharma and, 108, 109, 685–86, 687
  memory and, 108, 682–83
  objects of, 509
  preternatural knowledge and, 252
  on seventh level, 816
  two kinds of no-self and, 473–74
three families, 46, 180n11, 224, 369–70
threefold limpidity, 838
Three Jewels, 9, 145, 171, 254, 261, 667, 737. *See also* refuge
three kinds of acts, 107, 677
three kinds of enlightenment, 35, 82, 313–14, 420, 549, 550, 551, 552, 722
three kinds of individuals, 143, 144, 157
  concentration of, 84, 556–57
  diligence of, 87, 568
  potential of, 19, 223–24, 274
  refuge of, 182
  teaching Dharma to, 19, 225–27
three kinds of suffering, 241
  compassion for, 290, 602, 603, 604, 612, 623–24, 752
  knowledge of world and, 646
  suchness and, 761
  wisdom in understanding, 510
three kinds of thesis, 756
three pure levels, 121, 778, 779
  accomplishment on, 821, 831

  advanced interest on, 348
  attracting disciples from, 575
  birth on, 804–5
  boundless attitudes on, 596
  bringing others to, 275
  compassion on, 605
  four boundless attitudes on, 626
  four close mindfulnesses on, 658
  four genuine restraints on, 660
  indefatigability on, 641
  mastery on, 10, 51, 178–79, 406–7, 538
  memory on, 108, 682, 683
  nonconceptual gnosis on, 780
  nondeliberate sustained calm and profound insight on, 679
  realization on, 440
  shame and decency on, 632, 636–37
  signs of attaining, 69, 503
  teaching on, 57, 451
  two accumulations on, 654
three realities/natures, xvii, xx, 143, 144
  as devoid of production, 413
  direct perception of, 770–71
  five bases of knowable phenomena and, 396–98, 401, 404–5
  four truths and, 646, 762
  full knowledge of, 473–74
  indirect teachings and, 465–66
  intrinsic existence and, 410–12
  investigating, 50, 396–401
  realization of, 792, 793
  relationship between, 233–34
  suchness and, 761
  thatness of, 381–82
  three kinds of emptiness and, 509
three roots of virtue, 539, 559
three secrets, 10, 176
three spheres/concepts, 283, 332, 437n77, 824
  buddhas' speech and, 58, 461, 462
  of compassion, 605, 625
  complete purification of, 735
  in four boundless attitudes, 591
  freedom from, 65, 490
  nonconceptual gnosis and, 75, 523–24
  offerings and, 89, 579–80, 582, 584
  on path of seeing, 506
  realization of, 793
  sense of shame and, 636

six perfections and, 78, 530–32, 546, 547, 548, 549, 559, 570, 571, 653
skillful means and, 538
three supreme methods, 523–24
three times
  attracting disciples in, 88, 576
  as devoid of intrinsic existence, 410
  evenness of, 806, 807
  insatiable attitude toward, 537
  knowledge of, 123, 256, 794
  mirrorlike gnosis in, 325
  omnipresence in, 292
  vision of, 827
three trainings, 361–62, 374, 516
  diligence and, 542
  in following spiritual masters, 587
  six transcendental perfections and, 78, 529–30
  of spiritual masters, 585–86
  superior, 114, 160, 737, 738 (*see also* superior concentration; superior discipline; superior wisdom)
three vehicles, 5, 157, 162
  bodhisattvas' realization of, 9, 172–73
  differences between, xix
  diligence in, 87, 568
  dispelling others' doubts in, 224, 226
  inner science of, 422, 423, 642, 643, 644, 757, 787
  interest in, 130, 831–32
  Mahāyāna refuge and, 180
  maturation by, 268, 314
  potential for, 186, 189, 291
  presenting, 119, 762, 764–65
  refuge in, 180–82
  and single vehicle, intentions of, 52, 415
  six perfections and, 78, 530–32
  spiritual masters in, 91, 588
  teaching in accordance with, 58, 454–55, 456, 740
  three goals of, 420
three wisdoms, 360
  on eightfold path, 375
  Great Vehicle and, 197, 199, 202–3, 328
  objects of, 46, 367, 368–69
  in offerings, 90, 583
  in relying on spiritual masters, 589
  results of, 55, 442
  spiritual ambition and, 478–79
  suchness and, 761

in teaching Dharma, 57, 448–51
three worlds
  bodhisattvas' triumph over, 230
  defilements of, 59, 463, 464
  false imagination in, 400
  happiness in, 95, 615
  realms with and without light in, 700
  sameness of, 51, 407
  as simply/merely mind, 71, 384, 508
  suffering of, 623–24
tīrthikas, 155–56, 161, 259, 265, 459, 464
  ascetic practices of, 361
  bodhisattvas appearing as, 758
  compassion for, 601
  love in, 591–92
  mistaken interest in doctrines of, 347
  protection from, 285
  self, view of, 239, 242, 714–15, 720–21, 725
  subjugating, 132, 423, 456, 457n8, 837, 838
  views of, 410
training, 340
  in attracting disciples, 87, 573–74
  encouragement for, 356
  five aspects of, 79, 535–38
  five sciences on stage of, 422
  methods for, 145, 790
  results of, 733
transcendent perfections. *See* six transcendent perfections; ten transcendent perfections
transcendent state, 75, 450, 523
transformation, 120, 771–72
  diligence in, 87, 567
  of first level, 70, 506–7
  of perfect liberation, 51, 405–6, 409
  quality of, 31, 287–89
  seven attainments of, 34–35, 306–10
  superiority of buddhas, 31, 289–90
  ten divisions of, 31, 290–91
  ultimate, 73, 514
  uncontaminated state of, 403
transformation birth, 52, 417–18, 420
transitory composite, 716
  absence of self in, 239–40
  dispelling view of, 377, 780
  protection from view of, 30, 285
  transcending, 86, 566
transmigration, 90, 583, 584, 590, 665, 837

936 — INDEX

Tuṣita heaven, xv, xvii, 137, 212, 254, 313, 793, 804, 816
Twelve Branches of Excellent Speech
   as cause of realization, 50, 401–2
   classifying and analyzing, 67, 493–94
   contemplating names in, 67, 68, 493, 496
   contents of, 360, 377
   five sciences in, 118, 423, 756–60
   impartiality of, 314
   teaching, 449
   virtue of, 246
twelve hundred all-perceiving qualities, 34, 306–8
twelve links of dependent arising, 237, 243, 412, 760–61, 819
twelve sets of one hundred special qualities, 379–80, 405, 437
two accumulations, 372
   accomplishment of, 104, 653–54
   attentiveness and, 370
   bodhicitta and, 15, 16, 200, 202–3, 207, 210
   of bodhisattvas, 174, 215–16
   completion of, 33, 195, 300, 303
   at enlightenment, 29, 279–81, 331
   four boundless attitudes in completing, 92, 596
   function of, 104, 654
   going beyond, 244
   as infinite, 319
   interest with and without, 348
   lack of potential and, 194
   on level of earnest aspiration, 318
   in Listeners' and Great Vehicle, differences between, 5, 159, 305–6
   of listeners with unfixed potential, 418
   making offerings to complete, 89, 579–80, 582
   maturation of, 65, 490
   maturations from, 259, 264
   of others, bodhisattvas' help in completing, 115, 741
   on paths and levels, 491–92
   result of, 73, 288, 517
   shame and decency in completing, 100, 634
   six transcendent perfections and, 104, 425, 431, 652–53
   spiritual ambition and, 478–79
   strength of, as sign of realization, 823–24
   three doors in engaging, 522
two buddha bodies, 322, 372
two doors, 60, 470, 471
two extremes, 394
   dispelling, 51, 361, 407, 443–44
   liberation from, 10, 177, 178
   refutation of, 48, 386
   suchness as beyond, 296–97
   transcendent wisdom and, 548
two goals, 145, 146, 339
   accomplishment of, 112, 123, 728–29, 789–90
   aspiration prayers as causal factors, 108, 684, 685
   benefit of interest to, 42, 352–53, 356–57
   bodhicitta and, 15, 197–98, 205
   five powers and, 669
   four bases of miraculous powers and, 105, 662
   four boundless attitudes and, 626–27
   four close mindfulnesses and, 658
   fulfillment of, 29–30, 283–85, 287
   in Great Vehicle, distinction of, 6, 158, 159, 162–63, 172
   joy in attaining, 828
   knowledge of treatises and, 643
   manifestation body and, 37, 322
   potential and, 185
   practice for, 19, 20, 221–22, 228
   refuge and, 180
   sameness of, 19, 222–23
   six transcendent perfections and, 77, 527–28
   skillful means in attaining, 108, 680, 681
   steadfastness in accomplishing, 639
   three buddha bodies and, 38, 323
   two accumulations and, 104, 653–54
   See also benefiting beings
two kinds of no-self
   attainment of, 32, 296–97
   attentiveness to, 370, 610
   demonstration of, 444
   as distinction of Great Vehicle, 764
   four close mindfulnesses and, 658
   full knowledge of, 61, 473–74
   of individual, proof for, 21, 239–40
   listeners and bodhisattvas' realization of, 379
   in Listeners' and Great Vehicles,

differences between, 157, 158–59, 162, 236, 237, 522
nonconceptual gnosis of, 523
of phrases, names, letters, 373
rational application and, 763
realization of, 51, 61, 171, 172, 174, 199, 213, 237, 329, 407, 440, 475, 806–7
reflecting on, 244
suchness and, 761
three concentrations and, 108, 685–86
three realities and, 722
transcendent wisdom and, 544, 557
two obscurations
elimination of, 29, 213, 245–46, 279–81, 413, 476, 770
false imagination as support, 509
on fourth level, 829
freedom from, 15, 32, 199, 297–98, 514, 837
in Listeners' and Great Vehicles, differences between, 157, 303
mirrorlike gnosis and, 325
on path of seeing, 506
purification of, 37, 316–17, 380, 503, 513, 679–80
seeds of, destruction of, 31, 287–88
of three kinds of beings, 557
transcendent perfections and, 78, 529
transcendent wisdom and, 544, 557
two kinds of self and, 409
two purities, 321, 331, 841–42
Two Segments (Hevajra Tantra), 481
Two Stanza Incantation, 60, 470
two truths
acceptance of, 47, 383
bodhisattvas' teaching of, 452
distinguishing, 480
four noble truths and, 646
full knowledge of, 61, 473–74
investigating, 55, 445–46
in Madhyamaka view, 235
rational application and, 763–64
realization of, 123, 792–93
transcendent perfections and, 571–72
transcendent wisdom and, 552, 557, 561
union of, 490
unmistaken Dharma of, 59, 463, 464

Ultimate Emptiness, 724–25
ultimate excellence, 180, 526–27

ultimate reality, 753
attaining, as delivery from downfalls, 366
defining characteristics of, 21, 233–35
direct realization of, 180–81, 476
ignorance of, 47, 382
indirect teaching of, 59, 465–66
mind as, 63, 486
as nature of mind, 187
peace and birth on, 21, 242–43
of phenomena, 317
of saṃsāra and nirvāṇa, 243, 291
space-like, 477
as support for untainted aggregates, 819
ultimate teachings, 103, 414, 449, 462, 464–65, 647–48
ultimate truth
Cittamātra view of, 236
fully present reality as, 151, 403
impermanence and, 688
implied teaching of, 467
of individuals and phenomena, 329
joy in, 686
in Listeners' Vehicle, 363n9
mistaken views on, 444
perception and, 63, 484–85
realization of, 123, 200, 792
unity, elimination of concept of, 55, 443, 444
universal emperors, 758, 817
bodhisattvas born as, 125, 801, 803, 826
four perfections of, 9, 174, 175
rebirth as, 652, 658
seven attributes of, 671–75
wealth of, 732, 734, 751, 798, 824
Unraveling the Intent, 234, 444, 759–60, 761, 812
Uttarakuru, 219n17

Vaibhāṣika system, xxn5
Vairocana, 321
Vaiśravaṇa, 672
vajra awakening, 482
vajra-like concentration, 73, 192, 281, 514, 820
Vajrapāṇi, 176, 630
valid cognition
in establishing impermanence, 692, 713
in establishing no-self, 240, 715, 716, 722

valid cognition (*continued*)
  rational application and, 763
  repudiation of, 165
  in teaching Dharma, 451–52, 461, 756
  of thatness, 235
  three kinds, 642
Vast Activity tradition, xviiin1
Vasubandhu, xvi, 137, 144, 159n2, 219n17, 380. See also *Commentary on Ornament of the Mahāyāna Sūtras* (*Sūtrālaṃkārabhāṣya*)
Vātsīputrīyas, 714, 715, 718–19
Vehicle of Characteristics, 481, 483
veneration, 28, 90, 273, 583, 587
Verses Summarizing the Precious Qualities, 572, 622
views
  arrogant, 361
  correct, 143
  defiled, 376, 377
  perfectly pure, 127, 813
  realization of subtle, 123, 790, 791
  See also wrong views
Vimalacandra, 468
Vimalakīrti, 617
Vinaya Collection, 360–61
  classifications and etymology of, 45, 364–66
  contents of, 362
  discipline and, 540, 598
  learning in, 799
  of Listeners' and Great Vehicles, lack of contradiction in, 5, 155–56, 159, 160
virtues
  accumulation of, 468–69
  bodhicitta in increasing, 15, 18, 200, 214
  boundless, 29, 279–80
  definite duty of cultivating, 118, 751, 752
  delight in, 25, 26, 80, 261–62, 263, 265, 266, 271, 542
  of Dharma, 59, 284, 463–64
  diligence of, 87, 567
  establishing others in, 255
  four kinds, 10, 178–79, 191
  habituation to, 16, 202
  inferior, 14, 193
  and interest, relationship between, 345–46
  of Mahāyāna, superiority of, 13, 185
  mundane and supramundane, accomplishing, 118, 753
  as obstacles, 484
  of practice, 221–22
  as sign of potential, 13, 188–89
  totality of, 10, 177, 178
  vow to gather, 199
vows, 79, 657
  of bodhisattvas, 576
  breaking, 599
  impermanence of, 710
  maintaining, 113, 732–33
  on second level, 129, 828
  steadfastness regarding, 640
  supreme, 754
  three kinds (prātimokṣa, dhyāna, untainted), 541, 545, 570

Way of the Bodhisattva, The (*Bodhicaryāvatāra*, Śāntideva), xviii
wealth, 588
  bodhisattvas' generosity of, 85, 86, 88, 96, 562, 563–64, 576, 616–17, 782–83
  certainty regarding, 437
  concentration and, 106, 674
  generosity and, 79, 96, 539, 619
  lack of desire for, 90, 587
  nonattachment to, 116, 742, 743
  obstacles from lacking, 568–69
  relinquishment of, 113, 732–33, 824
wheel of Dharma, xvii, xx, 653, 817, xviiin1
White Lotus Sūtra of the Sacred Dharma, 307
wildness, antidotes to, 68, 496–97
wisdom
  accumulation of, 202
  of bodhisattvas, 20, 175, 229
  in Great Vehicle, distinction of, 158–59
  mundane and transcendent, distinctions between, 544
  nonconceptual, 62, 63, 480–83, 484–86
  of others, bodhisattvas' development of, 224
  power of, 667, 668–69
  self-cognizant, 6, 164
  of sharp mind, 26, 263–64
  steadfastness and, 101, 637–38, 639
  supramundane, 544
  supreme, bliss of, 10, 177

See also self-cognizant wisdom; superior wisdom
wisdom, transcendent, 6, 162, 174
  accumulation of wisdom and, 104, 652–53
  bodhicitta and, 208
  as cause of enlightenment, 39–40, 332–34
  defining characteristics of, 78, 532
  eight supreme aspects of, 85, 561
  etymology of, 79, 533, 534
  factors incompatible with, 81, 548
  four excellent qualities of, 83, 552
  in maturing others, 28, 273–74
  and other perfections, relationship between, 571
  as paramount among perfections, 118, 753, 754
  purity of, 84, 557
  subdivisions of, 80, 543–44, 571
  ten powers and, 667
wisdom perceptions, attainment of, 244
wisdom-vision, 5, 158
womb, realization of, 123, 793
world of desire
  attachment in, 600
  bodhisattvas' rebirth in, 551, 733, 745
  body's development in, 699
  consciousness in, 648
  elimination of defilements of, 501
  four boundless attitudes in, 595
  freedom from, 566
  gods of, 700
  listeners of unfixed potential and, 416–17, 418, 419
  meditation in, 498
  rebirth in, 92, 596, 666, 807
  shame and decency of, 631
  suffering of, 543
world of form, 227
  body's development in, 699
  boundless attitudes in, 625
  compassion for beings in, 601
  concentrations of, 666, 678 (*see also* four dhyānas)
  consciousness in, 648
  discipline in, 541n12
  four boundless attitudes in, 595–96
  gods of, 700
  interest and, 42, 353–55
  rebirth in, 543, 548n16, 596, 745
  shame and decency of, 631
world of formlessness, 227
  compassion for beings in, 601
  concentration of, 116, 668, 744, 745
  consciousness in, 648
  four boundless attitudes in, 595–96
  gods of, 700
  interest and, 42, 353–55
  rebirth in, 548n16
  shame and decency of, 631
  See also four absorptions of formless world
wrong views, 193, 468n18, 479n8, 555, 668, 791
  compassion for others', 229–30, 601, 799
  dispelling, 361, 377, 394–95, 815
  freedom from, 121, 782, 783
  protection from, 30, 286

yoga
  cause and nature of, 46, 371
  five indicative stages of, 50, 340–41, 401–4
  of mind, 91, 589
  of sustained calm and profound insight, 68, 107, 115, 121, 224, 394, 404, 431, 496, 678–80, 740, 783
  with three special points, 105, 661–62
Yogācāra (Yogic Practice), xviin1
Yogācāra Madhyamaka, 237–38

Padmakara Translation Group
Translations into English

The Adornment of the Middle Way. Shantarakshita and Mipham Rinpoche. Boston: Shambhala Publications, 2005, 2010.
Counsels from My Heart. Dudjom Rinpoche. Boston: Shambhala Publications, 2001, 2003.
Enlightened Courage. Dilgo Khyentse Rinpoche. Dordogne: Editions Padmakara, 1992; Ithaca, NY: Snow Lion Publications, 1994, 2006.
The Excellent Path of Enlightenment. Dilgo Khyentse Rinpoche. Dordogne: Editions Padmakara, 1987; Ithaca, NY: Snow Lion Publications, 1996.
Finding Rest in the Nature of the Mind: The Trilogy of Rest, Vol. 1. Longchenpa. Boulder: Shambhala Publications, 2017.
A Flash of Lightning in the Dark of Night. The Dalai Lama. Boston: Shambhala Publications, 1993. Republished as *For the Benefit of All Beings*. Boston: Shambhala Publications, 2009. Republished as *The Bodhisattva Guide*. Boulder: Shambhala Publications, 2017.
Food of Bodhisattvas. Shabkar Tsogdruk Rangdrol. Boston: Shambhala Publications, 2004.
A Garland of Views: A Guide to View, Meditation, and Result in the Nine Vehicles. Padmasambhava and Mipham Rinpoche. Boston: Shambhala Publications, 2015.
A Guide to the Words of My Perfect Teacher. Khenpo Ngawang Pelzang. Translated with Dipamkara. Boston: Shambhala Publications, 2004.
The Heart of Compassion. Dilgo Khyentse Rinpoche. Boston: Shambhala Publications, 2007.
The Heart Treasure of the Enlightened Ones. Dilgo Khyentse Rinpoche and Patrul Rinpoche. Boston: Shambhala Publications, 1992.
The Hundred Verses of Advice. Dilgo Khyentse Rinpoche and Padampa Sangye. Boston: Shambhala Publications, 2005.
Introduction to the Middle Way. Chandrakirti and Mipham Rinpoche. Boston: Shambhala Publications, 2002, 2004.
Journey to Enlightenment. Matthieu Ricard. New York: Aperture Foundation, 1996.
Lady of the Lotus-Born. Gyalwa Changchub and Namkhai Nyingpo. Boston: Shambhala Publications, 1999, 2002.

The Life of Shabkar: *The Autobiography of a Tibetan Yogin*. Albany, NY: SUNY Press, 1994; Ithaca, NY: Snow Lion Publications, 2001.
Nagarjuna's Letter to a Friend. Longchen Yeshe Dorje, Kangyur Rinpoche. Ithaca, NY: Snow Lion Publications, 2005.
The Nectar of Manjushri's Speech. Kunzang Pelden. Boston: Shambhala Publications, 2007, 2010.
The Root Stanzas on the Middle Way. Nagarjuna. Dordogne: Editions Padmakara, 2008.
A Torch Lighting the Way to Freedom. Dudjom Rinpoche, Jigdrel Yeshe Dorje. Boston: Shambhala Publications, 2011.
Treasury of Precious Qualities, Book One. Longchen Yeshe Dorje, Kangyur Rinpoche. Boston: Shambhala Publications, 2001. Revised version with root text by Jigme Lingpa, 2010.
Treasury of Precious Qualities, Book Two. Longchen Yeshe Dorje, Kangyur Rinpoche. Boston: Shambhala Publications, 2013.
The Way of the Bodhisattva (Bodhicharyavatara). Shantideva. Boston: Shambhala Publications, 1997, 2006, 2008.
White Lotus. Jamgön Mipham. Boston: Shambhala Publications, 2007.
The Wisdom Chapter: Jamgön Mipham's Commentary on the Ninth Chapter of The Way of the Bodhisattva. Jamgön Mipham. Boulder: Shambhala Publications, 2017.
Wisdom: Two Buddhist Commentaries. Khenchen Kunzang Pelden and Minyak Kunzang Sonam. Dordogne: Editions Padmakara, 1993, 1999.
The Wish-Fulfilling Jewel. Dilgo Khyentse Rinpoche. Boston: Shambhala Publications, 1988.
The Words of My Perfect Teacher. Patrul Rinpoche. Sacred Literature Series of the International Sacred Literature Trust. New York: HarperCollins, 1994; 2nd ed. Lanham, MD: AltaMira Press, 1998; Boston: Shambhala Publications, 1998; New Haven, CT: Yale University Press, 2010.
Zurchungpa's Testament. Zurchungpa and Dilgo Khyentse Rinpoche. Ithaca, NY: Snow Lion Publications, 2006.

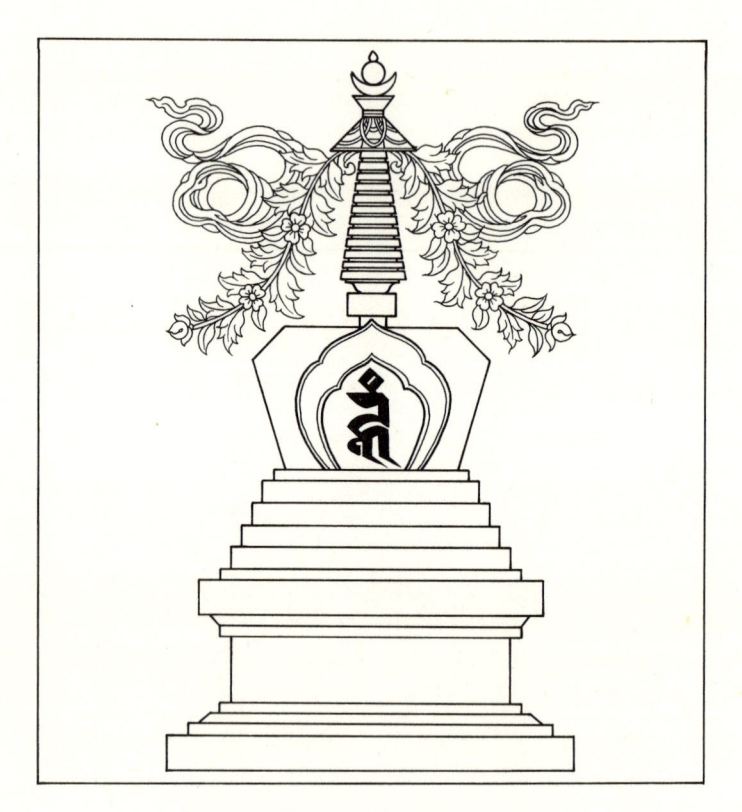

STŪPA OF SUPREME ENLIGHTENMENT